billylinguist@gn

THE ROUTLEDGE HANDBOOK OF DISCOURSE AND DISINFORMATION

This handbook offers a comprehensive overview of research into discourses of disinformation, misinformation, post-truth, alternative facts, hate speech, conspiracy theories, and "fake news".

Divided into two sections, it provides a detailed look at the methodological challenges and approaches for studying disinformation, along with a wide range of case studies covering everything from climate change denial to COVID-19 conspiracies. The studies address how discourses of disinformation are constructed and developed, what rhetorical and persuasive strategies they employ, how disinformation can be discerned from real news, and what steps we might take in order to create a more trustworthy news environment.

Authored by leading experts from around the world, and showcasing the most up-to-date methodological approaches to the topic, the volume makes a significant contribution to current linguistic research on politics and is an essential guide to the discourses of disinformation for advanced students and researchers of English language studies, linguistics, and media and communication studies.

Stefania M. Maci is Full Professor of English Language at the University of Bergamo, where she is the coordinator of the MA in Digital Humanities and Director of the Research Centre on Specialised Language. Her research is focussed on the study of the English language in academic and professional contexts.

Massimiliano Demata is Associate Professor of English Linguistics at the University of Turin. He has published monographs, papers, and book chapters on British and US political discourse, nationalism and discourse, populism, computer-mediated communication, and climate change refugees.

Mark McGlashan is Senior Lecturer in English Language at the Birmingham Institute of Media and English, Birmingham City University. Mark's research interests predominantly centre on the synthesis and application of methods from corpus linguistics and (critical) discourse studies to study a wide range of social issues, and his recent work has focussed on relationships between language and abuse. Mark is co-editor (with Professor John Mercer) of *Toxic Masculinity: Men, Meaning and Digital Media* (Routledge, 2023).

Philip Seargeant is Senior Lecturer in Applied Linguistics at the Open University, where he teaches and researches language and communication with a political focus on political discourse. His recent books include *The Art of Political Storytelling, Political Activism in the Linguistic Landscape,* and *Crisis Leadership: Boris Johnson and Political Persuasion during the Covid Pandemic.*

ROUTLEDGE HANDBOOKS IN APPLIED LINGUISTICS

Routledge Handbooks in Applied Linguistics provide comprehensive overviews of the key topics in applied linguistics. All entries for the handbooks are specially commissioned and written by leading scholars in the field. Clear, accessible and carefully edited *Routledge Handbooks in Applied Linguistics* are the ideal resource for both advanced undergraduates and postgraduate students.

THE ROUTLEDGE HANDBOOK OF CONTENT AND LANGUAGE INTEGRATED LEARNING
Edited by Darío Luis Banegas and Sandra Zappa-Hollman

THE ROUTLEDGE HANDBOOK OF APPLIED LINGUISTICS
Volume 1 Language Learning and Language Education, Second Edition
Edited by Li Wei, Zhu Hua, and James Simpson

THE ROUTLEDGE HANDBOOK OF APPLIED LINGUISTICS
Volume 2 Applied Linguistics in Action, Second Edition
Edited by Li Wei, Zhu Hua, and James Simpson

THE ROUTLEDGE HANDBOOK OF LANGUAGE POLICY AND PLANNING
Edited by Michele Gazzola, François Grin, Linda Cardinal, and Kathleen Heugh

THE ROUTLEDGE HANDBOOK OF MULTILINGUALISM
Second Edition
Edited by Carolyn McKinney, Pinky Makoe and Virginia Zavala

THE ROUTLEDGE HANDBOOK OF DISCOURSE AND DISINFORMATION
Edited by Stefania Maci, Massimiliano Demata, Mark McGlashan and Philip Seargeant

For a full list of titles in this series, please visit https://www.routledge.com/Routledge-Handbooks-in-Applied-Linguistics/book-series/RHAL

THE ROUTLEDGE HANDBOOK OF DISCOURSE AND DISINFORMATION

Edited by Stefania M. Maci, Massimiliano Demata, Mark McGlashan and Philip Seargeant

Routledge
Taylor & Francis Group

LONDON AND NEW YORK

Designed cover image: MHJ, Getty

First published 2024
by Routledge
4 Park Square, Milton Park, Abingdon, Oxon OX14 4RN

and by Routledge
605 Third Avenue, New York, NY 10158

Routledge is an imprint of the Taylor & Francis Group, an informa business

British Library Cataloguing-in-Publication Data
A catalogue record for this book is available from the British Library

ISBN: 978-1-032-12425-4 (hbk)
ISBN: 978-1-032-12428-5 (pbk)
ISBN: 978-1-003-22449-5 (ebk)

DOI: 10.4324/9781003224495

Typeset in Times New Roman
by Apex CoVantage, LLC

CONTENTS

Contents

FIGURES

TABLES

CONTRIBUTORS

Simone Abbiati is a PhD candidate in transcultural studies in the humanities at University of Bergamo ("Department of Excellence" research grant for Digital Humanities) and a visiting PhD student at Cambridge University (UK) and Stanford University (US). He is Associate Researcher at Cambridge Digital Humanities and Member of SIGHUM, the group of special interests of the Association for Computational Linguistics (ACL). His current research focuses on fiction that deals with politically sensitive spaces, such as the British-Irish border and the Basque Country. He explores the use of computational linguistics to extract spatial information from English contemporary fiction and testimonies from victims of terror groups (IRA, UDA, ETA, GAL) who have perpetrated violence in those areas. He is also investigating the use of transformer models for natural language processing tasks to investigate the stylistic variance in spatial expression and terror violence between fiction and actual testimonies.

Silje Susanne Alvestad is a researcher within and the PI of the Fakespeak project at the University of Oslo and the Language and Intelligence Academy at the Norwegian Defence University College. She holds a PhD in Slavic languages and linguistics from the University of Oslo. In 2014 she received H.M. the King of Norway's Gold Medal for outstanding dissertations within the humanities for her thesis. In her thesis she compares the use of verbal aspect in the imperative in 12 different Slavic languages. Alvestad has published internationally on topics as varied as Slavic aspect and noun phrases, morpho-phonological features of Biblical and modern Hebrew, evaluative language in academic discourse, and Ottoman Turkish versified glossaries. In 2019 she received NOK 12 million from the Research Council of Norway for her research project *Fakespeak – the language of fake news. Fake news detection based on linguistic cues.* Fakespeak is an interdisciplinary project involving linguists and computer scientists whose primary objective is to examine the language of fake news in English, Norwegian, and Russian and to see whether the inclusion of linguistic features can improve existing fake news detection systems. Within the Fakespeak project, she is responsible for deliveries in the Norwegian and Russian parts of the project, investigating the language of fake and genuine news in single-authored as well as general corpora.

Fatemeh Torabi Asr is a software engineer and data scientist specialised in natural language processing. Her recent research is focused on machine learning approaches to analysing large and diverse text datasets. Fatemeh is currently working at a Fintech company, Symend, and is still affiliated as a postdoctoral researcher with the Discourse Processing Lab at Simon Fraser University. She was awarded Simon Fraser University's President's Emerging Thought Leader Newsmaker of the Year in 2019 for her knowledge mobilization work on fake news detection and gender gap tracking.

Giuseppe Balirano, PhD in English linguistics, is Professor of English Linguistics and Translation at the University of Naples "L'Orientale". He is the current Director of the University Language Centre. His research interests and publications lie in the fields of multimodal critical discourse studies, humour, masculinity and queer studies, the discursive representation of organised crime and audio-visual translation. He is Director of the I-LanD, the Italian inter-university research centre for the linguistic investigation of identity and diversity in discourse and P.I. of the Monitoring group on hate speech online at UNIOR. He is BeTwiXt Series Director, publishing original monographs in the field of linguistics and communication studies. His most recent publications include *Re-Defining Gender, Sexuality, and Discourse in the Global Rise of Right-Wing Extremism* (2021, co-edited with R. Borba); *Homing in on Hate: Critical Discourse Studies of Hate Speech, Discrimination and Inequality in the Digital Age* (2020, co-edited with B. Hughes); *Food Across Cultures: Linguistic Insights in Transcultural Tastes* (2019, co-edited with S. Guzzo); *Miss Man: Languaging the Gendered Body* (2018, co-edited with O. Palusci); *Self-Narratives in Organizations: Transgender and Gender Non-Conforming Experiences* (2018, co-edited with P. Valerio and L.M. Sicca); *Queering Masculinities in Language and Culture* (2018, co-edited with P. Baker); Gar*daí & Badfellas: The Discursive Construction of Organised Crime in the Irish Media* (2017); *Humosexually Speaking: Laughter and the Intersections of Gender* (2016, co-edited with D. Chiaro); *Languaging Diversity* (2015, co-edited with M.C. Nisco); and *Masculinity and Representation: A Multimodal Critical Approach to Male Identity Constructions* (2014).

Marina Bondi is Professor of English Linguistics at the University of Modena and Reggio Emilia (Italy) and Founding Director of the CLAVIER centre (Corpus and Language Variation In English Research). Her research centres on textual, pragmatic, and phraseological aspects of academic and professional discourse across genres, discourse identities, and media.

Elinor Carmi is Lecturer in Data Politics and Social Justice at City, University of London. Dr. Carmi's work focuses on the politics of data, including data justice, data inequality, and feminist/queer approaches to data.

Paola Catenaccio is Full Professor of English Linguistics and Translation at Università degli Studi di Milano, where she has also served in several governance positions (Deputy Dean for Internationalisation, Degree Programme Coordinator, Head of Department). Her research interests lie primarily in the field of discourse analysis and pragmatics, which she has applied to a variety of domains in combination with other methodological perspectives (most notably corpus linguistics), adopting a multi-methods approach to linguistic research. She is especially interested in the linguistic and rhetorical dimensions of argumentation across media and modes and on identity construction and performance in and through language. She has published extensively on a vast array of topics in multiple domains, from legal to business and professional communication, from media discourse to the discourse of science and of scientific popularisation, to the rhetoric of conspiracy theorising. Her research has appeared in international journals and edited collections. She has also co-edited numerous books and special issues of journals. Among her most recent publications is a volume on *Ethics in Professional and Corporate Discourse: Linguistic Perspectives* (2021, with G. Garzone).

Dennis Chau is Senior Lecturer in the Department of Humanities, Language, and Translation at Hong Kong Metropolitan University. His current research interests include digital communication and language ideologies.

Isobelle Clarke is Leverhulme Trust Early Career Researcher in the Centre for Corpus Approaches to Social Science at Lancaster University. Isobelle specialises in the analysis of short texts. Her research interests include corpus linguistics, forensic linguistics, discourse analysis, and learner language. Her current project is aimed at understanding the linguistic mechanisms and repertoires of antiscience across pseudoscience and conspiracy websites on topics such as vaccination, climate change, stem cells, and genetically modified organisms.

Michelangelo Conoscenti is Professor of English Language and Linguistics at the University of Turin. His main research interests include the analysis of political and military discourse. He designed an approach, critical reverse language engineering to investigate military discourse. He has published a number of monographs, including *Language Engineering and Media Management Strategies in Recent Wars* (2004) and *The Reframer: An Analysis of Barack Obama's Political Discourse (2004–2010)* (2011). Other contributions on this topic are *Audience Architecture and Reverse Language Engineering: Problems and Opportunities for Social Media Intelligence and Digital Media Management Units* (forthcoming), *Europe at the Centre of Military Inform and Influence Activities: Implications for the European Public Debate* (2019), *NATO's Social Media Strategic Communication in the Making* (2018), *Big Data, Small Data, Broken Windows and Fear Discourse: Brexit, the EU and the Majority Illusion* (2018).

Chiara Degano (PhD) is Associate Professor of English Linguistics and Translation at Roma Tre University, Italy. Her research is centred on discourse analysis, integrated with the quantitative approach of corpus linguistics and with aspects of argumentation theory. She is Member of ILIAS – International Learned Institute for Argumentation Studies, and CLAVIER – Corpus and Language Variation in English Research Group, and sits on the editorial board of the *Journal of Argumentation in Context*. Within this framework she has focused on various strands of institutional communication, with special regard for media and political discourse. Other research interests include stylistics and translation. She has published three monographs: *Discorsi di guerra: il prologo del conflitto iracheno nella stampa britannica e italiana* [War Discourses: The Prologue to the Iraqi conflict in the British and Italian Press] (2008), *Discourse Analysis, Argumentation Theory and Corpus Linguistics. An Integrated Approach* (2012), and *Agreement in Argumentation. A Discursive Perspective* (2022, with F. Santulli).

Alison Duguid, Associate Professor of English Language and Linguistics at the University of Siena in the Department of Political, Social and Cognitive Studies, has worked in Italy as a language teacher and teacher trainer since 1977. Her research interests lie in the field of corpus assisted discourse studies (CADS) and discourse analysis. She has published analyses of a variety of text types: news discourse, including broadcast news, political discourse, and opinion pieces. She is interested in lexical priming, in particular forced priming, and evaluation as linguistic phenomena. She is a member of the SiBol group. She has written on absence, on public apologies and media evaluations, on evaluation in international TV news channels, and on the representations of class in British broadsheets and newspaper informalisation. Her publications include *Patterns and Meanings in Discourse* with Alan Partington and Charlotte Taylor.

Eleonora Esposito is a researcher at the Institute for Culture and Society (ICS) of the University of Navarra (Spain) and a Seconded National Expert at the European Institute for Gender Equality (EIGE). With an MA in cultural and postcolonial studies and a PhD in critical discourse studies, Eleonora has been investigating complex intersections between language, identity, and the digitalized society, in different global contexts, encompassing the EU, the Anglophone Caribbean, and the Middle East. A Marie Skłodowska-Curie Alumna, Eleonora was Principal Investigator of WONT-HATE (2019–2021), a project where she explored motives, forms, and impacts of online violence against women in EU politics. Her recent publications include the edited special issue of the *Journal of Language, Aggression and Conflict* titled "Critical Perspectives on Gender, Politics and Violence" (2021), and the monograph titled *Politics, Ethnicity and the Postcolonial Nation: A Critical Analysis of Political Discourse in the Caribbean* (John Benjamins, 2021).

Maria Grazia Guido is Full Professor of English Linguistics and Translation at the University of Salento (Italy), where she is Director of the Department of Humanities. She holds a PhD in English applied linguistics at the University of London Institute of Education. She is Director of the scientific journal *Lingue e Linguaggi*, top-rated as "A-class" by ANVUR (The National Agency for the Evaluation of Research and Universities), and she has been Coordinator (and Founder) of the International PhD Programme in "Modern and Classical Languages, Literatures and Cultures" at the University of Salento in collaboration with the University of Vienna. Her research interests are in cognitive-functional linguistics applied to English as a "Lingua Franca" (ELF) in intercultural communication, cognitive stylistics, and critical discourse analysis. Her monographs include *English as a Lingua Franca in Migrants' Trauma Narratives* (Palgrave Macmillan), *English as a Lingua Franca in Cross-cultural Immigration Domains* (Peter Lang), *Mediating Cultures* (LED), *The Acting Translator* (Lega).

Bronwen Hughes is Associate Professor of English Language and Linguistics at the Università degli Studi di Napoli, Parthenope. She has taught extensively in the fields of English for tourism, English for law, translation studies, and English for professional purposes at both undergraduate, postgraduate, and doctoral levels. She holds a PhD in linguistics and modern and comparative literature, and her research interests lie in the fields of translation as a tool for second language acquisition, cross-cultural media studies, gender diversity, and disability studies. In terms of methodological frameworks, she commonly employs the tools offered by CDA, conversation analysis, multimodal discourse analysis, and corpus linguistics. She has published several monographic works and numerous research articles, which appear in collected volumes.

Michael Humann is Training and Research Coordinator at the Critical and Major Incident (CAMI) group at the Department of Psychology, University of Liverpool. This work focuses on liaising with a range of partners and stakeholders, developing and delivering bespoke projects, as well as designing, developing, and delivering training, aimed at improving critical incident decision-making and developing expertise in policing and emergency response. Drawing on psychology, his work has focused on looking at performance in high-risk environments. This has resulted in the development of policy guidance, evaluation reports, and practical interventions, supporting decision-makers, agencies, and organisations. Some of these include: (i) development of evidence-based interventions for specialist policing areas (e.g. UK's Home Office, NCA), (ii) review and assessment of guidance for international cooperation (e.g. European Think Tank of Football Policing Experts, NFIP Network), (iii) training programmes for front-line officers (e.g. UK Cabinet Office, FBI, NCTP, CEPOL, CoE), and (iv) knowledge exchange and learning frameworks (e.g. UN's Simulation Training Network). He has developed various evaluation frameworks for a number of large-scale exercises, focused on multi-agency coordination, communication and deployment, as well as casualty interaction and training impact review.

Pietro Luigi Iaia is Associate Professor of English Linguistics and Translation at the University of Salento. His research interests are the cognitive-semantic, pragmatic, and sociocultural dimensions of multimodal translation; ELF variations in cross-cultural audio-visual discourse; Internet memes; and multimodal popularization.

Olivia Inwood recently submitted her PhD thesis at the School of the Arts and Media, University of New South Wales (UNSW). Her PhD research used methods in systemic functional linguistics to explore issues of mis/disinformation and deceptive communication on YouTube. During her PhD, she received an Australian Government Research Training Program Scholarship and additional research funding from the Commonwealth of Australia. She is currently Researcher at the School of Computing Technologies, RMIT University, working on a project using methods in systemic functional linguistics and natural language processing to analyse state-sponsored trolls on Twitter. She has research articles written with Associate Professor Michele Zappavigna published in *Discourse & Communication, Social Semiotics, Social Media + Society*, and *The Communication Review*.

Sylvia Jaworska is Professor of Language and Professional Communication at the University of Reading, UK. Her research explores language use and linguistic practices in professional settings, in particular in media, business, and health communication focusing on the ways in which language is used to persuade, manipulate, and perpetuate social stereotyping. She examines these areas using a combination of corpus linguistics and discourse analysis and has published on the topics in *Applied Linguistics, Language in Society, Discourse and Society, Journal of Pragmatics*, and many others. She is a co-author of *Language and Media* (Routledge, 2020).

Minhao Jin is an artificial intelligence professional with a strong background in natural language processing and big data analysis. He holds a BSc in computer science from the University of Liverpool and a master's degree in artificial intelligence from the University of Edinburgh.

Bente Kalsnes is Associate Professor at the Department of Communication of Kristiania University College. Her research interests include political communication, social media, disinformation, platform power. She received her PhD at the University of Oslo. She is the author of a book about fake news and disinformation (2019).

Elizaveta Kibisova is a PhD fellow within the Fakespeak project at the University of Oslo. She completed her master's programme in 2020 at the Higher School of Economics in Moscow and received a joint degree with the Arctic University of Norway. She has previously worked on theory and practice of translation, and the methodology of teaching Russian as a foreign language. In addition, she has collaborated on research projects such as SMARTool and the Russian Constructicon, web resources for L2 learners of Russian. Within the Fakespeak project, her primary focus is on the Russian language. She investigates the linguistic cues of deception in news media by building and analysing corpora of written fake and truthful news articles from various sources, including Russia-based news outlets and social media.

Carmen Lee is Associate Professor in the Department of English at Chinese University of Hong Kong. Her research interests include digital discourse and literacies, multilingualism, and more recently verbal aggression online. Her major publications include *Language Online* (2013, with David Barton) and *Multilingualism Online* (2017).

Sergio Maruenda-Bataller is Senior Lecturer of English Language and Linguistics at the University of Valencia, where he teaches critical discourse analysis, linguistics, and translation. He is also a member of the GenText research group, which fosters research on discourse, gender, and power. His main research interests are in (critical) discourse analysis, corpus linguistics, social and cognitive pragmatics, and translation. He has co-authored articles on naming practices and negotiation of meaning in newspaper discourse and on the linguistic representation of violence against women in Spanish and British contemporary newspapers, as well as book chapters on the role of news values in the discursive construction of violence against women in the press. His most recent publications are on Postfeminism in English teaching materials, the discursive construction of female victims in news reporting on gender-based violence, and the discourses of social inequality in the era of digital communication.

Mehrdad Mokhtari is an applied software engineer at the Berlinguette Group at the University of British Columbia. He utilises machine learning, including Bayesian optimisation and deep learning, to support robotics and science teams in their efforts to accelerate the development of clean energy materials.

Dylan Moore leads the Institute of Welsh Affairs' project on the media and democracy in Wales. He is also Editor of the IWA's magazine, *the welsh agenda*.

Elena Musi is Senior Lecturer (Associate Professor) in Communication and Media at the University of Liverpool where she is Program Lead of the MSc in Data Science and Communication. Her research interests rest at the interface between artificial intelligence and communication, including theoretical and applied argumentation, (mis)information, and the development of human computer interaction technologies to advance critical thinking skills. She has been PI on the UKRI ESRC project "Being Alone Together: Developing Fake News Immunity" (https://fakenewsimmunity.liverpool.ac.uk/), and she is currently PI of the EMIF-funded project "Leveraging Argument Technology for impartial fact-checking" (https://gulbenkian.pt/emifund/projects/leveraging-argument-technology-for-impartial-fact-checking-latif/).

Kay L. O'Halloran is Chair Professor and Head of Department of Communication and Media in the School of the Arts at the University of Liverpool. She is an internationally recognised leading academic in the field of multimodal analysis, involving the study of the interaction of language with other resources in texts, interactions, and events. A key focus of her work is the development of digital tools and techniques for multimodal analysis. Kay is developing mixed methods approaches that combine multimodal analysis, data mining, and visualisation for big data analytics within and across media platforms.

Roxanne H. Padley holds a PhD in linguistics and specialises in healthcare communication, interpreting, as well as language for specific purposes. She is Contract Professor at the Department of Medicine (University of Salerno) and at the Department of Letters, Philosophy, and Communication (University of Bergamo). She is also Lecturer in English for Academic Purposes at the University of Oxford Language Centre. Her research interests include English for specific purposes (scientific English), healthcare communication, and corpus-based discourse analysis. She has published and presented internationally on topics related to healthcare communication and English language teaching.

Gautam Pal is Research Fellow at the Department of Philological Medicine, King's College London. He works in collaboration with the National Health Service (NHS). His area of research is data science and natural language processing.

Tamsin Parnell is Research Assistant in Applied Linguistics at the University of Warwick, where she examines representations of higher education internationalisation in European Commission policy documents using corpus-based methods. She undertook her BA, MA, and PhD at the University of Nottingham, where she specialised in corpus linguistics and critical discourse analysis and worked on several health communication projects as a Research Assistant. Tamsin's PhD thesis focused on the discursive construction of British and European identities in the context of Brexit. She used corpus-assisted critical discourse analysis and a discourse analysis of narratives to examine representations of Britishness and Europeanness in pro-Brexit newspaper articles, UK Government documents, and semi-structured interviews with members of the public. She has published research on media representations of British division and discontent and national identity narratives and representations of European migrants in UK government documents, all within the context of Brexit. More broadly, Tamsin is interested in the discursive and social exclusion of socially disadvantaged groups such as refugees, asylum seekers, and people experiencing homelessness in periods of political and economic crisis. She is also interested in the application of corpus-assisted critical discourse analytical methods to political and media texts. To this end, Tamsin is currently examining the British media's discursive construction of homelessness in the context of the cost-of-living crisis.

Alan Partington, Professor of English Linguistics at Bologna University, was born in Manchester (UK) and studied at Oxford, Birmingham (supervisor Professor John Sinclair) and Siena Universities. His research interests include corpus research theory and methodology, corpus-assisted discourse study (CaDS) particularly into discourse strategies, modern diachronic language studies, evaluation and evaluative prosody, corpus-assisted stylistics, irony, wordplay, and metaphor. His publications include *Patterns and Meanings* (1998), *Patterns and Meanings in Discourse* (with Alison Duguid and Charlotte Taylor, 2013), both published by John Benjamins, and *The Linguistics of Political Discourse* (2003), *The Linguistics of Laughter* (2006), and *The Language of Persuasion in Politics* (with Charlotte Taylor, 2018), all published by Routledge. He was co-founder of the *SiBol* (Siena-Bologna) CaDS research group. In 2002 he inaugurated the international Corpora and Discourse Conference, now a biennial event. He was co-founder and first chief editor of the international *Journal of Corpora and Discourse*.

Nele Põldvere is Postdoctoral Fellow within the Fakespeak project at the University of Oslo. She completed her PhD in 2019 at Lund University, Sweden, where her research centred on spoken language and the combination of social and cognitive processes of meaning-making in English conversation. Her publications on this topic include *Advice in Conversation: Corpus Pragmatics Meets Mixed Methods* within the *Cambridge Elements in Pragmatics* series (2022, with Rachele De Felice and Carita Paradis). She is the recipient of an outstanding doctoral dissertation award from The Royal Swedish Academy of Letters, History, and Antiquities. Within the Fakespeak project, her main objective is to investigate differences in metaphorical and evaluative language use across fake and genuine news in English by drawing on insights from existing linguistic frameworks, such as conceptual metaphor theory and appraisal theory. She develops and uses large corpora for her investigations, most recently, the PolitiFact Corpus, a fake news corpus of written English texts from a variety of sources.

Farah Sabbah (PhD, Lancaster University, UK) is Consultant in Applied Linguistics and English Language Education. For the past 19 years, she has taught English and communication skills and held various educational leadership positions in centres and universities in Lebanon and Saudi Arabia.

Throughout her career, Dr. Sabbah has taught courses in English as a foreign language, English for specific purposes, and communication skills. She has also designed language and communication courses, most recently a course titled "Netiquette and the Language of Social Media". Between 2011 and 2013, she was the Instructional Coordinator and then Assistant Director of the INTERLINK Language Centres (Al Yamamah University, KSA). From 2019 to 2021, she was appointed as Director of the English Department at Phoenicia University, Lebanon, and then served as English Language and Applied Linguistics Consultant to the College of Arts and Sciences from 2021 to 2022.

Dr. Sabbah's research interests focus on critical discourse analysis of the media and teaching English as a foreign language in higher education. Her publications include a monograph, an article, and the contribution to this volume. She has also authored two chapters and two articles to be published in edited volumes and journals in 2023 and 2024.

Dr. Sabbah has presented her research at international conferences, including the Critical Approaches to Discourse Analysis across Disciplines conference and the Languaging Diversity conference. She is also Member of the International Higher Education Teaching and Learning Association (HETL). She has served on key committees in all of the higher education institutions in which she has worked, further demonstrating her commitment to effective teaching and communication.

Michele Sala, PhD (University of Bergamo), MA (Youngstown State University, Ohio), is Associate Professor in English Language and Translation at the University of Bergamo (Department of Foreign Languages, Literatures, and Cultures), where he teaches English linguistics and translation at graduate and undergraduate level. He is Member of AIA (Associazione Italiana di Anglistica), CERLIS (Centro di Ricerca sui Linguaggi Specialistici), CLAVIER (Corpus and Language Variation in English Research Group) and Member of the scientific and editorial board of the CERLIS Series (international peer-reviewed volumes on specialised languages). His research activity deals with language for specific purposes and, more specifically, the application of genre and discourse analytical methods to a corpus-based study of specialised texts in the domain of academic research, law, medicine, and applied linguistics (*English Language across Contexts, Media and Modes* [co-authored with S. Consonni], *Genre Variation in Academic Communication. Emerging Disciplinary Trends*, [co-edited with S.M. Maci]), *The Language of Medicine: Science, Practice and Academia*, and *Insights into Medical Communication* [both co-edited with M. Gotti and S.M. Maci]), as well as digital humanities (*Corpus Linguistics and Translation Tools for Digital Humanities* [co-edited with S.M. Maci]).

Leonardo Sanna has a PhD in digital humanities and digital communication, completed in 2022 at the University of Modena and Reggio Emilia. His primary expertise is within social media analysis, where he developed a methodology for studying filter bubbles and echo chambers from a linguistic perspective. He has been Visiting Fellow at the Digital Methods Initiative (DMI) at the University of Amsterdam, the University of Lorraine, and the New Sorbonne University Paris 3.

Donna Smith is Senior Lecturer in Politics at the Open University, Fellow of the Centre for Online and Distance Education, and Senior Fellow of the Higher Education Academy, focusing on politics and media, active citizenship, and teaching and learning.

Maite Taboada is Distinguished Professor in the Department of Linguistics at Simon Fraser University. She is a linguist working at the intersection of discourse analysis and computational linguistics. Her research interests within linguistics include discourse relations and evaluative language. In computational linguistics, she has worked on sentiment analysis, automatic moderation of online comments, and the language of misinformation. Her lab, the Discourse Processing Lab at SFU, has built the Gender Gap Tracker, an online tool to track the number of men and women quoted in Canadian mainstream news media.

Dr. Charlotte Taylor is Senior Lecturer in English Language and Linguistics at the University of Sussex. Her research is broadly concerned with the persuasive functions of language, and her current projects investigate discourses of migration, nostalgia in discourse and popular communication of science.

Simeon Yates is Professor of Digital Culture in the Department of Communications and Media at the University of Liverpool and Joint Director of the Digital Media and Society Research Institute. He has undertaken research on the social, political, and cultural impacts of digital media for over three decades. A major focus is on projects that address issues of digital inclusion and exclusion. He currently works with both academic and government colleagues to develop policy and interventions to support digital inclusion and digital literacies. This includes working with the UK's Department of Digital, Culture, Media, and Sport (DCMS); the UK's media regulator Ofcom; and the Welsh government as well as charity organisations such as the Good Things Foundation, Cwmpas in Wales, and SCVO in Scotland.

Michele Zappavigna is Associate Professor in the School of Arts and Media at the University of New South Wales. Her major research interest is in exploring ambient affiliation in the discourse of social media using social semiotic, multimodal, and corpus-based methods. She is a co-editor of the journal *Visual Communication*. Key books include *Searchable Talk: Hashtags and Social Media Metadiscourse* (2018, Bloomsbury) and *Discourse of Twitter and Social Media* (2012, Bloomsbury). Recent co-authored books include *Researching the Language of Social Media* (2014; 2022, Routledge) and *Modelling Paralanguage Using Systemic Functional Semiotics* (2021, Bloomsbury). Forthcoming in 2023 is *Emoji and Social Media Paralanguage* (Cambridge University Press) and *Innovations and Challenges in Social Media Discourse Analysis* (Routledge).

1

THE VARIOUS DIMENSIONS OF DISINFORMATION

An introduction

Stefania M. Maci, Massimiliano Demata, Philip Seargeant,
and Mark McGlashan

1 Framing

A discourse approach to disinformation

The term "fake news" is both a famous and controversial term in the public sphere of many countries. It became a defining feature for political and media discourse in the second half of the 2010s, and its effects are bound to be felt for a long time. Since then, "fake news" has become emblematic of a sense of crisis in contemporary political and social life. Along with related concepts such as "post-truth" and the "conspiracy theory", it speaks to a widespread worry about the fragile nature of truth in public discourse and how a culture of dishonesty appears to be undermining the social relations which provide the stability for a well-functioning democracy.

The term "fake news" is also a highly contested term as it has a number of distinct meanings and uses. It can refer to intentionally false news masquerading as legitimate news that can mislead readers (Allcott and Gentzkow, 2017) for either financial or ideological purposes. Indeed, on the one hand, fake and outrageous stories, when going viral, become clickbait and can be converted to advertising revenue (Tandoc et al., 2017). On the other hand, fake news is used to promote particular ideas either to favour some people or to discredit others (Allcott and Gentzkow, 2017). The term can also be used for attacking reporting that one does not like, perhaps the most famous case being former president of the United States of America Donald Trump calling "fake news" any news he did not like. Finally, the use of "fake news" also raises the issue of an increased scrutiny of the ways in which news journalism works, which has implications for how the news media presents reporting as legitimate as well as how the public perceive news media outlets as objective and reliable sources of information.

Lazer et al.'s (2018: 1094) definition of fake news as "fabricated information that mimics news media content in form but not in organisational process or intent" is probably the most well-established one in the academic literature. It should be noted that this conceptualization of fake news avoids directly connecting the concept to the ideas of truth or lies and emphasises both how this information formally imitates media content and how it has not been produced using the same procedures or with the same intentions as news produced by the media. As indicated by Miró-Llinares and Aguerri (2023) from this definition, it is clear that fake news is information that acquires the

DOI: 10.4324/9781003224495-1

characteristic of being *fake* because the producer does not use the same procedures or have the same intentions as the media. In other words, based on this approach, the "attribution of falsification is thus not at the level of the story, but at the level of the publisher" (Grinberg et al., 2019: 1). Furthermore, the term "fake news" as it is popularly used can be as problematic as the phenomena it refers to – it is often used, for example, as a propaganda tool to dismiss critical opinions. For this reason, it is mostly avoided as an analytic term in favour of "mis-" or "disinformation", even if it still occurs regularly in media and everyday discourse.

The complexities arising from the popularity of the term and its positioning as an emblem of contemporary political distress, along with the wide range of social domains in which its effects can be felt, means that it is studied across many different disciplines which focus on various different themes and use a variety of methodologies. An essential element in all instances of disinformation, however, is communication of information, and thus the creation, dissemination, and contestation of discourse. And it is this point which acts as the inception point for this *Handbook*, highlighting and examining the ways in which analysis of the discursive nature of disinformation is essential to our understanding of and ability to address the issues produced by the phenomenon.

A case study approach to disinformation

After the 2016 US presidential election, the terms "fake news" and "disinformation" came to be used interchangeably as a way to discuss the veracity of information found especially on online social networking platforms and the potential threats to social order that contested information can bring (Miró-Llinares and Aguerri, 2023). This is also due to the fact that in society, the term "fake news" has become a mechanism for undermining individual journalists and the professional media as a whole, which may not be related to the quality of journalism but, rather, to brand reporting that one disagrees with as "fake news". The term is also woefully inadequate to capture the variety of information "pollution" that stifles public discourse. Misleading content can take many forms: satire, clickbait, inaccurate captions, images or statistics, real content taken out of context, manipulated quotes and images, and made-up stories. Almost none of these details are captured by the term "fake news". For these two reasons, the term "fake news" should be avoided. Indeed, much of the discussion about information pollution mixes two terms: *misinformation* and *disinformation*. While there are certain generic properties and patterns that can be identified in the spread and effects of mis- and disinformation, "fake news" exact character and influence are always going to be tied closely to the context in which it exists. The media ecosystem which operates in a particular regional context, for example, will have a bearing on how information is shared within a community, while the cultural history of that community is also likely to influence how the information is interpreted. It is for these reasons – the multiplex meanings associated with the usage of the terms mis- and disinformation and "fake news", and the importance that context plays in the character and spread of these types of communication – that the *Handbook* takes a "case study" approach, surveying in detail a range of environs, practices, and events which are centred around the spread of disinformation.

2 Explanation of key concepts

It is worth distinguishing between true news and false news, and between news that is intentionally created, produced, or disseminated. While *disinformation* is false information that is deliberately passed on with the intention to deceive or otherwise cause harm, *misinformation* can be defined as false information disseminated by someone who believes it to be true (Wardle, 2020).[1]

Misinformation and disinformation have been an issue in the history of mass media for a long time. A notable example dates back to 1938, with Orson Welles' radio adaptation of *The War of the Worlds* (Tandoc et al., 2017; cf. also Cantril et al., 1940), which took the shape of a live news report, in a period when not only "the radio offered a more immediate communicative ethos" than any other forms of communication (Enli, 2016: 18) but also in which "[b]roadcast radio represented an unprecedented means of mass communication, and it required new media literacy skills to comprehend" (Enli, 2016: 28). Nowadays, just like in the US in the 1930s, a new form of mass communication which requires literacy skills is employed to spread information: social media.

The rise of social media, based on user-generated contents and many-to-many communication, represented a step forward in the democratisation of the public sphere, as information could be made potentially available to all Internet users: through social media, online information (and dis-/misinformation) reaches mass audiences. "An important facilitator of such distribution is how social media blur the conceptualization of information source" (Tandoc et al., 2017: 139), which is rarely verified by readers. In this process, while citizens can turn into participative-journalists (Wall, 2015) in the interaction with other people, if their post becomes viral – and therefore popular – it receives attention and is commented on whether it is true or not, in a self-fulfilling cycle, thus becoming legitimate news (Lokot and Diakopoulos, 2016).

A consequence of these new means of circulating information and opinion has been a rise in the prominence of extremist and, in some cases, even violent discourse, which is often linked to the use of fake news as a communication strategy deliberately used for strategic ends (McNair, 2018). For example, some extreme right-wing groups in several nations employ the language of protection for national tradition and culture to justify their anti-migration policies. Their racist ideologies become more acceptable to a wider public as they are conveyed through speeches that seem respectable and civil (van Dijk, 1992). Other groups use the same type of language to "protect" their children from official science, seen as going against traditional values and nature. This "weaponization" (Farhall et al., 2019: 4354) of the term, together with that of the synonyms "post-truth" and "alternative facts", has been appropriated by elite people around the world within the information ecosystem for strategic and persuasive purposes "to describe news organizations whose coverage they find disagreeable" (Wardle and Derakhshan, 2017: 5) and therefore diminish the individuals' trust in news media. It is clear that "fake news" is inextricably tied up to a range of problematic aspects of modern discourse, including propaganda, hate speech, conspiracy theories, to list a few of them. When these claims are pronounced by people with authority, for common people it becomes difficult to discern real news from fake news and elements of hatred that can be in elite's speech are not recognised even if they can be deemed harmful, because representatives of institutions never support their arguments with offensive language but rather with vague and ambiguous discourse (Sorial, 2013). As a consequence, these messages tend to be misinterpreted and become therefore acceptable and credible without recognising the underlying falsity or hatred.

Fake news shares a common terrain with conspiracy theories, undoubtedly one of the most popular and influential phenomena in the context of disinformation. Conspiracy theories commonly refer to a set of beliefs stigmatised as false, extravagant, totally irrational, and often dangerous to society as well as to individuals. They are "attempts to explain the ultimate causes of significant social and political events and circumstances with claims of secret plots by two or more powerful actors" (Douglas et al., 2019: 4). A conspiracy theory consists of a set of explanations on matters pertaining to politics, science, the economy, etc., for which the "official" explanations are not accepted. Such explanations are contained in the narratives proposed by the "epistemological authorities" (Uscinski, 2020), that is, those official social institutions, such as government, scientists, academia, media, which are in charge of constructing knowledge of all kinds. Conspiracy theories are said to be affected by "crippled epistemology" (Sunstein and Vermeule, 2009: 211), they are "unproven stories told as truth" (Bergmann, 2018: 6) or "bad science" and a pathology that affects some people whose conduct may damage other individuals or even society as a whole (Harambam, 2020: 14–16). While conspiracy theories are not new at all, there is little doubt that the current information environment, dominated by social media and networked communities, have made conspiracy theories extremely quick to launch and spread and, in turn, they can become very popular and heavily influence the public sphere.

Fake news, disinformation, and conspiracy theories are seen as thriving in a social and media environment which seem to be dominated by a general distrust in "official" news as well as all the information originating from "experts" of all kinds operating as part of the epistemological authorities. Scholars have tried to make sense of this new environment by using the term "post-truth", a paradigm whereby "emotion is claiming its primacy and truth is in retreat" (d'Ancona, 2017: 31). With post-truth, objective facts are subordinate to one's own personal beliefs and emotions and are discarded when they do not fit into one's own vision. This phenomenon has larger implications. As argued by McIntyre (2018), post-truth started with science denial but now engulfs many aspects of society and politics (see also Cooke, 2017).

One of the main functions for which the creation and circulation of disinformation is used is propaganda. Propaganda can be defined as a form of political persuasion which both manipulates and deceives its target audience. Although the word "propaganda" has not always had negative connotations, as the concept developed throughout the twentieth century, and was used extensively in the First, Second, and Cold Wars, it is now seen as a problematic form of political communication, associated especially with totalitarian regimes or those intent on perverting the workings of democracy. The spreading of disinformation can be a powerful propagandistic tactic in that it presents a false sense of reality which can be used either to bolster the image of those in or seeking power or undermine the critics and opponents of those in or seeking power. In this sense, propaganda is one of the purposes to which disinformation can be put, and many of the tactics available to the propagandist make use of disinformation as a resource.

Another concept having a close relationship with disinformation is hate speech. This is primarily a legal concept identifying speech which expresses or advocates violence against persons based on characteristics such as race, gender, sexual orientation, and so on. Precise definitions vary according to the different laws in different countries, and there is always a balancing act between free speech protections and the types of language use proscribed by hate speech legislation. One particular form of hate speech is to present false and derogatory information about a person or people with the intent to whip up prejudice against them. It is within this context that hate speech can become a relevant concept for discussing disinformation.

Undoubtedly, the removal of fake news and hate content from online platforms and society should focus on educating citizens and promoting policies to reduce social tensions. Yet a large problem in combating fake news is the lack of datasets. With this volume we hope to fill this gap. We would like to explain the reasons why *fake news*, *post-truth*, conspiracy theories, and *alternative facts* are so widespread in society and in what contexts, what is meant by them, what persuasive strategies are employed and why, how fake news can be discerned from real news, and how the latter can gain position in society.

3 So what?

In the early days of the media panic about "fake news", the editorial teams of news organisations liked to publish simple guides on how consumers could guard against being fooled by mendacious news stories and how a mixture of media literacy and critical thinking skills could be used to combat the problem. These often took the form of short lists of bullet points with advice on how to consume the news. The purpose behind these seems self-evident: "fake news" is a problem, and thus the identification of where, why, and how it happens is a first step in the process of stopping it from happening in the future. This approach was invariably highly simplistic, however, and often gave the impression that combatting the issues was something achievable by the individual were he or she just to follow these helpful guidelines.

The problem of "fake news" is, of course, far more complex than this. It can be broken down into different elements. There are the workings of the news and other information-communicating media ecosystems as these exist and operate in different locales. An understanding of the various political, economic, and practical forces which shape these ecosystems can provide insights into where reform can be targeted to attempt to align the functioning of the media environment with the ideals (e.g. liberal democracy, freedom of expression) upon which the political system of the state is built.

Secondly, there is media literacy and critical thinking competencies of the population. The generation, circulation, and application of information is a highly complex phenomenon which has immense bearing on how society operates. A simple distinction between "fake" and truthful news, or between legitimate and illegitimate information, does not exist, even if popular discourse around "fake news", with its prediction for extreme examples, would like to suggest it does. Instead, a critical citizenry needs to have an awareness of how knowledge, in the form of information, is produced, circulated, and used so that they are able to act on this in an informed way.

Finally, there are the ways the political system itself manages the flow of information within society. The news media, for instance, is often characterised as the "fourth estate" in liberal democracies, complementing the roles played by the legislative, the executive, and the judiciary. Laws protect, regulate, or constrain the ways in which information is communicated, and the complexion of these laws is one of the defining factors in the type of political system (e.g. liberal democracy, autocracy etc.).

To make the decisions needed to influence any or all of these elements, one first needs a detailed understanding of the ways in which mis- and disinformation are spread and used throughout society. Given the importance of the contextual factors which influence this spread and use, a case study approach can be particularly insightful. The scope of this *Handbook* therefore allows us to survey a broad range of such studies, as well as to examine and explicate the methodologies used for studying them.

4   Structure of the *Handbook*

As said previously, a major problem in combating fake news is the lack of datasets. This *Handbook* attempts to fill this gap by explaining the origin of the terms "fake news", "disinformation", "misinformation", "post-truth", and "alternative facts"; what is meant by them; the extent to which these terms are used in society; what persuasion strategies are used and why; how "fake news" can be distinguished from real news; and how the latter can gain prominence in society. As we will see, the chapters gathered in the *Handbook of Discourse and Disinformation* comprise foundational paradigm for discourse in the context of "fake news" that is large enough to support a variety of approaches, methods, and definitions related to the terms "fake news", "disinformation", and "misinformation" in their application to discourse. More specifically, the *Handbook* is divided into two main sections according to their relevance to linguists: (i) genres and methodologies, (ii) case studies, including (a) politics, (b) society, and (c) medicine. The two proposed sections provide a wide range of specific applications, showing how the concepts of fake news, misinformation, and disinformation are explored in a variety of contexts and for a wide range of applications. Case studies are used to show how the discourse on "fake news" is constructed, what persuasive strategies are used, and how misinformation is created. By using "fake news" models and state-of-the-art methodological approaches, the volume will also make a significant contribution to current linguistic research on the discourse of "fake news".

The first part, *Genres and methodologies*, focuses on some of the genres, such as headlines, memes and Twitter posts, and on different methodological approaches, such as multimodality, corpus analysis, AI, etc., that address how to approach the analysis of disinformation discourse and what kinds of data to use.

The first approach is offered by **Michele Sala**'s research, "The Expression of Bias in (Online) Newspaper Headlines". This research examines the genre of headlines in the US media and shows how bias can be embedded in the formulation of headlines in the US media, which thus become a possible means of codifying partial, distorted truths or falsehoods, either as forms of misinformation or disinformation. While headlines provide clues to the content and the angle from which the content is interpreted, due to the particular brevity of the genre, which requires processes of simplification of the content, they can convey forms of bias by favouring certain views over others, by foregrounding certain elements of information and giving them interpretive significance.

The second chapter by **Farah Sabbah**, "Critical Discourse Analysis Approaches to Investigating Fake News and Disinformation", shows models and frameworks developed by CDA to investigate the discursive strategies used in the production of fake news, the role of the social actor in the dissemination of false information, and the social action of labelling information as "fake news". This chapter presents CDA methods that can be used to study manipulation strategies of legitimation strategies used in the production of false information and the dissemination and labelling of false information as a social action. The study on the fictitious newsletter story "John Hopkins University confirms: You can be vaccinated with a PCR test, even without knowing" shows and demonstrates the CDA frameworks, models, and techniques that researchers can use to answer their research questions. Junior critical discourse analysts can use the models and theories presented as a guide for their own research on fake news and misinformation. More importantly, this chapter argues that critical analysis of the discourse on fake news and disinformation can add to the body of knowledge about the problems and concerns surrounding the phenomenon of fake news and disinformation in the digital age, while also producing potentially more complex frameworks and useful suggestions for dealing with them.

The quality of information and the spread of fake news, misinformation, and disinformation are the focus of **Bente Kalnes**' chapter, "Introducing Digital Source Criticism: A Method for Tackling Fake News and Disinformation". The author updates "source criticism" by analysing its modern twist and proposing the notion of "digital source criticism". She points out the enormous difficulties in assessing the authenticity of sources (and especially news sources) in the digital environment, even among professionals in the field (e.g. journalists), and addresses digital source criticism in its three components: sources, information, and technology. Using a case study (a tweet by former Swedish Prime Minister Carl Bildt that included a photo previously published in a different context), the author shows how easily the public can be misled with misinformation or disinformation and how urgent it is for journalists to use a critical toolkit to detect and avoid fake news.

Paola Catenaccio's contribution, titled "A Model for Understanding and Assessing Semi-Fake Scientific News Reporting", addresses the problem of misinformation in science reporting by identifying theoretical constructs that can help explain the phenomenon of "semi-fake" news, which refers to the reporting of scientific research that is at least partially misleading, even if it does not contain obvious falsehoods. The chapter offers an account of the discursive operations and cognitive phenomena involved in the communicative functioning of semi-fake news, which fall into the category of misinformation: precisely because they do not accurately reflect the intention of the text on which they are based, they convey information in ways that are often not only biased but also lead to conclusions that are not justified by the evidence originally presented.

The chapter by **Fatemeh Torabi Asr, Mehrdad Mokhtari,** and **Maite Taboada,** "Misinformation Detection in News Text: Automatic Methods and Data Limitations", attempts to detect whether or not a news article contains misinformation based on linguistic properties, while focusing on the difficulty of automatically detecting misinformation through natural language processing techniques. Although it is often claimed that the challenge of detecting misinformation on a large scale can be perfectly solved by machine learning and natural language processing, they claim that these approaches fail due to the lack of reliable annotated data. Their "stylometric" study identified certain trends in linguistic patterns in fake news articles. Some of these, such as n-grammes and semantic features, proved very useful in predictively classifying fake and real news articles; others, such as readability features, were rather less useful. They also contrasted feature-based classification models with deep-learning models and showed that feature-based models are better able to generalise across topics given the limited amount of data currently available, highlighting the need for automatic classification methods. Finally, they showed that test data could not be accurately classified when using data that had been tagged based on source reputation. This is a clear incentive for future data collection with trustworthy labelling and on a wide range of topics.

Sylvia Jaworska comes to a similar conclusion in her chapter, "Fakespeak in 280 Characters: Using a Corpus-Based Approach to Study the Language of Disinformation on Twitter", in which she demonstrates that the difference between legitimate and fake news is not so much one of content but is based on lexico-grammatical features. In her contribution, the author compares the language of serious news sites with the tweets of a disinformation site and thus fills a gap in the literature on the discourse of disinformation. By analysing a corpus of texts from the Associated Press, the British tabloid *Daily Mail*, and the tweets of the Russian Internet Research Agency (IRA), the notorious Russian troll factory, Jaworska, shows that serious news tends to use a formal style, while IRA uses a more colloquial and interpersonal style with a higher frequency of certain informal lexical expressions and interjections. In this sense, Jaworska offers a possible set of tools to distinguish between reliable information and fake disinformation.

A first approach to elaborating strategies to combat fake news is the contribution by **Pietro Luigi Iaia**, "Debunking Fake News through the Multimodal Composition of Internet Memes". Based on an empirical study with students from the University of Salento, Italy, Iaia applies the inoculation theory by showing how memes can be used to educate people to resist the persuasive power of fake news and develop a critical attitude towards information. The study shows that memes can be very effective in countering fake news on COVID-19 because of their multimodal text typology and humorous content. It is the multimodal composition of memes that activates inferential processes that lead addressees to question or reject the claims of fake news on social media: Iaia's chapter shows that antiscientific manipulation can be rejected and neutralised by creating a new epistemic foundation through engaging and often humorous multimodal messages. If the inoculation theory can be seen as an indirect way to inform on issues of disinformation – and thus help readers to fight against "fake news" – other methodological approaches can be applied in discourse to identify issues of disinformation also with the help of an artificial intelligence (AI). While these modalities are not exhaustive, they will deepen our understanding of current and relevant issues related to how disinformation is spread and how it can be distinguished from genuine knowledge. For example, **Stefania M. Maci and Simone Abbiati**'s chapter, "'*It's never about #ProLife, it's* *about punishment, hate, and religious repression*'. Polarising Discourses and Disinformation in the Abortion Debate on Twitter", provides an interesting reflection on how disinformation can be detected by an AI. In this study, questions about polarising discourse and disinformation in the abortion debate on Twitter are considered with the aim of automatically detecting the polarisation of attitudes based on discourse labels. When they attempted to instruct an AI to detect disinformation related to the abortion debate on Twitter over a period, from 1 January 2022 to 31 December 2022, they found that despite using a machine, the instruction could never be objective due to the researchers' ideological bias. Nevertheless, they found expressions of hate speech in relation to vilification: their preliminary results show that the more polarised the discourse, the more the group is misrepresented.

A different approach is taken by **Nele Põldvere, Elizaveta Kibisova,** and **Silje Susanne Alvestad** in their chapter, "Investigating the Language of Fake News Across Cultures", where they focus on the methodological issues, possibilities, and challenges of investigating the language of fake news across cultures. The authors refer to the Fakespeak project, a collaboration between linguists and computer scientists whose aim is first to identify the terminology and writing patterns used in fake news in English, Norwegian, and Russian and then to see if the results can be used to improve current fake news detection systems. When collecting data in the three languages representing the three different cultures (e.g. English in the US), there were a number of methodological problems that required creative solutions. The difficulties were somewhat different in each situation, with Norwegian and Russian users having particularly little access to "quality data" (compilations of real and fake news, each separately checked for validity by specialists) for a variety of reasons. The datasets produced so far by the Fakespeak project are extremely diverse. They range from large datasets with news published by numerous authors (so-called multiauthor datasets) to smaller datasets in which both fake and real news were written by one and the same author (single-author datasets). A number of data types are crucial for linguistic analyses of fake news that allow meaningful comparisons with real news, as well as for the subsequent development of automatic detection systems.

In the second part of the *Handbook*, case studies are presented that deal predominantly with issues or specific contexts related to the global and multicultural dimensions of disinformation: (a) politics, (b) society, and (c) medicine.

The "Politics" section begins with the chapter "Disinformation and Immigration Discourses" by **Charlotte Taylor** and focuses on the function of misinformation in discourses of immigration, which seems to be necessary to maintain the far right's constantly pessimistic view of mobility. Misinformation is examined here by considering the emergence of terms that do not make sense (such as "bogus asylum seekers") and the avoidance of terms that are true and legitimate (such as "refugees") in public discourses about immigration. Furthermore, the study looks at the myths that are closely related to current immigration discourses. These include both the myths that have been repeatedly debunked by social data and those that can be debunked by linguistic and historical studies (such as the fallacy that the UK has always been a welcoming nation). In both cases, the research shows how the maintenance of misinformation depends on the presence of contextual or salient information.

Apart from immigration, one of the main aspects of the disinformation revolves around the United Kingdom leaving the European Union. This topic is explored in the chapter "BREXIT and Disinformation" by **Tamsin Parnell**. This chapter examines the spread of problematic information related to the United Kingdom's withdrawal from the European Union (commonly referred to as Brexit). Specifically, it looks at three claims made during the EU referendum campaigns: that the UK transferred £350 million a week to the EU when it was a member, that Turkey would soon join the EU, and that the UK would be overrun by migrants due to the EU's migration policy (through the infamous "Breaking Point" poster). It also examines the phenomenon of Euromyths and their characterisation as disinformation. A case study is used to show that the Eurosceptic pro-Brexit press repeatedly spread disinformation about the EU at the time of the referendum.

The way politicians use strategies to delegitimise opponents is discussed by **Alan Partington** and **Alison Duguid** in their chapter, "New Dogs, Old Tricks. A Corpus-Assisted Study of the 'Art' of Delegitimisation in Modern Spoken Political Discourse", where instances of attempted delegitimisation of an opponent are analysed in a number of corpora of interactive spoken discourse. As the authors have noted, aggressive face attacks and attempts to delegitimise a questioner and/ or their questions are common in briefing discourse (Marakhovskaiia and Partington, 2019; Partington and Duguid, 2021) in order to divert attention from the information sought to the status of the information source. In this study, it is shown that delegitimisation is often accompanied by accusations of disinformation, fake news, or lying when a request triggers an assertion of unsubstantiated information, but also that it is often a response to a question on a topic that is the locus of disinformation.

A detailed overview of the nature of information warfare today and the role disinformation plays in it is offered by **Michelangelo Conoscenti** in his chapter, "The Military's Approach to the Information Environment". Since the public space in Europe is the target of military information and influence activities, the military and political contexts must be taken into account in order to better prepare public opinion for their influence. This would mean prioritising contrasting actions against information operations by foreign states that aim to politically influence public opinion in Europe. Despite the efforts of NATO to suggest specific solutions, its politico-military nature does not allow it to proactively lead change and transformation: NATO merely reacts by trying to adapt and accommodate scenarios within a traditional working model. The result is fragmented and incoherent communication, which is also shared and reflected by the European Union.

In their chapter "Attitudes About Propaganda and Disinformation: Identifying Discursive Personae in YouTube Comment Sections", **Michele Zappavigna** and **Olivia Inwood** focus on analysing social media users' attitudes in response to propaganda and disinformation. In their chapter, they use Martin and White's evaluation framework and Zappavigna's own concept of ambient affiliation to track users' comments on videos published by the YouTube channel Russia Today (RT) about the poisoning of Russian dissident Sergei Skripal. RT is known for spreading disinformation and conspiracy theories, and the analysis of user comments offers original insights into the nature of polarised discourse, with users employing very different linguistic devices to either praise or criticise RT's videos. The authors identify a number of discursive personae, that is, the generic identities that are grouped and represented in discourse (e.g. the nationalist persona or the conspiracy theory persona), and discuss the ways in which their evaluative and affiliative strategies are enacted in language.

The relationship between citizens' perspectives on the news media and their beliefs about politics, democracy, and their own political engagement is the focus of the chapter "Citizens' Perspectives on the News Media and Democracy: A Citizens' Panel Case Study from Wales" by **Philip Seargeant, Donna Smith,** and **Dylan Moore**. It offers an interesting perspective applied to the context of Welsh politics and the various challenges that arise in this context, both from a political, cultural, and media perspective and because of the nature of the union between Wales and the broader concept of the United Kingdom. The chapter reports on the process and findings of a citizens' panel research project conducted by the Open University and the Institute of Welsh Affairs in the first half of 2022. This research project explored how Welsh citizens' access to and understanding of media, news, and information in Wales could be improved, particularly in an era of "fake news". The chapter not only provides an insight into how Welsh citizens view the news media and democracy in the age of "fake news", but also outlines the challenges and opportunities associated with conducting a citizens' panel on a topic of this nature, which academics and policymakers can hopefully learn from.

The problem of disinformation affects all societal contexts. Indeed, a more in-depth focus on society is addressed in "Society", the second sub-section of the case studies. The contribution by **Sergio Maruenda-Bataller**, "(Dis)information and Ethical Guidelines: A Critical Discourse Analysis of News Reporting on Violence against Women", draws attention to gender-based violence and discusses the ways in which the media are (un)informed about violence against women. As a criminal phenomenon with profound social implications, violence against women has attracted much attention, and the media in many countries have developed certain guidelines for reporting on this type of violence in order to ensure greater visibility and sensitivity to the issue among the public. However, as the author argues, this kind of attention has often led to the spread of stereotypes about gender-based violence: the media still tends to portray violence against women as something women should be blamed for because they do not follow certain social rules. Lack of knowledge in the editorial offices and routine in news production are to blame for this phenomenon.

Aspects related to the strategies and effects of disinformation directed against women in politics, focusing on "image manipulation" and "false identity attribution", are covered in **Eleonora Esposito**'s chapter, "Online Gendered and Sexualised Disinformation Against Women in Politics". The chapter explores misinformation, gender, and violence at the intersection of politics and digital media, with a particular focus on gendered digital disinformation, that is, the digital dissemination of false or misleading information that attacks women on the basis of their identity as women. This type of disinformation uses visuality as the main feature of digital communication and is characterised by a high prevalence of sexualising and objectifying graphic content. Critically, it is explained as being rooted in traditional gender hierarchies and media sexism, which contributes to undermining the credibility and social acceptance of women in decision-making positions and discouraging them from participating in public debates.

Giuseppe Balirano and **Hughes Brownen** explore issues of disinformation in anti-LGBTIQ+ online discourses and the resulting claim that sexual diversity goes against the majority of traditional, ancestral, and religious values. Their chapter, "The Rainbow Conspiracy: A Corpus-Based Social Media Analysis of Anti-LGBTIQ+ Rhetoric in Digital Landscapes", shows how these narratives support the theory that a secret, large-scale gay lobby, like the proverbial Trojan horse, is slowly undermining traditional family values in order to contaminate all of humanity. This theory underlies an alleged disinformation campaign reportedly being carried out on most social media platforms. The author's corpus-based discourse-critical approach to the online fake news used and the online conspiracy texts collected on Twitter show that these harmful anti-LGBTIQ+ discourses can lead to the construction of an LGBTIQ+ conspiracy theory that harms a long-suffering minority.

The issue of conspiracy theories is also central to **Isobelle Clorke**'s research on climate change denial. In her chapter, "The Discourses of Climate Change Denialism Across Conspiracy and Pseudoscience Websites", Clarke examines the discourses of climate change denialism in a corpus of texts dealing with climate change and global warming on 186 websites and blogs known to promote pseudoscience and conspiracies. The research found that blogs and websites supporting pseudoscience and conspiracy theories all adopted strategies and arguments known to have been developed and disseminated by conservative think tanks (funded by the fossil fuel industry). The data also show that while overt climate change denial is widespread on these websites, the texts tend to downplay the severity of the problem. In contrast to overt denial, which is increasingly difficult to accept given the growing body of scientific data demonstrating anthropogenic climate change, downplaying the extent of climate change is considered a more subtle and persuasive tactic.

A different societal level in the analysis of disinformation is offered by **Chiara Degano** in her chapter, "Reframing of Fake in Art Discourse", which shows that unlike in the field of news or politics, where what is "fake" hardly receives positive press, art shows a different way. This chapter explores how discourse contributes to a problematisation of the notion of forgery in art. Using different genres of digital discourse, a repertoire of frames has been identified, each with its own specific pragmatic organisation and pointing to different attitudes, ideologies, and epistemological claims. One frame represents the orthodoxy according to which forgery is bad. The associated discursive scripts are those of crime reports, with crime as the consequence. Another marks an even greater shift, where forgery is overtly pursued as a critique of the logic of the art system. In this case, the discursive practices that expose the forgery become part of the artistic project that encompasses the channel through which these copies are offered for sale and the paratexts presented there. The attention drawn to the pragmatic conventions of discourse organisation in this field can reveal the underlying epistemologies. More broadly, the chapter contributes to exploring the discourses of the "culture industry", an area of subject discourse that, like most disciplines in the humanities, has received little attention in discourse and genre analysis.

The final, but not least important, subsection of Part 2, "Medicine", focuses mainly on the impact of COVID-19 on disinfodemic practices on our society.

Roxanne H. Padley's opening chapter, "Exploring Health-Related Misinformation, Disinformation and Fake News", provides some information and terminological issues around the topics of fake news, disinformation, and misinformation as they relate to health-related issues. While highlighting the rise of misinformation on a variety of topics, such as vaccinations, cancer, heart disease, other infectious diseases such as Zika and Ebola, the use of stem cells, abortion, and more recently the SARS-CoV-2 pandemic, Padley's contribution outlines some of the key issues surrounding misinformation both in a broader sense and in terms of its impact on people's health. In terms of future strategies to mitigate the problem, it is argued that the most effective strategy is to improve the digital health literacy of users in general to give them the tools they need to recognise misinformation.

The second contribution, by **Marina Bondi** and **Leonardo Sanna**, "The COVID-19 Infodemic on Twitter: Dialogic Contraction within the Echo Chambers", explores how the views of others are systematically rejected and instrumentalised to support one's own beliefs, particularly in Twitter discourse. Their study provides an analysis of language expressing the author's position based on the concept of engagement (Martin and White, 2005), which indicates the speaker's level of commitment to what is being expressed and expresses the speaker's stance in terms of opening and closing the dialogic space to external views. Using a corpus of tweets and a corpus of journalistic texts on the pandemic, the study shows that not only do certain markers dominate Twitter discourse (the adversative "but", the negative "no"/"not", and cognitive verbs such as "know" and "think"), but that it is also possible to identify patterns that are clear signals of explicit rejections, whether advocating or rejecting a position, and that the verbs are used as markers of ideological positioning.

The lockdown triggered by the global COVID-19 pandemic has shown the important role digital media have taken in our lives. However, as **Dennis Chau** and **Carmen Lee** argue in their paper titled "COVID-19 Parody Fake Voice Messages on WhatsApp", despite the many benefits offered by modern media, there is considerable evidence that these media have also helped to spread false and even malicious information about the disease. Their chapter explores how WhatsApp users in Hong Kong use parodied fake voice messages, an emerging audio-based digital genre that has not been thoroughly researched, to creatively counter misinformation.

A focus on the pedagogical implications related to COVID-19 and the spread of fake news is the main topic of **Maria Grazia Guido**'s chapter, "The Impact of COVID-19 Reports on Multicultural Young People's Social and Psychological Well-Being: Novel Experiential Metaphors in an ELF-Mediated Debate on Fake News". The author offers a case study of a group of university students from different countries who use ELF to discuss issues of social regulation during the pandemic. Their conversation is triggered by a shared reading of a popular science article speculating on the origins of the virus. The first draft does not particularly foreground the issue of disinformation.

The paper by **Elena Musi, Kay L. O'Halloran, Elinor Carmi, Michael Humann, Minhao Jin, Simeon Yates,** and **Gautam Pal** titled "Mapping Polylogical Discourse to Understand (Dis) Information Negotiation: The Case of the UK Events Research Programme" methodologically analyses polylogues where citizens, journalists, and politicians disseminate news claims while tracking potential sources of disinformation in digital media. This methodology is applied to the analysis of the discourse around the Events Research Programme (ERP) in the UK, followed by the examination of data resulting from a questionnaire that participants in the live events were asked to complete, with the aim of developing a methodology to identify how discourse can be shaped as a process to prevent the rise and spread of disinformation.

4 Conclusion

This *Handbook* provides an introduction to the concept of "fake news" from the perspective of applied linguistics and maps this concept from the angle of different disciplines (sociology, media, politics, science) in order to narrow it down linguistically and thus provide valid theoretical frameworks and methodological approaches with which to understand the mechanism triggering (dis-/mis-) information, post-truth, alternative facts, hate speech, and their rhetorical and persuasive strategies, in order to define an automatic model for detecting "fake news", and as scholars, to find a way to propose guidelines for more effective communication that can help laypeople distinguish false information from real information.

The volume is therefore a valuable resource for researchers and graduate, postgraduate, and undergraduate students as an introduction to the analysis of the discourse on "fake news" and disinformation in all applied linguistics courses.

Note

1 Wardle (2020: 71) claims that there exists a "third category, *malinformation*, which is information based in reality that is shared to do harm to a person, organization, or country. This term can refer to instances where private information is made public (e.g. revenge porn) or genuine imagery is reshared in the wrong context".

References

Allcott, H., and Gentzkow, M. (2017). "Social Media and Fake News in The 2016 Election." *Journal of Economic Perspectives*, 31(2), 211–236.
Bergmann, E. (2018). *Conspiracy and Populism: The Politics of Misinformation.* London: Palgrave.
Cantril, H., Gaudet, H., and Herzog, H. (1940). *Invasion from Mars.* Princeton: Princeton University Press.

Cooke, N. (2017). "Post-Truth, Truthiness, and Alternative Facts: Information Behavior and Critical Information Consumption for a New Age." *Library Quarterly*, 87(3), 211–221.

D'Ancona, M. (2017). *Post-Truth: The New War on Truth and How to Fight Back*. London: Ebury Press.

Douglas, K. M., Uscinski, J. E., Sutton, R. M., Cichocka, A., Nefes, T., Siang Ang, C., and Deravi, F. (2019). "Understanding Conspiracy Theories." *Advances in Political Psychology*, 40(1), 1–34.

Enli, G. (2016). *Mediated Authenticity: How the Media Constructs Reality*. Bern: Peter Lang.

Farhall, K., Carson, A., Wright, S., Gibbons, A., and Lukamto, W. (2019). "Political Elites' Use of Fake News Discourse Across Communications Platforms." *International Journal of Communication*, 13, 4353–4375.

Grinberg, N., Joseph, K., Friedland, L., Swire-Thompson, B., and Lazer, D. (2019). "Fake News on Twitter During the 2016 U.S. Presidential Election." *Science*, 363, 374–378.

Harambam, J. (2020). *Contemporary Conspiracy Culture. Truth and Knowledge in an Era of Epistemic Instability*. London and New York: Routledge.

Lazer, D. M., Baum, M. A., Benkler, Y., Berinsky, A. J., Greenhill, K. M., Menczer, F., Metzger, M. J., Nyhan, B., Pennycook, G., Rothschild, D., Schudson, M., Sloman, S. A., Sunstein, C. R., Thorson, E. A., Watts, D. J., and Zittrain, J. L. (2018). "The Science of Fake News." *Science*, 359(6380), 1094–1096.

Lokot, T., and Diakopoulos, N. (2016). "News Bots: Automating News and Information Dissemination on Twitter." *Digital Journalism*, 4(6), 682–699.

Marakhovskaiia, M., and Partington, A. (2019). "National Face and Facework in China's Foreign Policy: A Corpus Assisted Study of Chinese Foreign Affairs Press Conferences." *Bandung: Journal of the Global South*, 6, 105–131.

Martin, J. R., and White, P. R. (2005). *The Language of Evaluation*. London: Palgrave Macmillan.

McIntyre, L. (2018). *Post-Truth*. Boston: MIT Press.

McNair, B. (2018). *Fake News: Falsehood, Fabrication and Fantasy in Journalism*. Oxon, UK: Routledge.

Miró-Llinares, F., and Aguerri, J. C. (2023). "Misinformation about Fake News: A Systematic Critical Review of Empirical Studies on the Phenomenon and Its Status as a 'Threat'." *European Journal of Criminology*, 20(1), 356–374. https://doi.org/10.1177/1477370821994059

Partington, A., and Duguid, A. (2021). "Political Media Discourses." In E. Friginal and J. Hardy (eds.), *The Routledge Handbook of Corpus Approaches to Discourse Analysis*. New York: Routledge. ISBN 9780429259982

Sorial, S. (2013). "Free Speech, Hate Speech, and the Problem of (Manufactured) Authority." *Canadian Journal of Law and Society/Revue Canadienne Droit et Société*, 29(1), 59–75.

Sunstein, C. R., and Vermeule, A. (2009). "Conspiracy Theories: Causes and Cures." *Journal of Political Philosophy*, 17(2), 202–227.

Tandoc, E. C. T. Jr., Lim, Z. W., and Ling, R. (2017). "Defining 'Fake News'. A Typology of Scholarly Definitions." *Digital Journalism*, 6(3), 1–17.

Uscinski, J. E. (2020). *Conspiracy Theories. A Primer*. London: Rowman & Littlefield.

van Dijk, T. A. (1992). "Discourse and the Denial of Racism." *Discourse and Society*, 3(1), 87–118.

Wall, M. (2015). "Citizen Journalism: A Retrospective on What We Know, An Agenda for What We Don't." *Digital Journalism*, 3(6), 797–813.

Wardle, C. (2020). "Journalism and the New Information Ecosystem: Responsibilities and Challenges." In M. Zimdars and K. McLeod (eds.), *Fake News. Understanding Media and Misinformation in the Digital Age*. Cambridge, MA: MIT Press.

Wardle, C., and Derakhshan, H. (2017, September 27). "Information Disorder: Toward an Interdisciplinary Framework for Research and Policymaking." *The Council of Europe*. Retrieved from https://shorensteincenter.org/wp-content/uploads/2017/10/PREMS-162317-GBR-2018-Report-de%CC%81sinformation.pdf?x78124

PART I

Genres and methodologies

2

THE EXPRESSION OF BIAS IN (ONLINE) NEWSPAPER HEADLINES

Michele Sala

1 Introduction

This chapter discusses the manipulative potential of news headlines as the sites where – given the inherent brevity of the genre (allowing only for a limited number of words) and its syntactic and structural constraints (namely, the reduction of phrasal elements like preposition, auxiliaries, connectors, and discourse markers) – information is reduced or omitted, altered or distorted, simplified or generalised, not only for it to fit the requirements of the format but, possibly, also to misrepresent reality, influence interpretation, and foster ideologies. In this sense, headlines can be privileged and strategic vehicles for misinformation, disinformation, propaganda, or in general, the expression of tainted truths (Crossen 1994; Guess and Lyons 2020).

On this basis, this analysis sets out to investigate the codification of bias in headlines published on the webpages of US media outlets, notably when presenting current affairs, that is, events of general interests which – unlike political ideas and causes – would appear to allow little space, if any, for the expression of stance, judgement, or (dis)alignment. The case study for this analysis is the spin following the Oxford High School shooting (Michigan), where, on 30 November 2021, a teenage student, Ethan Crumbley, opened fire and killed four people. More specifically, the focus will be on headlines of articles reporting the legal actions taken against the parents of the boy and the school he attended for disregarding warning signs. The purpose is to identify the ways in which information can be manipulated in order to make it sound relevant, convincing, and, arguably, to corroborate given worldviews.

The assumption at the basis of this analysis is that, firstly, such a manipulative potential can be measured in terms of bias, that is, the favouring of given meanings over others, and secondly, that bias is not a matter of readers' or analysts' perception but can be established contrastively, that is, by comparing similar news from different sources.

For the sake of terminological precision, it should be pointed out that often terms such as fake news, fabrication, manipulation, propaganda, misinformation, and disinformation are broadly employed to refer to "all forms of untruth" (Macnamara 2020: 36), that is, all information that does not conform to our experience of or expectations about reality.

However, although contiguous in meaning, the concepts behind this terminology do differ on the basis of specific referential features. In fact, fake news is a highly evaluative label which points

DOI: 10.4324/9781003224495-3

to – and, notably, stigmatises – forms of falsehood meant to deceive readers in that "entirely fabricated and often partisan" (Pennycook et al. 2018: 1865), while fabrication is a less connotatively charged term with a similar meaning, namely, referring to news with "no factual basis" (Tandoc et al. 2018: 143; McNair 2018). Manipulation is both the act of altering information (Morgan 2018; Giusti and Piras 2018) and the effect of alignment (to be) produced on the reader (Gu et al. 2017), while propaganda refers to the act and outcome of intentionally misleading readers, often due to political agendas (Chomsky and Herman 1978; Woolley and Guilbeault 2017). Misinformation and disinformation are operative analytical categories denoting the act and effect of producing misleading information but on the basis of markedly different promptings: misinformation is the bending or (over-)simplification of reality meant to facilitate representation and interpretation regardless of the intent to mislead; disinformation, on the contrary, is deliberately intended to mislead, to make reality conform to expectation and align to ideology or agendas (Persily and Tucker 2020; Guess and Lyons 2020; Petratos 2021).

What makes all of these phenomena problematic in terms of reliability is, not only their degree of intentionality, but their bias. In fact, apart from ill-intention (even though often triggered by it), it is bias that guides (mis)representation of reality (Capone 2010; Jaffe 2009), which is then discursively codified by prioritising, maximising, and flaunting certain meanings while backgrounding, minimising, or concealing others. This, voluntarily or incidentally, contributes to tainting the truth and manipulating its perception. For this reason, studying bias and how it is textually realised can be useful in order to identify and understand the mechanisms of truth-bending and the forms that reader-misleading can take.

In the specific case of media communication, bias is generally defined as the absence of balance in news reporting (Baron 2006). When reporting an event, in fact, some stories are given the front page, and others are relegated to less prominent sections of the newspaper. Moreover,

> [r]eports can ignore or omit information inconsistent with the message of the story, "build up" information sources that corroborate the story, ignore or undermine information sources that contradict the message, or use colorful but misleading language and images that support the story. These types of information manipulation need not involve inaccuracies, but at the same time address "the narrative imperative".
>
> (Mullainathan and Shleifer 2002: 5–6)

The "narrative imperative" – the need to tell a memorable story that will attract readers, elicit an emotive response, and be easily remembered (Mullainathan and Shleifer 2005; Macnamara 2020) – is the basis for spin. Spin is "the twisting and stretching of truth" (Macnamara 2020: 96), whereby a complex fact is simplified and distilled and made to fit recognisable categories which, on the one hand, favour specific interests and views and, on the other, align "to reader's prior prejudices because this is one easy way to make stories memorable" (Mullainathan and Shleifer 2002: 10). In news reporting, the spin stage follows the breaking news stage, the latter being the site where an ongoing, evolving event is first introduced by a news outlet. As such, breaking stories contain very limited information (often from the same source, i.e. police, witnesses, newswire, etc.), only the main elements of the plot, if known (answering questions like what? who? when? where?) and are naturally open to updates.

The spin stage, instead, begins when updates become available (usually answering questions like why? how? thus providing a causal, chronological, and even moral dimension to the events, cf. Luengo 2012), and information is presented in ways which emphasise certain aspects over others for them to appear relevant with respect to ideas, values, expectations that may reflect partisan views. The spin stage is, therefore, an explanatory as well as evaluative and persuasive one: this is the stage where bias is vehicled and manipulation can be exerted, either intentionally or unintentionally. Precisely for this reason, the present chapter will focus exclusively on headlines used in the spin.

2 Newspaper headlines as (sub-)genre

Headlines are specific titling strategies. Titles are the textual handles anticipating information to be found in the full body of a text. They are the genre that confers cognitive relevance – in terms of informativeness and appeal (Blom and Hansen 2015) – to the ensuing text (cf. van Dijk 1988; Dor 2003). As such, titles are important markers of referential coherence and textual cohesion, embodying the "factuality of designation" – in fact, "how [could one] manage to handle anything, especially things fabricated from words, without verbal handles"? (Levin 1977: xxiii) – and enable writers to index and sequence contents, and also the readers to easily locate informative material when searching archives for specific texts, besides also contributing to priming the processing of text contents on their part (Geer and Kahn 1993; Blood and Phillips 2013; Hurst 2016). With the development of the Internet, these resources have also become important retrieval devices, in that they help users to find relevant contents through web searches (cf. Sala and Consonni 2019).

While titles can be generally defined as the "names" associated to given artefacts and events (books, films, songs, conferences, festivals, etc.), the label "headlines" refers specifically to titles used in news publications (both in their print and digital version) as "visual marks" (Kress and van Leeuwen 2001: 186) that are spatially and typographically distinguished from the main body of a text and are intended to anticipate its content.

The function of headlines is twofold: they both *inform* and *attract* readers (van Dijk 1988; Hartley 2005; Isani 2011). The informative function comprises two sub-functions, namely, a *referential* and a *framing* one. The referential sub-function accounts for the informative content of a formulation, while the framing refers to the type of stance and evaluation expressed or implicit in a formulation (Hartley 2005). For instance, the headline "How Police Justify Killing Drivers: The Vehicle Was a Weapon" (*New Your Times* 6/11/2021) introduces the content of the ensuing article (police's justification of a given act), on the one hand and, on the other, discloses element of negative evaluation concerning the reported event (note the verb *kill* rather that *shoot* or *target*). The attract function also includes two sub-functions, notably an *eye-catching* and a *persuasive* one. The former is meant to intrigue the reader and, mainly, stimulate their attention – this peculiarity has been defined as the "rhetoric of facticity" (Moncomble 2018: 32, typically found in "appealing, albeit inaccurate or misleading, headlines"), "crossword" effect (the perception of some puzzle to be solved, cf. Isani 2011) or "slogan" effect (due to the memorability of a given formulation, cf. Strutton and Roswinanto 2014). The persuasive sub-function, instead, is aimed at encouraging prospective readers to read the associated news article (Kronrod and Engel 2001) – for instance, in the example previously, as the effect of the unusual combination of the words *vehicle* and *weapon* and the desire to find out how they are connected.

From a structural point of view, headlines have to account for the reduced space allotted for their wording (usually an eight- to ten-item one-liner, Banko et al. 2000). As a consequence, in order to be appealing, they have to be extremely concise even if possibly informatively vague, at the level of ideation, and both engaging and recognisable, at the interpersonal level (Ifantidou 2009). The requirement of conciseness determines a way of using the language that is usually referred to as "headlinese" (Garst and Bernstein 1933; Mardh 1980), characterised by "minor sentences" (Crystal 1995), "economy grammar" (Halliday 2003) and "block language" (Firth 1957), where messages may consist of nominal clause, *wh*-clauses or prepositional phrases in isolation (Quirk et al. 1985: 846). Other syntactic peculiarities of headlines are the frequent omission of articles, determiners, prepositions, auxiliary verbs and the verb *be*, the use of heavy premodification, abbreviations, an unconventional punctuation, and a simplified tense system (McArthur 1992). These preferences contribute to defining a style which is elliptical (Firth 1957), where the emphasis conferred to nominal elements favours abstraction and vagueness (cf. Halliday 2003; Moncomble 2018; Ifantidou 2009). Such vagueness, however, does not automatically hinder interpretation. Headlinese, in fact, aims "to persuade the reader to read the news story through use of linguistic manipulation and decontextualisation designed to resist comprehension and prod, lure and incite the reader into reading the following body copy" (Isani 2011: 87). In fact, evidence (Collins et al. 1988; Marks 1995) seems to indicate that the potential effectiveness of headlines does not reside in vividness, explicitness, and precision, but rather in the motivation and the cognitive needs reader may have with respect to given contents (Strutton and Roswinanto 2014).

However, the operations of text reduction and content simplification typical of headlines produce a form of *notional hashtagging* by synthesising and reducing complex stories to general and memorable expressions – functioning as catch-phrases – whereby news stories and their contents are made easily recognisable, easily located on a newspaper page, and easily retrieved through web searches. These notional hashtags "encode multi-layered levels of culturally implicit references which are decoded – or not – according to the reader's degree of cultural integration into the mainstream fabric of society" (Isani 2011: 90, cf. Gallisson 1995). As such, they establish recognisable hierarchies of meaning based on both representational criteria and value-laden forms of stance.

The representational ones consist in interpretive models containing predefined roles, action, motives, and judgements (for instance, representing a given event as an *attack* or *attempted murder* activates a model where the idea of agency and intentionality are prioritised, while they would be concealed through labels like *incident* or *shooting*), or discursive indicators favouring certain readings (for instance, the use of domain-specific terms like *first-degree murder* and *involuntary manslaughter* would presuppose an expert reading of an event, while dynamic verbs like *shoot, kill,* or *wound* would anticipate a descriptive one). The expression of value-laden stance in headlines, on the other hand, will influence the perception of reality according to ideas like right vs wrong, normal vs abnormal, and civic vs anti-civic, which often reflect partisan views (Alexander 2003) – therefore a given event becomes relevant and newsworthy in that it violates principles which are held dear in either partisan worldview.

In consideration of these features, headlines are not only open to bias, but their structural constraints, discursive conditionings, and representational affordances (notably notional hashtags) favour the codification of some form of bias in order to enhance (the impression of) informative newsworthiness, maximise text attractiveness, and stimulate reader engagement.

3 Data and methods

3.1 Materials

The data for this analysis consists in a corpus of 675, where 504 headlines appeared on the official websites of different news outlets established and publishing in the US (whose URL identifier is generally *.com*, i.e. *www.nytimes.com*) and international outlets when their websites contain a full section dedicated, notably, to US current affairs. For the purpose of this analysis, the label "headline" refers to the entire formulation which is visible on the outlet's digital page – with no distinction between head and sub-head – that functions as (or is associated to) an active hyperlink redirecting readers to the related full article. The reason for this extended classification is that, irrespective of their generic category (head vs sub-head), it is arguably the language available in these formulations that will activate – and influence – expectations concerning the content, stimulate the readers' curiosity, and persuade them to process the ensuing article.

When collecting the sample for analysis, the outlet's ideological and political leaning was taken into consideration and classified according to the rankings provided by web sources measuring media bias, namely, *Media Bias/Fact Check* (https://mediabiasfactcheck.com), *AllSides* (www.all-sides.com/media-bias), *Ad Fontes Media* (https://adfontesmedia.com). By cross-referencing such classifications, five macro-groups are identified:

- Left bias (LB), for outlets which are openly to moderately biased towards progressive and liberal causes in terms of story selection and political affiliation and may resort to emotion and stereotyping in their news-making;
- Centre-left bias (CLB), for outlets which are generally informative and trustworthy (minimising, not excluding stereotyping and emotion) yet tending to favour liberal causes;
- Least biased (indicated here as NB, not to get confused with LB), for sources with minimal bias, whose reporting is generally factual and sourced and carried out without appeal to emotion, stereotypes, or loaded words;
- Centre-right bias (CRB), for sources which are slightly to moderately conservative and are generally trustworthy, with little resorting to stereotypes and emotion;
- Right bias (RB), for outlets which are moderately to openly biased toward conservative ideas and causes, which may resort to loaded words, emotion, and stereotyping.

The table here lists the outlets in the various bias groups.

Table 2.1 Outlets in the various bias groups

Liberal			Conservative	
LB	CLB	NB	CRB	RB
Alterner (AL)	ABC News (ABC)	AP News (AP)	Deseret News	Breitbart (BB)
Buzzfeed News	CBS News (CBS)	Axios (AX)	(DN)	The Blaze (BL)
(BF)	Guardian (GU)	BBC (BBC)	Intependent	Daily Caller (DC)
CNN (CNN)	NBC News (NBC)	CSM (CSM)	Review Journal	Daily Mail (DM)
Democracy Now	New York Times	NPR News	(IRJ)	Daily Wire (DW)
(DN)	(NYT)	(NPR)	New Your Post	Epoch Times (ET)
Daily Beast (DB)	Newsweek (NW)	Reuters (RE)	(NYP)	Foxnews (FX)
Huffington Post	Politico (PO)	The Hill (TH)	Real Clear Politics	National Review
(HP)	Time (TI)		(RCP)	(NR)
Intercept (IN)	Washington Post		Reason (RE)	Newsmax (NM)
Mother Jones (MJ)	(WP)		Wall Street	Post Millennial (PM)
MSNBC News	USAtoday (UT)		Journal (WSJ)	Washington
(MSN)			Washington Times	Examiner (WE)
Slate (SL)			(WT)	

Thematically, the corpus collects headlines related to the school shooting that took place at Oxford High school, Michigan, on 30 November 2021. The timeline of the related events (following the breaking news stage) is as follows: on that day, Ethan Crumbley, 15 years old, is identified as the suspect who opened fire and killed three students (a fourth will die on 1 December) and charged with first-degree murder and terrorism. On 3 December, the prosecutor charges Ethan's parents on counts of involuntary manslaughter, for having seen, having been informed (notably by the school officials) about signs of trouble on the part of their son, and not having taken the necessary precautions (for instance restraining from buying their son a gun). They manage to evade (3 December) and are eventually arrested after a few days' search (3 and 4 December). On 9 December, and again on 9 January 2022, lawsuits are filed by survivors of the shooting against Oxford Community Schools for "gross negligence" and for having ignored warning signs on the part of Ethan Crumbley prior to the shooting.

Headlines for our corpus have been found by typing in the search box available in all the outlets' websites the expressions "[Michigan] school shooting", "Oxford High", and "Crumbley", considered to be effective key terms to point to the case at stake (the ones likely to be used by readers to locate information relevant to the Michigan shooting). The time span of this corpus ranges from 30 November 2021 to 15 January 2022 (the date when the last set of headlines had been added to our corpus).

The material collected shows that the spin concerning the shooting was organised by emphasising different aspects of the event. One thread of spin, the narrative one, deals with outlining the chronological sequencing, or the storyline, and establishing causal links between different moments related of the event (1). The emotive thread would focus on the impact the event had on those who were directly affected by the shooting (victims, families of the victims, witnesses, etc.) (2). The evaluative thread is mainly intended to voice the comments and the reactions on the part of recognisable personalities or to express opinions about general principles, like gun control, parental responsibility, school safety, etc. (3). A fourth thread, the judicial one, details the legal measures taken against actors considered (directly or indirectly) responsible for the shooting (Ethan Crumbley, the Crumbleys, and the Michigan School district) (4). (Other themes were also found but thematically too varied for them to be considered as part of a coherent thread.)

1   Ethan Crumbley's "unusual" behaviour prior to the Michigan school shooting. (RB_DM)
2   Hero: Beloved High School Football Player Dies After Trying to Save Classmates from Deranged School Shooter. (LR_IJR)
3   Oxford High School shooting: Guns are more important than the motive. (LB_MSMBC)
4   Oxford High School shooting survivors' parents sue district for "reckless disregard" of students' safety. (RB_FX)

The distribution of headlines per thread is outlined in the table in the next section and, in order to favour comparison, has been indicated in terms of percentage calculated with respect to the total number of spin headlines for each outlet bias group.

The present analysis investigates only the judicial thread and, notably (due to space constraints), headlines reporting measures against parents and school (where the distribution is markedly more varied with respect to the Ethan sub-thread, where variation is contained, ranging between 15% and 20%). The focus on the judicial thread is not simply due to the fact that it is the one counting more headlines across outlets but will be worthwhile also for another reason that is central to this investigation.

Table 2.2 Distribution of headlines per dimension (the emphasis refers to the parts under investigation)

	Liberal Outlets			Conservative Outlets	
	LB	LCB	NB	RCB	RB
Narrative thread	22%	17%	25%	19%	19%
Emotive thread	6%	11%	5%	3%	14%
Evaluative thread	7%	12%	15%	20%	6%
Judicial thread					
Ethan	20%	15%	17%	15%	15%
Parents	25%	26%	18%	16%	14%
School	10%	15%	11%	23%	23%
Other	10%	4%	9%	4%	9%

As a matter of fact, while bias is inherent in the evaluative- and emotion-based texts, and is somehow presupposed in the narrative thread (with texts emphasising temporal and possibly causal links between events, of the type "post hoc ergo proper hoc"), in headlines reporting legal measures, the room for bias codification appears to be minimal, if any. It will be therefore interesting to see how forms of influence and manipulation are carried out when presenting contents apparently little open to bias.

3.2   Methods

The resources used to analyse bias in headlines are drawn from the Meta-Model theory (Bandler and Grinder 1975; Bandler et al. 1980; Katan 2004), a cognitive framework which studies human perception and linguistic representation. The main tenets of the theory are three processes by which the human mind makes sense of experiences (Bandler and Grinder 1975: 25–97):

- Deletion, by which some meanings are omitted from perception and textualisation because considered irrelevant, redundant, or easily recoverable (through comparative or simple deletion, unspecified nominal or verbal forms, or missing performatives, cf. Katan 2004: 133–150);
- Distortion, when experience is interpreted and classified with respect to – or made to fit – existing models (notably through nominalisation, presupposition, and the positing of causal relations, cf. Katan 2004: 151–160);
- Generalisation, where a single experience is taken to stand for a larger category (through universal quantifiers or terms with general referential indexes, Katan 2004: 130–132).

Given the specific discursive nature of headlines and their functions (and sub-functions), for the purpose of this analysis, these parameters require a further systematisation.

Deletion, in fact, may contain two sub-categories, namely, *substantial* and *informative* deletion. Through substantial deletion, whole chunks of information are omitted from textualisation. This becomes evident only comparatively, that is, by comparing headlines in different outlets: quantitatively different distributions of specific information will be indicative of this type of deletion. From a cognitive perspective, aspects which are frequently or systematically omitted are likely to be perceived as being less important than those frequently textualised. Informative deletion, instead, occurs when some informative elements in the headlines – not whole pieces of information – are omitted or when the argument of an expression is missing, typically the case of simple deletion (i.e. *responsible* [of what?], *guilty* [of what?], *to charge someone* [of what?]).

23

Distortion can be distinguished into *semantic* and *conceptual*. Semantic distortion can be found when actors or pieces of experience are represented through specific nominalisation (rather than hypernym), notably through terms pointing to roles and denoting specific actions (i.e. *gunman, shooter* rather than *boy* or *student, shooting* for *event*, etc.), or have marked emotive connotation (i.e. *tragedy, relief, shock,* etc.). This form of distortion is also realised through domain-specific terms (*suspect, count*) or conventional forms which will associate a given referent to a given domain (i.e. *first-degree murder, involuntary manslaughter* pointing to a legal framing of the event). Through conceptual distortion, instead, logical links are established between meanings through presupposition (when new information presupposes old information, i.e. *the shooting could have been prevented* → it was not prevented), through cause-effect relations (when correlation is presented as causation, i.e. *X was given a gun/the school ignored warning signs* → *days later the shooting took place*), or when evaluation- or emotion-based claims replace purely informative ones (*X is every parents' worst nightmare*).

Generalisation, as well, can be grouped into *semantic* and *conceptual*. Semantic generalisation occurs when terms with a general referential index or hypernyms are used to point to specific actors and roles (i.e. *teen, schooler, student* used to lexicalise the shooter; the terms *victim* used to refer to both those who died, those who were wounded as well as those who were present at the moment of the shooting) or verbs with very vague meaning used to lexicalise specific actions (when superordinate forms like *shoot, fire a gun* are employed instead of more specific ones such as *kill, wound*, etc.). Finally, through conceptual generalisation, specific events are lexicalised in terms of general phenomena, thus losing their specificity (*schools* [rather than one specific school] *should be held responsible for shootings; parents* [not only the Crumbleys] *should be charged for their kids' gun crime*).

The application of these parameters to the headlines in the judicial thread reveals some noticeable interconnection between the use of specific terms and expressions – owing to their function as notional hashtags – and given Meta-Model filtering, especially as regards deletion and distortion. This relationship seems to depend on four markedly different ways used by newsmakers to represent the legal action against either the Crumbleys or the school: namely, by emphasising either its facticity as a legal measure, which may result from processes of informative deletion; the counts behind it, evidenced through substantial distortion; the reasons leading to it, or personal opinion about it, both related to processes of conceptual distortion.

Informative deletion for measure. While substantial deletion, being a primarily quantitative phenomenon, can be assessed only by observing the distribution of headlines across outlets (as will be done, when relevant, in the analysis in the next section), informative deletion can be detected in those formulations describing the legal measures (through terms such as *charge, sue,* or *lawsuit*) without the specification of the count, the felony, or the motivations behind them. Omitting such details, on the one hand, prioritises emphasis on the actual action of taking measure and, on the other, may contribute to minimise the gravity or conceal the felony leading to such measures.

Substantial distortion for count. This form of alteration can be found in headlines which mention the count or the felony justifying the legal action and lexicalise such references through recognisable domain-specific formulations (*involuntary manslaughter, reckless disregards*) or mentions of disciplinary practices and concepts (*proceedings, evidence*) which establish a legal framing for the understanding of the content, thus conferring authoritativeness and legitimation to the legal action itself.

Conceptual distortion for reasons and opinion. This distortion can be found in headlines that, besides reporting legal actions, advance possible reasons or point to explanations meant to legitimate them, notably by forcing some alteration, for instance by presupposing cause-effect relations where mere co-occurrence or chronological sequencing would apply. Conceptual distortion characterises also those headlines where claims to the legitimacy of the legal action are found in opinions or comments expressed by individual directly or indirectly affected by the shooting, or involved in the legal proceedings, but also third parties or the newsmakers themselves.

As we see, measure and count headlines are likely to influence the readers' understanding on primarily informative grounds, by offering them informative material to consider and process (although partial and distorted). Reasons and opinion headlines, instead, may bias readers' interpretation on an interpersonal basis, that is, by suggesting or offering preferred ways through which to process given contents.

For the sake of completeness, it is interesting to notice that neither form of generalisation seems to be relevant for judicial headlines, and this can be explained by the very nature of the thread under investigation, which necessarily posits a judicial, domain-specific framing of events and actors (for the opposite reason, instead – that is, given the lack of details – semantic generalisation is likely to be favoured in the breaking news stage, while conceptual generalisation is found in the evaluative and emotive thread – although not analysed here – when contents are interpreted in terms of general principle or emotion).

4 Analysis and results

4.1 Parents-related headlines

As we have seen, the Crumbleys were charged on counts of involuntary manslaughter, for having ignored warning signs, not pulling their son from school, and having bought him a gun. Reference to the legal action against them are textualised as follows:

a Measure headlines (omitting specification of the felony), as in the examples here:

5 Parents Of Michigan School Shooting Suspect May *Face Charges* (RB_DW)
6 Parents of Oxford school shooting suspect Ethan Crumbley *charged*. (CRL_NYP)

b Count headlines (prioritising a domain-specific legal reading):

7 Parents of the Michigan school shooting suspect charged with *involuntary manslaughter*. (NB_NPR)
8 The Michigan School Shooting Suspect's Parents Have Been Charged With *Involuntary Manslaughter*. (LB_BF)

c Reasons headlines (favouring justifications for the accusation):

9 Why Ethan Crumbley's Parents Face Manslaughter Charges. James Crumbley bought the gun Ethan allegedly used in the November 30 shooting, but his wife is also facing charges of involuntary manslaughter. (CLB_NW)
10 *"Beyond negligence"*: Prosecutor weighs charges against accused Michigan school shooter's parents. (CRB_NYP)

d Opinion headlines (legitimating the charge by providing judgements as to its fairness, timeliness, exemplarity – or delegitimating it for the lack thereof):

11 Charging the parents in Michigan shooting *sends a powerful message*. (LB_CNN)
12 Oxford school shooting charges against parents spur debate: Who's at fault? There is no real debate the alleged shooter must pay. The much trickier question, is *what about his parents and the prosecutor's decision to file involuntary manslaughter charges against them*? (RB_FX)

25

Table 2.3 Distribution of parents-related headlines

		Liberal			Conservative	
	Type	LB	CLB	NB	CRB	RB
Informative Headlines	Measure	5%	6%	6%	6%	5%
	Count	9%	6%	4%	4%	4%
Interpersonal Headlines	Reasons	9%	8%	3%	3%	3%
	Opinion	2%	6%	5%	3%	2%
	Total %	25%	26%	18%	16%	14%

The frequencies of these headlines are organised in Table 2.3, expressed in terms of percentage on the total number of headlines per each bias group (i.e. 5% of LB headlines favour measure; 9% of LB headlines favour count, etc.), in order to facilitate comparison.

From a quantitative perspective, we can see a predominance of parents-related headlines – irrespective of the type – in more liberal outlets (where the majority of entries is above 5%), while in more conservative ones, such entries are less numerous (the majority being below 5%). This is a case of substantial deletion. Such a quantitative emphasis on the part of more liberal media headlines is likely to push forward the idea that – even before having reliable and detailed information about what they did – the Crumbleys possibly played a relevant part in what ended up being the shooting, while more conservative outlets, by allowing more limited space for this information, downplay parental role and responsibility.

In addition to that, if we consider the different distribution of informative and interpersonal headlines, we see that liberal outlets, and notably CLB headlines, are more prone to interpersonal engagement, leading the reader to accept the reasonableness of the charges, thus exerting control on interpretation, while conservative headlines tend to be mainly informative (even though the very act of omitting references to reasons for the charges could also be a way of controlling interpretation, by implying, for instance, lack of justification).

By observing the specific distributions per type, we notice that the percentage of measure headlines is similar for all outlets irrespective of their orientation (ranging from 5% to 6%). This is not surprising in that this is information that contributes to the understanding of the chronological sequencing of events (being the event that explains subsequent ones, i.e. The Crumbleys being placed in custody, their evading custody, the manhunt after them, etc.) and, as such, can hardly be omitted, for the sake of informativeness, completeness, and (perceived) objectivity.

Count and reasons headlines are found predominantly in more liberal outlets, hence readers, by simply looking at headlines, are provided more detailed information about and explanations for the actions against the Crumbleys. What is particularly noticeable when reading reasons headlines by LB and CLB is the emphasis placed on the parents buying guns (hence evoking the idea of gun possession – and the relative gun control vs gun right debate, notably a liberal cause vs conservative cause – as being related to their charges (9), rather than merely on parental negligence, which instead is the only element mentioned in the few reasons headlines by more conservative outlets (10).

Opinion headlines are mostly found in CLB and NB outlets, where usually evaluation is used to justify the charges against the parents (the idea in these outlets being that ignoring signs and, especially, offering guns to a "dangerous and disturbed" teenager is ill-advised, hence parents are to be held accountable for that – which is a form of conceptual distortion, establishing, again, an almost necessary link between the shooting and gun possession) (11). The fewer comments found in conservative headlines tend instead to express criticism towards legal measures targeting the parents (12), thus resisting automatic association between the shooting and the parents offering Ethan a gun. There are however some noticeable exceptions in conservative outlets, although very few, which go against this trend and express favourable appreciation for the charges, as in the examples here:

13 Criminal charges against Michigan school *shooter's parents justified.* Instead of getting their son the *professional help he needed,* James and Jennifer Crumbley *bought him a gun.* Ethan Crumbly then used it to allegedly murder four students at Oxford High School in Michigan. (RB_FX)

14 McCabe: Charges Against Parents *in Michigan School Shooting* Are Absolutely *Called For.* (RB_BB)

As we see, notably in (13), these headlines are markedly dissimilar from those in liberal outlets in that they aim at a contextualisation of the case (thus countering the gun-possession-leading-to-shootings framing evoked by LB and CLB): in this specific case, giving Ethan Crumbley a firearm is ill-advised on specific account of the fact the boy needed "professional help". This attempt at singling out the Crumbley case as not being paradigmatic – therefore not automatically interpretable as an evidence of the need of more restrictive gun control measures – is quite systematically carried out by conservative outlets also in narrative and evaluative thread headlines – not considered here – which counterclaim the generalisability of this case by pointing out that Ethan Crumbley was not an ordinary child (bullied and psychically disturbed, with behavioural health problems) and that the parents were neither ordinary nor good parents (they had legal records in Florida, they were reported by former neighbours for leaving their child home alone while out drinking, etc.) – see headlines like "Bullied Michigan high school shooter Ethan Crumbley" (RB_DM); "Prosecutor: Michigan school shooting suspect texted mom about demons, ghosts" (CRB_NYP); "Michigan high school gunman's parents had their own run-ins with law in Florida" (CRB_NYP); "Neighbor of Michigan school shooter, 15, claims she warned authorities that he was being neglected from the time he was eight when his parents would 'leave him home alone to go bar-hopping" (RB_DM).

4.2 School-related headlines

The school district was sued for negligence by the families of two survivors, on the claim that school officials were aware of warning signs concerning Ethan Crumbley (they found the drawing of a shooting and bullets in his possession days before the shooting) but underestimated them (allegedly Ethan convinced school officials that the drawing was for a video game) or downplayed their potential (after meeting with the Crumbleys on the subject of the drawing, school officials allowed the boy back to school, and no discipline was warranted).

The lexicalisation of the legal action is carried out via the same categories seen for parents headlines, namely, through:

a Measure headlines (deleting information about the type of lawsuit and what led to it), as can be seen in the cases here:

15 In Michigan School Shooting, the First *Lawsuit* Is Filed. The parents of two sisters who survived the Oxford High School shootings have filed a federal suit against the district and its officials. (CLB_NYT)

16 Parents of survivors *sue* Oxford Community Schools over shooting. (NB_AX)

b   Count Headlines (positing a legal framing):

17   Parents of Oxford High School Shooting Survivors Sue District *for Reckless Disregard*
18   Oxford School Officials Accused of Destroying Shooting *Evidence*: Lawyer. "Not only did defendants fail to take necessary steps to preserve the evidence, but they *willfully destructed the evidence* by deleting the webpages and social media accounts," attorney Nora Hanna. (RB_ET)

c   Reasons Headlines (conferring conceptual relevance to some elements, for instance the school's negligence, through which to interpret others, notably the lawsuits):

19   Ethan Crumbley *brought ammo, bird's head* to school before shooting: lawsuit. Ethan Crumbley brought ammo to high school the day before his alleged massacre and *administrators knew about the red flags, but failed to react.* (CRB_NYP)
20   Lawsuit faults administrators in Michigan school shooting. A civil lawsuit against Oxford High School accuses administrators of putting students in danger by allegedly *downplaying the accused gunman's actions* ahead of the shooting. Elise Preston reports. (CLB_CBS)

d   Opinion headlines (placing unwarranted emphasis on comments concerning the reasonableness – or lack of it – of the suit):

21   Sheriff: We Would Have Taken Guns *if Oxford School Had Alerted Us*. (RB_BB)
22   Andrew Pollack on Michigan Shooting: "*Arrest Those School Administrators* Who Let That Mentally Ill Kid go to His Classroom". Andrew Pollack said Oxford High School administrators in Michigan should be arrested for not preventing the school shooting despite "red flags". (RB_BB)

The distribution of the various types of headlines is listed in the table here, expressed in terms of percentage.

A general overview of the quantities reveals a predominance of school-related headlines in conservative outlets (where the majority of entries is above 5%), and conversely, scarcer references are to be found in outlets of other orientations, especially in NB and LB (where the majority of entries is below 5%). Also in this case, the significant variation of occurrences among outlets is mainly due to substantial deletion. The emphasis found in more conservative outlets seems to imply the accountability of the school for the shooting. The overall quantitative distribution is particularly interesting in that it is the reverse of what has been observed in parents-related headlines: the same emphasis that progressive outlets placed on parental responsibility (respectively 25% in LB and 26% in CLB) is here placed on school's responsibility (respectively in 23% of headlines in CRB and 23% in RB).

Table 2.4 Distribution of school-related headlines

		Liberal			Conservative	
	Type	*LB*	*CLB*	*NB*	*CRB*	*RB*
Informative Headlines	Measure	4%	5%	5%	6%	7%
	Count	–	1%	–	3%	4%
Interpersonal Headlines	Reasons	4%	5%	1%	7%	7%
	Opinion	2%	4%	5%	7%	5%
	Total %	10%	15%	11%	23%	23%

If we consider measure headlines, we notice a congruent distribution across the various outlets: as with the same category in parent-related headlines, this can easily be explained by the fact that such a piece of information cannot be left out by outlets aiming at providing relevant updates about events related to the shooting. However, the emphasis on the part of more conservative outlets on the possible shortcomings of the school become noticeable by looking at the specific distribution of informative vs interpersonal headlines. In fact, even though interpersonal headlines (reasons and opinion headlines) are overall the most frequent formulations used to point to the school's responsibility (7%+7% in CRB; 7%+5% in RB), this trend is balanced by a comparable percentage of informative headlines (6%+3% in CRB; 7%+4% in RB): as a consequence, readers of conservative outlets are not only pushed to consider and possibly accept the accountability of the school but are also offered referential elements which may substantiate this stance. Liberal outlets, instead, tend to privilege interpersonal headlines (4%+2% in LB; 5%+4% in CLB), where, as can be expected, negative meanings are formulated in elliptic and oblique ways (through conceptual distortion), that is, by avoiding lexicalising the school's shortcomings and the related evidence (23) or, on the other hand, by distorting interpretation and pointing out how difficult it is for schools to prevent this type of tragedies (24):

23 Lawsuit alleges Oxford High School administration *could have prevented* deadly school shooting. (LB_CNN)
24 What Can Schools Do About Disturbed Students? "*There is no* profile of a school shooter that is reliable" (CLB_NYT)

In general, the same ideas seen in parents headlines, loosely related to the dangers of having access to firearms – hence the problematicity of gun possession and gun right – are also evoked in school headlines, but in this case they are configured in markedly different terms. Conservative outlets tend to contrast the association *guns => shootings* – even though only evoked rather than lexicalised – by highlighting the situational specificity of the Michigan shooting (both in informative (18) and in interpersonal headlines (19), respectively) and by introducing – thorough a conceptual cause-effect distortion – a third element that takes apart such an association, namely, the school, which is here represented as not having recognised red flags, not having taken action, and notably, not having alerted the deputies who would have taken the boy's gun and prevented the shooting (i.e. *gun → school's ill-advised decisions → shooting*).

5   Conclusions

The Oxford High shooting was one of the deadliest US school shootings of the year 2021. As such, it has shocked the American public and triggered the need to be better informed about the event. This interest has hyped the media "narrative imperative" and contributed to the spinning of the news according to several thematic threads (narrative, judicial, emotive, and evaluative) over a relatively extended period of time (more than five weeks). Such news pieces are textually introduced by their relative headlines which, by their wording, are meant to attract the readers' attention and let them know in advance the type of information to be found in the ensuing text.

Given the dynamic of the event – a boy killing fellow students with a firearm legally bought by his parents and offered to him as a present – the event led itself to be framed quite naturally in the *gun control* vs *gun right* debate – which is particularly felt in the US and opposes liberal and conservative views – and to be interpreted as an evidence of the danger of owning firearms as opposed to merely being an accident only superficially related to it. Both positions (*gun possession is bad in that all shootings are carried out by people with guns* vs *gun possession is not bad because not all people owning guns carry out shootings*) – irrespective of their perceived reasonableness, or lack of it – are expressions of bias. Even a cursory observation of the material in the corpus indicates that purporting either position is the subtext and aim of several evaluative headlines (dealing with why gun possession is right vs wrong) and emotive headlines (expressing empathy vs disavowal towards those supporting either view), and also of a significant part of narrative headlines (informing readers as to if/how gun possession affected the shooting), where such debate is expressly referred to or simply evoked as necessary background knowledge, either to align with or to counterclaim.

The judicial thread – the one analysed in the chapter – by merely reporting, detailing, or commenting legal charges, would appear to be virtually bias-free or lie outside this debate. In reality, as we have seen, the different ways of textualising similar contents (by varyingly prioritising references to measure, count, reasons, or opinion) observed in outlets of different leaning and, especially, the forms of coherence and various trends found in outlets of the same leanings (favouring, for instance, informative over interpersonal headlines, or vice versa; providing specifications and offering framing or, conversely, omitting them) can be easily associated to the positioning of the various outlets in the gun debate as an expression of bias towards a given position. Moreover, precisely because of the expected little bias, headlines in this thread may be very strategic resources to influence interpretation, manipulate understanding, and lead readers to embrace either partisan position.

Even though it is hard to determine if certain forms of Meta-Model filtering, notably deletion and distortion, are purely due to the structural constraints of the format, or to the newsmaker's will to omit, minimise, or conversely, flaunt given readings – therefore, if it is virtually impossible to establish if they may be read as instances of misinformation or disinformation – judicial headlines can be effective manipulative resources in the gun-related debate, also in consideration of their priming potential, by which meanings prioritised in the headline are likely to be taken as relevant when processing the content of the ensuing article (Hurst 2016). As a consequence, while headlines from the same outlets or from outlets of the same orientation may appear as being thematically consistent, coherent among themselves, transparent as to the content and even truthful, their "truth" is, at best, a part of the truth, a partial truth, and as such a (more or less marked) expression of "un-truth".

References

Alexander, J. (ed.) (2003). *The Meanings of Social Life: A Cultural Sociology*, Oxford: OUP.

Bandler, R., Dilts, R., Delozier, J., and Grinder, J. (1980). *Neuro-Linguistic Programming: The Study of the Structure of Subjective Experience. Vol. 1*, Capitola, CA: Meta Publications, Inc.

Bandler, R., and Grinder, J. (1975). *The Structure of Magic I*, Palo Alto: Science and Behavior Books.

Banko, M., Mittal, V., and Witbrock, M. (2000). 'Headline generation based on statistical translation', in *Proceedings of the 38th Annual Meeting on Association for Computational Linguistics*, Stroudsburg: Association of Computational Linguistics, pp. 318–325.

Baron, D. (2006). 'Persistent media bias', *Journal of Public Economics* 90 (1–2), pp. 1–36.

Blom, J., and Hansen, K. (2015). 'Click bait: Forward-reference as lure in online news headlines', *Journal of Pragmatics* 76, pp. 87–100.

Blood, D., and Phillips, P. (2013). 'Economic headline news on the agenda: New approaches to understanding causes and effects', in *Communication and Democracy*, eds. M. McCombs, D. Shaw, and D. Weaver, London: Routledge, pp. 97–113.

Capone, A. (2010). 'Barack Obama's South Carolina speech', *Journal of Pragmatics* 42, pp. 2964–2977.

Chomsky, N., and Herman, E. (1978). *The Political Economy of Human Rights*, Boston: East End Press.

Collins, R., Taylor, S., and Wood, J. (1988). 'The vividness effect: Elusive or illusory?', *Journal of Experimental Social Psychology* 24 (1), pp. 1–18.

Crossen, C. (1994). *Tainted Truth. The Manipulation of Fact in America*, New York: Simon & Schuster.

Crystal, D. (1995). *The Cambridge Encyclopaedia of the English Language*, Cambridge: CUP.

Dor, D. (2003). 'On newspaper headlines as relevance optimizers', *Journal of Pragmatics* 35, pp. 695–721.

Firth, J. (1957). *Papers in Linguistics*, Oxford: OUP.

Gallisson, R. (1995). 'Les palimpsestes verbaux: des actualiseurs et révélateurs culturels remarquables pour publics étrangers', *Études de linguistique appliquée* 97, pp. 104–128.

Garst, R., and Bernstein, T. (1933). *Headlines And Deadlines: A Manual for Copy Editors*, New York: Columbia University Press.

Geer, J., and Kahn, K. (1993). 'Grabbing attention: An experimental investigation of headlines during campaigns', *Political Communication* 10 (2), pp. 175–191.

Giusti, S., and Piras, E. (eds) (2018). *Democracy and Fake News: Information Manipulation and Post-Truth Politics*, London: Routledge.

Gu, L., Kropotov, V., and Yarochkin, F. (2017). 'The fake news machine: How propagandists abuse the internet and manipulate the public', *Trend Micro* 5, pp. 1–85.

Guess, A., and Lyons, B. (2020). 'Misinformation, disinformation and online propaganda', in *Social Media and Democracy: The State of the Field, Prospects for Reform*, eds. N. Persily and J. Tucker, Cambridge: CUP, pp. 10–33.

Halliday, M.A.K. (2003). *On Language and Linguistics. Vol. III*, London: Continuum.

Hartley, J. (2005). 'To attract or to inform: What are titles for?', *Journal of Technical Writing and Communication* 35 (2), pp. 203–213.

Hurst, N. (2016). *To Clickbait or Not to Clickbait?: An Examination of Clickbait Headline Effects on Source Credibility* (Doctoral dissertation), University of Missouri-Columbia.

Ifantidou, E. (2009). 'Newspaper headlines and relevance: Ad hoc concepts in ad hoc contexts', *Journal of Pragmatics* 41 (4), pp. 699–720.

Isani, S. (2011). 'Of headlines & headlinese: Towards distinctive linguistic and pragmatic genericity', *ASp [Online]* 60. Available at: https://doi.org/10.4000/asp.2523 (last accessed January 15th, 2022).

Jaffe, A. (ed.) (2009). *Stance*, Oxford: OUP.

Katan, D. (2004). *Translating Cultures. An Introduction for Translators, Interpreters and Mediators*, Manchester: St. Jerome Publishing.

Kress, G., and van Leeuwen, T. (2001). 'Front pages: (The critical) analysis of newspaper layout', in *Approaches to Media Discourse*, ed. A. Bell and P. Garrett, Oxford: Blackwell Publishers, pp. 186–219.

Kronrod, A., and Engel, A. (2001). 'Accessibility theory and referring expressions in newspaper headlines', *Journal of Pragmatics* 33, pp. 683–699.

Levin, H. (1977). 'The title as a literary genre', *The Modern Language Review* 72 (4), pp. xxiii–xxxvi.

Luengo, M. (2012). 'Narrating civil society: A new theoretical perspective on journalistic autonomy', *Comunicación Y Sociedad* 25 (2), pp. 29–56.

Macnamara, J. (2020). *Beyond Post-Communication. Challenging Disinformation, Deception, and Manipulation*, Bern: Peter Lang.

Mardh, I. (1980). *Headlinese: On the Grammar of English Front Page Headlines*, Malmö: CWK Gleerup.

Marks, D. (1995). 'New directions for mental imagery research', *Journal of Mental Imagery* 19 (3–4), pp. 153–167.

McArthur, T. (1992). *The Oxford Companion to the English Language*, Oxford: Oxford University Press.

McNair, B. (2018). *Fake News Falsehood, Fabrication and Fantasy in Journalism*, London: Routledge.

Moncomble, F. (2018). 'The deviant syntax of headlinese and its role in the pragmatics of headlines', *E-rea* 15(2). Available at: https://journals.openedition.org/erea/6124 (last accessed on January 15th, 2022).

Morgan, S. (2018). 'Fake news, disinformation, manipulation and online tactics to undermine democracy', *Journal of Cyber Policy* 3 (1), pp. 39–43.

Mullainathan, S., and Shleifer, A. (2002). 'Media bias', *National Bureau of Economic Research Working Paper Series* (Unpublished paper). Available at: www.nber.org/system/files/working_papers/w9295/w9295.pdf (last accessed on January 15th, 2022).

Mullainathan, S., and Shleifer, A. (2005). 'The market for news', *The American Economic Review* 95 (4), pp. 1031–1053.

Pennycook, G., Cannon, T., and Rand, D. (2018). 'Prior exposure increases perceived accuracy of fake news', *Journal of Experimental Psychology* 147 (12), pp. 1865–1880.

Persily, N., and Tucker J. (eds) (2020). *Social Media and Democracy: The State of the Field, Prospects for Reform*, Cambridge: Cambridge University Press.

Petratos, P. (2021). 'Misinformation, disinformation, and fake news: Cyber risks to business', *Business Horizons* 64 (6), pp. 763–774.

Quirk, R., Greenbaum, R., Swartvik, J., and Leech, G. (1985). *A Comprehensive Grammar of the English Language*, London: Longman.

Sala, M., and Consonni, S. (2019). 'Titles in medicine and science popularization', in *Communicating Specialized Knowledge: Old Genres and New Media*, eds. M. Bondi, S. Cacchiani and S. Cavalieri, Newcastle upon Tyne: Cambridge Scholars Publishers, pp. 16–32.

Strutton, D., and Roswinanto, W. (2014). 'Can vague brand slogans promote desirable consumer responses?', *Journal of Product & Brand Management* 23 (4–5), pp. 282–294.

Tandoc, E., Lim, Z., and Ling, R. (2018). 'Defining "fake news". A typology of scholarly definitions', *Digital Journalism* 6 (2), pp. 137–153.

van Dijk, T. (1988). *News as Discourse*, Hillsdale: Lawrence Erlbaum Associates.

Woolley, S., and Guilbeault, D. (2017). *Computational Propaganda in the United States of America: Manufacturing Consensus Online*, Oxford: Project on Computational Propaganda.

3

CRITICAL DISCOURSE ANALYSIS APPROACHES TO INVESTIGATING FAKE NEWS AND DISINFORMATION

Farah Sabbah

Introduction

This chapter explores and demonstrates the potential and usefulness of critical discourse analysis (CDA) approaches in the analysis of fake news and disinformation to identify, explain, and challenge discursive strategies that might be used to convince audiences of false information or push the content creators' agenda. The chapter demonstrates the implementation of CDA frameworks and models for the analysis of fake news through the case of the fake newsletter "John Hopkins University confirms: You can be vaccinated with a *polymerase chain reaction (*PCR) test, even without knowing" (see Appendix). The qualitative approach of analysing one case of fake news is implemented, because case studies are suitable for answering "how" questions (Yin 2003) and are used to gain an understanding and knowledge of complex processes or phenomena in a particular context (Rozsahegyi, as cited in Ndame 2023). In this case, the phenomenon of fake news and disinformation is explored by analysing the language and rhetorical elements of the complex and multifaceted nature of texts.

Throughout history, people have fallen victim to false rumours, gossip, unfounded conspiracy theories, and false and/or exaggerated news pieces of journalism (Finneman and Thomas 2018; McGonagle 2017). However, the internet, online trolling, and self-publishing have caused the exponential growth of disinformation in terms of its "level, breadth, and speed" (Froehlich 2020: 37). As a result, in the digital era, people are deluged with false or misleading information on a daily basis. The results of a Pew Research Center 2019 survey of US adults show that the participants were very concerned about made-up news and information because of its negative effects on Americans' trust in their own government, political leaders' capacity to accomplish their work, and one another as citizens (Mitchell et al. 2019). The findings of the Pew Research Center study reaffirm that the news and information people consume affect their choices concerning politics, health, and finances (Rubin 2022). Therefore, the consumption of fake news and disinformation may have potentially harmful effects on people's lives when considering how these types of information have affected some people's eagerness to get vaccinated, for instance.

The phrase "fake news" was declared word of the year in 2017 by Collins Dictionary (Flood 2017), and in response to an increasing acknowledgement of the prevalence of fake news and disinformation, a large body of research has emerged (Abu Arqoub et al. 2020). A systematic review

DOI: 10.4324/9781003224495-4

conducted by Abu Arqoub et al. (2020) found that the majority of the studies on fake news were published in 2017 and 2018. Abu Arqoub et al. (2020) provide a possible explanation for this finding, which is that the phrase "fake news" became especially popular during the 2016 US presidential elections and since then, and Cunha et al.'s (2018) study found that the conceptualisation of fake news in news articles became more negative and focused more on politics after the elections. Fake news and disinformation deserve scholarly attention because they have been shown to have critical effects on our everyday political and social lives (Alba-Juez and Mackenzie 2019; Devereux and Power 2019; McGonagle 2017; Ribeiro and Ortellado 2018).

Fake news is a complex and nuanced phenomenon of disseminating false information. Most fake news is comprised of logical fallacies and an understated mixture of true and false information (Alba-Juez and Mackenzie 2019), and fake news also tends to present one-sided arguments that do not consider alternative points of view followed by a rebuttal as per the Toulmin model (Vamanu 2019). Through a critical reading of 34 academic articles that examined "fake news", published between 2003 and 2017, Tandoc et al. (2018)'s study yielded a typology of fake news that is based on the dimensions of facticity and intention. Tandoc et al. (2018) define facticity as "the degree to which fake news relies on facts" (p. 147), while intention refers to "the degree to which the creator of fake news intends to mislead" (p. 147). For example, the purpose of news satire television programs such *The Daily Show*, an American late-night talk show, is not deception but entertainment and humour, and the show is presented as a comedy show that starts with a disclaimer that it is not a real news show. Therefore, fake news is not always produced deliberately or with the intention to deceive. False information may simply result from an error, or what is referred to as "misinformation" (Alba-Juez and Mackenzie 2019; Froehlich 2020). "Disinformation", on the other hand, is false information that is deliberately created and disseminated to mislead the audience for various purposes (Alba-Juez and Mackenzie 2019; Bartlett 2020; Froehlich 2020). Allcott and Gentzkow (2017) define fake news as news articles that spread what would be referred to as "disinformation", albeit they do not use the term. An example of disinformation is what would later prove to be a completely fabricated story about the murder of an FBI agent involved in the Hillary Clinton email leaks, which implied Clinton's involvement in the murder (Alba-Juez and Mackenzie 2019).

Fake news and disinformation content are created and disseminated for myriad reasons. Allcott and Gentzkow (2017) identify two motives for producing fake news that spreads disinformation. The first reason is the financial incentive because they are sensational and thus draw the clicks of the audience, which in turn brings in advertising revenue. The second reason is that fake news that disseminates disinformation allows its creators to propagate certain ideas and gain backing for the people they support. Bartlett (2020: 17) suggests that disinformation is essentially driven by an agenda, stating that it is "deliberately false information, especially when supplied by a government or its agent to a foreign power or to the media, with the intention of influencing the policies or opinions of those who receive it".

Disinformation can achieve its purpose when it aligns with people's set of beliefs. People typically seek information that supports their beliefs and ignore or dispute those that oppose them because of "confirmation bias" (Krause et al. 2019), a form of unmotivated self-deception (Froehlich 2020). The internet exacerbates confirmation bias because both information and disinformation are equally and readily accessible. As Froehlich (2020: 38) explains,

> What is new in the Age of Disinformation is that anyone who believes anything can find support for it, no matter how ignorant, wrong, or true, whether it is a conspiracy theory, the flat-earth society, white supremacy, or aliens visiting earth. Google indifferently supplies both information and disinformation.

The conceptualization of fake news becomes more complex when considering that any news content may be considered fake news merely by questioning its veracity or accusing it of being false. Dalkir and Katz's (2020: XXVIII) definition of fake news, for example, is that it is "false, exaggerated, or other problematic news stories whose accuracy is questioned (though 'problematic' may be in the eye of the beholder, and different audiences may question a claim's accuracy for different reasons or motives)". Therefore, it is sufficient for news content to be *perceived* or constructed as fake for it to be considered as "fake news". The concern is labelling information as fake news may question information that stems from reliable sources, evidence, facts, and reason; such attacks on reliable information are amplified by a government that would label it as fake news if it does not align with its views (McGonagle 2017).

Much of the fake news and disinformation literature has investigated the subject through qualitative methods, and discourse analysis was found to be one of the most frequently used data collection techniques (Abu Arqoub et al. 2020). Information is, after all, shared mainly through the semiotic resources of language. This chapter argues that an analysis of the discourse of fake news and disinformation with a *critical* lens can contribute significantly to the literature on the issues and concerns surrounding the phenomenon of fake news and disinformation in the digital era while also potentially developing frameworks and actionable recommendations to combat this phenomenon. To pursue critical discourse analysis (CDA), a multidisciplinary approach (see Van Dijk 2001) that combines discourse analysis with theories and frameworks from other disciplines is highly recommended. Vamanu (2019), for example, analysed ten strategies for utilising fake news for propagandistic purposes based on a framework from argumentation theory that describes the ten dimensions of propaganda (Walton 2007) and critical discourse research (CDR) approaches, which refer to the German sociologist Reiner Keller's "Sociology of Knowledge Approach to Discourse" (SKAD) research program and critical discourse studies.

To achieve the purpose of this chapter, the CDA frameworks and models that analyse the discourse-pragmatic level, rhetoric, and context will be introduced and their implementation demonstrated through the article case study to answer research questions about the following aspects of the phenomenon of fake news and disinformation:

1 The strategies used in fake news and disinformation content to manipulate or mislead audiences;
2 The legitimation strategies used to validate fake news and disinformation.

The previously mentioned aspects of the phenomenon are analysed using the following CDA frameworks and models:

Appraisal theory

The appraisal framework presents the resources in English that describe the language of evaluation. Influenced by Halliday's systemic-functional linguistics model (Halliday and Matthiessen 2014), Martin and White (2005) developed the appraisal model situating it on the discourse-semantic level of language.

Argumentation strategies

Argumentation theory describes the rules for arguing rationally (Reisigl and Wodak 2005). Analysing faulty reasoning, or "logical fallacies" (Van Vleet 2021) and inference structures allows us to draw the premise and conclusion of an argument, or "argumentation schemes" (Walton 2007).

Legitimation strategies

Legitimation is the explanation or justification for certain practices by institutions such as the school system (Van Leeuwen 2007). Legitimation is achieved through strategies that support certain actions and views. Alternatively, certain strategies may be used to exclude or criticise memberships, views, actions, values, norms, and access to certain social resources, hence de-legitimised (Van Dijk 1998). Van Leeuwen (2007, 2008) developed a model for legitimation by describing four main strategies (authorisation, moral evaluation, rationalisation, and mythopoesis) that allow researchers to analyse the manner in which legitimation is constructed in discourse as well as reflect on issues pertaining to legitimation. This chapter considers the strategies that are used in fake news and disinformation content to legitimise the news content and strengthen its credibility.

The proliferation of fake news and disinformation in the media calls for immediate attention. The development of digital literacy and critical thinking skills can equip the individual with the tools for navigating through the digital world of information. In response to the fake news and disinformation phenomenon, for example, the International Federation of Library Association and Institutions published an infographic online on how to spot fake news with eight simple steps based on Factcheck.org's 2016 article on "How to Spot Fake News" (International Federation of Library Associations and Institutions 2017). The steps are as follows: (1) check the source, (2) read the whole story, not just the headline, (3) learn more about the author, (4) check the supporting information, (5) check that the story is not old news, (6) check if the article is meant to be satirical, (7) consider your biases, and (8) consult an expert. CDA provides a deeper understanding of fake news and disinformation content at the level of language, text, and discourse that can further educate and elaborate on the implementation of the aforementioned steps. As previously mentioned, fake news is also more nuanced than the mere dissemination of false information. The CDA frameworks, strategies, and models presented in this chapter were selected because they can provide valuable and in-depth understanding and insights into the conceptualization, language, rhetoric, and other semiotic characteristics of fake news and disinformation in terms of the strong emotions invoked as a persuasive strategy, its engagement with the audience in the text, the content's typically faulty logical reasoning, and the strategies used to validate if it's fake news. Moreover, the connections these characteristics have with the socio-political and historical background of the context in which they emerge may help policymakers, decision-makers, and various institutions gain insight into the phenomenon of fake news and disinformation, whilst considering its social and political repercussions.

The next section introduces CDA and how the "critical" aspect of this type of discourse analysis is key to investigating the social problem that a study chooses to focus on. The chapter then presents the article that is used as a case study for each of the selected CDA approaches and their application, followed by concluding remarks.

Critical discourse analysis

Critical discourse analysis (CDA) is a branch of linguistics that includes an array of approaches to analysing discourse, which are motivated by an identified social or political problem (Meyer 2001). This chapter adopts Fairclough et al.'s (2011: 2) definition of discourse as "an analytical category describing a vast array of meaning-making resources available to us" because it is broad enough to encompass all the linguistic and rhetorical features of oral and written texts. Nonlinguistic resources such as gestures, images, or any other multimedia aspect can be considered as well (Meyer 2001; Van Dijk 2001; Van Leeuwen 2008). CDA is distinguishable from other branches of linguistics in its conceptualisation of the relationship between language and society and its approach to methodology (Fairclough et al. 2011).

Fairclough et al. (2011: 2) consider discourse to be "socially influential", so discursive practices may yield ideological effects. Ideology is a complex concept to define for historical, political, and even ideological reasons (Van Dijk 1998). Van Dijk (1998)'s multidisciplinary theory of ideology incorporates Fairclough et al.'s (2011) understanding of the concept. According to Van Dijk (1998: 5), ideology is a "system of ideas" that have been considered to be within the realm of thought and belief, to be social in that it is often linked to "group interests, conflicts or struggle", and to be utilised "to legitimate or oppose power and dominance, or symbolize social problems and contradictions".

A key interest in discourse for CDA is its relationship to power because it can shape social structures and maintain pre-existing ones (Fairclough et al. 2011). CDA research considers the ideological, cultural, and social factors that comprise the context in addition to relationships *between* texts, that is, intertexuality (Meyer 2001). When discourse presents certain assumptions as common sense, even if they are false, it may reproduce stereotypes and assumptions that derive from hegemonic discourses such as sexist or racist discourse (Fairclough et al. 2011). The "critical" component of CDA originates from Marxist and Frankfurt School of critical theory and is a reference to *critique*, which serves to explain the problematic social phenomena and change them (Fairclough et al. 2011). Thus, the CDA research agenda is that of emancipation (Fairclough et al. 2011); it is to advocate for the underdogs, the oppressed, and the marginalised, and its research findings are also of practical value for the reader (Meyer 2001). Because of CDA's emancipatory agenda, critical discourse analysts aim for transparency by announcing their interests, political or otherwise (Fairclough et al. 2011).

CDA's activist agenda may be a departure from a distant and objective stance that other social sciences adopt, but the research is based on well-established approaches, theories, and methodologies derived from social science. CDA does not fixate on a particular theory or methodology; its methods originate from various disciplines, and the methods used are selected based on the topic being investigated (Fairclough et al. 2011). For example, the analytical and theoretical tools used to compare the representation of social actors involved in a particular event in two newspapers may be different from the persuasive strategies used in political speeches during the US elections, albeit both would require textual and/or multimodal analysis.

Since CDA recognises the power of discourse and its effect on social life, it would certainly consider the proliferation of fake news and disinformation as an alarming social issue that needs to be addressed. In fact, CDA studies heavily centre on the language of the media (see for example Bednarek and Caple 2017; Fowler 1991; Richardson 2017; Talbot 2007). The troubling effects of fake news and disinformation are at their core an issue of deception and manipulation of the masses that can lead to further polarisation of society and can heighten discrimination and othering leading to social conflicts such as the anti-vaccination movement that has been campaigning against vaccinations on social media (Maci 2019) and political polarisation during the 2016 US elections (Alba-Juez and Mackenzie 2019).

Before presenting the CDA approaches that can be used to research fake news and disinformation, it is important to note two key assumptions. The first is that strategies and social actions explored in this chapter operate based on the assumptions that texts are dialogical (Bakhtin 2010) and that the fake news content creators and the audience together co-construct fake news (Haw 2021). The second is that falsity cannot be interpreted at the linguistic level of semantics and grammar (Alba-Juez and Mackenzie 2019). Therefore, critical discourse analysts will need to analyse other aspects of a text, namely, the discourse-pragmatic level, rhetoric, and context, to interpret: (1) The ways in which ideologies, power, and inequalities are formulated in the discourse of fake news and disinformation through strategies of manipulation and legitimation; (2) the dialogic relationship between the fake news and disinformation text and its readers.

Critical discourse analysis approaches to analysing fake news and disinformation

Examples of the application of the critical discourse analysis approaches to analysing fake news and disinformation are derived from the fake newsletter titled "John Hopkins University confirms: You can be vaccinated with a PCR test, even without knowing" published on 13 April 2021 (see Appendix). A summary of the argument of the newsletter using the writer's point of view is what follows:

The World Health Organization (WHO) is insisting that all people around the world get vaccinated against the coronavirus disease of 2019 (COVID-19). But this is a ruse because they are in fact conspiring to inject people with a "vaccine" that genetically modifies people for the purpose of controlling the masses. Since there is growing resistance against the messenger ribonucleic acid (mRNA) vaccine, an alternative way of ensuring that people take the vaccine has been devised. A group of scientists from a reputable institution, John Hopkins University, has developed the technology that can be used to pursue the aforementioned plan. They have developed a microdevice called a "theragripper" that is administered through the rectum and passes through the gastrointestinal tract to attach itself to the tissue and autonomously release a drug. The theragripper is a star-shaped micro-device that can carry a drug and release it slowly in the body. Because it is an extremely small dust-like particle that can be administered via a swab, they will eventually begin to use this medical advancement to administer the vaccine orally, or possibly anally, under the pretense of administering a *PCR, a laboratory technique conducted* to test for the COVID-19 virus, thus carrying out the plan of the WHO masterminds. The establishment's [It is not quite clear if the article is referring to the WHO or the government here.] plan to have everyone vaccinated is for the purpose of practising human eugenics to control the masses.

The newsletter was published on the Dr. Leonard Coldwell website and posted on the social networking site, Facebook. Right below the headline is what appears to be the name of the publication: *Health Freedom*. A simple Google search shows that Coldwell has a strong social media presence and has published books. He is a highly controversial figure; one of the top search results is an article published by *Poynter* (2020) that fact-checked a video in which Dr. Coldwell claims that the coronavirus was created artificially as part of a conspiracy to insert chips in people. As for access to information, the sources cited in the newsletter are accessible to the public.

Appraisal theory

Martin and White's (2005) appraisal model consists of three systems: ATTITUDE, ENGAGEMENT, and GRADUATION. ATTITUDE refers to the language that explicitly or implicitly invokes the emotions (affect) triggered because of or towards an entity (e.g. people are **afraid**[1] [insecurity] of the vaccines), the judgements made about them (e.g. The WHO is **lying** [lack of veracity] to the public about the vaccines), and appreciation for the aesthetic and inanimate (e.g. The mRNA vaccine is **dangerous** [negative valuation]). ENGAGEMENT refers to the voice and the position of the writer or speaker as well as the attempt to position the reader or hearer vis-à-vis the subject of evaluation, therefore affecting the former's stance and attitude. The ENGAGEMENT system in the appraisal model is useful for analysing the writer's and putative reader's positioning vis-à-vis the text (Martin and White 2005). The propositions made in a text or utterance could be presented as expansive, acknowledging the multitude of explanations, or they may be presented as contractive, negating other possible explanations or points of view. Linguistic devices such as verbal and mental processes (e.g. ***claim, argue, said, believe***), adverbs (e.g. ***never, rarely, possibly***), and modals (e.g. ***may, will***) are commonly used to position the reader; for example, critics **believe** that the mRNA vaccine is dangerous [an expansive attribution of the proposition to the critics that simply conveys the views of others]. As for GRADUATION, it is the gradability of attitudinal meanings and the scaling of the engagement features of a text or utterance in terms of the writer/ speaker's intensity and commitment to the proposition; for example, I am **deeply** concerned about the effects of the vaccine.

In the fake newsletter, the claim is that mRNA vaccinations against COVID-19 in fact alter the genes "in order to patent or own" the people. This alleged conspiracy is described as "chilling", as is shown in the following sentences from the article:

(1) It seems like science fiction and is **chilling**, but the metohodes [sic] and techniques are available.
(2) [Subheading] Vaccinations increasingly scrutinized and the **chilling** alternative.
(3) What is particularly **chilling** is that the vast majority do not even know what the mRNA vaccine is doing in their bodies.

The adjective "chilling" invokes explicit feelings of fear and insecurity, especially when assuming a compliant reading position (Martin and White 2005) that is willing to consider or adopt the assumptions and the somewhat Orwellian narrative of the "establishment" that seeks to control the masses and suppress their freedom.

The WHO, and perhaps governments but this cannot be determined for sure, are accused of being unethical and immoral as can be analysed in the following sentence:

(4) Now several experts and former mainstream journalists like John O'Sullivan are warning that the massive PCR testing campaign could be a **WHO vaccination program in disguise**.

An attitudinal analysis of "WHO vaccination program in disguise" could be double-coded as a negative appreciation of the WHO vaccination program for its harmful effects or an indirect negative judgement of the WHO for its dishonesty.

The vilification of the WHO is juxtaposed with the positive judgement of its critics, as is shown in the examples here:

(5) Meanwhile, **resistance is emerging** even within the conventional medical community.
(6) Now several experts and former mainstream journalists like John O'Sullivan **are warning** that the massive PCR testing campaign could be a WHO vaccination program in disguise.

The journalists and experts are referred to as the "resistance" and "are warning" the public about the vaccination, which invokes positive judgement, as well as triggers feelings of insecurity in the putative audience. As for those who do not agree with this aforementioned narrative, they are judged negatively for their incapacity to believe or handle the bitter truth about the vaccination as example (7) shows:

(7) They simply **allow themselves to be blindly** vaccinated.

Because the vast majority of people do not know about the harmful effects of the mRNA vaccine, they are helpless and are victims of this conspiracy.

The conspiracy to vaccinate people without their knowledge or consent for the purposes of genetic modification is presented as a fact that is supported by scientific and historical evidence. Nevertheless, the reader is assumed to be sceptical because the article positions the reader as someone that needs to be persuaded in sentences such as examples (8) and (9):

(8) **It seems like science fiction and chilling, but** the metohodes [sic] and techniques are available.
(9) **If you can't imagine** the government administering toxins to you against your will and without your consent, think of all the horrific experiments on humans that were admitted afterwards and which, according to *Wikipedia*, [7] have continued well into modern times.

The mental processes in bold in examples (8) and (9) are a contractive engagement device that serves to counter those who may dismiss the claim that the mRNA vaccination program is a conspiracy to control the masses as implausible with the proposition that the scientific evidence, the John Hopkins published study, and the historical evidence exist.

Argumentation theory

The inclusion of argumentation theory in CDA approaches, particularly the discourse-historical approach (Reisigl and Wodak 2005; Wodak 2001), attests to the interdisciplinarity of CDA. The writer or speaker attempts to appeal to the audience's emotions, logic, or ethos. When an argument contains faulty reasoning, it is referred to as a "logical fallacy" (Van Vleet 2021). Logical fallacies can be categorized into formal or informal logical fallacies. In formal logical fallacies, a part of the structure of the argument is flawed. In informal logical fallacies, a part of the argument's content is flawed (Van Vleet 2021). This chapter tackles informal logical fallacies as it emerges in the everyday discourse of the media, such as ad hominem, which is an attempt to counter an opposing claim by attacking the opposer's character rather than the argument (Walton 2007). Argumentation schemes are helpful in analysing informal logical fallacies (Walton 2007). Argumentation schemes are structures that allow inferences to be made about the premise and conclusion of common arguments made in the discourse of everyday life and more specialised contexts such as law and science (Walton 2007), such as an argument that is supported by expert opinion, which translates to "if the statement is made by an expert, then the statement is true". Despite the fact that fake news may mention sources and evidence to support a claim, the reader may not be diligent enough to pay attention to the way the information is synthesised or check the credibility of the sources mentioned (Alba-Juez and Mackenzie 2019).

The article serves as an example of how true and false information can be combined and presented as "evidence", as the piece of disinformation that the article uses to support its claim is that the microdevices called "theragrippers" have been developed to slowly release the drugs in the body and can be administered with a cotton swab. The picture obtained from the study, or perhaps O'Sullivan's article, shows a swab that contains theragrippers, but the swab was actually used to merely illustrate the micro size of the theragrippers. In fact, the scientific journal article clearly states that the theragrippers in this experiment were administered rectally through endoscopy on animals (Ghosh et al. 2020), but this detail is not mentioned in the newsletter. Instead, it is suddenly brought to the reader's attention that the PCR test can be performed anally, as is the case in China. The combination of this aforementioned true and false information is used to support the claim that people will be asked to conduct the PCR test rectally to in fact vaccinate them without their knowledge, and that vaccination will harm them and alter their DNA.

Two logical fallacies that can be identified in the article are ad hominem and slippery slope. A rhetorical analysis of the fake newsletter article shows that the writer committed an ad hominem to support the claim that the public may be secretly vaccinated. The article accuses the WHO and the authorities of planning to conduct gene therapy based on a very ill-supported assumption that the mRNA vaccine is in fact not a vaccine but a drug that will modify our genetic makeup and that there is a conspiracy to have the masses vaccinated without their knowledge. Another type of faulty logic found in the article is the slippery slope. A slippery slope is a logical fallacy that is committed when a writer or speaker argues that a certain event or action will yield a series of events that lead to a terrible result (Van Vleet 2021). In the newsletter, the line of reasoning is that scientists have created a device that will help certain patients by improving the effectiveness of long-term drug delivery, so the WHO will use the device to vaccinate people under the false pretense of testing for COVID-19.

The article assumes ill-intent on behalf of the WHO. The text does not show that this assumption is based on concrete evidence, but by relying on the argument from example and fear appeal argument argumentation schemes. Example (10) is an instance of argument from example:

(10) The Nazis, for example, disguised eugenics as "hereditary health science" or "hereditary care" to make it attractive to the masses, and today the same sick agenda is sold to us with a new "vaccine" to save us from a supposed "pandemic".

Not only is this example supposed to support the claim that the WHO wants to practice human eugenics, but it is indirectly portraying the WHO and its intentions negatively by comparing it to the Nazis. And example (11) is an instance of the fear appeal argument argumentation scheme:

(11) *Dr. Carrie Madej*, [12] a specialist in internal medicine with over 19 years of experience, states that the COVID-19 vaccine could actually be a Trojan horse to patent humans because it alters our DNA.

The COVID-19 vaccine is compared to a Trojan horse, a threat disguised as a blessing, triggering fear of danger and harm.

As demonstrated in the appraisal theory and argumentation theory sections, a variety of strategies may be implemented in fake news to deceive, mislead, or simply persuade audiences to take a particular course of action. Researchers who choose to investigate the strategies used to make fake news content credible and legitimate in the minds of the audience may find Van Leeuwen's legitimation strategies useful.

Legitimation strategies

Legitimation is the act of justifying or explaining a social practice or policy, usually by institutions (Van Leeuwen 2007). Van Leeuwen (2007, 2008) developed a model for legitimation by describing four main strategies that allow researchers to analyse the manner in which legitimation is constructed in discourse as well as reflect on issues pertaining to legitimation. The model includes four main strategies: authorisation, moral evaluation, rationalisation, and mythopoesis. The authorisation strategy is legitimation established by referring to an authority; for example, "The Principal of the school announced that all the students had to attend school on Saturday". Moral evaluation is a strategy for legitimation that relies on our values and morals that people consider a reference to judge an individual, action, or entity as good or bad; for example, "This policy threatens free speech". Rationalization is a strategy that legitimises social practice through references to its purpose(s) and effects or the norm; for example, "Getting vaccinated is going to protect us from the virus". As for mythopoesis, it is the act of storytelling that focuses on moral or cautionary tales that the reader should learn from or consider as a means of understanding the instance of discourse at hand; for example, "Learn from history how to prepare for future epidemics".

An analysis of the legitimation strategies utilised in a text aids in answering the following question: what makes fake news and disinformation appear credible to the reader? Igwebuike and Chimuanya (2021), for example, conducted a study that identified the authorisation legitimation strategy to be most frequently employed in the validation of false information covering the 2019 Nigerian elections that were shared on WhatsApp, Facebook, and Twitter, the implication being that the authority and status of the person whom the fake news is attributed to may play a role in its credibility.

The first legitimation strategy considered here, authority, may be achieved by referring to an individual who is considered an authority figure because of their perceived expertise and/or position in a social situation or context. In news reports, for example, experts are typically quoted to provide context for the event and help the reader "make sense" of the event. Certain members of the medical community were quoted in the newsletter. Mary Holland who is the "Vice President and Chief Advocate of the Children's Health Defense Organization" was quoted. Her credentials play a role in legitimation because the verbal process "warns" that introduces the quote triggers a sense of alarm towards COVID-19 vaccinations. Holland's expertise also authorises her to demonise the WHO for allegedly conspiring to vaccinate everyone without their knowledge. Van Leeuwen (2008) suggests looking for verbal processes that contain modals of obligation, as is present in example (12):

(12) Experienced physician and epidemiologist, Dr. Wolfgang Wodarg, stated in a censored *interview* with Rubikon, "Actually, this 'promising' vaccine **should be PROHIBITED** for the vast majority of people because it is genetic engineering!"

The modal of obligation "should be" comes from a position of authority, that is, Wodarg's experience and specialisation. Van Leeuwen (2008) also mentions that expert authority may be qualified shown in example (13):

(13) Now **several** experts and former mainstream journalists like John O'Sullivan **are warning** that the massive PCR testing campaign could be a WHO vaccination program in disguise.

The qualifier "several" strengthens the authorisation effect when it is combined with the verbal process "are warning".

Moral evaluation is another legitimation strategy that uses language to trigger a moral concept in the minds of readers subconsciously (Van Leeuwen 2007, 2008). Moral evaluation can be identified through a combination of linguistic analysis and the discourse analyst's "commonsense cultural knowledge" (Van Leeuwen 2008:110). Van Leeuwen (2008) mentions evaluative adjectives that "play a key role in moral evaluation legitimation" (110). A typical construction, Van Leeuwen argues, is an adjective that modifies a nominal group; the nominal group is the head of a clause that can be realised in the form of a nominalised reference to a practice, as shown in example (14):

(14) But the masterminds at WHO continue to insist on an **unrealistic vaccination rate** of at least 70 percent.

The evaluative adjective "unrealistic" modifies the nominal group "vaccination rate". Another construction may be an attribute in a relational clause that includes the practice such as the attribute "unknown" in example (15) extracted from a quote in the article by Mary Holland, vice president and chief advocate of the Children's Health Defense Organization:

(15) "The long-term damage is completely **unknown**".

Moral evaluation can also be analysed in instances of abstraction, which are abstract representations of a practice that is moralised by making connections between them and moral discourses (Van Leeuwen 2008). A combination of authority legitimation and moral evaluation appears in example (16):

(16) Resistance is forming even within the orthodox medical establishment.

The medical practitioners represent the expert authority who support the claim that vaccinations are harmful. Therefore, "resistance" is a nominalisation that is an abstract, indirect reference to the immoral practice of harming others as well as the moral obligation of standing up for what is right. This suppressed reference to the medical practitioners could also be analysed as a form of resistance. Moral evaluation may also be realised using an explicit or implicit analogy. An analogy can trigger legitimation explicitly through comparison or implicitly through the transfer of the positive or negative values of one social practice to the social practice or activity that is being legitimised. In this fake news article, for example, the claim that the WHO is deceiving people into getting vaccinated through PCR tests is an instance of explicit analogy expressed through the similarity conjunction "like" in example (17):

(17) It seems **like** science fiction and is chilling.

Implicit analogies are used as well through the word "disguise", as in example (18):

(18) But because common sense instinctively resists such interventions, the establishment has always endeavored to **disguise** its true intentions with misleading labels.

The word "disguise" functions as a metaphor that signals deception based on those who disguise themselves in order not to be caught.

A third legitimation strategy is the rationalization legitimation strategy. Van Leeuwen (2007, 2008) distinguishes between two types of rationality: instrumental and theoretical rationality. Instrumental rationality "legitimizes practices by reference to their goals, uses, and effects", while theoretical rationality "legitimizes practice by reference to a natural order of things" (Van Leeuwen 2008: 113). Analysing instrumental rationality involves an analysis of the purpose of the practice. An example of instrumental rationality is the accusation that what the article vaguely refers to as the "establishment" of practising human eugenics for the purpose of controlling the masses. In this last sentence of the article, the "establishment's" efforts to deceive the masses are compared to the Nazi's efforts to conceal their human eugenic endeavours (see example 10). The analyst will need to analyse the text at the pragmatic level aided by quotation marks. Therefore, it can be considered an indication that the author questions the purpose and function of the vaccine and insinuates that the pandemic is merely a ruse for a conspiracy plan. Theoretical rationality focuses on whether or not the practice follows the norm or natural order. This article legitimises the concern towards the mRNA vaccine and the refusal to take it because it was not developed in a typical manner as expressed in example (19):

(19) "Because vaccines have been developed so quickly and clinical trials are so short, the long-term damage is completely unknown".

The final legitimation strategy that Van Leeuwen (2007, 2008) describes is mythopoesis, which is essentially storytelling. Through moral or cautionary tales, certain social practices and activities are legitimised through narratives that remind the reader that adhering to legitimate social practices is rewarded and that engaging in illegitimate ones leads to an unfortunate ending. In this fake news article, the reader is reminded of the historical events involving human eugenics whose victims are the members of society who were deceived by governments to participate in their projects. One example cited in the article is presented as a fact that is listed in its reference list is presented in example (20):

(20) In 2007, the CDC [8] even admitted that between 1955 and 1963, 10–30 million citizens were infected with the carcinogen SV40 via polio vaccination.

This "scandal" serves as a cautionary tale on how vaccinations have been used to harm the public.

Conclusion

Fake news has been shown to cause deep polarisation within a society, which causes social conflict (Alba-Juez and Mackenzie 2019; Dalkir and Katz 2020; Maci 2019). A critical discourse analysis of confirmed fake news pieces and false information can describe the strategies used to create these effects. The purpose of this chapter is to showcase the CDA approaches, frameworks, and models for analysing disinformation and fake news. The areas of inquiry relating to fake news and disinformation that CDA has been demonstrated as capable of investigating are strategies of manipulation and persuasion and legitimation strategies for validating fake news. The chapter has showcased three models and frameworks developed by main contributors to CDA scholarship to investigate strategies that can be analysed in fake news and disinformation, but they are by no means exclusive to critically investigating the discourse of fake news and disinformation.

CDA approaches create systematic and contextualised avenues for critically analysing fake news and disinformation that reveal the obvious as well as tacit elements of fakeness and non-credibility. This chapter stresses that CDA research on disinformation and fake news can make valuable contributions to the fake news literature and participate in an intellectual movement against the unjust hegemonic effects of fake news and disinformation; it can educate the general public on how to be more critical readers and thinkers in order to become more conscious of biases, logical fallacies, and confront their own beliefs and assumptions about the world and the sources that they trust. CDA researchers should continue to explore other approaches to address questions about fake news and disinformation in a digitally connected, complex world.

APPENDIX

JOHNS HOPKINS UNIVERSITY CONFIRMS: YOU CAN BE VACCINATED WITH A PCR TEST, EVEN WITHOUT KNOWING

13 April 2021 | Health Freedom | 0 comments

In January 2019, the WHO defined the growing number of vaccination critics as one of the top ten threats to global health, and since the unprecedented Corona vaccination fiasco, the number of vaccination refusers has truly multiplied.

Meanwhile, resistance is forming even within the orthodox medical establishment. But the masterminds of the WHO continue to insist on an unrealistic vaccination coverage rate of at least 70 percent.

In this article, Jan Walter describes, with extensive source citations, which techniques are possible to still vaccinate the population, when people are becoming increasingly critical of vaccinations. This is only fuelled by the continuing pressure for mass "vaccination" against a nonlethal disease for 99.8% of people, with a new type of "vaccine" that is actually gene therapy by means of mRNA. It seems like science fiction and is chilling, but the metohodes and techniques are available. There question is how far do we let it get?

Vaccinations increasingly scrutinized and the chilling alternative

In January 2019, *WHO* [1] defined the growing number of vaccine critics as one of the ten greatest threats to global health, and since the unprecedented corona vaccination *fiasco* [2], the number of vaccine refusers has really multiplied. Meanwhile, resistance is emerging even within the conventional medical community. But the masterminds at WHO continue to insist on an unrealistic vaccination rate of at least 70%.

Now several experts and former mainstream journalists like John O'Sullivan are warning that the massive PCR testing campaign could be a WHO vaccination programme in disguise. (see *Principia Scientific*) [3] O'Sullivan is referring to a new technology developed at Johns Hopkins University that is supposed to make it possible to carry out covert vaccinations through a PCR test. (See Johns Hopkins Universitiy) [4]

Inspired by a parasitic worm that digs its sharp teeth into the intestines of its host, Johns Hopkins researchers have developed tiny, star-shaped micro-devices that attach to the intestinal mucosa and can deliver drugs into the body.

45

These tiny devices, known as "Theragrippers", are made of metal and a thin film that changes shape. They are covered with heat-sensitive kerosene wax and each no larger than a dust particle. (See Figure 3.1)

When the kerosene coating on the Theragripper reaches body temperature, the devices close autonomously and clamp onto the wall of the colon. Because of the sealing action, the tiny, six-pointed devices burrow into the mucosa and attach to the colon, where they are held and gradually release their drug load to the body. Eventually, the Theragripper lose their grip on the tissue and are removed from the colon through normal gastrointestinal muscle function.

Note: According to Johns Hopkins University, Theragrippers are actually administered with a cotton swab. (see Figure 3.2)

The Johns Hopkins University research team published positive results from an animal study as a cover article in *Science Advances* on 28 October 2020 [5], confirming that the new technology works flawlessly:

Here we report that GI parasite-inspired active mechanochemical therapeutic grabs, or theragrippers, can survive 24 hours in the gastrointestinal tract of live animals by autonomously adhering to mucosal tissue. We also observe a remarkable six-fold increase in elimination half-life when using ripper-mediated delivery of the model analgesic ketorolac tromethamine. These results provide excellent evidence that shape-shifting and self-locking microdevices improve the effectiveness of long-term drug delivery.

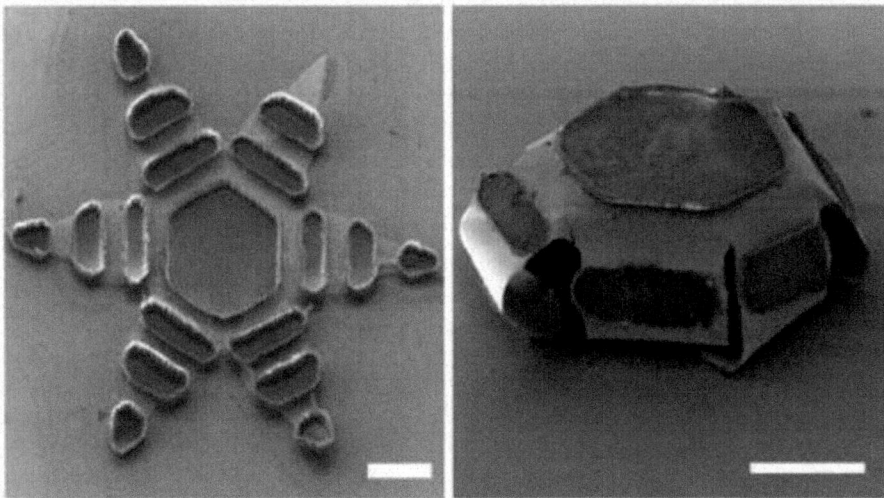

When an open theragripper, left, is exposed to internal body temperatures, it closes on the instestinal wall. In the gripper's center is a space for a small dose of a drug.

Figure 3.1   Theragripper images

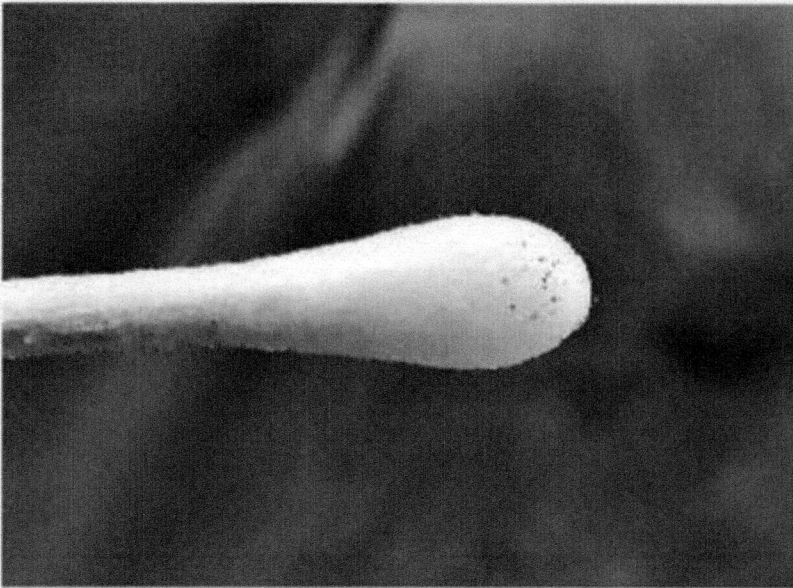

A theragripper is about the size of a speck of dust. This swab contains dozens of the tiny devices.

Figure 3.2   Theragrippers on a cotton swab

Coincidentally, the PCR test in China is now also performed anally because the reliability of the results is said to be better and of course this practice is immediately supported in the Western mainstream media. (See *Business Insider*) [6]

Note: If you can't imagine the government administering toxins to you against your will and without your consent, think of all the horrific experiments on humans that were admitted afterwards and which, according to *Wikipedia*, [7] have continued well into modern times. In 2007, the CDC [8] even admitted that between 1955 and 1963, 10–30 million citizens were infected with the carcinogen SV40 via polio vaccination.

The vaccination that is not a vaccination, but gene therapy

In a revealing *video conference* [9] with Dr. Judy Mikovits, Robert Kennedy Jr. and Dr. David Martin, it is explained that the mRNA vaccine, by the legal definition, is not a vaccine at all. It is falsely called a vaccine to hide the fact that the purported vaccine is, in fact, a gene therapy. Experienced physician and epidemiologist, Dr. Wolfgang Wodarg, stated in a censored *interview* with Rubikon, "Actually, this 'promising' vaccine should be PROHIBITED for the vast majority of people because it is genetic engineering!" Mary Holland, Vice President and Chief Advocate of the Children's Health Defense Organization, warns, "New vaccine technologies will likely lead to new types of vaccine harms. Since there has never been an approved mRNA vaccine, we really don't know what such damage will look like. Because vaccines have been developed so quickly and clinical trials are so short, the long-term damage is completely unknown".

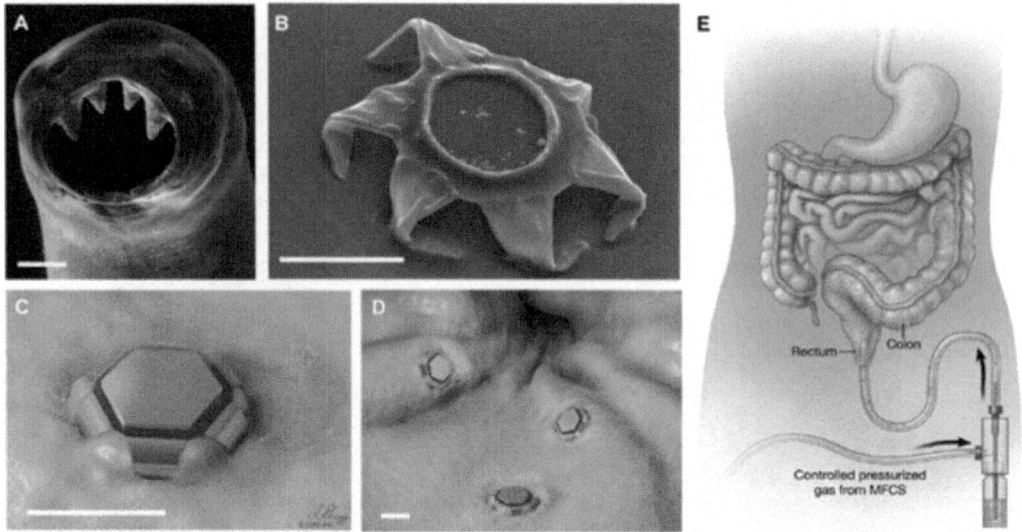

Figure 3.3   Shape-shifting Theragripper as self-locking drug delivery devices

What is particularly chilling is that the vast majority do not even know what the mRNA vaccine is doing in their bodies. They simply allow themselves to be blindly vaccinated, and this despite the fact that more and more independent and even orthodox medical experts are warning against it. (See doctors from around the world *warn against* mRNA vaccination) [10] In this context, it should not be forgotten that the American company modeRNA Therapeutics was founded in 2010 not as a vaccine manufacturer, but as a GenTech company. The example of the many Monsanto scandals makes it crystal clear that genetic engineering does not serve to protect species, but rather to gain power. The hidden agenda is to genetically modify species in order to patent or own them. Former U.S. Secretary of State Henry Kissinger once said, "Whoever controls the seed controls the world" (See Press Portal) [11].

What's next? Are they going to patent our bodies after they genetically engineer us with the mRNA vaccine?

Dr. Carrie Madej, [12] a specialist in internal medicine with over 19 years of experience, states that the COVID-19 vaccine could actually be a Trojan horse to patent humans because it alters our DNA. According to an Article published in the British science journal Phys.org in January 2020 [13], it is confirmed that modified RNA has a direct impact on our DNA. The following passage is particularly alarming: "Several research groups are now working together to investigate what effect this may have on the DNA molecule. We already know that R-loop regions are associated with DNA sequences that contain active genes, and that this can lead to chromosome breaks and the loss of genetic information". Also alarming is the fact that leading vaccine manufacturers such as Pfizer are warning their subjects not to reproduce after vaccination (see Pfizer, p. 132) [14 PDF] By doing so, the pharmaceutical company is confirming that the mRNA vaccine can have negative effects on human reproduction and is being vaccinated in spite of it!

Conclusion: Anyone who knows a little history knows that **genetic experimentation** and **human experimentation** are nothing new. Although modern **eugenics** has its origins in the nineteenth century, the ideas, measures and justifications of state and social interventions and influences on reproduction have been known since ancient times. They can already be found in Plato's "Politeia", which, however, is limited to state selection and education. In the Renaissance, corresponding lines of thought can be found in the social utopian writings "Utopia" by Thomas Morus, "Nova Atlantis" by Francis Bacon and "La città del Sole" by Tommaso Campanella. But because common sense instinctively resists such interventions, the establishment has always endeavored to disguise its true intentions with misleading labels. The Nazis, for example, disguised eugenics as "hereditary health science" or "hereditary care" to make it attractive to the masses, and today the same sick agenda is sold to us with a new "vaccine" to save us from a supposed "pandemic".

Sources

[1] https://web.archive.org/web/20200812085538/www.who.int/news-room/feature-stories/ten-threats-to-global-health-in-2019

[2] www.legitim.ch/post/schockierende-bilder-beh%C3%B6rden-verschweigen-massenhaft-corona-impfsch%C3%A4den

[3] https://principia-scientific.com/are-pcr-tests-secret-vaccines/

[4] https://hub.jhu.edu/2020/11/25/theragripper-gi-tract-medicine-delivery/

[5] https://advances.sciencemag.org/content/6/44/eabb4133

[6] www.businessinsider.com/microbiology-professor-china-anal-swab-test-covid-19-makes-sense-2021-1?r=MX&IR=T

[7] https://en.wikipedia.org/wiki/Human_subject_research

[8] http://web.archive.org/web/20110307094146/www.cdc.gov/vaccinesafety/updates/archive/polio_and_cancer_factsheet.htm

[9] www.bitchute.com/video/4fVFgHXPELoO/

[10] https://tinyurl.com/y32qpl74

[11] www.presseportal.de/pm/62556/3331518

[12] https://banthis.tv/watch?id=5f176746677a7f01e9302af6

[13] https://phys.org/news/2020-01-rna-effect-dna.html

[14] PDF] https://pfe-pfizercom-d8-prod.s3.amazonaws.com/2020-11/C4591001_Clinical_Protocol_Nov2020.pdf

Originally posted: https://tapnewswire.com/2021/04/johns-hopkins-university-confirms-you-can-be-vaccinated-with-a-pcr-test-even-without-knowing

Note

1 The words or phrases that are analyzed in all the examples in this chapter were bolded for the reader's reference.

Further reading

Mackenzie, J.L. and Alba-Juez, L., eds., 2019. *Emotion in Discourse* (Vol. 302). Amsterdam: John Benjamins Publishing Company. (For further study of emotion processes in discourse).

Reisigl, M., 2018. The discourse-historical approach. In J. Flowerdew and J. E. Richardson (Eds.), *The Routledge Handbook of Critical Discourse Studies*. London: Routledge. (A well-established model that emphasises the importance of incorporating the historical context into the analysis).

References

Abu Arqoub, O., Elega, A.A., Efe Özad, B., Dwikat, H. and Oloyede, F.A., 2020. Mapping the scholarship of fake news research: A systematic review. *Journalism Practice*, pp. 1–31. https://doi.org/ 10.1080/ 17512786.2020.1805791

Alba-Juez, L. and Mackenzie, J.L., 2019. Emotion, lies, and "bullshit" in journalistic discourse: The case of fake news. *Ibérica: Revista de la Asociación Europea de Lenguas para Fines Específicos (AELFE), 38*, pp. 17–50.

Allcott, H. and Gentzkow, M., 2017. Social media and fake news in the 2016 election. *Journal of Economic Perspectives, 31*(2), pp. 211–236. https://doi.org/10.1257/jep.31.2.211

Bakhtin, M.M., 2010. *The Dialogic Imagination: Four Essays*. Austin: University of Texas Press.

Bartlett, J.C., 2020. Information literacy and science misinformation. In *Navigating Fake News, Alternative Facts, and Misinformation in a Post-Truth World*. Hershey, PA: IGI Global, pp. 1–17.

Bednarek, M. and Caple, H., 2017. *The Discourse of News Values: How News Organizations Create Newsworthiness*. Oxford: Oxford University Press.

Cunha, E., Magno, G., Caetano, J., Teixeira, D. and Almeida, V., 2018, September. Fake news as we feel it: perception and conceptualization of the term "fake news" in the media. In *International Conference on Social Informatics* (pp. 151–166). Springer, Cham.

Dalkir, K. and Katz, R., eds., 2020. *Navigating Fake News, Alternative Facts, and Misinformation in a Post-Truth World*. Hershey, PA: IGI Global.

Devereux, E. and Power, M.J., 2019. Fake news? A critical analysis of the 'Welfare cheats, cheat us all' campaign in Ireland. *Critical Discourse Studies, 16*(3), pp. 347–362. https://doi.org/10.1080/17405904.2019 .1568898

Fairclough, N., Mulderrig, J. and Wodak, R., 2011. Critical discourse analysis. In T.A. Van Dijk (Ed.), *Discourse Studies: A Multidisciplinary Introduction* (2nd ed.). London: SAGE Publications Ltd., pp. 357–378. https://doi.org/10.4135/9781446289068.n17 (Accessed 12 February 2022).

Finneman, T. and Thomas, R.J., 2018. A family of falsehoods: Deception, media hoaxes and fake news. *Newspaper Research Journal, 39*(3), pp. 350–361. https://doi.org/10.1177/0739532918796228

Flood, A., 2017, November 2. Fake news is 'very real' word of the year for 2017. *The Guardian*. Retrieved from: www.theguardian.com/books/2017/nov/02/fake-news-is-very-real-word-of-the-year-for-2017

Fowler, R., 1991. *Language in the News: Discourse and Ideology in the Press*. London: Routledge.

Froehlich, T.J., 2020. Ten lessons for the age of disinformation. In *Navigating Fake News, Alternative Facts, and Misinformation in a Post-Truth World*. Hershey, PA: IGI Global, pp. 36–88.

Ghosh, A., Li, L., Xu, L., Dash, R.P., Gupta, N., Lam, J., Jin, Q., Akshintala, V., Pahapale, G., Liu, W. and Sarkar, A., 2020. Gastrointestinal-resident, shape-changing microdevices extend drug release in vivo. *Science Advances, 6*(44), p. eabb4133. https://doi.org//10.1126/sciadv.abb4133

Halliday, M.A.K. and Matthiessen, C.M., 2014. *An Introduction to Functional Grammar*. London: Routledge.

Haw, A.L., 2021. Audience constructions of fake news in Australian media representations of asylum seekers: A critical discourse perspective. *Journal of Language and Politics, 20*(5), pp. 761–782. https://doi.org/ 10.1075/jlp.21028.haw

Igwebuike, E.E. and Chimuanya, L., 2021. Legitimating falsehood in social media: A discourse analysis of political fake news. *Discourse & Communication, 15*(1), pp. 42–58. https://doi.org/10.1177/1750481320961659

International Federation of Library Associations and Institutions, 2017. How to spot fake news. Retrieved from: https://repository.ifla.org/handle/123456789/167 (Accessed 18 July 2023).

Krause, N.M., Wirz, C.D., Scheufele, D.A. and Xenos, M.A., 2019. Fake news. In *Journalism and Truth in an Age of Social Media* (pp. 58–78). Oxford: Oxford University Press.

Maci, S.M., 2019. Discourse strategies of fake news in the anti-vax campaign. *Lingue Culture Mediazioni-Languages Cultures Mediation (LCM Journal), 6*(1), pp. 15–43. https://doi.org/10.7358/lcm-2019-001-maci

Martin, J.R. and White, P.R., 2005. *The Language of Evaluation*. Gordonsville: Palgrave Macmillan.

McGonagle, T., 2017. "Fake news" False fears or real concerns? *Netherlands Quarterly of Human Rights, 35*(4), pp. 203–209. https://doi.org/10.1177/0924051917738685

Meyer, M., 2001. Between theory, method, and politics: Positioning of the approaches to CDA. In R. Wodak and M. Meyer (Eds.), *Methods of Critical Discourse Analysis, 113*. London: Sage Publications, pp. 14–31.

Mitchell, A., Gottfried, J., Stocking, G., Walker, M. and Fedeli, S., 2019. Many Americans say made-up news is a critical problem that needs to be fixed. *Pew Research Center*, 5 June. Retrieved from: www.

pewresearch.org/journalism/2019/06/05/many-americans-say-made-up-news-is-a-critical-problem-that-needs-to-be-fixed/ (Accessed 29 March 2023).

Ndame, T., 2023. Case study. In J.M. Okoko, S. Tunison and K.D. Walker (Eds.), *Varieties of Qualitative Research Methods: Selected Contextual Perspectives'*. Cham: Springer Nature, pp. 67–72. https://doi.org/10.1007/978-3-031-04394-9

Poynter, 2020. *Misleading: Dr. Leonard Coldwell: Coronavirus Was Created Artificially for Mass Chipping.* Retrieved from: www.poynter.org/?ifcn_misinformation=dr-leonard-coldwell-coronavirus-was-created-artificially-for-mass-chipping (Accessed 7 March 2022).

Reisigl, M. and Wodak, R., 2005. *Discourse and Discrimination: Rhetorics of Racism and Antisemitism.* London: Routledge.

Ribeiro, M.M. and Ortellado, P., 2018. Fake News: What it is and how to deal with it. *The International Journal of Human Rights*, 27, pp. 69–81.

Richardson, J.E., 2017. *Analysing Newspapers: An Approach from Critical Discourse Analysis.* London: Bloomsbury Publishing.

Rubin, V.L., 2022. *Misinformation and Disinformation: Detecting Fakes with the Eye and AI.* Springer Nature. https://doi.org/10.1007/978-3-030-95656-1

Talbot, M., 2007. *Media Discourse: Representation and Interaction.* Edinburgh: Edinburgh University Press.

Tandoc Jr., E.C., Lim, Z.W. and Ling, R., 2018. Defining "fake news" a typology of scholarly definitions. *Digital Journalism*, 6(2), pp. 137–153. https://doi.org/10.1080/21670811.2017.1360143

Vamanu, I., 2019. Fake news and propaganda: A critical discourse research perspective. *Open Information Science*, 3(1), pp. 197–208. https://doi.org/10.1515/opis-2019-0014

Van Dijk, T.A., 1998. *Ideology: A Multidisciplinary Approach.* London: SAGE Publications Ltd. Retrieved from: https://search-ebscohost-com.ezproxy.lau.edu.lb:2443/login.aspx?direct=true&db=e000xww&AN=518847&site=ehost-live (Accessed 30 March 2023).

Van Dijk, T.A., 2001. Multidisciplinary CDA: A plea for diversity. In R. Wodak and M. Meyer (Eds.), *Methods of Critical Discourse Analysis, 113.* London: Sage Publications, pp. 95–120.

Van Leeuwen, T., 2007. Legitimation in discourse and communication. *Discourse & Communication*, 1(1), pp. 91–112. https://doi.org/10.1177/1750481307071986

Van Leeuwen, T., 2008. *Discourse and Practice: New Tools for Critical Discourse Analysis.* Oxford: Oxford University Press.

Van Vleet, J.E., 2021. *Informal Logical Fallacies: A Brief Guide.* Lanham, MD: Hamilton Books.

Walton, D., 2007. *Media Argumentation: Dialectic, Persuasion and Rhetoric.* Cambridge: Cambridge University Press.

Wodak, R., 2001. The discourse-historical approach. In R. Wodak and M. Meyer (Eds.), *Methods of Critical Discourse Analysis.* London: Sage Publications, pp. 63–94.

Yin, R.K., 2003. *Case Study Research: Design and Methods* (3rd ed.). Thousand Oaks, CA: Sage Publications.

4

INTRODUCING DIGITAL SOURCE CRITICISM

A method for tackling fake news and disinformation

Bente Kalsnes

Introduction

The production and distribution of fake news and mis- and disinformation have created additional challenges for journalists and fact checkers who daily examine the veracity of information from different sources (Wardle and Derekshan 2017; Kalsnes 2018). Source criticism has been both a method and a practice for journalists in the Nordic countries for several decades (Allern 2018), and with the digital turn, digital source criticism is developing as a useful approach to tackle the spread of misinformation online. Historically, source criticism offers several methodological concepts and steps to reveal a source's tendency (or bias) and potential information value, and digital sources require new methods, tools, and practices to assess information typically used by journalists. This chapter will outline what digital source criticism is and how it can be used when assessing claims in general and specifically within journalism, such as investigative journalism and fact-checking. But before discussing digital source criticism and its characteristics, I will start by introducing the original term – source criticism – and how it relates to journalism. Source criticism is a term and an approach that has a long tradition within history research. Digital source criticism, on the other side, is a rather new term that has developed alongside the development of Internet and different digital communication technologies. Before we focus on digital source criticism, we need to look at the historic roots of this concept.

Source criticism

Source criticism can be defined as a method or a process of evaluating an information source (Alexanderson 2012) and can be described as a way of testing the credibility of the information. The term *source criticism* originates from the German word *quellenkritik*, which is called *kildekritikk* in Norwegian, *kildekritik* in Danish, and *källkritik* in Swedish. The term *criticism* has evolved from the Greek term *kritike tekhne*, which means "the art of judgement", thus it does not imply to give negative views of something or someone, but more neutrally to evaluate a source's credibility (Allern 2018). Source criticism draws on the legacy of Leopold von Ranke, the nineteenth-century German historian who developed source criticism as a method within historiography (Allern 2018: 53). Ranke is regarded as the father of modern professional history, who introduced the archive as

DOI: 10.4324/9781003224495-5

the historian's habitat and rigorous fact-checking as the essence of the historian's craft (Fickers et al. 2017:1). He is said to be responsible for the archival turn at the end of the nineteenth century. Source criticism has been described as a method developed within history and biblical studies to differentiate between fact-based sources from none-fact-based sources (Leth and Thurén 2000). The function of sources was to provide knowledge about reality, but as stated by Leth and Thuren, historians have experienced a range of challenges, ranging from how sources can be forged, manipulated, or too distant from the original event. Sources are not of equal weight; some sources are more relevant, and other sources must be excluded. Thus, we can argue that source criticism is an epistemological approach which raises questions about how knowledge is obtained and how we can evaluate information sources. To use an example from Scandinavian historians in the nineteenth century, it was believed all historical accounts were informed by the subjective view of their authors, and source criticism was deemed as the best method to create distinction between sources based on their trustworthiness (Edelberg and Simonsen 2015: 218). Source criticism has developed in several directions and the concept has different meanings across cultural and disciplinary contexts. In English-speaking countries, source criticism usually refers to the evaluation of information in historical, especially religious texts (e.g. Viviano 1999). The concept is also increasingly referred to within library and information studies, where it is used as an umbrella term for various methods for evaluating information sources (Hjørland 2012). It is common within history studies to differentiate between different kinds of sources: primary sources, secondary sources, and tertiary sources. While the primary source is the original source, secondary and tertiary sources are one or more sources away from the original source. While history studies mainly have focused on primary sources, other fields of society will use a broader set of sources to get information and knowledge to identify what are the facts (Leth and Thurén 2000). Another way to differentiate between how to examine sources is to differentiate between internal and external source criticism (Koch and Kinder-Kurlanda 2020): while external source criticism focuses on the creation, appearance, and authenticity of a source, internal source criticism focuses on the evidential value that can be attributed to a particular source: what does the source have to say about a topic?

Here we refer to source criticism as it has been developed in Germany and Scandinavia during the twentieth century. Source criticism has been such a central approach among Scandinavian historians that is has been deemed "a foundational mind-set among professional historians" (Edelberg and Simonsen 2015: 231). Source review or examination could be other terms to describe the process, according to historian Knut Kjeldstadli (Allern 2018: 51). This implies a functional and hermeneutic understanding of source criticism. In its modern version, the concept of source criticism implies a hermeneutic view on the relationship between news and truth, and as such, it represents an alternative to the more positivist notions of information verification often found in investigative journalism and fact-checking (Steensen et al. 2022). The catalyst for modern source criticism was the German philosopher Hans-Georg Gadamer and his book *Truth and Method* (*Wahrheit und Methode*, in German), published in 1960. Gadamer argued that truth in relation to human and social life is not an objective entity but an evolving understanding based on interpretations and reinterpretations of the sources of information we have available. The human sciences relate to "modes of experience in which a truth is communicated that cannot be verified by the methodological means proper to science" (Gadamer 2013: xxi; Steensen et al. 2022). In other words, truth, in relation to social life (the kinds of truth that journalism mostly deals with), cannot be accomplished through a material, positivist view on sources and the information they convey, as the nineteenth-century developers of source criticism believed. To Gadamer, truth is irrevocably connected to interpretation and understanding. A phenomenon in the social world cannot be understood without interpretation, and an understanding of that phenomenon will therefore always be coloured by the interpreter. Interpretation and understanding do not constitute a linear process but rather a circular movement in which an interpretation is always guided by a degree of under-standing, which in turn leads to new interpretations and new understandings in a potential never-ending loop. In Scandinavia, the central position of source criticism and interpretation has been called "fundamentalism" (Torstendahl 2005), but also that source criticism has been foundational "not by solving everything but by positing subjective agency as a central problem to contend with in Scandinavian history" (Edelberg and Simonsen 2015: 217). A source – whether it is a tweet, a written document, an image, registry data, an interview subject, a video, an audio recording, or any other kind of source – will be influenced by the originator's "horizon of understanding" (Gadamer 2013) – the situation of origin, the wider sociocultural context of that situation, the genre and language applied, and so forth. This is what within the vocabulary of source criticism is labelled "tendency" or bias. All sources have a tendency, and an important task when performing source criticism is to reveal this tendency and assess how it affects the source's information value. Tendencies can be intentional or unintentional; they can be related to human bias, genre attributes, or technological affordances; and they can be black-boxed in algorithms (Diakopoulos 2015). Be-cause of such tendencies, it is impossible within the hermeneutics of source criticism to determine a source's credibility based on an assumed existence of a true-false scale – it is only possible to assess whether the source's originator express themself in accordance with what they *believe* to be true (Ankersborg 2007: 110). Within source criticism in history studies, four questions are crucial to ask (Kjeldstadli 2007): *whom did what where and when?* By using source criticism, we can determine whether the information is probable, trustworthy, credible, and rooted in reality. When investigating the trustworthiness of a source, four additional questions are recommended to ad-dress (Uppsala University Library 2019):

- **Authenticity** – Is the source what it claims to be? Who is the publisher?
- **Time** – Is the information up-to-date? Has the website been updated? Is there a more recent edition of the book?
- **Dependency** – Is the source independent, or does it depend on other sources? Is the source a primary, secondary, or tertiary source?
- **Tendency** – Does the information contain values and opinions of the author? Does the source portray people and events in a neutral way? Is one specific perspective (like one side of a conflict) favoured in the text?

Nevertheless, this approach is not sufficient in a digital environment where it is easier to modify, falsify, and manipulate information than ever before. The digital turn and the spread of disinforma-tion demands further development of source criticism, both as a method and practice for journal-ists. Thus, I would like to introduce digital source criticism as a way to describe the upskilling and reorientation that is needed to evaluate digital sources.

Digital source criticism

Adding the prefix "digital" to "source criticism" means that the traditional way of questioning the authenticity of a source – finding out who created it, when, how, for what purpose, and in what context (Drucker 2011) – is no longer enough. Different types of sources require different assess-ments, as well as different questions of origin and materiality (Pfanzelter et al. 2021). The system-atic inquiry into the origins and creation of sources requires news approaches when the sources are digital. Thus, the transformation from analogue to digital affects the epistemological value and qualities of sources. To identify the sources which can give correct knowledge of reality is still the purpose of digital source criticism. But while source criticism within history studies was mainly focused on identifying primary sources, source criticism on the Internet is building on a wider set of different sources (Leth and Thurén 2000), as well as a complex set of infrastructure. Next, we will look at how new communication technology impacts sources, information and context, and some of the arising challenges.

First, the digital turn has made it less obvious what is a *source*. It can still be a document, a book, or a person, as was the case in more analogue times, but it can also be email messages, digital photographs, websites, databases, metadata, to mention a few relevant objects (Owens and Padilla 2021). Digital sources have different qualities than analogue sources, and "digital objects' embeddedness in particular information environments" is a crucial factor for source criticism that needs to be taken into account (Föhr 2018, cited in Koch and Kinder-Kurlanda 2020: 4). For example, algorithms impact what information is produced, how it is presented, and who is able to see it, thus the medium's embeddedness is also necessary to take into account when examining digital sources. Richard Rogers has argued for the need to follow the evolving methods of a technology or a medium, such as web crawling, crowd sourcing, tag clouds, or visualisations in order to learn how they handle hits, likes, tags, date stamps, and other web-native objects (Rogers 2013). Similarly, Koch and Kinder-Kurlanda argue that digital source criticism should be applied to social media platforms, Internet of Things, self-tracking, citizen science, social media metrics, data of public administrations, to mention a few types of digital data sources (2020).

Second, another challenge is how *information* can be remixed, manipulated, or erased, as addressed by Gilliland-Swetland (2000) when she mentions that digital information is not only high-volume but also dynamic. When applying source criticism to digital objects, this challenge arises out of the objects' volatility and concerns the question of authenticity. The endless possibilities of cloning, remixing, or adjusting digital objects challenges the idea of authenticity of sources. In some fields, which are highly affined to authenticity of sources, new approaches for creating mechanisms to prove authenticity of digital objects are increasingly installed, that is, digital object identifier (DOI), version management, and researcher's identification systems as elements of research repositories or platforms (Koch and Kinder-Kurlanda 2020).

Third, new communication technology makes it easy to take information out of its original *context*. Information can be authentic in itself, but if placed in another context, the information can become misleading or downright false. Only in particular cases do we have version controls as an integral element of the platform infrastructure, for example, on Wikipedia or in blockchain technology, a system to store information which is very difficult to change or hack (Al-Saqaf and Edwardsson 2019). A crucial dimension of source criticism is the authenticity of data or information, which can be translated into the concept of data integrity, that is, the maintenance and assurance of the accuracy and the consistency of data over its life cycle (Koch and Kinder-Kurlanda 2020). Thus, we are not only questioning the authenticity and provenances of sources but also investigating the integrity of source.

Fourth, *technology* itself impacts information in numerous ways. Communication technology carries a set of affordances that essentially condition what is possible to do with the technology or a platform, yet these affordances do not determine how platforms or technologies are used (Westlund et al. 2022). Affordance theory, as first introduced by Gibson (1979), stresses how a specific materiality carries both opportunities for action and constraints, while users can engage with in different ways. This approach draws attention to how technologies and platforms interrelate with humans in socio-technical infrastructures. Digital platforms and networks have many different affordances, some have been identified as persistence, visibility, spreadability, and searchability

(Boyd 2014). In other contexts, particularly related to the spread of mis- and disinformation, another set of affordances are highlighted: automation, algorithms, and anonymity (Woolley and Howard 2019). These affordances allow for a new type of computational propaganda: "data driven techniques and tools like automation (bots) and algorithms (decision-making code) allow small group of actors to megaphone highly specific and sometime abusive and false information into mainstream online environment" (Woolley and Howard 2019: 7). This type of manipulation of information is particularly important for journalists to detect and disclose. Digital source criticism can be used for this purpose.

While source criticism is usually understood as a "basic method for the critical evaluation of historical sources" (Edelberg and Simonsen 2015: 215), here, we define that digital source criticism is the systematic method or process for the critical evaluation of digital information. In the next section, we will discuss in more details how this approach can be used within journalism.

Digital source criticism for journalists

Digital source criticism is often mentioned within history and educational studies (i.e. Koch and Kinder-Kurlanda 2020; Francke et al. 2011; Nygren and Guath 2022; Marttunen et al. 2021), typically in connection with terms such as digital literacy, media literacy, information literacy, and source credibility. As argued by Nygren and Guath (2022), media and information literacy (MIL) can be conceptualized as an umbrella term that includes multiple literacies that are useful and necessary to navigate online information (Carlsson 2019; Koltay 2011a, 2011b). Interesting enough, digital source criticism is seldom mentioned in media and journalism studies, with some few exceptions (Carlsson 2018; Grut 2021). In Nordic media literature, (digital) source criticism is identified as an integrated part of media and information literacy studies, which are described as

> the knowledge of how media, platforms and networks functions, how meaning is created in the media society, about human rights and ethics, how the media and communication system is organized, about actors' different objectives and their consequences (i.e. propaganda, misinformation and advertising), about the economy and structure of the media and communication industry, about technology and its effects (i.e. algorithms).
>
> (Carlsson 2018, my translation)

In general, source criticism is not a commonly used concept within international media and journalism studies. Terms such as verification and debunking are much more frequently applied, particularly in Anglo-American studies. Nevertheless, I will argue they differ somewhat from source criticism, and here I will explain why. Kovach and Rosenstiel calls journalism "the discipline of verification" (2007), and studies suggest that verification is a norm held in high regard by journalists, even though opinions among journalists related to what competences it takes to verify pieces of information vary greatly (Brandtzaeg et al. 2016; Shapiro et al. 2013). Checking claims stated by politicians or other prominent people is a central component within fact-checking, and claims are often rated along a "truth-o-meter", ranging from verdicts such as true to false or what the American fact-checker Politifact calls "pants on fire" (Holan 2018). As mentioned by Steensen et al. (2022), the word "verification" inevitably carries with it some discursive baggage from its origin in logical positivism and the later development of the hypothetico-deductive method (Popper 2005). The concept of verification is therefore developed and discursively framed within methods of the natural sciences and a formal regime of hypothesis-testing, which, while it may perfectly reflect scientific practice (Kuhn 2012), conforms even less well to systems of knowledge production in the sociocultural domain to which journalism belongs (Steensen et al. 2022). Along the same lines as verification, we find the term (and journalistic practise) called "debunking", which can be described as the journalistic practise of fighting viral online misinformation such as conspiracy theories, doctored images, and bogus news reports (Saldaña and Vu 2022). This is a new form of accountability journalism developing in the aftermath of a growing public concern about online misinformation. Journalists and fact-checkers, both existing outlets and especially new entrants to the field, have increasingly embraced debunking work (Graves 2017). Nevertheless, I will argue that both verification and debunking are more narrow approaches than digital source criticism when journalists are dealing with digital sources. Based on the previously mentioned definition – *digital source criticism is the systematic method or process for the critical evaluation of digital information* – I will look more closely at the four main components of digital source criticism: source, information, context, and technology, which I present in Figure 4.1:

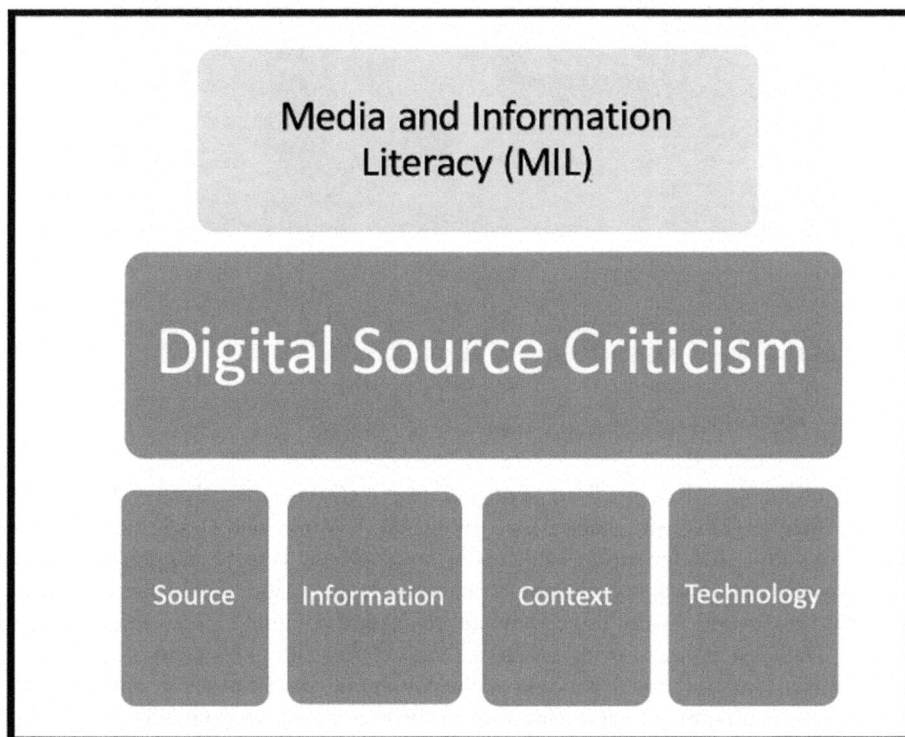

Figure 4.1 The components of digital source criticism

The Norwegian author and journalist Ståle Grut (2021) has written about how journalists can use digital source criticism as a method before, during, and after publishing a story (2021). To explain how digital source criticism can be used in journalism, I will use a tweet as an example and discuss how digital source criticism can impact the work process of journalists. I have selected a tweet by Carl Bildt, the previous Swedish prime minister, which received a lot of attention because the tweet misrepresented current events in Ukraine (Bildt 2022).

It was later revealed that the picture was indeed from Ukraine, but not from the same year or context (Devlin and Sardarizadeh 2022). Here, we assume that Bildt was spreading this picture

Carl Bildt ✔
@carlbildt

···

There are photos that will be with us for a long time.

1:30 PM · Feb 26, 2022 · Tweetbot for iOS

7,544 Retweets   **538** Quote Tweets   **45.8K** Likes

Figure 4.2   Carl Bilt's misrepresentation of Ukraine events on Twitter

with good intention, but still, it is a form of misinformation (information that is false, but not created with the intention of causing harm), done by mistake (Wardle and Derekshan 2017). Misinformation differs from disinformation, which is information that is false and deliberately created to harm a person, social group, organisation, or country. In the Twitter discussion or "thread" following the picture, several Twitter users were correcting and pointing to the origin of the picture, back in 2016. The open nature of many social media platforms allows for everyone to share information, also misinformation, and depending on the community guidelines and content moderation practices, misinformation might get a widespread distribution on a social media platform, potentially creating a type of viral hoax. Next, we will look at how the four main components of digital source criticism – source, information, context, and technology – can help us examine the tweet.

Source

A *source* can be a person, a document, a picture, but it can also be a social media account, a TikTok video, or a hacked email account. Here, Carl Bildt is the source of the tweet. As the co-chair of the European Council on Foreign Relations and as Sweden's former prime minister and foreign minister, Bildt enjoys high international credibility. Additionally, he has a large following on Twitter (745K) and is thus able to reach a large audience within a short timespan. His account had the official approval mark on Twitter, the blue Verify badge next to his name when the picture was shared, which indicates that the account is authentic. In order to receive the Verify badge, the user needs to identify with Twitter in order to be verified, which Bildt had done. It should be noted that after Twitter's new CEO, Elon Musk, changed the policy for the Verify badge and turned it into a subscription service, Bildt no longer had the Verify badge as this chapter went into print. Nevertheless, a high-profiled politician can also make mistakes. In this case, Carl Bildt was sharing a picture of two children standing on the side of the road, greeting a convoy of Ukrainian forces heading into battle. The picture generated thousands of likes and shares on social media. And even though it could have depicted the situation in Ukraine in the spring of 2022, the picture was taken by a photographer for the Ukrainian defence ministry who was later dismissed over allegations that he had staged some of his combat images, as documented by BBC (Devlin and Sardarizadeh 2022) and the Norwegian fact-checking organisation Faktisk (Lindin 2022). Previous research has demonstrated that high-profiled people, such as politicians and celebrities, have extra responsibilities when it comes to avoiding sharing mis- and disinformation (Nielsen 2021; Kalsnes et al. 2021). They are not necessarily very frequent spreader of mis- or disinformation, but when they do, they reach a larger audience than most other social media users. Therefore, it is of particular importance that they carefully check the authenticity of the information they share. That is also the case for journalists writing about content shared by different types of celebrities – it should be checked. The picture got fact-checked by several fact-checkers, among them Reuters, who concluded that the picture was shot in another context, thus a miscaptioned picture from 2016 (Reuters 2022).

Information

In order to check the authenticity of the *information,* in this case the picture of two children in front of a Ukrainian military convoy, journalists can do reverse image searches to check if the picture has been used before. Services such as *TinEye, RevEye,* and *Google Image Search* allow for users to check the origin of an image and previous publication or versions. *WeVerify InVid,* as well as *YouTube Data Viewer*, are technologies that extract data from YouTube videos, such as all the thumbnails to facilitate a reverse image search, and the exact upload time to facilitate analysis of original video source vs copies (Westlund et al. 2022). A reverse image search would have revealed that the image is six years old, not a depiction from the current war in Ukraine. Other parameters we can use in order to examine the authenticity of information, according to Koch and Kinder-Kurlanda (2020: 274), is "persistence (where published, long-term accessibility, etc.), dating (date of publishing, changes, etc.), authorship (identifiability, intention), addressee (recognition, relation to author), content (indicators for authenticity), and relations (references, indications, hyperlinks)". Here, we have information about persistence (where the tweet was published – Twitter – but not the original picture), date (26/2/2022), authorship (Carl Bildt, sympathising with the Ukrainian side in the war started by Russia), addressee (Bildt's followers), content (no indication of the image's origin from the tweet), or relations (no hyperlinks or references in the tweet). In order to examine these parameters (as well as the authenticity and integrity of digital information in general), it is necessary to do both internal and external source criticism. As previously mentioned, internal source criticism is an in-depth "textual" analysis of the source as such, while external source criticism is the contextualisation of the source (De Leeuw and Van Gorp 2019).

Context

An image can be perfectly authentic, without any technical manipulation, but shot in another context than the information describing the picture, thus it misinforms the user. Carl Bildt did not connect the picture directly with the Ukrainian defence but had a rather philosophical comment on it: "There are photos that will be with us a long time". The tweeted picture could have depicted the current war, but as mentioned, the context was wrong. To decide whether an image depicts the right context, several procedures can be done. In order to examine the context, it is necessary to conduct external source criticism (Koch and Kinder-Kurlanda 2020). External source criticism can be based on the five *W* questions: who, where, when, what, why (Kjeldstadli 2007) – thus contextual questions about the situation. When and where was the picture taken, by whom, for what purpose? How was the weather on the day the photo was shot? Is the landscape correct, according to the area it supposedly depicts? In a digital environment, another approach is to do a *horizontal* digital reading and search across many (web) pages, not only *vertical* reading and search within one (web)page (Grut 2021: 26–27; McGrew et al. 2017). Grut calls this *network reading* due to the fact that it is necessary to check the network surrounding a piece of information in order to evaluate the credibility (Grut 2021: 27). Other researchers have called this technique *laterally reading* (Nygren and Guath 2022). Network reading can be employed when checking a tweet such as the one mentioned previously.

Technology

As our society becomes increasingly datafied, the tools that are developed for the collection, cleaning, processing, and presenting of such data influence knowledge production. Technology might impact how a source or a piece of information is presented, amplified, or hidden. Due to Carl Bildt's large Twitter following, his tweets will in general get substantial visibility in Twitter's algorithms and recommendation systems. This tweet in particular received 7,500 retweets, 540 quote tweets and 45.8K likes – engagement affordances that drives visibility and amplification. Recently, several scholars have argued that it in addition to digital source criticism, "digital tool criticism" is needed: in addition to answering to the five *W*s (who, what, where, when, why), digital tool criticism also requires the important additional question "How". How does the tool work? (De Leeuw and Van Gorp 2019). While some differentiate between terms such as digital source criticism, tool criticism, algorithmic criticism, and interface criticism, others call for reflexivity by considering the entire "technical stack", which includes infrastructure, platform, software, algorithms, data, and interface (Es et al. 2018). In our tweet previously, Bildt's user account is verified, as previously mentioned. This is an affordance that Twitter has developed in light of previous inauthentic and manipulative behaviour on the platform (Jain et al. 2016).

Twitter makes most of its content publicly available, and thus it can be monitored and analysed through a set of third-party technologies available to monitor information flows (such as the Twitter API). There are numerous tools for gathering information on Twitter users. *Tweetdeck* enables users to search and analyse content on Twitter and is a specific tool for Twitter, but it is available for use by diverse actors (Westlund et al. 2022). Other tools to examine content on Twitter is *AccountAnalysis*, which offers details about when and what type of content different accounts publish, what accounts they interact with, and what websites they share; *Botometer* analyses the activity of a Twitter account and gives it a score, where higher scores indicate more bot-like activity; *TinfoLeaks* help Twitter users by using tweet and image information; *Foller.me* offers tools to analyse the most popular words used; *Hoaxy* visualises Twitter conversations by topic, illuminating influential accounts and the origins of hashtags, to mention a few of the tools and technologies available to conduct digital source criticism on sources and information on Twitter (Westlund et al. 2022). In the case of this tweet, journalists could have used a tool such as *AccountAnalysis to* analyse how many people and within which group of users the tweet was spread. Additionally, the software *Tableau* could be used to visualise how the misinformation in Bildt's tweet was spread in the network of users.

Conclusion

The ease of manipulating information and spreading it to a global audience requires new methods and approaches for examining digital sources and information. Deep fakes, chat robots producing text, and AI-developed images are just some of the recent developments that make it more challenging to examine the authenticity of information and to decide what is true or not. Access to credible news and skills to navigate and detect biased and fake information have been highlighted as a pivotal democratic and educational challenge (Nygren and Brounéus 2018). Source material is always related to its source, the situation of origin, and the wider sociocultural context of the situation of origin (Steensen et al. 2022), and digital information and sources have other qualities and characteristics than what is typical for analogue information. Citizens, organisations, institutions, and particularly journalists need to be able to identify and determine the trustworthiness of different information sources. I have argued that in order to examine digital sources, it requires different tools, methods, and approaches than analogue sources. This chapter has discussed how digital source criticism can be one such method and approach for journalists and everyone else who needs to examine the authenticity of digital information. Verification and debunking are established methods within fact-checking and investigative reporting (Graves 2017), with roots from logical positivism and the later development of the hypothetico-deductive method. I have argued that digital source criticism allows for a more holistic approach encompassing a range of procedures and attitudes in order to check the sources, the information, the context, and the technology. As we have discussed here, digital information and sources must be understood in the specific (social, cultural, political, economical) context they appear in, as well as the technological context. Technologies have specific affordances or qualities, impacting how information is produced, presented, selected, and amplified, and this needs to be taken into account when evaluating information. As stated by Melvin Kranzberg long before today's digital communication technologies environment, "technology is neither good nor bad; nor is it neutral" (Kranzberg 1986: 545). Technology relies on a set of underlying mechanism, algorithm and programmed choices, therefore it is important to understand "the worldview built into our tools" (Graham et al. 2015: 54; Fridlund 2020). The way technologies and platforms interrelate with humans in socio-technical infrastructures, which are far from neutral, must be taken into account when assessing digital sources. Detecting and fighting mis- and disinformation are complex tasks, but digital source criticism offers an assorted methodological and practical toolbox to tackle complex information challenges.

References

Allern, S. (2018). *Journalistikk og kildekritisk analyse*. Oslo: Cappelen Damm Akademisk.

Alexanderson, K. (2012). *Källkritik på Internet*. Available at: https://iis.se/docs/Kallkritik-pa-Internet.pdf (Accessed 20 June 2022).

Al-Saqaf, W. and Edwardsson, M. P. (2019). Could blockchain save journalism? An explorative study of blockchain's potential to make journalism a more sustainable business. In Ragnedda, M. and Destefanis, G. (eds.), *Blockchain and Web 3.0*. London: Routledge, pp. 97–114.

Ankersborg, V. (2007). *Kildekritik i et samfundsvidenskabeligt perspektiv*. Frederiksberg: Forlaget samfundslitteratur.

Bildt, C. (2022). *Tweet*. Available at: https://twitter.com/carlbildt/status/1497549571232342019 (Accessed 3 August 2022).

Boyd, D. (2014). *It's Complicated: The Social Lives of Networked Teens*. New Haven, CT: Yale University Press.

Brandtzaeg, P. B., Lüders, M., Spangenberg, J., Rath-Wiggins, L. and Følstad, A. (2016). Emerging journalistic verification practices concerning social media. *Journalism Practice*, 10(3), 323–342.

Carlsson, U. (2018). *Medie- och informationskunnighet (MIK) i den digitala tidsåldern: En demokratifråga: Kartläggning, analys, reflektioner*. Available at: http://urn.kb.se/resolve?urn=urn:nbn:se:norden:org:diva-5321 (Accessed May 10 2022).

Carlsson, U. (2019). *Understanding Media and Information Literacy MIL in the Digital Age: A Question of Democracy*. Gothenburg: University of Gothenburg.

De Leeuw, S. and Van Gorp, J. (2019). Texts as data III: Digital TV archives. In H. Van den Bulck, M. Puppis, K. Donders, and L. Van Audenhove (eds.), *The Palgrave Handbook of Methods for Media Policy Research*. Cham: Springer International Publishing, pp. 277–293.

Devlin, K. and Sardarizadeh, S. (2022). Ukraine invasion: Misleading claims continue to go viral. *BBC*. Available at: www.bbc.com/news/60554910 (Accessed 13 August).

Diakopoulos, N. (2015). Algorithmic accountability: Journalistic investigation of computational power structures. *Digital Journalism*, 3(3), 398–415.

Drucker, J. (2011). Humanities approaches to graphical display. *Digital Humanities Quarterly*, 5(1).

Edelberg, P. and Simonsen, D. G. (2015). Changing the subject. *Scandinavian Journal of History*, 40, 215–238.

Es, K.V., Wieringa, M. and Schäfer, M.T. (2018). Tool criticism: From digital methods to digital methodology. *International Conference on Web Studies, Paris*, October 3–5, 2018. Paris. Available at: https://doi.org/10.1145/3240431.3240436 (Accessed 29 May).

Fickers, A., Scagliola, S. and O'Dwye, A. (2017). *Exploring the Origin and Use of the Term "Digital Source Criticism"*. Available at: https://ranke2.uni.lu/de/define-dsc/skilltraining.html (Accessed 3 June 2022).

Föhr, P. (2018). *Historische Quellenkritik im Digitalen Zeitalter*. Dissertation. Basel: Universität Basel.

Francke, H., Sundin, O. and Limberg, L. (2011). Debating credibility: The shaping of information literacies in upper secondary schools. *Journal of Documentation*, 67(4), 675–694.

Fridlund, M. (2020) "Digital history 1.5: A middle way between normal and paradigmatic digital historical research." In Fridlund, M., Oiva, M. and Paju, P. (eds.), *Digital Histories. Emergent Approaches within the New Digital History*. Helsinki: Helsinki University Press, pp. 69–88. Available at: http://doi.org/10.2307/j.ctv1c9hpt8.9 (Accessed 15 March 2022).

Gadamer, H. G. (2013). *Truth and Method*. London and New York: Bloomsbury Academic.

Gibson, J. J. (1979). *The Ecological Approach to Visual Perception*. New York and London: Psychology Press.

Gilliland-Swetland, A. J. (2000). *Enduring Paradigm, New Opportunities. The Value of the Archival Perspective in the Digital Environment*. Washington, DC: Council on Library and Information Resources.

Graham, S., Milligan, I. and Weingart, S. (2015). *Exploring Big Historical Data: The Historian's Macroscope*. 2nd ed. London: Imperial College Press.

Graves, L. (2017). Anatomy of a fact check: Objective practice and the contested epistemology of fact checking. *Communication, Culture and Critique*, 10, 518–537.

Grut, S. (2021). *Digital kildekritikk. En innføring i digitale kilder, brukerskapt innhold og graving i åpne kilder for journalister og mediestudenter*. Oslo: Gyldendal.

Hjørland, B. (2012). Methods for evaluating information sources: An annotated catalogue. *Journal of Information Science*, 38(3), 258–268. https://doi.org/10.1177/0165551512439178

Holan, A. D. (2018). The principles of the truth-o-meter: PolitiFact's methodology for independent fact-checking. *PolitiFact*. Available at: www.politifact.com/article/2018/feb/12/principles-truth-o-meter-politifacts-methodology-i/#Truth-O-Meter%20ratings (Accessed 20 September 2022).

Jain, S., Sharma, V. and Kaushal, R. (2016). Towards automated real-time detection of misinformation on Twitter. *2016 International Conference on Advances in Computing, Communications and Informatics (ICACCI)*, pp. 2015–2020. http://doi.org/10.1109/ICACCI.2016.7732347.

Kalsnes, B. (2018). Fake news. In *Oxford Research Encyclopedia of Communication*. Available at: https://oxfordre.com/communication/display/10.1093/acrefore/9780190228613.001.0001/acrefore-9780190228613-e-809;jsessionid=9582BEDBDB307FB621BC1D26332C6BA2 (Accessed March 2022).

Kalsnes, B., Falasca, K. and Kammer, A. (2021). Scandinavian political journalism in a time of fake news and disinformation. In *Power, Communication, and Politics in the Nordic Countries*. Gothenburg: Nordicom, University of Gothenburg, pp. 283–304. https://doi.org/10.48335/9789188855299-14

Kjeldstadli, K. (2007). *Fortida er ikke som den en gang var*. Oslo: Universitetsforlaget.

Koch, G. and Kinder-Kurlanda, K. (2020). Source criticism of data platform logics on the Internet. *Historical Social Research*, 45(3), 270–287. https://doi.org/10.12759/hsr.45.2020.3.270-287

Koltay, T. (2011a). The media and the literacies: Media literacy, information literacy, digital literacy. *Media, Culture & Society*, 33(2), 211–221. https://doi.org/10.1177/0163443710393382

Koltay, T. (2011b). New media and literacies: Amateurs vs. Professionals. *First Monday*, 16(1). https://journals.uic.edu/ojs/index.php/fm/article/download/3206/2748

Kovach, B. and Rosenstiel, T. (2007). *The Elements of Journalism: What Newspeople Should Know and the Public Should Expect*. New York: Three Rivers Press.

Kranzberg, M. (1986). Technology and history: "Kranzberg's laws". *Technology and Culture*, 27, 544–560.

Kuhn, T. S. (2012). *The Structure of Scientific Revolutions* (4th ed.). Chicago: University of Chicago Press.

Leth, G. and Thurén, T. (2000). *Källkritik för Internett*. Available at: https://web.archive.org/web/20070716001651/www.psycdef.se/Global/PDF/Publikationer/kallkritid%20for%20internet.pdf (Accessed 20 March 2023).

Lindin, I. K. (2022). Dette bildet er gammelt og tatt ut av sammenheng. *Faktisk*. Available at: www.faktisk.no/artikler/zmlog/dette-bildet-er-gammelt-og-tatt-ut-av-sammenheng (Accessed 28 August 2022).

Marttunen, M., Salminen, T. and Utriainen, J. (2021). Student evaluations of the credibility and argumentation of online sources. *The Journal of Educational Research*, 114(3), 294–305.

McGrew, S., Ortega, T., Breakstone, J. and Wineburg, S. (2017). The challenge that's bigger than fake news. Civic reasoning in a social media environment. *American Federation of Teachers*. Available at: www.aft.org/ae/fall2017/mcgrew_ortega_breakstone_wineburg (Accessed 4 August 2022).

Nielsen, R. K. (2021). How evidence can help us fight against COVID-19 misinformation. *Reuters Institute*. Available at: https://reutersinstitute.politics.ox.ac.uk/news/how-evidence-can-help-us-fight-against-covid-19-misinformation (Accessed 21 May 2022).

Nygren, T. and Brounéus, F. (2018). The news evaluator: Evidence-based innovations to promote digital civic literacy. In Andersson, Y., Dalquist, U. and Ohlsson, J. (eds.), *Youth and News in a Digital Media Environment*. Gothenburg: Nordicom.

Nygren, T. and Guath, M. (2022). Students evaluating and corroborating digital news. *Scandinavian Journal of Educational Research*, 66(4), 549–565. http://doi.org/10.1080/00313831.2021.1897876

Owens, T. and Padilla, T. (2021). Digital sources and digital archives: Historical evidence in the digital age. *International Journal of Digital Humanities*, 1(3), 325–341. http://doi.org/10.1007/s42803-020-00028-7

Pfanzelter, E., Oberbichler, S., Marjanen, J., Langlais, P. C. and Hechl, S. (2021). Digital interfaces of historical newspapers: Opportunities, restrictions and recommendations. *Journal of Data Mining & Digital Humanities (HistoInformatics)*. https://doi.org/10.48550/arXiv.2006.02679

Popper, K. (2005). *The Logic of Scientific Discovery*. London and New York: Routledge.

Reuters Fact Check (2022). *Fact Check-Photo of Children Saluting Ukrainian Tanks Dates Back to 2016*. Available at: www.reuters.com/article/factcheck-ukraine-russia-idUSL1N2V10DO (Accessed 25 May 2022).

Rogers, R. (2013). *Digital Methods*. London: MIT Press.

Saldaña, M. and Vu, H. T. (2022). You are fake news! Factors impacting journalists' debunking behaviors on social media. *Digital Journalism*, 10, 823–842.

Shapiro, I., Brin, C., Bédard-Brûlé, I. and Mychajlowycz, K. (2013). Verification as a strategic ritual. *Journalism Practice*, 7(6), 657–673. https://doi.org/10.1080/17512786.2013.765638

Steensen, S., Belair-Gagnon, V., Graves, L., Kalsnes, B. and Westlund, O. (2022). Journalism and source criticism. Revised approaches to assessing truth-claims. *Journalism Studies*, 1–19. http://doi.org/10.1080/1461670X.2022.2140446

Torstendahl, R. (2005). Källkritik, metod och vetenskap. *Historisk Tidskrift*, 125(2), 2–10.

Uppsala University Library. (2019). *Söktips och sökteknik*. Uppsala: Uppsala Universitet. Available at: https://libguides.ub.uu.se/sok (Accessed 20 April 2022).

Viviano, P. A. (1999). Source criticism. In McKenzie, S. L. and Haynes, S. L. (eds.), *To Each Its Own Meaning. An Introduction to Biblical Criticisms and Their Application*. Leiden: Westminister John Know Press, pp. 35–57.

Wardle, C. and Derekshan, H. (2017). *Information Disorder: Toward an Interdisciplinary Framework for Research and Policy Making*. Strasbourg: Council of Europe. Available at: https://rm.coe.int/information-disorder-toward-an- (Accessed May 12 2022).

Westlund, O. T., Larsen, R., Graves, L., Kavtaradze, L. and Steensen, S. (2022). Technologies and fact-checking: A sociotechnical mapping. In Correia, J. C. and Jerónimo, P. (eds.), *Disinformation Studies: Perspectives from an Emerging Field*. Covilhã: Lab Communication & Arts, pp. 193–227.

Woolley, S. and Howard, P. N. (2019). *Computational Propaganda: Political Parties, Politicians, and Political Manipulation on Social Media*. New York: Oxford University Press.

5

A MODEL FOR UNDERSTANDING AND ASSESSING SEMI-FAKE SCIENTIFIC NEWS REPORTING

Paola Catenaccio

0 Introduction

This chapter addresses the issue of misinformation in scientific news reporting by identifying theoretical constructs which can help explain the phenomenon of "semi-fake" news in this domain, and testing the suitability of such constructs to explain the misleading character of a selected news sample reporting on COVID-19-related research. By semi-fake news is meant, following Musi and Reed (2022), news which provides accounts of scientific research that are at least in part misleading (deliberately or otherwise) even while not containing any blatant falsehoods.

The study is to be seen within the broader context of the contemporary phenomenon of fake news, which all but dominates today's news discourse. Fake news has a long and well-documented history (see, amongst others, Gorbach 2018 and Watson 2018), but it was after the 2016 US election that it rose to prominence in media discourse (cf. Allcott and Gentzkow 2017). The COVID-19 pandemic which engulfed the world in 2020 further heightened interest in the phenomenon, as the "infodemic" of fake, misleading, and unverified news which developed parallel to the pandemic was found to be even less manageable, and possibly more contagious, than the pandemic itself.

Within this scenario, the very term "fake news" can in fact be in itself misleading. In its common usage, the label is used to indicate different – albeit related – phenomena, ranging from fabrication of facts or details, to inaccurate reporting of factually true events, to biased, though technically not necessarily false, accounts. In this sense, a broad definition of fake news is that of "false information that is spread, regardless of whether there is intent to mislead" (Dictionary.com *ad vocem*, discussed in Sherman 2018). On the other hand, Gelfert (2018: 84) has argued that the phrase "should be reserved for cases of deliberate presentation of (typically) false or misleading claims as news, where these are misleading *by design*". Regardless of the label adopted, the phenomenon has been attracting increasing attention (Ha et al. 2021), giving rise to a growing body of literature aimed at identifying the characterising features of fake news in its various forms, both at a textual and discursive level, and in terms of its dissemination patterns – an aspect which is the more important in light of the fact that social media are the prime vectors for its spread.

Defining fake news is no easy task (Tandoc et al. 2018), nor is it easy to univocally describe the characterising features. One of the problems with this task is that there is often a continuum between deliberate disinformation and possibly inadvertent misinformation (Rubin 2019); as a

DOI: 10.4324/9781003224495-6

result, any distinction which aims to identify clear-cut boundaries between the two is bound to fail. For instance, misinformation may develop from originally true information by subtly varying it through partial selection, de- or recontextualization, or by carrying out other textual or discursive operations which may cause the original message to be substantially altered, sometimes to the point of qualifying as "fake" or at least misleading. This process is a well-known phenomenon in journalism, where "dynamic transfer-and-transformation of something from one discourse/text-in-context . . . to another" (Linell 2009: 144–145) is common and leads to "textual change, such as simplification, condensation, elaboration, and refocusing" (Linell 1998: 155) that may – though does not have to – lead to a substantial altering of the information conveyed.

With specific reference to scientific news reporting, of which COVID-related news is an instance, it has been observed that "certain content categories such as health and medicine . . . require prior knowledge on the topic and some uncertainty is associated with it"[1] (Ha et al. 2021: 293). As Garzone (2020: 171–172) points out following Bauman and Briggs (1990), the need to make highly specialised knowledge accessible to the general public calls for extensive "decontextualization (or de-centering) and recentering of information and knowledge" (Garzone 2020: 272). This process "inevitably involves transformations, changes in orientation towards authoritative voices, shifts in referential and indexical frames etc." (*ibidem*), all of which can be considered as conditions potentially facilitating misrepresentation, whether deliberate or otherwise. While the resulting popularised news cannot be defined as "fake" in the sense of "fabricated", it can well be misleading and encourage readers to draw conclusions that are not aligned with the source on which the popularised text is based.

The fact that misleading news contains information which is not technically false can pose challenges to its categorisation along the fake-trustworthy continuum. Such challenges are generally recognised not only in the scientific literature on fake news but also by fact-checking sites such as Snopes.com, Healthfeedback.org, Politifact.com, Fullfact.org, and FactChecker.com, which are the most widely used sources of information to verify the truthfulness of claims found in news outlet or on social media. For instance, PolitiFact.com, which is devoted to fact-checking of political statements (admittedly different from scientific information, but in the age of pandemic, science is indeed often seen as political), uses a "truth-o-meter" to rate claims along the entire false-true continuum, from "false" to "mostly false", to "half-true", to "mostly true" and "true" (cf. Vlachos and Riedel 2014 5-point veracity scale), and includes a "pants-on-fire" label for completely fabricated, ridiculous news and a "full flop" one which exposes politicians' false promises. As Rashkin et al. (2017: 2931) point out, the "graded notion of truthfulness" used by PolitiFact introduces an added element of complication, as it acknowledges that "falsehoods often arise from subtle differences in phrasing rather than outright fabrication" (Rashkin et al. 2017: 2931, following Rubin et al. 2015).

Against this backdrop, this chapter puts forth a proposal for the analysis of news which are not patently false or fabricated, but which are nonetheless misleading, with specific reference to news reporting on scientific findings. The aim is to identify a theoretically sound framework for the investigation of semi-fake scientific news capable of "explaining the roots of misinformation" (Musi et al. 2022: 4) and to test its validity by applying it to a case study. Potential applications of the framework are also discussed, with specific reference to the identification of best practices in scientific journalism, to the potential of the framework for aiding in the development of media literacy, and to the development of methods for the identification of misleading news reporting. The chapter is organised as follows: Section 1 presents some key principles of scientific popularization relevant to the analysis of misleading scientific news, and argues, on the basis of a recent study by Musi and Reed (2022), for an argumentation-based approach to the analysis of semi-fake news as fallacious claims; Section 2 outlines three theoretical constructs/approaches which hold explanatory power for an account of semi-fake news as arising from fallacious argumentation – namely, the notions of relevance, framing, and misrepresentation of intentions; Section 3 provides a short account of the roots of misinformation in a piece of fake news based on the theoretical constructs outlined in Section 2. Finally, Section 4 offers some provisional conclusions and suggestions for future research.

1 Misleading news as fallacious claims

As mentioned previously, scientific journalism is a domain particularly prone to misinformation because of the sheer complexity of the topics dealt with. The need to make scientific research both comprehensible and relevant to the general public calls for extensive recontextualization so as to enhance the relevance of the scientific discovery for the intended audience. In order "to arouse as much interest as possible in readers" (Garzone 2014: 91), it is common for some aspects to be prioritised over others, in a process of "selective knowledge transformation" (Nikitina 2020), which can give rise to partial and incomplete at best, but also ideologically biased and even deliberately manipulated accounts of the original information (van Dijk 1998; Fairclough 2014; Garzone 2018).

Even leaving aside deliberate disinformation (i.e. the spreading of knowingly fabricated information with the intention to deceive the audience), the problem of misinformation remains a serious one. As Musi and Reed (2022: 353) point out following Kyriakidou et al. (2020), while readers appear to be able to recognise fabricated news such as conspiracy theories fairly easily, they are much less likely to identify the misleading character of, say, partially or inaccurately presented information. Musi and Reed call the latter "semi-fake news", that is, news that is "not constructed by the authors with the deliberate intention of dis-informing the audience" (Musi and Reed 2022: 353) and which can therefore be argued to fall within the definition of misinformation. The label "semi-fake news" (as opposed to more common "misinformation") highlights the uncertain status which often characterises this type of news, and the difficulty that is sometimes encountered in deciding whether a piece of news is genuine or not due to the fact that it is partly true but nonetheless misleading. As they further specify,

> semi-fake news articles do not contain fabricated information intended to represent states of affairs known by the authors to be in conflict with reality. However, they may contain propositions presented as assertions backed up by sources partially valid or anyways not sufficient to draw conclusions presented as factual. . . . The lack of misleading intention and fabricated news make semi-fake news good candidates to appear on trustworthy news sources.
>
> (Musi and Reed 2022: 353)

The authors conclude that "even if conveying information less far from truth than patently false information", semi-fake news is "more pernicious at a large scale" because it can more easily pass for trustworthy and truthful. This makes it all the more important – but also all the more challenging – to study it.

Because the key problem with semi-fake news is that it makes claims which lack adequate backing, Musi and Reed call for an argumentation-based approach for the identification and analysis of semi-fake news. Argumentation theory provides a suitable framework for assessing if the arguments provided in support of a given claim warrant the conclusions drawn by the claim itself. If a claim is adequately supported, the news in which it occurs can be considered reliable. If not, it is to be considered fallacious, even though the supporting claims are not mendacious in themselves, and regardless of the intentions of the news producer.

In line with this conceptualization of semi-fake news as fallacious arguments, Musi and Reed propose a fallacy theory-informed method for its analysis. Real-life arguments can contain informal fallacies, that is, incorrect forms of reasoning occurring in natural language which are not bound exclusively to rules of logical correctness (as is the case for logical fallacies), but take into consideration content and context. Although incorrect from a purely logical perspective, informal fallacies may be acceptable under specific contextual circumstances (see Walton 1987: 3) and indeed may fail to be recognised even when they do lead to fallacious conclusions. Consider, for instance, the different but equally potentially misleading ways in which the findings of a 2020 study on the impact of COVID-19 infection on male fertility were announced by two news providers:

(1a) COVID may affect fertility by reducing men's sperm counts, study finds.
(1b) COVID-19 could impact male fertility for months after recovery.

The study (Donders et al. 2022) on which both articles (which will be discussed more in detail in Section 3) are based had found that one month immediately after recovery, a percentage of men who had contracted COVID-19 had decreased sperm count and motility. For the greatest majority of the men affected, sperm quality had substantially improved at two months from recovery, though in a minority of cases the problem persisted. The study concluded that COVID-19 infection appeared to affect male fertility in the short term, that recovery could be expected within three months, and that more research was needed to verify whether long-term effects might be experienced by a minority of men.

The first thing that can be noticed is that neither headline states clearly that the impact of COVID-19 on fertility is temporary, with substantial signs of improvement being detectable as early as two months after recovery without any need for treatment. On the contrary, both lend themselves to the interpretation that the impact may be permanent (1a) or at least long-lasting (1b). As for the articles, the one introduced by headline (1a) correctly reports the findings of the original study, including information about the lack of evidence regarding the possibility of long-term effects for a minority of men. While the headline, as pointed out previously, does not specify that the effects on fertility are limited in time and tend to get resolved, this is clarified in the body of the article. On the other hand, the article introduced by headline (1b) omits details of the findings (most notably, it fails to adequately report the improvement in sperm quality at two months from recovery), and while it does provide a quote stating that "it's not time to sound the alarm", it insists that "it could take time to recover" without quantifying the time required, and rather suggesting that the duration of the impairment is unknown and full recovery uncertain. While the body of article (1a) faithfully reflects the conclusions of the research, that of article (1b) misrepresents the findings by not disclosing the improvements found in men's sperm tested at two months from recovery and omitting the researchers' claim that recovery was generally expected within three months.

The misrepresentation in (1b) can hardly be flagged as fake news. It can, however, be misleading in so far as it provides ambiguous information regarding the timeframe for presumed recovery and fails to explicitly mention evidence indicating that the impairment was indeed only temporary for the greatest majority of the men included in the study. It may also well be that the misrepresentation is not intentional. As Musi and Reed observe, the authors of semi-fake news most likely act in good faith, "commit[ting] genuine flaws in the processes of interpreting the available evidence and/or presenting it in the most informative way" (Musi and Reed 2022: 354). This seems to be the case for article (1b), as shall be shown in Section 3; nonetheless, the article does encourage the inference that the impact of COVID-19 infection on male fertility is substantial and lasting – a claim which is not warranted by the research findings it is reporting on.

Because of this, the claim made in article (1b) can be considered at least partly fallacious. The fallacy in (1b) is one which, following Tindale's (2007) taxonomy, Musi and Reed classify as one of diversion (i.e. it has to do with "relevance and (mis)representation of sources" (Musi and Reed 2022: 366); in this specific case, the fallacy is one of bias – some evidence is suppressed so as to accent one aspect of the argument in the service of a preferred interpretation. In their thorough analysis of 220 news stories flagged as "fake" by fact-checking websites, Musi and Reed found strategies of diversion (which in their taxonomy include *cherry-picking, strawman arguments, false authority*, and *red herrings*) to be the most frequent ones in aggregate terms. The most frequent single strategy was *evading the burden of proof*, which falls into the category of structural fallacies (fallacies having to do with the "presence and quantity of evidence supporting the claim"); *vagueness*, which belongs to the category of language fallacies (having to do with "(un)clear narratives"), was also quite frequent, while logical fallacies (fallacies related to "(un)sound reasonings in drawing conclusions from available evidence") were less represented (Musi and Reed 2022: 360 and 366).

Fallacies of diversion are especially difficult to spot because they require comparison with the sources they use to make their point. While structural, language, and logical fallacies come with text-internal cues, strategies of diversion build an apparently sound case out of selective evidence and require comparison with other texts in order to be identified with certainty. In the case of scientific news reporting, such comparison can be especially challenging, because an in-depth reading of the source text – access to which is often restricted anyway – is generally beyond the capabilities of the average reader. The lack of clear cues drastically reduces the chances that readers spot inconsistencies or imprecisions that may lead them to raise critical questions challenging the narrative put forth by the news producer.

Of course, material selection, re-contextualisation, and re-framing are not always or necessarily fallacious strategies. However, they may lead to misinformation, whether deliberately or inadvertently. In particular, in the case of scientific news which taps into issues that are the object of controversy, it may be tempting for news producers to present research findings in ways which fuel the controversy, as this is known to attract readers.

In the next section I will briefly discuss three theoretical constructs which can be useful for a better understanding of diversion strategies and their role in misinformation: the notion of relevance (Sperber and Wilson 1986), the concept of framing (Entman 1993), and the role of misrepresentation of intention in the argumentative fallacies implicated in misleading science reporting (Walton and Macagno 2010).

2 Relevance, framing, and misrepresentation of intention

2.1 *Relevance*

Relevance theory (Sperber and Wilson 1986) is a pragmatic theory of cognition developed with the specific purpose of providing a psychologically realistic account of how human communication works. As Wilson and Sperber (1998: 8) put it, "human cognition is relevance-oriented" and "we pay attention to information that seems relevant for us". This holds true of all kinds of input, not necessarily and not only verbal. For instance, if I hear a horn honking as I am about to cross a street, I will likely interpret it as a warning. When applied to human communication, relevance theory posits that understanding an utterance means understanding our interlocutor's communicative intentions. As Wilson and Sperber (2002) summarize,

> Relevance theory may be seen as an attempt to work out in detail one of Grice's central claims: that an essential feature of most human communication, both verbal and non-verbal,

is the expression and recognition of intentions (Grice 1989: Essays 1–7, 14, 18; Retrospective Epilogue). . . . According to the inferential model, a communicator provides evidence of her intention to convey a certain meaning, which is inferred by the audience on the basis of the evidence provided.

(Wilson and Sperber 2002: 249)

Key to relevance theory is the assumption that relevance is a trade-off between effort and effect and that cognition tends to maximise it; this means that when receiving an input, we tend to focus on the components of such input that provide us with information that is (1) relevant to the contextual circumstances at hand and (2) readily inferable. More specifically, "relevance theory claims that what makes an input worth picking out from the mass of competing stimuli is not just that it is relevant, but that it is more relevant than any alternative input available to us at that time" (Wilson and Sperber 2002: 253), and that "the greater the effort of perception, memory and inference required, the less rewarding the input will be to process, and hence the less deserving of our attention", leading to relevance being best assessed "in terms of cognitive effects and processing effort" (Wilson and Sperber 2002: 253).

In communication, it is in the interest of the communicator to make the input as explicit as possible by providing an "ostensive stimulus . . . designed to attract an audience's attention and focus it on the communicator's meaning". The use of an ostensive stimulus "may create precise and predictable expectations of relevance not raised by other stimuli" (Wilson and Sperber 2002: 256). On their part, the receiver of a message is called upon to mobilize "an appropriate set of contextual assumptions" (Wilson and Sperber 2002: 258):

[V]erbal comprehension starts with the recovery of a linguistically encoded sentence meaning, which must be contextually enriched in a variety of ways to yield a full-fledged speaker's meaning. There may be ambiguities and referential ambivalences to resolve, ellipses to interpret, and other underdeterminacies of explicit content to deal with. There may be implicatures to identify, illocutionary indeterminacies to resolve, metaphors and ironies to interpret. . . . The hearer should take the linguistically encoded sentence meaning; following a path of least effort, he should enrich it at the explicit level and complement it at the implicit level until the resulting interpretation meets his expectation of relevance.

(Wilson and Sperber 2002: 258)

When encoding a message, a communicator will construct his or her message in such a way as to facilitate the retrieval of his or her communicative intentions and maximise the relevance of the information which needs to be understood in order to ensure that their retrieval is correct. The more ostensible the stimulus, the easier it will be for the audience to correctly infer the [pragmatic] meaning of the message.

2.2   *Framing*

This is where the notion of framing comes into play. This notion has a long and varied history, having been used in multiple independent, though interrelated domains. For the purposes of this discussion, the most relevant definition of framing is the one provided by Entman (1993):

To frame is to select some aspects of a perceived reality and make them more salient in a communicating context, in such a way as to promote a particular problem definition, causal interpretation, moral evaluation, and/or treatment recommendation for the item described.

(Entman 1993: 52)

Through framing, certain aspects of a given situation can be foregrounded, thus making them more textually prominent and facilitating their understanding as carrying greater relevance – against the receiver's background assumptions – than other aspects, which may or may not be mentioned alongside them. In a relevance-theoretical perspective, framing cues relevance and facilitates the retrieval of the encoder's stance and positioning in respect of the subject matter discussed – and, ultimately, of the communicative intentions encoded in it.

Within the field of media studies, the notion of framing has a well-established history (de Vreese 2005). In communicative terms, frames are configurations of discursive coordinates used to "activate" preferred versions of information, views, and events. They do so by providing "schemata of interpretation" (Goffman 1974), which guide our understanding of a given issue, factor, or episode. With reference to relevance theory, frames can be argued to reduce the cognitive effort required to process a given piece information, thus encouraging its perception as relevant. Entman (1993) argues that frames reside in several "locations": the communicator, the text, the receiver, and the culture. This means that they exist in the minds of the participants in a communicative event (though they are not always shared; there can indeed be a frame mismatch in communication), may (but need not) be explicitly encoded in texts, and are at their most powerful when they are shared on the societal level, as they can function as shortcuts for interpreting reality. This, again, fits with the pragmatic assumption, central to relevance theory, that relevance is co-constructed by message producers and receivers.

The role of frames in facilitating processing has been widely emphasised. Gitlin (1980: 7), for instance, defines frames as "persistent patterns of cognition, interpretation and presentation, of selection, emphasis and exclusion by which symbol handlers routinely organize discourse". For Gamson and Modigliani (1989: 3), frames are "interpretative packages" that give meaning to an issue. At the core of this package is "a central organizing idea, or frame, for making sense of relevant events, suggesting what is at issue" (Gamson and Modigliani 1989: 3). In this sense, frames "define problems", "diagnose causes", "make moral judgments", and "suggest remedies" (Entman 1993), activating knowledge and stimulating "stocks of cultural morals and values" (Cappella and Jamieson 1997: 47). In this sense, framing can be argued to be argumentative in nature, designed as it is for promoting a preferred view of a given event.

By reason of the persuasive implications of framing, the notion has been used – amongst others – to explore ideological bias (cf. Entman 2010), which can be seen as a form of manipulation, though not one which necessarily leads to misinformation. However, it can easily be seen how the concept can also be used to investigate the way in which by means of textual operations certain core facts can be (mis)represented in such a way as to convey remarkably different information, to the extent that some of these representations may be defined as misleading.

Based on the previous discussion, it is possible to state that framing cues relevance, which, in turn, is fundamental to enable the retrieval of the intended meaning of a given message.

Now, if we go back to our original concern, that is, the need to devise a method for addressing and explaining the nature of semi-fake news, we can see that, in the case of misleading news resulting from diversion fallacies, selection, relevance, and intention are central concepts. In fallacies from diversion, claims made by another party (in an argumentative debate, the opponent) are subjected to strategic selection (and possibly, but not necessarily, linguistic alteration) and turned into the central element of an alternative argument making a different claim. They are, in other words, fallacies related to quotation – whether because quotation is selective to the point of being fallacious, or because it is a misquotation. Diversion strategies such as *red herring* (distracting attention from the object of discussion by drawing attention to an irrelevant topic) and *strawman* (misrepresenting an opponent's position so as to more easily attack it) lift claims out of their original context and embed them in a different context where they are used to cue (entirely) different interpretations – interpretations which contrast with, or at least diverge from, the ones which were within the communicative intentions of the original utterer. And here lies the problem: the reported news betrays the communicative intentions embedded in the source text by encouraging, through the manipulation of relevance (though not of facts), inferences which are not invoked nor licensed by the original text.

2.3 Misrepresentation of intention

The role of the misrepresentation of intention in fallacious reasoning has been exhaustively discussed by Walton and Macagno (2010) in their discussion of the fallacy of *wrenching from context*. Wrenching from context is "a fallacy in which there are two or more parties engaged in argumentation and one has interpreted or represented the position of another in an improper way that has failed to take the context of the other's statement into account" (Walton and Macagno 2010: 284). The strategy involves "a distortion of the other's position and is based on ambiguity arising from emphasis on a particular aspect of a quotation" (Walton and Macagno 2010: 284); it differs from, for instance, selection bias (which is normal and expected in media reporting) because it involves a greater degree of deceptive manipulation. Wrenching from context does not involve misquotation: the quotation is correct, but it is embedded in a different context in such a way as to distort the original meaning.

One aspect of wrenching from context which Walton and Macagno (2010) emphasise as being distinctive of this fallacy is that, differently, for instance, from other strategies involving quotation, such as *strawman*, in wrenching from context the misrepresented quotation may report not the opponent's, but rather a third party's words. This makes this fallacy especially interesting in the context of the analysis of fallacious scientific reporting, because the faulty reasoning involved in the practice is not necessarily meant to attack the utterer of the quote, but rather misrepresents the position of a third party (the original research authors) in order to put forth a claim which is different from the one made in the original text.

Quoting Van Eemeren and Grootendorst (1992), Walton and Macagno point out that "the determination of a text sense is made primarily by the comprehension of the speaker's intentions" (Walton and Macagno 2010: 303), and argue that the fallacies arising from wrenching from context can be interpreted as being caused by a wrong attribution of intent (*ibid.*). In misleading scientific news reporting, the original sense of text from which the quote is lifted is altered to serve a different communicative purpose. The strategy is particularly convenient for the arguer because it exempts him or her from the burden of proof, shifting it to the utterer of the original utterance: after all, the reporter is quoting from a research paper whose authors remain responsible for its content.

Walton and Macagno's discussion of wrenching from context also provides useful insights into the reason why it is so difficult to find reliable linguistic indicators of misleading, but not fabricated, news. The discursive strategies involved in wrenching from context are not fallacious *per se*. As the two authors point out,

> an omission of context may not be fallacious at all if it does not bring about a distortion in meaning used to attack an arguer or draw a wrong conclusion from what was supposedly said. Nor is bias always fallacious. Nor is selective quotation always fallacious. Nor is paraphrase always fallacious.
>
> (Walton and Macagno 2010: 315)

However, "such factors may be fallacious, if additional conditions are met" – the key condition being, specifically, the misrepresentation of intent.

Of course, if the intent of the utterer of the original utterance is the benchmark against which to assess the validity of an argument, recognising a fallacious claim without having access to the source of the quote becomes near impossible. In the case of scientific discourse and popularisation, the very inaccessibility of the original information to the general public is a factor that inhibits the identification of the fallaciousness of semi-fake news.

3   An analysis of not-quite-fake-but-misleading news

In this section, I discuss a piece of misleading news based on the theoretical considerations outlined previously. The piece of scientific research I have selected for the analysis is the one already briefly discussed in Section 1, where I highlighted the misleading nature of the headline of two news articles reporting on the same findings. In this section, I will compare the abstract of the original research paper (Text 1) with an example of accurate reporting despite the misleading headline (Text 1a), and one of misleading reporting (Text 1b), and will describe the aspects of Text (1b) which make it fallacious in light of the notions of framing, relevance, and misrepresentation of intentions outlined previously.

Text (1)

Sperm quality and absence of SARS-CoV-2 RNA in semen after COVID-19 infection: a prospective, observational study and validation of the SpermCOVID test

Objective: To study the contagiousness of sperm and its influence on fertility after recovery from COVID-19 infection.

Design: Prospective cohort study.

Setting: University medical center.

Patient(s): One hundred twenty Belgian men who had recovered from proven COVID-19 infection.

Intervention(s): No intervention was performed.

Main outcome measure(s): Semen quality was assessed using the World Health Organisation criteria. DNA damage to sperm cells was assessed by quantifying the DNA fragmentation index and the high density stainability. Finally antibodies against SARS-CoV2 spike-1 antigen, nuclear and S1-receptor binding domain were measured by Elisa and chemilumenscent microparticle immunoassays, respectively.

Result(s): SARS-CoV-2 RNA was not detected in semen during the period shortly after infection nor at a later time. Mean progressive motility was reduced in 60% of men tested shortly (<1 month) after COVID-19 infection, 37% of men tested 1 to 2 months after COVID-19 infection, and 28% of men tested >2 months after COVID-19 infection. Mean sperm count was reduced in 37% of men tested shortly (<1 month) after COVID-19 infection, 29% of men tested 1 to 2 months after COVID-19 infection, and 6% of men tested >2 months after COVID-19 infection. The severity of COVID-19 infection and the presence of fever were not correlated with sperm characteristics, but there were strong correlations between sperm abnormalities and the titers of SARS-CoV-2 IgG antibody against spike 1 and the receptor-binding domain of spike 1, but not against nucleotide, in serum. High levels of antisperm antibodies developed in three men (2.5%).

Conclusion(s): Semen is not infectious with SARS-CoV-2 at 1 week or more after COVID-19 infection (mean, 53 days). However, couples with a desire for pregnancy should be warned that sperm quality after COVID-19 infection can be suboptimal. The estimated recovery time is 3 months,

---

but further follow-up studies are under way to confirm this and to determine if permanent damage occurred in a minority of men.

Keywords: DNA fragmentation index; infertility; real-time quantitative PCR; test validation; transmission risk.

The abstract in Text (1) conforms to the conventional structure of the genre, which is highlighted by its breakdown into its component moves, each with its own subheading. To determine the text sense (i.e. its meaning grounded in its intentions and derived from the contextual reading of single utterances), the Objective and Conclusion(s) sections appear to be the most relevant, with the Result(s) section providing supporting evidence. The contents of the abstract can be further schematized as follows:

As can be seen, the study aimed to answer two separate research questions, one related to sperm contagiousness, the other to the possible effects of COVID-19 infection on fertility. RQ1 is answered in a straightforward manner: the research showed no signs of sperm contagiousness; the answer to RQ2, by contrast, consists of three separate but interconnected claims, with the sense of the text (i.e. its meaning as intended by the authors) emerging from all three of them (and not from each of them separately, though, of course, they are all independently valid). This suggests that for the results to be faithfully reported in a news article, all three claims must be represented. Missing out on any of them would result in misrepresentation of the intentions of the original authors.

Let us now consider text (1a), which appeared on a US news channel. As the news provider refused to grant permission to reproduce the full article, its content and textual organisation can only be schematically summarised here. Figures 5.1–5.2 shows what claims made in the abstract occur in the news article. Claims that are fully reported are highlighted in dark grey; claims that are only partially reported are highlighted in light grey; unreported claims are not highlighted.

Selection strategies are quite clearly at play in the news report. First of all, the article only discusses the results pertaining to RQ2. That this should be the case is not unusual, given the unproblematic findings concerning sperm contagiousness and the greater potential relevance of fertility issues for the general public, coupled with the broader interest for such issues also in relation to the much discussed alleged effects of COVID-19 vaccines on both female and male fertility, which

RQ1: contagiousness of sperm　　**RQ2: influence on fertility after recovery from COVID-19 infection**

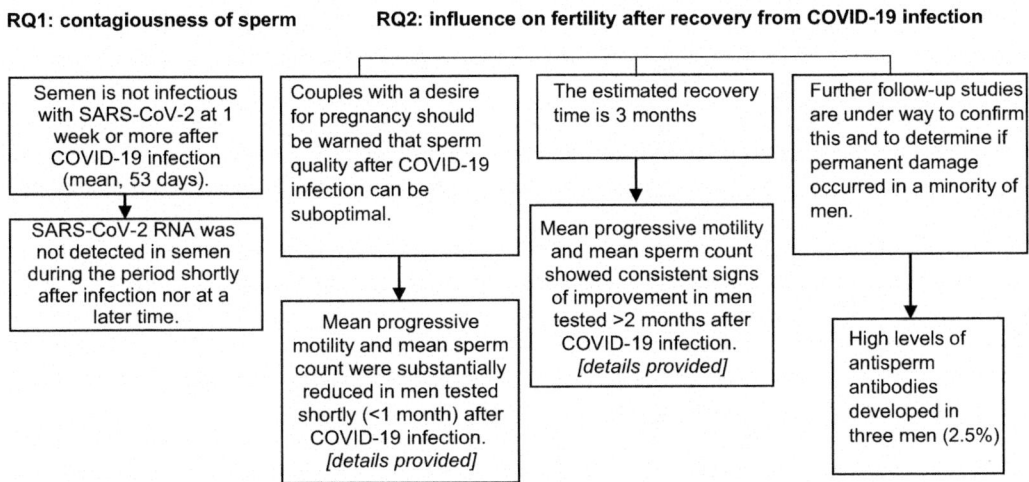

Figure 5.1　Schematic representation of the claims and supporting arguments in Text 1

RQ1: contagiousness of sperm   **RQ2: influence on fertility after recovery from COVID-19 infection**

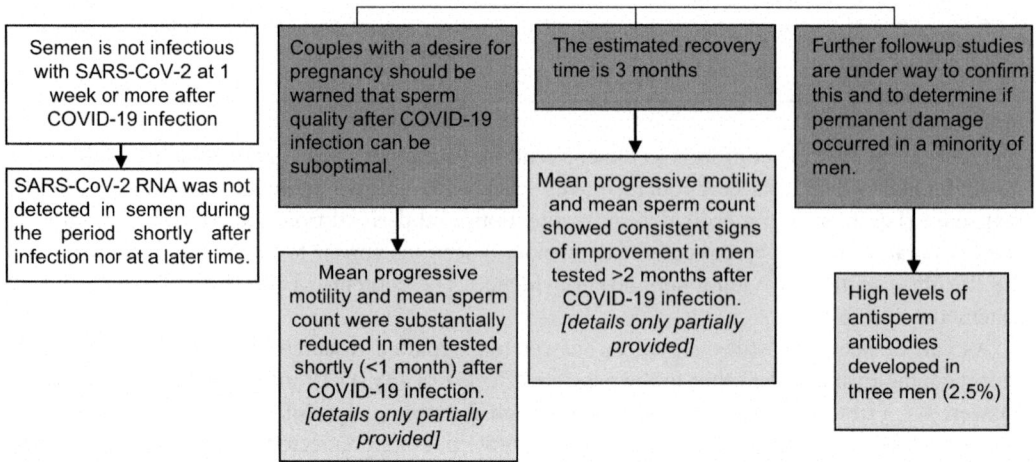

Figure 5.2 Claims reported in Text (1a)

had contributed to vaccine hesitancy in the months prior to the publication of the research. The article, in other words, focuses on the main takeaway of the research, that is, that people should be aware of the possible decrease in sperm quality in the period immediately following COVID-19 infection. This point is made twice in the article, at the beginning and at the end – both of them strong points of focus. As for the rest of the contents, not all the details of the findings are reported with the same exhaustiveness; however, the three interlocking claims constituting the conclusions conveying the intention of the research writers are all present. Overall, the article faithfully conveys the findings and implications of the original research, providing a truthful account even while omitting some of the details. The exclusive focus on fertility is the result of framing choices, and the provision of details, albeit partial ones, is in the service of optimal relevance aimed at aiding readers to accept the validity of the research authors' conclusions.

Let us now turn to Text (1b), also published by a US news provider. The contents of the text are schematically summarised in Figure 5.3. As can be seen, the article reproduces claims relating to both RQ1 and RQ2, but supporting details are for the most part missing, and the findings pertaining to RQ2 are only partially reported:

The bulk of the article is occupied by findings relating to the fertility impact of COVID-19 infection. This is similar to what was seen in Text (1a); differently from Text (1a), however, Text (1b) does not suppress the findings relating to RQ1, even though it does background them, only mentioning them in the closing.

With regard to the findings concerning infertility, only the first of the three interlocked claims is correctly reported. In argumentative terms, this could arguably be considered a form of cherry-picking, that is, of only selecting the evidence which supports a preferred interpretation. In light of the discussion of the fallacy of wrenching from context offered in Section 2.3, however, I would be inclined to assign this selective use of quotation to this fallacy. In terms of framing, the emphasis is placed exclusively on the finding relating to the measurements taken soon after recovery, and while the article does state that the decrease in sperm count and quality "is most severe early after infection", it fails to mention the subsequent improvement, which hinders readers' perception of its relevance. It may be argued that the existence of a subsequent improvement is implied by the

RQ1: contagiousness of sperm　　　　**RQ2: influence on fertility after recovery from COVID-19 infection**

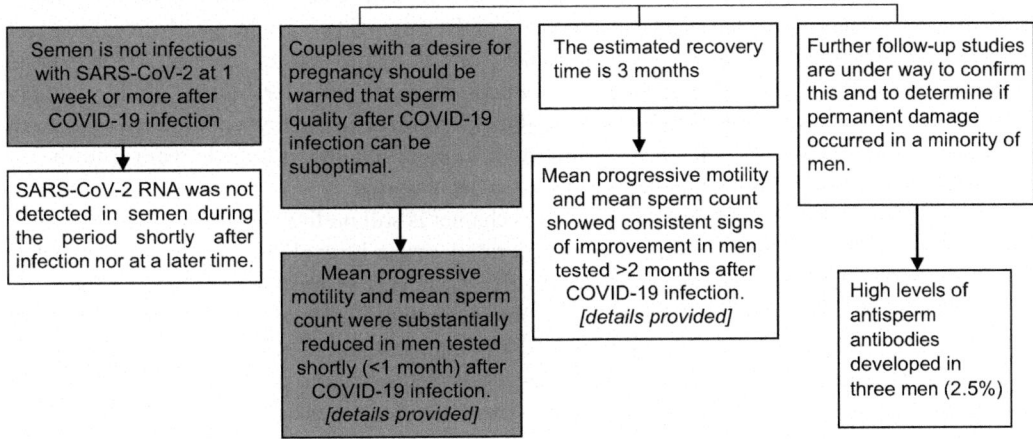

Semen is not infectious with SARS-CoV-2 at 1 week or more after COVID-19 infection	Couples with a desire for pregnancy should be warned that sperm quality after COVID-19 infection can be suboptimal.	The estimated recovery time is 3 months	Further follow-up studies are under way to confirm this and to determine if permanent damage occurred in a minority of men.
SARS-CoV-2 RNA was not detected in semen during the period shortly after infection nor at a later time.	Mean progressive motility and mean sperm count were substantially reduced in men tested shortly (<1 month) after COVID-19 infection. *[details provided]*	Mean progressive motility and mean sperm count showed consistent signs of improvement in men tested >2 months after COVID-19 infection. *[details provided]*	High levels of antisperm antibodies developed in three men (2.5%)

Figure 5.3　Claims reported in Text (1b)

phrase "*most* severe *early after infection*", which carries the implicature that there is a time, which is not early after infection, when sperm quality is not as impaired. In accordance with the tenets of relevance theory, information that is inferable but not foregrounded or at least explicitly stated requires, however, a supplement of cognitive processing which goes counter to the principle of least effort underpinning the notion of optimal relevance. Thus, while no false information is provided, suppression of information, combined with the introduction of the linguistically ambiguous expression "for months", which is conventionally used to indicate an unacceptably long time, in the headline ("COVID-19 could impact male fertility *for months* after recovery"), encourages an interpretation which departs from the intentions and commitment encoded in the original article, with effects on the reader that can be confusing at best and misleading at worst.

4　Conclusions

In this chapter I have attempted to offer an account of the discursive operations and cognitive phenomena involved in the communicative functioning of semi-fake news, that is, news stories which are not quite fake but which qualify as potentially, when not factually, misleading – at least to a certain extent. While they cannot be defined as disinformation by reason of the fact that they do not deliberately aim at inducing false beliefs in readers, they do fall into the category of misinformation: by failing to represent accurately the intention of the text on which they are based, they convey information in a way which is often not simply biased but conducive to inferences which are unwarranted by the evidence originally provided. As highlighted in the introduction, this type of misinformation is particularly dangerous because it is difficult to spot and often equally difficult to explain.

In order to explain semi-fake news, I have relied on three different but interrelated concepts: (1) the concept of framing; (2) the notion of cognitive relevance as posited in relevance theory; and (3) the argumentative fallacy of wrenching from context, which entails a selective use of quotations that fail to convey the "text sense" as intended by the authors of the source text on which the popularised version is based, thus misrepresenting their intention.

Framing rests on selection. Selection *per se* is not only not necessarily fallacious but inevitable, and indeed necessary, in scientific popularisation. When selective use of a source text fails – deliberately or otherwise – to reflect the intentions of the original text producers, the resulting text may end up warranting inferences which were not licensed by the original text and which may be misleading. Even when the popularised text contains implicit (but inferable) information which may be used, if effectively retrieved, to realign the claims made in the text with the ones put forth in the source text, lack of "ostensive stimuli" will in most likelihood impede them from being perceived as relevant, thus leading to their dismissal as marginal.

The account of semi-fake news outlined in this chapter is still preliminary and requires theoretical refining, as well as further testing to more accurately assess its explanatory power. Its potential applications are, however, manifold. Most notably, the notion of misrepresentation of intention could be usefully deployed in the service of establishing quality standards for scientific reporting to be used not only to assess the quality of media popularisations of science but also in training courses for prospective scientific journalists. Raising awareness about the risks of a fallacious use of selection (in itself a routine practice in journalism) may help avoid unintentional misinformation. The notions of relevance, framing and manipulation of intentions could also be used in media and digital literacy courses to enhance understanding of the reasons why a given piece of news is to be considered semi-fake. As for the identification of semi-fake news, the analysis of samples of truthful and semi-fake science news reporting conducted in Section 3 suggests that, even in the absence of a direct comparison with the original piece of research, comparing the way in which the same piece of news is reported across different media may provide insights into potential distortions which exceed the degree of bias which is to be normally expected in news reporting, especially in the case of controversial news. Devising methods to automatically retrieve and compare multiple news on the same scientific findings may provide a heuristic tool for flagging potential semi-fake news for further probing and assessment.

Semi-fake news represents a huge challenge to effective scientific popularisation. It is hoped that this study has provided some useful insights for a better understanding of the processes at play in their construction and reception, and that it will pave the way for more in-depth inquiries into this phenomenon.

Note

1 Among the research on misinformation in the domain of health and medicine, Ha, Andreu Perez, and Ray quote Seltzer et al.'s (2017) study of misinformation during a Zica outbreak, Shelby and Ernst (2013) and Zimet et al. (2013) research on misinformation on vaccines, and Bryant and Levi's (2012), Chipeta et al. (2010), Rowlands' (2011) and Tobin's (2008) studies on contraception, abortion, and women's health. To this list they add studies on misinformation in environmental science and climate change (Bedford 2010; van der Linden et al. 2017) – all particularly controversial domains where the politicisation of the debate can easily lead to deliberate manipulation and, hence, purposeful misinformation.

References

Allcott, H., and Gentzkow, M. 2017. Social media and fake news in the 2016 election. *Journal of Economic Perspectives* 31(2): 211–236. http://doi.org/10.1257/jep.31.2.211.

Bauman, R., and Briggs, G. 1990. Poetics and performance as critical perspectives on language and social life. *Annual Review of Anthropology* ix: 59–88.

Bedford, D. 2010. Agnotology as a teaching tool: Learning climate science by studying misinformation. *Journal of Geography* 109: 159–165.

Bryant, A. G., and Levi, E. E. 2012. Abortion misinformation from crisis pregnancy centers in North Carolina. *Contraception* 86: 752–756.

Cappella, J. N., and Jamieson, K. H. 1997. *Spiral of cynicism. The press and the public good*. New York: Oxford University Press.

Chipeta, E. K., Chimwaza, W., and Kalilani-Phiri, L. 2010. Contraceptive knowledge, beliefs and attitudes in rural Malawi: Misinformation, misbeliefs and misperceptions. *Malawi Medical Journal* 22: 38–41.

de Vreese, C. H. 2005. News framing: Theory and typology. *Information Design Journal + Document Design* 13(1): 51–62.

Donders, G. G. G., Bosmans, E., Reumers, J., Donders, F., Jonckheere, J., Salembier, G., Stern, N., Jacquemyn, Y., Ombelet, W., and Depuydt, C. E. 2022. Sperm quality and absence of SARS-CoV-2 RNA in semen after COVID-19 infection: A prospective, observational study and validation of the SpermCOVID test. *Fertility and Sterility* 117(2): 287–296.

Entman, R. M. 1993. Framing: Toward clarification of a fractured paradigm. *Journal of Communication* 43(4): 51–58.

Entman, R. M. 2010. Media framing biases and political power: Explaining slant in news of campaign 2008. *Journalism* 11(4): 389–408.

Fairclough, N. 2014. *Language and Power*. London: Longman.

Gamson, W. A., and Modigliani, A. 1989. Media discourse and public opinion on nuclear power: A constructionist approach. *American Journal of Sociology* 95: 1–37.

Garzone, G. 2014. News production and scientific knowledge: Exploring popularization as a process. In Caliendo, G., and Bongo, G. (eds.), *The Language of Popularization: Die Sprache der Popularisierung*. Bern: Peter Lang, pp. 73–107.

Garzone, G. 2018. Scientific knowledge and legislative drafting: Focus on surrogacy laws. *Lingue Culture Mediazioni/Languages Cultures Mediation* 5(1): 9–36.

Garzone, G. 2020. *Specialized Communication and Popularization in English*. Roma: Carocci Editore.

Gelfert, A. 2018. Fake news: A definition. *Informal Logic* 38(1): 84–117.

Gitlin, T. 1980. *The Whole World is Watching*. Berkeley: University of California Press.

Goffman, E. 1974. *Frame Analysis: An Essay on the Organization of Experience*. London: Harper and Row.

Gorbach, J. 2018. Not your grandpa's hoax: A comparative history of fake news. *American Journalism* 35(2): 236–249.

Grice, H. P. 1989. *Studies in the Way of Words*. Cambridge, MA: Harvard University Press.

Ha, L., Andreu Perez, L., and Ray, R. 2021. Mapping recent development in scholarship on fake news and misinformation, 2008 to 2017: Disciplinary contribution, topics, and impact. *American Behavioral Scientist* 65(2): 290–315. https://doi.org/10.1177/0002764219869402

Kyriakidou, M., Morani, M., Soo, N., et al. 2020. Government and media misinformation about COVID-19 is confusing the public. In *LSE COVID-19 Blog*. Available at: https://blogs.lse.ac.uk/covid19/2020/05/07/government-and-media-misinformation-about-covid-19-is-confusing-the-public/ (accessed 1 June 2021).

Linell, P. 1998. *Approaching Dialogue: Talk, Interaction and Contexts in Dialogical Perspectives*. Amsterdam: Benjamins. https://doi.org/10.1075/impact.3

Linell, P. 2009. Discourse across boundaries: On recontextualizations and the blending of voices in Professional discourse. *Text* 18(2): 143–158.

Musi, E., Aloumpi, M., Carmi, E., Yates, S., and O'Halloran, K. 2022. Developing fake news immunity: Fallacies as misinformation triggers during the pandemic. *Online Journal of Communication and Media Technologies* 12(3): e202217.

Musi, E., and Reed, C. 2022. From fallacies to semifake news: Improving the identification of misinformation triggers across digital media. *Discourse and Society* 33(3): 349–370.

Nikitina, J. 2020. Representation of gene-editing in British and Italian newspapers. A cross-linguistic corpus-assisted discourse study. *Lingue & Linguaggi* 34: 51–75.

Rashkin, H., Choi, E., Jang, J. Y., Volkova, S., and Choi, Y. 2017. Truth of varying shades: Analyzing language in fake news and political fact-checking 2017. In *Proceedings of the 2017 Conference on Empirical Methods in Natural Language Processing*. Copenhagen, Denmark, pp. 2931–2937, September 7–11, 2017.

Rowlands, S. 2011. Misinformation on abortion. *European Journal of Contraception & Reproductive Health Care* 16: 233–240.

Rubin, V. L. 2019. Disinformation and misinformation triangle: A conceptual model for "fake news" epidemic, causal factors and interventions. *Journal of Documentation* 75(5): 1013–1034.

Rubin, V. L., Chen, Y., and Conroy, N. J. 2015. Deception detection for news: Three types of fakes. *Proceedings of the Association for Information Science and Technology* 52(1): 1–4.

Seltzer, E. K., Horst-Martz, E., Lu, M., and Merchant, R. M. 2017. Public sentiment and discourse about Zika virus on Instagram. *Public Health* 150: 170–175.

Shelby, A., and Ernst, K. 2013. Story and science: How providers and parents can utilize storytelling to combat anti-vaccine misinformation. *Human Vaccines & Immunotherapeutics* 9: 1795–1801.

Sherman, E. 2018, November 26. *Dictionary.com's Word of the Year is "Misinformation": A Slap at High Tech.* Available at: http://fortune.com/2018/11/26/misinformation-dictionary-com-word-year-misinformation-social-media-tech/

Sperber, D., and Wilson, D. 1986. *Relevance: Communication and Cognition.* Oxford: Blackwell.

Tandoc, E. C. Jr., Wei Lim, Z., and Ling, R. 2018. Defining "fake news": A typology of scholarly definitions. *Digital Journalism* 6(2): 137–153.

Tindale, C. W. 2007. *Fallacies and Argument Appraisal.* Cambridge: Cambridge University Press. https://doi.org/10.1017/CBO9780511806544

Tobin, H. J. 2008. Confronting misinformation on abortion: Informed consent, deference, and fetal pain laws. *Columbia Journal of Gender & Law* 17(1). Available at: https://ssrn.com/abstract=1174297

van der Linden, S., Leiserowitz, A., Rosenthal, S., and Maibach, E. 2017. Inoculating the public against misinformation about climate change. *Global Challenges* 1(2): 1600008.

van Dijk, T. 1998. *Ideology: A Multi-disciplinary Approach.* Thousand Oaks, CA: Sage.

Van Eemeren, F., and Grootendorst, R. 1992. *Argumentation, Communication, and Fallacies.* Hillsdale: Lawrence Erlbaum Associates.

Vlachos, A., and Riedel, S. 2014. Fact checking: Task definition and dataset construction. In *Proceedings of the ACL 2014 Workshop on Language Technologies and Computational Social Science.* Baltimore, MD: Association for Computational Linguistics, 18–22.

Walton, D. 1987. *Informal Fallacies: Towards a Theory of Argument Criticisms.* Amsterdam: John Benjamins.

Walton, D., and Macagno, F. 2010. Wrenching from context: The manipulation of commitments. *Argumentation* 24(3): 283–317.

Watson, C. A. 2018. Information literacy in a fake/false news world: An overview of the characteristics of fake news and its historical development. *International Journal of Legal Information* 46(2): 93–96.

Wilson, D., and Sperber, D. 1998. Pragmatic and time. In Carston, R. (ed.), *Relevance Theory.* Amsterdam: John Benjamins.

Wilson, D., and Sperber, D. 2002. Relevance theory. In Horn, L., and Ward, G. (eds.), *Handbook of Pragmatics.* Oxford: Blackwell, pp. 249–290.

Zimet, G. D., Rosberger, Z., Fisher, W. A., Perez, S., and Stupiansky, N. W. 2013. Beliefs, behaviors and HPV vaccine: Correcting the myths and the misinformation. *Preventive Medicine*, 57, 414–418.

6

MISINFORMATION DETECTION IN NEWS TEXT

Automatic methods and data limitations

Fatemeh Torabi Asr, Mehrdad Mokhtari, and Maite Taboada

1   Introduction: the problem of detecting the language of misinformation

A major vulnerability of public discourse online – a fast, unbound, and often anonymous medium – is the increased susceptibility to deception. When we started this research, in 2017, "fake news" was an accusation against some news organisations and a small area of research in the academic community. Just a few short years of political turmoil across the globe, a pandemic, and a climate crisis have brought misinformation to the forefront of public discourse and to the attention of many researchers.

Fake news has been defined in different ways, such as "news articles that are intentionally and verifiably false, and could mislead readers" (Allcott and Gentzkow, 2017). We find "misinformation" (wrong information) and "disinformation" (wrong information with the intention to deceive) more accurate terms for scientific research as compared to "fake news", which is frequently used in political discourse and media stories (for definitions, see Habgood-Coote, 2019; Tandoc Jr et al., 2018; Wardle and Derakhshan, 2017). The subject of our study is false information in news text, regardless of the distributing source's intention, thus misinformation in its general sense, which can manifest itself as rumours and hoaxes, propaganda, or even false information in mainstream news publications.

The research community turned its attention to the phenomenon in 2015 and 2016 (Connolly et al., 2016; Perrott, 2016), with two comprehensive studies published in 2018 (Lazer et al., 2018; Vosoughi et al., 2018). The latter in particular clearly established the danger of misinformation: Fake news stories are particularly dangerous because they not only tend to reach a larger audience but also penetrate into social networks nearly ten times faster than fact-based news (Vosoughi et al., 2018).

The current trends to combat the misinformation problem take three main approaches: educate the public, carry out manual checking, or perform automatic classification. Educating the public involves encouraging readers to check the source of the story, its distribution (who has shared it, how many times), or to run it by fact-checking websites. This is certainly necessary, but it will not be enough. Organised manual checking, before or after publication, is a possibility, but it is also not a realistic solution, given the fast spread of misinformation that Vosoughi et al. (2018) found. Approaches from machine learning, computational linguistics, and natural language processing (NLP) show promise, in that they can perform automatic classification and can help complement the efforts of fact-checking sites. The promise is that we will be able to detect fake news stories

DOI: 10.4324/9781003224495-7

automatically, before they have a chance to spread and do harm. The process of fact-checking can be modelled as a series of NLP tasks, from identifying claims and rumours to comparing information and producing fact-checking verdicts and justifications (Guo et al., 2022). In this chapter, we explore the deployment of a specific NLP task, text classification.

One of the important challenges in automatic misinformation detection using modern NLP techniques is data (Asr and Taboada, 2018, 2019). Annotation of fake news is a resource-demanding and particularly sensitive task because of the wide spectrum of public opinions about who exactly is a reliable source, including established news organisations. The majority of automatic systems built to identify fake news rely on training data (news articles) labelled with respect to the credibility or the general reputations of the sources, that is, domains/user accounts (Fogg et al., 2001; Horne et al., 2018; Nørregaard et al., 2019; Rashkin et al., 2017; Volkova et al., 2017; Yang et al., 2017). Even though some of these studies try to identify fake news based on linguistic cues, what they eventually model is the publisher's general writing style (e.g. common writing features of the publishing websites) rather than the linguistic similarities of the articles containing false information.

For example, Rashkin et al. (2017) collected news articles from websites that they categorized as general publishers of hoax, propaganda, satire, or trusted (mainstream) news. They showed that a classifier trained on news articles from some of these websites could identify news from other websites from the same category, thus learning the general linguistic characteristics of each type of publisher. Detecting the style of a news article in terms of belonging to coarse categories such as satire, propaganda, hoax, or trusted mainstream outlets is an interesting task, but not exactly what we would like to do in our battle against fake news. The goal of our paper is to pursue a slightly different and hypothetically more difficult task, namely, detecting, based on linguistic properties, whether or not a news article contains false information. This is useful, because the approach could then work across different sites, regardless of publisher.

In terms of methodology, we focus on a content-based approach to news text classification. Rather than using contextual metadata such as user activity features, network cues, or credibility of the publishing sources, we assess the feasibility of detecting misinformation by examining the content of the article, that is, the text itself. This puts our work in the category of *style-based* fake news detection, as opposed to *context-based* or *knowledge-based* detection (Potthast et al., 2018) and in the area of language-based detection (Lugea, 2021). The hypothesis behind our approach is that deception in news has its own style, that is, a language for misinformation. If the language of news articles with true vs false content is different, then we should be able to detect misinformation even with no access to metadata or a universal knowledge base about which facts are true.

In order to investigate this hypothesis, we explore a variety of data collections and state-of-the-art text classification techniques. We test both classic feature-based models and modern deep learning classifiers. Big data is required for robust performance and especially in the case of deep learning models. Unfortunately, however, available datasets for automatic misinformation detection are either small in size but accurate in labels, or large in size but labelled based on source reputation. To address the lack of data, we leverage fact-checking websites and collect news articles that these fact-checkers have labelled as false and true. These collections are still much smaller than standard benchmark datasets in text classification. Therefore, we also test two transfer learning approaches:

- Label transfer: using a large dataset of reputation-based labelled news articles as training data and considering news articles from generally known fake publishers as "false" and that of mainstream publishers as "true" (mapping propaganda, hoax, and satire in Rashkin's data to "false" and the trusted category to "true").

- Knowledge transfer: using a relatively small dataset of fact-checked news articles as training data in combination with a pretrained language model based on deep learning techniques for text classification.

In both training settings, we tune model parameters on a validation set and then test on reliably labelled news articles, which have been individually fact-checked and rated as true or false. Our test datasets are either sampled from the same distribution of the training data (mixed claims/topics/headlines) or a different distribution (unseen claims/topics/headlines). Our experiments show that a "classic" feature-based model trained on the small but fact-checked dataset would generalise better and achieve a higher accuracy on unseen topics. The knowledge transfer model, which uses a pretrained language model as its linguistics backbone, can fine-tune itself to the small training data and achieve a higher accuracy on test data from a similar distribution. However, this model does not generalise well to unseen topics. Finally, the label transfer technique that uses large training data collected from categorized publishers does not distinguish between false and true news articles in a fact-checked test dataset and has a large bias towards labelling anything as fake news. This suggests that reputation-based labelling, despite its potential to easily provide us with big data, is not suitable for misinformation detection in terms of veracity checking. Error analysis reveals that, for a robust and scalable classification, we would need more fact-checked news articles from a variety of topics and balanced across labels.

The contributions of this approach are twofold, in data and in methods. In data, we explore the right amount and type of data necessary to reliably train misinformation classification methods and release a mid-size dataset for the task. In terms of methods, we first conduct a feature analysis on false and true news articles and then build and evaluate a variety of text classifiers for predictive modelling. Above all, we see these experiments as a cautionary tale on the use of NLP and machine learning techniques on data that has not been properly collected and examined.

2 Related work

Many of the studies in detecting misinformation apply what we may call "classic" machine learning methods, that is, supervised classification with a variety of features. The features range from surface characteristics such as document length and n-gram frequency to specific types of semantic classes (e.g. subjectivity and emotion markers), syntactic features (e.g. depth of syntactic tree and frequency of each part of speech) and discourse-level features (Afroz et al., 2012; Conroy et al., 2015; Horne and Adali, 2017; Pérez-Rosas and Mihalcea, 2015; Rashkin et al., 2017; Rubin et al., 2015; Ruchansky et al., 2017; Volkova et al., 2017). Some of these studies have been characterised as stylometric (Przybyla, 2020), in that they use the style of the language as an indicator of misinformation.

Algorithms deployed in this type of supervised learning are often Support Vector Machines (SVMs), with a feature engineering and feature selection process. Performance in these approaches tends to plateau as data increases, showing that features are useful with smaller amounts of data, but performance increases stall at some point as amount of available data increases. Therefore, these methods are considered to have an important limitation (Ng, 2011).

A second set of studies use modern neural network models. In cases where large amounts of data are available, deep neural network models tend to achieve more impressive results. Deep learning has, in general, taken over many natural language processing tasks, at least in domains where large-scale training data is available. Deep learning models in NLP usually rely on word vectors and embedded representations. Although it is possible to extract embeddings from domain data, most methods rely on pretrained embeddings (Le and Mikolov, 2014; Pennington et al.,

2014). Models in deep learning include recurrent neural networks (RNNs), convolutional neural networks (CNNs), and attention models (Conneau et al., 2017; Lai et al., 2015; Le and Mikolov, 2014; Medvedeva et al., 2017; Yang et al., 2016; Zhang et al., 2015). They perform slightly differently, depending on the task and the type of data. In general, the task tends to be a binary classification task (i.e. is this text X or Y?). In our case, whether the text in question is an instance of fake news/misinformation or an instance of reliable, fact-based news. For this task, what RNNs do is encode sequential information in the articles, modelling short text semantics. CNNs are composed of convolution and pooling layers, providing an abstraction of the input. CNNs are useful in tasks where presence or absence of features is a more distinguishing factor than their location or order, and work well when classifying longer text. For instance, CNNs are helpful in sentiment analysis of product reviews, where the distinguishing features between positive and negative reviews may be the relative frequency or presence of positive and negative words (Dos Santos and Gatti, 2014; Kucharski, 2016; Ouyang et al., 2015).

The issue with many of these studies is the data collection methodology. Many of the existing datasets use publisher/website reputation as the main criterion for collection (Przybyla, 2020). A website is assumed to be a "fake news publisher" as a whole, with no individual labelling of data. It is often the case, however, that these publishers mix truth with lies, publishing relatively true stories, or republishing stories from reputable sources. It is also the case, albeit much less frequently, that reputable websites may inadvertently publish inaccurate information (Fichtner, 2018; Mantzarlis, 2017). In fact, this fundamental distinction between focusing on fake news outlets vs fake news stories may be the source of much confusion about how much misinformation is actually circulating (Ruths, 2019).

The solution to the unreliability of publishers is to label each news article individually as to whether it is reliable or not. This kind of data is rare, and it is difficult to assign such labels as the task requires professional expertise and background knowledge.

Small existing datasets include a collection by Allcott and Gentzkow (2017), who annotated 156 articles by manually consulting three fact-checking websites (Snopes, Politifact, and Buzz-feed) and downloading the source page of the debunked rumours and the 40 articles annotated by the Credibility Coalition (Zhang et al., 2018). Most other data is either short statements rather than full articles (Wang, 2017), satirical news articles rather than misinformation (Rubin et al., 2016), annotations for stance (Thorne et al., 2018), or articles that were modified to be made untrue (Pérez-Rosas et al., 2017). The dataset from Shu et al. (2020) comes closest to the requirements for this task as it was crawled from fact-checking websites (but not validated after scraping).

In summary, although a few different types of datasets exist, none of them contain a large enough number of both fake and legitimate news articles, which is the type of data that we need to learn to classify misinformation (as opposed to classifying stance, headlines, or satire). For this reason, we collected our own data, using fact-checking websites, as we describe in the next section.

3   Quality data for misinformation detection

We have established that a reliably labelled collection of false and true news articles needs to be individually labelled, not scraped from specific websites. To achieve this individual labelling, we leverage fact-checking websites to collect news articles with false and true content. We use the following:

- A dataset of news articles on the topic of US election in 2016 from a BuzzFeed study;
- A dataset that we collect by harvesting the Snopes fact-checking pages and downloading the source text of the news articles.

3.1 *BuzzFeed data*

The first source of information that we used to harvest full news articles is a BuzzFeed collection of links to Facebook posts, originally compiled for a study around the 2016 US election (Silverman et al., 2016). It includes links to posts from nine Facebook pages (three right-wing, three left-wing, and three mainstream publishers) and manual annotation of the veracity of individual posts by an instructed group of raters. The dataset of links with user interaction information is available via Kaggle (www.kaggle.com/mrisdal/fact-checking-facebook-politics-pages). Unfortunately, only the Facebook link is available there, not the full article. We took each individual link, followed it to the Facebook page, and then followed the link to the original post. We scraped the webpage of the original post to extract the full text of each article, which we cleaned of HTML tags and any other extraneous material. Veracity labels come in a four-way classification scheme, including *mostly true, mixture of true and false, mostly false*, and *containing no factual content*. This dataset contains 1,380 articles. We refer to this collection as the *Buzzfeed USE* dataset.

We also use a collection of Buzzfeed selected top fake news of the year 2017 for test purposes in our classification experiments. A similar scraping process was performed to get the content of the news articles in this collection. We refer to it as the *Buzzfeed Top* dataset, and it contains 33 news articles with false content (note that this dataset is not balanced, as it contains only fake news stories). Both of the Buzzfeed datasets have been published in our previous work (Asr and Taboada, 2018, 2019). The following dataset is a new contribution.

3.2 *Snopes data*

The second source we used for collecting news texts with veracity labels is the Snopes fact-checking website. Snopes is one of the oldest and most well-known rumour debunking websites, run by a team of expert editors. In addition to finding rumours and mentioning distributing sources, they provide elaborate explanations of the rumour and its effects. News articles collected from Snopes come with a fine-grained labelling (*true, mostly true, mixture of true and false, mostly false*, and *false*). The diagram in Figure 6.1 shows the process of data collection from Snopes fact-checking pages.

The challenge with using Snopes is that the site does not reproduce the entire text of the false or debunked news article; it instead publishes an article discussing a false story or rumour. The structure of a Snopes article is the investigation of a claim, rumour, or story that has been contested. Snopes then discusses the content of that contested story, including a number of links, some to the source of the false story, some to sites that debunk the story, or other links for extra information on the topic. Our task, then, was to follow those links and, for instance, in the case of a "false" label on the Snopes site, to find the link containing the full article with the false story. The entire process involved, for each claim ("true" or "false"), scraping the discussed claim, the veracity scoring of the claim according to the Snopes labelling system, and the links to the source of the claim. Given that the scraped data might be noisy (e.g. other links on the webpage might be harvested but do not necessarily point to the source news article), a verification step is required afterwards.

We first cleaned the data by removing exact duplicates, texts that were too short, noisy (i.e. advertisements), or texts that were scraped from outdated links (pages showing a message like "this content has been removed"). We then verified the alignment between the discussed claim and the scraped body text of each article by crowd sourcing annotators on the Figure Eight platform (now part of Appen). During this process, we gave more than 4,000 texts and supposedly associated headlines to the annotators and asked them to select the alignment of the text with respect to the headline. If the alignment was right, they would next label the body text (which we scraped from the source article) as *supporting* the given headline (which we scraped from the Snopes

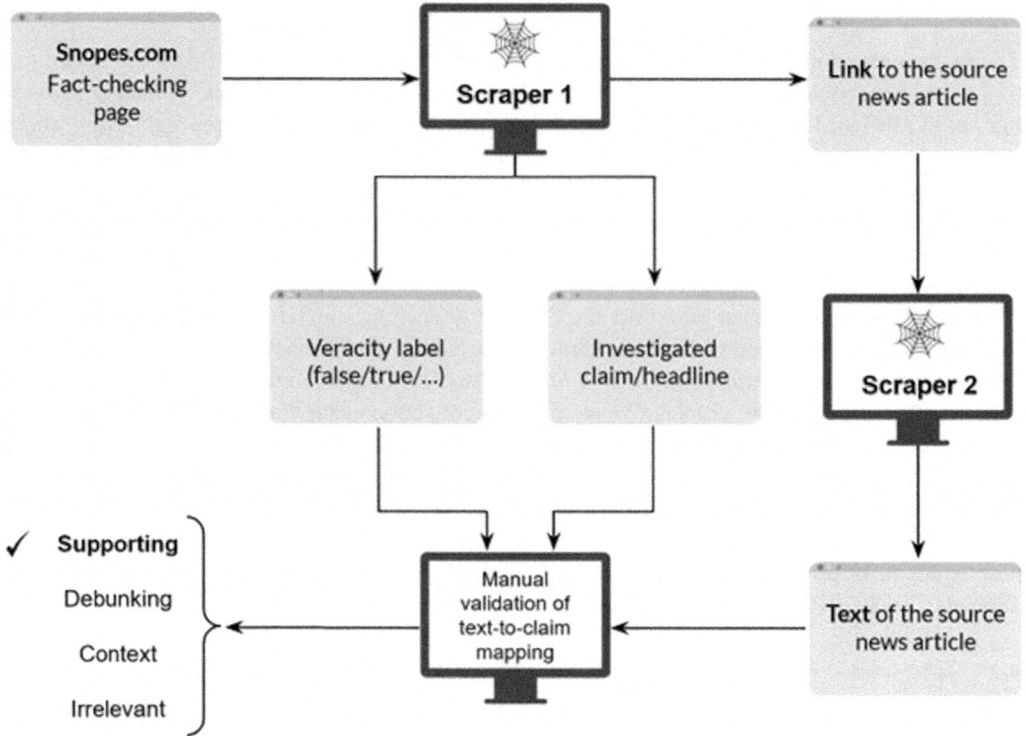

Figure 6.1   Data scraping and validation process

fact-checking page). Otherwise, they would choose one of the other answers (*debunking* the head-line, *context* information, or *irrelevant* text). Finally, we filtered all items that had the "supporting" label, which were the actual source of the debunked rumours. We refer to this dataset as the *Snopes Silver* dataset because it is annotated by crowd workers rather than in-house experts (which would make it Gold; see next section). The data contains 2,075 articles (1,425 false, 160 mostly false, 231 mixture, 17 mostly true, and 242 true items). This dataset is publicly available on our lab reposi-tory (https://github.com/sfu-discourse-lab/MisInfoText).

Before conducting the crowd sourced experiments on the automatically collected Snopes articles, we picked a semi-randomly selected set of the scraped articles and verified their association with the claims and veracity labels with the help of two annotators in our lab. Two annotators performed inde-pendent assessment of the claim and the article supposedly containing that claim. A third annotator, one of the authors of this chapter, examined each claim and article and solved any disagreements. This data includes a total of 118 news articles (17 false, 27 mostly false, 26 mixture, 26 mostly true, and 22 true items). We refer to this dataset as the *Snopes Gold* dataset, as it was more carefully curated within our lab. We have also referred to a superset collection containing these items as the Snopes312 dataset in previous work (Asr and Taboada, 2018, 2019). We made sure that the Gold dataset included a bal-anced number of articles from each veracity label and that the claims/news headlines in this smaller set did not overlap with our Silver dataset. These decisions were made so we could use the Gold dataset both as training material for crowd-source annotation and as test data (unseen claims) in our automatic text classification experiments, which will be presented in the following sections.

When we use these datasets in our experiments, we remove the "mixture" items and build a false and true category by collapsing the finer grained distinctions. This gives us a total of 1,649 false and 1,349 true items.

4 Analysing linguistic features in false and true news

The first step towards understanding the linguistic differences between false and true news articles involves conducting a feature analysis. In this section we look closely at the linguistic differences between the two datasets of news text that we introduced in the previous section and also the differences between the true and false items in each dataset. In order to conduct a feature analysis experiment, we studied five main categories of linguistic features ranging from surface properties of the text to measures of readability.

- **Surface text features.** We consider the surface properties of a text such as length and punctuation frequency. Previous work in text classification has found correlations between such features and whether the text is an instance of fake or mainstream news (Biyani et al., 2016; Horne and Adali, 2017). We employ the following surface properties of the text: number of characters, words, and sentences; proportion of punctuation; uppercase characters; and average sentence length in terms of number of words.
- **N-grams.** Short sequences of words, known as n-grams, have a long history in NLP. In text classification, models using n-gram features have been vastly successful, and they have set a difficult baseline even for modern deep learning models (Zhang et al., 2015). They represent an approximation of phrases appearing in a text, and their frequencies across documents within a corpus can be informative with regard to the similarities and differences across texts. We use the TF-IDF (term frequency-inverse document frequency) scored n-grams generated by the scikit-learn python library to visualise and understand the topic differences between fake and real news articles.
- **Semantic features.** The frequency of words coming from a specific semantic category, such as negative polarity words, words related to religion, sex, feelings, body, money, and work, can provide useful information about a text. Studies on deceptive text and fake news have used such features to try and find distributional differences between lies and truthful statements (Biyani et al., 2016; Pérez-Rosas et al., 2017; Pérez-Rosas and Mihalcea, 2015; Rashkin et al., 2017; Rubin et al., 2016). We consider a large set of semantic lexicons, where words are assigned to specific semantic categories, in order to extract semantic features from each text document. We include all lexicons from the *LIWC* (Linguistic Inquiry and Word Count) inventory (Pennebaker et al., 2015) as well as a set of lexicons for markers of subjectivity and biased language (Recasens et al., 2013; Wilson et al., 2005).
- **Syntactic features.** Syntactic properties of text have been used for text classification in a variety of domains, including deception detection (Mukherjee et al., 2013; Pérez-Rosas et al., 2017; Pérez-Rosas and Mihalcea, 2015; Post and Bergsma, 2013). We use the proportional frequency of each part of speech tag from the universal POS tagset of the NLTK library. This tagset includes 12 general tags, including NOUN, PRON, ADJ, ADV, VERB, ADP, NUM, PRT, DET, X, CONJ, and punctuation.
- **Readability features.** Measures of text coherence such as readability indices have shown to be helpful features for text classification and particularly in deception detection (Pérez-Rosas et al., 2017; Pérez-Rosas and Mihalcea, 2015). We extracted the readability indices of each text with the help of the *textstat* python library, which gives us a number for each of the following measures:

Flesch reading ease, Smog index, Coleman-Liau index, Linsear write formula, Dale-Chall readability score, automated readability index, Flesch Kincaid grade, and Gunning Fog score.

In order to provide a clear overview of the important features, we compute each of the cited feature sets for the Buzzfeed and Snopes datasets separately. We expect overlapping patterns between the two datasets in terms of the differences between the false and true news instances.

For each dataset, we first mapped all "false" and "mostly false" items to one label, that is, "false" and "true" and "mostly true" to "true". We also removed "mixture" items to avoid basing our analysis on edge cases. We then combined all documents of the false class and all documents of the true class so we can compute the average value of each feature for each class of news articles. We then provide two quantitative measures to discuss the importance of a given feature: (1) the proportional average value of the feature in false to true news articles and (2) the p-value of a correlation analysis that reveals whether the feature value difference between the false and true categories is statistically significant. We compute the p-value based on the recursive feature elimination (RFE) method of the scikit-learn python library, applied to each feature set separately, and present the most discriminating features (*p-value* < 0.001) in the result tables.

Table 6.1 shows some of the features that help distinguish between false and true news articles. All listed features in this table are significantly more frequent in one of the two categories. The rows within each feature set are sorted in ascending order based on the ratio of occurrences in false

Table 6.1 Important features for distinguishing true from false news articles; only overlaps between Buzzfeed and Snopes Silver datasets are included here. Shaded rows are features of false news articles.

Feature Category	Feature	Ratio False/True	P-value
Surface	num punc/num char	0.926844562	0.001331224
Semantic lexicon	comparative forms	0.947737051	0.020227509
	negative HuLui	1.133089752	0.00267177
	negative mpqa	1.192098625	0.000864263
	modal adverbs	1.298092007	0.005319897
	manner adverbs	1.35698137	0.001742446
Semantic LIWC	apostro	0.648061274	0.002444304
	work	0.876750931	0.00999914
	Sixltr	0.940804067	0.033111439
	cogproc	1.06101936	0.057419697
	pronoun	1.070951735	0.029411617
	auxverb	1.077592026	1.077592026
	adverb	1.110034072	1.077592026
	they	1.151274939	0.066116507
	bio	1.224761165	0.041183623
	anx	1.383614276	0.097296795
	sexual	2.753109267	0.060287064
Syntactic	NOUN	0.970826348	0.021800144
	VERB	1.034897463	1.034897463
	PRT	1.040020625	0.097773857
	ADV	1.093310376	0.000661848
	PRON	1.094581886	0.011254044

news articles to that of the true news articles within the Snopes dataset. In this table, we only kept rows that had the same pattern in the Buzzfeed dataset to avoid confusion. Two separate tables for each of the two datasets are available in the Appendix. Shaded rows in the table refer to the general features of false news articles, and rows with no background colour are those that occur more often in true news articles.

In general, the textual features reveal that false news in both datasets were on average shorter than true news and contained fewer punctuation marks. However, in the Buzzfeed data only the proportion of punctuation came out as a statistically significant marker. Therefore, other surface features are not listed in the table.

With the large number of semantic features considered in our analysis, it is not surprising to see a handful of them emerging as distinguishing features for content veracity. We find both subjectivity markers and LIWC properties in the list of helpful features. Among the lexicon-based features, we find more negative polarity words in false news compared to true news. We also find a relatively larger proportion of adverbs and, in particular, modal and manner adverbs in false news. A higher usage of comparative forms is, however, a marker of true news. Based on our analysis of LIWC features, words related to sex, death, anxiety, biological, and cognitive processes frequently occur in false news articles; whereas in true news, we found a larger proportion of words related to work and money. These patterns reveal how true and false news articles may differ in the distribution of topics and headlines. While true news articles usually discuss serious and more abstract topics, false news is more focused on topics that can quickly capture the reader's attention. Texts in the true category seem to contain longer words (Sixltr means word with more than six letters) and more apostrophes (previously also captured as more punctuation in true news). These features may reveal the more sophisticated writing style of true news, which normally appear on a moderated website with editor supervision.

Finally, the syntactic feature analysis shows that true news contains a larger proportion of nouns and numbers (the latter only significant in Snopes data); whereas false news contains more adverbs, particles, and pronouns. Looking more closely at the usage of pronouns, we find that in false news most pronouns refer to the plural third person "they", whereas in true news the first person pronoun "I" is relatively more frequent (the latter pattern significant only in Snopes data). This can be attributed to the use of direct quotations or self-mention of the reporter in true news, as opposed to repeated mention of other entities in false news, perhaps a sign of othering certain groups of people (Riggins, 1997).

Extracting the most important n-grams is a challenging task due to the large number of such features. Moreover, by examining the individual n-grams, one can hardly infer a general pattern regarding the differences they reveal between false and true news articles. In order to examine the n-grams most specific to each dataset, we first combined the Snopes Silver and the Buzzfeed USE corpora and then extracted 100 n-grams that occurred in less than half of all the documents (to avoid corpus-specific stop words) but in more than three documents within the combined corpus. We then analysed these unigrams the same way as other feature types: we calculated the false to true proportion of each unigram and filtered those with highest and lowest values and a *p-value* < 1 according to the recursive feature elimination method. The list of most discriminating unigrams based on this technique is provided in Table 6.2.

The majority of high-score unigrams marking the true news articles are focused around the topic of the US election. This is expected, given the fact that most true examples in the combined dataset come from the Buzzfeed USE corpus, which includes news related to the US presidential candidates and events around the 2016 election. The Snopes data includes a variety

Table 6.2 TF-IDF unigram features with highest proportion in true (top) vs false news (bottom) within the combined corpus (Snopes Silver and Buzzfeed USE)

Feature	Avg. in True	Avg. in False	Ratio False/True	P-value
debate	0.066639	0.011568	0.173589	1.18E-50
voters	0.043444	0.009592	0.220792	2.48E-31
clinton	0.114134	0.031633	0.277158	2.71E-72
presidential	0.065025	0.019048	0.29294	8.90E-56
campaign	0.075448	0.022253	0.294945	1.77E-52
republican	0.062131	0.019052	0.306639	1.74E-46
hillary	0.074586	0.023268	0.311959	5.28E-53
donald	0.087009	0.032008	0.367873	1.74E-62
trump	0.150655	0.063265	0.419935	4.73E-67
vote	0.036512	0.018449	0.505276	1.03E-08
election	0.041777	0.021478	0.514117	7.42E-12
today	0.025932	0.036286	1.399304	4.85E-04
year	0.044547	0.06537	1.467454	8.41E-10
come	0.02743	0.040592	1.479861	3.47E-06
family	0.029711	0.044435	1.495613	2.58E-05
home	0.026483	0.041189	1.555327	9.89E-06
school	0.021147	0.034088	1.611911	2.88E-04
world	0.03383	0.056416	1.667639	5.27E-10
use	0.027951	0.049615	1.775065	1.07E-09
children	0.023254	0.043545	1.872602	3.24E-08
old	0.024174	0.047418	1.96152	3.68E-13

of topics, and most false articles come from this dataset; that is why the high-score unigrams in the false class come from a more diverse and general vocabulary, as it is evident from the table. Now, this imbalance in terms of topic vocabulary between the two classes of news articles may raise a challenge for building predictive models based on the presented data: if we train a model on this dataset, the classifier may overfit to fine-grained lexical features rather than high-level properties of the text, and this may result in weak generalisation and low accuracy on collections of false/true news articles with a different topic distribution. We will discuss this further in the next section.

5 Misinformation detection through text classification

A variety of different machine learning techniques have been applied to text classification problems such as sentiment analysis, product review classification, authorship recognition, and deception detection in text (Eisenstein, 2019; Hovy, 2020). These methods include classic feature-based classification algorithms and deep neural network models, which instead of using features exploit pretrained word embeddings or language models. Deep learning models usually achieve a higher accuracy compared to traditional classifiers such as support vector machines using engineered features, but they require more training data to converge. In a situation where training data is scarce, such as the case of misinformation detection, classic feature-based algorithms may be preferred over deep learning. For example, Zhang et al. (2015) showed that the classic TF-IDF model worked better than a variety of deep learning models if less than a million training records were available.

In this section, we explore the performance of different text classification techniques when used in combination with our data for detecting false from true news articles. We employ both a classic method, that is, a support vector machine classifier with linguistic features, and a deep learning model, BERT (Devlin et al., 2019). We train them on different slices of our collected data and examine their generalisation power on several test datasets. We also consider a setup with larger training data that has been labelled based on the reputation of the publishing sources rather than fact-checking of each individual news article. These experiments will help us reveal the pros and cons of each classification technique and draw future directions especially for collecting more and better quality data.

5.1 Models

Feature-based model. We use a support vector machine classifier (SVM) from the scikit-learn python library with all the linguistic features that we introduced and analysed in the previous section. These features include surface text features, TF-IDF scored n-grams, semantic category features, syntactic features (parts of speech counts), and readability scores. Both the TF-IDF vectorizer and the SVM classifier had a set of parameters that we tuned through cross validation on training data. The best values for parameters of the TF-IDF vectorizer were max-df=0.5, min-df=5, n-gram-range=(1,2) and sublinear-tf=True. Best parameter values for the SVM were penalty="l2", tol=1e-3, and others set to default.

Deep learning model (BERT). In order to apply deep learning to the task of misinformation detection, we use a well-known language representation model in sentence classification tasks such as sentiment analysis or fact-checking. BERT, which stands for Bidirectional Encoder Representations from Transformers (Devlin et al., 2019), is based on a transformers architecture (Vaswani et al., 2017). BERT-base, the model that is used in this article, comprises 12 transformer layers, where every transformer layer accepts a list of token embeddings and generates the same number of embeddings with the same hidden size on the output. The output of the last transformer layer of the classification token (a special token that is added for classification purposes) will be applied to feed a classifier. We use the PyTorch implementation of the pretrained BERT model in Python using the transformer library of *Hugging Face* (Wolf et al., 2019). The BERT model was trained on Wikipedia articles with 1 million steps for 40 epochs, with batch size of 256 on 8 GPUs for 6.5 days. Due to the large number of parameters and layers in a BERT network and the high risk of overfitting, we fine-tune this pretrained BERT model. To fine-tune, we train the entire pretrained model on our training data and feed the output to a softmax classifier to compute logits. We optimize the main hyperparameter values, including the dropout rate, batch size, optimizer learning rate, and the number of epochs based on the average area under curve (AUC) score from cross-validation on training data. The best values for the parameters of the BERT-based model were dropout = 0.35, batch size = 12, learning rate = 1e-5 (Adam optimizer). We utilised the maximum sequence length of 512 and tried between 4 and 15 training epochs. With the smaller training data, higher epoch numbers (around 12) gave us better results (lower validation and training loss). However, with larger training data size the performance plateaued after about five epochs, so we keep that as the accepted parameter. It is also worth mentioning that smaller training data are more prone to suffer from overfitting, resulting in larger validation losses with the same hyperparameter values. Table C.6.7 in the Appendix includes our best range of hyperparameters for the BERT-base model.

Table 6.3 Number of samples taken from each collection (Snopes Silver and BuzzFeed USE) to prepare our two different training datasets: the *small balanced* and *large mixed* samples

Dataset	False Items	True Items	Small Balanced Sample	Large Mixed Sample
Snopes Silver	1, 585	259	2 * 259	2 * 1, 300
Buzzfeed USE	64	1, 090	2 * 64	
Total	1, 649	1, 349	646	2, 600

5.2   Data preparation

While building a predictive model for any detection task, it is important to spend time preparing data by removing noise and balancing the samples for the prediction classes. Our observation during feature analysis of the datasets showed a topic imbalance across datasets and, most importantly, across target classes (false and true news articles), as we have shown in other work (Asr and Taboada, 2019). Therefore, we decided to consider two different data scenarios in our text classification experiments. Table 6.3 shows how we sample the Buzzfeed USE and Snopes Silver datasets for preparation of training data with two approaches. We consider two training data scenarios, one with a small balanced training data and another with a relatively large but mixed training data. For sampling the small and balanced dataset, we randomly picked 64 items from each class within the Buzzfeed USE dataset, because its false class only contains this many items. This was in principle to make sure that data from a focused topic (the US election) is represented in both false and true classes in the balanced dataset. We take a similar approach in sampling from the Snopes Silver data, by picking 259 items from each class. The total number of items in our small and balanced dataset is 646 news articles. Second, we consider a larger training dataset, that is, we put together all true and false news articles from the Snopes and Buzzfeed datasets and then sample 1,300 items per class from this collection, which totals 2,600 news articles. This dataset is about four times larger than our small sample, but it is unbalanced with respect to the distribution of topics across false and true news articles.

As test data, instead of sampling from the same data sources, which may result in an artificially high accuracy, we consider three separate test datasets. These are all datasets that have been manually checked for the content veracity of individual news articles. The first obvious choice is the Snopes Gold data that we described in the section on data collection (Section 3). Apart from having been verified manually, this dataset has the nice feature of including nonoverlapping news headlines with the Snopes Silver data. Performance on this dataset would tell us about the generalisation power of a model to new topics and headlines.

The second test data is Buzzfeed Top, which contains the 33 top fake news of the year collected by the Buzzfeed agency from Snopes fact-checking pages (see Asr and Taboada (2018) for more details on this data). This dataset only includes false news and may have some overlap with topics in our training data, therefore should be an easy benchmark for all the models.

The third dataset is the collection of false and true celebrity related news articles collected and published by Pérez-Rosas et al. (2017), the Celebrity dataset. This dataset has two nice characteristics: it is focused on the specific domain of celebrity stories, which may be less frequent in our training data, so it may reflect the generalisation power of the models better; furthermore, this dataset contains a balanced number of false and true news articles on preselected matched topics (for instance, the same number of false and true articles about Jenifer Aniston's personal life!). Performance of our models on this last test dataset would be representative of cross-domain classification performance on real data.

As a separate kind of benchmark, we compare the performance of the same models on larger data that has been labelled based on the reputation of the publishing sources rather than based on the veracity of individual news articles. This method serves as the baseline in our experiments. We adopt Rashkin et al. (2017)'s dataset of propaganda, hoax, satire, and trusted news articles, scraped automatically from websites based on their reputation. In order to map this data to our scheme of false and true news, we combine all items from propaganda, hoax, and satire and sample 4,000 news articles from this combination and label them as *false* news. We then sample 4,000 articles from the trusted items and label them as *true*. That is why we call this data scenario the *mapped* data condition.

5.3   Experimental setup

In all the experiments across the three data scenarios, we first train a model on the training data and then test it on the three held-out test datasets. We report the performance of the model both on training data itself (to show the quality of the fit) and each of the test datasets by measuring the weighted F1-score (weighted average of the precision and recall for the false and true classes). As we mentioned before, parameter tuning is performed by cross-validation on training data prior to retraining on the entire set and the actual experiments.

For experiments using the SVM classifier, we present results on several feature sets to show the helpfulness of each feature category. We found a general trend that the TF-IDF n-grams were the best single set of features, followed by the semantic category features and the syntactic features. The readability and surface textual features came out as the least helpful ones for predictive modelling. In order to present the most relevant results, we picked the best feature setups and will report the outcome of these across different data scenarios.

The BERT model (Devlin et al., 2019), as introduced earlier in this section, is a state-of-the-art language model for NLP. This model was published in 2018 by researchers at Google AI. It contains 110M parameters and 12 transformer layers, which makes BERT training a hard task. Training a BERT model from scratch on a small set of data would greatly increase the likelihood of overfitting, the expensive computational costs aside. To avoid this problem, we take advantage of pretrained BERT models that were trained on Wikipedia articles (https://github.com/google-research/bert). This language model is pretrained on two NLP tasks: masked language modelling and next sentence prediction (Devlin et al., 2019). In this study, we fine-tuned the BERT pretrained model in two different scenarios, however report results only for the second one. In the first approach, we froze the entire BERT architecture and attached one hidden-layer feed forward neural network as our classifier and trained this new model. During fine-tuning, we only updated the weights of the last attached layer. In the second method, we train the entire pretrained model on our train data and feed the output to a softmax classifier to compute logits. The optimized hyperparameter values, which led to the results in Table 6.4, can be found in Appendix C.

Finally, we would like to mention that based on repeated experiments with a variety of parameter values with both the SVM and the BERT models, the final results depend also on the data sampling and the random effects present in both models. We report the most stable results in the paper rather than performing an aggressive brute force parameter tuning to obtain the highest possible score from a model.

Table 6.4 Performance of different text classification models in various data scenarios measured by F1-score on training data as well as three test datasets

Data scenario	Model	Train	BuzzTop	SnopesGold	Celeb
Rashkin mapped	SVM N-gram	98	94	55	57
(8,000 train items)	SVM N-gram+Sem	96	94	52	57
	SVM N-gram+Sem+Syn	96	90	54	58
	SVM All features	92	86	56	57
	BERT	93	**97**	58	57
Large mixed (2,600	SVM N-gram	86	**97**	54	50
train items)	SVM N-gram+Sem SVM	85	**97**	54	50
	N-gram+Sem+Syn	85	**97**	54	52
	SVM All features	83	85	50	52
	BERT	80	91	56	49
Small balanced (646	SVM N-gram	97	88	66	64
train items)	SVM N-gram+Sem SVM	93	88	**70**	**65**
	N-gram+Sem+Syn	84	88	**70**	**65**
	SVM All features	91	95	59	56
	BERT	64	68	59	54

5.4   Results

The results of all our text classification experiments are presented in Table 6.4. Let us start with the model that we consider as our baseline, that is, using the linguistic features of the news articles belonging to propaganda, hoax, and satire to predict whether an article contains false or true information. Experiments with an SVM using this type of approximate training data are categorized under the Rashkin mapped scenario in the table. A high training accuracy in these experiments is not surprising given both the large training data and that the validation split belonging to the same distribution of news articles. Training accuracy above 90% is indicative of a good fit to the domain data: The classifier learned very well the linguistic features appearing across all publications of trusted sources and those of the so-called fake news publishers. Now the question is whether such a model can generalise its knowledge to the detection of true from false content. Surprisingly, we see that using any of the presented feature sets, such as only the n-gram features, the model does very well in labelling fake news articles in the Buzzfeed Top dataset. However, the performance of the model drops drastically when it comes to Snopes Gold and Celebrity data. We investigated the reason for this and realised that the classifier is highly biased towards labelling anything as fake news (i.e. mapped to *false*), therefore the majority of the items within the Buzzfeed Top data as well as in the other two datasets were given the false label. Given the equal number of items from both classes in the training data, one possible explanation for the classifier's bias could be that the items of the false class were a better representative of the language data that we see in the test sets; in other words, these items could have covered a larger number of topics, more varied vocabulary and writing styles. This distributional characteristic can be due to the more diverse sources of online news scraped for the fake items than for real items (mainstream trusted news) in Rashkin's data.

Overall, the low F-scores obtained on the Snopes Gold and Celebrity data provides some evidence that reputation-based data collection may not be the best strategy when the target task is to detect false from true content. While the classifier seems to be good at detecting fake news (as a general label for propaganda, hoax, and satire), it cannot tell when an article with a similar style is written based on facts. Therefore, the features of deception that we would like to capture for misinformation detection at the level of individual articles have not been learned in this scenario.

Next, let us examine the models that were trained on our large mixed dataset. A relatively smaller training fit is obtained in the experiments using this dataset as training material, which is expected given the smaller size of it compared to Rashkin's data. Evaluation of the models on the test datasets shows a similar pattern: performance on Buzzfeed Top is high, but when it comes to distinguishing true news articles (in Snopes Gold and Celebrity collections), the classifier shows a negative bias. This observation has a similar explanation to the one we just provided for the mapped data scenario. Most true items in the large mix dataset come from the Buzzfeed USE dataset, which is focused on a narrow topic. Therefore, more variance will be captured for the false class with more various items in it coming from the Snopes Silver collection, and the classifier would later assign the false label to the majority of test items. Recall from the previous section that this was the main reason for us to sample equal number of items from the two datasets to build a balanced training dataset.

Finally, we review the results of our experiments using the best quality training data, that is, a small but balanced set of news articles with reliable labels. In this data scenario, we get a better fit on training data and a better generalisation on the test sets for all models except for BERT. Using the n-gram, semantic, and syntactic features would give us the best cross-domain generalisation reflected in the 70% and 65% F1-score on the Snopes Gold and the Celebrity dataset. Adding the readability and surface textual features provides better results on the Buzzfeed Top items, which may have overlap in topic, headline, and even entire body content with some of the training items (this can also be viewed as a type of over-fitting to the training data, which decreases the generalisation power of the model).

A comparison between the classification results obtained from the BERT model and the SVM models shows the superiority of the feature-based approach with the currently available training data. Deep learning text classification techniques in general need a large amount of training data, and that is what we are still lacking for the task of misinformation detection. An intriguing possibility is the application of hybrid methods, as proposed by Rohera et al. (2022), who found that a Naive Bayes algorithm obtained the highest recall in their experiments, whereas a deep learning model (LSTM) had the highest accuracy. A combination of those two methods, depending on which parameter we want to maximise, shows promise.

In summary, our results speak in favour of a hybrid approach based on both linguistic feature analysis and deep neural network models, and always taking into consideration the size and composition of the data. And above all, the results suggest that more reliably labelled data, in the form of full news articles, is needed for this particular problem.

6 Conclusion

We have investigated the problem of misinformation in news text from a linguistic perspective, using natural language processing and text classification techniques. The contributions can be summarized as the following:

- We built a dataset of false and true news articles by scraping the Snopes fact-checking pages, tracking the links to the original publisher of the news headlines and collected the body text. We also used crowdsourcing to verify the alignment between each news article and the headline labelled for veracity by the fact-checker, to make sure the data is of good quality. The Snopes Silver collection contains 1,844 texts; it has been introduced in our previous work and a small sample of it, that is, the Snopes Gold, was used in our previous experiments (Asr and Taboada,

2019). The complete collection with crowdsourced stance data is available from our lab page (www.sfu.ca/discourse-lab).

- We analysed the previous dataset and the Buzzfeed USE dataset (from our previous work) for linguistic features indicative of false content and provided significant tests on what types of features were most discriminatory between false and true news articles.
- We conducted experiments on automatic misinformation detection using a variety of text classification techniques. By doing so, we established a new baseline for this NLP task and clarified the type of data and features that can offer the best accuracy both in within-domain and cross-domain predictions.

Our experiments show that the veracity and linguistic characteristics of a text are correlated, but high-quality training data is required to develop an accurate and scalable misinformation detection system. In particular, data should be well-distributed across topics and sources, balanced across different levels of factuality, and reliably labelled based on individual articles rather than the reputation of publishing sources, because dubious websites may publish or republish factual news articles, making the data noisy.

In terms of the machine learning techniques, we found that the classic feature-based SVM model was superior across all data scenarios. Especially in a small but balanced training data scenario, the models showed a more robust behaviour, that is, they generalised better on the test news articles with unseen headlines and claims. Based on our analysis and feature ablation study, the best features were n-grams, semantic category features, and part of speech tags. Surface textual features and readability features were less effective in classification. We also found, using the same algorithm and linguistic features, that big data labelled based on reputation of the sources or big data with unbalanced topic distribution would not enhance the final system accuracy, in particular in cross-domain evaluation.

Finally, we tried a deep learning model with a pretraining phase, which helped deal with the small size of training data to some extent. However, the results show that the data we currently have is not enough to benefit from the potentials of a deep learning model. We believe that better accuracy can be obtained with an improved dataset, not only in terms of quantity but also in terms of quality. Quality improvements can be achieved with a sufficiently large collection of news articles from a variety of topics distributed in a balanced manner across the false and true target classes. Otherwise, the classifier can easily become biased towards assigning false or true labels to any unseen test item (as it was shown through our classification experiments in the larger data scenario). A larger question is whether BERT and similar deep learning architectures are truly the best tools for all classification problems. Church et al. (2021) argue that some NLP problems may be better addressed with "older rule-based systems".

Our new dataset and the properties we found for a quality dataset based on repeated experiments contribute to opening up the bottleneck in the NLP approach to misinformation detection, but more data and more contributions in the public domain are necessary. We urge researchers and, more importantly, internet and social media platforms, to share and make available such datasets for research.

Appendix A
DISCRIMINATIVE FEATURES IN BUZZFEED USE DATA

Table A.6.5 Discriminative features in Buzzfeed data

Feature Category	Feature	Ratio false/true	P-value
Surface	num punc/num char	0.824111622	1.07E-07
Semantic lexicon	comparative forms.txt	0.847129838	0.000312741
Semantic lexicon	negative mpqa.txt	1.170890719	0.039175394
Semantic lexicon	negative-HuLui.txt	1.191929819	0.003812285
Semantic lexicon	assertives hooper1975.txt	1.204042781	0.025607042
Semantic lexicon	factives hooper1975.txt	1.210492088	0.075483432
Semantic lexicon	modal adverbs.txt	1.250324586	0.08518351
Semantic lexicon	neutral mpqa.txt	1.262506856	0.008025674
Semantic lexicon	manner adverbs.txt	1.285541793	0.070899584
Semantic lexicon	implicatives karttunen1971.txt	1.402833634	0.003614918
Semantic LIWC	Apostro	0.285518503	0.029453081
Semantic LIWC	i	0.597079036	0.019747465
Semantic LIWC	male	0.774133673	0.042933602
Semantic LIWC	posemo	0.84567739	0.086936016
Semantic LIWC	work	0.846851239	0.082703344
Semantic LIWC	time	0.849324655	0.008926775
Semantic LIWC	Sixltr	0.909433348	0.052975401
Semantic LIWC	relativ	0.938080123	0.059859233
Semantic LIWC	Dic	1.038763776	0.017908327
Semantic LIWC	function	1.058609143	0.000492969
Semantic LIWC	conj	1.08800601	0.026463843
Semantic LIWC	pronoun	1.0995215	0.045389199
Semantic LIWC	verb	1.12184365	0.043788628
Semantic LIWC	auxverb	1.1262107	0.091416299
Semantic LIWC	focuspresent	1.141192519	0.021681326
Semantic LIWC	adverb	1.152874365	0.009971697
Semantic LIWC	ipron	1.166344782	0.001385981
Semantic LIWC	cogproc	1.168456841	0.000735018

(Continued)

Table 6.5 (Continued)

Feature Category	Feature	Ratio false/true	P-value
Semantic LIWC	insight	1.219253872	0.033014437
Semantic LIWC	quant	1.254843046	0.000564555
Semantic LIWC	we	1.300643709	0.085971532
Semantic LIWC	tentat	1.326261041	0.000128842
Semantic LIWC	certain	1.369503643	0.000657455
Semantic LIWC	bio	1.523506626	0.006427043
Semantic LIWC	they	1.669499824	4.83E-07
Semantic LIWC	health	1.763599914	0.007421396
Semantic LIWC	anx	1.936134338	0.01550405
Semantic LIWC	sexual	3.069336627	0.027490318
Syntactic	NOUN	0.934513783	0.000113056
Syntactic	DET	1.052851775	0.033674456
Syntactic	VERB	1.061155645	0.001962608
Syntactic	PRT	1.073478103	0.098291531
Syntactic	ADV	1.185689806	2.21E-05
Readability	Linsear write formula	0.758426991	0.000619185
Readability	Automated readability index	0.86367538	0.000692822
Readability	Flesch Kincaid grade	0.864976275	0.000797506
Readability	Gunning fog	0.891185015	0.002323244
Readability	Smog index	0.928396971	0.002329779
Readability	Flesch reading ease	1.097455733	0.004082952

Appendix B

DISCRIMINATIVE FEATURES IN SNOPES SILVER DATA

Table B.6.6 Discriminative features in Snopes Silver data

Feature Category	Feature	Ratio False/True	P-value
Surface	num char	0.832909412	0.007837336
Surface	num punc/num char	0.926844562	0.001331224
Surface	num sentence	0.772084384	0.00088547
Semantic lexicon	comparative forms.txt	0.947737051	0.020227509
Semantic lexicon	negative-HuLui.txt	1.133089752	0.00267177
Semantic lexicon	negative mpqa.txt	1.192098625	0.000864263
Semantic lexicon	modal adverbs.txt	1.298092007	0.005319897
Semantic lexicon	manner adverbs.txt	1.35698137	0.001742446
Semantic LIWC	allPunc	0.648061274	0.002444304
Semantic LIWC	apostro	0.648061274	0.002444304
Semantic LIWC	money	0.69778316	0.001087094
Semantic LIWC	work	0.876750931	0.00999914
Semantic LIWC	sixltr	0.940804067	0.033111439
Semantic LIWC	article	0.953846799	0.013036009
Semantic LIWC	cogproc	1.06101936	0.057419697
Semantic LIWC	pronoun	1.070951735	0.029411617
Semantic LIWC	time	1.076314329	0.029136756
Semantic LIWC	compare	1.077072577	0.039553518
Semantic LIWC	auxverb	1.077592026	0.093201528
Semantic LIWC	adverb	1.110034072	0.00311221
Semantic LIWC	ppron	1.123737701	0.014012724
Semantic LIWC	cause	1.12805548	0.038490645
Semantic LIWC	certain	1.141792908	0.032021603
Semantic LIWC	they	1.151274939	0.066116507
Semantic LIWC	male	1.199129633	0.039660435
Semantic LIWC	bio	1.224761165	0.041183623
Semantic LIWC	body	1.328246174	0.041617951
Semantic LIWC	anx	1.383614276	0.097296795
Semantic LIWC	death	1.601757888	0.022198678

(Continued)

Table 6.6 (Continued)

Feature Category	Feature	Ratio False/True	P-value
Semantic LIWC	sexual	2.753109267	0.060287064
Syntactic	NUM	0.905802493	0.06678729
Syntactic	DET	0.962340276	0.009099241
Syntactic	NOUN	0.970826348	0.021800144
Syntactic	VERB	1.034897463	0.008362629
Syntactic	PRT	1.040020625	0.097773857
Syntactic	ADV	1.093310376	0.000661848
Syntactic	PRON	1.094581886	0.011254044

Appendix C
FINE-TUNED BERT MODEL OPTIMIZED HYPERPARAMETERS

Table C.6.7 Fine-tuned BERT model hyperparameters

Hyperparameters	Tested range	Best range
Sequence Length	256–512	360–512
Number of epochs	3–15	4–12
Batch size	4–16	8–12
Dropout rate	0–0.5	0.25–0.35
Learning rate (Adam optimizer)	1E-6–1E-4	1E-5–5E-5
Warm-up steps	0–500	0–500

References

Afroz, S., Brennan, M., Greenstadt, R., 2012. Detecting hoaxes, frauds, and deception in writing style online. In: *Proceedings of IEEE Symposium on Security and Privacy*. San Francisco: Institute for Electrical and Electronics Engineers, pp. 461–475.

Allcott, H., Gentzkow, M., 2017. Social media and fake news in the 2016 election. *Journal of Economic Perspectives* 31, 211–236.

Asr, F. T., Taboada, M., 2018. The data challenge in misinformation detection: Source reputation vs. content veracity. In: *Proceedings of the First Workshop on Fact Extraction and VERification (FEVER), Conference on Empirical Methods in Natural Language Processing*. Brussels: Association for Computational Linguistics, pp. 10–15.

Asr, F. T., Taboada, M., 2019. Big data and quality data for fake news and misinformation detection. *Big Data & Society*, January–June 2019: 1–14.

Biyani, P., Tsioutsiouliklis, K., Blackmer, J., 2016. "8 amazing secrets for getting more clicks": Detecting clickbaits in news streams using article informality. In: *Proceedings of the 30th AAAI Conference on Artificial Intelligence*. Phoenix: Association for the Advancement of Artificial Intelligence, pp. 94–100.

Church, K. W., Chen, Z., Ma, Y., 2021. Emerging trends: A gentle introduction to fine-tuning. *Natural Language Engineering* 27 (6), 763–778.

Conneau, A., Schwenk, H., Barrault, L., LeCun, Y., 2017. Very deep convolutional networks for text classification. In: *Proceedings of the 15th Conference of the European Chapter of the Association for Computational Linguistics*. Valencia: Association for Computational Linguistics, pp. 1107–1116.

Connolly, K., Chrisafis, A., McPherson, P., Kirchgaessner, S., Haas, B., Phillips, D., Hunt, E., Safi, M., 2016, December 2. Fake news: An insidious trend that's fast becoming a global problem. *The Guardian*. www.theguardian.com/media/2016/dec/02/fake-news-facebook-us-election-around-the-world.

Conroy, N. J., Rubin, V. L., Chen, Y., 2015. Automatic deception detection: Methods for finding fake news. In: *Proceedings of the Conference of the Association for Information Science and Technology*. Vol. 52. St. Louis: Association for Information Science and Technology, pp. 1–4.

Devlin, J., Chang, M.-W., Lee, K., Toutanova, K., 2019. BERT: Pre-training of deep bidirectional transformers for language understanding. In: *Proceedings of the 2019 Conference of the North American Chapter of the Association for Computational Linguistics*. Minneapolis: Association for Computational Linguistics, pp. 4171–4186.

Dos Santos, C., Gatti, M., 2014. Deep convolutional neural networks for sentiment analysis of short texts. In: *Proceedings of COLING 2014, the 25th International Conference on Computational Linguistics*. Dublin: Association for Computational Linguistics, pp. 69–78.

Eisenstein, J., 2019. Introduction to Natural Language Processing. MIT Press, Cambridge, MA.

Fichtner, U., December 20, 2018. Der Spiegel reveals internal fraud. *Der Spiegel*. www.spiegel.de/international/zeitgeist/claas-relotius-reporter-forgery-scandal-a-1244755.html.

Fogg, B. J., Marshall, J., Laraki, O., Osipovich, A., Varma, C., Fang, N., Paul, J., Rangnekar, A., Shon, J., Swani, P., Treinen, M., 2001. What makes web sites credible? A report on a large quantitative study. In: *Proceedings of the SIGCHI Conference on Human Factors in Computing Systems*. Seattle: Association for Computing Machinery, pp. 61–68.

Guo, Z., Schlichtkrull, M., Vlachos, A., 2022. A survey on automated fact-checking. *Transactions of the Association for Computational Linguistics* 10, 178–206.

Habgood-Coote, J., 2019. Stop talking about fake news! *Inquiry* 62 (9–10), 1033–1065.

Horne, B. D., Adali, S., 2017. This just in: Fake news packs a lot in title, uses simpler, repetitive content in text body, more similar to satire than real news. *arXiv preprint arXiv:1703.09398*.

Horne, B. D., Khedr, S., Adali, S., 2018. Sampling the news producers: A large news and feature data set for the study of the complex media landscape. In: *Proceedings of the Twelfth International AAAI Conference on Web and Social Media*. Palo Alto: Association for the Advancement of Artificial Intelligence, pp. 518–527.

Hovy, D., 2020. *Text Analysis in Python for Social Scientists*. Cambridge: Cambridge University Press.

Kucharski, A., 2016. Post-truth: Study epidemiology of fake news. *Nature* 540 (7634), 525–525.

Lai, S., Xu, L., Liu, K., Zhao, J., 2015. Recurrent convolutional neural networks for text classification. In: *Proceedings of AAAI Conference on Artificial Intelligence*. Austin: Association for the Advancement of Artificial Intelligence, pp. 2267–2273.

Lazer, D., Baum, M. A., Benkler, Y., Berinsky, A. J., Greenhill, K. M., Menczer, F., Metzger, M. J., Nyhan, B., Pennycook, G., Rothschild, D., Schudson, M., Sloman, S. A., Sunstein, C. R., Thorson, E. A., Watts, D. J., Zittrain, J. L., 2018. The science of fake news. *Science* 359 (6380), 1094–1096.

Le, Q., Mikolov, T., 2014. Distributed representations of sentences and documents. In: *Proceedings of the 31st International Conference on Machine Learning*. Beijing: International Machine Learning Society, pp. II–1188–II–1196.

Lugea, J., 2021. Linguistic approaches to fake news detection. In: Deepak, P., Chakraborty, T., Long, C., Kumar, S. G. (Eds.), *Data Science for Fake News: Surveys and Perspectives*. Cham: Springer, pp. 287–302.

Mantzarlis, A., 2017, December 18. Not fake news, just plain wrong: Top media corrections of 2017. *Poynter News*. www.poynter.org/news/not-fake-news-just-plain-wrong-top-media-corrections-2017.

Medvedeva, M., Kroon, M., Plank, B., 2017. When sparse traditional models outperform dense neural networks: The curious case of discriminating between similar languages. In: *Proceedings of the 4th Workshop on NLP for Similar Languages, Varieties and Dialects (VarDial)*. Valencia: Association for Computational Linguistics, pp. 156–163.

Mukherjee, A., Venkataraman, V., Liu, B., Glance, N., 2013. Fake review detection: Classification and analysis of real and pseudo reviews. In: *Technical Report UIC-CS-2013–03*. Chicago: University of Illinois at Chicago.

Ng, A., 2011. Why is deep learning taking off? *Technical Report Coursera*. www.coursera.org/lecture/neural-networks-deep-learning/why-is-deep-learning-taking-off-praGm.

Nørregaard, J., Horne, B. D., Adalı, S., 2019. NELA-GT-2018: A large multi-labelled news dataset for the study of misinformation in news articles. In: *Proceedings of AAAI Conference on Web and Social Media*. Munich: Association for the Advancement of Artificial Intelligence, pp. 630–638.

Ouyang, X., Zhou, P., Li, C. H., Liu, L., 2015. Sentiment analysis using convolutional neural network. In: *2015 IEEE International Conference on Computer and Information Technology; Ubiquitous Computing and Communications; Dependable, Autonomic and Secure Computing; Pervasive Intelligence and Computing*. Liverpool: Institute for Electrical and Electronics Engineers, pp. 2359–2364.

Pennebaker, J. W., Boyd, R. L., Jordan, K., Blackburn, K., 2015. The development and psychometric properties of LIWC 2015. In: *Technical Report*. Austin: University of Texas at Austin.

Pennington, J., Socher, R., Manning, C. D., 2014. Glove: Global vectors for word representation. In: *Proceedings of the Conference on Empirical Methods in Natural Language Processing*. Doha: Association for Computational Linguistics, pp. 1532–1543.

Pérez-Rosas, V., Kleinberg, B., Lefevre, A., Mihalcea, R., 2017. Automatic detection of fake news. *arXiv preprint arXiv:1708.07104*.

Pérez-Rosas, V., Mihalcea, R., 2015. Experiments in open domain deception detection. In: *Proceedings of the Conference on Empirical Methods in Natural Language Processing*. Lisbon: Association for Computational Linguistics, pp. 1120–1125.

Perrott, K., 2016. A fake news on social media influenced US election voters, experts say. *ABC 26*. www.abc.net.au/news/2016-11-14/fake-news-would-have-influenced-us-election-experts-say/8024660.

Post, M., Bergsma, S., 2013. Explicit and implicit syntactic features for text classification. In: *Proceedings of the 51st Annual Meeting of the Association for Computational Linguistics*. Vol. 2. Sofia: Association for Computational Linguistics, pp. 866–872.

Potthast, M., Kiesel, J., Reinartz, K., Bevendorff, J., Stein, B., 2018. A stylometric inquiry into hyperpartisan and fake news. In: *Proceedings of the 56th Annual Meeting of the Association for Computational Linguistics*. Melbourne: Association for Computational Linguistics, pp. 231–240.

Przybyla, P., 2020. Capturing the style of fake news. In: *Proceedings of AAAI Conference on Artificial Intelligence*. Vol. 34. New York: Association for the Advancement of Artificial Intelligence, pp. 490–497.

Rashkin, H., Choi, E., Jang, J. Y., Volkova, S., Choi, Y., 2017. Truth of varying shades: Analyzing language in fake news and political fact-checking. In: *Proceedings of the 2017 Conference on Empirical Methods in Natural Language Processing*. Copenhagen: Association for Computational Linguistics, pp. 2921–2927.

Recasens, M., Danescu-Niculescu-Mizil, C., Jurafsky, D., 2013. Linguistic models for analyzing and detecting biased language. In: *Proceedings of the Conference of the Association for Computational Linguistics*. Sofia: Association for Computational Linguistics, pp. 1650–1659.

Riggins, S. H., 1997. The rhetoric of othering. In: Riggins, S. H. (Ed.), *The Language and Politics of Exclusion*. Thousand Oaks, CA: Sage, pp. 1–30.

Rohera, D., Shethna, H., Patel, K., Thakker, U., Tanwar, S., Gupta, R., Hong, W. C., Sharma, R., 2022. A taxonomy of fake news classification techniques: Survey and implementation aspects. *IEEE Access* 10, 30367–30394.

Rubin, V. L., Chen, Y., Conroy, N. J., 2015. Deception detection for news: Three types of fakes. In: *Proceedings of the Conference of the Association for Information Science and Technology*. Vol. 52. St. Louis: Association for Information Science and Technology, pp. 1–4.

Rubin, V. L., Conroy, N. J., Chen, Y., Cornwell, S., 2016. Fake news or truth? Using satirical cues to detect potentially misleading news. In: *Proceedings of NAACL-HLT*. San Diego: Association for Computational Linguistics, pp. 7–17.

Ruchansky, N., Seo, S., Liu, Y., 2017. CSI: A hybrid deep model for fake news detection. In: *Proceedings of the 2017 ACM on Conference on Information and Knowledge Management*. Singapore: Association for Computing Machinery, pp. 797–806.

Ruths, D., 2019. The misinformation machine. *Science* 363 (6425), 348–348.

Shu, K., Mahudeswaran, D., Wang, S., Lee, D., Liu, H., 2020. FakeNewsNet: A data repository with news content, social context, and spatiotemporal information for studying fake news on social media. *Big Data* 8 (3), 171–188.

Silverman, C., Strapagiel, L., Shaban, H., Hall, E., Singer-Vine, J., 2016, October 20. Hyperpartisan Facebook pages are publishing false and misleading information at an alarming rate. *BuzzFeed News*. www.buzzfeed.com/craigsilverman/partisan-fb-pages-analysis.

Tandoc Jr., E. C., Lim, Z. W., Ling, R., 2018. Defining "fake news": A typology of scholarly definitions. *Digital Journalism* 6 (2), 137–153.

Thorne, J., Vlachos, A., Christodoulopoulos, C., Mittal, A., 2018. FEVER: A large-scale dataset for Fact Extraction and VERification. In: *Proceedings of the 2018 Conference of the North American Chapter of the Association for Computational Linguistics: Human Language Technologies*. Vol. 1 (Long Papers). New Orleans: Association for Computational Linguistics, pp. 809–819.

Vaswani, A., Shazeer, N., Parmar, N., Uszkoreit, J., Jones, L., Gomez, A. N., Kaiser, L. U., Polosukhin, I., 2017. Attention is all you need. In: Guyon, I., Luxburg, U. V., Bengio, S., Wallach, H., Fergus, R., Vishwanathan, S., Garnett, R. (Eds.), *Advances in Neural Information Processing Systems*. Vol. 30. Curran Associates, Inc., pp. 5998–6008. https://proceedings.neurips.cc/paper/2017/file/3f5ee243547dee91fbd05 3c1c4a845aa-Paper.pdf

Volkova, S., Shaffer, K., Jang, J. Y., Hodas, N., 2017. Separating facts from fiction: Linguistic models to classify suspicious and trusted news posts on Twitter. In: *Proceedings of the 55th Annual Meeting of the Association for Computational Linguistics*. Vol. 2. Vancouver: Association for Computational Linguistics, pp. 647–653.

Vosoughi, S., Roy, D., Aral, S., 2018. The spread of true and false news online. *Science* 359 (6380), 1146–1151.

Wang, W. Y., 2017. 'Liar, liar pants on fire': A new benchmark dataset for fake news detection. In: *Proceedings of the 55th Annual Meeting of the Association for Computational Linguistics*. Vol. 2. Vancouver: Association for Computational Linguistics, pp. 422–426.

Wardle, C., Derakhshan, H., 2017. Information disorder: Toward an interdisciplinary framework for research and policy making. *Report*. Strasbourg: Council of Europe.

Wilson, T., Wiebe, J., Hoffmann, P., 2005. Recognizing contextual polarity in phrase-level sentiment analysis. In: *Proceedings of the Conference on Human Language Technology and Empirical Methods in Natural Language Processing*. Vancouver: Association for Computational Linguistics, pp. 347–354.

Wolf, T., Debut, L., Sanh, V., Chaumond, J., Delangue, C., Moi, A., Cistac, P., Rault, T., Louf, R., Funtowicz, M., Brew, J., 2019. Huggingface's transformers: State-of-the-art natural language processing. *ArXiv abs/1910.03771*.

Yang, F., Mukherjee, A., Dragut, E., 2017. Satirical news detection and analysis using attention mechanism and linguistic features. In: *Proceedings of the 2017 Conference on Empirical Methods in Natural Language Processing*. Copenhagen: Association for Computational Linguistics, pp. 1979–1989.

Yang, Z., Yang, D., Dyer, C., He, X., Smola, A., Hovy, E., 2016. Hierarchical attention networks for document classification. In: *Proceedings of the 2016 Conference of the North American Chapter of the Association for Computational Linguistics: Human Language Technologies*. Vancouver: Association for Computational Linguistics, pp. 1480–1489.

Zhang, A. X., Ranganathan, A., Metz, S. E., Appling, S., Sehat, C. M., Gilmore, N., Adams, N. B., Vincent, E., Lee, J., Robbins, M., 2018. A structured response to misinformation: Defining and annotating credibility indicators in news articles. In: *Proceedings of the The Web Conference 2018.* Lyon: Association for Computing Machinery, pp. 603–612.

Zhang, A. X., Zhao, J., LeCun, Y., 2015. Character-level convolutional networks for text classification. In: *Proceedings of the 28th International Conference on Neural Information Processing Systems*. Montréal: Curran Associates, pp. 649–657.

7

FAKESPEAK IN 280 CHARACTERS

Exploring the language of disinformation on Twitter through a comparative corpus-based approach

Sylvia Jaworska

1 Introduction

Despite the original hopes for the Internet to become the vehicle for democratising communications and societies, things have not entirely turned out this way. The affordances of the digital have empowered more horizontal and wider participation giving voice to people who were previously excluded or marginalised in mainstream communications (Castells 2007). They have also enabled opportunities for creating bonds and for expanding existing communities around common interests and values, some of which brought about positive changes in society. The Arab spring, the #metoo campaign, or #BlackLivesMatter are some examples of global socio-political activism that have been powered by the affordances of the digital.

Yet the same affordances have also intensified social ills. Although ordinary people can now participate in creating, curating, and spreading information from the bottom-up, research shows that the digital space is largely occupied by the traditionally rich and famous who already hold positions of power and influence in society (e.g. Goodman and Jaworska 2020). Furthermore, digital media users also tend to operate in so-called "echo chambers" driven by algorithms that separate audiences into information bubbles, in which existing biases are often spread and reinforced. The digital "siloisation" of information has intensified polarisation, stirring acrimony and violence as the case of the Capitol Riot on 6 January 2021 has demonstrated.

Many of the negative impacts of digital communication have been fuelled by the increase in disinformation. Social media platforms with their affordance of many-to-many communication in real-time and ease of use have become a fertile ground for the spread of disinformation influencing public perceptions and decision-making. A particularly damaging form of online disinformation are fake news that have proliferated in recent years (Linvill and Warren 2020). Aside from influencing significant political or other events, fake news disturbs some of the fundamental values that people hold, for example, what counts as truth or credible voice whom we can trust. In doing so, fake news works to confuse and make us unsure what or whom to believe and therefore more susceptible to manipulation and exploitation (Jones et al. 2020).

Given the huge amount of fake news circulated on social media and its often fateful effects on society and individuals, a great deal of research has been dedicated to the development of

DOI: 10.4324/9781003224495-8

automatic detection systems to combat the spread of fake contents (e.g. Zhang and Ghorbani 2020). Yet the volume, velocity, and diversity of fake news pose challenges for automated detection delivering results with partial successes (Zhang and Ghorbani 2020). Research on automated systems for the detection of fake news is important when it comes to the reduction of the spread of disinformation online. Yet this research has so far provided little advice for online users on how to distinguish fake news from verified facts. This is a critical matter in light of the volume and diversity of disinformation to which social media users are exposed on a daily basis, and the fact that fake news is likely to appear alongside contents that are not necessarily misleading (Maci 2019). How to work one's way through this rolling "staccato" of messages and distinguish "good" from "bad" apples in everyday media consumption remains a challenge.

What users read as fake news are essentially texts composed of words, phrases, and sentences. In this way, fake news does not differ from other types of online media news. A question arises whether there are any specific language features in fake news that might give rise to suspicion and help differentiate false information from legitimate news. Research concerned with the detection of fake news has paid a great deal of attention to the contents of fake messages yet offers only general insights into the language use therein. For example, features such as functional words, symbols, punctuation, numbers, and adverbs have been identified as occurring quite frequently in fake news. But this kind of language features in legitimate news too. A more helpful way to differentiate between fake and verified news would be to understand something about the details behind categories such as symbols, pronouns, or punctuation, specifically what kind of items feature prominently in these categories in fake news but are less frequently employed or perhaps absent in legitimate contents. Such a comparison might better reveal language features that are specific to fake news and help online users distinguish fact-checked contents from disinformation.

This chapter endeavours to respond to this challenge by exploring a corpus of fake news spread on Twitter in 2016 and 2017 by the Russian Internet Research Agency (IRA) also known as the Russian troll factory. The corpus of fake news is compared with verified news tweets produced by the international news agency Associated Press (AP) and more sensationalist news tweets disseminated by the British middle-range tabloid the *Daily Mail*. The comparison is performed employing the techniques of a corpus-based approach to discourse, specifically the tool of keyword analysis, which has been successfully used in past research to identify distinctive lexico-grammatical features of various genres or registers (e.g. Xiao and McEnery 2005; Friginal 2009; Breeze 2019). Research has shown that the difference between, for example, telling lies vs telling truth sits not so much in the content of what is told but in the style or the *how* of telling (Galasiński 2000). Identifying distinctive lexico-grammatical features of fake news can therefore shed light on the particularities and peculiarities of its style, allowing researchers to better understand how disinformation is linguistically constructed and how to better recognise misleading contents. Therefore, this chapter pursues two major goals; first, it showcases how a keyword analysis can be effectively used to identify distinctive language features of disinformation online; secondly, it endeavours to raise awareness of the particularities and peculiarities of the language of fake news that might help foster critical (social) media literacy.

2   Fake news: what do we know about the language of exploitative deception online?

Despite the simplicity of the term *fake news*, this type of content is not so easy to define because of the diversity of discourse forms and formats that it encompasses. A broad definition of fake news includes any kind of false claims ranging from gossip, rumours, lies, false advertising to political propaganda, sensationalist news and satire. Yet fake news seems to have particular characteristics that make them somewhat different, for example, from a satire. The difference lies in the intention. Fake news fabricates false claims with the purpose to mislead; this type of content is intentionally false (Lugea 2021) and disseminated *en masse* in the service of a particular ideology or for financial gains (Maci 2019). In contrast to satire or benign kidding, which are quite pervasive in media or everyday communicative practices, fake news is an example of exploitative deception that aims to gain an advantage for the deceiver at all cost (Galasiński 2000). This is the narrower definition of fake news, and this definition is considered in this chapter too, since the fake news under investigation has been confirmed to be deliberately manufactured and spread to large social media audiences with the purpose of sowing disinformation and polarising public conversations (Linvill and Warren 2020).

Because fake news presents a huge problem with potentially harmful consequences to individuals and societies, a great deal of research has been dedicated to the detection of fake news on social media sites. Using machine learning and/or AI techniques, researchers in computer science have devised systems for automatic detection of fake contents, some of which have led to relative successes (Zhang and Ghorbani 2020). Yet the velocity and variety of fake news present an ongoing challenge for computational research concerned with automatic detection of false contents. In their systematic literature review, de Beer and Matthee (2020) identified that 34% of studies on fake news detection were interested in language and used a linguistic approach. Yet what is termed "linguistic" in those studies refers mostly to natural language processing (NLP) techniques. Although NLP procedures have something in common with approaches adopted in linguistics (e.g. the use of part-of-speech tagging), studies using NLP are rarely concerned with detailed analyses of language. The dominant approaches underpinned by NLP and used so far include the Bag of Words (BoW) approach or semantic analyses performed using linguistic inquiry and word count (LIWC) tool (Lugea 2021). Studies using these approaches provide some useful insights into the language features of fake news. For example, using BoW Dey et al. (2018) identified superlatives and terms of abuse as distinctive features of false claims made by Donald Trump. Using LIWC, Rashkin et al. (2017) compared fake news with legitimate news articles and found that exaggeration was used more frequently in false contents, while numbers, comparatives, and reporting verbs in verified news. Pérez-Rosas et al. (2017) too used LIWC to examine differences and similarities between legitimate and fake news and identified social and positive words, expressions of certainty, and the focus on the present and future actions as more prominent in fake than verified contents. Fake news writers seemed also to use more verbs, adverbs, and punctuation characters, whereas fact-checked news relied more on nouns pointing to cognitive processes, for example, "cause", "insights", or "discrepancy".

While studies using NLP techniques highlight some interesting language features of fake news, there are several issues with this kind of research. First, it rarely takes into account the intricacies of contextual variables, especially those of register, genre, or style. Often short online sensationalist fake news, for example tweets, are compared with long and elaborate articles from highbrow newspapers (Dey et al. 2018) or use data crowdsourced through Amazon Turk (Pérez-Rosas et al. 2017). Secondly and in most cases, an NLP approach is used alongside machine learning or other computational techniques with language analysis being secondary or complementary to the overall analysis. Although a variety of language features are identified, they are rarely reported in full and mostly aggregated in larger categories, for example, punctuation, symbols or swearwords, to assist with an automated fake news detection at the level of content. For example, Pérez-Rosas et al. (2017) identified the use of punctuation as a prominent feature of fake contents, yet what specific kinds of punctuation marks were employed more frequently by fake news writers than professional journalists was not shown.

In linguistics too, research on fake news presents a niche despite a vast number of studies exploring language use across media formats and contexts (e.g. Jones et al. 2020; Bednarek and Caple 2017; Zappavigna 2018). While linguists have a good understanding of what kind of language makes a story a news and what kind of discursive processes are involved in news production, including specific language features, we still know little about the distinctive linguistic characteristics of fake news. Maci's (2019) research on language and semiotic strategies employed in fake news about vaccinations offers first important insights into the language of misleading contents disseminated online in the context of health communication. Using a combination of critical discourse analysis (CDA) with a corpus-based and a semiotic approach, the study examines a corpus of 16,768 tweets produced by the #anti-vax campaign. The textual analysis has shown that the anti-vax tweet producers overwhelmingly employed nouns such as "death", "danger", "risk", and "children" and adjectives such as "dangerous" and "adverse" to create a strong imaginary of harm and danger affecting the vulnerable people in society. This was underpinned by the use of large numbers (e.g. 630%, 97% of people, 50 million people) to amplify the supposedly negative effects of vaccinations, while no links to actual research were provided. Maci's (2019) findings highlight that it is not just a specific linguistic category, such as numbers, that is, prominent in fake news, but precisely the specific kind of items that belong to the category such as exaggerated statistics that can tell us more about the kind of language used in disinformation online.

Exploring the context of political communication online in Nigeria, Igwebuike and Chimuanya (2021) study legitimation in fake news manufactured for political agitation. The researchers found that authorisation was the most commonly used legitimation strategy followed by moralisation and rationalisation. While these strategies are used in legitimate contents too, the authors have shown that in fake news, overwhelmingly expert and role model authority was employed underpinned by emotive language and direct appeals to emotions as well as hate speech and coercive verbs. The authors emphasise the harmful and politically destabilising effects of fake news because of its capacity to instil fear and incite hatred amongst various ethnic and religious groups.

Given that fake news on social media sites is a fairly recent phenomenon, it is perhaps not surprising that linguistic research on this form of online disinformation is still in its infancy. The two aforementioned studies set important research directions showing how detailed linguistic and discursive insights can point to specific language features of fake news. Similar to Maci (2019) and using a corpus-based approach, this chapter endeavours to contribute to this slowly growing body of knowledge by exploring the differences between fake, legitimate, and sensationalist news tweets. The purpose of this chapter is to offer insights into the distinctive features of the language of fake news as compared with legitimate and sensationalist contents with the view to raise awareness of the linguistic specificities of fake news, which in turn might contribute to fostering critical (social) media literacy.

3   Data and methods

This section summarises the main datasets and procedures involved in the keyword analysis adopted to study the language of fake news on Twitter. It begins by outlining the details of the three corpora under investigation.

3.1   *Corpora*

The data under study involves three corpora of news disseminated on Twitter: the FN-Corpus, which consists of a set of fake news spread in 2016 and 2017; the AP-Corpus, which includes

Table 7.1 Twitter news corpora and their sizes

Corpus	No of Tweets	Number of Words
FN-Corpus	10,000	96,676
AP-Corpus	1,950	33,925
DM-Corpus	1,707	26,923

fact-checked tweets produced by the Associated Press (AP); and the DM-Corpus, which comprises news tweets disseminated by the mid-range British tabloid the *Daily Mail* (DM). Table 7.1 presents the size of the corpora in terms of the number of tweets and words.

The corpus of fake news includes tweets disseminated by fake accounts set up by the Russian Internet Research Agency (IRA) also known as the Russian troll factory or Russian troll farm. IRA is a company that engaged in social media influence by manufacturing fake news in order to sow disinformation and manipulate social media audiences. The ultimate goal was to influence outcomes of important political events in the ways that align with Kremlin's agenda. This has been regarded as the most significant state-sponsored foreign influence operation of the social media age, and there is some evidence suggesting that the activities of the troll factory have impacted outcomes of political events especially in US (e.g. Linvill and Warren 2020).

The data for the FN-Corpus was downloaded from the platform github, on which tweets produced by the IRA are stored (the full dataset can be accessed here: https://github.com/fivethirtyeight/russian-troll-tweets). In 2017, Twitter identified some 2,848 accounts associated with IRA. Subsequently, almost 3 million tweets produced by these accounts were removed but also made available to researchers on github in August 2018. This data presents a unique opportunity to examine strategies of disinformation, including the kind of language that is used to manufacture fake news in 280 characters. The data are available in 13 batches (saved as csv files), each including between 180,000 and 250,000 tweets. To create a smaller sample to analyse using the linguistic software programme Sketch Engine, 1,000 tweets in English were randomly selected from the first ten csv files to create the FN-corpus of 10,000 tweets (96,676 words).

Since the boundary between fake, verified, and even sensationalist news can be blurry, and the different types of contents often appear side by side on social media feeds, this study compares a corpus of fakes news tweets to verified news tweets from the Associated Press (AP) as well as the middle-range tabloid the *Daily Mail*. The AP is one of the largest news organisations in the world and employs a rigorous fact-checking on its social media contents. In contrast, the *Daily Mail*, which has more than 2 million readers in the UK and around 25 million unique visitors on its online site per month, is known for its sensationalist style; it has been criticised for poor fact-checking, which led to its removal from Wikipedia with the Wikipedia editors deeming the news group unreliable as a news source (Jackson 2017).

To compile the AP-Corpus, tweets produced between November 2019 and January 2020 by the AP were collected from the AP handle @AP using a python script. This produced a sample of 1,950 tweets (33,925 words), which were subsequently cleaned (the html links were removed) and saved in a txt file. The same procedures and timeframe were adopted to collect data from the handle @DailyMailUK, which retrieved 1,707 tweets (26,923 words) for the DM-Corpus. Arguably, it would have been ideal to have all tweets collected from the same period of time, yet due to the later release of the IRA data and restrictions put in place by Twitter when it comes to collecting historical data, this was not possible. This was not deemed too big a problem since the aim was to reveal language features of fake news independent of the topic of tweets.

3.2 Methods

The goal of this study was to offer more detailed insights into linguistic features of fake news that in some ways are distinctive to this type of "news" discourse. To this end, a corpus-based approach, specifically keyword analysis, was employed to explore the three corpora described previously. In corpus-linguistic terms, a corpus is a large collection of language data available electronically for quantitative and qualitative analyses (McEnery and Hardie 2012). A corpus is usually interrogated using a specialist linguistic software programme, and most of the widely available ones offer a wider range of tools, including automatic frequency counts, part of speech tagging, fast retrieval of concordance lines, collocations, and keywords. The advantage of using a specialist software programme to explore a large corpus lies in its capacity to reveal patterns of language use systematically and more accurately pointing to salient or less salient tendencies that might simply be missed in a manual analysis, which is normally based on reading relevant text data. It also takes much less time. Yet it needs to be pointed out that most researchers, who use a corpus-based approach, do not stop the analysis at the point of retrieval of quantitative outputs; frequency counts, collocations, or keywords are almost always explored in greater detail by engaging with the data qualitatively, for example, through close reading of concordance lines or larger text extracts, and/or categorising data in some ways. Often, various analytical and theoretical frameworks are employed to explore one topic and a triangulation of methods, data, and techniques is performed to offer richer, complementary, and comparative perspectives (e.g. Baker and Egbert 2016; Kinloch and Jaworska 2020). This study follows this practice in that two analytical tools are employed, that of single keywords and key parts of speech (PoS) to interrogate three corpora for comparative purposes; a selection of salient PoS is then further explored qualitatively through reading concordance lines.

A corpus-based approach defines keywords as words that are unusually frequent in one corpus (i.e. a focus corpus) as compared to another (i.e. a reference corpus). Such words are deemed representative of a particular topic, style, or register (Egbert and Biber 2019). The unusualness is determined by comparing frequencies of words in two corpora and using a range of filters to establish which ones are keywords. This can include metrics such as log-likelihood to determine statistically significant differences or effect size statistics to determine the magnitude of difference (Gabrielatos and Marchi 2012). Researchers also apply a specific frequency cut-off point, and some call for a stronger consideration of dispersion when identifying keywords (Egbert and Biber 2019). It is important to note that the choices which the researcher makes to retrieve keywords influence the results, that is, what kind of words are identified as key. Not only the metrics and other filters but also the choice of the reference corpus is important since the kind of texts included in the comparator can determine the outputs on the keyword list. Recent studies have shown that the more similar the reference corpus is to the focus corpus in terms of the text types, genre, or register, the more specific differences are highlighted (Pojanapunya and Todd 2021).

The first reference corpus selected for this study is the AP corpus of fact-checked news tweets. Because AP tweets are similar in purpose (information and/or comments on newsworthy events, people, or incidents) and produced in the same media context (Twitter), it was felt that this is a good comparator to reveal specific linguistic features of fake news allowing insights into how fake news writers use language on Twitter as opposed to professional journalists who follow the journalistic code of conduct. The second reference corpus is that of tweets produced by the middle-range tabloid the *Daily Mail*. Since fake news often resemble a sensationalist style of writing, it was felt important to explore the extent to which they might still differ from news tweets produced by tabloids to show potential ways in which social media users could distinguish between sensationalist and utterly fake contents.

A keyword analysis is normally based on the retrieval of single lexical items that are often categorised into thematic domains (e.g. Baker et al. 2013; Jaworska and Kinloch 2018). While singular words and a categorisation into themes can point to topical features of a particular discourse type and tell us a great deal about the way in which a topic is discussed, the topic in itself was felt less relevant since both fake and validated news are often about the same issues, events, and people that are largely considered newsworthy at a particular point of time. The difference is in *how* they construct those. Previous research has shown that exploring larger grammatical categories, for example, key parts of speech (PoS) can be productive for identifying lexico-grammatical features distinctive of a register, genre, or style (e.g. Breeze 2019). Therefore, the decision was made to focus not only on single keywords but also on distinctive or key PoS and the most frequent items that represent the top PoS.

The analysis proceeded as follows: all three corpora were uploaded onto the software programme Sketch Engine (SE), which was employed to retrieve keywords. SE calculates keyness based on a normalised frequency ratio with a simple math parameter added to account for the zero problem in divisions (more information can be obtained from: www.sketchengine.eu/documentation/simple-maths/). The keyness score calculated in this way simply tells us how many times an item X is more frequently used in corpus Y as opposed to corpus Z. For the purpose of the analysis, the simple math parameter was set at 100 to include not too rare and not too general keywords, and the minimum frequency of 50 was set as the cut-off point. Results of the analysis are discussed in Section 4.

4   Results

This section presents the key findings that emerged from the comparative corpus-based analysis. To give a flavour of the fake news data, Section 4.1 discusses the top 30 keywords (single lexical items) that were identified in comparisons with AP-Corpus and DM-Corpus. Section 4.2. focuses on the top ten key PoS and zooms in to the most frequent items "sitting" under the top three distinctive PoS.

4.1   *Distinctive lexical features of fakespeak on Twitter*

Table 7.2 shows the top 30 most distinctive (lemmatised) keywords identified in the FN-Corpus as compared with verified news tweets from AP. Several characteristics of fake news discourse become evident. First, many of the distinctive lexical items are colloquial terms ("cop") and swearwords ("fuck", "shit"). Amongst the top 30 keywords, there are also words with strongly negative or pejorative meanings, such as "traitor", "racist", and "hate", whose use can be associated with an emotionally charged and hostile style. In the FN corpus, the word "traitor" was mostly used to describe representatives of the Democratic Party of US, who were directly accused of betraying their country. This kind of pejorative and emotionally charged words were absent from the AP tweets. Another prominent feature is the use of abbreviations commonly employed in digital writing, such as "lol" as well as a range of non-standard features including contractions such as "wanna", "ya", "u", omission of apostrophes ("dont", "Im") or final consonants ("juss"). These features are typical of informal writing in the digital but certainly not of legitimate tweet news as they have zero frequencies in the AP-Corpus.

The discourse of fake news on Twitter seems also much more personal and relational as evidenced by the frequent employment of personal pronouns and possessive determiners in plural and singular ("me", "I", "Im", "my", "we", "your", "you", "u"). And while some of the pronouns ("I"

Table 7.2 Top 30 most distinctive keywords in the FN-Corpus as compared to the AP-Corpus

Item	Freq. in FN	Freq. in AP	Relative freq. in FN	Relative freq. in AP	Keyness Score
1. cop	418	0	*3,164*	*0*	32.6
2. ya	260	1	*1,968*	*24*	16.7
3. lol	151	0	*1,143*	*0*	12.4
4. fuck	127	0	*961*	*0*	10.6
5. oh	108	0	*817*	*0*	9.2
6. me	351	10	*2,656*	*242*	8.1
7. racist	109	1	*825*	*24*	7.5
8. shit	79	0	*598*	*0*	7.0
9. your	381	14	*2,883*	*338*	6.8
10. god	76	0	*575*	*0*	6.8
11. I	1,349	60	*10,209*	*1,449*	6.7
12. Hillary	74	0	*560*	*0*	6.6
13. wanna	73	0	*552*	*0*	6.5
14. liberal	72	0	*545*	*0*	6.4
15. my	432	18	*3,269*	*435*	6.3
16. juss	69	0	*522*	*0*	6.2
17. you	1,136	54	*8,597*	*1,304*	6.2
18. Trump	68	0	*515*	*0*	6.1
19. dont	64	0	*484*	*0*	5.8
20. wow	60	0	*454*	*0*	5.5
21. traitor	58	0	*439*	*0*	5.4
22. we	550	29	*4,163*	*701*	5.3
23. so	353	18	*2,672*	*435*	5.2
24. u	119	4	*901*	*97*	5.1
25. Obama	86	2	*651*	*48*	5.1
26. Im	53	0	*401*	*0*	5.0
27. black	334	18	*2,528*	*435*	4.9
28. hate	82	2	*621*	*48*	4.9
29. remember	50	0	*378*	*0*	4.8
30. nigga	50	0	*363*	*0*	4.6

and "we") are used in the AP tweets as well, their frequencies are much lower with the possessive determiners ("my" and "your") and the personal pronoun "me" almost negligible. The personal and informal style is also emphasised by the unusually frequent occurrence of interjections "oh" and "wow", which tend to mimic speech and express surprise. Interestingly, the adverb "so" came up as one of the top keywords too. "So" is a distinctive feature of informal conversations and can function as a linking adverbial used in the initial position to structure talk (Biber et al. 1999). It can also act as an amplifier of other adjectives or adverbs. "So" was used 353 in the FN-Corpus, of which 219 times as an amplifier of an adjective or adverb; the most frequent items intensified by "so" were "much", "many", "true", and "hard". On the list, we also find proper nouns that point to important political figures ("Hilary", "Obama", "Trump"); their distinctiveness in the FN-corpus has to do with the fact that they were frequently mentioned in the fake news at the time. Having AP tweets from the same period (2017–2018) might have reduced their keyness score.

A very similar list of items was produced when comparing the FN-Corpus with the DM-Corpus just with slightly different ranks (see Table 7.3). Here too, colloquial and slang terms, swearwords,

Table 7.3 Top 30 most distinctive keywords in the FN-Corpus as compared to the DM-Corpus

Item	Freq. in FN	Freq. in DM	Relative Freq. in FN	Relative Freq. in DM	Keyness score
1. ya	260	0	1,968	0	20.7
2. lol	151	0	1,143	0	12.4
3. we	550	9	4,163	295	10.8
4. fuck	127	0	961	0	10.6
5. me	351	5	2,656	164	10.4
6. your	381	6	2,883	197	10.1
7. you	1,136	27	8,597	886	8.8
8. here	96	0	727	0	8.3
9. I	1,349	36	10,209	1,181	8.0
10. my	432	10	3,269	328	7.9
11. cop	418	10	3,164	328	7.6
12. u	119	1	901	33	7.5
13. black	334	8	2,528	262	7.2
14. shit	79	0	598	0	7.0
15. our	163	3	1,234	98	6.7
16. wanna	73	0	552	0	6.5
17. juss	69	0	522	0	6.2
18. Trump	68	0	515	0	6.1
19. nothing	67	0	507	0	6.1
20. should	171	4	1,294	131	6.0
21. problem	65	0	492	0	5.9
22. guy	64	0	484	0	5.8
23. dont	64	0	484	0	5.8
24. hey	61	0	462	0	5.6
25. racist	109	2	825	66	5.6
26. oh	108	2	817	66	5.5
27. today	106	2	802	66	5.4
28. traitor	58	0	439	0	5.4
29. so	353	13	2,672	427	5.3
30. no	306	11	2,316	361	5.2

abbreviations, non-standard writing features, personal pronouns and possessive determiners as well as the adverb "so" topped the list. This suggests that even in comparison with tweets produced by a news group known for a more sensationalist style of writing, these features of personal and informal discourse are distinctive to the style of fake news on Twitter.

4.2 Distinctive PoS of fake news on Twitter

The analysis of keywords in the FN-Corpus highlights some distinctive lexical features of fake news on Twitter in comparison with legitimate news tweets produced by the established news organisation the AP and the middle-ranged tabloid the *Daily Mail*. Yet from a list of isolated 30 or even 100 words, it is difficult to judge what the overall style of the genre or register in question is. Since styles or genres are essentially aggregates of distinctive lexico-grammatical features, that is, parts of speech, an analysis of key PoS was performed to offer more comprehensive insights into the features of the style of fake news (Breeze 2019).

Table 7.4 The top ten key PoS in the FN-Corpus in comparison with the AP-Corpus

PoS Tag	Category	Freq. in FN	Freq. in AP	Relative freq. in FN	Relative freq. in AP	Keyness Score
UH	*interjections*	206	7	*1,559*	*169*	6.2
SYM	*symbols including non-standard punctuation*	1,302	72	*9,854*	*1,739*	5.4
PP	*personal pronouns*	5,696	680	*43,108*	*16,426*	2.6
VB	*verb "be", base form*	513	71	*3,882*	*1715*	2.2
SENT	*standard sentence-final punctuation marks*	5,868	911	*44,410*	*22,006*	2.0
RB	*adverbs*	4,990	804	*37,765*	*19,422*	1.9
VVP	*verbs, present, not 3rd pers.*	2,501	410	*18,928*	*9,904*	1.9
EX	*existentials*	128	21	*969*	*507*	1.8
WRB	*wh-adverbs*	810	146	*6,130*	*3,527*	1.7
VV	*verb, base form*	4,021	818	*30,432*	*19,760*	1.5

Table 7.4 lists the top 10 PoS tags that were identified as key in the FN-corpus as compared to the AP-Corpus, while Table 7.5 shows a comparison with the DM-Corpus. As can be seen, the comparisons deliver very similar results. The only difference is that compared to the DM, fake news writers use more predeterminers (e.g. "all", "such") that can act as emphasisers, and they seem to rely more on the auxiliary "have" mostly in the present perfect, which situates past events in the present – something that writers of DM news tweets do very rarely. On the other hand, the AP seems to use more verbs especially in the present tense. Otherwise, the top 10 key PoS are the same, suggesting that fake news writers employ a set of specific language features that differ from both fact-checked and the more sensationalist news tweets. For reasons of space, only three PoS categories are discussed in more detail, and those include the ones that occur at least twice as often in fake news as compared to the AP and DM news tweet. The focus is on interjections, symbols, including non-standard punctuation, and personal pronouns.

As Table 7.4 and 7.5 show, one of the most distinctive PoS in the FN-corpus are interjections, of which "oh" (freq. 87), "hey" (39), and "yes!" (20) are the most frequent ones. This kind of feature is almost negligible in the two other corpora. Interjections are typical features of informal conversations. Although they have long been seen primarily as means of expressing emotions, research in pragmatics has shown that they fulfil a variety of functions that go beyond emotive responses (Norrick 2009). For example, they can act as discourse markers initiating a turn, signalling a contrast or elaboration and in combinations with other inserts often from fixed or routine expressions (Norrick 2009). "Oh" is one of the most frequently used interjections in spoken English and never in formal registers; it usually conveys the feeling of unexpectedness, surprise, or fear (Biber et al. 1999), but it can also function as a discourse marker signalling a joint focus of attention and shared knowledge (Schiffrin 1987). In the FN-corpus, "oh" too is the most frequent interjection employed mostly in combination with other lexical items, including "shit", "wait", "God", "yes", "boy" to express surprise but also to confirm a certain state of knowledge – mostly events that are evaluated negatively. Similar to spoken conversations, in which interjections are often used as turn initiators, in the fake news tweets studied here, they almost always appear at the beginning of the tweet (see Examples 1–3):

1   Oh yes @EnemyWithin? Any Buddhist terrorists?
2   OH BOY Hillary and Obama are Joining Forces and Its SAD #ABISS
3   Oh Shit! #Texas Cops Now Pull You Over For Driving Safely To Reward You

Table 7.5 The top ten key PoS in the FN-Corpus in comparison with the DM-Corpus

PoS Tag	Category	Freq. in FN	Freq. in DM	Relative Freq. in FN	Relative Freq. in DM	Keyness Score
SENT	standard sentence-final punctuation marks	5,868	101	44,410	3,314	13.0
EX	existentials	128	0	969	0	10.7
PDT	predeterminer	97	0	734	0	8.3
SYM	symbols including non-standard punctuation	1,302	52	9,854	1,706	5.5
UH	interjections	206	7	1,559	230	5.0
VHP	verb have, sing. present, non-3d	294	22	2,225	722	2.8
VVP	verbs, present, not 3rd pers.	2,501	234	18,928	7,678	2.4
WRB	wh-adverbs	810	83	6,130	2,723	2.2
RB	adverbs	4,990	536	37,765	17,587	2.1
PP	personal pronouns	5,696	643	43,108	21,098	2.0

Table 7.6 The top ten symbols in the FN-Corpus in comparison with the AP and DM corpora

FN-Corpus			AP-Corpus		DM-Corpus	
	Freq.	Relative Freq.	Freq.	Relative Freq.	Freq.	Relative Freq.
1. &	201	2,077	15	442	8	297
2. /	161	1,664	7	206	4	149
3. @	141	1,457	1	29	14	520
4. *	103	1,064	0	0	18	669
5. !!!	100	1,033	0	0	2	74
6. !!	55	568	0	0	0	0
7. %	48	496	8	236	10	371
8. ???	46	475	0	0	0	0
9. ?!	39	403	0	0	0	0
10. ??	32	331	0	0	0	0

"Oh" is often used in combination with expletives, exclamation markers, or capitalised words possibly to attract readers' attention; in doing so, it negatively "pre-evaluates" for the reader the follow-up content priming them to interpret the message as a piece of bad news.

Symbols were the second most distinctive PoS tag, which is not surprising given that Twitter users tend to use a variety of symbols, including hashtags and mentions. Yet the FN-corpus was compared to two other corpora of news tweets, and the fact that symbols are still identified as particularly distinctive seems to suggest that fake news writers employ them more frequently than legitimate journalists. Table 7.6 shows the top 10 standalone symbols that fake news writers use and compares their occurrences in the two other corpora.

While certain standard symbols such as "&", "/", or "%" are used across all three datasets, they have a much lower proportional frequency in the AP and DM news tweets. Others, specifically those that can be considered non-standard punctuation, such as double or triple exclamations or question marks as well as combinations of the two, are largely absent from legitimate news tweets.

Exclamation marks are used in writing to give an extra emphasis to the expressed contents; repeating the symbol strengthens this effect, as the examples of tweets here show:

4   @Breaking911 Build that wall!!
5   @realDonaldTrump We support you, Mr. President!!!
6   HAPPENING NOW: St. Louis rioters put a little kid on police car to help smash it. This is outrageous!!! #STLVerdict

In the standard punctuation, a single question mark is used at the end of a sentence to mark it as a question. Double, triple, or multiple question marks can be considered non-standard punctuations; in the FN-corpus, their use seems to signal a heightened level of emotion, mostly of negative ones, including scepticism, disbelief, or outrage. Examples 7–9 illustrate this pattern:

7   Can our #black #president do at least smth to stop this??? #PoliceBrutality #policeviolence
8   WTF?? Refugees With TB Are Interviewing at Starbucks #ABISS
9   WHAT??? Liberal Media Advising Parents to IGNORE Gender Science!

A combination of exclamation with question marks fulfils similar functions; they too are mostly used to intensify the feeling of disbelief or anger:

10   WTF?! California is Choosing ILLEGALS Over the American Middle Class
11   SERIOUSLY?! Rosie ODonnell APOLOGIZES to Kim Jong-Un!
12   The Clintons stole 6 billions dollars that was meant to rebuild Haiti. When will the Clinton corruption stop?! #CrookedHillary #CrookedBill

Often this kind of non-standard punctuation is used just after the initial word, which is, at times capitalised, as shown in Examples 8, 9, 10 and 11. The capitalisation of the initial item, which is normally short or abbreviated ("WHAT", "WTF"), makes the item stand out to possibly attract attention. This kind of feature was absent from the AP and DM tweets.

Another distinctive PoS was that of personal pronouns suggesting that the style of fake news tweets is possibly more relational. Table 7.7 shows the top ten personal pronouns used in the FN-Corpus and, as previously, compares their occurrences in the AP and DM corpora.

Table 7.7 The top ten personal pronouns in the FN-Corpus in comparison with the AP and DM corpora

FN-Corpus			*AP-Corpus*		*DM-Corpus*	
	Freq.	*Relative Freq.*	*Freq.*	*Relative Freq.*	*Freq.*	*Relative Freq.*
1. I	1,217	*12,588*	62	*1,828*	36	*1,337*
2. you	1,135	*11,740*	54	*1,592*	27	*1,003*
3. we	550	*5,689*	29	*855*	9	*334*
4. they	411	*4,251*	95	*2,800*	49	*1,820*
5. he	378	*3,910*	135	*3,979*	168	*6,240*
6. me	325	*3,362*	10	*295*	5	*186*
7. she	170	*1,758*	73	*2,152*	165	*6,129*
8. us*	151	*1,562*	7	*206*	1	*37*
9. him	152	*1,572*	10	*295*	38	*1,411*
10. them	125	*1,293*	8	*236*	14	*520*

*Excludes instances of US referring to the United States of America.

"I" and "you" are the most frequent personal pronouns in fake news tweets – used almost seven times more often than in the AP and nine times more than in the DM news tweets. Both pronouns are a typical feature of informal conversations, in which they are employed to refer to the speaker and the addressee, creating an interpersonal relationship. "You" is also used extensively in advertising to give an impression of informality and to create a sense of connection – a feature which is known as synthetic personalisation (Fairclough 2001). Research in cognitive narratology has shown that readers feel more emotionally involved if they are addressed personally (e.g. Brunyé et al. 2011), and higher emotional engagement and connection can stimulate viral sharing (Nikolinakou and Whitehill King 2018). Previous linguistic research on digital advertising, specifically on native ads, has shown that personal pronouns and mostly "you" as a form of synthetic personalisation are a distinctive feature of contents that are purposefully created to "go viral" (Jaworska 2020). The extensive use of both pronouns in the fake news tweets studied here suggests that similar to native advertising, their style is more "synthetically" personalised and more engaging and clickbait-y (see Examples 13–15) in comparison with fact-checked and even sensationalist news tweets, which seem to use "I" and "you" minimally.

13 #ObamaNextJob? I wouldn't hire that man to shovel horseshit . . .
14 You'll Melt When You See What Happens When This Cat's Favorite Human Plays The Piano
15 WOW! This Viral Photo From Hurricane Harvey Will Leave You SPEECHLESS!

Interestingly, the pronoun "you" was often used in fake news that were prompting Twitter users to contribute to a hashtag, and some were rather playful and humorous in tone, as the examples of tweets here show:

16 #RuinADinnerInOnePhrase Why do you look so pretty on tinder?
17 #SurvivalGuideToThanksgiving Lots of exercise all year & zero carbs. Be the skinniest motherfucking turkey ever & you'll live another year
18 #RealLifeMagicSpells Honey we have to talk. Makes you divorced

This might be a deliberate strategy to increase the engagement with fake accounts and the likelihood of the contents being shared widely. It is not just political topics, expletives, and exclamation marks but also humour and invitations to (verbal) challenges that fake news writers employ to attract attention to their tweets and make them more share-able.

5 Discussion and conclusions

This chapter showcases how a corpus-based analysis, and specifically the tool of keyword, can be productively used to identify features of the language of disinformation that can help distinguish fake news from fact-checked or ever sensationalist contents. As the analysis has shown, fake news writers employ a set of specific linguistic devices, including the interjections "oh", "hey", and "yes!", various non-standard punctuation marks such as double and triple question and exclamation marks as well as their combinations often with capitalisation for extra emphasis. Fake news writers also create a more personalised, conversational, and engaging style of communication, as evidenced by the extensive use of two personal pronouns "I" and "you" with their tweets often resembling the clickbait-y style of native ads. The use of non-standard spelling and abbreviations associated with informal digital communication ("lol", "u", "dont") and expletives often in combination with non-standard orthographic marks is also distinctive to fake news. The analysis undertaken for the purpose of this chapter was motivated not just by linguistic but also pedagogical reasons. Showing and discussing language features that are distinctive to fake news, for example, in the context of English education in secondary schools and universities can raise critical awareness of the language style of such contents amongst younger generations of social media users, sensitize them to strategies used in disinformation, and in doing so, hopefully make them less susceptible to manipulation and exploitation.

Despite the ubiquity and variety of fake news in the digital, linguistic research on this disinformation phenomenon remains scarce. While this chapter offers some initial insights into distinctive lexico-grammatical features of fakespeak in 208 characters, there are several dimensions of the discourse of fake news, including pragmatic and multimodal aspects that warrant further linguistic investigations. Corpus linguistic approaches are particularly suited to an analysis of fake news, since fake news come in large numbers. Yet quantitative insights are not enough, and a combination of corpus approaches with analytical frameworks from pragmatics, media linguistics, critical discourse analysis, and multimodality would deepen our understanding of the strategies that fake news writers employ to sow disinformation and manipulate social media users.

References

Baker, P. and Egbert, J. (2016) "Introduction," in P. Baker and J. Egbert (eds.), *Triangulating Methodological Approaches in Corpus-Linguistic Research*, London: Routledge, pp. 1–19.

Baker, P., Gabrielatos, C. and McEnery, T. (2013) *Discourse Analysis and Media Attitudes*, Cambridge: Cambridge University Press.

Bednarek, M. and Caple, H. (2017) *The Discourse of News Values*, Oxford: Oxford University Press.

Biber, D., Johansson, S., Leech, G., Conrad, S. and Finegan, E. (1999) *Longman Grammar of Spoken and Written English*, Harlow: Longman.

Breeze, R. (2019) "Part-of-speech patterns in legal genres: Text-internal dynamics from a corpus-based perspective," in T. Fanego and P. Rodríguez-Puente (eds.), *Corpus-Based Research on Variation in English Legal Discourse*, Amsterdam: Benjamins, pp. 79–103.

Brunyé, T.T., Ditman, T., Mahoney, C.R. and Taylor, H.A. (2011) "Better you than I: Perspectives and emotion simulation during narrative comprehension," *Journal of Cognitive Psychology* 23(5) 659–666.

Castells, M. (2007) "Communication, power and counter-power in the network society," *International Journal of Communication* 1 238–266.

De Beer, D. and Matthee, M. (2020) "Approaches to identify fake news: A systematic literature review," *Integrated Science in Digital Age 2020* 136 13–22.

Dey, A., Rafi, R.Z., Hasan Parash, S., Arko, S.K. and Chakrabarty, A. (2018) "Fake news pattern recognition using linguistic analysis," in *Joint 7th International Conference on Informatics, Electronics & Vision (ICIEV) and 2018 2nd International Conference on Imaging*, Vision & Pattern Recognition (icIVPR), Kitakyushu, Japan, pp. 305–309.

Egbert, J. and Biber, D. (2019) "Incorporating text dispersion into keyword analyses," *Corpora* 14(1) 77–104.

Fairclough, N. (2001) *Language and Power* (2nd ed.), London: Longman.

Friginal, E. (2009) *The Language of Outsourced Call Centres: A Corpus-Based Study of Cross-Cultural Interaction*, Amsterdam: Benjamins.

Gabrielatos, C. and Marchi, A. (2012) "Keyness: Appropriate metrics and practical issues," *CADS International Conference 2012*. 13–14 September, University of Bologna, Italy. http://repository.edgehill.ac.uk/4196/1/Gabrielatos%26Marchi-Keyness-CADS2012.pdf

Galasiński, D. (2000) *The Language of Deception: A Discourse Analytical Study*, London: Sage.

Goodman, M. and Jaworska, S. (2020) "Mapping digital foodscapes: Digital food influencers and the grammars of good food," *Geoforum* 117 183–193.

Igwebuike, E.E. and Chimuanya, L. (2021) "Legitimating falsehood in social media: A discourse analysis of political fake news," *Discourse & Communication* 15(1) 42–58.

Jackson, J. (2017) "Wikipedia bans Daily Mail as 'unreliable' source," *The Guardian*, 8 February 2017, www.theguardian.com/technology/2017/feb/08/wikipedia-bans-daily-mail-as-unreliable-source-for-website

Jaworska, S. (2020) "Discourse of advertising," in E. Friginal and J. Hardy (eds.), *The Routledge Handbook of Corpus Approaches to Discourse Analysis*, London: Routledge, pp. 428–444.

Jaworska, S. and Kinloch, K. (2018) "Using multiple data sets," in C. Taylor and A. Marchi (eds.), *Corpus Approaches to Discourse: A Critical Review*, London: Routledge, pp. 110–129.

Jones, R., Jaworska, S. and Aslan, E. (2020) *Language and Media*, London: Routledge.

Kinloch, K. and Jaworska, S. (2020) "Using a comparative corpus-assisted approach to study health and illness discourses across domains: The case of postnatal depression (PND) in lay, medical and media texts," in Z. Demjen (ed.) *Applying Linguistics in Illness and Healthcare Contexts*, London: Bloomsbury, pp. 73–98.

Linvill, D.L. and Warren, P.L. (2020) "Troll factories: Manufacturing specialized disinformation on Twitter," *Political Communication* 37(4) 447–467.

Lugea, J. (2021) "Linguistic approaches to fake news detection," in D. Padmanabhan, T. Chakraborty, C. Long, and S. Kumar (eds.) *Data Science for Fake News: Surveys and Perspectives*, Cham: Springer, pp. 287–302.

Maci, S. (2019) "Discourse strategies of fake news in the anti-vax campaign," *Lingue Culture Mediazioni – Languages Cultures Mediation* 6(1) 15–43.

McEnery, T. and Hardie, A. (2012) *Corpus Linguistics. Method, Theory and Practice*, Cambridge: Cambridge University Press.

Nikolinakou, A. and Whitehill King, K. (2018) "Viral video ads: Emotional triggers and social media virality," *Psychology and Marketing* 35 715–726.

Norrick, N. (2009) "Interjections as pragmatic markers," *Journal of Pragmatics* 41 866–891.

Pérez-Rosas, V., Kleinberg, B., Lefevre, A. and Mihalcea, R. (2017) "Automatic detection of fake news," in *Proceedings of the 27th International Conference on Computational Linguistics*, Santa Fe, New Mexico, pp. 3391–3401, https://aclanthology.org/C18-1287/

Pojanapunya, P. and Todd, R. (2021) "The influence of the benchmark corpus on keyword analysis," *Register Studies* 3(1) 88–114.

Rashkin, H., Choi, E., Jang, J.Y., Volkova, S. and Choi, Y. (2017) "Truth of varying shades: Analysing language in fake news and political fact checking," in *Proceedings of the 2017 Conference On Empirical Methods in Natural Language Processing*, Copenhagen, Denmark, pp. 2921–2927, https://aclanthology.org/D17-1317/

Schiffrin, D. (1987) *Discourse Markers*, Cambridge: Cambridge University Press.

Xiao, Z. and McEnery, A. (2005) "Two approaches to genre analysis: Three genres in modern American English," *Journal of English Linguistics* 33(1) 62–82.

Zappavigna, M. (2018) *Discourse of Twitter and Social Media*, London: Bloomsbury.

Zhang, X. and Ghorbani, A. (2020) "An overview of online fake news: Characterization, detection, and discussion," *Information Processing and Management* 57 1–26.

8

DEBUNKING FAKE NEWS THROUGH THE MULTIMODAL COMPOSITION OF INTERNET MEMES

Pietro Luigi Iaia

Introduction

After becoming the buzzword of the year in 2017, owing to the increase of its influence and diffusion after the American presidential election of 2016 (Vamanu 2019), fake news is preserving and perhaps extending its pervasiveness in the personal and public spheres, following the outbreak of the COVID-19 pandemic. Discussion about the origin of the virus, its treatment, as well as the production of and inoculation with vaccines are just some of the themes of the counterfactual pieces of news that are shared through social media posts. The proliferation of fake news was contaminating the fight against SARS-CoV-2, and it was detrimental to official information sources, whose credibility was eventually undermined. In addition, the combination of the escalation of disinformation and the harsh and almost constant debate that is involving – among others – physicians, virologists, and politicians is contributing to the distortion of our perception of the state of the emergency and the circulation of the virus (Krause et al. 2020). This situation is raising people's vulnerability, for it has become easier to believe the most sensational accounts or to fall victim to click bait (Allcot and Gentzkow 2017). Research has addressed fake news from distinct – and yet interacting – perspectives, enquiring into the outset of the phenomenon, which dates back to the nineteenth century, and investigating the strategies of production, transmission, and neutralisation of misinformation. Interesting attempts to redress fake news are represented by the actualisations of the so-called inoculation theory (van der Linden et al. 2020: 3), whereby audiences are trained to resist the "sinister form of mass persuasion" (Nyilasy 2019) at issue, by exposing them to rebuttal strategies delivered through engaging, interactive, and multimedia text types. This chapter reports on a specific application of inoculation theory by means of Internet memes. This approach was devised at the University of Salento, where a number of undergraduate students from modern literatures were involved in a ten-hour workshop that focused on the critical analysis of the multimodal discourse of memes and of the discourse of fake news, as well as on the creation of original compositions using words and images aiming to pursue positive – and more beneficial – objectives. The viral texts are usually exchanged over the Internet to spread disinformation, offensive messages, and humour. In contrast, the students' creations are designed to attract the viewers' interest before proposing to them facts and notions about the COVID-19 pandemic from reliable sources, trying to counteract harmful and controversial communication.

DOI: 10.4324/9781003224495-9

The following section will describe the main features of fake news and of the humorous discourse of memes, along with the objectives of the "Memerizing" approach, which is the umbrella term labelling the unconventional applications of those text types that have been produced so far (Iaia 2020). After detailing the characteristics of the subjects who produced the examined memes, the research method, main objective, and hypothesis, this chapter will illustrate the multimodal strategies of inoculation with which the selected samples are imbued.

Inoculation of memes against fake news

Fake news and memes have online communication and the Internet as their shared privileged floor of transmission. Memes represent cultural units that gain influence and propagate themselves through online transmission and imitation (Bulatovic 2019). Their structure is usually "relatively complex [and] multi-layered" (Laineste and Voolaid 2016) since they are characterised by peculiar interactions between images and words in order to produce typically a joke (Davison 2012). As concerns fake news, it is a phenomenon that emerged in the nineteenth century (Montgomery-McGovern 1898) and has appeared over the years on different media, from newspapers and magazines to television, but it is online social networking that has "enabled purveyors of fake news to target specific audiences" (Gelfert 2018: 86). Misinformation about the COVID-19 pandemic "widely" circulates online (Bakir and McStay 2017: 1) through the publication of false statements (Klein and Wueller 2017: 6) whose "parasitic" nature is reflected by their mimicking "the look and feel" of mainstream media and sources (Gelfert 2018: 91; see also Marsh et al. 2016; Rapp 2016). If the Italian scenario is considered, two examples can be mentioned: *Il Fatto Quotidaino* and *KontroKultura*. Both titles make some of the most distinguishing features of disinformation explicit. The former is characterised by a hardly visible switch between vowels "a" and "i"; in turn, this creates a pun that urges distracted readers to think that they are approaching news from the credible website *Il Fatto Quotidiano* (which may be rendered as "The Daily *Fact*" where "daily" means "*quotidiano*", whereas "*quotidaino*" does not exist as a word in standard Italian). The latter denominates an online place which is self-appointed as a repository for items of knowledge, news, and experience ("*cultura*", "culture", misspelt as *Kultura*) that are "against" ("contro", misspelt as *Kontro*) or alternative to the official reports. The degree of mystification is high over the Internet because of the lack of mediation or guidance from TV show hosts, journalists, or comedians – the "gatekeepers" (Westerman et al. 2014) – who normally comment on fake news and help receivers acknowledge the roots of disinformation. A case in point is the Italian comedy-news programme *Striscia la notizia* ("*Slithering news*"), which stages satirical interviews with politicians or other personalities using deepfakes (Kietzmann et al. 2020). This decision was criticised (Duello 2019; Puente 2019), claiming that viewers could be cheated. Yet the renowned nature of the show, the constant activation of "canned laughter" record tracks, and the fact that *Striscia la notizia* has been on air on a trusted mainstream media channel for 34 years can work towards educating viewers to separate consciously what is the actual representation of current facts from what is their reinterpretation for humorous purposes. What is more, the staff's helping hand is confirmed by a video having been uploaded, on the show's website, revealing how their deepfakes are made. In different circumstances, when consumed exclusively online and by itself, fake news contributes to the expansion of "a worse informed populace" (Levy 2017: 20) who select and believe specific sources without any form of guidance and who prefer websites that use over-the-top headlines, depict dramatic associations between words and pictures, imitate the titles and structure of more reliable sources (as has just been described), and contain articles that fuel readers' fears. The impossibility of rebutting misinformation, along with the inability to compare what one reads with trustworthy accounts of the same reality induce in recipients the acquisition of wrong beliefs about the external world, leading – which is worse – to shape their behaviour in their social communities and even their epistemic world (Cheney and Seyfarth 2007; Camp 2009).

In order to counteract such negative outcomes, researchers have delved into the rules of the construction of fake news, intending to uncover the basics of the tactics of persuasion before using them to their advantage. This is the rationale behind inoculation theory, which aims to fight deceitful texts by developing tools – such as the original creations under examination – that are used to attract addressees before assisting them in improving their familiarity with how fake news is assembled, or in accessing stories that reveal to what extent misinformation is untrustworthy. In so doing, people's defence – their antibodies – would be built up. The approach stems from the theory of "psychological inoculation", which takes the "practice of vaccination . . . into the realm of resistance to persuasion" (van der Linden et al. 2020: 3), aiming to trigger positive responses, such as enhancing one's critical thinking (Compton 2013), or disarming the negative effects of spreading fake news. Actualizations of inoculation theory have included educational video games or other interactive media whose primary function is to allow receivers to reach different epistemic destinations. In the case study presented here, inoculation targets the "unhealthy state" (Compton 2020) of those who are reached by fake and sensational stories over the Internet (Brady et al. 2017), where memes reign currently (Blank 2013; Laineste and Voolaid 2016). These subjects are exposed to novel memes that, instead, aim to counteract the fallacies and psychological negative effects (Richards and Banas 2015; Cook et al. 2017) of conspiratorial reasoning (van der Linden 2015). This study is the latest product of the "Memerizing" approach, which was developed at the University of Salento for the purpose of inventing innovative and more engaging means to assist general audiences in increasing their secondary knowledge (Iaia 2019) or in learning foreign languages (Iaia 2020). The hypothesis behind the "Memerizing" approach is that audience interest can be piqued by means of appealing multi-semiotic hybridizations between specialised and humorous discourses, or between foreign-language learning and humorous discourses. The ease of replication and adaptation of memes (Milner 2013; Laineste and Voolaid 2016; Baysac 2017) and the fact that these text types are gaining appreciation and acclaim as a mainstream phenomenon (Gil 2020) are thought of as properties that can encourage participants' direct involvement and interactions (Mills 2012: 289), thus empowering them to acquire and absorb the new pieces of information more easily (Purnama 2017). As far as this chapter is concerned, memes ought to overturn the habits of authors of fake news. The latter are aware of the potential readers' epistemic and cognitive biases; hence, fabrication in fake news is tailored to the implied receivers' knowledge and their bewilderment ensuing from the amplification of available sources. As regards this study, it is true that the viral texts at issue are seen as communication means with which addressees are familiar. Actually, their role as mere decoys is exploited to summon online viewers, who run into memes that, unexpectedly, attempt to instruct them on how to re-evaluate the reliability and truthfulness of disinformation.

An essential element to attain this functional goal is humour, which can contribute to the achievement of the viewers' "positive reception" (Masek et al. 2019), but also to the reinforcement of the sense of community permeating digital groups. Groups that can be both synchronous and asynchronous, which are subordinate to the anticipation of sharing interests or beliefs (Sumi and Mase 2002). Humour in memes is produced by means of the following approaches (Taecharungroj and Nueangjamnong 2015): (1) affiliation, when producers try to enhance relationships between members of the same communities; (2) self-enhancing; and (3) self-defeating, whereby disparaging messages are transmitted relying upon clashes and contrasts between people from different sociocultural and linguistic contexts; and (4) aggressive, when jokes are authored disregarding their effects on who or what their target is. The examined corpus of memes resorts to types (1), (2), and (3). At the same time, the preservation of virtual and transient groups of people sharing interests is exploited because this is what pushes web users to visit the same websites or to consult a restricted pool of sources (van Schalkwyk et al. 2020). The perception of belonging to a restricted group of people who access "hidden" and unofficial truths informs the readers' vanity (Soghoian 2007; Pham 2015), and the original creations seize upon the latter form of self-awareness. First, the memes' multimodal composition feeds the readers' self-perception of "being right", or "knowing best", or of approaching alternative representations of reality, which, in fact, spread antiscientific and anti-vaccination attitude (Leask 2015; Bennato 2017). The aim is to gain the receivers' trust. Then, the analysis of the association between words and images and the reception of humour would lead to the recipients' realisation that the particular multimedia item is, in fact, making fun of specific beliefs. The reaction to such unexpected intent would be one of curiosity about the rationale of the messages, eventually urging viewers to get further information – and to approach the viewpoint opposing disinformation.

Method, research hypothesis, and objective

The memes under investigation were produced by 26 undergraduate students in modern literatures from the University of Salento. The workshop was meant to attract the students' attention and increase their interest in foreign languages and translation thanks to the adoption of text types that participants could perceive closer to their daily experience. Although this chapter discusses the creations of twenty-six students, we think that the results do shed light on alternative approaches to the exploitation of the multimodal compositions of memes. At the same time, we acknowledge that further studies are essential to test the research hypothesis by involving more subjects, such as people from different sociocultural and linguistic backgrounds, or with different levels of education.

The workshop under discussion was structured as follows: three hours were dedicated to the theoretical presentation of the main issues pertaining to multimodality, in order to provide participants with an essential background illustrating the making of meaning by means of the interaction between linguistic and extralinguistic dimensions. Then, two hours were dedicated to the discussion of the main types of memes, their structures and humorous discourse. It emerged that subjects had already produced and shared those texts, in particular to comment on some events from TV series or reality TV programmes, or other current affairs. In fact, some of the templates that were picked by the students were unknown to the researcher who devised the practical application of this project. In the rest of the workshop, participants freely established working groups and developed the objects of the upcoming analysis, and they were also free to produce memes in English or Italian. Those who created memes in English said that their choices reflected the universal nature of the texts, since they are diffused disregarding the interactants' native languages and provenance. Twenty-five memes were created; most of them are of the "image-macro" type, where a central image is surrounded by written captions, or where the semiotic resources are juxtaposed, whereas two are in the format called "Graphics Interchange Format" (GIF), which defines short animations. In one, the character from a film is looking menacingly at a razor (meme (1) in the following section); the other (meme (2)) shows a man sweating copiously before the appearance of the verbal captions. The overall result is a sequence of associations that create the incongruities and script oppositions originating humour (Veatch 1998; Attardo 2001).

Eleven samples will be examined. They deal with the following fake news items (FNIs, arranged in alphabetical order), ranging from false strategies of prevention to the distinctive elements of misinformation about vaccines (Maci 2019), such as the hidden content in a serum, or its side effects:

Table 8.1 Association between fake news items and the examined corpus of memes

FNI 1	Connection between vaccines and breast enlargement	Meme (11)
FNI 2	Connection between vaccines and infertility	Meme (10)
FNI 3	Drinking alcohol as a prevention strategy	Memes (3) and (4)
FNI 4	Drinking chlorine dioxide as a prevention strategy	Meme (5)
FNI 5	Eating garlic as a prevention strategy	Meme (6)
FNI 6	Paracetamol as a cure for COVID-19	Meme (7)
FNI 7	Shaving as a prevention strategy	Meme (1)
FNI 8	Sweating as a prevention strategy	Memes (2) and (9)

Meme (8) is not included in Table 8.1 because it adopts a slightly different approach, which is nonetheless worth considering in the following analysis. The design of this activity is meant to represent one of the "[n]ew tools and methods" pursuing prevention against counterfeit news items. They can be "text, images, videos, or audio" (Kalsnes 2018: 15) whereby people are "immunize[d] . . . against misinformation" about the current pandemic and other forms of conspiracy (van der Linden et al. 2020). The decision to use a group of subjects where people who frequently communicate online and consume online texts were heavily represented was expected to encourage a "bottom-up" form of creation that, in accordance with the main research hypothesis, could function as another way to prolong the effects of immunization thanks to "booster shots" (Maertens et al. 2020) reinforcing rebuttal of counterfactual stories (Schmid and Betsch 2019).

Analysis

The analysis will comment on the multimodal strategies of communication of the counterfactual value of the fake news items that were selected by the students who were participants in this research. The interaction between words, images, and humour, in the subjects' creations, is meant to prompt the desired interpretation on the part of receivers, who are expected to change their beliefs and attitudes about the objects of disinformation. Precisely, by resorting to nonsensical, exaggerated, and even derogatory depictions, the authors of the selected samples attempt to suggest to recipients that it is not worth believing sensational and irrational claims. The multimodal compositions of the examples target the Internet users' vanity and interests, urging readers to identify themselves, first, with whom or what is being displayed, thus fortifying the interactants' connection. Yet once the semantic potential of the creations is accessed – namely, labelling the stories and behaviours as unpopular – the addressees' puzzlement is expected to leave them questioning the convenience of following misinformation, thus stimulating their curiosity about the reasons behind the unexpected negative evaluation.

The 11 objects of investigation are divided into two batches, which will be explored in the following sections: the first deals with the surmised forms of prevention from contagion; the other regards vaccines and their side effects.

Memes exposing fake news about COVID-19 prevention

The official indications regarding avoiding catching COVID-19 suggest wearing a mask or avoiding close contacts with other people (CDC 2022), since coronavirus particles are mainly transmitted "via respiratory droplets . . . including aerosols produced when coughing and speaking" (ECDC 2020). At the same time, misinformation has been spread that consuming alcohol, shaving

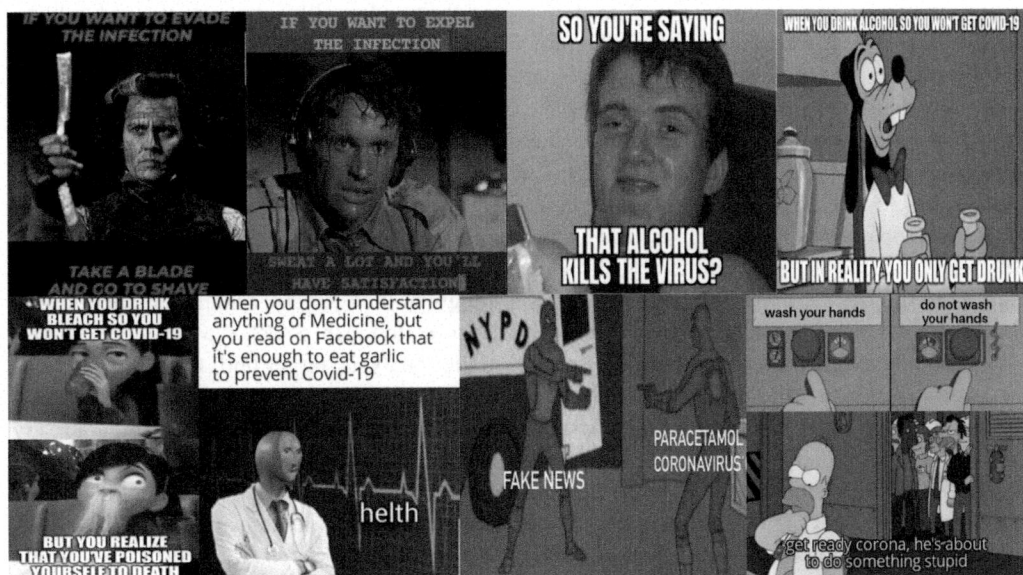

Figure 8.1   Memes (1)–(4) (top row, from left to right) and memes (5)–(8) (bottom row, from left to right)

facial hair, drinking chlorine dioxide, or sweating may provide protection from contagion. These claims are not true, and all of them are contained in the fake news items that the first group of memes, reproduced in Figure 8.1, tries to counteract:

From a general perspective, multimodal compositions in (1)–(8) seek the activation of close connection with potential receivers, so as not to be perceived initially as messages that do not belong to the epistemic community of online viewers. In light of this, most of the memes from the first group resort to intratextual references to the most famous templates (e.g. (3) and (6)), or to intertextual links to films and animated series (e.g. (1), (2), and (8)), hopefully attracting the younger recipients' interests, for the latter are those who most use – and re-use – viral texts online. Memes (1) and (2) aim to instil doubt about the belief that "a very bushy beard" may create "an improper seal with the mask" (Schimelpfening 2021). Yet according to Dr. Amesh Adalja, there is "no evidence that having a beard" increases one's vulnerability (Bowman and Donevan 2020), and to express the irrational nature of the concern, an intertextual reference to the film *Sweeney Todd: The Demon Barber of Fleet Street* (Tim Burton 2007) and black humour interact. The images and linguistic features of (1) contribute to the activation of the predicted inferential processes. One of the tools that are employed by subjects is the insertion of sentences whose semantic and communicative dimensions are unveiled only after being associated with the extralinguistic pieces. Another implement is the tenor of the captions, which aim to close psychological and social distances between senders and addressees. In (1), when the multimodal reading commences and only the top margin is watched, viewers are invited to know one of the paths that are available to "evade the infection". The authors of the examined meme purport that, as they move to the picture, receivers are likely to shift from a positive evaluation of the fake news, which they may already know, to the unforeseen and unpleasant feelings arising from looking at the menacing-looking "Demon Barber", Benjamin Barker, who ends up murdering his customers to revenge his loved one's death. The invitation hence exhibits the particular consequences of shaving. To be precise, by means of exaggeration, the multimodal composition insinuates that one had better keep his beard and follow other indications against contagion. The delivery of the senders' illocutionary force should be successful even if one had not watched the movie, and this is due to Barker's blood-covered face and appearance. It follows that the visual element is prevalent in the activation of inferencing; something that is true with respect to (2) as well, although its tone is more light-hearted, as can be deduced by its linguistic features such as the rhyme between the nouns "infection" and "satisfaction". Sarcasm fuels the relationship that is activated between the meme and the fake news it counteracts. At first, the object of the false news story seems to be supported. Actually, the represented participant, that is, the traumatized ex-fighter pilot Ted Striker, from the film *Airplane!* (Jim Abrahams et al. 1980), is meant to reveal the connotative dimension of the multimodal composition. Accordingly, the hyperbolic composition should guide the viewers' acknowledgment of the questionable nature of the claim about sweating as a protection from SARS-CoV-2.

Memes (1) and (2), along with all the samples under analysis, target both those who believe fake news and those who are aware of disinformation. The latter type of recipients would find them amusing ways to confirm the inconsistencies and anti-scientific positions that they already know. The former, on the other hand, may be urged to re-consider their favourable reception of the content of the false stories, owing to the derogatory depictions. They are more explicit in memes (3), (4), (5), (6), and (8), opposing other counterfactual prevention strategies ((3)-(6)) or having an educational intent supporting effective protection (object (8)). Memes (3) and (4) reveal that drinking alcohol does not limit infection, and the irrationality of that hypothesis is evoked by the multimodal reading of the messages. In the third sample, the Really High Guy (as the person from the homonymous template is called) is posing an illogical question to the "you" who is watching his picture. Viewers accustomed to meme sharing know that the young man is virally associated with useless and completely senseless questions, and this is expected to stimulate readers' curiosity. The same inferential processes are sought through the assemblage of resources in example (4). Tenor, again, serves the addressees' identification, for the informal two-part sentence calls out recipients ("you"). In the first part, Goofy's face mirrors the viewers' reaction to the unbelievable and shocking realisation that alcohol – whose abuse leads to negative consequences – prevents infection. Actually, the ending caption reveals that "alcohol as a form of prevention" is another example of fake news, hence the animated character's expression is alternatively connoted, in a way that reminds one of the Really High Guy. Meme (5) makes use of similar inferential strategies. In it, Violet – another character from an animated film, *Incredibles 2* (Brad Bird 2018) – drinks some liquid and then expels it out through her nose. Her astonishment makes sense if images are considered along with what is written, which makes the actual shade of meaning explicit. Sample (5), resorting to intertextual references and direct tone, as occurred in the previous texts, addresses the "social media rumours" promoting fake cures such as "drinking bleach" (Capatides 2020), which exemplify one of the greatest threats posed by spreading misinformation. Readers of disinformation may be led to very harmful and even deadly consequences, as is conveyed by the image in (5), as well as by the second part of the caption. Authors opted for simplification and generalisation of language, which are typical lexical characteristics of popularization. They are visible in "bleach", substituting "chlorine dioxide", as well as in "poisoned yourself to death". Even though chlorine dioxide is not bleach, that form of generalisation is tailored to the envisaged viewers, for both compounds are confused online and even on mainstream media reporting on that fake news. Hence, recipients are likely to have already heard about this dangerous suggestion, and such linguistic reformulation is evidence of what was discussed in the sections presenting the theoretical and methodological backgrounds of this research. Variations of language uses with which implied readers are familiar, along with the recipients' epistemic limits or shared experience and interests, are wittingly employed and turned to the inoculators' advantage.

The definition of garlic as a life-saver and the antiscientific movement are part of that experience, and both are contested by meme (6), which displays another way to indicate the nonsensical nature of the features of misinformation. The human-like character in (6) is dressed like a doctor, but one of the main words, "health", is purposely misspelled as "helth". This choice conveys the authors' illocutionary force multimodally, since the cognitive opposition informing humour is delivered by means of the interaction between words and images. Finally, (8) tries to counteract the general consequences of fake news – without disapproving one report in particular – by spreading knowledge of an effective prevention strategy, which is washing one's hands. In order to increase interest towards the meme, the students still adopt audience-tailored intertextuality. Meme (8) replicates one of the scenes from "Homer to the Max", an episode of *The Simpsons* (Matt Groening 1989–present), when Homer Simpson is sad because everyone compares him to the homonymous character from the fictitious TV series *Police Cops*, who acts stupidly. The original utterance is adapted to the illocutionary force, insofar as Homer has to choose between washing his hands or not – and his choice may lead him "to do something stupid".

To conclude the analysis of the first group of texts, meme (7) addresses the use of paracetamol as a cure for coronavirus. That active ingredient does not treat the infection but can be used against high temperature, as per NHS (2022) guidelines. The wrong consideration of paracetamol as a cure is reproduced by two Spider Men indicating each other. Although there is no direct relationship between Spider Man and the story, or between Spider Man and paracetamol, meme (7)'s authors claim that the scene that is exhibited in the examined figure would achieve two main goals. Subjects believe that the "universal nature" of the fictional character can succeed in attracting the widest number of potential receivers, whereas the multimodal link between words and images is expected to ease the evaluation of the counterfactuality of considering paracetamol as a specific cure for SARS-Cov-2. Intertextuality, replicability, and adaptation are in all the memes that were produced – even in the ones that are not commented on in this chapter. It follows that memes can be rearranged in order to serve the delivery of senders' intentionality. Indeed, the participants in this research have selected the visual frames and templates that were deemed as the most appropriate ones to forward their message to the widest group of recipients. In addition, despite the different pictures that were added to the compositions, some shared elements can be highlighted. The most evident aspects are the explicit reference to the wrong habits and beliefs as something to ridicule, before explaining the reasons illustrating the truth, as well as the visual association between people trusting fake news and the disparaged character in the multimodal pattern. This stance becomes transparent when the entire message is received. At that moment, in the creators' opinion, the potential identification between readers and the represented participants would be interrupted, since the latter are made fun of because of their beliefs. The inferential reading that, in the subjects' view, is activated by the discussed memes could be represented as follows ("+>" means "implicates"):

1 Recipients are regular Internet users.
2 1. +> Recipients know memes and fake news about COVID-19.
3 Due to 2., recipients are attracted by the multimodal compositions, and they may identify themselves with the represented participants, due to their perception of belonging to the same community of shared interests.
4 The association between linguistic and extralinguistic dimensions reveals the disparaging nature of the stance.
5 Due to 4., recipients access the illocutionary force, and their identification is interrupted.
6 5. +> Recipients may be urged to delve into the reasons behind the multimodal compositions.

Figure 8.2 Memes (9)–(11) (from left to right)

Similar inferential processes are prompted by the second group of memes. It is dedicated to the false beliefs about vaccines, and its analysis is in the following section.

Memes exposing fake news about vaccines

The three memes against misinformation about vaccines, reproduced in Figure 8.2, respectively oppose scepticism about inoculation, the association between vaccines and infertility issues, and an alleged side effect:

Memes (9) and (10) provide further proof of the shared characteristics in the original creations. In particular, they adapt two of the most diffused templates, and the former also activates an intertextual reference to the animated movie *Godzilla: King of the Monsters* (Michael Dougherty 2019). Both traits validate the participants' expertise regarding the examined communication means and the audience-specific quality of humour and multimodal compositions. The selection and adaptation of the best-known templates originate from the senders' anticipation of what serves the delivery of their intentionality, along with the achievement of the benefit of inoculation of multimedia. In accordance with the research hypothesis, the expected benefits are to debunk fake news through memes, or to attract the readers' attention before guiding them towards an article rebutting fake news.

Meme (9)'s template is titled *Three-Headed Dragon*, and it is used to foreground the best option(s) out of three alternatives. As can be inferred from Figure 8.2, three dragons are multimodally associated with three objects, three people, or as in the examined case, three actions. The combination between words and images aims to develop a left-to-right multimodal reading whereby the last pick becomes the butt of the disparaging representation and delineates what receivers do not need to follow. The Italian captions interact with the illustration, notifying addressees that "taking swabs" and "getting vaccinated" are the most appropriate solutions to prevent the infection, whereas "doing sports" in order to sweat is useless, since it is not true that "sweat eliminates the virus", reiterating the standpoint of the students who created meme (2). The second meme exemplifies the functional reinterpretation of the template *Girl Asking Santa for Unreasonable Gifts*. In (10), a little girl is talking to Santa Claus, setting a humorous scene by means of an "expected/unexpected" opposition (Attardo 2001). The child asks for a dragon as a gift, but since it is impossible to find one (the "expected" situation), Santa Claus invites her to "be realistic". The little girl, then, wishes for a vaccine, which she connotes by talking about one of its surmised side effects – infertility. The dialogue hints at a video shared on social media, which shows "an 'insider' at GlaxoSmithKline". The person reveals that a COVID-19 vaccine was manufactured despite containing "chemicals that will eventually cause 'an explosion of infertility'" (Reuters 2020). The news agency Reuters (2020) has explained why the clip spreads misinformation, and the untruthfulness of the story is unveiled multimodally by the closing exchange. Santa Claus' look reveals his puzzlement, which increases to the point that he accepts venturing into the search for a dragon. The "unexpected" twist – the man's query about the colour of the desired dragon – triggers humour.

The last meme relies on the value of the visual representation almost exclusively. The fake news being debunked is the purported side effect causing enlargement of breast size (Morgan 2021; Sinclair 2022). Multimodal composition in (11) tries to convince readers of the counterfactuality of the claim by gathering three seemingly unrelated images. The captions read, from top to bottom, and from left to right, "The anti-Covid vaccine increases breast size"; "Expectation"; "Reality". The pictures that are included do not make the sample suitable for an international diffusion; nonetheless, they are worth dissecting in order to enquire into the multimodal strategies of interpretation informing the receivers' inferencing. As for one's "Expectation", the reader can see the Italian reality TV personality Francesca Cipriani, who has undergone several cosmetic surgery procedures, including breast augmentation. When the column "Reality" is examined, a picture of a gear level and a photo of a man reversing his car can be seen. They do not seem to have any connection with what is written and, especially, with the content of the fake news. In fact, this juxtaposition plays on a colloquial epithet, according to which "*avere la retromarcia*" ("shifting into reverse") denotes an extra-small cup size. The latter, in Italian, is informally known as "*prima [taglia]*", "first size", and the innuendo stems from the fact that if only the adjective "*prima*" is uttered, one may refer to the first gear and the first size. As happened with the previous samples, meme (11) builds an audience-tailored multimodal composition, where language uses and reference to Internet sensations (Francesca Cipriani) feed the sense of community of Internet users, which is eventually turned to the authors' advantage. Attracting viewers and raising their interest first, and only then, when their interest is aroused, urging them to discover more about the underlying truth.

Conclusions

This chapter has discussed an application of inoculation theory, consisting in devising multimodal compositions of image-macro memes in order to debunk the most diffused fake news about COVID-19. The examined memes were produced by a number of undergraduate students from the University of Salento, who were elected as the most appropriate participants to explore the potential innovative – and more positive – adoptions of the interactions between words and images that constantly propagate over the Internet. The objects of investigation, adhering to the features of other actualizations of inoculation theory, resort to interactive and viral text types to present virtual interlocutors with unexpected representations of their beliefs. The aims are to counteract antiscientific manipulation, as well as to endeavour to facilitate retention in the readers' memory of the novel epistemic achievement by means of unconventional and engaging multimodal messages (Pfau et al. 2005). The meme-specific instances of humorous discourse were adopted to attract the receivers' interest, before guiding them towards the anticipated interpretation of the multimodal compositions. This interpretation mostly leans on the viewers' vanity and preference for pop-culture references or sensational stories, raising their curiosity and hopefully guiding them to acknowledge the irrational roots of misinformation.

Future development of this research should follow two main paths. First, the creation of other samples would help enquire into whether the shared traits that are highlighted by this research depend on the authors' sociocultural background or, instead, stem from their expertise in the elaboration and re-elaboration of the discussed texts. The other route is assessing the reception and effect of one's exposure to the booster shots that were analysed. The execution of tests aiding to evaluate the extent to which the subjects' expectation and knowledge about the content of fake news change, as well as to measure the tangible contribution of multimodality and creativity to favourable cognitive modifications would support and increase the available data on resistance to misleading information (Basol et al. 2020). No one reads in fake news that inoculation against COVID-19 can keep people alive. One may read in future news that inoculation against disinformation can keep people safe.

References

Allcot, H., and Gentzkow, M. (2017) "Social Media and Fake News in the 2016 Election," *Journal of Economic Perspectives* 31(2) 211–236.

Attardo, S. (2001) *Humorous Texts: A Semantic and Pragmatic Analysis*, Berlin and New York: Mouton de Gruyter.

Bakir, V., and McStay, A. (2017) "Fake News and the Economy of Emotions: Problems, Causes, Solutions," *Digital Journalism* 6(2) 154–175.

Basol, M., Roozenbeek, J., and van der Linden, S. (2020) "Good News about Bad News: Gamified Inoculation Boosts Confidence and Cognitive Immunity against Fake News," *Journal of Cognition* 3(1) 1–9.

Baysac, P.E.G. (2017) "Laughter in Class: Humorous Memes in 21st Century Learning," *Journal of Social Sciences* 6 267–281.

Bennato, D. (2017) "The Shift from Public Science Communication to Public Relations: The Vaxxed Case," *Journal of Science Communication* 16(2) 1–11.

Blank, T.J. (2013) *Folk Humour, Celebrity Culture, and Mass-Mediated Disasters in the Digital Age*, Madison: University of Wisconsin Press.

Bowman, E., and Donevan, C. (2020) "Should You Shave Your Quarantine Beard?," *NPR*. www.npr.org/sections/coronavirus-live-updates/2020/04/09/830238952/should-you-shave-your-quarantine-beard?t=1642411586122&t=1645291121229.

Brady, W.J., Wills, J.A., Jost, J.T., Tucker, J.A., and Van Bavel, J.J. (2017) "Emotion Shapes the Diffusion of Moralized Content in Social Networks," *Proceedings of the National Academy of Science of the United States of America* 114 7313–7318.

Bulatovic, M. (2019) "The Imitation Game: The Memefication of Political Discourse," *European View* 18(2) 250–253.

Camp, E. (2009) "A Language of Baboon Thought?," in R. Lurz (ed.), *Philosophy of Animal Minds*, New York: Cambridge University Press.

Capatides, C. (2020) "Coronavirus Cannot Be Cured by Drinking Bleach or Snorting Cocaine, Despite Social Media Rumors," *CBS News*. www.cbsnews.com/news/coronavirus-drinking-bleach-cocaine-false-rumors-social-media/.

Center for Disease Control and Prevention (2022) *How to Protect Yourself & Others*. www.cdc.gov/coronavirus/2019-ncov/prevent-getting-sick/prevention.html.

Cheney, D.L., and Seyfarth, R.M. (2007) *Baboon Metaphysics: The Evolution of a Social Mind*, Chicago: University of Chicago Press.

Compton, J. (2013) "Inoculation Theory," in J.P. Dillard and L. Sehn (eds.), *The SAGE Handbook of Persuasion: Developments in Theory and Practice*, Thousand Oaks, CA: SAGE Publications.

Compton, J. (2020) "Prophylactic versus Therapeutic Inoculation Treatments for Resistance to Influence," *Communication Theory* 30 330–343.

Cook, J., Lewandowsky, S., and Ecker, U.K.H. (2017) "Neutralizing Misinformation through Inoculation: Exposing Misleading Argumentation Techniques Reduces Their Influence," *PLoS ONE* 12(5) 1–21.

Davison, P. (2012) "The Language of Internet Memes," in M. Mandiberg (ed.), *The Social Media Reader*, New York: New York University Press.

Duello, G.M. (2019) "Antonio Ricci sul deepfake e l'imitazione di Matteo Renzi e Matteo Salvini: Perfetto e inquietante," *Fanpage.it*. https://tv.fanpage.it/antonio-ricci-sul-deepfake-e-limitazione-di-matteo-renzi-e-matteo-salvini-perfetto-e-inquietante/.

European Center for Disease Prevention and Control (2020) *Transmission of COVID-19*. www.ecdc.europa. eu/en/covid-19/latest-evidence/transmission.

Gelfert, A. (2018) "Fake News: A Definition," *Informal Logic* 38(1) 84–117.

Gil, P. (2020) "What is a Meme? Examples of Popular, Funny Memes," *Lifewire*. www.lifewire.com/ what-is-a-meme-2483702.

Iaia, P.L. (2019) "Memerizing Popularization. Multimodal Discourse Hybridization and Reformulation of Specialized Knowledge for Young-Adult Receivers and Web Users," in *International Conference "Specialized Discourse and Multimedia"*, University of Salento, Lecce (Italy), February 14–16, 2019.

Iaia, P.L. (2020) "Memerizing Language Learning: Educational Connotation of Image-Macro Memes," in *International Virtual Conference on Language and Literature Proceeding*, Malang: UPT Bahasa.

Kalsnes, B. (2018) "Fake News," *Oxford Research Encyclopedias, Communication* 1–21.

Kietzmann, J., Lee, L.W., McCarthy, I.P., and Kietzmann, T.C. (2020) "Deepfakes: Trick or Treat?," *Business Horizons* 63(2) 135–146.

Klein, D.O., and Wueller, J.R. (2017) "Fake News: A Legal Perspective," *Journal of Internet Law* 20(10) 5–13.

Krause, N.M., Freiling, I., Beets, B., and Brossard, D. (2020) "Fact-Checking as Risk Communication: The Multi-Layered Risk of Misinformation in Times of COVID-19," *Journal of Risk Research* 7(8) 1052–1059.

Laineste, L., and Voolaid, P. (2016) "Laughing across Borders: Intertextuality of Internet Memes," *European Journal of Humour Research* 4(4) 26–49.

Leask, J. (2015) "Should We Do Battle With Antivaccination Activists?," *Public Health Reseach and Practice* 25(2) e2521515.

Levy, N. (2017) "The Bad News about Fake News," *Social Epistemology Review and Reply Collective* 6(8) 20–36.

Maci, S. (2019) "Discourse Strategies of Fake News in the Anti-Vax Campaign," *Lingue Culture Mediazioni* 6(1) 15–43.

Maertens, R., Roozenbeek, J., Basol, M., and van der Linden, S. (2020) "Long-Term Effectiveness of Inoculation against Misinformation: Three Longitudinal Experiments," *Journal of Experimental Psychology Applied* 27(1) 1–16.

Marsh, E.J., Cantor, A.D., and Brashier, N.M. (2016) "Believing that Humans Swallow Spiders in Their Sleep: False Beliefs as Side Effects of the Processes that Support Accurate Knowledge," *Psychology of Learning and Motivation* 64 93–132.

Masek, A., Hashim, S., and Ismail, A. (2019) "Integration of the Humour Approach with Student's Engagement in Teaching and Learning Sessions," *Journal of Education for Teaching* 45 228–233.

Mills, A.J. (2012) "Virality in Social Media: The SPIN Framework," *Journal of Public Affairs* 12(2) 162–169.

Milner, R.M. (2013) "FC-156 Hacking the Social: Internet Memes, Identity Antagonism, and the Logic of Lulz," *The Fibreculture Journal* 22 62–92.

Montgomery-McGovern, J.B. (1898) "An Important Phase of Gutter Journalism: Faking," *Arena* 19(99) 240–253.

Morgan, L. (2021) "People are Reporting an Increase in Boob Size after Receiving the Covid Vaccine, Here's What's *Actually* Going On," *Glamour*. www.glamourmagazine.co.uk/article/covid-vaccine-breast-size-increase.

National Health Service (2022) *How to Look After Yourself at Home if You Have Coronavirus (COVID-19)*. www. nhs.uk/conditions/coronavirus-covid-19/self-isolation-and-treatment/how-to-treat-symptoms-at-home/.

Nyilasy, G. (2019) "Fake News: When the Dark Side of Persuasion Takes Over," *International Journal of Advertising* 38(2) 336–342.

Pfau, M., Ivanov, B., Houston, B., Haigh, M., Sims, J., Gilchrist, E., Russell, J., Wigley, S., Eckstein, J., and Richert, N. (2005) "Inoculation and Mental Processing: The Instrumental Role of Associative Networks in the Process of Resistance to Counterattitudinal Influence," *Communication Monographs* 72 414–441.

Pham, M.-H. (2015) "I Click and Post and Breathe, Waiting for Others to See What I See: On #feministselfies, Outfit Photos, and Networked Vanity," *Fashion Theory* 19 221–241.

Puente, D. (2019) "I pessimi deepfake di *Striscia la Notizia* su Renzi e Salvini: Perché sono pericolosi," *Open*. www. open.online/2019/09/25/i-pessimi-deepfake-di-striscia-la-notizia-su-renzi-e-salvini-perche-sono-pericolosi/.

Purnama, A.D. (2017) "Incorporating Memes and Instagram to Enhance Student's Participation," *Language and Language Teaching Journal* 20(1) 1–14.

Rapp, D.N. (2016) "The Consequences of Reading Inaccurate Information," *Current Directions in Psychological Science* 25 281–285.

Reuters (2020) *Fact Check: A Coronavirus Vaccine that Makes Everyone Infertile Has Not Been Approved for Use.* www.reuters.com/article/uk-factcheck-covid-vaccine-causing-infer-idUSKBN25H20G

Richards, A.S., and Banas, J.A. (2015) "Inoculating against Reactance to Persuasive Health Messages," *Health Communication* 30(5) 451–460.

Schimelpfening, N. (2021) "Why Your Beard May Be Increasing Your COVID-19 Risk," *Healthline*. www.healthline.com/health-news/why-your-beard-may-be-increasing-your-covid-19-risk

Schmid, P., and Betsch, C. (2019) "Effective Strategies for Rebutting Science Denialism in Public Discussions," *Nature Human Behaviour* 3 931–939.

Sinclair, A. (2022) "Am I Just Hallucinating? Women Reporting Unexpected Side Effect of Pfizer COVID-19 Vaccine as Breasts and Lymph Nodes Swell," *7News*. https://7news.com.au/lifestyle/am-i-just-hallucinating-women-reporting-unexpected-side-effect-of-pfizer-covid-19-vaccine-as-breasts-and-lymph-nodes-swell-c-3511092

Soghoian, C. (2007) "The Problem of Anonymous Vanity Searches," *SSRN*. https://papers.ssrn.com/sol3/papers.cfm?abstract_id=953673

Sumi, Y., and Mase, K. (2002) "Supporting the Awareness of Shared Interests and Experiences in Communities," *International Journal of Human-Computer Studies* 56(1) 127–146.

Taecharungroj, V., and Nueangjamnong, P. (2015) "Humour 2.0: Styles and Types of Humour and Virality of Memes on Facebook," *Journal of Creative Communication* 10(3) 288–302.

Vamanu, I. (2019) "Fake News and Propaganda: A Critical Discourse Research Perspective," *Open Information Science* 3 197–208.

van der Linden, S. (2015) "The Conspiracy-Effect: Exposure to Conspiracy Theories (about Global Warming) Decreases Pro-Social Behavior and Science Acceptance," *Personality and Individual Differences* 87 171–173.

van der Linden, S., Roozenbeek, J., and Compton, J. (2020) "Inoculating against Fake News about COVID-19," *Frontiers in Psychology* 11 1–7.

van Schalkwyk, F., Dudek, J., and Costas, R. (2020) "Communities of Shared Interests and Cognitive Bridges: The Case of the Anti-Vaccination Movement of Twitter," *Scientometrics* 125 1499–1516.

Veatch, T.C. (1998) "A Theory of Humor," *Humor* 11(2) 161–215.

Westerman, D., Spence, P.R., and Van Der Heide, B. (2014) "Social Media as Information Source: Recency of Updates and Credibility of Information," *Journal of Computer-Mediated Communication* 2(1) 171–183.

Audiovisual texts

Abrahams, J., Zucker, D., and Zucker, J. (1980) *Airplane!*

Bird, B. (2018) *Incredibles 2.*

Burton, T. (2007). *Sweeney Todd: The Demon Barber of Fleet Street.*

Dougherty, M. (2019) *Godzilla: King of the Monsters.*

Groening, M. (1989–present). *The Simpsons.*

9

"IT'S NEVER ABOUT #PROLIFE, IT'S ABOUT PUNISHMENT, HATE, AND RELIGIOUS REPRESSION". POLARISING DISCOURSES AND DISINFORMATION IN THE ABORTION DEBATE ON TWITTER[1]

Stefania M. Maci and Simone Abbiati

1 Introduction

1.1 Alternative narratives

Alternative narratives focused on issues with either unknown or undesirable consequences that existed before the Internet era (Sharevski et al. 2023). In the 1980s, for example, the KGB initiated an information warfare campaign called "Operation Infektion", spreading the rumour that HIV/AIDS was a misguided American biological weapon, to undermine US credibility during the Cold War (Boghardt 2009). At the same time, the tobacco industry in the United States developed a disinformation scheme to systematically distort and downplay the link between tobacco use and cancer (Reed et al. 2021). Although these campaigns were clearly aimed at misleading, the scope and dissemination of the alternative health narratives were limited to a number of outlets and fabricated publications: at the time, there were few sources and fake journals producing alternative health narratives (Sharevski et al. 2023). The Internet and social media have now become the means by which information with quality discrepancies can reach the public (Zielinski 2021), to such an extent that its amplification can have uncontrollable consequences even for known and treatable health problems. For example, the heinous (and retracted) 1998 article by Wakefield et al. attempting to link administration of the measles, mumps, and rubella vaccine to autism (Wakefield et al. 1998) caused such a backlash in public immunisation that several measles outbreaks occurred 20 years later. Disinformation about the Ebola and Zika viruses also overshadowed evidence-based health information and led to greater vaccination hesitancy for fear of negative health consequences and death (Donato 2015; Wood 2018). Such vaccination hesitancy was observed

DOI: 10.4324/9781003224495-10

on a global scale during the recent COVID-19 pandemic, leading to an unprecedented spread of COVID-19 disinformation (Pullan and Dey 2021). Misleading health information not only about vaccines and communicable diseases but also about cancer, heart disease, and other conditions has led to the spread of alternative narratives (Wang et al. 2019). As underlined by Sharevski et al. (2023), the uncontrollable consequences in these cases are not a general aversion to treatment but the search for alternative and unproven treatments for these diseases. In this context, the medical community considers as misinformation the opposition to the consensus of what the medical community defines as accurate and evidence-based information (Swire-Thompson and Lazer 2020). In response, attention has been focused on addressing health-disinformation by examining the harms that result from disinformation (Southwell et al. 2019; Loomba et al. 2021) and by prebunking and debunking disinformation (Kirchner and Reuter 2020; Lewandowsky et al. 2020; Pennycook and Rand 2021) so that people's ability to spot and resist manipulation techniques can be improved.

1.2   Alternative narratives about abortion

With regard to abortion, women who have abortions face a societal culture in which not only disapproval and stigmatisation but also disinformation about the risks and consequences of abortion are widespread (Littman et al. 2009).

Religious-led campaigns and political negotiations have helped spread disinformation about abortion to such an extent that in some Central American states, the right to abortion has been abolished even when it was necessary to save the life or health of a pregnant woman (Feigenblatt Rojas 2022). Digital technologies have played an important role in spreading and amplifying religious messages, often based on disinformation: religion reporting was a conduit for the spread of disinformation through fact-based news outlets. In addition, the press repeated religious disinformation twice as often as nonreligious disinformation (Feigenblatt Rojas 2022).

In the USA, crisis pregnancy centres discourage women from having an abortion by providing misleading or false information about abortion (Bryant et al. 2014). Well, 80% of crisis pregnancy centres websites apparently contain misleading or inaccurate information regarding the risks associated with abortion, which is alarming because many US states currently list (and sometimes fund) these organisations as places to seek information on alternatives to abortion (Bryant et al. 2014). As Sharevski et al. (2023) correctly note, 70.1% of women obtain information about abortion on the Internet. Disinformation about abortion on the Internet thus takes many forms and users generally have difficulty identifying inaccuracies in the relevant alternative representations.

1.3   The abortion debate

In the USA, in particular, the abortion debate is a contentious issue in politics and society, resulting in dramatically different abortion regulations in US states (nearly 800 bills about abortion were introduced across the United States in the period 2009–2013; cf. Roberti 2021). While the Democratic Party has generally protected access to abortion and facilitated access to contraception since 1976, the Republican Party has traditionally pushed to restrict access to abortion or ban abortion depending on the stage of pregnancy (Wilson 2020). This has led to two different ideological positions: the anti-abortion movement maintains that the foetus has a right to life; the abortion rights movement advocates for patient autonomy and choice. Most Americans agree with some of the positions of both sides in the dispute, which has been portrayed in the past as a dispute between pro-abortion and pro-life advocates (Saad 2011).

The 1973 US Supreme Court decisions *Roe v. Wade* and *Doe v. Bolton* decriminalised abortion nationwide and established a woman's constitutional right to have an abortion. This decision has been controversial ever since, with anti-abortion advocates arguing that it should be overturned. Precisely because of this, over the past several decades, many states have passed laws restricting access to abortion, which have included mandatory waiting periods, requirements for parental consent, and limitations on funding for abortion services. In 2022, *Dobbs v. Jackson Women's Health Organisation* (JWHO) overturned *Roe v. Casey*. This removed the United States Constitution's protection of abortion rights and allowed individual states to control all elements of abortion not already covered by federal law (Mangan and Breuninger 2022). In addition, this decision

> could have reverberations at the global level in two ways. First, anti-equality governments and anti-equality NGOs [non governmental organisations] working to undermine and dismantle human rights protections and support for SRHR [sexual and reproductive health and rights] might use this as an opportunity to argue that the decision represents a lack of consensus and legitimacy on SRHR during negotiations on UN resolutions. Second, this decision might undermine the U.S. government's ability to play a leadership role in global spaces on abortion.
>
> (Kaufman et al. 2022: 24)

The proliferation of abortion disinformation following the Supreme Court's decision to overturn *Roe v. Wade* banning legal abortion in the US highlights a gap in scientific attention not only to individual health- and abortion-related disinformation (Sharevski et al. 2023) but also to the long-running controversy over abortion, which has always touched on its moral, legal, medical, and religious aspects (Groome 2017; Osborne et al. 2022). The issue is most clearly polarised among supporters of self-proclaimed "pro-choice" and "pro-life" groups in English-speaking countries. The "pro-life" group argues that a foetus is a human being deserving of legal protection regardless of the mother's will, while the "pro-choice" group emphasises a woman's right to bodily autonomy (Osborne et al. 2022). Both terms are considered loaded in the mainstream media (Martin 2010), where terms like "abortion rights" or "pro-lifers" are generally preferred.

The Supreme Court's ruling in *Dobbs v. JWHO* appears to have had an effect on the debate about abortion around Europe, especially after the rise of the right-wing party. In Italy, for instance, the ongoing controversy over abortion laws and efforts by certain conservative legislators to restrict access to the procedure has been more and more debated (Carlo 2022; Roberts 2022). Although Italy does not currently have an active abortion ban proposal (Italy now allows abortions up to 90 days into a pregnancy; beyond that, it is only legal if the mother's life is in danger or if the foetus is abnormal; cf. Law 194/78), abortion regulations in Italy started to be the focus of increasingly intense criticism and debate since the fall of 2022. While certain conservative and religious groups in Italy have pushed for tougher restrictions on abortion, others have argued that access to the procedure should be widened. Earlier, conservative and Catholic politicians opposed the 2018 plan (AOGOI 2018), which would have taken Italy closer to other European nations by allowing abortions up to 14 weeks of pregnancy, claiming it would result in the "massacre of innocents". Right-wing political group Fratelli d'Italia (Brothers of Italy) members put out a plan in February 2021 that would tighten abortion regulations and mandate counselling and a waiting time for women seeking the operation. Women's rights organisations and proponents of reproductive freedom strongly opposed the idea, claiming that it would be detrimental to women's autonomy and health (Carboni 2023).

1.4 Disinformation and polarised discourses about abortion

Disinformation in the abortion debate is usually centred around these aspects:

1 False or exaggerated claims about the risks of abortion: anti-abortion groups may spread misleading information about the health risks of abortion, such as claiming that it leads to an increased risk of breast cancer or infertility (McElroy 2014; Montoya et al. 2022. See also Rowlands 2011).
2 Misleading doctored images and videos: groups or individuals may share deepfake doctored images or videos designed to manipulate public opinion on abortion (Shin and Lee 2022; cf also Lee and Shin 2022).
3 Conspiracy theories about the motivations of abortion advocates: some anti-abortion groups may spread conspiracy theories about the motivations of abortion advocates, such as claiming that they are part of a larger plot to destroy the nation (Cichocka 2020), to reduce the world's population (Ophir 2022) or that they are profiting off of the sale of foetal tissue found in COVID-19 vaccines (Petrušić and Rapić 2022).

To this, the rhetorical strategy of *vilification* must be added (Vanderford 1989), which is used to construct the enemy as both powerful and vulnerable, offering movement members urgency, empowerment, reward, and sustained engagement. As claimed by Vanderford (1989), vilification, used to discredit opponents as spurious and malicious proponents, was pervasive in the rhetoric of both the pro-life (anti-abortion) and pro-choice (pro-abortion) movements in Minnesota between 1973 and 1980. Both movements characterise their opponents as elitist conspirators whose influence is based on the abuse of powerful authorities and whose motives are tyrannical and unjust. Indeed, while formulating a specific adversarial force, vilification casts opponents in a negative light, attributing them a diabolic motivation (Vanderford 1989: 166–167). As vilification in the abortion debate has been used by both pro-choice and pro-life parties, it seems that it is used to encourage, shape, and sustain activism on both sides: enemies are simultaneously powerful and vulnerable, violate democratic principles and their purpose in uncorrect and dictatorial (Vanderford 1989).

It is clear that the polarisation between pro-abortion and anti-abortion positions is underlined by the spread of disinformation and, nowadays, on social media platforms in particular. Although social media platforms like Twitter have given millions of people the opportunity to share truthful information, they also facilitate the spread of false information, which often spreads faster than true information (Karami et al. 2021). In an age of disinformation, polarisation, and blowtorch politics, 20% of the US population believe that the government, media, and finance in the US are controlled by a group of Satan worshippers who are running a worldwide child sex trade, which damage, amongst others, the relationship between patients and their caregivers and hinder access to reproductive health care (Ibrahim 2022). This, of course, is a misleading version of the social reality and contributes to feeding the disinformation ecosystem by reinforcing biased messages with expressive patterns and polarising practices (Palau-Sampio 2022). As claimed by Wardle and Derakhshan (2018), misleading representation of reality can be realised according to the level of falseness and/or intent to cause harm: *mis*-information (false, but not created to harm); *dis*-information (deliberately created to harm); and *mal*information (based on reality, but used to inflict harm). The intention to deceive is what differentiates disinformation from genres such as satire or parody (Tandoc et al. 2018). Information disorder becomes even more problematic when connected to a highly polarised and fragmented public sphere (Palau-Sampio 2022). A scale of "issue polarisation" can even be constructed, accounting for the extremity, constraint, and salience of societal issues (Mason 2016), in this case related to abortion. Mouw and Sobel (2001: 914) make a difference between the state of polarisation and the process of polarisation. While polarisation as a state "refers to the extent to which views on a matter are opposed in reference to some theoretical maximum", polarisation as a process "refers to the increase in such opposition overtime". Furthermore,

> activists on both sides of the abortion dispute attempt to coerce consent by relying on rhetorical distortions and emotional appeals, with the modern media exacerbating matters by encouraging superficial and confrontational discourse. Thus, the debate over abortion is reduced to a struggle over inflammatory images that limits the possibilities for compromise.
>
> (Mouw and Sobel 2001: 916)

It is true that Mouw and Sobel's (2001) results indicate no increase in polarisation in abortion attitudes up to 2000; however, as pointed by Chang et al. (2023), attitudes over abortion have been triggered by the recent normative developments, which have caused increased discussions, many of which occurred on social media platforms. When mobilisation for collective action is prompted, online debates provide tangible effects on the public opinion.

1.5 Aim

Chang et al. (2023) offer the first dataset collected from Twitter (74 million tweets) on the abortion rights debate in the United States following the United States Supreme Court's decision to overturn the 1973 *Roe v. Wade* verdict. Chang et al. (2023) underline the importance that social media have for society, as they allow citizens to express their opinions, mobilise for collective action, and offer online debates that impact not only public opinion but also political participation, media coverage, and policymaking processes. Drawing on Chang et al. (2023), and being aware that attitudes and stance are nowadays expressed on such social media as Twitter, the aim of this chapter it to detect the following:

- What, if any, linguistic patterns are used in the discourse of disinformation and hate speech about abortion in Twitter and the extent to which these reveal attitude;
- Whether there exists any relationship between disinformation, hate speech, and discourse polarisation about the abortion debate.

In answering these research questions, we tried to automatically identify (a) disinformation on the basis of content correctness vs fake news and (b) stance and polarisation on the basis of discourse labelling. For this purpose, this chapter will be developed as follows: after this *Introduction*, Section 2 describes the methodological approach for Twitter scraping, language modelling, sentiment analysis, hate speech, and stance detection, while data analysis is presented in Section 4, which is followed by the discussion and conclusion (Section 5). The preliminary results show that it is extremely easy to find polarised discourse and that the more polarised discourse is, the more misrepresented the group is – which ultimately, is a form of disinformation. However, the detection of correctness is not so simple due to the fact that the instruction to the AI has been given by the research team: we have become aware that in this investigation researchers' bias cannot be avoided, which has an impact on the ideological perspective about abortion.

2. Methodology

2.1 Twitter scraping and first remarks

The tweet scraping process was possible thanks to the Twint library, a Twitter scraping tool programmed in Python that enables tweet extraction without relying on Twitter's API and thus avoiding API scraping limitations. Twint uses Twitter's search operators to allow the researcher to collect tweets from particular users or tweets about specific topics using hashtags, expressions, or other tweet metadata (such as date, user, geo-location, among others). After conducting an initial search on Twitter threads dealing with the topic of abortion or with the overturn of *Roe v. Wade*, we chose six keywords and four hashtags that seemed the most representative in relation to the abortion debate:

- "abortion";
- "anti-abortion";
- "prolife";[2]
- "prochoice";
- "abortionright";
- "RoeVWade";
- "#abortion";
- "#mybodymychoice";
- "#abortionrightsarehumanrights";
- "#abortionishealthcare".

To refine the precision of the tweet extraction process, the script was run over intervals of two days and iterated ten times over those two days for each pair of days from 1 January to 31 December 2022. In this way, we were able to extract a total corpus of 166,180 tweets (4,281,681 words), consisting of one tweet every 80 seconds for the entire year. The time span of one year seemed to be a reasonable period of time for checking both the immediate response to the announcement of the Supreme Court (which was given on Friday, 24 June 2022) and any change in abortion discourse from before to after the overturn of the decision.

After having scraped the tweets, we randomly[3] selected a sample of 8,309 tweets (i.e. 5% of the total corpus), which were then read, to perform an initial analysis in relation to issues of disinformation in the abortion debate. Our hypothesis was we would find incorrect medical information regarding the abortion procedure. We expected to find incorrect information regarding at least the following topics of which we knew the content correctness:

- Vaccines containing aborted cells: some vaccines are made using cell lines that were derived from aborted foetal tissue many decades ago, and these cell lines are still used in vaccine production today (i.e. HEK 293 cells). It is worth noticing that these cell lines are not the same as foetal tissue or organs, and the cells have been replicated in labs and used in research for decades (Graham et al. 1977; Hu et al. 2018; Corbett et al. 2020).
- Abortion never being medically necessary: in fact, ectopic pregnancies are for instance a potentially life-threatening condition (Murray et al. 2005; Panelli et al. 2015).
- Safety of abortion reversal pills (Redd et al. 2023).

The purpose would be that of finding a sample of tweets containing disinformation so as to instruct an AI to automatically detect disinformation in the whole corpus. Interestingly, we did not find a consistent number of tweet occurrences reporting medically inaccurate or misleadingly represented information (only 7 (0.08%) tweets out of 8,309 tweets contained disinformation); we, on the contrary, found a ubiquitous presence of group misrepresentation: in a form of vilification, both the pro-choice and pro-life side tends to represent the other group by assuming inaccurate and exaggerated implications. For instance, we found pro-choice individuals suggesting that being anti-abortion means being anti-women *tout-court* or pro-life individuals suggesting that being pro-abortion means not caring about the lives of any infant. This exacerbates singular views and leads to stronger polarisation. As vilification and polarisation can be seen as a form of reality misrepresentation, and hence of disinformation, we decided to focus on this connotation and investigate patterns of polarisation in group misrepresentation rather than disinformation regarding medical inaccuracies.

To do so, we decided to process our corpus using two pretrained transformer models to perform sentiment analysis, hate speech detection and automatic stance detection. Instead of training the models from scratch, we adopted the perspective of transfer learning (Pan and Yang 2010; Raffel et al. 2019) for machine learning, which is a common strategy to leverage pretrained language models in new machine learning pipelines. Transfer learning assumes that if two language models are developed to perform similar tasks, then generalised knowledge can be shared between them. This approach reduces the resources and amount of labelled data required to train new models, which was essential in our case due to the scarcity of already labelled abortion tweets. To defend the validity of our methodology and understand how LMs can be used for automatic tweet labelling, we will (a) introduce language models and the transformer architecture, (b) introduce a specific implementation of transformer called BERT, and (c) explain how BERT can be leveraged for automatic labelling.

2.2   *Language models and transformers*[4]

In simple words, a language model (LM) is a mathematical model that computes the probability a sequence of words W_1 (word 1) to W_n (word n) can be jointly present in a sentence (Manning and Schütze 1999). This computation (known as a *chain rule of probability*) is based on the probability one word x_i can be in the sentence given the presence of previous words in the sentence (Jurafsky and Martin 2000), thanks to statistical methods such as maximum likelihood estimation. These probabilities can then be used to build mathematical models of language with which to generate new sentences, predict the likelihood of a sentence given another linguistic sequence, or compute similarity between sequences of words (Bengio et al. 2003). To do so, the language model needs to follow a training process on a very large corpus of text, such as books, articles, and web pages. Once trained, the language model can generate new text that is similar in style and content to the original corpus or predict whether another portion of text is mathematically similar to the data it was trained on (Goodfellow et al. 2016). Language modelling is primarily associated with natural language processing (NLP), which has recently been revolutionised by a new LM architecture called transformer, a type of deep learning[5] model architecture that was initially introduced by Vaswani et al. (2017) to perform machine translation.[6]

The model comprises two main parts: an encoder and a decoder. The encoder takes the input text and produces a sequence of word vectors or *embeddings*[7] that capture the meaning of each word and its position in the text. The decoder then uses these embeddings to generate the output text, one word at a time. The transformer also incorporates an attention mechanism,[8] which helps the decoder to focus on the most important parts of the input text while generating the output text.

Although transformers were initially designed for machine translation, they can also be used for various labelling tasks such as hate speech detection, political stance detection, and sentiment analysis. To explain how to use this architecture for such tasks, we need to focus on a specific type of transformer.

2.3 Bidirectional encoder representations from transformers (BERT)

Within the transformers domain, one of the state-of-the-art architectures is Google's BERT (bidirectional encoder representations from transformers),[9] a model introduced in 2018 and designed to understand the contextual relationships between words in a sentence or piece of text by training it on large amounts of text data. BERT associates vectors with words and sentences through a two-step process involving two tasks: the *masked language modelling* and the *next sentence prediction*.

The *masked language modelling* randomly masks some of the input words in a sentence, and then trains the BERT model to predict what those masked words mean on the basis of the meanings of the other words in the sentence. This allows BERT to capture complex relationships between words and the context in which they appear.

With the *next sentence prediction* task, BERT predicts whether two given sentences are logically connected or not. In this way, BERT is able to retain linguistic information both about relationships between words and about relationships between sentences.

2.4 BERT as a transformer for automatic labelling

Both BERT (and in general transformers) has been useful for many other NLP tasks (Wolf et al. 2020), including labelling thanks to the *fine-tuning process*, that is, using a pretrained machine learning model and adjusting it to improve its performance on a specific task or domain by training the model on a smaller set of task-specific dataset, while keeping the majority of the original pretrained model intact. BERT can therefore associate sentences with labels based on the mathematical similarity of the vectors of input sentences with sentences from a manually labelled dataset. Once the fine-tuned model is trained on a dataset, it can be used to label new, unseen data. In our case, the pretrained BERT model was fine-tuned on three tweet datasets manually labelled for sentiment, hate speech, and stance regarding abortion. Thus, we were able to devise different models to assign different labels based on three tasks at hand.

2.5 LMs for sentiment analysis, hate speech, and stance detection

To perform automatic labelling, we used three pretrained language models (LMs) stored in the Hugging Face Repository[10] that were fine-tuned for hate speech detection, abortion stance detection, and sentiment analysis.

The first model we deployed is a fine-tuned version of one of the models first presented by Daniel Loureiro et al. (2022) as part of the TimeLMs project, which presented a set of language models specialised for diachronic Twitter data. The original model from the TimeLMs project was fine-tuned on ~124 million tweets from January 2018 to December 2021, starting from the baseline RoBERTa model (Liu et al. 2019). The model was then subjected to a further fine-tuning process on a dataset of 9,000 annotated tweets to improve the model for sentiment analysis according to the TweetEval benchmark, which enables comparative assessment and tweet classification tasks (Barbieri et al. 2020). In this way, all tweets could be assigned a three-part label, that is, positivity, negativity, and neutrality, expressed as a percentage.

After performing sentiment analysis, we used a ByT5-based model (Xue et al. 2022) fine-tuned on a dataset of 31,962 tweets that were manually annotated and categorised as either "hate speech" or "no hate speech". We used this second pretrained language model to automatically tag our data with a positive ("hate speech") or negative ("no hate speech") label. Finally, we performed automatic detection of stance and attitudes using one of the language models (LMs) presented by Camacho-Collados et al. (2022). This LM is a transformer-based implementation trained on Twitter data (Barbieri et al. 2020; Loureiro et al. 2022) and fine-tuned using a dataset presented in Mohammad et al. (2016), which consisted of 4,870 tweets manually labelled according to their stance on abortion. This third model assigned a triple label to each tweet and categorised them as "pro-abortion" "anti-abortion", or "not clearly identifiable".

Tweets resulting from this collection were then uploaded to Sketch Engine for linguistic analysis.

3 Data analysis

3.1 *Evaluating correctness: an ethical problem*

In the first step of our analysis, we tried to evaluate the correctness of the tweet information in relation to abortion. We first tried to deploy different pretrained models[11] after reviewing the reference literature for fake news and disinformation detection methods (Ahmed et al. 2021; Pérez-Rosas et al. 2017; Pérez-Rosas and Mihalcea 2015; Shu et al. 2017; Wang 2017). Regardless of the declared technical efficiency of the different models, the predictions assigned to our tweets were not satisfactory. In fact, for such an opinionated topic as abortion, several problems can interfere with the machine learning process. More specifically, when machine learning algorithms give incorrect labels, that could be due to different reasons:

1 Limited training data: since language models are statistical replication data on which they were trained, they are only as good as the data on which they were trained. If the training data are limited or have strong biases, the model may not be able to produce the desired results and end up replicating the biases of the training data (Caliskan et al. 2017; Bolukbasi et al. 2016; Hovy and Spruit 2016; Jo and Gebru 2020).
2 Lack of context: language models may not always have access to enough contextual information to accurately predict the next word or phrase in a sentence. In our case, we were performing a linguistic analysis and did not take into consideration other types of metadata (account reliability, images/videos posted with the tweets, etc.) (Kiros et al. 2014; Tamkin et al. 2021).
3 Inadequate algorithms: the algorithms used to train and run language models may not be sophisticated enough to accurately capture the complexity and variability of natural language. There are many different types of algorithms used in language modelling, ranging from simple n-gram models to more complex neural network-based models. However, not all algorithms are equally effective or appropriate for all types of language tasks.
4 Ambiguity in language: natural language is often ambiguous and can have multiple interpretations, depending on the context. Language models may struggle to accurately disambiguate language, leading to errors in output due to lexical, syntactic, or semantic ambiguity. In cases where the semantics of linguistic structures are not transparent, they may contradict fundamental laws of computability, resulting in the possibility of automatic emulation and language modelling becoming "uncomputable" (Merrill et al. 2021).

In our study, the labelling errors were mainly caused by the fact that we were dealing with semantic ambiguity around the topic of abortion, which is in itself ethically controversial. When we read the sample of our corpus, we were unsure how to evaluate the correctness of specific tweets.

We could understand and be confident in our assessment of medical inaccuracies that lead to fake news, so we initially thought to focus on those. However, during the labelling process, we found that there were few tweets that reported medical inaccuracies, and we also tended to label extreme tweets that expressed individual viewpoints as "fake". For example, the statement "Abortion is murder" (or even more extreme tweets such as "Abortion is genocide" or "Abortion is the leading cause of death in the U.S.") could be classified as "fake" from one perspective, whereas from the perspective of those who believe that life begins at conception, the interruption of a pregnancy would be considered the termination of a human life. The definition of "fake" or "incorrect" would then become a matter of debate for them. The same could happen with opposing viewpoints, where tweets such as "opposing abortion means forcing women to get pregnant after rape, and therefore defending rape" could be labelled as "fake" because the logical implications could be seen as false. However, from the perspective of pro-choice advocates, our labelling choice could be objectionable because denying abortion causes a victim of rape to bear the pregnancy, regardless of the ethical and moral implications involved. These cases are complex and controversial, leading to an equally complex labelling process. In addition, it is important to point out that LMs and machine learning systems do not have the ability, nor should they be given the responsibility to sort out such an emotionally charged issue. The solution to the complexity of the labelling process, which would create a good dataset for fine-tuning our corpus, must be found outside the language. Attempting to expand the dataset to force meaning extraction would lead us to repeat our bias, as any LM would end up finding what was taught using the fine-tuned labelled dataset. Furthermore, if we try to respect different viewpoints and avoid bias, and create a dataset that labels both extreme positions as "fake", the model will not be able to use facts to determine which position is more agreeable or accurate. Instead, the model will detect linguistic polarisation. While this may seem an interesting result, recognising the limitations of AI can help us to focus on a surprising avenue of inquiry. Linguistic polarisation, the phenomenon associated with hard-to-label tweets, is related to disinformation in that it does not help resolve the debate over abortion, but further complicates the discussion by attributing to the opposing group views that they would not agree with if asked directly. This realisation contributed to our decision to focus on disinformation and polarisation.

When researching this topic, we must bear in our minds that AI systems are statistical models trained on existing data which may inadvertently reflect the biases and opinions of their creators. If language models are a statistical representation of linguistic systems, then they present the same linguistic relativity of natural languages (*Carroll* 1956). In other words, if language models are linguistic systems, then researchers' biases shape those systems, and consequently their language models inadvertently transfer their biases to others. In our case, this means that language models cannot distinguish what might be called "fake news" or disinformation, regardless of the complexity of our AI model. While we were able to efficiently assess polarisation with language models, classifying abortion news as "fake" or "not fake", "informed" or "disinformed" was problematic from the outset for news that went beyond medical inaccuracies. Our personal position on the abortion debate could easily influence our perception of what we consider "fake" and thus the instructions we give our AI. Using language models to assess correctness necessarily reflects the bias of the texts used to train the model, and expanding the corpus will not solve the problem. The problem should be addressed outside the language.

3.2 Polarisation

As to the analysis about discourse polarisation, we consider the results obtained with the AI models to be more reliable. Firstly, using the first LM described in the previous section, we were able to assign a label to each tweet in the corpus according to its stance. Each tweet was assigned a value

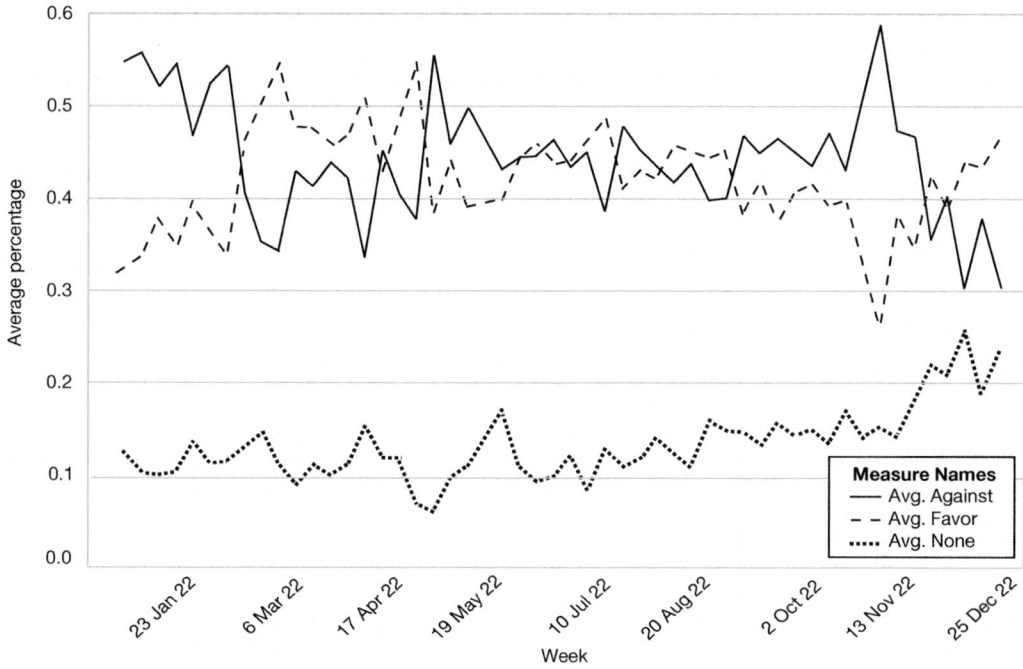

Figure 9.1 Average trend of abortion debate positions per week

for "against", "for", or "none" (the third category was used in cases where it was not possible to assign the tweet to the other two positions). This was done based on the similarity of each tweet to the
tweets in the dataset to which the pretrained model was matched. The dataset consisted of manually
labelled tweets about abortion that were classified into the three categories of interest (against, for,
none). The greater the mathematical similarity of a tweet to a manually labelled tweet in the dataset,
the higher the assigned value to indicate the relevance of the tweet to a particular category. In this
way, the category that received the highest value was used as the label for the tweet.

The results of this first labelling process (which are statistically significant, with p-value≤0.01)
are visualised in Figure 9.1. On the y-axis, we have the percentage of tweets per stance normalised per week. In other words, the chart represents the total number of tweets per day with a label
against/favour/none out of the total number of tweets per day, averaged over the number of days
of the week. On the x-axis, we have the weeks of the year. For example, during the first week of
January 2022, 55.9% of the tweets in our corpus are against abortion, 32.4% of the tweets are in
favour of abortion, and 11.7% are not recognised by the LM as relevant for an individual stance.

In our corpus, the two investigated stances ("in favour of abortion" and "against abortion",
respectively corresponding to the "pro-choice" and "pro-life" groups) are relatively balanced
throughout the year, with none of them prevailing over the other. However, as can be seen in
Figure 9.1, in three different periods of the year, that is, March–April, June and November, the
lines representing the tweets in favour of abortion and the tweets against abortion are exactly one
the opposite of the other. More precisely:

- In the March–April period, the "in favour of abortion" stance found in the collected tweets
  seems to prevail over the pro-life stance;

- Around the time of the court overturn (24 June 2022), the two positions tend to be evenly distributed: around 44% of the tweets are in favour of abortion, around 44% of the tweets are against it, and 12% of tweets adopt a neutral position, as they are neither pro or against abortion;
- During the first week of November (when the voters from California, Michigan, Vermont, Kentucky, and Montana decided on abortion-related ballot measures and came down in favour of abortion rights), the stance supporting the tweets against abortion increased and almost reached 60% of the overall tweets collected in that period.

We decided to focus on this three time-span (March–April; June; November), to investigate whether abortion discourse changed according to the predominance of one's stance over the other. We then processed our corpus with the LM for sentiment analysis presented in the previous paragraph, assigning a threefold percentage value (for positivity, neutrality, and negativity, regardless of the ideological position) and a predominant sentiment label to each tweet. This strategy allowed us to investigate both the overall sentiment trends per week and evaluate the intensity of sentiment per tweet, indicating the level of polarisation in discourse about abortion. In other words, the higher the value for a sentiment category in the threefold label, the closer its linguistic similarity to tweets labelled as positive, negative, or neutral in the training dataset, resulting in a more emotionally charged and polarised discourse. The results are shown in Figure 9.2.

Figure 9.2 shows the median value of sentiment intensity for each day of the year. The x-axis represents the days of the year. For simplicity, we have only indicated the first day of each month,

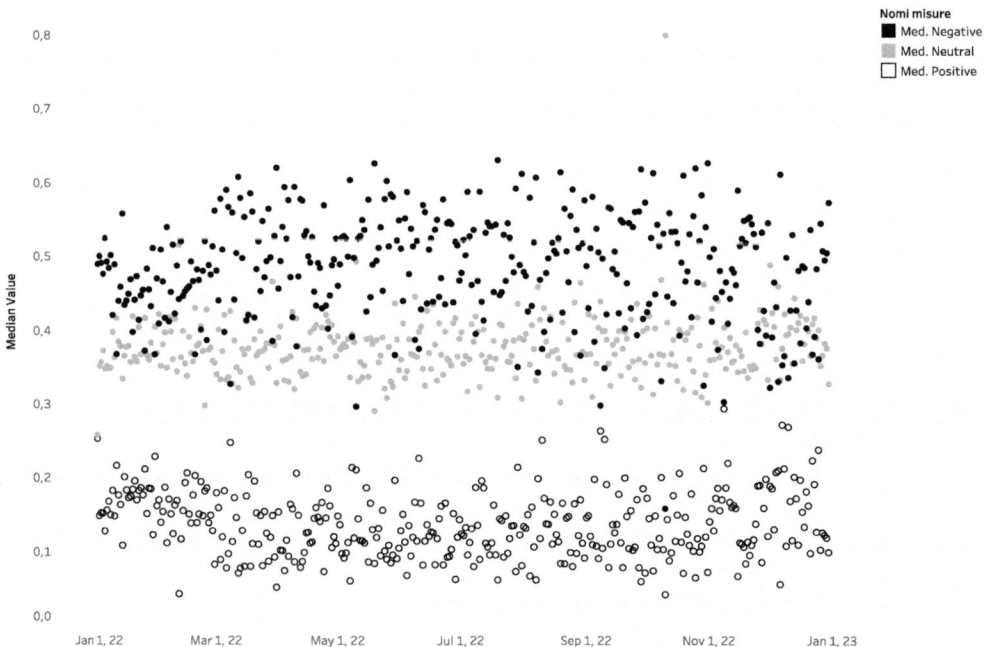

Tracciati di Med. Negative,Med. NeutraleMed. Positive per Date giorno. Il colore mostra i dettagli relativi a Med. Negative,Med. NeutraleMed. Positive.

Figure 9.2 Median sentiment per week of the year 2022

but the results are shown for all 365 days. The y-axis displays three points for each day: one in green indicating the median value for positivity, one in yellow indicating the median value for neutrality, and one in red indicating the median value for negativity. The graph shows that negativity is consistently more intense throughout the year, indicating that the discourse is most polarised in negative sentiment.

If we look at the sentiment polarisation, we must underline that positivity, negativity, and neutrality do not correspond to the ideological stance (i.e. pro-choice or pro-life) of the tweets but rather to the way in which discourse is polarised, with either a negative or positive sentiment, regardless of the ideological positioning. We can see that in the three periods under investigation:

- Neuter sentiment is constant, representing from 4% to 6% of the tweets;
- Negative sentiment reaches a peak in March–April (8.62%) and November (9.8%), while in June, negativity has the same occurrence as neuter tweets and is about 4.39%;
- Positive sentiment is particularly present in March–April (1.52%) and in November (1.8%) and is less than 1% in June.

If we overlap sentiment analysis with pro-choice/pro-life tweets, we can see that a change in the stance of the tweets is underlined by negativity, which augments in both groups.

As sentiment polarisation is consistently more intense towards negativity, we have decided to investigate the tweets from our three reference time periods (March–April, June, and November) that display a higher level of negativity, which we suppose is an indicator of hate speech.

At this point, we applied the third language model introduced in the previous section to automatically detect hate speech. By doing this, we could focus our analysis on those negatively polarised tweets (included in the three periods of interest) that our model identified as "hate speech", for a total of 19,525 tweets. We cross-checked the resulting tweets because we saw that the label "hate speech" could also be found with a positive stance, which was not supposed to be collected. The overall number of hate-speech-labelled tweets (8199) thus found in the previously indicated span of time is as follows:

- 6,255 tweets in March–April;
- 799 tweets in June;
- 1,145 tweets in November.

Tweets have been classified according to whether they express a position in favour of abortion, against it, or if they are neuter, as can be seen in Table 9.1:

Table 9.1 Breakdown of tweets in the three investigated period

	Tweets	*Tokens*	*Types*
PRO-LIFE	2,497	84,453	66,179
PRO-CHOICE	5,087	174,393	142,999
NEUTER	615	22,780	17,037
TOTAL	**8,199**	**281,626**	**226,215**

A manual analysis of the hate speech tweets has suggested the presence of an identical syntactic pattern *X is Y* realised as a simile; such pattern semantically reveals two distinct ways of processes of vilification and, consequently, polarisation. This was then checked for confirmation with the *Word Sketch* tool of Sketch Engine.

The first pattern can be defined as the *misrepresentation of arguments*. It is linked to the pro-life group and operates at a nominal level. In this case, vilification is often accomplished through a misrepresentation of abortion itself, rather than through direct mention of the opposing group: abortion is "evil", is "murder", or a "killing". This results in a form of vilification aimed at stigmatising the pro-choice movement ideology. This can be illustrated by examining some examples (our emphasis here and there):

(1) Abortion is **the greatest evil** of our time.
(2) There is an **actual murder** in this video but Twitter can't remove it because Twitter employees **think it's not murder**.
(3) Democrats want abortion up until the moment of birth. That would be **murder** by the constitution.
(4) You need to stop them before they start **the killing**.

The emerging implications result in a form of misrepresentation that serves to further demonise the opposition's belief. This type of vilification is achieved by linking or substituting the noun "abortion" with a strongly connoted noun or nominalized constituent such as "the killing". Such a misrepresentation can be accomplished through the use of copulative constituents that present different degrees of intensity (such as "to be", "would be", or indications that "abortion is thought to be something"), as can be seen in examples (5) and (6):

(5) Abortion is **child slaughter**!
(6) Abortion is a **holocaust** on a grander scale than any Nazi ever could have dreamed

However, regardless of the intensity of the linking verb used to potentially attenuate or enhance the vilification process, the subject ("abortion") always occurs a simile where the second term of comparison is strongly negatively connotated: this implies indirect vilification of the opposing group. Moreover, since the pattern we found in these tweets often correlates with a shorter tweet length, this results in a more impactful negativity for the reader, as the vilification is displayed without explanation and without being linked to any other topic. As a result, the reader becomes solely focused on the vilification.

The second pattern of disinformation can be defined as the *misrepresentation of people* and is characteristic of the pro-choice representatives. By using a simile, this pattern mainly misrepresents the adversarial group by linking them to other groups not directly involved with abortion: in this process character assassination is performed with the aim of discrediting the adversarial group and ruining their reputation by associating them with another culturally negatively connoted group, as in the following examples:

(7) Those "pro-life" traitors in the GOP who are more **pro-Russia** than they are pro-democracy.
(8) Anti-abortion politicians don't give a damn that they are backwards, **pro-death**, medically ignorant laws are harming people.
(9) They are **pro-forced birth**; that's it.
(10) Pro life? No, they are **pro gun**, **pro profit** and **anti-women** at all costs.

This narrative does not facilitate the mediation between the pro-choice and pro-live groups because it shifts the focus to another topic, thereby increasing polarisation: pro-choice people are "pro-Russia", "pro-death", "pro-forced birth", "pro gun", "pro profit", and "anti women". The use of predicativity resulting from the pattern *X is PRO-Y people* suggests that in these tweets, attention is posed on the definition of the adversarial group as what the pro-choice group is not. As can be seen in the examples previously, this linguistic pattern operates at an adjectival level and often involves hyphenated compound nouns. Such a pattern seems to stem from the use of hyphenated nouns (*PRO-Y people*) as slogans, which in a way is similar to the one found in the pro-life and anti-abortion discourse. However, while in the pro-life group the copula introduces a negatively connoted nominal group referring to an argument, in the pro-choice group, the nominal group introduced by the copula results in a hyphenated compound noun referring to a different (and negatively connoted) group of people.

We then used Word Sketch from Sketch Engine to retrieve the two patterns in the three periods of interest. The results are shown in Table 9.2. For each of the two periods we considered, the number of times the patterns of interest were found is indicated. We did this to hypothesise an interpretation of how those patterns are used by each of the two groups and to check whether there is any relationship with the change in dominant political stance that we described at the beginning of paragraph 3.2.: do these patterns of disinformation correspond to a particular political stance? How are they utilised?

Based on the findings presented in the table, it appears that "misrepresentation of people" is a prevalent rhetorical pattern used by the pro-choice movement against the pro-life movement. Conversely, the pattern of "misrepresentation of pattern" is more frequently used by the pro-life movement against the pro-choice movement.

A first noteworthy observation is that during the months of March and April, when the pro-choice movement makes substantial use of "misrepresentation of arguments", public opinion tends to shift in favour of abortion. This suggests that the pro-choice movement is able to effectively counter the "abortion is murder" rhetoric of the pro-life movement by offering an alternative misrepresentation linguistic strategy. During this time period, the pro-choice movement uses "misrepresentation of argument" to attribute an intentionality between the "killing" or death of pregnant women and the pro-life movement, in the event that anti-abortion laws were to be passed. This allows the pro-choice movement to develop a more persuasive linguistic strategy to counteract the misrepresentations made by the opposing side. There is another data point that supports this suggestion. During the month of November, when the pro-life movement surpasses the pro-choice, the latter still uses the "misrepresentation of people" pattern against the pro-life movement, but the "misrepresentation of arguments" pattern does not appear to be as effective. This suggests that the "misrepresentation of argument" pattern carries greater political weight than "misrepresentation of people" strategy, in terms of the effectiveness of rhetorical discourse.

An additional observation that can be drawn from the data at hand is that during the March–April period, there is also a high incidence of the "misrepresentation of people" pattern, used by the pro-choice movement. In the month when the pro-choice movement prevails over the pro-life movement, "misrepresentation of people" is particularly numerous, leading to a highly negative

Table 9.2 Breakdown of patterns per stance in the three investigated period

Period	Pattern 1 (misrepresentation of arguments)		Pattern 2 (misrepresentation of people)	
March–April	Pro-life:[12] 38	Pro-choice:[13] 37	Pro-life:[14] 5	Pro-choice:[15] 126
June	Pro-life:[16] 7	Pro-choice: 0	Pro-life:[17] 5	Pro-choice:[18] 21
November	Pro-life:[19] 11	Pro-choice:[20] 3	Pro-life:[21] 3	Pro-choice:[22] 41

rhetoric that associates the opposing group with a variety of other groups that are seen as limiting the rights of minorities.

4   Discussion and conclusion

The purpose of this chapter is to identify any linguistic patterns used in the discourse of misinformation and hate speech about abortion on Twitter, if any, and the degree to which these reveal attitudes. We also want to determine whether there is any connection between misinformation, hate speech, and discourse polarisation regarding the abortion debate. We therefore used an AI to automatically determine (a) disinformation based on content accuracy vs false news, and (b) attitude and polarisation based on discourse labelling in order to respond to these study questions. However, as can be seen in section 2, the detection of correctness in relation to (a) is not as straightforward due to the fact that the AI was instructed by the research team's instructions: we have realised that in this investigation, it is impossible to avoid the bias of the researchers, which affects the ideological perspective on abortion.

As vilification and polarisation can be seen as a form of reality misrepresentation, and hence of disinformation, we decided to focus on this connotation and investigate patterns of polarisation in group misrepresentation rather than disinformation regarding inaccuracies. With regard to (b), our findings suggest that it is extremely easy to find polarised discourse and that the more polarised discourse is, the more misrepresented the group is – which ultimately, is a form of disinformation. The linguistic analysis of misrepresentation has revealed that negative polarisation is realised with a simile constructed on an *X is Y* pattern by the pro-life group and an *X is PRO-Y people* pattern by the pro-choice group, which, respectively, construe either a misrepresentation of the issue or a misrepresentation of the group.

The kind of misinformation that thus arises in both cases, while not "fake news" in the sense of "incoherent events", is a misrepresentation of the opposing group. In other words, members of both groups would not agree to be described as they are by the other group using the terms found in the corpus: neither would pro-lifers agree to be described as "forced birth advocates" etc., nor would pro-choicers agree to be described (indirectly) as "murderers", "Nazis", etc.

The difference between the two ways of misrepresenting the other is that abortion supporters are indirectly vilified by their misrepresentation of abortion. Abortion supporters directly insult by their misrepresentation of abortion supporters.

Notes

1 Both authors conceived the present chapter. Stefania Maci has written the *Introduction* and the *Conclusion*, and supervised the *Data Analysis* section. Simone Abbiati developed the algorithm to instruct the various AIs employed to scrape tweets, label it, and collect the corpus. He also wrote the *Methodology* section and contributed significantly (90%) to the proper development and writing of the *Data Analysis* section.

2 Twitter does not allow any tweet scraping by using hyphenated words. For this reason, the keywords "prolife" and "prochoice" have been written as one-word.

3 We used a Python script that implemented the functions "time" and "random". The algorithm generated a random value based on the current time and then selected a tweet from our corpus whose index was equal to the randomly generated value. We calculated 5% of the entire corpus and then extracted the corresponding number of random tweets.

4 Explaining the computational aspects necessary to carry out this investigation goes beyond the scopes of this chapter. For this reason, here, we will explain the processes in a simplified way. For technical details, see Vaswani et al. (2017).

5 Deep learning is a specific type of machine learning that involves the use of multiple layers of nodes, or "neurons" (McCulloch and Pitts 1943) to learn complex patterns and relationships from data. While in machine learning we teach a computer program to perform a task by giving it examples and letting it learn from those examples, deep learning uses neural networks, which are systems of interconnected nodes that work together to process and analyse data. Each layer of neurons takes an input, analyses the data in a specific way, and then uses the result of one layer as the input to the next layer. This allows the neural network to learn increasingly complex features of the data as it goes through each layer, and the intermediate layers are called "hidden layers".

6 The Transformer is a "neural sequence transduction" model, which is a type of machine learning task that involves transforming one sequence of data into another sequence of data by leveraging on neural networks. It has an encoder-decoder structure, which means that the input sequence (e.g. a sentence) is first processed by an encoder, which converts it into a fixed-length vector representation (i.e. the word represented in number for being processed by an AI), also known as the "hidden state" or "context vector". This vector is then passed on to the decoder, which generates an output sequence (e.g. a translated sentence) based on the encoded information. For instance, in the case of translation, the Transformer takes as input the sequence W_n "I like my place because it is cosy" in the encoder and the already translated sequence W_{n-1} "adoro la mia casa perché è" (without the Italian adjective corresponding to cosy) in the decoder, to output the word that in the target language has the highest probability of being correct ("accogliente").

7 Since computers can only understand numbers, a "vectorizing" process is used to transform words/tokens into vectors. In this process, each tokenized word is assigned to a position in a high-dimensional space called an embedding space, where similar tokens have similar meanings. In simple words, these vectors (or *embeddings*) are numerical representations of words that capture their semantic and syntactic meaning. In a typical word embedding model, each word is represented by a single high-dimensional vector, where each dimension represents a particular aspect of the word's meaning. In modern NLP, the dimensionality of the vectors can range from a few hundred to several thousands. For the technical explanation, refer to Mikolov et al. (2013).

8 In simple words, the attention mechanism is a technique used in neural networks to help the model selectively focus on relevant parts of the input sequence when making predictions. It allows the model to weigh the importance of different parts of the sequence based on their relevance to the current prediction, similar to how a person might pay closer attention to certain words or phrases in a sentence to better understand the context. This helps the model achieve a more nuanced understanding of the relationships between the input and output, particularly in natural language processing tasks where context is crucial. For technical details, see Vaswani et al. (2017).

9 BERT is a type of neural network. The original BERT model released by Google in 2018 was trained on a large text corpus (various collections of books and book excerpts) as well as on the entire English Wikipedia dataset (containing a wide range of articles on various topics), called BooksCorpus, which consists of over 3 billion words. The Bidirectional Transformer architecture differs from standard Transformer architecture because it allows for information flow in both directions by using two separate layers of self-attention that process the input sequence in both directions. This enables the model to have access to both past and future context when making predictions, which can improve its accuracy (Devlin et al. 2019).

10 Hugging Face is an open-source software company, specialised in natural language processing (NLP), which offers a comprehensive suite of NLP tools and libraries to the research and development communities. Their best known offering is the Transformers library, which provides state-of-the-art pretrained models and tools for creating, training, and using NLP models.

11 We experimented the following language models (LMs) from Hugging Face's repository: "ghanashyam-vtatti/roberta-fake-news" based on RoBERTa (Liu et al. 2019) and fine-tuned on the Kaggle dataset presented by Clément Bisaillon (www.kaggle.com/clmentbisaillon), which consists of 44,920 entries labelled as "fake news" or "not fake news"; and "jy46604790/Fake-News-Bert-Detect," based on RoBERTa and fine-tuned on 44,898 news articles (https://huggingface.co/spaces/jy46604790/Fake-News-Recognition). Although the datasets used for fine-tuning covered different topics from abortion, we hypothesised that fake news could have been conveyed with similar linguistic patterns, as theorised by Pérez-Rosa et al. (2017).

12 Abortion is associated with: murder (17); eugenics (4); genocide (1), killing (11); homicide (4); slaughter (1).

13 Being pro-life is parallelled to murder of pregnant women (2); (intention to) killing pregnant women (34); killing trans people (1).

14 Pro-life mocks the "misrepresentation of people" pattern to define themselves as: anti-moral decadence (1); anti-gender re-definition (1); anti-white violence (1).

15 Pro-lifers are associated with: anti-trans (9), anti-lesbian (2); anti-choice (4), anti-gay (10), anti-civil rights, anti-brown, anti-women (4), anti-poor; anti-sex education laws; anti-interracial marriage, anti-same sex marriage; anti-birth control; anti-health care; anti-increased social program, anti-affordable healthcare, anti-childcare; anti-black; anti-family; anti-LGBT (11); pro-white; anti-critical race theory; anti-gay marriage (3); anti-gay parents; anti-immigrant; anti-anything not white; anti-gender equality; anti-everything; anti-drug reform; anti-assisted dying; anti-critical race theory (2); anti-communist; anti-child support; anti-vaccine (6); anti-women's rights; antiscience (2); anti-"woke"; anti-left; anti-queer legislation; anti-sex; anti-mask (2); anti-feminist; anti-immigrant; anti-medicare; anti-race; anti-nerodivergents; anti-vegan; anti-COVID vaccination; anti-EU; pro-underage marriage; pro-conversion therapy; pro-controlling women; pro-abuse; pro-medical neglect; pro-policing the bodies; pro-controlling women's rights; pro-guns (3); pro-white preservation (2); pro-forced birth (3); pro-pregnancy; pro-pedophiles; pro-fetus; pro-males in female only; pro-death to women; pro-punishing women for getting pregnant; pro-throw women in jail for miscarriage; pro-gender pay gap; pro-child marriage; pro-cop; pro-fascism; pro-narcan protesters; anti-environment; pro-keeping women and minorities in their place; pro-white privilege; pro-2A (3); pro-(selective)lives.
16 Abortion is paralleled to murder (3), killing (3); holocaust (1).
17 Pro-life mock the "misrepresentation of people" pattern, and define themselves anti-gay agenda (1); anti-wokeness (1); anti-leftists schools that silence their speech (1); anti-tech curving their speech (1). And they also use the same pattern towards pro-choicers, calling them anti-Christmas (1).
18 The pro-lifers are associated with: pro-revenge (1); pro-gun (3); pro-gun right (1); anti-choice (1); anti-woman (2); anti women rights (1); anti-black lives matter (1); anti-trans (2); anti-gay (2); anti-intersectional feminism (1); anti- LGBTQ+ (2); anti-contraceptive (1); pro-insurrection (1); pro-gun lobby (1); pro-death (2).
19 Abortion is paralleled to: murder (6), killing (4), eugenics (1).
20 Pro-choicers affirm that being pro-file equals: murder in the name of god (1); killing women (2).
21 Pro-lifers are associated with: anti-choice (1), pro-death (1), pro-death cult (1).
22 Pro-lifers are associated with: pro-control; pro-birth; pro-forced birth; pro-gun; pro-profit; pro-lie; pro-banning books in schools; pro-fascism; pro-racism; anti-vax; anti-COVID injections; anti-black (3); anti-student debt relief; anti-gun control; anti-climate change; anti-women issues; anti-same sex marriage (2); anti-face masks; anti-trans; anti-LGBTQ (3); anti-American; anti-science; anti-social security; anti-working people; anti-interracial laws; anti-voting rights; anti-health; anti-Jew; anti-gay, anti-Muslim; anti-union; anti-democracy (2); anti-equal rights.

References

Ahmed, Alim Al Ayub, Aljarbouh, Ayman, Donepudi, Praveen, and Cho, Myung (2021). "Detecting Fake News using Machine Learning: A Systematic Literature Review". *Psychology* 58, 1932 1939.
Associazione Italiana Ostetrici Ginecologi Ospedalieri Italiani (2018). *Aborto, per il neo senatore leghista Simone Pillon resta un reato: "La legge 194 ha bisogno di un tagliando. Più risorse per prevenire e dissuadere le donne che vogliono abortire"*. www.aogoi.it/notiziario/archivio-news/aborto-pillon/
Barbieri, Francesco, Camacho-Collados, Jose, Neves, Leonardo, and Espinosa-Anke, Luis (2020). "Tweet-Eval: Unified Benchmark and Comparative Evaluation for Tweet Classification". *Arvix*. https://doi.org/10.48550/arxiv.2010.12421
Bengio, Yoshua, Ducharme, Réjean, Vincent, Pascal, and Jauvin, Christian (2003). "A Neural Probabilistic Language Model". *Journal of Machine Learning Research* 3, 1137–1155.
Boghardt, Thomas (2009). *Operation INFEKTION: Soviet Bloc Intelligence and Its AIDS Disinformation Campaign*. www.cia.gov/library/center-for-the-study-of-intelligence/csi-publications/csi-studies/studies/vol53no4/soviet-bloc-intelligence-and-its-aids.html
Bolukbasi, Tolga, Chang, Kai-Wei, Zou, James, Saligrama, Venkatesh, and Kalai, Adam (2016). "Man is to Computer Programmer as Woman is to Homemaker? Debiasing Word Embeddings". In *Proceedings of the 30th International Conference on Neural Information Processing Systems (NIPS'16)*, Red Hook, NY, Curran Associates Inc., 4356–4364.
Bryant, Amy G., Narasimhan, Subasri, Bryant-Comstock, Katelin, and Levi, Erika E. (2014). "Crisis Pregnancy Center Websites: Information, Misinformation and Disinformation". *Contraception* 90(6), 601–605. https://doi.org/10.1016/j.contraception.2014.07.003

Caliskan, Aylin, Bryson, Joanna J., and Narayanan, Arvind (2017). "Semantics Derived Automatically from Language Corpora Contain Human-Like Biases". *Science* 356(6334), 183–186.

Camacho-Collados, Jose, Rezaee, Kiamehr, Riahi, Talayeh, Ushio, Asahi, Loureiro, Daniel, Antypas, Dimosthenis, Boisson, Joanne, Anke, Luis Espinosa, Liu, Fangyu, and Martínez Cámara, Eugenio (2022). "TweetNLP: Cutting-Edge Natural Language Processing for Social Media". *Proceedings of the The 2022 Conference on Empirical Methods in Natural Language Processing: System Demonstrations*, Abu Dhabi, Association for Computational Linguistics, 38–49.

Carboni, Kevin (2023). "La destra ha presentato quattro proposte di legge contro l'aborto". In *Wired*. www. wired.it/article/aborto-legge-menia-fratelli-italia/

Carlo, Andrea (2022). "Getting an Abortion in Italy Can be Difficult. Is it about to Get Much Tougher?" *My Europe*, Last modifies September 29, 2022. www.euronews.com/my-europe/2022/08/04/getting-an-abortion-in-italy-can-be-difficult-is-it-about-to-get-much-tougher

Carroll, John B. (ed.) (1956) Language, Thought and Reality. Selected Writings of Benjamin Lee Whorf, Cambridge, MA: MIT Press.

Chang, Rong-Ching, Rao, Ashwin, Zhong, Qiankun, Wojcieszak, Magdalena, and Lerman, Kristina (2023). "#RoeOverturned: Twitter Dataset on the Abortion Rights Controversy". *Computers and Society (cs. CY), Social and Information Networks (cs.SI) arXiv* 2302.01439 [cs.CY]. https://doi.org/10.48550/arXiv.2302.01439

Cichocka, Aleksandra (2020). "To Counter Conspiracy Theories, Boost Well-Being". *Nature* 587, 177.

Corbett, Kizzmekia S., Edwards, Darin K., Leist, Sarah R., Abiona, Olubukola M., Boyoglu-Barnum, Seyhan, Gillespie, Rebecca A., Himansu, Sunny, Schäfer, Alexandra, Ziwawo, Cynthia T., DiPiazza, Anthony T., Dinnon, Kenneth H., Elbashir, Sayda M., Shaw, Christine A., Woods, Angela, Fritch, Ethan J., Martinez, David R., Bock, Kevin W., Minai, Mahnaz, Nagata, Bianca M., Hutchinson, Geoffrey B., Wu, Kai, Henry, Carole, Bahl, Kapil, Garcia-Dominguez, Dario, Ma, LingZhi, Renzi, Isabella, KongWing-Pui, Schmidt, Stephen D., Wang, Lingshu, Zhang, Yi, Phung, Emily, Chang, Lauren A., Loomis, Rebecca J., Altaras, Nedim Emil, Narayanan, Elisabeth, Metkar, Mihir, Presnyak, Vlad, Liu, Cuiping, Louder, Mark K., Shi, Wei, Leung, Kwanyee, Yang, Eun Sung, West, Ande, Gully, Kendra L., Stevens, Laura J., Wang, Nianshuang, Wrapp, Daniel, Doria-Rose, Nicole A., Stewart-Jones, Guillaume, Bennett, Hamilton, Alvarado, Gabriela S., Nason, Martha C., Ruckwardt, Tracy J., McLellan, Jason S., Denison, Mark R., Chappell, James D., Moore, Ian N., Morabito, Kaitlyn M., Mascola, John R., Baric, Ralph S., Carfi, Andrea, and Graham, Barney S. (2020). "SARS-CoV-2 mRNA Vaccine Design Enabled By Prototype Pathogen Preparedness". *Nature* 586(7830), 567–571. http://doi.org/10.1038/s41586-020-2622-0.

Devlin, Jacob, Chang, Ming-Wei, Lee, Kenton, and Toutanova, Kristina (2019). "BERT: Pre-training of Deep Bidirectional Transformers for Language Understanding". *ArXiv* abs/1810.04805

Donato, Anthony A. (2015). "YouTube as a Source of Information on Ebola Virus Disease". *North American Journal of Medical Sciences* 7(7), 306.

Feigenblatt Rojas, Hazel (2022). *Religion Coverage as a Conduit for Disinformation and Exclusion in Latin America*. Unpublished PhD thesis. https://drum.lib.umd.edu/handle/1903/29225

Goodfellow, Ian J., Bengio, Yoshua, and Courville, Aaron (2016). *Deep Learning*, Cambridge, MA: MIT Press.

Graham, Frank L., Smiley, James R., Russell, William C., and Nairn, St R. (1977). "Characteristics of a Human Cell Line Transformed by DNA from Human Adenovirus Type 5". *Journal of General Virology* 36(1), 59–74. http://doi.org/10.1099/0022-1317-36-1-59.

Groome, Thomas (2017). "To Win Again, Democrats Must Stop Being the Abortion Party". *The New York Times*, March 27, 2017. www.nytimes.com/2017/03/27/opinion/to-win-again-democrats-must-stop-being-the-abortion-party.html

Hovy, Dirk, and Spruit, Shannon L. (2016). "The Social Impact of Natural Language Processing". In *Proceedings of the 54th Annual Meeting of the Association for Computational Linguistics (Volume 2: Short Papers)*, Berlin, Germany, Association for Computational Linguistics, 591–598.

Hu, Jianwen, Han, Jizhong, Li, Haoran, Zhang, Xian, Liu, Lan Lan, Chen, Fei, and Zeng, Bin (2018). "Human Embryonic Kidney 293 Cells: A Vehicle for Biopharmaceutical Manufacturing, Structural Biology, and Electrophysiology". *Cells Tissues Organs* 205(1), 1–8.

Ibrahim, Tod (2022). "Confronting Disinformation, Polarization, and Demagoguery. ASN Executive Vice President's Update". *ASN Kidney News Online* 14(5), 8–9.

Jo, Eun Seo and Gebru, Timnit (2020). "Lessons from Archives: Strategies for Collecting Sociocultural Data in Machine Learning". In *Proceedings of the 2020 Conference on Fairness, Accountability, and Transparency,* New York, NY: Association for Computing Machinery 306–316.

149

Jurafsky, Daniel, and Martin, James H. (2000). "Speech and Language Processing: An Introduction to Natural Language Processing". In *Computational Linguistics, and Speech Recognition*, Upper Saddle River, NJ: Prentice Hall PTR.

Karami, Amir, Lundy, Morgan, Webb, Frank, Turner-McGrievy, Gabrielle, McKeever, Brooke W., and Mc-Keever, Robert (2021). "Identifying and Analyzing Health-Related Themes in Disinformation Shared by Conservative and Liberal Russian Trolls on Twitter". *International Journal of Environmental Research and Public Health* 18(4), 2159. http://doi.org/10.3390/ijerph18042159.

Kaufman, Risa, Brown, Rebecca, Catalina, Martínez Coral, Jacob, Jihan, Onyango, Martin, and Thomasen, Katrine (2022). "Global Impacts of Dobbs v. Jackson Women's Health Organization and Abortion Regression in the United States". *Sexual and Reproductive Health Matters* 30(1), 22–31.

Kirchner, Jan, and Reuter, Christian (2020). "Countering Fake News: A Comparison of Possible Solutions Regarding User Acceptance and Effectiveness". *Proceedings of the ACM on Human-Computer Interaction* 4(CSCW2A), 1–27.

Kiros, Ryan, Salakhutdinov, Ruslan, and Zemel, Rich (2014). "Multimodal Neural Language Models". *Proceedings of the 31st International Conference on Machine Learning* 32(2), 595–603.

Law 194/78. *Norme per la tutela sociale della maternita' e sull'interruzione volontaria della gravidanza.* www.trovanorme.salute.gov.it/norme/dettaglioAtto?id=22302

Lee, Jiyoung, and Shin, Soo Yun (2022). "Something that They Never Said: Multimodal Disinformation and Source Vividness in Understanding the Power of AI-Enabled Deepfake News". *Media Psychology* 25(4), 531–546. http://doi.org/10.1080/15213269.2021.2007489

Lewandowsky, Stephan, Cook, John, Ecker, Ullrich, Albarracin, Dolores, Amazeen, Michelle, Kendou, Panayiota, Lombardi, Doug, Newman, Eryn, Pennycook, Gordon, Porter, Ethan, Rand, David G., Rapp, David N., Reifler, Jason, Roozenbeek, Jon, Schmid, Philipp, Seifert, Colleen M., Sinatra, Gale M., Swire-Thompson, Briony, van der Linden, Sander, Vraga, Emily K., Wood, Thomas J., and Zaragoza, Maria S. (2020). *The Debunking Handbook.* https://sks.to/db2020. http://doi.org/10.17910/b7.1182

Littman, Lisa L., Zarcadoolas, Christina, and Jacobs, Adam R. (2009). "Introducing Abortion Patients to a Culture of Support: A Pilot Study". *Archives of Womens' Mental Health* 12(6), 419–431. http://doi.org/10.1007/s00737-009-0095-0

Liu, Yinhan, Ott, Myle, Goyal, Naman, Du, Jingfei, Joshi, Mandar, Chen, Danqi, Levy, Omer, Lewis, Mike, Zettlemoyer, Luke, and Stoyanov, Veselin. (2019). "RoBERTa: A Robustly Optimized BERT Pretraining Approach". *ArXiv.* http://arxiv.org/abs/1907.11692

Loomba, Sahil, de Figueiredo, Alexandre, Piatek, Simon J., de Graaf, Kristen, and Larson, Heidi J. (2021). "Measuring the Impact of COVID-19 Vaccine Misinformation on Vaccination Intent in the UK and USA". *Nature Human Behaviour* 5(3), 337–348.

Loureiro, Daniel, Barbieri, Francesco, Neves, Leonardo, EspinosaAnke, Luis, and Camacho-collados, Jose (2022). "TimeLMs: Diachronic Language Models from Twitter". In *Proceedings of the 60th Annual Meeting of the Association for Computational Linguistics: System Demonstrations*, Dublin, Ireland, Association for Computational Linguistics, 251–260.

Mangan, Dan, and Breuninger, Kevin (2022). "Supreme Court Overturns Roe v. Wade, Ending 50 Years of Federal Abortion Rights". *CNBC*, June 24, 2022. www.cnbc.com/2022/06/24/roe-v-wade-overturned-by-supreme-court-ending-federal-abortion-rights.html

Manning, Chris D., and Schütze, Hinrich (1999). *Foundations of Statistical Natural Language Processing*, Cambridge, MA: MIT Press.

Martin, Paul (2010). "Hyperbole". *The Wall Street Journal* 23(1). www.wsj.com/articles/vol-23-no-1-hyperbole-01557859513?tesla=y#_=_

Mason, Lilliana (2016). "A Cross-Cutting Calm: How Social Sorting Drives Affective Polarization". *Public Opinion Quarterly* 80(S1), 351–377. https://doi.org/10.1093/poq/nfw001

McCulloch, Warren S., and Pitts, Walter. (1943). "A Logical Calculus of the Ideas Immanent in Nervous Activity". *Bulletin of Mathematical Biophysics* 5(1–2), 115–133.

McElroy, Meagan (2014). "Protecting Pregnant Pennsylvanians: Public Funding of Crisis Pregnancy Centers". *University of Pittsburgh Law Review* 76, 451.

Merrill, W.C., Goldberg, Y., Schwartz, R., and Smith, N.A. (2021). "Provable Limitations of Acquiring Meaning from Ungrounded Form: What Will Future Language Models Understand?". *Transactions of the Association for Computational Linguistics* 9, 1047–1060.

Mikolov, Tomas, Chen, Kai, Corrado, Greg, and Dean, Jeffrey (2013). "Efficient Estimation of Word Representations in Vector Space". *ArXiv arXiv:1301.3781.*

Mohammad, S., Kiritchenko, S., Sobhani, P., Zhu, X., and Cherry, C. (2016). "SemEval-2016 Task 6: Detecting Stance in Tweets". In *Proceedings of the 10th International Workshop on Semantic Evaluation (SemEval-2016)*, San Diego, CA, Association for Computational Linguistics, 31–41.

Montoya, Melissa N., Judge-Golden, Colleen, and Swartz, Jonas J. (2022). "The Problems with Crisis Pregnancy Centers: Reviewing the Literature and Identifying New Directions for Future Research". *International Journal of Women's Health* 14, 757–763. http://doi.org/10.2147/IJWH.S288861

Mouw, Ted, and Sobel, Michael E. (2001). "Culture Wars and Opinion Polarization: The Case of Abortion". *American Journal of Sociology* 106(4), 913–943.

Murray, Heather, Baakdah, Hanadi, Bardell, Trevor, and Tulandi, Togas (2005). "Diagnosis and Treatment of Ectopic Pregnancy". *Canadian Medical Association Journal* 173(8), 905–912.

Ophir, Yotam, Pruden, Meredith L., Walter, Dror, Lokmanoglu, Ayse D., Tebaldi, Catherine, and Wang, Rui (2022). "Weaponizing Reproductive Rights: A Mixed-Method Analysis of White Nationalists' Discussion of Abortions Online". *Information, Communication & Society*. http://doi.org/10.1080/1369118X.2022.207765

Osborne, Danny, Huang, Yanshu, Overall, Nickola C., Sutton, Robbie M., Petterson, Aino, Douglas, Karen M., Davies, Paul G., and Sibley, Chris G. (2022). "Abortion Attitudes: An Overview of Demographic and Ideological Differences". *Political Psychology* 43, 29–76. http://doi.org/10.1111/pops.12803

Palau-Sampio, Dolors (2022). "Pseudo-Media Disinformation Patterns: Polarised Discourse, Clickbait and Twisted Journalistic Mimicry". *Journalism Practice*. http://doi.org/10.1080/17512786.2022.2126992

Pan, Sinno J., and Yang, Qiang (2010), "A Survey on Transfer Learning". *IEEE Transactions on Knowledge and Data Engineering* 22(10), 1345–1359.

Panelli, Danielle M., Phillips, Catherine H., and Brady, Paula C. (2015). "Incidence, Diagnosis and Management of Tubal and Nontubal Ectopic Pregnancies: A Review". *Fertility Research and Practice* 1, 15. https://doi.org/10.1186/s40738-015-0008-z

Pennycook, G., and Rand, D. G. (2021). "The Psychology of Fake News". *Trends in Cognitive Sciences* 25(5), 388–402. https://doi.org/10.1016/j.tics.2021.02.007

Pérez-Rosas, Veronica, Kleinberg, Bennet, Lefevre, Alexandra, and Mihalcea, Rada. (2017). "Automatic Detection of Fake News". *Proceedings of the 27th International Conference on Computational Linguistics*, Santa Fe, New Mexico, Association for Computational Linguistics, 3391–3401

Pérez-Rosas, Veronica, and Mihalcea, Rada (2015). "Experiments in Open Domain Deception Detection". *Proceedings of the 2015 Conference on Empirical Methods in Natural Language Processing*, Lisbon, Association for Computational Linguistics, 1120–1125.

Petrušić, Bruno, and Rapić, Darko (2022). "Conspiracy Theories and Fake News within (Critical) Religious Education". *Learning and Teaching Challenges in the Context of Pandemic and Migration*, 167–178. https://ojs.kbf.unist.hr/index.php/proceedings/issue/view/35

Pullan, Samuel, and Dey, Mrinalini (2021). "Vaccine Hesitancy and Anti-Vaccination in the Time of COVID-19: A Google Trends Analysis". *Vaccine* 39(14), 1877–1881.

Raffel, Colin, Shazeer, Noam, Roberts, Adam, Lee, Katherine, Narang, Sharam, Matena, Michael, Zhou, Yanqi, Li, Wei, and Liu, Peter J. (2019). "Exploring the Limits of Transfer Learning with a Unified Text-to-Text Transformer". *arXiv arXiv:1910.10683*.

Redd, Sara K., AbiSamra, Roula, Blake, Sarah C., Komro, Kelli A., Neal, Rachel, Rice, Whitney S., and Hall, Kelli S. (2023). "Medication Abortion 'Reversal' Laws: How Unsound Science Paved the Way for Dangerous Abortion Policy". *American Journal of Public Health* 113, 202–212.

Reed, Genna, Hendlin, Yogi, Desikan, Anita, MacKinney, Taryn, Berman, Emily, and Goldman, Gretchen T. (2021). "The Disinformation Playbook: How Industry Manipulates the Science-Policy Process – And How to Restore Scientific Integrity". *Journal of Public Health Policy* 42(4), 622–634.

Roberti, Amanda M. (2021). "'Women Deserve Better:' The Use of the Pro-Woman Frame in Anti-abortion Policies in U.S. States". *Journal of Women, Politics & Policy* 42(3), 207–224. http://doi.org/10.1080/1554477X.2021.1925478

Roberts, Hanna (2022). "Italy Slowly Erodes Abortion Access, Riding US Wave". *Politico*. May 23, 2022. www.politico.eu/article/italy-abortion-access-erodes-riding-united-states-wave/

Rowlands, Sam (2011). "Misinformation on Abortion". *European Journal of Contraception and Reproductive Health Care* 16(4), 233–240. http://doi.org/10.3109/13625187.2011.570883

Saad, Lydia (2011). "Plenty of Common Ground Found in Abortion Debate". *Gallup*. https://news.gallup.com/poll/148880/Plenty-Common-Ground-Found-Abortion-Debate.aspx

Sharevski, Filipo, Loop, Jennifer Vander, Jachim, Peter, Devine, Amy, and Pieroni, Emma (2023). "Abortion Misinformation on TikTok: Rampant Content, Lax Moderation, and Vivid User Experiences". *arXiv*. https://doi.org/10.48550/arxiv.2301.05128

Shin, Soo Yun, and Lee, Jiyoung (2022). "The Effect of Deepfake Video on News Credibility and Corrective Influence of Cost-Based Knowledge about Deepfakes". *Digital Journalism* 10(3), 412–432. http://doi.org /10.1080/21670811.2022.2026797

Shu, Kai, Sliva, Amy, Wang, Suhang, Tang, Jiliang, and Liu, Huan (2017). "Fake News Detection on Social Media: A Data Mining Perspective". *SIGKDD Exploration Newsletter* 19, 22–36.

Southwell, Brian G., Niederdeppe, Jeff, Cappella, Joseph N., Gaysynsky, Anna, Kelley, Dannielle E., Oh, April, Peterson, Emily B., and Chou, Wen-Ying Sylvia (2019). "Misinformation as a Misunderstood Challenge to Public Health". *American Journal of Preventive Medicine* 57(2), 282–285.

Swire-Thompson, Briony, and Lazer, David (2020). "Public Health and Online Misinformation: Challenges and Recommendations". *Annual Review of Public Health* 41, 433–451.

Tamkin, Aalex, Brundage, Miles, Clark, Jack, and Ganguli, Deep (2021). "Understanding the Capabilities, Limitations, and Societal Impact of Large Language Models". *ArXiv, arXiv:2102.02503*. https://doi. org/10.48550/arXiv.2102.02503

Tandoc Jr., Edson. C., Lim, Zheng W., and Ling, Richard (2018). "Defining 'Fake News'. A Typology of Scholarly Definitions". *Digital Journalism* 6(2), 137–153. http://doi.org/10.1080/21670811.2017.1360143

Vanderford, Marsha L. (1989). "Vilification and Social Movements: A Case Study of Pro-life and Pro-choice Rhetoric". *Quarterly Journal of Speech* 75(2), 166–182. http://doi.org/10.1080/00335638909383870

Vaswani, Ashish, Shazeer, Noam, Parmar, Niki, Uszkoreit, Jakob, Jones, Llion, Gomez, Aidan N., Kaiser, Łukasz, and Polosukhin, Illia (2017). "Attention is All You Need". In *Proceedings of the 31st International Conference on Neural Information Processing Systems (NIPS'17)*, Red Hook, NY, Curran Associates Inc., 6000–6010.

Wakefield, Andrew, Murch, Simon H., Anthony, Andrew, Linnell, John, Casson, David H., Malik, Mohsin, Berelowitz, Mark, Dhillon, Amar P., Thomson, Michael A., Harvey, Peter, Valentine, Alan, Davies, Susan E., and Walker-Smith, John A. (1998). "Ileal-Lymphoid-Nodular Hyperplasia, Non-Specific Colitis, and Pervasive Developmental Disorder in Children". *The Lancet* 351(9103), 637–641.

Wang, William Yang (2017). "'Liar, Liar Pants on Fire': A New Benchmark Dataset for Fake News Detection". *Proceedings of the 55th Annual Meeting of the Association for Computational Linguistics (Volume 2: Short Papers)*, Vancouver, Canada. Association for Computational Linguistics, 422–426.

Wang, Yuxi, McKee, Martin, Torbica, Aleksandra, and Stuckler, David (2019). "Systematic Literature Review on the Spread of Health-related Misinformation on Social Media". *Social Science & Medicine* 240, 112552. http://doi.org/10.1016/j.socscimed.2019.112552.

Wardle, Claire, and Derakhshan, Hossein (2018). *Information Disorder: Toward an Interdisciplinary Framework for Research and Policy Making*, Strasbourg: Council of Europe.

Wilson, Joshua C. (2020). "Striving to Rollback or Protect Roe: State Legislation and the Trump-Era Politics of Abortion". *Publius: The Journal of Federalism* 50(3), 370–397. http://doi.org/10.1093/publius/pjaa015

Wolf, Thomas, Debut, Lisandre, Sanh, Victor, Chaumond, Julien, Delangue, Clement, Moi, Anthony, Cistac, Pierric, Rault, Tim, Louf, Remi, Funtowicz, Morgan, Davison, Joe, Shleifer, Sam, Von Platen, Patrick, Ma, Clara, Jernite, Yacine, Plu, Julien, Xu, Canwen, Le Scao, Teven, Gugger, Sylvain, Drame, Mariama, Lhoest, Quentin, and Rush, Alexander (2020). "Transformers: State-of-the-Art Natural Language Processing". In *Proceedings of the 2020 Conference on Empirical Methods in Natural Language Processing: System Demonstrations*, Association for Computational Linguistic, 38–45. https://aclanthology.org/2020.emnlp-demos.6/

Wood, Michael J. (2018). "Propagating and Debunking Conspiracy Theories on Twitter During the 2015–2016 Zika Virus Outbreak". *Cyberpsychology, Behavior, and Social Networking* 21(8), 485–490.

Xue, Linting, Barua, Aditya, Constant, Noah, Al-Rfou, Rami, Narang, Sharan, Kale, Mihir, Roberts, Adam, and Raffel, Colin (2022). "ByT5: Towards a Token-Free Future with Pre-trained Byte-to-Byte Models". *Transactions of the Association for Computational Linguistics* 10, 291–306.

Zielinski, Chris (2021). "Infodemics and Infodemiology: A Short History, a Long Future". *Revista Panamericana Salud Pública* 45, e40.

10

INVESTIGATING THE LANGUAGE OF FAKE NEWS ACROSS CULTURES

Nele Põldvere, Elizaveta Kibisova, and Silje Susanne Alvestad

Introduction

In this chapter, we present and discuss the methodological challenges and opportunities of the linguistic investigation of fake news across languages and cultures – specifically, English in the USA, and Norwegian and Russian in Norway and Russia, respectively. By doing so, we draw heavily on our work on the Fakespeak project, an interdisciplinary project on the language of fake news involving linguists and computer scientists. We start by defining fake news as understood in Fakespeak. Then, we provide the state-of-the-art of the fake news problem in the three cultures in question as well as current work on linguistic approaches to detecting fake news. Finally, we present the methodological considerations of conducting fake news research in English, Norwegian, and Russian, based on our experience with collecting data for Fakespeak.

In Fakespeak, we define "fake news" as news items that are meant to be deceptive and in which case the author knows them to be false (see e.g. Horne and Adalı 2017: 2). This corresponds to the notion of *disinformation* in related work. For reasons that will become clear later, in our definition we also include *misinformation*, which may be inadvertent (see Grieve and Woodfield 2023 for a recent typology of fake news). Furthermore, "news" in our case also includes social media posts where important information about current events may be distributed to millions of people. Fakespeak was developed against the background of, i.a., Jamieson's (2018) conclusion that Russian involvement most likely tilted the 2016 US presidential election in favour of Donald Trump. The primary aim of the project is to investigate the language and style of fake news (i.e. "fakespeak") in English, Norwegian, and Russian. A secondary goal is to help news editors, journalists, fact-checkers and other stakeholders detect fake news in a more accurate, efficient, and timely way than what is currently possible through the automation of the defining linguistic features of fake news.

Some anecdotal evidence that the procedure of conducting fake news research will be different in English, Norwegian, and Russian can be found in Google Trends, a website which tracks the popularity of Google's searches across regions and languages (see https://trends.google.com). While such trends cannot be used as scientific evidence, they provide interesting first insights into the rise and spread of fake news in the USA, Norway, and Russia. Thus, a quick comparison of the trends for the fake news topic shows, firstly, that in the USA and Norway, there was a surge in interest in fake news after the 2016 US presidential election, while Russia was relatively unaffected

DOI: 10.4324/9781003224495-11

(but not uninvolved) in this regard and, secondly, that the election still marks the peak in the USA, while both Norway and Russia peaked during the first year (2020) of the COVID-19 pandemic. Unsurprisingly, interest in fake news saw an increase in Russia immediately after the start of the war in Ukraine in February 2022, although, as we will show later, this does not necessarily mean that the topic provides a particularly fruitful ground for fake news research in Russian. Therefore, the trends in the public's engagement with discourses around fake news across the three cultures are reflected in some of the methodological challenges and opportunities that we have encountered in Fakespeak so far.

The fake news problem across languages and cultures

In the English part of Fakespeak, we focus on the USA. This is largely because of the sheer size of their news media and the contentious relationship of the American public with its news distributors. Seen by many as the "the leader of the free world", the USA's leadership in world affairs has increasingly come into question due to internal fighting over key issues (e.g. gun control, mask mandates, abortion), increased hyperpartisanship at national and state levels, and low levels of public trust in the news media, as shown by various surveys. According to a recent survey by the Reuters Institute (Newman et al. 2021), only 29% of Americans trust most news most of the time, which places the USA at the bottom of a list of over 40 countries.

It is well-known that much of the fake news problem in the USA today can be traced back to Donald Trump's ascendancy to the American presidency. While fake news existed well before 2016, Trump is often credited with taking it to the mainstream (e.g. Allcott and Gentzkow 2017). During Trump's time in office, fake news became a political tool used to publicly attack and discredit certain news outlets. This stirred up "heated discussions on social media platforms regarding media credibility and bias" (Li and Su 2020: 2), which in turn have become fertile breeding grounds for deep state conspiracy theories such as Pizzagate (a theory about a child sex ring within the Democratic Party) and the 2020 US presidential election fraud. Facebook and other platforms have taken steps to combat such fake news peddlers, for example, by shutting down fake accounts and teaming up with third-party fact-checking services (e.g. PolitiFact). However, the speed with which fake news spreads online, and people's resistance to change their minds when proven wrong (Mosleh et al. 2021), continues to be a problem. Thus, the period between the two elections and beyond provides a fruitful ground for fake news research in English.

As for Norway and Norwegians, in the Reuters survey mentioned previously, Norway ranks as number six: 57% of the respondents trust most news most of the time. This suggests that for Norwegians, there is relatively little fake news around to be investigated. Considering that fake news is one means of trying to influence an election result (cf. the 2016 US presidential election mentioned previously), in one study researchers investigated the activities on selected digital platforms (open Facebook groups, Twitter, and traditional and alternative media) in connection with the 2019 Norwegian regional elections (Grøtan et al. 2019). The authors concluded that there were no clear signs of any attempts by foreign actors to influence the election outcome. It is perhaps for these reasons that, currently, there is only one fact-checking service in Norway – Faktisk.no (www.faktisk.no), established in 2017. It presents itself as ideal and independent, and it is owned by the biggest news organisations in the country. Faktisk fact-checks claims put forth in traditional media as well as marginal forums by politicians and other prominent figures in the public domain.

As far as Russia and Russians are concerned, our focus is on media outlets based in Russia, although as of 2023 the current situation is such that references to Russian-speaking fact-checking services in neighbouring countries are inevitable. As illustrated by the Google Trends results in the previous section, the peak numbers of searches on the topic of fake news in Russia in recent years have been due to the COVID-19 pandemic and the invasion of Ukraine. The periods with the highest levels of engagement follow the implementation of a set of federal laws against fake news. In 2020, a new law made the dissemination of unreliable information administratively and criminally punishable. The law was promoted as a means of fighting the uncontrollable spread of fake news around COVID-19 and related topics in traditional and social media. However, the law is reportedly being used to impose additional restrictions on media and activism under the pretext of the pandemic (Repucci and Slipowitz 2020). In 2022, against the backdrop of the Russian invasion of Ukraine, another set of laws was signed, which made publications about the actions of the Russian Armed Forces criminally punishable. The implementation of this law has further affected the freedom of expression in Russia, as many Russian media outlets have been forced to stop covering the invasion, suspend operations, or stop working altogether. Additionally, the law triggered the mass exodus of foreign media from the country as well as the moving abroad of several Russian news offices. In view of these circumstances and the general state of independent journalism in Russia, the study of fake news in Russia is a complex, yet rewarding, endeavour.

Linguistic approaches to detecting fake news

The imminent threat of fake news to modern democracies requires a multifaceted approach, addressing all aspects of the content, spread, and characteristic features of this type of news. Here, we focus on what in natural language processing is called the style-based approach or fake news detection based on linguistic features. The goal of the style-based approach is to identify the most important linguistic differences between fake and genuine news as a basis for the development of automatic fake news detection systems. Due to the large amount of data needed for this task, so far the focus has been on linguistic features that can be identified with relative ease and/or using existing tools (e.g. parts-of-speech and semantic information, syntactic dependency relations, sentiment orientation; see Feng et al. 2012; Potthast et al. 2018; Rashkin et al. 2017, among others). These studies have found systematic differences in the language and style of fake news compared to genuine news, with the former being characterised by more negative and intense emotions, as exemplified by intensifiers and negative sentiment words as well as the more frequent use of verbs and adjectives.

Grieve and Woodfield (2023) have taken it a step further and proposed a theoretical linguistic framework for the analysis of fake news. Their study draws on Register Analysis (Biber 1988), which posits that there are systematic structural differences between contexts of language use due to the different communicative goals of the speakers/writers. Thus, if the communicative function of genuine news is to inform, the function of fake news must be to deceive. A common distinction in Register Analysis is between informational and involved styles of communication. The former tends to contain more nouns and noun modifiers and is common in registers with dense styles of communication such as news reportage; involved styles of communication, however, are characterised by a more frequent use of verbs, pronouns, and adjectives and are common in spontaneous conversation with lower information density. Indeed, Grieve and Woodfield's (2023) study reflected those tendencies. Based on an analysis of 49 grammatical features in English, the authors found that, while the genuine news items shared features with informational styles of communication, the fake news items were more similar to involved styles of communication, through the use of, for example, emphatics, present tense verbs, and predicative adjectives.

The availability of quality data is highly important for linguistic analyses of fake news. Following Asr and Taboada (2019), we define quality data as large collections of fake and genuine news individually labelled for veracity by experts, such as academics trained in the area or journalists working for fact-checking services. This contrasts with many datasets in natural language processing where the fake news items have been identified based on the reputation of the source (e.g. Rashkin et al. 2017). The problem with this approach is that there is no one-to-one correspondence between truth content and source reputation: even well-known fake news outlets get it right every so often. By drawing on the veracity labels of the individual news items instead, we can ensure a more reliable classification of fake and genuine news for automatic detection. Moreover, Asr and Taboada (2019: 5) argue for the need to harvest full texts of the news items to build robust models, because "text classification relies mainly on the linguistic characteristics of longer text" rather than short statements or claims, as is often the case in fake news datasets.

Grieve and Woodfield (2023) identify two further problems, namely, (i) the lack of metadata about the news items and (ii) fuzzy boundaries between the notions of misinformation and disinformation. Firstly, access to metadata such as register, news outlet, and authorship is important for us to be able to control for confounding variables. Individual differences between authors, in particular, are a major source of variation in Register Analysis, and therefore care should be taken to compare like with like. Secondly, a similar problem arises when misinformation or false information (including inadvertent mistakes) is conflated with disinformation or intentionally deceptive information (see Stahl 2006 for the particular terms), because the difference in the communicative intent of the authors further confounds the linguistic results. To address these problems, Grieve and Woodfield (2023) based their analysis on the writings of one author only, Jayson Blair, who was known for having produced both fake and genuine news for *The New York Times* in the early 2000s. A detailed investigation by *The New York Times* and Blair's own admissions of guilt made it clear at the time that Blair's fake news was the result of intentional deception driven primarily by personal gains. This provided Grieve and Woodfield (2023) with a highly controlled corpus, 56,982 words in total, which was particularly well suited for the analysis of deceptive language in the news media. The articles were collected from LexisNexis, a large archive of newspapers and periodicals.

It follows that linguistic detection of fake news is no easy feat; for robust and reliable analyses, the dataset needs to meet several criteria, some of which are quite contradictory. For example, while collecting news items from one author only (e.g. Jayson Blair) ensures a highly controlled dataset, it would be difficult to find a comparable case where the fake and genuine news samples are large enough to draw meaningful comparisons, let alone be used for the development of automatic systems (but see next section for a Norwegian equivalent). Corpora such as Jayson Blair's also raise questions about the generalisability of the linguistic results to new data, even within the same genre, because "there are many different ways in which journalists can lie" (Grieve and Woodfield 2023). Our solution in the Fakespeak project is to build and make available a variety of different datasets. Users can choose which dataset works best for their purposes, or they can use the datasets in tandem to reach a more comprehensive understanding of the defining linguistic features of fake news. The two major data types are the *single-authored dataset* (fake and genuine news collected from the same author) and the *general dataset* (news produced by a mix of authors), with a third, *hybrid* type for datasets where several authors have produced both fake and genuine news (also referred to as the *multiauthored dataset*). However, although the datasets were built based on similar criteria, the specific methodological considerations were quite different across the three languages of Fakespeak.

Methodological considerations in English, Norwegian, and Russian

In this section, we present the methodological considerations of investigating the language of fake news in English, Norwegian, and Russian, with a focus on the US context for English. In each case, we report on (i) the most important datasets that are currently available for linguistic analyses of fake news and (ii) the methodological challenges and opportunities of developing new datasets within Fakespeak, including a variety of single-authored, multiauthored, and general datasets.

English

Of the three languages included in this chapter, English poses the least challenges in terms of the availability of fake news datasets; in fact, listing them all would go beyond the scope of this chapter (but see Asr and Taboada 2019 for an overview). Therefore, we focus our discussion on one dataset only, namely, MisInfoText (Asr and Taboada 2019). We chose MisInfoText because (i) it meets the criteria for quality data for linguistic analysis in the previous section: it contains large collections of full texts of both fake and genuine news individually labelled for veracity by experts, and because (ii) it forms the basis for the development of English datasets, multiauthored and general, in Fakespeak. MisInfoText relies on well-known fact-checking websites for its data, such as Buzzfeed, Snopes, PolitiFact, and Emergent, whereby the fake and genuine news stories have been extracted in their original form from the websites (see also Allcott and Gentzkow 2017 for Buzzfeed, Snopes, and PolitiFact, and Ferreira and Vlachos 2016 for Emergent). This ensures a diversity of the news topics. Moreover, MisInfoText relies on the veracity labels assigned by journalists, which go beyond the two-way distinction between fake and genuine news and include finer-grained labels such as "mostly true" and "mostly false".

To extract data from the websites, both manual and automatic procedures were required in MisInfoText. This was because not all the external links in the websites' articles were the supporting sources of the claims. Instead, most of them provided contextual information for the fact-checking of the claim and therefore had to be manually removed (Asr and Taboada 2019: 8–9). The result was a combination of "gold" datasets such as Buzzfeed (1,380 articles) and Snopes (145 articles) and unverified but larger datasets such as PolitiFact and Emergent (so-called "silver" datasets). Moreover, MisInfoText provides access to metadata information about the content of the external links (e.g. the name of the author), which was extracted automatically. The cited features make MisInfoText an excellent dataset on which to build new fake news datasets within Fakespeak. Not only does it allow us to draw on prior data collection procedures to build a general dataset covering more recent events (e.g. the 2020 US presidential election, Black Lives Matter, COVID-19), but it also gives us access to authors who may have produced both fake and genuine news for the multiauthored dataset, to complement the Jayson Blair corpus. At the same time, the new datasets can address some of the limitations of MisInfoText.

The development of the multiauthored dataset in Fakespeak was based primarily on the metadata information about authors in MisInfoText. We used the unverified versions of the datasets to access a larger number of authors. A small number of news items were extracted from Fakespeak's own general dataset. Following the Jayson Blair corpus, we limited our searches to one genre only, in this case, online news websites, which we expected to contain more instances of fake news than traditional newspapers such as *The New York Times*. In addition, the fake and genuine news articles by the same author had to have been published in the same news outlet, as with Jayson Blair. There was no lower limit on the number of articles. An author qualified if they had produced at least one fake news article and one genuine news article, labelled either "false"/"mostly false" or "true"/"mostly true" by the fact-checkers, thus excluding indeterminate labels such as "mixed". The searches gave us seven authors, with two to fourteen articles per author and 13,391 words for the whole dataset (8,185 words for fake news and 5,206 words for genuine news). The data are from 2011–2022 and include such US-based news outlets as *Mediaite* and *Washington Press* as well as well-known fake news websites such as *The Gateway Pundit*.

The main challenges of collecting data for the multiauthored dataset were (i) finding a considerable number of authors who met the criteria in the previous paragraph and (ii) the lack of access to information about the authors' communicative intent to distinguish misinformation from disinformation. Firstly, despite searching among a large pool of authors, the resulting dataset is still quite small both in terms of the number of authors and the number of articles per author. While it may be the case that some of the authors in our data have engaged in long-term deception of the public and thus have produced a sizable oeuvre of both fake and genuine news articles over time, this was not captured by the fact-checking websites. One reason for this may be that such authors tend to write for well-known fake news websites (e.g. *The Gateway Pundit*), and so their tendency to produce inaccurate or misleading content means that their genuine news articles, which would provide a comparable sample, are seldom picked up by the fact-checkers. We will have to address these gaps in future expansions of our dataset, for example, by carrying out our own fact-checks of the articles.

The data collection procedure for the multiauthored dataset was further complicated by the fact that much of the metadata about the authors in MisInfoText is incomplete. This is due to the automatic extraction of the metadata from the external websites whereby what has been picked up from the websites is not always the author's full name but a part of their name (e.g. Edward), their title (e.g. policy analyst), their workplace (e.g. *Las Vegas Review*) or the date of publication (e.g. posted March). These had to be manually corrected by us.

The second main challenge of collecting data for the multiauthored dataset was the lack of access to information about the authors' communicative intent to distinguish misinformation from disinformation. This is different from Jayson Blair, whose intent to deceive was established by *The New York Times*' investigation as well as Blair's own admissions of guilt (see e.g. Blair 2004 for his autobiography). There have been similar cases of breaches of journalistic standards and the spread of fake news which have come under public scrutiny in recent decades, for example, from Boris Johnson's time as a journalist; however, none of them come close to Blair in terms of volume and therefore would not have provided a better alternative.

This said, a close inspection of our data gives us reason to believe that most of the fake news articles in the multiauthored dataset are instances of disinformation rather than misinformation. For one, they have been published in news websites which are partisan in nature (e.g. the right-wing *Gateway Pundit*), and therefore they are in line with the ideological motivation underlying the production of fake news. Specifically, such "fake news providers produce fake news to promote particular ideas or people that they favor, often by discrediting others" (Tandoc et al. 2018: 138; cf. Allcott and Gentzkow 2017). According to Sousa-Silva (2022), a useful way to discredit the opposing party is to attribute to them negative actions, even if untrue. This is illustrated in our data by the following claim by *The Gateway Pundit*, "(Joe) Biden imports oil from Iran", which, according to PolitiFact, was a misrepresentation of the actual events (the oil was seized, not bought) and was labelled "mostly false". It should also be noted that none of the fake news articles in our data contain a correction, which is often added when an author has made an inadvertent mistake. Therefore, we believe that the dataset that we have built is by and large a dataset of disinformation, although some verification of the circumstances around the fake news articles is required in each case.

The procedure for collecting data for the general dataset was based on that of MisInfoText but with a few modifications to address some of the limitations of the earlier dataset. Among the many fact-checking websites available for English, we chose PolitiFact for our data (see www. politifact.com). PolitiFact has a relatively simple structure, making it suitable for automatic extraction, and there seems to be some balance in terms of partisanship. This is indicated by the fact that allegations of political bias have come both from left-leaning and right-leaning media outlets.

Unfortunately, there is no way for us to determine whether the claims fact-checked by Politi-Fact are intentionally deceptive or not, although their effect on public discourse can be damaging either way. Owing to its size, the compilation of the general dataset in Fakespeak is still ongoing. Thus, the discussion is based on the challenges of extracting a pilot sample from PolitiFact, which comprises 907 news stories, 185,171 words in total. There is a great deal of overlap between our challenges and those of Asr and Taboada (2019) in relation to MisInfoText. Here, we focus on two challenges which have not previously been reported on, namely, (i) the fact that many of the supporting sources of the claims in PolitiFact correspond not to textual material but to visual material, which poses a challenge for linguistic analyses of fake news in the strict sense, and (ii) the extraction of accurate data, including metadata, from the external sources.

Firstly, the presence of visual material in the supporting sources of the claims in PolitiFact is a challenge for the Fakespeak project, which focuses primarily on fake news that has been written down. After all, the fake news detection systems developed within the project will be based on text only, although multimodal feature extraction has shown promising results (see e.g. Nakamura et al. 2020 and references therein). However, this poses a problem for Fakespeak because a large number of fake news stories today, including those fact-checked by PolitiFact, are produced and propagated via visual means. Fake news distributed in this way can take the form of images and videos (including deepfakes where the media has been manipulated), i.e. some combination of (moving) images or videos combined with text, or any other visual material that conveys false information. A quick search for the ten most recent claims by PolitiFact (as of 5 July 2022) revealed that three of them were based on a video (e.g. "This is the 911 call placed by the migrants trapped in the truck found in San Antonio, Texas"). While the video may be accompanied by text, this text may not necessarily correspond to the claim, thus introducing noise to the data.

Yet other claims in PolitiFact are taken from speeches and interviews that have been written down but that come with no assurances that the transcripts are detailed enough for linguistic analyses. To address the previous challenges, we used PolitiFact's metadata information about each news story to filter out those stories that contained certain words, such as "ad", "press conference", "radio", "TV", "debate", etc. Naturally, such an approach was not completely reliable, sometimes missing out on relevant textual material and sometimes letting visual material seep in, but it considerably reduced the amount of manual work.

The second main challenge of collecting data for the general dataset concerns the extraction of accurate data from the external sources. By data, we mean the news story itself and its title, as well as the name of the author and the date of publication, as is also provided in MisInfoText. In addition, our dataset contains information about genre and news outlet (e.g. news and blog – *The Gateway Pundit*; social media – Facebook) to allow for genre-specific investigations in future. As previously mentioned, some of the metadata information in MisInfoText is often incomplete or at times inaccurate. This is due to the fact that the external links contain diverse structures, which pose a challenge for automatic extraction. In the hope that this information may have been stored in a systematic way by PolitiFact, or any other fact-checking service for that matter, we reached out to them to ask about the possibility of gaining access to such archives. While we never received a response from PolitiFact, the negative responses from many of the other services indicated to us that, unfortunately, data storage does not seem to be part and parcel of the procedure of fact-checking today.

Therefore, we carried out manual extraction of the data from the external sources. Manual work of this kind requires a lot of effort and is very time-consuming, but it had several advantages. Not only did it give us control over the accuracy of the (meta)data, but it also allowed us to extract data that would otherwise have gone unnoticed. For example, an increasingly common way to distribute false information on Facebook is to embed one's post in an image, presumably to attract attention by other users and/or to evade detection by automatic systems, such as the one set up by Facebook in collaboration with PolitiFact. It gets even more complicated when the post in the image is accompanied by an additional comment by the same user, which, however, does not correspond to PolitiFact's claim. Automatic extraction would likely have failed in such cases, so our manual approach provided a useful alternative.

In sum, then, the outlook for conducting fake news research in English is promising. There are several datasets that can be used, although not all of them are suitable for linguistic analyses of fake news, which require large collections of individually labelled fake and genuine news stories with the appropriate metadata. The datasets developed within Fakespeak offer several alternatives. Users can combine the Jayson Blair corpus with the multiauthored dataset to improve the generalisability of the former, and both datasets can further be combined with the general dataset for a more comprehensive analysis of the language of fake news in English.

Norwegian

For Norwegian, there are currently no available datasets for the linguistic analysis of fake news, so we have had to build such datasets ourselves. Thus, we are currently building three datasets – two single-authored and one general dataset – based on available articles that have not yet been gathered in a systematic way. Even though this is work in progress, the situation seems promising.

Compiling datasets in the Norwegian context, we have encountered the following overall challenges: (i) since Norwegian is a small language, the number and types of potential datasets to analyse linguistically are limited, and (ii) the datasets are relatively small. For the larger of the two single-authored datasets in Fakespeak, a challenge is also that the fake news sample involves plagiarism and various (other) kinds of dishonest reporting, in addition to fabrication. The latter point is related to the general challenge mentioned for English previously, and it also holds for the general dataset in Norwegian – namely, the fuzzy boundaries between the notions of misinformation and disinformation. Also, the intent of the authors in the general dataset is unclear. Here, we present the Norwegian datasets in view of these challenges.

The first Norwegian dataset is the smaller of the two single-authored datasets in Fakespeak, the *Folkeopplysningen* ("The enlightenment of the people") dataset. In 2019, Norway held regional elections, and in connection with the school elections, the team behind the TV series *Folkeopplysningen* wanted to see whether they could influence the election results at a particular upper secondary school. As part of this controversial experiment, the team exposed the pupils at the school to fake news articles that were published on the Facebook accounts of two fake digital newspapers, 12 days prior to the election. The fake news articles were entirely fabricated and written by journalists. A first challenge for us was that several of the articles in the *Folkeopplysningen* material were written by a journalist for whom a reference sample of genuine news articles would not have been possible to find, since they had been working for radio and television. Secondly, some articles were co-authored. We discarded these two groups of fake articles, which left us with 2,755 words of entirely fabricated news articles. As for the reference set, the journalist in question had written for several newspapers. We decided to select texts the journalist had written for one of Norway's largest newspapers, as they shared most characteristics with the fabricated texts in terms of length (one A4-page, approximately), topic (regional and national politics and events), and style (popular, as opposed to, for example, a style with a lot of vocabulary from economy and business). The result is a single-authored dataset in which the fake news articles are entirely fabricated and from a fictitious news source, whereas the corresponding sample of genuine news comprises authentic articles from one newspaper. The dataset comprises approximately 6,000 words in total.

The second and the larger single-authored dataset in Fakespeak is from one of Norway's leading newspapers. Some years ago, a tip from a reader set off an internal investigation into the works of a particular journalist, and it was discovered that around 40 of the 160 articles (mainly feature articles on culture) authored by this journalist for the newspaper between 2007 and 2015 involved some kind of ingenuousness, such as plagiarism or fabrication. At first, this seemed like the Norwegian version of the Jayson Blair case, equalling even in size. However, while the Jayson Blair case was much spoken about in the US public domain and the data were easily accessible, in the Norwegian case little was said from the side of the newspaper management about the scandal, even though the disingenuous articles were listed with details about what exactly in them was fraudulent. Also, it has been difficult for us to get access to the material. The newspaper operates with a paywall, and the relevant issues could not be accessed from the University of Oslo Library, for example. After a lot of time and effort, the newspaper itself granted access to their archive for one project team member for a limited period of time. Thus, we are currently working on building a Norwegian single-authored dataset of the size of the Jayson Blair corpus.

As briefly mentioned previously, however, the fake news sample in this case consists of articles that are not (necessarily) disingenuous in their entirety, only partially. In some articles, some sources are invented but their claims are true, while in others the opposite may be the case. In yet other articles, parts have been plagiarised from other newspapers or magazines. This may have consequences for how the computer scientists in the Fakespeak project will work with the material, as one and the same model should perhaps not be trained both on articles that are fake in their entirety and articles that are only partially fake.

The third Norwegian dataset in Fakespeak is a general one obtained from the fact-checking service Faktisk, mentioned previously. This dataset so far consists of approximately 200 articles containing claims that have been fact-checked. The sources of the claims vary from social media platforms such as Facebook and Twitter to news websites such as *VG*, *Aftenposten*, *Dagbladet* and *Nettavisen*, some of the most widely read newspapers in Norway, via personal blogs and broadcasting sites such as NRK (Norwegian Broadcasting Corporation) and NTB (Norwegian News Agency). Most of the claims are from Facebook with the NRK close behind. The length of the articles also varies, from claims consisting of just one sentence to proper news articles with around four to eight paragraphs of text. The articles cover the time period from 2014 until 2021, with the most articles being from 2017 to 2020. The topics include health, politicians, political parties, celebrities, culture, the European Union, and past events such as 9/11. The main challenge of compiling the general dataset has been the amount of manual work that is required. Faktisk did not have an archive of original full-text fact-checked articles or posts to share with us, so we have had to trace the original articles manually based on the 423 URLs we originally received. The procedure has been complicated by several factors: (i) the link to the original article may be missing; (ii) the claim may have been edited out of the article after the article was fact-checked, so that the link in the data points to the now edited article without the claim; (iii) the link may point to a deleted article; and (iv) the article may be behind a paywall.

Summing up, we are working to build three Norwegian datasets: one smaller single-authored dataset in which the fake news articles are fabricated in their entirety, one larger single-authored dataset in which the fake news articles are partially disingenuous, and one general dataset in which fake news takes the shape of claims or whole articles from various sources, debunked by Norway's only fact-checking service. The three datasets are distinct in other ways, too. For example, in the general Faktisk dataset, a claim may be false while the rest of the article is true, while in the larger single-authored dataset, a claim may be correct while the rest, or parts of it, is false. Thus, if computer scientists train one and the same model on both datasets, the results may be untrustworthy. For this reason, two distinct models may be needed to be trained on each dataset. Similarly, a linguistic analysis of the *Folkeopplysningen* dataset alone, which may be the "purest" of the Norwegian datasets, may render interesting results, but the dataset is too small to be used on its own. Thus, for more robust analyses, it is important to combine several datasets.

Russian

The compilation of Russian datasets for the Fakespeak project is in its early stages. As far as we know, there are no available Russian datasets similar to the Jayson Blair corpus that could be used as a single-authored dataset, or as collections of several authors for a multiauthored dataset. The only general dataset that is available was created 2017–2019 (Zaynutdinova et al. 2019). This dataset can be used for preliminary observations, but it has some limitations, such as the fact that the veracity of its entries partially relies on source reputation and that the language of fake news in Russia has probably changed over the past few years, especially during the Russia–Ukraine war. For these reasons, we are now exploring opportunities for building a general dataset of a higher quality ourselves. In addition to the challenges that have already been described in relation to English and Norwegian in the previous subsections, the war in Ukraine and the legal restrictions on the freedom of expression in Russia pose several methodological challenges that require extra time and effort to resolve: (i) the limited number of articles that provide original news statements and (ii) the surge of propagandistic texts with little credibility, both in news media and fact-checking.

Firstly, both the war and the current legislation limit the journalists' opportunities to investigate and publish original stories. On the one hand, military actions and restrictions prevent many journalists from going on-site to explore the events first-hand; a lot of information regarding the armies is classified. On the other hand, the retaliatory measures that have been imposed prevent many journalists from reporting any information about the war that differs from the official line, that is, information published or confirmed by official government sources such as the Ministry of Defence or the Kremlin (the Russian Government) press service. Thus, many journalists have no other choice but to reproduce news reports from other sources either by citing or paraphrasing the source without confirming or disproving it. The Latvia-based Russian-language news website Meduza offers disclaimers to all war reports based on official statements from Russian and Ukrainian armed forces, thus warning the reader to consider with caution any information provided by the official representatives of the parties to the conflict, arguing that in times of war it is impossible to verify the information. Most Russian media outlets do not provide any disclaimers. Since such texts are not original, they are not suitable for linguistic analyses of deception. Even if they are fake, the possible intent to deceive would belong to the author of the original claim, not the reporters.

Secondly, using fact-checking services has proven to be an effective strategy for building datasets of fake news in English and Norwegian. This approach is also applicable to the Russian data but requires additional scrutiny. Since the implementation of laws against fake news, the development of fact-checking in Russia has slowed down considerably, compared to its popularity in the past two years: in 2020 alone, at least three new fact-checking services were launched. Provereno. Media (https://provereno.media) claimed to be the first fact-checking service in Russia, followed by Fakecheck.ru and the Yandex.Zen media platform, which has introduced a fact-checking service for its publications (https://yandex.ru/support/zen/requirements/fact-checking.html). At the time of writing this chapter, however, Fakecheck.ru has ceased to release their public investigations and closed their website. Yandex.Zen has not announced any changes in their operations, but it only provides internal fact-checks of its authors and does not have any openly accessible archive. Provereno.Media continues to function as a fact-checking website, but its web domain, the servers, and part of its editorial staff were situated outside of Russia already from the outset. In 2022, its creator and manager Ilya Ber announced that he has moved to Lithuania, so we will from now on treat this resource as operating outside of Russia.

The outcome of the Kremlin policy of presenting the invasion and the army in a positive light is the emergence of unreliable journalistic investigations, tendentious fact-checking websites, and accounts of questionable credibility on social media. Such "news" items or "fact-checkers" often use propaganda techniques such as exaggeration, minimisation, oversimplification, and quite often, appeal to authority (for a list of propaganda techniques, see e.g. Da San Martino et al. 2019). Not necessarily all fake, even the fact-checking initiatives can be biased and selective in their ways of including material. The most vivid example is War on Fakes – an anonymous fact-checking website and Telegram channel. Its authors declare that they "don't do politics" but "consider it important to provide unbiased information about what is happening in Ukraine and on the territories of Donbass", because they "do not want ordinary people to feel anxious and panicked because of information wars" (War on Fakes 2022). With the first post published 24 February 2022, just a few hours after the start of the invasion, this Telegram channel currently lists more than 700,000 subscribers. Managers of other Russian-speaking fact-checking services have claimed in an interview to Delfi.lv, a Latvian news outlet, that the work of such initiatives has little in common with the fundamental principles of fact-checking, and they suspect the initiatives are affiliated with Russian state bodies (Fedkevich 2022). The surge of propaganda in Russia poses a serious methodological challenge for us: it makes it difficult to distinguish between what might be presented online as fake news as opposed to what is fake in the light of reasonable evidence, a fact which can be resolved by making use of fact-checking services outside of Russia.

The fact-checking websites outside of Russia are based in neighbouring countries such as the already mentioned Provereno.media in Lithuania, the Estonian Propastop (www.propastop.org), the Ukrainian StopFake (www.stopfake.org/ru), and the Kazakh FactCheck.kz (https://factcheck.kz). Meduza (https://meduza.io/razbor), primarily a news outlet, also has a section on investigations that potentially can be used to search for fake news. Since they are based abroad, the fact-checking websites are not under Russian legislation, although they review Russian news outlets. However, the problem of verifying war events remains unsolved. Even without Russian propagandistic influence, there is still a lack of on-site sources and possibilities for verification in the combat zones. A possible way to resolve this challenge is to shift the focus to topics and events that have already received some retrospection, such as COVID-19. Another method that we are considering is to cross-check between several fact-checking services and to monitor users' reactions to news on social media. This requires a lot of time and effort, but it allows us to build a quality dataset for the linguistic analysis of fake news in Russian.

Therefore, conducting fake news research in Russian is a demanding task. Recent events, such as the Russian invasion of Ukraine and the fake news legislation implemented in Russia over the past few years, have made it particularly challenging. However, with a carefully designed approach to fact-checking, it seems possible to build a dataset on the topic of COVID-19 or other recent events. It is especially important that we develop our own methodology of fake news detection and verification that includes multiple reference checks, instead of relying on the decisions made by particular fact-checkers only.

Conclusion

In this chapter, we have discussed the topic of investigating the language of fake news across three cultures – English in the USA, and Norwegian and Russian in Norway and Russia, respectively. All three languages and cultures suffer from a lack of quality data (collections of fake and genuine news individually labelled for veracity by experts) for linguistic analyses of fake news. Therefore, within the Fakespeak project we have built several datasets, some single- and multiauthored and some general, which we are currently preparing for release to the public. Some of the challenges associated with investigating the language of fake news are culture-specific (e.g. the lack of reliable news sources in Russia), while others are common across the cultures. One common challenge that has emerged during the compilation of the datasets in Fakespeak is that almost none of the fact-checking services of interest have been able to share with us archives of the fact-checked articles. We have thus had to trace the articles manually, a hugely time-consuming task that is also often fruitless, as shown previously. Given that researchers and fact-checkers work towards the common goal of reducing the spread of fake news, the lack of archives by the fact-checking services is striking. This said, we are optimistic about the opportunities of doing fake news research across English, Norwegian, and Russian and the future development of automatic fake news detection systems based on the defining linguistic features in each language.

Acknowledgements

We are thankful to Jack Grieve and Helena Woodfield for giving us access to the Jayson Blair corpus. We also wish to thank Kristoffer Egeberg and Jari Bakken at Faktisk for providing us with the URLs of their fact-checked articles, to Lasse Nederhoed at Teddy TV for sending us the fabricated articles for the televised *Folkeopplysningen* experiment, to the editors of the Norwegian newspaper we mention for granting us access to their archive, and to Zia Uddin, Aleena Thomas, and Håkon Bjørn Due for their work on the English and Norwegian datasets. This research was made possible thanks to the Research Council of Norway, project ID 302573.

References

Allcott, H. and Gentzkow, M. (2017) "Social media and fake news in the 2016 election," *Journal of Economic Perspectives* 31(2), pp. 211–236. http://doi.org/10.1257/jep.31.2.211.

Asr, F. T. and Taboada, M. (2019) "Big Data and quality data for fake news and misinformation detection," *Big Data & Society* 6(1). http://doi.org/10.1177/2053951719843310.

Biber, D. (1988) *Variation across Speech and Writing*, Cambridge: Cambridge University Press.

Blair, J. (2004) *Burning Down My Master's House: My Life at The New York Times*, Beverly Hills, CA: New Millennium Press.

Da San Martino, G., Yu, S., Barrón-Cedeño, A., Petrov, R. and Nakov, P. (2019) "Fine-grained analysis of propaganda in news article," in *Proceedings of EMNLP-IJCNLP 2019*, pp. 5636–5646, Hong Kong: Association for Computational Linguistics.

Fedkevich, D. (2022) "'Etu voynu myi proigryivaem.' Pochemu 'zakon o feykah' navsegda izmenil rossiyskiy faktcheking," *Delfi*, 19 April. Available at: www.delfi.lv/a/54255082 (Accessed: 7 July 2022).

Feng, S., Banerjee, R. and Choi, Y. (2012) "Syntactic stylometry for deception detection," in *Proceedings of ACL '12*, pp. 171–175, Jeju Island, Korea: Association for Computational Linguistics.

Ferreira, W. and Vlachos, A. (2016) "Emergent: A novel data-set for stance classification," in *Proceedings of the NAACL-HLT 2016*, pp. 1163–1168, San Diego, CA: Association for Computational Linguistics.

Grieve, J. and Woodfield, H. (2023) *The Language of Fake News*, Cambridge Elements in Forensic Linguistics, Cambridge: Cambridge University Press.

Grøtan, T. O., Fiskvik, J., Halland Haro, P., Auran, P. G., Mathisen, B. M., Karlsen, G. H., Magin, M. and Bae Brandtzæg, P. (2019) *På leting etter utenlandsk informasjonspåvirkning. En analyse av det norske kommunestyre- og fylkestingsvalget 2019*, Oslo: SINTEF Digital.

Horne, B. D. and Adalı, S. (2017) "This just in: Fake news packs a lot in title, uses simpler, repetitive content in text body, more similar to satire than real news," in *Proceedings of AAAI*, San Francisco: Association for the Advancement of Artificial Intelligence.

Jamieson, K. H. (2018) *Cyberwar: How Russian Hackers and Trolls Helped Elect a President*, Oxford: Oxford University Press.

Li, J. and Su, M.-H. (2020) "Real talk about fake news: Identity language and disconnected networks of the US public's 'fake news' discourse on Twitter," *Social Media + Society* 6(2). http://doi.org/10.1177/2056305120916841.

Mosleh, M., Martel, C., Eckles, D. and Rand, D. (2021) "Perverse downstream consequences of debunking: Being corrected by another user for posting false political news increases subsequent sharing of low quality, partisan, and toxic content in a Twitter field experiment," in *Proceedings of CHI '21*, pp. 1–13, Yokohama, Japan: Association for Computing Machinery.

Nakamura, K., Levy, S. and Wang, W. Y. (2020) "r/Fakeddit: A new multimodal benchmark dataset for fine-grained fake news detection," in *Proceedings of LREC 2020*, pp. 6149–6157, Marseille, France: European Language Resources Association.

Newman, N., Fletcher, R., Schulz, A., Andi, S., Robertson, C. T. and Nielsen, R. K. (2021) *Reuters Institute Digital News Report 2021*, Oxford: Reuters Institute.

Potthast, M., Kiesel, J., Reinartz, K., Bevendorff, J. and Stein, B. (2018) "A stylometric inquiry into hyperpartisan and fake news," in *Proceedings of ACL '18*, pp. 231–240, Melbourne, Australia: Association for Computational Linguistics.

Rashkin, H., Choi, E., Jang, J. Y., Volkova, S. and Choi, Y. (2017) "Truth of varying shades: Analyzing language in fake news and political fact-checking," in *Proceedings of ACL '17*, pp. 2931–2937, Copenhagen, Denmark: Association for Computational Linguistics.

Repucci, S. and Slipowitz, A. (2020) *Democracy under Lockdown: The Impact of COVID-19 on the Global Struggle for Freedom*, Washington, DC: Freedom House.

Sousa-Silva, R. (2022) "Fighting the fake: A forensic linguistic analysis to fake news detection," *International Journal for the Semiotics of Law* 35, pp. 2409–2433. http://doi.org/10.1007/s11196-022-09901-w.

Stahl, B. C. (2006) "On the difference or equality of information, misinformation, and disinformation: A critical research perspective," *Informing Science: The International Journal of an Emerging Transdiscipline* 9, pp. 83–96. http://doi.org/10.28945/473.

Tandoc Jr, E. C., Lim, Z. W. and Ling, R. (2018) "Defining 'fake news': A typology of scholarly definitions," *Digital Journalism* 6(2), pp. 137–153. http://doi.org/10.1080/21670811.2017.1360143.

War on Fakes. (2022) Available at: https://waronfakes.com (Accessed: 7 July 2022).

Zaynutdinova, A., Pisarevskaya, D., Zubov, M. and Makarov, I. (2019) "Deception Detection in Online Media," in *Proceedings of EEML 2019*, pp. 121–127, Perm, Russia: National Research University Higher School of Economics.

PART II

Case studies

A. Politics

11

DISINFORMATION AND IMMIGRATION DISCOURSES

Charlotte Taylor

1 Introduction

As seen throughout the chapters in this handbook, there is not a single agreed-upon definition of disinformation, and indeed there is debate on the processes of definition (e.g. Ó Fathaigh et al. 2021). The European Commission (2018) defines disinformation as "verifiably false or misleading information that is created, presented and disseminated for economic gain or to intentionally deceive the public, and may cause public harm". The key components which are typically shared across definitions are veracity, deception, and intention. However, when we start to look at disinformation in the context of public discourses, that core element of intention becomes a challenge because we have multiple production roles. In Goffman's terms (1981: 226), we must consider the *animator* – "the sounding box", the *author* – "the agent who scripts the lines", and the *principal* – "the party to whose position the words attest". In the case of media and political discourse, journalists, digital content creators, speech writers, etc. routinely script text representing a specific position which is not their own and which may be reproduced by an animator. So whose intentionality must we consider? The journalist or sub-editor who reproduces a known falsehood, or the editor or proprietor (*principal*) whom the journalist believes wants that narrative to be spread? Furthermore, intertextuality is core to both discourse types; the speech made by the politician becomes part of the media debate and vice versa. In this case, if a deception is intentionally produced by one participant and spread by others who lack the intent to deceive, should we stop considering it disinformation and reclassify it as misinformation? This would seem highly counterintuitive considering how information is shared on social media and that the intention of the original author would have included an expectation that it would be animated by many others. Furthermore, the nature of discourse is that it relies on replication of "common sense", which may involve the *animation* of disinformation at multiple and banal levels. Therefore, in the context of this chapter, misinformation will be used to refer to false information which is reproduced in media and political discourses in relation to migration at a point where the falsehood is widely known.

The form which disinformation takes may also vary. Wardle (2017, in Bakir and McStay 2018: 155) identifies seven types of mis- and disinformation which range along a cline from fabricated content (100% false and designed to deceive), manipulated content (genuine information is modified to deceive), imposter content (genuine sources are impersonated), false content (genuine content is shared with false contextual information), misleading content, false connection (when headlines

DOI: 10.4324/9781003224495-14

don't support the content) to satire or parody. Key points here are the recognition that content is often unlikely to be wholly false, which again presents a challenge for identification.

The reasons for disinformation have also attracted extensive attention. According to Allcott and Gentzkow (2017) these are most commonly either financial (fake news can achieve maximum newsworthiness through a disregard for truth) and/or ideological as it promotes specific versions of reality. This twofold function is acknowledged in the European Commission definition, which notes the potential for financial gain to the disinformation promoter as well as the potential for harm to others. Mourão and Robertson (2019: 16) go on to note that "fake news as misinformation is only a small part of a larger phenomenon of increasing polarization, fragmentation and identity politics" and thus it must be seen within a wider context.

The topicality of disinformation relates to both the spread and impact. There is widespread agreement that disinformation may be facilitated by social media, which may provide greater reach, spread, and visibility. Furthermore, social media offer a range of resources for the spread, as Culloty and Suiter (2021b: 224) set out, social media may facilitate disinformation tactics of appropriation of existing hashtags, decontextualising new stories, use of memes, automated bots. Regarding impact, previous work shows a correlation between misinformation consumption and populist voting (e.g. Cantarella et al. 2023 on the Italian 2018 elections), and this has particularly strong effects for the topic of this chapter: immigration discourse.

The topic of this chapter is specifically regarding *immigration* discourses, rather than *migration* discourses, because emigration is largely absent from public discourses of migration in the UK context on which I will mostly be drawing. To use the term *migration* discourses when only actually discussing *immigration* discourses risks colluding in this public narrative which holds that only immigration is salient and newsworthy, and this, in turn, feeds into the core myth of migration in the UK context (and further afield), which is that there is a stable and static host population who are essentially different from a mobile and erratic Other (discussed further later).

The problematization of immigration has become a core component in populist and (far)right rhetoric and is framed as one of the many "culture wars" on which these divisive politics depend. This also means that immigration is particularly salient in discussion of disinformation. As Culloty and Suiter (2021a: 316) note, anti-immigrant disinformation is a mainstay of far-right communication because it reinforces the core ideology of exclusion and nativist supremacy. Therefore, we have a nexus where immigration is salient to the far-right, which in turn is a major provider of disinformation. Moreover, as I will argue later, disinformation is not simply an associated problem but is absolutely necessary to maintain the consistently negative representation of mobility and that core myth of difference to which I alluded previously. These negative representations, facilitated by disinformation, as always with powerful discourses, have social and physical effects for all those affected, from the fear engendered in those identifying as "host" populations, to the discrimination and xenophobia leveled at those seen as migrant Others.

2 Disinformation and naming practices

2.1 Naming as choice

In its most basic linguistic form, we can identify disinformation in the way in which people who move are named. This is sometimes dismissed as trivial, but as Mautner (2016: 156) says, "the way labels . . . are used reflects social attitudes, perspectives and categorizations. And the labels, in turn, shape the way in which social structures and relationships are perceived". Thus, the principal reason why names matter is that they fulfil the central role of discourse in both reflecting and *shaping* perceptions of social realities. The act of naming is a choice is two senses: first, in that "there are always different ways of saying the same thing, and they are not accidental alternatives. Differences in expression carry ideological distinction (and thus differences in representation)" (Fowler 1991: 4), and second, in that the act of naming is an act of categorization which brings the category into being. Furthermore, in the case of immigration discourses, the highly persuasive trope of binary categorization (Davies 2012) is often employed in the naming choices. Frequent binary categorization of immigrants might include nationality (e.g. EU vs non-EU) or legal status (regular vs irregular), and these categories can look like common sense but Goodman and Speer (2007: 180) remind us that

> other ways of categorizing asylum seekers could be in terms of those who have fled a country in which the British army is involved and those who have not, or in terms of those who have come from ex-British colonies and those who have not

and this absence of alternative binaries lays bare the constructed nature of those categories which have become normalised.

2.2 Use of delegitimising terms

One overt way in which disinformation may occur in naming choices is through the use of delegitimating terms as in (1) spoken by the then UK prime minister.

(1) We can't have a situation where we are collectively spending £6 million a day on hotels for *illegal asylum seekers* (Sunak, April 2023, my italics).

This term *illegal asylum seekers* is an instance of disinformation as there is no such thing, and indeed as far back as 2003, the (now defunct) Press Complaints Commission in the UK sanctioned a newspaper for using the phrase and ruled that it was inaccurate, stating that "An asylum seeker is someone currently seeking refugee status or humanitarian protection; there can be no such thing in law as an illegal asylum seeker".

As Figure 11.1 shows, in the period from the 1980s into the 1990s, the constructed opposition of "real" vs "fake" refugees was a common binary in parliamentary discourse. We can see three clear spikes in frequency for both terms in that central period indicating that they were being used together, as shown in example (2).

(2) We should strengthen our internal safeguards against *bogus asylum seekers*. I stress the word "bogus", because *genuine asylum seekers* will always be welcome in the United Kingdom, as is our tradition (Evans, Conservative 1992, my italics).

As Figure 11.1 shows, the binary link between these two names loosened in the 1990s, following or coinciding with criticism of the lack of veracity, and the framing of refugees or asylum as "false" generally reduced.

In its place, as Figure 11.2 shows, came the binary of the *real asylum seeker* vs *the economic migrant* with spikes of both terms occurring from 2015 onwards.

Here we are looking at patterns of use among members of Parliament, and so we can assume that they are aware of the veracity of the terms they use and that these are not "one-offs". While the speakers in this later period rarely overtly use *illegal* or *false*, they invoke this disinformational

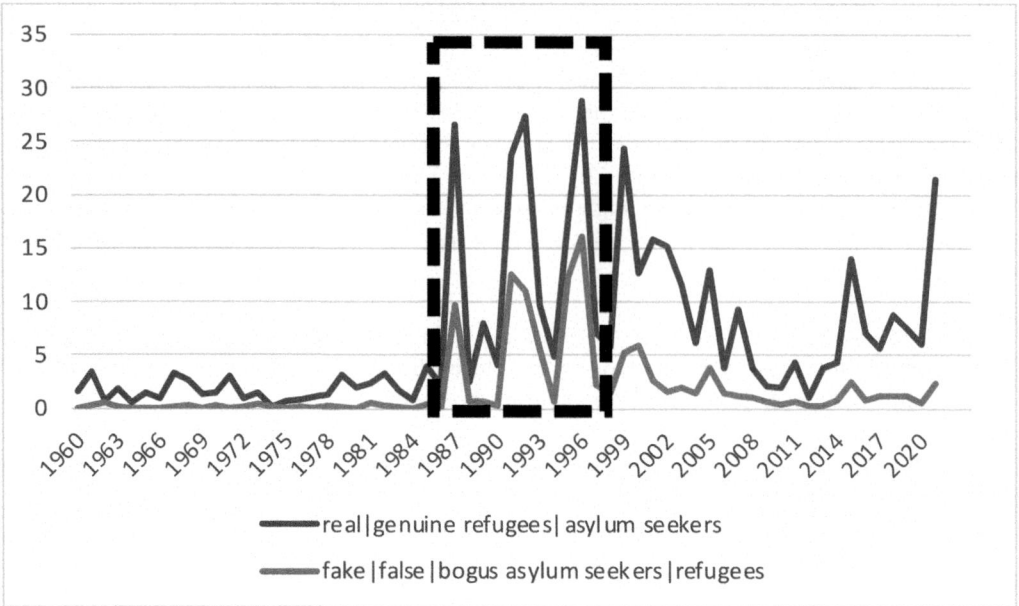

Figure 11.1   Frequency of the binary real vs fake in UK parliamentary discourse

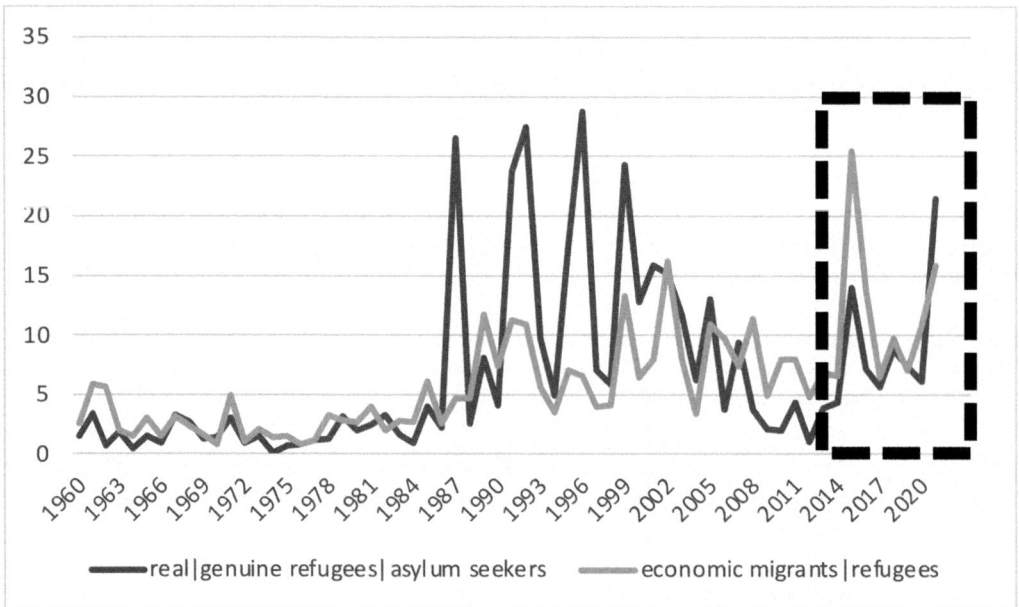

Figure 11.2   Frequency of the binary real vs economic migrant in UK parliamentary discourse

framing through the use of *real* and *genuine*, which presupposes the existence of a non-genuine counterpart. In each case, we might note that the frequency of binary opposition spikes as a long-standing Conservative government approaches a general election (1992, 1997, and 2024), and indeed there seems to be an upsurge even in the blatantly disinformational use of *illegal* and *bogus* in the most recent period, as illustrated in (1) and (3), though we do not yet have sufficient data to verify whether this is a pattern.

(3) We must strike a balance between being tough on those *bogus claimants* who are jumping the queue and gaming our system, and *genuine refugees* who really need our help (Loughton, Conservative, March 2023, my italics).

As might be expected, these terms are also used in the press, and their use aligns on newspaper type (tabloid) and political orientation (right-wing). Gabrielatos and Baker (2008) find that one-third of the newspapers in their corpus of articles from 1996 to 2005 account for three-quarters of all occurrences of these overly disinformation terms, and the newspapers most likely to use these terms were the right-wing tabloids the *Sun* (twice as frequent as the second ranking) and *Express*, followed by Labour-supporting tabloids *People, Daily Star*.

2.3   Avoidance of legitimising names

As a counterpart to the spread of disinformation through the use of factually inaccurate del-egitimising names, we might also note the avoidance of factually accurate legitimising terms. Here we move into the territory of absence, which is always difficult to pin down, but the pattern has been sufficiently strong in relation to migration discourses that previous research has shown how this avoidance occurs and indeed is deliberately implemented. In the Austral-ian context, Hodge (2015: 125) describes how an Australian immigration minister "instructed departmental and detention centre staff to refer publicly to asylum seekers as 'illegal arrivals' or 'illegal maritime arrivals'". Therefore, their legitimate legal status is misrepresented in overt disinformation. Goodman et al. (2017) analyse the UK press and show how UK media portrayals of the humanitarian crisis in Mediterranean countries were briefly affected by the publication of a shocking photo of a drowned child. In the immediate aftermath, the papers moved to prefer the naming choice *refugee*, acknowledging the suffering and rights of the people involved, before moving back to the wider encompassing label *migrant*, which ob-scures those rights. We may consider *refugee* to be the most legitimating name because it has a specific legal meaning as protected by the 1951 Refugee Convention (UN General Assembly). As Figure 11.3 shows, the term *refugees*, like relatively sympathetic terms such as *exiles* and *boat people*, has been on the decline in UK public discourse.

However, this is not indicative of a decline in applications for asylum in the UK, as shown in Figure 11.4. What Figures 11.3 and 11.4 show, in conjunction, is that the legitimating term *refu-gees* is not used where it could be used; in other words, we can see an absence.

In fact, the avoidance is even more marked than these charts appear. If we consider Table 11.1, which reports findings from the SiBol corpus of UK newspapers alongside asylum statistics (Asylum and resettlement datasets 2023), we can see that when the terms *refugees* and *asylum seekers* are used in the UK press, they are often used to discuss displaced people elsewhere in the world (e.g. *Rohingya refugees* have mostly sought asylum in Bangladesh) or elsewhere in time (e.g. the references to *Jewish refugees* are largely with reference to 1940s Europe). We can also

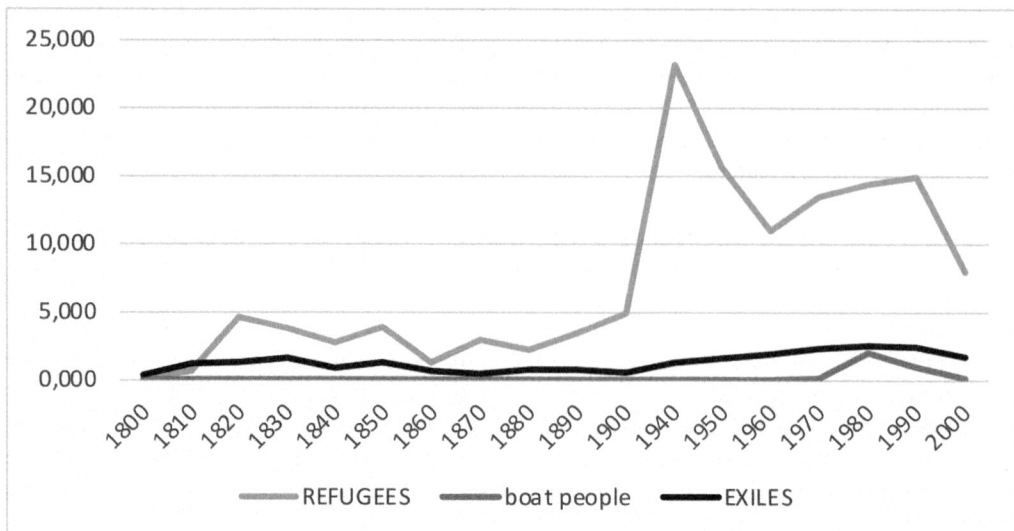

Figure 11.3 Frequency of naming choices in *The Times* newspaper

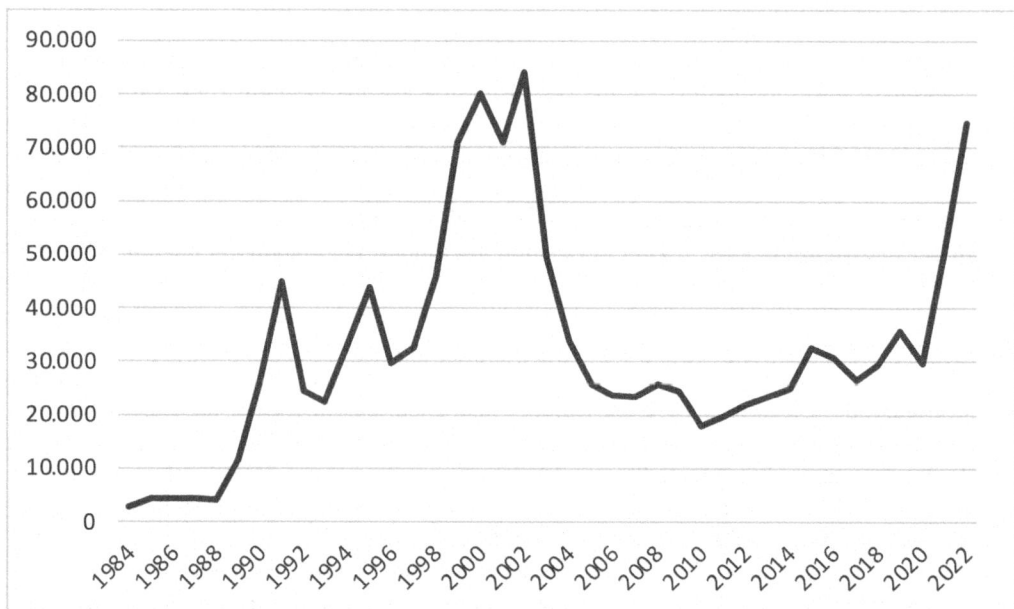

Figure 11.4 Asylum applications and initial decisions UK 1984–2022 (based on data in Sturge 2023)

gather further evidence of the avoidance by looking at the collocates of another naming choice: *immigrant*. In the press in 2021, the most salient collocates of *migrant* were *boats, crossings, Channel, crossing, undocumented, Haitian, unaccompanied, crossed, refugees, smugglers*. These terms point towards a major news story in 2021 which regarded an alleged crisis in relation to small boats crossing the Channel to the UK. The UK government's own statistics show that 90%

176

Table 11.1 Comparison of nationalities seeking asylum and national/ethnic modifiers in the UK press in 2021

Most Frequent Nationality in Asylum Applications in the UK 2021	Most Frequent Modifiers of Refugees in 2021 UK Press	Most Frequent Modifiers of Asylum Seekers in 2021 UK Press
Iran	*Afghan*	*Afghan*
Iraq	*Syrian*	*Cameroonian*
Albania	*Rohingya*	*Haitian*
Eritrea	*Palestinian*	*Tamil*
Syria	*Jewish*	*African*

of people who reached the UK in this way went on to claim asylum (Irregular migration to the UK 2023). In other words, they are *asylum seekers* – but that legitimating term is avoided.

This functions as disinformation because the people who are legally recognised as asylum seekers and refugees are denied those names – typically in favour of delegitimating names such as *migrant* or *immigrant* (for which the most frequent words immediately to the left in the 2021 corpus of UK newspapers are *illegal* and *undocumented*). This avoidance of the legitimating term where it applies also feeds into a myth of the "deserving vs undeserving" or "good vs bad migrant" – a myth in which the good migrant is consistently temporally or geographically dislocated from the speaker.

These examples of patterns of use serve to show how even the names that are used to describe people who move may be part of a disinformation choice that is not immediately apparent. However, these choices do not occur in isolation; they typically feed into macro stories – or myth.

3   Disinformation and myth

Following Kelsey (2016, inter alia), myth is here understood as a discursive practice which is not synonymous with deceit or disinformation. Myth is rather a form of social storytelling in which stories undergo a degree of simplification or "flattening out" to enable them to obtain archetypical status. Myths "carry ideology and express it through the theatrics and dramatisation of storytelling" (Kelsey 2016: 975). The key relationship between myth in this sense and disinformation is that disinformation serves the maintenance of a strong and simple myth such as the central or foundational myth that I alluded to earlier, which is one that asserts there is such a thing as a static host population which is intrinsically different to the mobile Other. These myths are the culmination and cumulation of many narratives. In the migration context, these "narratives are stories developed through communicative practices including framing, codifying, selecting, omitting, and silencing in order to offer a specific view on migration or migrants or a country's migration history" (Sahin-Mencutek 2020: 4). And these stories are powerful; according to Maneri (2023: 70), "mass-mediated narratives are probably the most compelling way to naturalise a certain cognitive and emotional landscape of migration". Once stories build into myths; they are naturalised, taken for granted, and part of the common-sense folklore. Disinformation then serves to maintain migration myths which would crumble in the light of facts. Indeed, a French study found that the most shared fake news relating to migrants were regarded criminal acts supposedly committed by migrants (30%), social benefits claimed by migrants (20%), and the idea of a migrant invasion (19%) (reported in Mas 2018). In other words, the most popular narratives that were verified as being based on disinformation all fed into an existing myth of immigrants representing a threat to a host population; disinformation is not new information, it appears.

3.1 Contemporary myths

Previous work shows a remarkable consensus on the negativity of dominant immigration narratives. For instance, Bakamo Social (2018) analysed five immigration narratives present on social media in 28 European countries in 2017–2018. Overall, they found that humanitarian narratives were the most frequent (49.9%); security narrative (25.9%); identity narrative (15.3%); economic narrative (8%); demographics narrative (1%). They report that the identity and security narratives provided the frame for an us versus them macro narrative, or myth as we are terming it here. In the UK context, the dominant frame was security (46.5%) and the humanitarian narratives peaked in discussion of the Windrush scandal and USA policies – sympathy was for those temporally and geographically dislocated.

We can observe the dominance of these negative framings simply at the level of collocates – the words which go together with names. Figure 11.5 visualises the collocates of four terms used to refer to people who move over the period 2010–2020 in UK parliamentary discourse. The larger the word in the image, the stronger the association.

We can immediately see a narrative of legality with *genuine* collocating with both *refugees* and *asylum seekers*, thus implicitly positing the existence of "non-genuine", as discussed previously. In the case of *asylum seekers*, the categorisation as "non-genuine" is also overt with *bogus* appearing. In the collocates of *migrants* and *immigrants*, *illegal* dominates and *economic* is also a strong collocates for *migrants* referring to delegitimizing framing.

If we look at the 2021 press, the collocates of *asylum seeker* focus on economic narratives (the ten strongest collocates include *housed, resource, accommodating*), those for *migrant* focus on a security narrative (*boats, crossings, Channel, crossing, crossed*), and those for *immigrants* include both elements (*undocumented, visas, illegal,* and *welfare*). Previous research (Taylor 2014) has also shown how public discourses in the UK emphasise the alleged pull factors of the UK for migration with metaphors such as *honey pot* and *magnet* being used to describe the relationship of the nation to the migrant.

Cumulatively, these narratives about economic pressures, security risk, and unique attraction of the host country contribute to a myth of threat from the Other. As Neidhardt and Butcher (2022) report, "[i]ndividual instances advanced by migration opponents and opportunists are generally consistent with some 'established' narrative, with each story seeking not so much to convince about a particular incident as to reinforce the plausibility of the stereotypes". These in turn may feed wider concerns about large-scale future change and the image of the future. What a textual analysis cannot show us is whether this constitutes disinformation, and for that we have to step outside the corpus or text to the numerous resources supplied by colleagues in the social sciences, fact-checking websites (e.g. https://fullfact.org/immigration/), and the government's own statistics. For instance, while the UK government and press focused great amounts of attention on the "threat" of Channel boat crossings, their own data showed, as mentioned previously, that the people making these crossing were asylum seekers, that most requests were recognised as legitimate, and that in fact they accounted for under half (45%) of all asylum requests. In light of these facts, the positioning of the phenomenon as an "invasion of our southern coast" by the Home Secretary Suella Braverman in 2022 is clearly disinformation. As was the assertion by the Home Secretary Priti Patel in 2021 that "70% of individuals on small boats are single men who are effectively economic migrants. They are not genuine asylum seekers" (in the latter case, when pushed the Home Office made no attempt to provide data to back up the falsehood).

What is absent in migration discourses also helps to maintain myths, and this too can support disinformation. Maneri (2023) reports that analysis of news stories about the "refugee crisis" across six European countries found only a threat frame with no examples of stories falling into a benefits frame. As he emphasises, "dominant frames tell a lot about how migration and

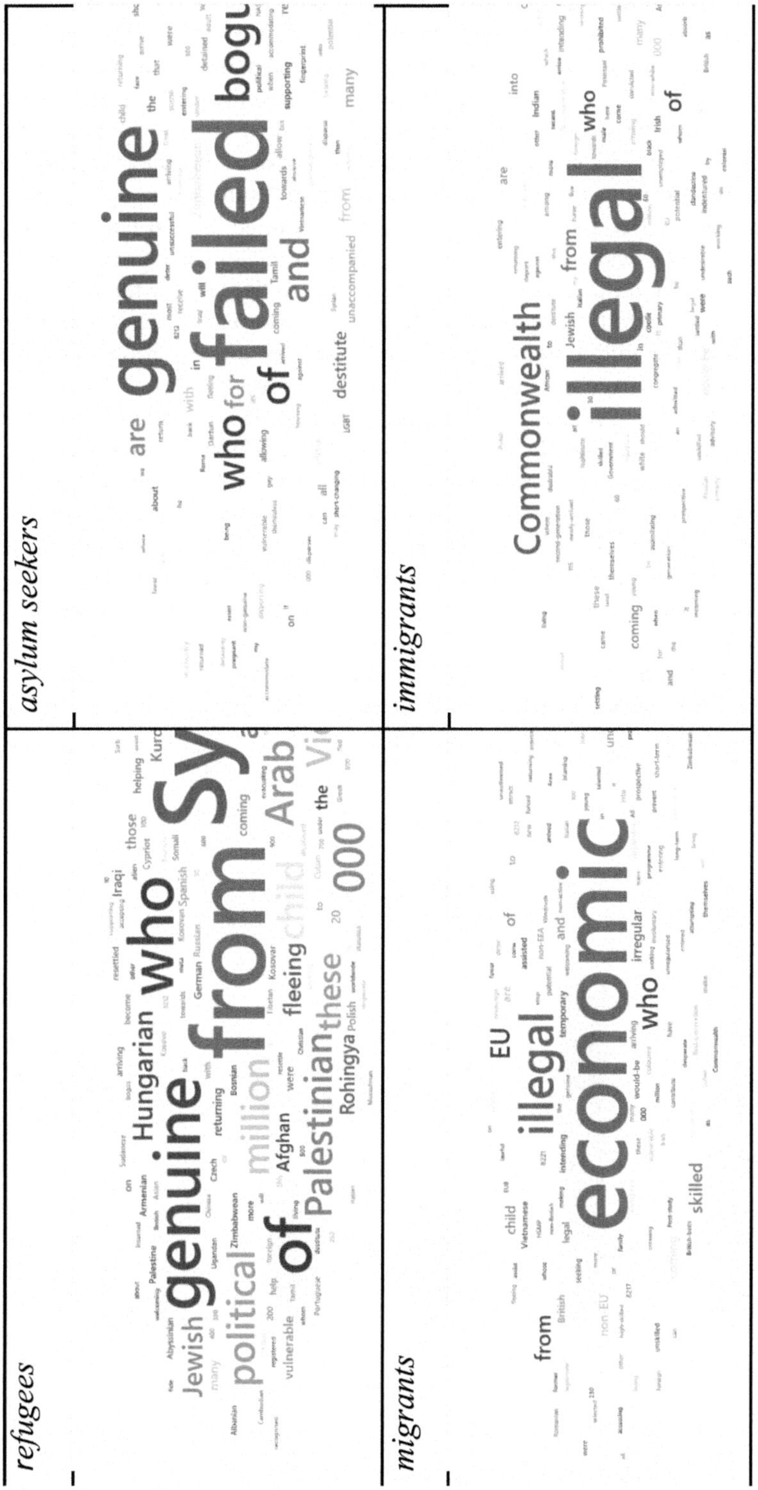

Figure 11.5 Visualisation of collocates 2010–2020 in UK parliamentary discourse

asylum are made meaningful, but the same goes for missing frames and narratives" (2023: 21), and disinformation may also be achieved through the suppression of information. To take a contemporary UK-based example, the Conservative government in the run up to the 2024 elections pursued a narrative of being "tough on immigration" and attempted to pass an "Illegal immigration bill" (itself an example of disinformation through naming as it refers to people travelling to the UK to request asylum, which is not illegal). The bill proposed that the UK would only accept applications for asylum from people who arrived through "safe and legal routes". However, what was not present in that public-facing narrative was an admission that (a) UK law states that a person must be physically present in the UK in order to claim asylum or (b) UK law make no provision for any person to come (or apply to come) to the UK for the purpose of making an asylum claim. This type of disinformation through absence and silence (Schröter and Taylor 2017) presents particular difficulties for processes of textual identification whether manual or automated. We might also consider example (1) in which the UK Prime Minister referred to "collectively *spending £6 million a day* on hotels for illegal asylum seekers" (my italics). What is absent and meaningful here are the reasons why the UK government chooses to provide hotel accommodation. For instance, asylum seekers may be housed in hotels in the UK for long periods because the UK has underfunded the process of reviewing applications, as evidenced by its 2021 status as the country with the second-largest backlog of applications to process in Europe – despite receiving less than a third of the number of applications for the country with the highest backlog (Germany) (Migration Observatory 2023). Other salient information might include the fact that the UK is unusually restrictive in regulations around whether asylum seekers may work and therefore support themselves. For instance, in the UK people cannot apply to work until they have been waiting over 12 months for their application to be reviewed – in Canada, they can look for work immediately (Gower et al. 2022).

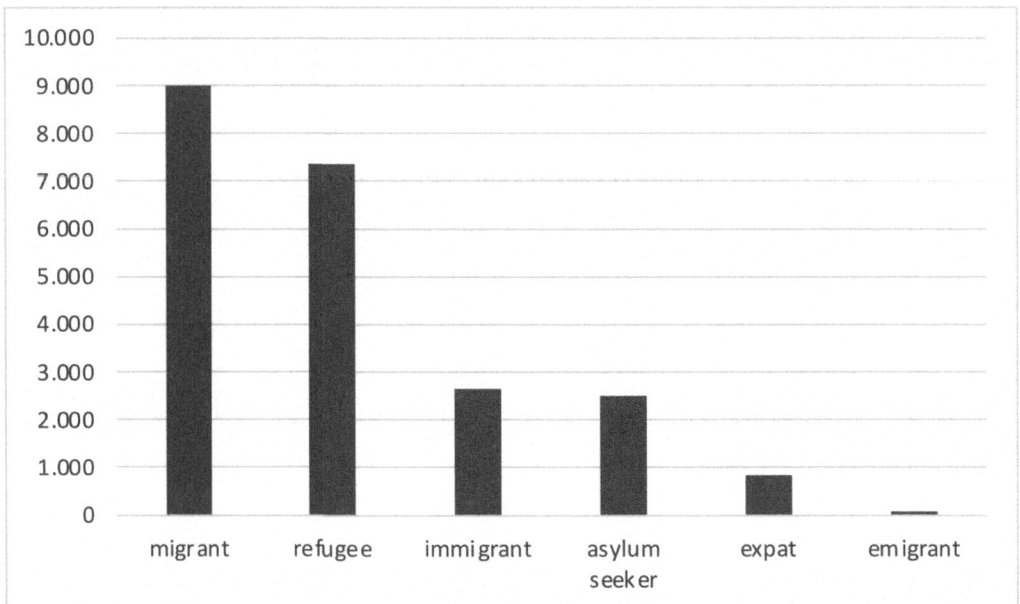

Figure 11.6 Frequency of migrant names in UK newspapers 2021

The spread of these myths of the "undeserving migrant" is also facilitated by the discursive news value (Bednarek and Caple 2017) of negativity, often characterised as the basic news value, and "[c]onsequently, news stories about refugees and immigrants tend to focus on crime, public unrest, and violence resulting in a perpetual flow of 'bad news' about immigrants and refugees (Philo et al. 2013)" (Culloty and Suiter 2021b: 322).

Looking at absence from a broader perspective, a central element in relation to public discourse of migration in the UK is *emigration*, as shown in Figure 11.6.

Although outward migration from the UK has remained relatively stable at around 350,000–400,000 per year with a gradual increase in more recent times (Migration Statistics 2022), it is not considered newsworthy in the 2021 press. Furthermore, even when outward migration is mentioned, it rarely refers to people leaving the UK in the here and now. For example, a sample analysis of the mentions of *emigrants* in UK press showed that just 4% referred to people leaving the UK at the time of writing in 2000–2009, and 11% in 2010–2018. This absence helps to foreground the myth that "we" are not like "them" because the mobility of the "us" group is suppressed.

3.2   Historical myths

The stories which are told about immigration also draw on historical myths and, in particular, those based on nostalgia. Research has indicated that collective nostalgia correlates with positive attitude to an in-group (Wildschut et al. 2014) and hostility to an out-group (Cheung et al. 2018), which makes it a rhetorically useful device in anti-immigration discourses. Furthermore, feelings of nostalgia are associated with times of uncertainty and across the EU "nostalgic types seem to be more fearful of immigrants and the consequences of migration" (De Vries and Hoffman 2018: 3). They found that those who felt nostalgic were more likely to agree with statements such as "immigrants take jobs away from natives" and "recent immigrants do not want to fit into society", and to disagree with statements such as "immigration is good for the economy" and "immigrants enrich cultural life". Similar findings were reported in a study based in the Netherlands (Smeekes and Verkuyten 2015) which found that feelings of national nostalgia significantly and positively correlated with feelings of displacement caused by immigrants (e.g. "Native Dutch are slowly losing the Netherlands to newcomers") and feelings of discontinuity caused by Muslims (e.g. "Muslims' way of life threatens the continuity of Dutch identity"). More specifically, nostalgia is likely to infuse contemporary (far)right myths about migration as the very idea of a time pre-migration relies on a myth of past monoculture and "pure" society (Mols and Jetten 2014). So we can envisage nostalgia interacting with disinformation about immigration in two ways: first, those experiencing nostalgia appear primed to being receptive to negative sentiment about immigration, and second, nostalgia is required to maintain the anti-immigration myth of the static "us" threatened by the mobile Other.

There are two recurring myths in this vein: the first asserts a proud tradition of positive attitude towards immigrants, and the second tells a story about how "these" immigrants who are here and now are qualitatively different to past immigrants. The UK prime minister drew on both of these, shown in example (4), when writing in a right-wing tabloid.

(4) THE UK has a *proud history of welcoming* those most in need – with thousands opening their homes to Ukrainian refugees in the last year and providing help to those fleeing from persecution in Hong Kong. *But* those arriving on small boats aren't directly fleeing a war-torn country or facing an imminent threat to life (Sunak, Sun 2023, my italics).

This is a textbook example of how the *proud history* trope is used to justify current hostility – note the assertion of past behaviour followed by the adversative conjunction *but*. The statement can be interrogated as disinformation on two levels. First, is it true that those arriving are not refugees? No, according to the government's own data cited previously. Second, is it true that the UK has a proud history? Here work in historiography helps us to unpick the rhetoric as it has been repeatedly shown that immigrants to the UK through time have been the target of institutional hostility (e.g. Kushner 2006 on refugees). Example (4) also illustrates the second trope as the target of the hostility (*those arriving in small boats*) are framed in opposition to those *in need*. This is something I interrogated in Taylor (2020), which was a detailed study of how the government drew on these two tropes in responding to criticism of how their "hostile environment" immigration policy had damaged the lives of British-Caribbean citizens who moved to the UK in the period 1940s–1970s (often referred to as the *Windrush generation*). The government repeatedly drew on the *proud tradition* to reject accusations of racism or xenophobia, as shown in example (5), and framed the current "undeserving" immigrants in opposition to the temporally distant "deserving" migrants, shown in example (6).

(5) The United Kingdom has *a proud history of welcoming arrivals* from around the world. We have long held open the door to those who want to come and help build a better country. . . . We would not be the country that we are today without the men and the women who crossed oceans to come here *legally*, to make their homes, to work hard, to pay taxes, to raise their families. And we all know it. Which is why the whole country was shocked by the unacceptable treatment experienced by some members of *the Windrush generation* (Javid, Home Secretary 2019).
(6) May I make the point that my constituents in Kettering, while recognising the value of the *Windrush generation* 100%, want the Government to crack down as hard as they can on *illegal immigration*? (Hollobone, Conservative 2018, my italics).

To test the rhetoric that these two groups (the Windrush generation and those framed as illegal immigrants) were indeed qualitatively different and that the UK has a proud history of welcome, I compared the metaphors used in parliamentary debate and mainstream newspaper (the *Times*) to frame (a) the Windrush generation in 2018, (b) those framed as illegal immigrants in 2018, (c) the Windrush generation in the 1950s. If the rhetoric were accurate, if there were no disinformation, we could hypothesise a close match between the language used to describe the Windrush generation in the 1950s and the Windrush generation 2018 (they are the same people) and a large difference to the language used to frame *illegal immigrants* in 2018. What I actually found was the opposite. Metaphors of WATER, INVASION, ANIMALS, and COMMODITIES linked the representation of the Windrush generation in the 1950s with that of illegalised immigrants in 2018; they occupy similar discursive roles. In contrast, there was *no* overlap in the metaphors used to describe the Windrush generation in the 1950s and the same people in 2018. So those government assertions about the warm welcome at the point of arrival and the intrinsic difference between the groups fall apart – and are revealed as disinformation, which serves to maintain that myth of difference.

As in the previous discussions, what is absent also helps to maintain these myths. Here, we can consider the absence of a collective memory of how outward migrants from the UK were represented and treated. As I show in Taylor (2021), those UK citizens who emigrated in the nineteenth and twentieth centuries were described using the same metaphors as the so-called illegal immigrants today, with metaphors of WATER, shown in (7), and COMMODITY, shown in (8), dominating in parliamentary and press discourse.

(7) I suggest that to stimulate the *flow* of suitable emigrants to Australia he might consider paying entirely the passage of suitable boys who are approved by his Department (Crowder 1938, italics).

(8) The female emigrants *sent out* from workhouses in 1857 had been most unsatisfactory to the colony of South Australia; so much so that the colony had ceased to use the agency of the Board, in *procuring* female emigrants (Childers 1860, my italics).

These metaphorical representations remove all agency from the people who move and reduce them to commodities for trade. Yet this image of how outward migration from the UK was perceived within the UK itself rarely makes it into public discourses – to do so would challenge that myth of difference – and so we have a false representation through absence.

4 Conclusions

In this chapter, I have attempted to synthesise previous research to show how immigration discourses are structured by myths, which in turn are underpinned by disinformation. The forms that disinformation may take are varied, ranging from the use of a name that obscures the legal status of an individual, to an outright lie about a specific statistic, to the omission of essential contextualizing information required to interpret an event. I have also attempted to argue that any attempt to analyse disinformation needs to systematically integrate absence and consider the structural role that silencing can play.

The effects of disinformation in immigration discourses are felt by both the imaginary static population who are encouraged to feel vulnerable and the mobile population who are positioned as aggressors. This type of polarisation opens up division and there is also negative impact on society as whole, as Teano (2021: 37) argues "the amplification of the populist and xenophobic rhetoric can be detrimental to democratic and humanitarian processes and values" and disinformation undermines journalism's legitimacy. However, what previous research suggests is that disinformation is not introducing new information so much as supporting existing myths and narratives, which are themselves unsupported by evidence. In some ways this is reassuring as it constrains the power of disinformation. But on the other, it makes it difficult to tackle because myths are powerful and persuasive.

In terms of future research, one issue for the linguist or discourse analyst is that disinformation in immigration discourses can only be identified by going outside the text, and so ideally it requires a multidisciplinary enterprise. Key areas for research include the systematic and comparative analysis of disinformation in public discourses of immigration – including multimodal representations. These should examine both individual claims (e.g. Juhász and Szicherle 2017 on the disinformation linking a rise in rape statistics in Sweden to immigration) and broader narratives. Research is also needed into the persuasive devices used to communicate disinformation. For instance, the role of humour and irony as deniable means of communicating prejudice. A crucial follow-up area is reception and literacy as we currently know relatively little about how the verified elements of disinformation are read by consumers of the press, social media content, and political discourse.

Equally important will be the dissemination of these findings; how do we most effectively show disinformation to be just that? Who should we talk to? For this, we need to build on work in disinformation more broadly to try and find what makes some audiences receptive to disinformation and what effectively raises awareness of misinformation. For instance, Greene and Murphy (2021) find that generic warnings about misinformation have no effects on behaviour, and Hameleers (2023) suggests that raising awareness of disinformation may have a negative impact on people's trust in news and information more generally. We may need to think of approaching diverse audiences in diverse ways. In the first instance, taking responsibility inside the academic community and being aware of how these wider discourses (unconsciously) impact scholarship, as well as overtly addressing misinformation. Kushner (2006: 232) says that "unless historians and popularisers of the past in the world of heritage normalize and problematize the responses to and experiences of refugees in Britain, it will continue to be easy to distort past", and the same must apply to those of us working on discourse and rhetoric. Second, when we identify disinformation in these discourses, we can follow the existing local processes to call the producers to account, particularly in the case of mainstream media discourse. As Culloty and Suiter (2021b: 325) state, "[w]hile the online environment is flooded with disinformation, mainstream news media remain highly influential. It is vital that these outlets offer audiences a comprehensive and accurate understanding of issues relating to immigration and avoid platforming extremist views for sensational coverage", and we can contribute to that accuracy by holding them to account. Third, while the politicians who intentionally spread disinformation are unlikely to be receptive – and may even appreciate their message being boosted through criticism – the nature of discourse means that others may have found themselves acting as *animators* in Goffman's terms and would be receptive. Fourth, for public communication, we may need to see how our research can enable us to identify and communicate alternative narratives, following Boswell and Hampshire (2017), who claim that

> politicians who want to challenge ignorance and prejudice need to construct narratives about immigration and its place in our society which draw on existing public philosophies of openness and inclusion. These public philosophies do exist and they have been mobilized in the recent past. They can and should be resuscitated.

Related chapters

- Chapter 3: Critical Discourse Analysis Approaches to Investigating Fake News and Disinformation.
- Chapter 7: Fakespeak in 280 Characters: Exploring the Language of Disinformation on Twitter through a Comparative Corpus-Based Approach.
- Chapter 12: Brexit and Disinformation.

Further reading

The following all address the topic of disinformation and immigration discourses from a more political science perspective. They are particularly helpful in understanding the mechanisms for the spread of disinformation facts (especially the role of digital media) and the actors involved.

1 Culloty, E. & J. Suiter. 2021. Anti-immigration disinformation. In *The Routledge Companion to Media Disinformation*. Routledge pp. 221–230.

2   Neidhardt, A & P. Butcher. 2022. Disinformation on Migration: How Lies, Half-Truths, and Mischaracterizations Spread. *Migration Policy Institute.* www.migrationpolicy.org/article/disinformation-migration-how-fake-news-spreads
3   Teano, F. 2021. Fake news and the spread of disinformation regarding migration. In *Riace: Local impact of a case of self-valorisation of migrant labour in the frame of the global compact.* transform! europe pp. 37–48 www.transform-network.net/fileadmin/user_upload/riace.local_impact_of_a_case_of_self-valorisation_of_migrant_labour_in_the_frame_of_the_global_compact.pdf#page=37

References

Allcott, H. and Gentzkow, M. (2017). Social media and fake news in the 2016 election. *Journal of Economic Perspectives*, 31(2), 211–236.

Asylum and resettlement datasets. (23 February 2023). www.gov.uk/government/statistical-data-sets/asylum-and-resettlement-datasets

Bakamo Social. (2018). *Migration Narratives in Europe in 2018.* https://drive.google.com/drive/u/0/folders/1oDArtrfU7dqIJPgAt03DakZF6T8unPET

Bakir, V. and McStay, A. (2018). Fake news and the economy of emotions: Problems, causes, solutions. *Digital Journalism*, 6(2), 154–175.

Bednarek, M. and Caple, H. (2017). *The Discourse of News Values: How News Organizations Create Newsworthiness.* Oxford University Press.

Boswell, C. and Hampshire, J. (2 March 2017). Taking back control of ideas: How politicians can shape public debates on immigration. *LSE BPP.* https://blogs.lse.ac.uk/politicsandpolicy/taking-back-control-of-ideas-immigration-debate/

Cantarella, M., Fraccaroli, N. and Volpe, R. (2023). Does fake news affect voting behaviour?. *Research Policy*, 52(1), 104628.

Cheung, W. Y., Wildschut, T. and Sedikides, C. (2018). Autobiographical memory functions of nostalgia in comparison to rumination and counterfactual thinking: Similarity and uniqueness. *Memory*, 26(2), 229–237.

Culloty, E. and Suiter, J. (2021a). How online disinformation and far-right activism is shaping public debates on immigration. In McAuliffe, M. (Ed.) *Research Handbook on International Migration and Digital Technology* (pp. 316–329). Edward Elgar Publishing.

Culloty, E. and Suiter, J. (2021b). Anti-immigration disinformation. In Tumber, H., and Waisbord, S. (Eds.) *The Routledge Companion to Media Disinformation and Populism* (pp. 221–230). Routledge.

Davies, M. (2012). *Oppositions and Ideology in News Discourse.* Bloomsbury.

De Vries, C. E. and Hoffmann, I. (2018). *The Power of the Past.* How Nostalgia Shapes European Public Opinion. http://aei.pitt.edu/102425/1/eupinions_Nostalgia.pdf

Fowler, R. (1991). *Language in the News: Discourse and Ideology in the Press.* Routledge.

Gabrielatos, C. and Baker, P. (2008). Fleeing, sneaking, flooding: A corpus analysis of discursive constructions of refugees and asylum seekers in the UK press, 1996–2005. *Journal of English Linguistics*, 36(1), 5–38.

Goffman, E. (1981). *Forms of Talk.* University of Pennsylvania Press.

Goodman, S. and Speer, S. A. (2007). Category use in the construction of asylum seekers. *Critical Discourse Studies*, 4(2), 165–185.

Goodman, S., Sirriyeh, A. and McMahon, S. (2017). The evolving (re) categorisations of refugees throughout the "refugee/migrant crisis". *Journal of Community & Applied Social Psychology*, 27(2), 105–114.

Gower, M., McKinney, C. J. and Meade, L. (2022). Asylum seekers: The permission to work policy. *House of Commons Library.* https://researchbriefings.files.parliament.uk/documents/SN01908/SN01908.pdf

Greene, C. M. and Murphy, G. (2021). Quantifying the effects of fake news on behavior: Evidence from a study of COVID-19 misinformation. *Journal of Experimental Psychology: Applied*, 27(4), 773–784. https://doi.org/10.1037/xap0000371

Hameleers, M. (2023). The (un)intended consequences of emphasizing the threats of mis-and disinformation. *Media and Communication*, 11(2).

Hodge, P. (2015). A grievable life? The criminalisation and securing of asylum seeker bodies in the 'violent frames' of Australia's Operation Sovereign Borders. *Geoforum*, 58, 122–131.

Irregular migration to the UK, year ending December 2022. (2023). www.gov.uk/government/statistics/irregular-migration-to-the-uk-year-ending-december-2022/irregular-migration-to-the-uk-year-ending-december-2022#:~:text=The%20majority%20of%20small%20boat%20arrivals%20claim%20asylum.,in%20the%20UK%20in%202022.

Juhász, A. and Szicherle, P. (2017). The political effects of migration-related fake news, disinformation and conspiracy theories in Europe. *Friedrich Ebert Stiftung, Political Capital.* https://politicalcapital.hu/pc-admin/source/documents/FES_PC_FakeNewsMigrationStudy_EN_20170607.pdf

Kelsey, D. (2016). The myth of the "Blitz spirit" in British newspaper responses to the July 7th bombings. *Social Semiotics*, 23(1), 83–99.

Kushner, T. (2006). *Remembering Refugees: Then and Now.* Manchester University Press.

Maneri, M. (2023). A comparative analysis of migration narratives in traditional and social media. *BRIDGES Working Papers 11.* www.bridges-migration.eu/wp-content/uploads/2023/02/BRIDGES-Working-Papers-11_WP3-Comparative-report.pdf

Mas, L. (2018). How fake images spread racist stereotypes about migrants across the globe. *The Observers, France 24*, 5 January 2018. https://observers.france24.com/en/20180105-fake-images-racist-stereotypes-migrants

Mautner, G. (2016). Checks and balances: How corpus linguistics can contribute to CDA. In Wodak, R., and Meyer, M. (Eds.) *Methods of Critical Discourse Studies* (3rd ed., pp. 154–179). Sage.

Migration Observatory (5 April 2023). *The UK's Asylum Backlog.* https://migrationobservatory.ox.ac.uk/resources/briefings/the-uks-asylum-backlog/#:~:text=At%20the%20end%20of%202021,an%20important%20driver%20of%20backlog

Migration Statistics (24 November 2022). https://commonslibrary.parliament.uk/research-briefings/sn06077/

Mols, F. and Jetten, J. (2014). No guts, no glory: How framing the collective past paves the way for anti-immigrant sentiments. *International Journal of Intercultural Relations*, 43, 74–86.

Mourão, R. R. and Robertson, C. T. (2019). Fake news as discursive integration: An analysis of sites that publish false, misleading, hyperpartisan and sensational information. *Journalism Studies*, 20(14), 2077–2095.

Neidhardt, A. H. and Butcher, P. (2022). Disinformation on migration: How lies, half truths, and mischaracterizations spread. *Migration Information Source.* Migration Policy Institute. https://www.migrationpolicy.org/article/disinformation-migration-how-fake-news-spreads

Ó Fathaigh, R., Helberger, N. and Appelman, N. (2021). The perils of legally defining disinformation. *Internet Policy Review*, 10(4), 2022–2040. Press Complaints Commission (code republished https://editorscode.org.uk/guidance_notes_7.php)

Philo, G., Briant, E. and Donald, P. (2013). *Bad News for Refugees.* Pluto Press.

Sahin-Mencutek, Z. (2020). Migration narratives in policy and politics. Working papers. *Ryerson Centre for Immigration and Settlement (RCIS) and the CERC in Migration and Integration.* www.torontomu.ca/centre-for-immigration-and-settlement/publications/working-papers/

Schröter, M. and Taylor, C. (Eds.). (2017). *Exploring Silence and Absence in Discourse: Empirical Approaches.* Palgrave Macmillan.

Smeekes, A. and Verkuyten, M. (2015). The presence of the past: Identity continuity and group dynamics. *European Review of Social Psychology*, 26(1), 162–202.

Sturge, G. (2023). Asylum statistics. *House of Commons Library Research Briefing*, 1 March 2023. https://researchbriefings.files.parliament.uk/documents/SN01403/SN01403.pdf

Taylor, C. (2014). Investigating the representation of migrants in the UK and Italian press: A cross-linguistic corpus-assisted discourse analysis. *International Journal of Corpus Linguistics*, 19(3), 368–400.

Taylor, C. (2020). Representing the Windrush generation: Metaphor in discourses then and now. *Critical Discourse Studies*, 17(1), 1–21.

Taylor, C. (2021). Metaphors of migration over time. *Discourse & Society*, 32(4), 463–481.

Teano, F. 2021. Fake news and the spread of disinformation regarding migration. In *Riace: Local Impact of a Case of Self-Valorisation of Migrant Labour in the Frame of the Global Compact.* transform! europe pp. 37–48. www.transform-network.net/fileadmin/user_upload/riace.local_impact_of_a_case_of_self-valorisation_of_migrant_labour_in_the_frame_of_the_global_compact.pdf#page=37

Wardle, C. (2017). Fake news. It's complicated. *First Draft.* https://medium.com/1st-draft/fake-news-its-complicated-d0f773766c79

Wildschut, T., Bruder, M., Robertson, S., van Tilburg, W. A. and Sedikides, C. (2014). Collective nostalgia: A group-level emotion that confers unique benefits on the group. *Journal of Personality and Social Psychology*, 107(5), 844.

12

BREXIT AND DISINFORMATION

Tamsin Parnell

Introduction

On 20 February 2016, then British prime minister David Cameron announced the date of the referendum on the United Kingdom's (UK) membership of the European Union (EU). The announcement came after Cameron had tried to negotiate a new deal with the EU over the UK's place in the bloc. Partly a response to divisions over EU membership in Cameron's party, the Conservatives, the referendum also reflected party-internal concerns that voters would opt for the populist, right-wing United Kingdom Independence Party (UKIP) in the next General Election (Hobolt, 2016; Swales, 2016; Cooper, 2021). Adding to these factors was the decades-long Eurosceptic sentiment in Britain which had contributed to the UK's reputation as the EU's "awkward partner" (George, 1990). Eurosceptic, in this case, refers to "an opposition to UK membership of the European Union and its antecedents" (Harmsen and Spiering, 2004: 16).

In the months that followed Cameron's announcement, several political campaigns vied for public attention and support. On the Remain side, there was Britain Stronger in Europe and the In campaign (which later became the BSIE campaign). Supported by David Cameron, major business interests, trade unions, and many foreign leaders (Hobolt, 2016), the cross-party BSIE campaign sought to persuade voters to remain in the EU based largely on the idea that it would be better for the British economy (Zappettini, 2019). On the other side, there were two political campaigns: Leave.EU and Vote Leave. Both aimed to become the official leave group, but Vote Leave was designated the formal campaign by the Electoral Commission on 13 April 2016. The Vote Leave campaign was spearheaded by Conservative MPs Michael Gove and Boris Johnson, and Labour MP Gisela Stuart. These political actors told the public that leaving the EU would save the UK £350 million a week, ensure the country had control over its borders, and allow the UK to produce and apply its own laws (Vote Leave, 2016). Remain supporting activists accused Leavers of lying about the money the UK would save by leaving. This accusation was later supported by the independent fact-checker Full Fact, whose researchers concluded that the £350 million figure was incorrect because it did not take into account the rebate the UK received (Full Fact, 2017). Those who wanted to leave accused Remainers of embarking on "Project Fear" by catastrophising the effects of withdrawing the UK's membership (see, for example, Habib, 2019; Elphicke, 2019). Both campaigns were negative, with Remainers predicting economic disaster if the UK voted

DOI: 10.4324/9781003224495-15

Leave, and the Leave campaign claiming that when Turkey joined the EU,[1] which was allegedly imminent, the UK would see a steep rise in its immigration levels. Ultimately, the campaigns were characterised by "exaggeration, and the use of dubious facts and figures on both sides, but particularly by the Leave campaign" (Cassidy, 2020: 54).

After weeks of intense and divided campaigning, Britons went to the polls. On 24 June 2016, the public in Britain awoke to the news that the nation had voted by 51.9% (17,410,742 votes) to leave the EU, with a turnout of 72.2%. The Leave vote has been interpreted since in a variety of ways, including as "a revolt of the economically left behinds" and as the result of resurging English nationalism (Chan et al., 2020: 830). The former theory propounds that Brexit was a vote against globalisation (Coyle, 2016; O'Rourke, 2016), with Remainers being the younger, more highly educated "winners of globalisation" (Hobolt, 2016) and Leavers being the so-called losers of globalisation (Andreouli, 2020). The latter interpretation posits that "Brexit voters . . . are motivated by identity, not economics" (Kaufmann, 2016: n.p.). Whatever the motivation for the vote, both the campaigns and the result revealed "deep disunity among citizens and widespread distrust of authority" (Wincott, 2019: 15). Indeed, in the lead up to the referendum vote, 46% of respondents said they thought politicians across the campaign debates were "mostly telling lies" (Whatukthinks, 2016; Marshall and Drieschova, 2018).

Such public sentiment is not without basis; research has shown that misleading claims were circulating before and after the vote. For instance, the former fact-checking non-profit First Draft identified a range of Brexit-related assertions that could be considered part of a broader deluge of "misleading tweets, dodgy maths, deceptively-framed narratives and outright lies" on social media (First Draft, 2019: n.p.). There is also evidence that misperceptions circulated among laypeople. The Policy Institute at King's College London, working in partnership with Ipsos MORI and UK in a Changing Europe, ran a survey of over 2,200 people aged 18–75 in Great Britain on misperception of immigration and Brexit realities (Policy Institute at King's and Ipsos MORI, 2018). The survey showed that there were "significant misperceptions on some key facts around Brexit" (ibid.: n.p.), particularly around immigration. It found that only 29% of respondents correctly asserted that immigrants pay more in taxes than they receive in welfare benefits and services, for instance (ibid.: n.p.).

The aftermath of the Brexit vote has been a turbulent time for the UK. David Cameron resigned as prime minister, with Conservative MP and former Home Secretary Theresa May eventually taking his place. May failed to get her Withdrawal Agreement (the terms upon which the UK would leave the EU) through Parliament, ultimately resigning too. Conservative MP Boris Johnson then became prime minister; he tried to speed up the Brexit process by proroguing (suspending) Parliament, an act which was judged to be unlawful by the British Supreme Court. While Boris Johnson's Withdrawal Agreement was accepted by MPs and Britain left the European Union in January 2020, there have been further tensions in British politics. Notably, Johnson resigned in 2022 after he and other politicians attended parties while the country was in lockdown due to the COVID-19 pandemic. These events have undoubtedly contributed to the low levels of trust in politicians in contemporary Britain (Curtice, Hudson and Montagu, 2020).

As this necessarily cursory summary of the socio-political context surrounding Brexit reveals, the UK's withdrawal from the EU has highlighted polarisation in the UK, which has been fuelled by both traditional (see Parnell, 2021, 2022) and social media (North, Piwek and Joinson, 2021). In this chapter, I consider a specific part of the Brexit process, namely, the use of disinformation used in political campaigns related to Brexit. I begin by defining disinformation and related terms, such as "fake news" and "post-truth politics", and then discuss "problematic information" (Jack, 2017) in the Brexit context before considering the phenomenon of the so-called

"Euromyths" (see Henkel, 2018). Finally, I present a case study of disinformation in the Brexit context by examining (a) the presence of the claim that the UK sent £350 million a week to the EU and (b) the Euromyth of the bent banana in a corpus of articles published by the pro-Brexit press between June and July 2016.

Defining disinformation and related terms

Problematic information refers to information that is "inaccurate, misleading, inappropriately attributed, or altogether fabricated" (Jack, 2017: 1). Within the realms of problematic information, there is a constellation of terms such as "fake news", post-truth politics, and disinformation. Given that they are somewhat conceptually fuzzy and often conflated in the public sphere (Freelon and Wells, 2020), it is important to consider definitions of disinformation and related terms. "Fake news", together with misinformation and disinformation, is a form of disruptive communication facing contemporary democracies (Bennett and Livingston, 2020). The phrase "fake news" is often avoided by scholars because it is "woefully inadequate to describe the complex phenomena of information pollution" and has "begun to be appropriated by politicians" such as former US president Donald Trump, who applied the term to unfavourable news coverage from mainstream media outlets (Wardle and Derakhshan, 2017: 5; Höller, 2021). Indeed, in its *Interim Report on disinformation and "fake news"*, the Digital, Culture, Media, and Sport Committee recommended that the UK Government reject the term "fake news" (DCMS, 2018). Given the scholarly caution about the term being a floating signifier (Farkas and Schou, 2018), I will avoid using the phrase "fake news" in this chapter, except where it has been applied to the Brexit context by other scholars (for example, Höller, 2021). Attempting to provide a systematic account of different forms of disruptive communication while moving away from the "fake news" label, Wardle and Derakhshan (2017) propose the terms misinformation and malinformation. Misinformation is false information that is not intentionally distributed, while malinformation can be rooted in facts but published to induce damage (Wardle and Derakhshan, 2017).

Adding to the number of related terms, Gaber and Fisher (2022) theorise the idea of "strategic lying". The authors state that strategic lying involves the use of misleading content in the context of a political campaign; its goal is to set the campaign agenda and prime an issue (Gaber and Fisher, 2022). The veracity of the strategic lie is "irrelevant" – on the contrary, "the more outlandish the claim, the more likely it is to attract widespread attention" (Gaber and Fisher, 2022: 462). Like strategic lying, post-truth politics is "a politics which seeks to emit messages into the public domain which will lead to emotionally charged reactions, with the goal of having them spread widely and without concern for the accuracy of the messages provided" (Marshall and Drieschova, 2018: 90). Marshall and Drieschova (2018) argue that the EU referendum heralded a new age of post-truth politics in which facts and expertise were not the primary concern for most people (although Birks [2021] argues that this is not necessarily a new phenomenon). They posit that post-truth politics has been made possible because of technological innovation and rising distrust in politicians, traditional media, and expert knowledge. Somewhat confusingly, Marshall and Drieschova (2018) and Gaber and Fisher (2022) offer the same Brexit-related claims to exemplify "strategic lying" and "post-truth politics": the allegation that the UK sends £350 million a week to the EU, and the assertion that Turkey will soon be joining the EU. While this does little to help demystify the concepts, it points to some consensus surrounding what can be considered "problematic information" in the Brexit context.

Perhaps a more established term in the literature (although equally discursively contested), *disinformation* has been variously defined as "intentionally factually incorrect news that is published to deceive and misinform its reader" (Dance, 2019: n.p.) and "combinations of images and texts, drawing on elements of truthful representations, used to spread misleading, inaccurate or false information designed to cause harm" (Faulkner, Guy and Vis, 2021: 200). These definitions usefully capture some important features of disinformation: it does not just involve language, and it intentionally deceives. To add to these features, Freelon and Wells (2020) outline three crucial criteria: (1) deception, (2) potential for harm, and (3) an intent to harm. Disinformation "seeks to stimulate emotional responses that make one feel less secure and take action accordingly" (Trithara, 2020: 2) and sits at the intersection between false and harmful content (Höller, 2021). Perhaps the most encompassing definition of disinformation, and the one which I follow in this chapter, comes from Bennett and Livingston (2020: 3): "[I]ntentional falsehoods or distortions, often spread as news, to advance political goals such as discrediting opponents, disrupting policy debates, influencing voters, inflaming social conflicts, or creating a general backdrop of confusion and information paralysis".

According to Bennett and Livingston (2020: 10), disinformation as a phenomenon is caused by a crisis of legitimacy in authoritative institutions which developed from the "growing emptiness" of mainstream political discourses. A similar argument is also made for the prevalence of "post-truth politics", where Marshall and Drieschova [2018] position the Iraq war, the 2008 recession, and the 2009 expenses scandal as events affecting the levels of trust in contemporary authoritative institutions in the UK. A crisis of legitimacy might easily be identified in the UK in the Brexit context, where politicians such as Michael Gove have proclaimed that the public has "had enough of experts" (Financial Times, 2016: n.p.), and research has reported on "widespread distrust of authority" (Wincott, 2019: 15) and record low levels of trust in politicians (Curtice, Hudson and Montagu, 2020). Adding to the crisis of legitimacy theory, Freelon and Wells (2020: 146) acknowledge the effect of "deep political contentiousness and polarisation" on both falling trust in the media and engagement in and consumption of disinformation. Division is certainly rife in the UK in the post-Brexit era (Wincott, 2019), with the identities of Remainer and Leaver becoming a new political cleavage (Kelley, 2019). Despite the relevance of disinformation to the current political climate in the UK, it is important to remember that disinformation is not a new phenomenon – it is simply the case that, due to digital platforms, intentionally false information can spread faster and further than ever before (Margolin, 2020).

"Problematic information" and Brexit

Although problematic information is not a new phenomenon in the UK, it is often discussed in the context of the EU membership referendum of 2016. While scholars use different terms to describe them (e.g. "post-truth politics", "strategic lying", "propaganda"), there are three claims made during the Brexit campaigns that tend to be used to illustrate problematic information surrounding Brexit. Cooper (2021: 399) refers to these claims as "at best misleading and at worst disinformation and propaganda".

The first claim is that the UK sent £350 million a week to the European Union that could be spent on the National Health Service if the country left the EU. The assertion, which was plastered on the side of the Vote Leave campaign bus, was officially misleading because it used the "maximum possible conceptualisation" of the costs facing the UK because of its EU membership while ignoring the rebate and other money that the UK received from the EU (Rose, 2017: 556; Full Fact, 2017). Between 20 February 2016 and 25 June 2016, there were 396 UK media stories which mentioned the £350 million figure close to the NHS (Cooper, 2016).[2] Perhaps unsurprisingly, then, despite being incorrect, an opinion poll conducted by Whatukthinks (2016) found that 47%

of respondents thought the claim was accurate (Cassidy, 2020). Cromby (2019: 64) contends that many who encountered the claim "lacked either the education, knowledge, time, analytic skills, confidence, or motivation to interrogate the assertion", and so they relied on politicians and the media for information, where the claim was repeated. Even when Remainers and/or fact-checking institutions tried to contest the claim with a more accurate figure, it merely reinforced the idea that the cost of EU membership was high (Shipman, 2017), and so the Leave campaign dominated the terms of the debate. The £350 million figure was ultimately concerning for democracy because "the obfuscation of facts makes it more difficult for citizens to access the relevant information" (Reid, 2019: 624) necessary to vote in referenda. It also showed, as is often the case with problematic information, that even when falsehoods are debunked, they can still shape people's attitudes (Marwick and Lewis, 2017).

The second example of problematic information is the "Breaking Point" poster that was created by the Leave.EU campaign and unveiled by Nigel Farage (then of UKIP) the week before the referendum. The poster depicted a long, winding queue of non-white men alongside the headline "Breaking Point: The EU has failed us all".

The picture was, in fact, of Syrian migrants at the border between Croatia and Slovenia and so depicted people who would struggle to enter the UK given that it had not signed the Schengen Agreement (Cooper, 2021). It was, therefore, a misrepresentation of UK migration and likely an "attempt to stir racial animus among a subset of Leave voters" (Reid, 2019: 630). Even though the poster did not depict people migrating to the UK, the text superimposed on the image linked UK immigration levels to EU policy, implying that inward migration from the EU is a "non-white phenomenon" that mainly involves young males and enables terrorists to enter the country (Morrison, 2016: 66). Reid (2019: 631) argues that the "Breaking Point" poster is problematic because it could shift public opinion towards the exclusion of certain groups from the deliberative process by "erod[ing] the stigma attached" to racist or socially exclusionary views (Reid, 2019: 631).

Figure 12.1   "Breaking point", UKIP poster

Source: United Kingdom Independence Party (2016) under the CC licence

The final claim that is often highlighted in discussions of problematic information surrounding Brexit is the suggestion that Turkey would soon be joining the EU and, as a result, a population of 76 million would have access to the UK. This claim began to be associated with EU membership when UKIP dedicated its three-and-a-half-minute party broadcast (www.youtube.com/watch?v=nnrFddSJWsk) to the alleged dangers of Turkey's potential membership in 2016 (Ker-Lindsay, 2018). The party implied that Turkey's accession was only five years away and that the UK should leave the EU before it happened (Ker-Lindsay, 2018). Even though the broadcast was criticised (Ker-Lindsay, 2018), the claim that Turkey would soon be joining the EU was picked up by the Vote Leave campaign on its website (Vote Leave, 2016). Although Turkey had begun talks to accede in 2005, progress had been "slow and stormy" (Cooper, 2021: 405), making it unlikely that Turkey would join the EU anytime soon. Despite this, Turkey was often associated with immigration in the UK national press during the EU referendum process (Moore and Ramsay, 2017). Of the 461 articles that mentioned Turkey, 109 were negative, framing the country and its citizens in terms of criminality or the pressure they would place on UK services if allowed to join the EU (Moore and Ramsay, 2017; Cooper, 2021).

The success of these three messages was "embedded deeply in the history of UK populism, which had manifested itself as English exceptionalism and anti-European feeling for decades" (Cooper, 2021: 399). While the specific messages discussed here might have been novel formulations of anti-EU rhetoric, they likely reinforced much longer, more well-developed anxieties and concerns about Britain and its relationship with the European Union. This is particularly problematic: if people accept information that reinforces their ideologies, even if it is inaccurate, there is a polarising effect which can reduce "the common ground on which reasoned debate" can take place (DCMS, 2019: 5). This, in turn, may have the potential to threaten democracy (Reid, 2019).

As Hinde (2017) points out, politicians were not solely to blame for disseminating the misleading statements outlined in the previous section, the UK press also played a role. While many right-wing newspapers actively advocated for the UK to leave the EU (e.g. *The Daily Express, Daily Mail, The Telegraph)*, the BBC (British Broadcasting Corporation) – the UK's national broadcaster – often gave equal time to Leave and Remain claims in the name of neutrality; truths and falsehoods on both sides were given equal weight. Resultingly, the three claims outlined previously were repeated over and over across print and broadcast media platforms. Ultimately, spreading falsehoods could undermine the media's credibility, leading to a further crisis of legitimacy, as well as weakening the political knowledge of citizens (Marwick and Lewis, 2017).

But can we refer to the three claims as disinformation? After all, as Hinde (2017: 84) recognises, "in all political campaigns there are debates about facts, allegations of lying and actual blatant untruths". It is useful here to recap Bennett and Livingston's (2020) definition of information, which includes the following features:

1 Intentional falsehoods or distortions;
2 Spread as news;
3 Used to enhance political goals.

All three claims meet this definition of disinformation, given that they were clearly false, reported on *as* news and *by* news outlets, and used to discredit the Remain campaign and persuade the UK public to vote Leave. But were they intentionally spread? Hinde (2017: 85) cites the multi-millionaire backer of Vote Leave, Aaron Banks, as saying that facts do not work and that you (as political campaigners) have "got to connect with people emotionally". Arguably, this quote indicates a move away from facts in the Leave campaign. Many core Leave campaigners backtracked on the £350 million claim after the vote, with Nigel Farage calling it a "mistake". Walking back on the claim suggests that it was used solely to fulfil a political goal: to influence the public to vote Leave. I would contend, then, that the three claims do indeed constitute disinformation, although I recognise that scholars such as Birks (2021) would characterise them as propaganda.

In addition to these three central claims, studies have explored other aspects of problematic information in relation to Brexit (e.g. Cervi and Carrillo-Andrade, 2019), generally finding that "values were being contested [in the referendum] rather than facts" (Gillet, 2017: n.p.). For instance, Höller (2021) considers the role of politicians in the spread of "fake news" surrounding Brexit. He finds that, through their tweets, both Boris Johnson and Nigel Farage shared multiple misleading arguments. For example, when tweeting about the UK's payments to the EU, Johnson argued that "it is perfectly reasonable to use the £350 million figure – actually it is an underestimate". As we have seen, this is inaccurate because the £350 million figure was *overestimating* the amount the UK sent to the EU. Meanwhile, Farage posted several tweets warning that Turkey would imminently join the EU, which, as Höller (2021) concludes, is misleading. Ultimately, Höller's (2021) study supports the view that politicians' direct use of social media can contribute to the dissemination of disinformation.

Euromyths

There is another type of discourse relating to Brexit that has been labelled disinformation: the Euromyth. Euromyths, as they have been termed by the European Commission (EC), are news stories, often published by the right-wing British press, which report on EU activities or directives which seemingly "defy 'common sense'" (Stanyer, 2007: 134). The exaggerated or invented stories typically focus on "trivial matters" (Henkel, 2021a: 10) or "petty rules" (Stanyer, 2007: 134), such as the abnormal curvature of bananas or the banning of certain flavours of potato crisps (Irwin and Tominc, 2023). The foundation of the Euromyth has been linked to former British journalist turned Conservative MP and PM Boris Johnson (of Vote Leave), who was Brussels correspondent for the *Daily Telegraph* in the 1990s and often wrote stories about EU officials in a mocking tone (Hinde, 2017). As this suggests, the Euromyth reports are not solely the fare of tabloids, they are also found in broadsheets (Cross, 2008; Martin, 1996). To refute the misleading media coverage of its directives, the EC created an A-Z Euromyth index in which it monitored and responded to stories between 1992 and 2018. Although the website has now been archived, it remains accessible through the online archive Wayback Machine.[3]

The Euromyths blog responded to the initial publication of Euromyths, but it did not account for how these stories have become part of more sustained Eurosceptic conceptualisations of the European Union (Usherwood, 2013) and how they were intertextually alluded to during the coverage of Brexit. For instance, in the 1990s, the Euromyth blog refuted media claims that it had banned bent bananas (Henkel, 2021a). Yet three days before the 23 June EU referendum in 2016, *Daily Star Online* (2016) published an article in which it asked, "Will we say adiós, au revoir and auf wiedersehen to Brussels bigwigs who have a say from everything from the shape of our bananas to how many immigrants shack up here?"[4] Similarly, Henkel (2018: 88) cites a *Daily Mail* claim that "we laughed when they tried to ban prawn-flavoured crisps". The assertion that the EU tried to ban certain flavours of crisps was alluded to again in 2017, when *Express Online* told readers to "imagine a childhood without licking the salt and vinegar flavour off your fingers".

These examples illustrate that the Euromyths are not one-off misunderstandings about Brussels' decision-making but are part of a longer-term Eurosceptic discourse of the EU as an interfering bureaucracy. Indeed, as Irwin and Tominc (2023) state, the Eurosceptic and right-wing newspapers have *systematically* reported on these EU-related myths as a way of distinguishing between a British in-group and an EU out-group.

In her book on Euromyths, Henkel (2021a) makes the case for these stories as a form of disinformation. She considers three different definitions of disinformation, one from Wardle and Derakhshan (2017), another from Bennett and Livingston (2018), and a third from the EC (2018). Conceptualising Euromyths as false news stories that were deliberately created and intended to harm the reputation of the European Union, thereby advancing the political goals of Eurosceptics, Henkel (2021a) contends that Euromyths fit firmly within the sphere of disinformation. However, there is the caveat, as Henkel (2021a) admits, that classifying Euromyths as untrue relies purely on the often-complicated refutations of the EC as published in their Euromyths index. Although the EC, according to Henkel (2021a), followed internationally recognised principles of fact-checking, their refutations were sometimes ambiguous and did not always outright reject the claims made by the British press as false. Indeed, compared to the simplicity of the Euromythic claims, the EC's rebuttals often appeared convoluted. Although we should remain cautious in homogenising all Euromyths as falsehoods, then, it is not far-fetched to claim, as Henkel (2021a: 155) does, that the news stories often amount to "a distortion, a wilful exaggeration, or misleading selection of facts" with arguably similarly worrying consequences for democracy. Indeed, some Euromyths, such as the claim that the EU tried to ban bendy bananas, have been openly debunked not just by the European Parliament (2016), but also by newspapers such as *The Guardian* (Henley, 2016), giving further credibility to their categorisation as disinformation.

A case study: the circulation of the £350 million claim and the Euromyth of bendy bananas in the British pro-Brexit press during Brexit

The following case study uses a corpus of 733 articles (666,734 words) published between June and July 2016 in five pro-Brexit newspapers and their online counterparts: *The Sun, The Daily Express, Daily Telegraph, Daily Mail,* and *Daily Star*. The articles were collected from LexisNexis.

The £350 million claim

I was interested in the degree to which the £350 million claim was reported on by the pro-Brexit press around the time of the EU membership referendum, so I searched the corpus for the phrases "350 million" and "350m". This search returned 40 mentions (in 36 articles) across the months of June and July. Of those, some 26 mentions were repetitions of the claim that the UK sent £350 million to the EU, either without recognition that the figure was incorrect or with a rebuttal to the assertion that the figure was incorrect. Most often the claim appeared in the verbatim reporting of speeches by Leave campaigners, but this was not always the case. One might argue, then, that the pro-Brexit press amplified the claim by not fact-checking it *and* by repeating it in their articles. Examples from the newspapers included not only pieces published by journalists, as in Extract (1), but also letters from the public, as shown in Extract (2). The inclusion of the letter from the public tells readers that their views are shared by other voters and suggests that the claim reached and was influential for some voters. Notably, the parenthesis in Extract (2) suggests that even with the acknowledgement that the figure did not include the rebate, it was still being circulated and accepted as accurate by laypeople.

1 This is the latest doomsday message from an EU country increasingly worried about losing £350 million gross figure that Brussels syphons off from British taxpayers every week (*Express Online*, 2016).
2 SIR – I look forward to the additional contribution of £350 million per week (in real terms) to the NHS budget (*Daily Telegraph*, 2016).

A further 23 articles acknowledged that £350 million was an inaccurate figure, but importantly, these articles tended to be published *after* the Leave vote as reflections on the campaign. Arguably, then, this corrective information was not necessarily being made widely available to readers at the time of voting by the pro-Brexit press. For example, Extract (3) was published two days after the referendum vote. The scare quotes around the verb "lied" reveal a reluctance to characterise the figure as disinformation. More importantly, Extract (3) seems to indicate that the "lie" was not the figure itself, but the claim that this money, once recuperated, would be given directly to the NHS. Even when the claim is challenged, then, it is only partially corrected.

3 Other voters were dismayed when they admitted that they felt "lied" to by the Leave campaign. Ukip leader Nigel Farage admitted that it was a "mistake" for the leave campaign to claim that the weekly £350 million saved from EU contributions would go to the NHS (*Daily Star*, 2016).

There are other discursive strategies that further contribute to the downplaying of corrective information about the £350 million claim. One strategy is to present the figure as a question, as though the veracity of the figure is still open to contestation, as Example (4), published in July 2016, demonstrates:

4 Would Brexit liberate £350 million a week for the NHS? Or would it dent the public finances just as the health service needs more public money? (*Daily Telegraph*, 2016).

In this extract from a guest opinion piece by the Chief Executive of NHS England, Simon Stevens, the £350 million figure is presented as part of a rhetorical question that contemplates the claims made by both campaign groups about financing the NHS. By including a viewpoint from the Remain side ("dent the public finances just as the health service needs more public money"), as well as the Leave side, the writer perpetuates the idea that the figure was just one side of an argument rather than an inaccuracy. In other words, the writer frames the falsehood as just part of politics. As Birks (2021: 391) recognises, if reporting of political campaigning suggests that *all* candidates are being untruthful in some way, voters "may conclude that they are not in a position to demand veracity via the choice they have been given".

A similar downplaying of the inaccuracy of the figure is featured in *Telegraph Online*, where journalist Allison Pearson does not acknowledge that the figure is incorrect, even while representing it as "hotly disputed" (see Example 5). The verb "disputed" plays into the idea that there is no "truth", just two sides disagreeing on what is a fact. The verb phrase "slow to admit", while indexing reluctance, downplays the deliberate nature of the disinformation, which was undoubtedly intended, in Bennett and Livingston's (2020) terms, to "enhance political goals":

5 B is for . . . Boris, Brexit and Battlebus. Throughout the campaign, Boris tamped down his Inner Tigger, perhaps because he harbours serious hopes of running the country at the end of it all. The shout on the side of the Leave battlebus – "We send the EU £350 million a week" – became the referendum's most hotly disputed statistic because Brexiteers were slow to admit it was a gross rather than a net figure (*Telegraph Online*, 2016).

We see from this short case study, then, that the £350 million claim was reported on and amplified at the time of the referendum and its immediate aftermath and was often not widely challenged by the pro-Brexit press until after the Leave vote. This finding suggests that it was not just politicians and campaigners who were responsible for the spread of misleading, "problematic information" (Jack, 2017), but that the Eurosceptic media also had a part to play.

Euromyths: bent bananas

For the remainder of this case study, I focus specifically on the bent banana claim. As Henkel (2021b) outlines, the Eurosceptic media claimed in the 1990s that the EU was banning bent bananas. The EC refuted the claim on its Euromyth blog, established to rebut some of the claims made about EC's directives; Henkel (2021b) uses this refutation to characterise the Euromyth as disinformation (although Irwin and Tominc [2023: n.p.] refer to it as "a vehicle of a political myth"). I was particularly interested in whether this "myth" played a part in pro-Brexit media coverage of the EU membership referendum, so I searched my corpus of pro-Brexit media articles from June and July 2016 and found that the Euromythic claim is intertextually alluded to ten times (across eight articles). This low figure suggests that the Euromyth of the bent banana was not particularly prevalent during the campaign. However, a closer look at the Examples (6) and (7) reveals that the Euromyth has become part of a broader British Eurosceptic discourse:

6 This goes far beyond frustration at diktats on banana curvature. The EU has started to deform our government (*MailOnline*, 2016).
7 Will we say adiós, au revoir and auf wiedersehen to Brussels bigwigs who have a say from everything from the shape of our bananas to how many immigrants shack up here? (*Daily Star Online*, 2016).

These examples seem to lack the joking tone characteristic of the original Euromythic stories (see Henkel, 2021a; Irwin and Tominc, 2023), although the *Daily Star Online* does express a degree of playfulness through the Spanish, French, and German phrases for "goodbye". What *is* recognisable across these extracts is the Eurosceptic terminology of "diktats" and "bigwigs" and the populist expression of "frustration" towards the so-called European elites and their directives. I contend that what is happening here is akin to what Irwin and Tominc (2023) find in their study of the original Euromyths: the myth is constantly repeated and passed on unquestioningly, becoming, through time, part of a representation of the EU that can be evoked without being directly discussed. In these examples, the bendy banana myth is only minimally alluded to through the noun phrases "banana curvature" and "shape of our bananas" – the journalists do not explain what they are referring to. Instead, it is expected that readers will recognise the allusion and be primed to associate this (arguably disinformative) allusion with the broader Eurosceptic discourse to which "diktats" and "bigwigs" belongs. We might conclude, then, that disinformation has become part of the broader Eurosceptic pro-Brexit treatment in contemporary UK discourses about the EU.

Conclusion

This chapter has explored the prevalence of problematic information in the Brexit context. Following a brief introduction to the socio-political background of Brexit, it has outlined the conceptually fuzzy constellation of terms surrounding disinformation. It has introduced the phenomenon of the Euromyth as a news story that focuses on seemingly trivial regulations that the EC has allegedly imposed on the UK. Through two case studies exploring disinformation and the Euromyth in the British pro-Brexit press, the chapter has revealed that disinformation has become part of contemporary pro-Brexit representations of the EU.

Notes

1 Turkey began accession talks in 2005, but progress had slowed to the point that "it seemed inconceivable that it could possibly join any time before 2030" (Ker-Lindsay, 2018: n.p.).
2 According to Cooper (2021: 407), the search was conducted on Lexis Nexis using the search terms "£350m near/25 NHS (i.e. between 25 words, within the same paragraph between 20 February 2016 and 25 June 2016. Search results included newspapers, web-based publications, video, news transcripts, audio, news, magazines, and journals based in the UK and Northern Ireland".
3 See https://web.archive.org/web/20200131192225/https://blogs.ec.europa.eu/ECintheUK/euromyths-a-z-index/.
4 www.dailystar.co.uk/news/latest-news/eu-referendum-brexit-decision-day-17096143.

References

Andreouli, E. (2020). Lay rhetoric on Brexit. In: Demasi, M. A., Burke, S. and Tileaga, C. (eds.) *Political Communication*. Switzerland: Palgrave Studies in Discursive Psychology, pp. 63–87.

Bennett, W. L. and Livingston, S. (2018). The disinformation order: Disruptive communication and the decline of democratic institutions. *European Journal of Communication*, 33(2): 122–139.

Bennett, W. L. and Livingston, S. (eds.) (2020). *The Disinformation Age: Politics, Technology, and Disruptive Communication in the United States*. Cambridge: Cambridge University Press.

Birks, J. (2021). Fact-checking false claims and propaganda in the age of post-truth politics: The Brexit referendum. In: Rawnsley, G. D., Ma, Y. and Pothong, K. (eds.) *Research Handbook on Political Propaganda*. Cheltenham: Elgaronline, pp. 390–404.

Cassidy, J. (2020). How post-truth politics transformed and shaped the outcome of the 2016 Brexit referendum. In: Giusti, S. and Piras, E. (eds.) *Democracy and Fake News. Information Manipulation and Post-Truth Politics*. London: Routledge, pp. 53–63.

Cervi, L. and Carrillo-Andrade, A. (2019). Post-truth and disinformation: Using discourse analysis to understand the creation of emotional and rival narratives in Brexit. *ComHumanitas: Revista Científica de Comunicación*, 10(2): 125–149.

Chan, T. W., Henderson, M., Sironi, M. and Kawalerowicz, J. (2020). Understanding the social and cultural bases of Brexit. *The British Journal of Sociology*, 71(5): 830–851.

Cooper, G. (2021). Populist rhetoric and media disinformation in the 2016 UK Brexit referendum. In: Tumber, H. and Waisbord, S. (eds.) *The Routledge Companion to Media Disinformation and Populism*. London: Routledge, pp. 397–410.

Coyle, D. (2016). Brexit and globalization. In: Baldwin, R. (ed.) *Brexit Beckons: Thinking Ahead by Leading Economists*. London: Centre for Economic Policy Research Press, pp. 23–28.

Cromby, J. (2019). The myths of Brexit. *Journal of Community and Applied Social Psychology*, 29(1): 56–66.

Cross, S. (2008). Hippoglossus hippoglossus and chips: Twice please love? Adventures in the underbelly of Euromyths. In Keeble, R. (ed.) *Communication Ethics Now*. Leicester: Troubador Publisihing Ltd, pp. 52–57.

Curtice, J., Hudson, N. and Montagu, I. (eds.) (2020). *British Social Attitudes: The 37th Report*. London: The National Centre for Social Research.

Daily Star (2016). *'I Kinda Regret My Vote' Brexiteers Suffer from 'Bregret' After Voting Leave*. Available at: www.dailystar.co.uk/news/latest-news/regret-vote-brexiteers-suffer-bregret-17098529. [Date accessed: 23/3/23].

Daily Star Online (2016). *Countdown Begins to EU D-Day: Brits Braced for Most Important Vote in Modern Times*. Available at: www.dailystar.co.uk/news/latest-news/eu-referendum-brexit-decision-day-17096143. [Date accessed: 23/3/23].

Dance, W. (2019). Disinformation online: Social media user's motivations for sharing 'fake news'. *Science in Parliament*, 75(2).

Digital, Culture, Media and Sport Committee (2018). *Disinformation and "Fake News": Interim Report, HC 363*. Available at: https://publications.parliament.uk/pa/cm201719/cmselect/cmcumeds/363/363.pdf [Date accessed: 23/3/23].

Digital, Culture, Media and Sport Committee (2019). *Disinformation and 'Fake News': Final Report, HC 1791*. Available at: https://publications.parliament.uk/pa/cm201719/cmselect/cmcumeds/1791/1791.pdf [Date accessed: 23/3/23].

Elphicke, C. (2019). The ghost of Project Fear is back again, but Britain stands ready for Brexit. *BrexitCentral*, 8 July. Available at: https://brexitcentral.com/the-ghost-of-project-fear-is-back-again-but-britain-stands-ready-for-brexit/.

European Commission (2018). A multi-dimensional approach to disinformation. *Report of the Independent High Level Group on Fake News and Online Disinformation*. Available at: https://data.europa.eu/doi/10.2759/739290.

European Parliament (2016). Bendy Bananas – the myth to end all myths. *European Parliament Liaison Office in the United Kingdom*. Available at: www.europarl.europa.eu/unitedkingdom/en/news-and-press-releases/euromyths/bendybananas.html.

Farkas, J. and Schou, J. (2018). Fake news as a floating signifier: Hegemony, antagonism and the politics of falsehood. *Javnost – The Public*, 25(3): 298–314.

Faulkner, S., Guy, H. and Vis, F. (2021). Right-wing populism, visual disinformation, and Brexit: From the UKIP 'Breaking Point' poster to the aftermath of the London Westminster bridge attack. In: Tumber, H. and Waisbord, S. (eds.) *The Routledge Companion to Media Disinformation and Populism*. London: Routledge, pp. 198–208.

Financial Times (2016). *Britain Has Had Enough of Experts, Says Gove*. Available at: www.ft.com/content/3be49734-29cb-11e6-83e4-abc22d5d108c.

First Draft (2019). *Brexit: The False, Misleading and Suspicious Claims CrossCheck Has Uncovered so Far*. Available at: https://firstdraftnews.org/articles/brexit-the-false-misleading-and-suspicious-claims-crosscheck-has-uncovered/.

Freelon, D. and Wells, C. (2020). Disinformation as political communication. *Political Communication*, 37(2): 145–156.

Full Fact (2017). *£350 Million EU Claim "a Clear Misuse of Official Statistics"*. Available at: https://fullfact.org/europe/350-million-week-boris-johnson-statistics-authority-misuse/.

Gaber, I. and Fisher, C. (2022). "Strategic lying": The case of Brexit and the 2019 UK election. *The International Journal of Press/Politics*, 27(2): 460–477.

George, S. (1990). *An Awkward Partner: Britain in the European Community*. Oxford: Oxford University Press.

Gillett, G. (2017). *The Myth of Post-Truth Politics*. Available at: https://georgegillett.com/2017/04/20/the-myth-of-post-truth-politics/.

Habib, B. (2019). The Success of Brexit Britain Has Left Project Fear on its Deathbed. *Telegraph Online*, 20 September. Available at: www.telegraph.co.uk/politics/2019/09/20/success-brexit-britain-has-left-project-fear-deathbed/.

Harmsen, R. and Spiering, M. (2004). *Euroscepticism: Party Politics, National Identity and European Integration*. Amsterdam: Rodopi.

Henkel, I. (2018). How the Laughing, Irreverent Briton Trumped Fact-Checking: An Analysis of Fake News in British Newspaper Stories about the EU. *Journalism Education*, 6(3): 87–97.

Henkel, I. (2021a). *Destructive Storytelling. Disinformation and the Eurosceptic Myth that Shaped Brexit*. Switzerland: Palgrave Macmillan.

Henkel, I. (2021b). Ideology and Disinformation. How False News Stories Contributed to Brexit. In López-García, G., Palau-Sampio, D., Palomo, B., Campos-Domínguez, E. and Masip, P. (eds.) *Politics of Disinformation: The Influence of Fake News on the Public Sphere*. London: Wiley, pp. 79–90.

Henley, J. (2016). Is the EU Really Dictating the Shape of Your Bananas? *The Guardian*. Available at: www.theguardian.com/politics/2016/may/11/boris-johnson-launches-the-vote-leave-battlebus-in-cornwall.

Hinde, S. (2017). Brexit and the media. *Hermès, La Revue*, 77(1): 80–86.

Hobolt, S. B. (2016). The Brexit vote: A divided nation, a divided continent. *Journal of European Public Policy*, 23(9): 1259–1277.

Höller, M. (2021). The human component in social media and fake news: The performance of UK Opinion Leaders on Twitter during the Brexit campaign. *European Journal of English Studies*, 25(1): 80–95.

Irwin, M. and Tominc, A. (2023). How the bendy banana became a symbol of anti-EU sentiment: British media, political mythology and populism. In: Fakazis, L. and Fürsich, E. (eds.) *The Political Relevance of Food Media & Journalism: Beyond Review and Recipes*. London: Routledge.

Jack, C. (2017). Lexicon of lies: Terms for problematic information. *Data & Society Research Institute*. Available at: https://datasociety.net/wp-content/uploads/2017/08/DataAndSociety_LexiconofLies.pdf.

Kaufmann, E. (2016). It's NOT the economy, stupid: Brexit as a story of personal values. *LSE Blog*. Available at: http://eprints.lse.ac.uk/69138/1/blogs.lse.ac.uk-Its%20NOT%20the%20economy%20stupid%20Brexit%20as%20a%20story%20of%20personal%20values.pdf.

Kelley, N. (2019). *British social attitudes survey: Britain's shifting identities and attitudes*, 36. London: National Centre for Research.

Ker-Lindsay, J. (2018). Turkey's EU accession as a factor in the 2016 Brexit referendum. *Turkish Studies*, 19(1): 1–22.

Margolin, E. (2020). 10 tips for reporting on disinformation. *Data & Society*. Available at: https://datasociety.net/library/10-tips-for-reporting-on-disinformation/.

Marshall, H. and Drieschova, A. (2018). Post-truth politics in the UK's Brexit referendum. *New Perspectives*, 26(3): 89–106.

Martin, G. (1996). Euromythology and Britain in Europe. *European Business Journal*, 8(2): 26–31.

Marwick, A. and Lewis, R. (2017). Media manipulation and disinformation online. *Data & Society Research Institute*. Available at: https://datasociety.net/pubs/oh/DataAndSociety_MediaManipulationAnd-DisinformationOnline.pdf.

Moore, M. and Ramsay, G. (eds.) (2017). *UK Media Coverage of the 2016 EU Referendum Campaign*. Technical Report. London: The Policy Institute, King's College London.

Morrison, J. (2016). Break-point for Brexit? How UKIP's image of 'hate' set race discourse reeling back decades. In: Moore, M. and Ramsay, G. (eds.) *UK Media Coverage of the 2016 EU Referendum Campaign*. Technical Report. London: The Policy Institute, King's College London.

North, S., Piwek, L., & Joinson, A. (2021). Battle for Britain: Analyzing events as drivers of political tribalism in Twitter discussions of Brexit. *Policy & Internet*, 13(2): 185–208.

O'Rourke, K. (2016). The lesson from Brexit is that too much market and too little state invites a backlash. *LSE Blog*. Available at: http://eprints.lse.ac.uk/70302/1/blogs.lse.ac.uk-The%20lesson%20from%20Brexit%20is%20that%20too%20much%20market%20and%20too%20little%20state%20invites%20a%20backlash.pdf.

Parnell, T. (2021). Humiliating and dividing the nation in the British pro-Brexit press: A corpus-assisted analysis. *Critical Discourse Studies*: 1–17.

Parnell, T. (2022). 'Tinpot revolutionary agitation': Framing Brexit-related demonstrations in the British Pro-Brexit press. *Critical Approaches to Discourse Analysis Across Disciplines*, 14(1): 45–62.

Policy Institute at King's and Ipsos MORI (2018). *Brexit Misperceptions*. Available at: www.kcl.ac.uk/policy-institute/assets/brexit-misperceptions.pdf.

Reid, A. (2019). Buses and breaking pint: Freedom of expression and the 'Brexit' campaign. *Ethical Theory and Moral Practice*, 22: 623–637.

Rose, J. (2017). Brexit, Trump and post-truth politics. *Public Integrity*, 19(6): 555–558.

Shipman, T. (2017). *All Out War: The Full Story of Brexit* (revised ed.). London: William Collins.

Stanyer, J. (2007). *Modern Political Communications: Mediated Politics in Uncertain Terms*. Cambridge: Polity.

Swales, K. (2016). *Understanding the Leave Vote*. London: NatCen Social Research. Available at: http://natcen.ac.uk/media/1319222/natcen_brexplanations-report-final-web2.pdf.

Trithara, D. (2020). Securitizing disinformation: The case of westminster's digital, culture, media and sport committee. *Democracy and Security*: 1–28.

Usherwood, S. (2013). The power of Euromyths shows that there needs to be a more substantial effort to change the debate on the EU. *European Politics and Policy at LSE*. Available at: http://eprints.lse.ac.uk/49153/1/__Libfile_repository_Content_LSE%20EUROPP_2013_February%202013_TO_DO_blogs.lse.ac.uk-The_power_of_Euromyths_shows_that_there_needs_to_be_a_more_substantial_effort_to_change_the_debate_on.pdf.

Vote Leave (2016). *Why Should I Vote Leave*. Available at: www.voteleavetakecontrol.org/why_vote_leave.html.

Wardle, C. and Derakhshan, H. (2017). Information disorder: Toward an interdisciplinary framework for research and policymaking. *Council of Europe Report*, 27.

Whatukthinks (2016). *Are Politicians from Both the Leave and Remain Campaign Mostly Telling Truth or Lies?*. Available at: https://whatukthinks.org/eu/questions/8070/.

Wincott, D. (2019). Brexit and the state of the United Kingdom. In: Diamond, P., Nedergaard, P. and Rosamond, B. (eds.) *The Routledge Handbook of the Politics of Brexit*. London: Routledge, pp. 15–26.

Zappettini, F. (2019). The Brexit referendum: How trade and immigration in the discourses of the official campaigns have legitimised a toxic (inter)national logic. *Critical Discourse Studies*, 16(4): 403–419.

13

NEW DOGS, OLD TRICKS. A CORPUS-ASSISTED STUDY OF THE "ART" OF DELEGITIMISATION IN MODERN SPOKEN POLITICAL DISCOURSE

Alison Duguid and Alan Partington

1   Introduction: delegitimising an opponent's *ethos* or *face*

Delegitimisation can be defined as "[t]he action or process of treating someone as not having legal or moral authority" (Macmillan Dictionary online 2021). Delegitimisation in the field of politics, usually performed through the employment of various argumentative strategies can be defined as "the attempt to discredit the right or ability of an opponent to make a certain claim or argument or to hold a certain power" (Partington and Taylor 2018: 76). It is the tactic used to discourage people from being vaccinated against the COVID-19 pandemic, and it lies behind the label of climate "denier" (with the obvious echo of "Holocaust denier") or "feminazi" or "mansplaining" or "remoaner".[1] It is a call to ignore information and to avoid the need to examine any counter-argument or inconvenient data. By delegitimising the sources of information, denying its validity in a number of ways, the path to disinformation is made smooth.

The practise of attempted delegitimisation is as old as all attempts at persuasion in the public arena; indeed, it is strongly advocated by Aristotle in his major work on *Rhetoric* (2012). His first overarching categorisation of the skills required of any public orator, his "three Parts" of rhetoric, are the abilities to appeal to *logos* (reason), to *pathos* (the emotions), and to project a positive *ethos* (a public character or *persona*) (*Rhetoric* I.ii. 3–6). By "public orator" we can intend an individual not necessarily of intimate acquaintance with their audience, which would include politicians, lawyers, and *epideictic* speakers, that is, orators of "praise" and "blame", which today we might identify for instance in advertising and press-release copy-writers, and even obituary writers and funeral speakers.

The greatest of these three Parts is *ethos*, argues Aristotle, for (to paraphrase St. Paul, *Corinthians*) if you cannot project positive *ethos*, you may speak with the soundest of reason and the sincerest of emotions, but it profits you nothing. However, in practice, in most attempted acts of political persuasion, appeals to *logos*, *pathos*, and *ethos* are employed in combination. A celebrated example is the opening of Shakespeare's Mark Antony's funeral oration (*Julius Caesar* III: 2) in which the speaker first establishes his *ethos* as an honest, simple Roman speaking to his "fellow countrymen" (see *affective face*),

DOI: 10.4324/9781003224495-16

appeals to reason by recalling Caesar's exploits in enriching Rome – but any appeal to the self-interest of the audience is also an appeal to *pathos* – and appeals directly to pathos by confessing his love for his mentor and questioning why his audience does not love him too. In the meantime, he both establishes Caesar's *ethos* as a faithful servant of the Roman people and insinuates, by repeated irony, that Caesar's enemies have the *ethos* of dishonourable men.

In recent times, a number of linguists have attempted to update the terminology of Aristotle's basic analysis and apply the notions to forms of communication either not envisaged by Aristotle or not yet invented in his day.

The most influential reformulation of Aristotle's *ethos* and its integration into modern sociolinguistics is Goffman's theorising of the presentation of the "self" to others as *performances*, followed by Brown and Levinson's 1987 description of face and face-work theory. Goffman's basic insight is that human social interaction has many of the features of *performance*, not only in the kind of public arenas (politics and law) that interested Aristotle (and interest us in this chapter), but also in more private interactions. We all perform or "play" a number of different roles, adopt a number of *personae*. Brown and Levinson argue that the most important performance task, or face-work as they term it, is the construction and maintenance of an effective *ethos* or face in each situation and, when necessary, to be able to either bolster or attack the face of others.

Partington subdivides *ethos* or face into two separate categories, those of *competence* and *affective* face (2006: 95, 97–8). Competence face is one's image as well-informed, an expert, in control and authoritative. Affective face is one's image as likeable, good-humoured, normal, "one of us". However, one problem that politicians have is that the two kinds of face are not fully compatible; it is not always possible to project an image of authority and expertise at the same time as one of a normal, easy-going person. It is a political skill to know when to prioritise one over the other in front of an audience. And of course, in actual practise, many accusations attack both kinds of face. In terms of the theme of this volume, for instance, allegations of lying or spreading disinformation can attack both someone's competence face (their information is unreliable) as well as their affective face (they are unlikeable cheats).

Another vital strand in this research is evaluation theory and practice (Hunston and Thompson 2000). Evaluation, in its briefest definition, is "the indication of whether the speaker thinks that something is good or bad" (Thompson 1996: 65), and of course, "good" and "bad" can come in an infinite variety of ways. Partington, Duguid and Taylor (2013: 45–46) argue that evaluating is a basic human (even animal) instinct, and it is also fundamental to persuasion, the process of getting others to share one's evaluations. *Ethos*, or face-work, and evaluation are thus used in unison. In the political sphere a speaker will work at projecting an evaluatively positive face and stating or insinuating that their opponents is negative in some way. A recent example is the UK Labour Party's 2019 General Election slogan "For the many, not the few". Like much political language, this is not principally a statement of *logos* (most slogans provide no evidence), it is to a degree an emotional appeal, but it is principally a projection of a positive *ethos* for the Labour party and a negative one for its opponents, thus an attempted delegitimisation of their political interests and intentions. The resurrection of Aristotle's notion of *ethos* is useful in our interpretation because it is clear how such a slogan itself rests upon a set of unspoken positive *ethical* values (or evaluations) about equality and social justice. Not dissimilar is US Senator Sanders 2016 Democratic Primaries slogan "Not for Sale", projecting positively evaluated face and ethical values of honesty and incorruptibility, meanwhile delegitimising his opponent (Hillary Clinton) by insinuating opposite ethical evaluations of her. When candidate Donald Trump tweeted repeatedly about the *fake*, *dishonest*, etc. liberal media (Napoletano and Aiezza 2018), he was attacking their *logos*, their truth-content, but at the same time undermining their *ethos*, their right to have a central voice in the public arena.[2]

This chapter presents an analysis of instances of attempted delegitimisations of an opponent in a set of corpora of interactive spoken discourse, namely, recent Chinese Foreign Affairs Ministry press briefings, in which a professional spokesperson (or "podium") responds to questions from journalists relating to foreign policy. The present authors had already noted in earlier studies that aggressive face-attacks and attempts at delegitimising a questioner and/or their question were common in briefings discourse (Marakhovskaiia and Partington 2019; Partington and Duguid 2021), diverting attention from the information requested to the status of the source of that information. We shall see that the delegitimisation often includes the accusation of disinformation, fake news, or lying, where an inquiry triggers assertions about groundless or baseless information but also that it is frequently a reaction to a question on a topic which is the site of disinformation.[3]

In the concluding section we consider the ethics of *ethos*; are there limits to acceptable delegitimisation in political arenas, and if so, what might they be?

2   Corpora

A corpus approach is useful in analysing such an issue as it allows us, through quantitative data, to identify repeated instances of lexical patterns in a discourse type and through qualitative analysis these patterns can be identified as part of a communicative strategy. Salient individual lexical items or grammatical structures can be grouped into sets which reveal particular language behaviours. A list of lexical items can together form part of a group of features which, in turn, are related to a particular linguistic phenomenon such as face-threatening or face-bolstering acts, or to features of modality which relate to subjective attitudes. The regularities are identified by comparison and the pinpointing of salience through keyness analysis, which can reveal salient speech acts such as criticism or praise. In such cases, delegitimisation can be seen as both an aggressive and a defensive technique for dealing with undesirable information in political discourse. Comparison and contrast are important ways of highlighting lexical patterns, so more than one corpus will be employed in this study.

The main corpora used in this analysis are three corpora of press briefings of the Chinese Ministry for Foreign Affairs (CMFA), dating from 2016 (CMFA-16), 2018 (CMFA-18), and 2020 (CMFA-20). The official transcriptions of every briefing in each of these years was downloaded manually from the CMFA's website. The briefings questions from the Chinese press are posed in (Mandarin) Chinese, and translations are made available in several languages, including English, French, Russian, and Arabic, all of which are posted on the CMFA site. The spokesperson generally responds in Chinese with the occasional comment in English when appropriate (e.g. a quotation or the reading of a short text in English).

CMFA-16 consists of 236 briefings, comprising 270,000 word tokens. CMFA-18 consists of 223 briefings comprising 359,226 tokens. CMFA-20 contains 230 briefings comprising 575,992 tokens. One novelty of the 2020 data is the identification of the news organisation asking the questions (e.g. Reuters, CCTV). Having datasets from three different time periods allows us to track changes in topic and perhaps also kinds of face-work.

Further examples of delegimisation, which we examine later, were found in a corpus of speeches by and interviews with Donald Trump (interviews, speeches, and tweets between 2015 to 2017, 68 texts, comprising 387,879 tokens; the tweets were all contained in one file containing 146,272 tokens).

3 Delegitimisation strategies in Chinese Ministry of Foreign Affairs press briefings

3.1 CMFA briefings in 2016: national delegitimisation

In the first corpus-assisted research on CMFA briefings, Marakhovskaiia and Partington (2019) looked at ways in which the spokespersons of the CMFA treated the *ethos* or face of other national actors or organisations over the course of 2016, using the English language transcripts on CMFA website. The main methodology employed was the compilation of frequency lists of one- to five-word n-grams and then concordancing items with negative evaluation likely to be site of a delegitimisation strategy. They uncovered a number of instances of open delegitimisation, including the following rebuke (our emphasis):

(1) Q: The New York-based Human Rights Watch issued a report on human rights in Tibet on May 22, bashing the Chinese government's fiercer oppression in Tibet. Do you have any comment?

Podium: I have **no comment on** this report released by the **so-called** human rights organization. How many of them have been to China, Tibet particularly? What do they know about the real life in Tibet? We hope they would take an objective and fair look at China.

The podium delegitimises the competence face of HRW as lacking knowledge and objectivity. A refusal to comment is a common strategy of podiums; it attacks not only the *logos* – the contents, the information, of the report, which are, in fact ignored – but the *ethos* of those who produced it, as not worthy of a reply.

Over 2016 the podium uses "I . . .", "we . . .", and "the Chinese side" *has/have no comment on* eight occasions, five times in 2018, and six times in 2020 (see next section). As mentioned, ignoring or purporting to ignore a question can both delegitimise the question and be a considerable face-threat to the source of the question (the journalist is sometimes the source but often the vehicle rather than the party responsible for the question).

The epithet *so-called* is a sort of "all-purpose" delegitimiser; it attempts to dismiss the *ethos* or standing of whoever or whatever it is applied to. It is used by the podium 70 times in CFMA-16, often preceding items in distancing quotation marks, for example, "so-called 'diplomatic ties' with Taiwan", "the so-called 'freedom of the press'". It occurs 82 times in the 2018, 100 times in the 2019, and 118 in the 2020. Among the frequent clusters we find *Taiwan and diplomatic ties, freedom of the press, human rights issue, Hong Kong autonomy, debt trap*. Here is a further instance:

(2) Q: When meeting with the Dalai Lama in the White House, US President Barack Obama said that he supported Tibet in protecting its own religion and culture. What's your comment?

Podium: As I pointed out yesterday, Tibetan affairs fall entirely within China's domestic affairs which brook no foreign interference. The 14th Dalai Lama is not a pure religious figure, but a political exile that has long been engaged in anti-China separatist campaigns under the cloak of religion. The **so-called "middle path"** he peddles boils down to "independence of Tibet". The US's meddling with China's domestic affairs will inevitably inflict harm on bilateral mutual trust and cooperation.

China projects its own negative-face claims by insisting that "China's domestic affairs" must be free from "foreign interference". It attacks the *ethos* or face of the Dalai Lama as a "political exile" engaged in "anti-China separatist campaigns". Note too how the term "independence", which normally has a much more positive evaluative prosody than "separatist" is placed in distancing quotes. By maintaining that the Dalai Lama engages in politics "under the cloak of religion", the podium is accusing him of hypocrisy and even of plotting against China, a serious attack on his affective face. The item *peddles* has a highly negative evaluative prosody (Partington 1998: 70–73). Finally, the US's positive face is criticised in the accusation of *meddling* (eight occurrences in CFMA-16, see also Section 3.4); others accused of *meddling* include the UK, the G7, and more vaguely, "countries not directly concerned". The defence of China's face, the *pathos* appeal to Chinese patriotism, and the frequent emotional attacks on foreign groups of various sorts, is a thread which runs throughout all three of our CMFA corpora.

Not surprisingly, many allegations emanating from official US sources were treated to detailed delegitimisation. It was also noticeable that many of the journalists' questions were related to the topic of China's relations with what we might call its "near neighbours", see Table 13.1.

Analysing the mentions of *Japan* revealed a very particular strategy of delegitimisation, which the authors termed "history-shaming". The two countries are locked in several current territorial and maritime disputes, but the CMFA-16 podium frequently resorts to delegitimising Japan itself with constant reference to Japan's invasions of China in the 1930s and 1940s. Japan is mentioned repeatedly in conjunction with items such as Japanese "war crimes" (18), Japan's "war of aggression" (10), China's "war of resistance" (4), the "Nanjing massacre" of 1937 "8 occurrences), "Japanese militarism" (12):

(3) Podium: Today marks the 75th anniversary of Japan's sneak raid on the Pearl Harbor and the breakout of the Pacific War. That war of aggression waged by the Japanese militarists inflicted grave sufferings on people in regional countries, those in the Asian victimized countries in particular. The international community keeps watching whether Japan can view that part of history in a sincere and accurate way.

On China's part, we believe that upholding international justice and the international order established following WWII is very important. What is also important is that Japan show a right attitude toward history and the crimes against humanity committed by Japanese militarists and take concrete actions to win the trust of people in China and other victimized countries of Asia.

Japan's national affective face is attacked with open criticism and even insult "sneak raid" (*sneak* has a worse evaluation than, say, *surprise*), "war of aggression", "Japanese militarists", "crimes against humanity", and so on. Japan's face is further pressured by the demand that Japan show "a right attitude" (presumably of contrition) towards their crimes.[4] The podium enhances China's

Table 13.1 The number of mentions of China's neighbours in the full corpus of briefings Chinese Foreign Affairs, 2016

China's Neighbours Mentioned in the DFA Corpus	No of Mentions
Democratic People's Republic of Korea (North Korea)	375
Republic of Korea (South Korea)	301
Taiwan	295
Tibet (Dalai Lama)	45 (32)
Hong Kong	91
Japan	304

ethos by claiming the mantle of the upholders of international justice and order. It reinforces this face-claim further by claiming to speak for "the international community". From the evidence of example (3) and others, it can be assumed that the real strategic purpose of such history-shaming is – and "whaboutery" – to delegitimise Japan's current territorial and maritime claims.

3.2   Keyness and self-presentation in 2018

Key items are items which are identified by the Wordsmith software as frequent in one corpus with respect to the other. The exploration of key items provides a useful way of characterising certain aspects of a collection of texts, for example, frequent topics, phraseologies, and even level of formality. Wordsmith tools (Version 7; Scott 2016) provides us with a great deal of potentially interesting data with three alternative measurements, namely, log likelihood, log ratio, and a BIC score, measuring respectively: keyness in terms of statistical significance, effect size, and trustworthiness of the comparison. Items were selected for examination when salient on all three measurements. Such keyword comparison provides us with some fairly clear differences between the various corpora.

In a previous study (on the importance on studying what is *absent* from discourse), Partington and Duguid (2021) performed a contrastive study of the press briefings held at the Chinese Foreign Affairs Ministry (the previously mentioned CMFA-18), and at the US State Department (USSD-18), the US foreign affairs ministry, for the year 2018 using transcripts downloaded from the relative official websites. The various US or Chinese podium's words are interpreted by the press as government policy, and are also frequently interpreted by foreign administrations as official US or Chinese policy.

A number of key items were found in the PRC data, which were either entirely or almost entirely absent from the USSD data. All of these items express positive evaluation, and all represent China's political actions in a form of self-promotion or self-legitimisation; one set of CMFA-18 key items share the semantic feature "communality", sometimes marked morphologically by the prefixes *co-* and *con-* (e.g. *cooperation, consensus, concerted, cooperative, community, conference, consultation, consultations, shared, inclusive, inclusiveness, synergy*), all highlighting the value of cooperation and joint action, seen as *beneficial, fruitful, positive*, and *friendly*, expressing aspirations about desired outcomes or praise (usually self-praise by the CMFA) for actions taken and how they were taken. We find again frequent strong *pathos* appeals to Chinese patriotism.

It was noticeable, however, that there were relatively few items of clearly negative evaluation, that is, possible sites of delegitimisation, in the CMFA-18 keywords. It is interesting, therefore, to examine exactly what is disapproved of and for what the CMFA was prepared to reprove *others*. We found a set of items related to certain speech acts (characterised by them as *accusations)* and two terms of evaluation (*groundless and irresponsible)* which were employed to rebut accusations made about Chinese foreign policy, thus delegitimising remarks the CMFA disapprove of, remarks perceived as attacks on China's collective competence or affective face. In this case the grounds of the rebuttal are that the speech acts were without foundation, and thus basically disinformation, or that whatever the *logos* or truth-value, the possible deleterious effects of such speech acts made them reprehensible.

3.3   2020, a year of China-related sensitivities

Since 2018, a series of events and shifts in the geopolitical situation (including the COVID-19 pandemic and the question of its origins, conflicts over Hong Kong and Taiwan, events in the South China Sea, controversy surrounding the Chinese Belt and Road strategy, the Huawei issue, the continuing trade tensions with the US and others and diplomatic tensions with Australia) have exercised negative effects on the relationship between the PRC and several other foreign powers. We therefore decided to examine the CMFA press briefings throughout 2020 to ascertain whether the relationship between the questioners and the podium had become more confrontational and whether the podiums were more aggressive or defensive, less or more liable to self-congratulate, and especially, if accusations against the ruling Chinese Communist Party were made, what forms of delegitimisation of such accusations were employed by podiums, noting where they relate to forms of disinformation.

In order to test whether there are repeated regularities of form which could highlight the ways in which delegitimisation takes place in this institutional discourse type, we first applied the methodology of examining the keyword lists for CMFA-20 compared with CMFA-18 and indeed did find greater evidence of negative evaluation and attacks on the national face and *ethos* of other countries, mainly the US, but also Australia and Canada. As an illocutionary act, delegitimisation is discernible as the intent to discredit both the words, actions, and reputations of other protagonists, through criticism and disapproval, contradiction and challenge, to rebut accusations and delegitimise remarks the speakers disapprove of, and to respond to a perceived face-threat with a counter face-threat.

In Section 3.1 we noted the podium's use of *I have no comment on* to dismiss a question topic. It was used five times in 2018, and six times in 2020, including the following, in which both the competence (they are irrational) and affective (they are unjust and China-phobic) faces of "some politicians in Australia" are severely attacked:

(4) Zhao Lijian: We noted relevant reports and have **no comment** on Australia's domestic affairs. I want to point out that for a while, some politicians in Australia seem to be suffering from **paranoia**, dominated by **China-phobia** and conjectures to the extent of **losing all sense of rationality** and justice. Under the guise of "values", they often make **groundless accusations** against China in domestic politics, stigmatize and demonize normal personnel exchanges and cooperation with China, and poison the atmosphere of bilateral relations. This is totally unconstructive and **irresponsible**. China is firmly opposed to this. (29/06/2020)

Perhaps more aggressive still is the podium declaring he will not even *waste* his time considering a question about an interview with US secretary of state Pompeo:

(5) Zhao Lijian: This US politician has been a **lying blabbermouth**. It's **a waste of time** to comment on his fabrications.

It may be noted that *groundless accusations* and *lying* are related to the concept of disinformation. Figure 13.1 is a collection of ways in which the podium in the CMFA-20 refuses to "waste time" on answering a question.

The aggressive process through which language is used to invalidate the opponents' arguments and authority is a particularly evident strategy of delegitimisation and a deliberate strategy of rebuttal.

day-to-day work to spread lies about China. I don't think more time shall be wasted today to refute his meaningless lies. We should start our weekend i
of bias and capable of nothing but churning out inflammatory lies. I see no point in wasting my breath on refuting its nonsense. Global Times: Former Florida s
facts and the common understanding of the international community. Every minute wasted on smearing and complaining would be better spent on enhancing (
are just groundless and absurd. The answer, I believe, is self-evident. Let's not waste our time on this. AFP: Some reports say that the China-India-Russia
, smears and blame games cannot make up for lost time. More lies will only waste more time and lead to more lives lost. A word of advice to these politi
Republic has just published a press release for "disinfection". We don't want to waste more time on refuting Pompeo's lies. Perhaps some of you can do n
Lijian: I refuted this politician's comments multiple times last week. I don't want to waste our time on him again today. BBC: A question on the BNO passports
this article. It's just a patchwork of distorted pieces with faulty logic. I don't want to waste too much time refuting it. By re-posting such an article on their officia
the blame to others while neglecting serious problems at home. We hope he will waste the valuable time no more. AFP: Protesters continue demonstrations

Figure 13.1 Concordance list of *waste** in CMFA-20

3.4 Keyness and an escalation of delegitimisation in 2020

Given the events of 2020, it is unsurprising that the top keywords for 2020 (using CMFA-18 as the reference corpus) are pandemic-related, but a further series of salient items, a set of negative evaluations, appear in the keywords list. On examination, they can all be seen to participate in a set of phraseologies used to delegitimise the bearers of criticism. For the most part they consist of labelling strategies in which critical speech acts are characterised in such a way as to discredit them, rather than respond to or engage with them.

This is an attack strategy in which the criticism is undermined on a number of grounds: the grounds of lack of legitimacy or authoritativeness, for example, in the frequently occurring item *rumours*; there is also a substantial number of accusations of systematic unfairness and prejudice, in the use of items, for example, *bias, ideological, stigmatization, stigmatize, discriminatory, hypocrisy, discrimination*; in addition, there are accusations which revolve around an abuse of power, for example, *bullying, attacking, abusing, interfering*, and a set which implies hidden or hostile intentions: *manipulation, politicizing, pretext, spreading, spread, smearing, smear, smears*. Finally, criticism is dismissed on the grounds of a lack of veracity (thus accusing the accusers of dishonesty, undermining as previously noted, both their *logos* and *ethos* and both their competence and affective faces), for example, *lie, lies, disinformation*. Any one of these parameters can be combined with any of the others, each key item appearing alongside others in the co-text, occurring in a minimum of 26 and a maximum of 96 texts. Many more which come under the same categories occur with some frequency in the wordlists (again with the criterion of appearing in at least 5% of texts).

The phrases exemplify the line which the CMFA has decided to take in the face of criticism, the communication strategy to adopt when the administration is perceived as being under attack; even a mild question on a sensitive topic can provoke this response strategy.

We might hypothesise that the increase in the use of such phraseologies used as delegitimisers from 2018 to 2020 is related to the increase in the number of sensitive topics. In the 2018 corpus, 25% of these items were completely absent, another 25% were found only once.

3.5 The main strategies

The following categories are characterisations of the main grounds for the negative evaluations with a delegitimising purpose. Examples are given of the items in the keywords list and of further items found in the wordlist:

A   Delegitimisation through **assertions of bad intentions, intentions to wound for malicious purposes**. The definition of *smear*, for instance, is "**to try to** damage someone's reputation by telling lies" (Macmillan's online dictionary).

   Among the keywords we found: *smear, smearing, hypocrisy, pretext*.
   The following were present in the frequency wordlist: *malicious, maliciously, undermining, denigrate, denigration, slander, slanders, hypocritical*.

B   Delegitimisation through **accusations of unfairness or bias**.

   Among the keywords we found: *discrimination, bias, discriminatory, ideological, stigamtization*.
   The following were present in the wordlist: *distorted, distortion, hostility, hype-up*.

C   Delegitimisation through **accusation of abuse of power, of interference** – the strong preying on the weak, attacking negative face: that one's freedom of action and freedom from imposition be respected (Brown and Levinson 1987: 129–130) freedom of movement, territory, or interests:

Among the keywords we found: *bullying, attacking, abusing, interfering.*
The item *meddling* was present in the wordlist.

The bullying accusation is interesting as it suggests a position of weakness, which is hardly logically objective. China has a growing economy, a large territory and population, great technological and military capabilities, and yet it uses a word associated with the small and weak. Bullying is defined as behaviour that "frightens or hurts someone smaller or weaker" (Macmillan's online dictionary). This strategy is exemplified by the "history-shaming" of Japan as the regional bully (harking back to the 1930s). It is designed to appeal to emotions, thus delegitimising some alleged bully on the grounds of both *pathos* and *ethos*.

D Delegitimisation through **questioning the authoritativeness of the proposition,** questionable right to speak, a very direct attack on *ethos*, that is, the right to have any voice:

Rumor, in the keywords and *rumors* in the wordlist.

E Delegitimisation through **accusations of falsehood**. The items have "lack of veracity" in their inherent meaning.

Among the keywords we found: *disinformation, lies, lie, erroneous.*
The wordlists contained the following: *misrepresenting, fabricating, falsely, fake, wrong.*

F Delegitimisation by **attacks on opponents' alleged personal characteristics** proposed in terms of personal "defects". These can range from their sex, height, colouring, their religion, and nothing whatsoever to do with their ability or politics, which sometimes could even be construed as discrimination against minorities (see Section 4.2).

The label *fake news*, famously associated with Donald Trump, falls within category E. We might see it as another "all-purpose" delegitimiser, an accusation of disinformation, used to refute all manner of unfavourable comments. It is used 24 times by the CMFA in 2020, compared to only 7 occurrences in CMFA-18, and none in CMFA-16 (see Figure 13.2 *fake*).

and untenable accusations exemplify disinformation **and fake news.** The State Council Information Office of t
. Could you confirm that? Wang Wenbin: It's nothing **but fake news** aimed to smear China, which only indicat
and the AU Commission chairperson. It is nothing **but fake news** cooked by Western media and has long
. What we oppose is ideological bias towards **China, fake news** in the name of press freedom, and violati
of the press, cherish their credibility and refrain from **citing fake news** or made-up stories. Second, on Novemb
: For quite some time Pompeo has been busy **concocting fake news** to vilify China and drive a wedge betweer
Pompeo have been spreading fallacies on Xinjiang, **creating "fake news",** wantonly criticizing China's Xinjiang p
have the basic sense to make proper judgments and **discern fake news.** It is dreadful and highly dangerous to bel
allegation of "China bugging the AU headquarters" **is fake news** 100 percent, and has been rejected by th
that the Japanese government has openly stated that this **is fake news** and reiterated its commitment to the 197:
this? Wang Wenbin: It was groundless rumor and **malicious fake news.** If you trace the European reports to their
after another on Xinjiang. They cooked up all kinds **of fake news** from "re-education camps" to "forced lab
Taiwan leader Tsai Ing-wen were not true at all, a piece **of fake news** that was previously released by Taiwan's
in Russia's Far East Region has long been **proven fake news.** It is irresponsible for certain media to us
I said is a principle. Any country and individual should **reject fake news.** This is something indisputable. Q: I feel
relevant social media platforms 621 times in 2019 to **remove fake news** and unverified information targeting the H
to defeat the COVID-19 pandemic. By dispelling **rumors, fake news,** and messages of hate and division, the I
Xinjiang before, but he seems to be blindfolded by **some fake news** and his judgment was clouded by falsehc
be able to see the facts as they are and jointly reject **such fake news.** AFP: The Cambodian King Norodom Sih
so-called "sources". The sole purpose of fabricating **such fake news** is to sabotage the good cooperation betw
to Beijing earlier. However, an Italian journalist found it **was fake news** after investigation. The author of the artic
and her son did not die in a Urumqi hospital. So that **was fake news.** And yet Mihrigul was brought to a US Se

Figure 13.2 Concordance list of *fake news* in CMFA 2020

Given that many of these lexical items are polysemous, some of them could be placed in more than one category. For example, *rumour*, is defined by Macmillan's online dictionary as "unofficial information that may or may not be true" so that it falls into both category D and category E. The main distinction being lack of authoritativeness (the part highlighted by Macmillan's use of "unofficial"). Similarly, *pretext* (defined as "a reason you pretend to have in order to hide your real reason or intention" contains elements of categories A, D, and E. Disinformation (false information that is intended to make people believe something which is not true) contains elements of categories A (i.e. intentions) and E, truth value. However, the strategies are more clearly identifiable when the context is analysed. Here are three sample concordance lines from CMFA-20 to illustrate how the terms can be interwoven (letters in brackets refer to the category).

(6) **Q:** And the second question, the Australian Strategic Policy Institute said China is transferring Uighurs out of vocational education and training centers and into factories to serve as forced labor. Do you have any response to this?

A: As to your second question, what it said is simply **baseless** (D, E). It is just another **fabricated** (A, E) and **biased** (B) accusation on Xinjiang by this institution to show its allegiance to the **anti-China** (B) forces in the US and **smear** (A) China's counter-terrorism and de-radicalization measures in Xinjiang.

(7) **Q:** Secondly, I wanted to talk a little bit about the nature of the people that have been targeted by the U.S. side. The people are basically vice chairpersons of the NPC, which would suggest that the Trump administration is gradually targeting more and more senior Chinese officials with sanctions. I'd like to ask if you have any comment on this trend and how might that be reflected in the countermeasures that China will take?

A: **Anti-China** (B) extremists in the United States, headed by Pompeo, have totally **lost their minds** (D) in their **unscrupulous** (A) political crackdown on China. They cling to the **old Cold War thinking** (D) and **ideological prejudice** (B), look at China's development and China-US relations from the perspective of zero-sum game, regard China as an opponent or even an enemy, and **attack** (C) the system and path chosen by the Chinese people. As for their true motive, in fact, many international media have already seen it through, and they do make a point in commenting that this is "last-day madness". They seek to consolidate their legacy of containing China and leave little wriggle room for the new administration to adjust it in the future. This wrong practice seriously **tramples on** (C) the basic norms of international relations, **harms the interests** (C) of the Chinese side

(8) Q: According to reports, White House Trade and Manufacturing Policy Director Peter Navarro said in a recent interview that China produced the coronavirus in a biological lab and used it as a weapon. He added, "They deliberately allowed Chinese nationals to come to the United States, Italy, and everywhere in between, who were infected, while they were locking down their own transportation network". Do you have any comment?

A: Mr. Navarro is a habitual **liar** (E) and **rumor-monger** (D) who has been **spreading a "political virus"** (A) to **stigmatize** (B) China under the **pretext** (A) of the pandemic.

We should note that the items *spread* and *spreading* used literally refer to the pandemic, but in 20% of the former and for 41% of the occurrences of the latter, the terms are used metaphorically to label criticism; both *rumors* and *disinformation* are collocates of *spread* and *spreading*, and sometimes the metaphor is made explicit, as in example 8. The term *disinformation* itself occurs 111 times in the 2020 corpus (as opposed to 6 in the 2019 corpus) in 46 different briefing texts. Among the collocates we find *China, China's Russia, pandemic, coronavirus, EU, US, Xinjiang, Chinese, Iran.*

We might also add that the delegitimisation is frequently enhanced with other pragmatic moves, in particular "pushback", resistance or opposition as a response, in which accusations are turned back on the accuser (as, for instance in example [1], where Human Rights Watch is accused of ignorance, and example [4] where "Australia" is accused of Sinophobia and example [10] where the US is accused of genocide). Another element which often accompanies a delegitimising strategy is that of a threat of negative repercussions and retaliation.

(9) The US side should immediately redress its mistakes, stop its **political discrimination** and **unjustified suppression** against Chinese media and journalists, and guarantee that the safety, property, press freedom, and other legitimate rights and interests of these Chinese journalists will not be **violated** and their normal reporting activities not affected. **If the US refuses to correct its course and insists on taking more wrong steps, China is faced with no other choice but doing what is necessary and legitimate to safeguard its rights and interests.**

The same topics recur so that it becomes clear, over the year, which are the trigger areas of questioning with consequent delegitimisation of the question or the source responsible for the question. There are some indications as to the most contested areas: the key item *interference*, an indication that the CMFA feels their negative face has been threatened, is a common collocate of *Hong Kong*, as are *interfering* and *meddling*. *Xinjiang* cooccurs frequently with *pretext*. As so often in CADS, quantitative findings can indicate where to look for the qualitative details.

As the US Secretary of State in 2020, Mr Pompeo's name comes up frequently and is a key item. He comes in for a great deal of delegitimisation since it is his comments which are the base of the journalists' questions and which provoke numerous distinctly undiplomatic responses. Accusing a diplomatic counterpart of *evil intentions, hysteria, lying, cheating, stealing, malign intent, ugly and malicious intentions* is not understated diplomatic language (see Figure 13.3). Both his competence face and his affective face are attacked. He is delegitimised

placed on the wrong thing, I believe they are now walking on an erroneous and dangerous path. Pompeo is ambitious but as a Chinese saying goes, "it is important to know one's ow undermine China-US relations and normal exchanges and cooperation. The evil intentions of Pompeo and others have been seen through by the world since long ago, and their re response in light of the development of the situation. China Daily: US Secretary of State Mike Pompeo continued to make groundless accusations against China during his press . Do you have any comment? Hua Chunying: In disregard of basic facts and moral integrity, Pompeo, as a habitual liar, has tried every possible means to smear China day after d marine debris and over-fishing. Do you have a comment on this? Zhao Lijian: The remarks of Pompeo disregard facts and confuse right and wrong. It was a vicious attempt to mis rejected by insightful people from all communities in the US. Once again we urge the like of Pompeo to discard Cold War mentality and ideological bias, respect facts, stop fabric to Pakistan.â€ Do you have any comment? Zhao Lijian: Some US politicians, especially Mr. Pompeo, are using every possible occasion to smear China. China enjoys traditional China. China enjoys traditional friendly relations with Laos, Montenegro and Pakistan, so Mr. Pompeo, why not stop wasting energy? Today, I would like to take Laos as an examp . What is China's response? Zhao Lijian: Out of ideological prejudice and political self-interest, Pompeo has repeatedly stigmatized and discredited China, exaggerated the so-calle wanton accusations against other countries? Out of ideological bias and political expediency, Pompeo has repeatedly slandered and smeared China, even endorsing a cult like Fa has repeatedly slandered and smeared China, even endorsing a cult like Falun Gong. We urge Pompeo to respect the facts and stop fabricating all kinds of China-related lies. Other people. Out of ideological bias and political expediency, Some U.S. politicians, such as Pompeo, deliberately undermined the cultural and educational exchanges and coop the Chinese government on these issues. Do you have any comment on this? Zhao Lijian: Pompeo is proud of "lying, cheating and stealing". We urge Pompeo and his like to respect to Pakistan.â€ Do you have any comment? Zhao Lijian: Some US politicians, especially Mr. Pompeo, are using every possible occasion to smear China. China enjoys traditional all kinds of lie to viciously attack the CPC, hype up ideological confrontation. The hysteria of Pompeo and his like will only rally the Chinese people's greater support for the CPC a you have any response to this? Zhao Lijian: For some time, several U.S. politicians including Pompeo has been making all kinds of lie to viciously attack the CPC, hype up ideolog . Such regressive behavior is bound to be rejected by both peoples and history. We urge Pompeo and his like to stop concocting lies to undermine China-US relations and stop , above-board and beyond reproach. By making an issue out of China's United Front work, Pompeo and Pottinger are trying to discredit China's political system and disrupt nor "United Front work" to infiltrate other countries. Do you have any comment? Wang Wenbin: Pompeo and Pottinger's remarks, filled with distortion of facts, are malicious slander on its own presumption and only reveals the sinister thinking and malign intent of the likes of Pompeo. Third, the MOU signed by the two sides was proposed by the United States against Muslims in the American society. Out of ideological bias and selfish political agenda, Pompeo and his like are taking religious freedom as a pretext to slander other countri affairs. It is an unpopular move that is denounced by the international community. We urge Pompeo to stop fabricating clumsy lies on China and stop meddling in China's interna . Lying, cheating and slandering will never stand a chance of stopping the wheel of the history. Pompeo and his likes will go down in history with reputation shattered and credibility s China and the Communist Party of China. What is China's comment on this? Wang Wenbin: Pompeo has been using his endless political lies to smear and attack China, so typic the Taiwan Strait. His ugly and malicious intentions have been laid bare for all to despise. Pompeo should know that China will resolutely fight back against all attempts that un of it very clearly. Over a period of time, anti-China extremists in the United States, headed by Pompeo, have totally lost their minds in their unscrupulous political crackdown on Ch States has become increasingly unpopular as a result of misguided foreign policies led by Pompeo and his likes. According to a recent survey by the European Council on Fore the threat from the Chinese Communist Party. Do you have any comment? Wang Wenbin: Pompeo is a habitual liar who respects no facts and wantonly smears China on every

Figure 13.3 Concordance list of *Pompeo* in CMFA 2020

at all three of Aristotle's ground, of *logos* – his arguments are flawed – of *pathos* – he is full of evil anti-China intent and the podium appeals to Chinese patriotism – and of *ethos* – he has no right to a voice on China's affairs.

These keywords and phrases, then, form the core of a number of illocutionary acts. Here is a limited list of the most frequent illocutionary acts which the key items perform. The first five exemplify a variety of **accusations**:

- You have hostile intentions, so any criticisms are illegitimate (see example 10, 13).
- You are biased, so your criticisms are unfair and thus illegitimate (see example 11, 13).
- You are exercising power in an abusive way in affairs in which you have no legitimate rights (see examples (11, 14).
- The authority and authoritativeness of your criticisms are dubious and thus illegitimate (see example 10, 13).
- Your criticisms are illegitimate because they are simply untrue (See example 11, 13, 14).

While the last three comprise a diversionary tactic which is often called "whataboutery",[5] a warning, and lastly a direct threat:

- Other countries do the same thing or worse and so do you, so why pick on us? (see example 10, and note the history-shaming).
- Your lies will be found out (see example 12, 13).
- If you don't stop, we will have to retaliate (see example 14).

(10) We have repeatedly stated China's position on issues relating to Xinjiang. The **so-called** "genocide" is a **rumor** deli**berately started** by some **anti-China** forces and a **farce** to **discredit China**. As a matter of fact, from 2010 to 2018, the Uyghur population in Xinjiang grew from 10.17 million to 12.72 million, an increase of 2.55 million or 25 percent, higher than the 14 percent for the whole population in Xinjiang, and much higher than the 2 percent for the Han population. So I wonder what evidence the Senators have to back their genocide allegation? **What we do see is that the US government slashed the population of Native Americans from 5 million to 250,000 by its large-scale exiling, assimilating and killing policies. Isn't that genocide?**

(11) We urge certain U.S. politicians to respect facts and stop **weaving lies** and **interfering** in China's internal affairs with Xinjiang as a **pretext**.

(12) The Chinese people cannot be beaten down. China doesn't provoke troubles, but we never flinch when trouble comes our way. I'd like to remind Pompeo and his like that **anti-Communist** and **anti-China** political **manipulation** is a lost cause. The more they **lie and cheat,** the more people with judgment and sense of justice will see through their **true intention.**

(13) Let me reiterate that China is the biggest **victim** of **disinformation.** China always opposes the **fabrication** and **dissemination of disinformation.** The United Nations and WHO have repeatedly called on all countries to strengthen solidarity and cooperation to combat **disinformation.** We call on the international community to enhance solidarity and coordination, jointly reject **disinformation,** so that those **political viruses** such as **rumors** and **slanders** and the perpetrators and **manipulators behind the scene** will have **no place to hide.**

As for the more frequent use of Twitter by Chinese diplomats, I think it's nothing strange. This is an era of new media. Just as many foreign diplomats and journalists in China use WeChat and Weibo, Chinese diplomats have taken Twitter as a channel and platform to communicate with people in other countries.

Meanwhile, some foreign media and social platforms are fraught with **lies** and **rumors** against China. In the dark and ugly world of **disinformation**, it is necessary for some people, including Chinese diplomats, to speak in a truthful, objective and impartial manner, like striking a match in the dark night to bring some light. **Anyone who is not playing deaf and dumb will be able to see the truth**.

(14) I would like to stress that China has always adhered to an independent foreign policy of peace. Aggressiveness is not our tradition, neither is bending our knee. In the face of hegemony and **bullying**, Mao Zedong once said, "**We will not attack unless we are attacked, if we are attacked, we will certainly counterattack**". China does not provoke trouble, but **will never flinch** when trouble comes their way. We will not yield to coercion and blackmailing. If some people call China's diplomacy "wolf-warrior diplomacy" just because we fight back and speak the truth in the face of **unscrupulous attacks, slanders and denigration**, I don't see any problem in living with that "wolf-warrior" title, as long as we are fighting for China's sovereignty, security and development interests, national dignity and honor, and international fairness and justice.

Essentially there is a defensive and reactive core to these delegitimisations; the CCP presents itself as being above suspicion and more or less untouchable, but it often goes on the back foot on sensitive issues. One of the concerns of the CMFA is to underline the legitimacy of the CCP's actions. We note that for the item *legitimate*, the clusters include many phrases in which the spokespersons assert the legitimacy of their reactions and responses to any attempt to criticise the CCP or to interfere in its sphere of sovereignty (*legitimate and necessary, safeguard the legitimate, necessary response, justified self-defence, justified reaction, legitimate self-defence*); in other words it reacts as if its negative face is being threatened and exhibits considerable concern for its own freedom of action and sovereignty. It does not intend to be held accountable by others and often responds using delegitimising moves.

In essence, press briefings are examples of accountability in action. The CMFA does not brook any questions about these sensitive issues because they are being asked to account for contested actions. On the issue of accountability, it is interesting to note that the Trump presidency interrupted the practice of daily press briefings for almost a year, starting in August 2018. Accusing the media of anti-government bias and spreading "fake news" (yet another example of attempted delegitimisation), it "de-platformed" itself so as not to have to answer awkward questions both in the White House and in the State Department, an especially radical way of avoiding accountability.

4   Concluding remarks

In terms of the framework of this Handbook, delegitimisation is clearly not coterminous with disinformation, but there can be considerable overlap, especially when the attempted act of delegitimisation includes deliberate falsehoods. We have also seen in this chapter that the accusation of spreading falsehoods is one of the most common delegitimising accusations.[6] Indeed, Aristotle even recommended it as a highly effective rhetorical strategy in political discourse.

While the CMFA corpora contain some fairly sophisticated lexis to perform the act of delegitimisation, the Trump corpus mentioned section 2, in comparison, contains many examples of his propensity for very simple legitimising and delegitimising responses, for instance, using *nice* and *nasty*:

(15) Q Mr. President, Melania Trump announced the reopening of the White House Visitors Office. . . . And she does a lot of great work for the country as well. Can you tell us a little bit about what First Lady Melania Trump does for the country?

THE PRESIDENT: Now, that's what I call a **nice** question. That is very **nice**. Who are you with?

A question implying Trump was mishandling the US COVID testing programme (by a CNN reporter) received the following frigid response:

(16) [. . .] instead of asking a **nasty** snarky question like that you should ask a real question.

The question and questioner are both delegitimised; if a question is labelled not real, then the interviewee frees themselves from any obligation to reply. It is a warning to others that disinformation is to be expected from such a questioner.

However, some questions remain.

4.1 *Evidentiality and attribution, giving evidence for one's accusations*

Claims of lying or disinformation are often made without supplying any evidence, which casts a cloud over both their truth-value and their ethical acceptability. In many of the examples previously, speakers *aver* the face-threat, that is, they issue it with their own voice. On other occasions, however, it is *attributed* to another source. In the following, the accuser feels that it is enough to attribute the delegitimisation to a general but unspecified "they":

(17) If this stuff is true about Russia, Ukraine, China, other countries, Iraq – If this is true, then he's a corrupt politician. So don't give me the stuff about how you're this innocent baby. Joe, they're calling you a corrupt politician (Trump 2020).

Whereas, in the following, the competence of both major UK parties is not judged credible by a high status independent third party (the Institute for Fiscal Studies):

(18) The IFS think-tank has looked at both Labour and Conservative [spending] proposals and said neither are credible, how do you respond to that? (Etchingham, journalist 2019)

which makes the face-threatening allegation much more legitimate and harder to dodge. And perhaps the most serious of face-threats is when the delegitimisation is presented as emanating from one's own side (Mr Corbyn at the time was Labour Party leader, the reference to "the most successful Labour PM" is to Mr Blair):

(19) What's happened to your party, Mr Corbyn, that the most successful Labour Prime Minister in history cannot back you to move into Number Ten? (Robinson, journalist, 2019)

4.2   Other debatable types

There are, of course, evaluation strategies which contain more content than an emotive reaction signalling approval or disapproval like the vague terms *nice* and *nasty*. In the 2020 CMFA press briefings in particular, every act of evaluation is an addition to a system of values which adds specific meanings and information about the grounds for the evaluation. It makes clear a value system but also makes explicit relationships and affiliations, a key purpose of foreign affairs briefings.

Some delegitimising terms are more relevant than others. Attempts to delegitimise by criticising an individual's appearance or mannerisms – from Trump's complexion, to Berlusconi's stature, to Hillary Clinton's voice ("Shrillary") – the staple of satirical comedy, are frequent and facile, but they do not address relevant matters in political discourse.

Not all *ad hominem* delegitimisations are equally invalid; a climate campaigner who owns a private jet is open to accusations of hypocrisy at the very least. Politicians are fair game, but family members? What if those family members are happy to expose themselves on talk shows, or make money commercialising products? Is there a distinction to be made between delegitimisation as a genuine attempt to persuade others and when it is firing up one's own base, as in Clinton's notorious "basket of deplorables" jibe; contempt being perhaps the *least* successful of persuasive techniques (Brooks 2019)?

Finally, we mentioned previously the strategy of "whataboutery" or distracting from an issue by pointing to some other. In the CMFA briefings, questions about human rights in China were often countered by podium remarks on, for instance, civil unrest and inequalities in the USA, logically a non-sequitur but which can have considerable emotional appeal. And what if there are degrees of whataboutery? Is the CMFA podium's response to a question on Chinese militarism by commenting on US militarism a complete non-sequitur? All these are questions which are easier to pose than to answer, but they are vital questions. At the time of writing, a former US president, using the rhetoric of insurrection, has attempted to delegitimise the outcome of a national election, with disinformation about the result, but this is the topic for another paper.

In conclusion then, we have used corpus data to examine the illocutionary act of delegitimisation in political discourse. In particular we have looked at a particular discourse type, CCP foreign affairs press briefings, and examined how this particular strategy has increased proportionately over time. This insight came from analysing quantitative data by interrogating the corpus with Wordsmith text analysis software. Negative evaluation has increased and the lexical items were seen to be the core of a set of accusations, formulaic acts of delegitimisation, often upscaled and intensified to a surprising extent. Subsequent qualitative analysis revealed a variety of strategies brought to bear to answer questions on a rather limited set of topics and protagonists with strategies seeking to undermine the legitimacy of the source in terms of hostile intentions, systematic unfairness and prejudice, abuse of power or bullying, and questionable authority and bias. A considerable number of salient items (*disinformation, lie, lies*) form the core of accusations of untruth, clustering together with items such as *slander, groundless, baseless, misinformation, propaganda, rumours*. It appears that such accusations of disinformation are a significant strategy in the Chinese Ministry of Foreign Affairs rebuttals or reactions to questions on sensitive topics and part of a more general tendency to delegitimise when it felt it was being called to account (usually, unsurprisingly, by representatives of non-Chinese media).

Notes

1   "Mansplaining" is a derogatory portmanteau word combining "man" and "explaining". "Remoaner" is a derogatory term coined in UK politics by "Brexiters" to refer to someone who wishes the UK to remain a member of the European Union.

2 Trump himself has claimed that, ironically, part of the reason for his electoral success was the publicity he received given the furious reaction of the same media to his strategy of attacking their legitimacy (Trump and Schwartz 2015: 11–14).

3 Topic areas contested with reciprocal accusations of disinformation or concerned with legislating against disinformation might be gauged by the number of hits (English language scholarly articles) resulting from a simple Google Scholar search term inquiry (carried out in February 2023):
Search terms Scholarly articles
US + disinformation 207,000
Disinformation 150,000
UK + disinformation 80,900
China + disinformation 64,100
EU + disinformation 55,400
Russia + disinformation 54,000
Covid 19 + disinformation 52,000
Climate change + disinformation 40,200
Brexit + disinformation 20,800
Hong Kong + disinformation 19,500
Taiwan + disinformation 16,600
Tibet + disinformation 4,590
Xinjiang + disinformation 2,790

4 According to a dedicated Wikipedia page ("List of war apology statements issued by Japan"), between 1957 and 2013 representatives of various Japanese administrations have in fact issued no less than 52 apologies for its belligerence in the 1930s and 1940s, the following being fairly typical:
"Japan's conduct caused tremendous damage and suffering to the people of many countries, including China, and the Prime Minister expressed his feeling of deep remorse and stated his heartfelt apology" (PM Ryutaro Hashimoto 1997).

5 https://en.wikipedia.org/wiki/Whataboutism.

6 As noted *disinformation* is a keyword in the 2020 CMFA corpus with respect to CMFA 2019.

Dictionaries

Macmillan Dictionary. [Online] Available at: www.macmillandictionary.com/dictionary/british/delegitimization [Accessed: 02/02/2021].

References

Aristotle. (2012) *The Art of Rhetoric*, London: HarperCollins.

Brooks, A. (2019) *Love Your Enemies: How Decent People Can Save America from the Culture of Contempt*, New York: HarperCollins.

Brown, P. and Levinson, S. (1987) *Politeness: Some Universals in Language Use*, Cambridge: Cambridge University Press.

Hunston, S. and Thompson, G. (eds.) (2000) *Evaluation in Text*, Oxford: Oxford University Press.

Marakhovskaiia, M. and Partington, A. (2019) 'National Face and Facework in China's Foreign Policy: A Corpus Assisted Study of Chinese Foreign Affairs Press Conferences', *Bandung: Journal of the Global South* 6, 105–131.

Napoletano, A. and Aiezza, M.-C. (2018) 'The press war in the post-truth era: A corpus-assisted CDA of the discourse of US political analysts on Trump's figure and policy', *Textus* 31(1), 91–118.

Partington, A. (1998) *Patterns and Meanings*, Amsterdam: John Benjamins.

Partington, A. (2006) *The Linguistics of Laughter*, London: Routledge.

Partington, A. and Duguid, A. (2021) 'Political media discourses', in E. Friginal and J. Hardy (eds.), *The Routledge Handbook of Corpus Approaches to Discourse Analysis*, New York: Routledge. ISBN 9780429259982

Partington, A., Duguid, A. and Taylor, C. (2013) *Patterns and Meanings in Discourse*, Amsterdam: John Benjamins.

Partington, A. and Taylor, C. (2018) *The Language of Persuasion in Politics*, London and New York: Routledge. ISBN: 9781138038479
Scott, M. (2016) *WordSmith Tools Version 7*, Stroud: Lexical Analysis Software.
Thompson, G. (1996) *Introducing Functional Grammar*, London: Arnold.
Trump, D. (2020) *Second Presidential Debate*, October 22nd, 2020, Belmont University, Nashville (TN).
Trump, D. and Schwartz, T. 2015. *The Art of the Deal,* New York: Random House.

14

THE MILITARY'S APPROACH TO THE INFORMATION ENVIRONMENT

Michelangelo Conoscenti

Introduction

The US Capitol attack of 2021 and the Ukraine war of 2022 have shown that conflict involves different clusters of populations and affects its public discourses, disclosing the fact that military information operations, and techniques, are now present in our everyday life, although we do not have a conscious perception of the problem. The 2008 economic crisis, the consequent rise of populist movements, the COVID pandemic, and *social media* have greatly contributed to polluting the information environment, making it impossible, for non-specialists to detect when and where these operations are taking place. Whatever the topic under discussion, public opinion is split into almost equal factions contesting reciprocal ideas with divisive debates. This is so true that whether it is election time or war communication, campaigns target the 3 to 7% of swinger voters, or biconceptuals, as Lakoff (2008: 69–74) named them, who are vital to obtaining consensus. Furthermore, these campaigns frequently rely on disinformation. With the rise of social media, disinformation campaigns are increasingly easier and cheaper to pull off than in past decades. As a consequence, the military consider communication a way to control the environment of operations and establish supremacy over the enemy, even in peacetime. To them,

> the *Information Environment* is the space within which opponents mass and manoeuvre information, often in careful coordination with physical assets, to gain advantage within an Information-heavy Complex Problems. It is not a single entity, as the term implies, but rather a composite of the global Information Environment and many Information-heavy Complex Problems related to distinct problem sets with national security relevance.
>
> (Ehlers and Blannin 2020)

Several labels have been used to denominate, at the doctrinal level, these activities: *information operations*, *psychological operations*, and more recently, *Inform and Influence Activities*. Therefore, it is evident that so-called *fake news* is not such a recent phenomenon in the military environment. The spread of social media has only amplified the potential to generate different kinds of information. Disinformation, misinformation, malinformation, fake news, deep fakes, and information disorder are the variables one has to consider to properly frame these phenomena. To save time and space, please

DOI: 10.4324/9781003224495-17

refer to the Council of Europe (2017) and UNESCO (2018) for the discussion of these general terms. Specific military terminology will be discussed in the next section.

Recently, the European and, more generally, the Western public information space has been targeted by Russian Inform and Influence Activities which aim to determine the public debate and orientate decision-makers and the public's attitudes towards sensitive issues. In this chapter, a detailed discussion of the military doctrines on the topic, and the exposure of the main principles of information operations and psychological operations, will advocate the need to generate resilience to these military interferences to make public opinion aware of their role in everyday life. This is why scholars argue that a better understanding of how to stop these campaigns from poisoning our information ecosystems and societies is sorely needed. Kelly and François (2018) have uncovered, employing a graphic analysis of filter bubbles, how polarisation is exploited by Russian Inform and Influence Activities. Instead of trying to force their messages into the mainstream, they target polarised communities. The false personas engage with real people to build credibility. Once their influence has been established, they introduce new viewpoints and amplify divisive and inflammatory narratives that are already circulating. They use the community's language quirks and cater to its obsessions to influence national politics. Thus, the "language of the (virtual) neighbourhood" is vital to influence what is a war on information.

Since to a given information operation, there will be an equivalent counteroperation, one of the problems of this period is that propaganda tends to be turned against its users, like a boomerang. For instance, terms such as *humanitarian intervention, legitimate military target, collateral damage, casualties*, have all been used in 2022 by Putin; unfortunately, in the past, they have been used by us, today's opponents, to explain unpleasant events in which Western democracies have operated without a UN resolution and which have thus been subject to the scrutiny of the International Criminal Court. This is one of the Russians' techniques. Finding inconsistencies and divisive arguments in the other's field so that everything is relativized, thus putting the adversary's system of values in crisis, calling into question, and into doubt, everything. A by-product of this is the rise and spread of conspiracy theories. This is made easier when the adversary's field enjoys a degree of freedom that allows for an open debate on the actions taken by governments and military institutions. This crystallises in a self-destructive syndrome that emerges behind the hypocritical pacifism that reads, "Neither NATO nor Russia". As Rampini (2022, my translation) puts it:

> It is the ideological demobilization of the West: it has long concentrated on trying itself, criminalizing its history, blaming itself for the horrors of imperialism. Only its own, of course: Russian or Chinese imperialisms do not count. If all the evil in the world can be traced back to us, why should we have watched over who wants to bring us to our knees? . . . if the only militarism to have disseminated suffering on the planet is ours?

Daines (2022) has summarised this idea, stating as follows:

> The global rise of authoritarianism is a pressing strategic problem for the United States and its like-minded allies. Chinese and Russian authoritarianism threaten the liberal order from without. Simultaneously, democratic backsliding in the U.S. and Europe undermines liberalism from within.

But this discarding process is incomplete because another fundamental element of the terminology under discussion is missing, namely, *target selection*. When, not only does the utterer of these statements do nothing to avoid or reduce *civilian casualties*, terrible *collateral damage* of war operations, but repeatedly, he targets civilians, then they become *targeted killings*. Thus, the other terminologies indicated previously no longer apply or exist. They are made void by this intentional derogatory action. The relativization process is halted, and it is not possible to have doubts with the excuse of "it must be understood who did something first and who did after".

Keeping the public information environment clean and safe from toxic communication is paramount. Since the strategies enacted by key players – states, institutions, and lobbyists – have their roots in military doctrine and they fit into a post-ideological context where people are persuaded that everything is relative and nothing is better than anything else, we need to clarify the terminology used to describe these phenomena. Given the nature of these, the military are quite secretive about the way they are operationalised. This contribution relies on the author's activities as an academic coordinator of NATO's Working Groups on information operations and psychological operations complemented by original research on the role of language in these activities. Although most of these are protected by nondisclosure agreements, and given the characteristics of this contribution, some confidential sources will be treated according to the Chatham House Rule:

> When a meeting, or part thereof, is held under the Chatham House Rule, participants are free to use the information received, but neither the identity nor the affiliation of the speaker(s), nor that of any other participant, may be revealed.
>
> (Chatham House)

Furthermore, given the situation at the moment of writing, April 2022, the *Custodians of the Doctrine* of several Allied Armed Forces, for the sake of a clearer discussion, have guaranteed access to the latest versions of relevant documents.

Methodology

To document the evolution of language engineering techniques (Conoscenti 2004) in the last 25 years and how and to what extent they have been reframed in the West, an analysis of military discourse methodology combined with a blend of ethnography of communication and netnography is used (Kozinet et al. 2014). Netnography, a specific type of social media research that analyses interactions in digital communications contexts, allows a thorough investigation of the military doctrinal discourse, with specific attention to the information environment. More precisely, quantitative (corpus linguistics) and qualitative analyses are conducted on a corpus of 314 doctrinal documents from 1996 to 2022 published by NATO, US, and UK Armed Forces and covering information operations, psychological operations, *civil-military cooperation, public diplomacy*, and *public affairs* areas. This blend of methodologies helps to identify recurring themes, variants of definitions, and mapping their relevant semantic areas. The corpus is integrated with publications on Russian and Chinese doctrine and the observation of online discourses communities targeted by information operations.

Terminology review: NATO, US, and UK doctrines

The **INTRODUCTION** shows that even a preliminary discussion of this subject resorts to several military terms that pervade today's public discourse. Although some of the military language engineering activities (Conoscenti 2004) at the base of the processes we observe generate in the domain of public relations, the overlap of civilian and military techniques and terminology is well documented. Thus, we start considering the most relevant terms for our discussion. First of all, today's military view of *command and control warfare* has undergone a fundamental change. *Communication and information systems* are now the base, the foundation, together with *all-source intelligence*, of the system upon which the traditional pillars of war rest: (a) *physical destruction*, (b) *operations security*, (c) psychological operations, (d) military deception, (e) *electronic warfare*. To support this building, *NGOs*, civil-military cooperation, and media are paramount. To properly understand the military doctrinal approach to information operations, it must be remembered that they are part of *military operations*:

> A sequence of coordinated actions with a defined purpose. Note(s): 1. NATO operations are military. 2. NATO operations contribute to a wider approach including non-military actions.
>
> (NATO 2021: 95)

We have thus several specific operations that take place in a *battlespace*:

> The environment, factors and conditions that must be understood to apply combat power, protect a force or complete a mission successfully.
>
> (NATO 2021: 19)

More specifically, they operate in an *information environment*:

> An environment comprised of the information itself, the individuals, organizations and systems that receive, process and convey the information, and the cognitive, virtual and physical space in which this occurs.
>
> (NATO 2021: 68)

The complexity of the doctrine is such that this definition has gained the "NATO Agreed" status only in 2020. It must be noted that information environment now includes the *cognitive aspect*, thus implying the importance of the language (spoken, written, visual) used in information operations activities. Since military ones are framed in a strategy, the role of *strategic communications* is paramount:

> In the NATO military context, the integration of communication capabilities and information staff function with other military activities, to understand and shape the information environment, in support of NATO strategic aims and objectives.
>
> (NATO 2021: 123)

Even this definition has been given the status of NATO Agreed quite recently, in 2017. In 2015 NATO delivered the first draft for use (version 9.1.21) of the *Strategic Communications Handbook*. This is a kind of work-in-progress document that has undergone an 18-month test to consider all the lessons identified during exercises and experimentation. The definition of *strategic communications* is the following:

> The coordinated and appropriate use of NATO communications activities and capabilities – Public Diplomacy, Public Affairs (PA), Military Public Affairs, Information Operations

(Info Ops) and Psychological Operations (PSYOPS), as appropriate – in support of Alliance policies, operations and activities, and in order to advance NATO's aims.

(NATO 2015: 6)

In this matryoshka-like definition, each function evokes another one without clearly defining who does what. It can be noted that the 2021 military definition tries to make the operational use of the concept easier, although not necessarily doctrinally more efficient. This is the reason why, as discussed later, a debate between all the mentioned functions is still active to establish the hierarchy entailed by this confusing definition (Lin 2020b). Michaels (2013) has demonstrated the existence of a discourse trap, a worldwide phenomenon in which the discourses and associated terminology devised for political or military reasons can entrap policymakers by motivating or constraining their actions. Michaels discusses how, during a conflict, the politics of terminology can constitute an important battlefield in its own right. He maintains that the language of war had a direct impact on US strategy and operations, and not necessarily a positive one. As we will see, this holds for military mediated communication.

Having explained the basic reference terms, we now turn to the first key term, *information operations*:

A staff function to analyse, plan, assess and integrate information activities to create desired effects on the will, understanding and capability of adversaries, potential adversaries and audiences in support of mission objectives.

(NATO 2021: 68)

It must be noted that this definition is less "aggressive" than the US Department of Defense (2021: 104) one:

The integrated employment, during military operations, of information-related capabilities in concert with other lines of operation to influence, disrupt, corrupt, or usurp the decision-making of adversaries and potential adversaries while protecting our own. Also called IO. See also electromagnetic warfare; military deception; military information support operations; operations security.

In three years, the US Army has changed the title of *FM (Field Manual) 3–13*, the source of the definition, from *Inform and Influence Activities* to *Information Operations*, signalling a dramatic change of perspective. It is important to note the absence of the concept in the NATO doctrine. Given the impact of social media on information operations, a common definition has not yet been agreed upon, and it indicates an incredible effort of adaptation to the new information environment. FM 3–13 (2013) for the first time tried to unify the information operations and the psychological operations under a common denomination and conceptual framework. The 2013 definition was generic enough to allow different interpretations and left the room for Commanders' understanding, entailing several possible operational options with a focus on the communicative side:

Inform and influence activities is the integration of designated information-related capabilities in order to synchronize themes, messages, and actions with operations to inform United States and global audiences, influence foreign audiences, and affect adversary and enemy decision-making.

(Department of the Army 2013: 11)

As it can be understood, several possible interpretations, a form of free will, are not suitable for the military since hierarchical ranks govern their organisation. These generate a specific discourse system that considers orders as the only accepted form of communication. Orders, by definition, are normative and, to guarantee the efficiency of the chain of command, do not envisage the possibility of objection and thus dialogic conversation. As a consequence, forms of communication that encourage dialogue or misinterpretation of orders are considered a potential threat to the specific discourse system. Lin (2020a, 2020b) discusses the doctrinal and conceptual confusions within DoD policy regarding these concepts and the 2021 US and NATO definitions seem an attempt at avoiding such problems. The difference is not to be taken for granted at all. National sensitivities, interests, and approaches to war are reflected in the doctrine, that is, they prioritise in different ways the object of the activities themselves and the way they are carried out. This is why the British in their *UK Terminology Supplement to NATOTerm* have added an important entry, *Media Ops*:

> The military information activity that offers accurate and timely information to nominated audiences through the media, in order to achieve the desired communications effect and build consent for UK national objectives, while maintaining operations security and personal security.
>
> (The Development, Concepts and Doctrine Centre 2022: 37)

The British, unlike the NATO doctrine, deem it vital to distinguish the national elements and audiences, thus keeping a discretional margin on the subtle difference that is implied when internal audiences can be targeted, transforming them into the subject of propaganda activities. Normally, they should not. This tenet was made void for the first time during the Kosovo war when NATO directed propaganda to internal audiences (Conoscenti 2004: 34). The grey areas these definitions generate is a blurred information environment where citizens are not sure, anymore, if what they receive as information, that could influence them, anyway, is, technically, propaganda.

This is possible because psychological operations are defined as follows:

> Planned activities using methods of communication and other means directed at approved audiences in order to influence perceptions, attitudes and behaviour, affecting the achievement of political and military objectives.
>
> (NATO 2021: 105)

Psychological operations are a strategic option in the range of operations that can be resorted to. They have been present in the AAP-06 since 1994, although their definition was reviewed and modified in January 2013. Again, the US *FM 3.05–30 Psychological Operations* documents this. Three roles are of interest to our discussion (Department of the Army 2005: 10):

ROLES OF PSYOP

1–7. To execute their mission, PSYOP Soldiers perform the following five traditional roles to meet the intent of the supported commander:

- Influence foreign populations by expressing information subjectively to influence attitudes and behavior, and to obtain compliance, noninterference, or other desired behavioral

changes. These actions facilitate military operations, minimize needless loss of life and collateral damage, and further the objectives of the supported commander, the United States, and its allies.
- Provide public information to foreign populations to support humanitarian activities, restore or reinforce legitimacy, ease suffering, and maintain or restore civil order. Providing public information supports and amplifies the effects of other capabilities and activities such as civil military operations (CMO).
- Counter enemy propaganda, misinformation, disinformation, and opposing information to portray friendly intent and actions correctly and positively for foreign TAs, thus denying others the ability to polarize public opinion and political will against the United States and its allies.

Several elements of interest could be highlighted from these roles, but we focus on *expressing information subjectively* and in the absence of NATO's *approved audiences*, while specific attention to *foreign* populations/audiences is evident. Irrespective of their nature, the military can apply to them the psychological operations six-step influence cycle on behaviour. The first is the information transmission. This makes sure that (1) a possibility of perception is achieved. The audience is targeted through the most effective medium to guarantee that (2) the subject becomes aware that a certain idea/notion is available in the information environment. This will generate (3) a creative reflection on the idea, that is, the cognitive resources of the target audience are activated so that (4) the making of a decision is possible so that the audience assumes the desired attitude. Finally, (5) a sensible behaviour is generated.

These doctrinal differences show evidence of the current strain that NATO and its national components are facing in the frequent production of *joint publications*, field manuals, and *strategic concepts*. Institutions are generating these to keep pace with a fast-evolving scenario where public opinion is more and more aware of the complex mechanisms of International Relations. Recent US doctrine, like other NATO joint publications, tends to bypass some of these problems. Nonetheless, they show that the whole institutional body, unlike its adversaries, is not proactively leading the change and transformation but simply reacts to them by trying to adjust and accommodate them within a traditional working model. The result is fragmentary and incoherent communication easily threatened by foreign authoritarian regimes. The next two sections are devoted to this specific aspect.

Terminology and doctrine review: China

Investigating Chinese and Russian doctrine is not easy. Setting aside the difficulty of the respective languages, few doctrinal documents are available, and most of the literature relies on translations, confidential reports, first-hand experiences, and specific case studies. This is so because NATO, the US, and the UK are an exception having their information operations and *information warfare* doctrine unclassified and available on the Internet. Hence, current information about Chinese and Russian policy and doctrine is not freely available.

Chinese doctrine on information operations began in 1991 after the US victory in the First Gulf War. From that point on, the People's Liberation Army began to develop its concepts of information operations and information warfare that show distinctive Chinese traits:

As with all its military theories and strategic perspectives, Chinese traditional wisdom and strategic thought are applied to all new concepts and precepts originating from the US, Russia or elsewhere.

(Anand 2006)

According to Yadav (2021), the ultimate aim of the Chinese information warfare strategy (信息战战略, Xìnxī zhàn zhànlüè) is *information dominance* (信息权 Xìnxīquan). One of the goals, as we will see later, is to gather sensitive information from the adversary by conducting cyber espionage and psychological operations. The People's Liberation Army has emphasised the development of its *Three Warfares* strategy in its operational planning since at least 2003:

> Three Warfares is comprised of psychological warfare, public opinion warfare, and legal warfare. Psychological warfare uses propaganda, deception, threats, and coercion to affect the adversary's decision-making capability. Public opinion warfare disseminates information for public consumption to guide and influence public opinion and gain support from domestic and international audiences. Legal warfare uses international and domestic laws to gain international support, manage political repercussions, and sway target audiences.
>
> (DoD 2019: 112)

The Chinese Defence White Paper of 2008 *Informatized warfare of China* clears the principles of the implementation of information warfare within the People's Liberation Army. The Department of the Army (2021: 75) reports the following:

> In keeping with the teachings of Sun Tzu, the PLA considers information operations to be at least as important – if not more important – than maneuver or firepower. Deception, trickery, and concealment are to be employed extensively throughout the information operations campaign in order to manipulate the enemy commander's state of mind, the morale of enemy troops, and the enemy's understanding of the battlefield to the PLA's advantage.

The Chinese Information Warfare strategy is strategically implemented by carrying out information operations across global cyberspace. They can be further classified, into *Offensive Information Operations* and *Defensive Information Operations*. The Chinese doctrine has an aggressive approach to the problem. Substantive destruction and the use of hard weapons to destroy enemy headquarters, command posts, and command and control warfare information centres are paramount. Information operations are treated as a kinetical asset making the boundary between physical and psychological attack very thin or undetectable. This is made clear by the definition of *information attack*:

> Any IW activity intended to weaken or deprive the enemy of control of information. Information attack is the primary means by which information warfare is won, and it is the key to achieving information superiority. There are four subcategories of information attack: electromagnetic attack, network attack, psychological attack, and physical attack. Of note, the psychological attack is considered both a form of information attack and its own unique campaign; it is unclear what the relationship is between the two.
>
> (Department of the Army 2021: 76)

In 2015, the People's Liberation Army created the *Strategic Support Force*. Since then space, cyber, electronic, and psychological warfare missions are coordinated by a single command. This confirms that information dominance is key to winning conflicts. This could be done by denying or disrupting the use of communications equipment of its competitors. Thus, it is psychological warfare that encompasses all the information operations activities that we have discussed in Western doctrine. These are activities wherein a combatant employs information and media to target human thought, emotion, and spirit, at the tactical level. The People's Liberation Army views psychological warfare as the operational element of the fundamental reason for conflict: a contest of wills. Psychological warfare is considered a fourth operational mode, in addition to land, air, and sea warfare. This is an element in common with the more recent Command and Control Warfare doctrine, although it must be noted that

> the PLA appears to categorize domains in much the same way as does the United States, but its categorization of psychological warfare as an operational mode is unique. It is unclear how operational modes differ from domains.
>
> (Department of the Army 2021: 78)

We can say that Chinese psychological warfare displays four primary characteristics: (1) a central role, (2) concurrent hard-kill and soft-kill techniques, (3) long duration, (4) vast scope. The long duration element is the one that reflects the Chinese attitude to time. A historical cycle can be interpreted as meaningful when it lasts 144 years (12 by 12, a Chinese magic formula). As a consequence, psychological warfare commences long before formal hostilities begin, and it continues long after they are concluded. It is ultimately tied to a nation's collective morale, unity, and spirit, and so it lasts a far longer period than do tactical or even strategic military operations.

The 2020 DoD report confirms that a cornerstone of China's strategy includes appealing to overseas Chinese citizens to advance party objectives through soft power and to conduct inform and influence activities on behalf of China. Furthermore, it harnesses academia and educational institutions, think tanks, and media to advance its soft power campaign in support of China's security interests. For example, Chinese students abroad and academic organisations are used to spread the party's narrative on Tibet and the Dalai Lama. Chinese Students and Scholars Associations and Confucius Institutes organise events to support China's sovereignty claims and lodge complaints and organise protests against academic institutions that conduct activities that differ from China's policies.

> China uses its cyber capabilities to not only support intelligence collection against U.S. diplomatic, economic, academic, and defense industrial base sectors, but also to exfiltrate sensitive information from the defense industrial base to gain military advantage. The targeted information can benefit China's defense high-technology industries, support China's military modernization, provide the CCP insights into U.S. leadership perspectives, and enable diplomatic negotiations, such as those supporting the One Belt, One Road initiative.
>
> (Department of Defense 2020: 84)

Terminology and doctrine review: Russia

This section attempts to summarise what is known about the Russian attitude towards the information environment. As far as Russia is concerned, Giles (2016), Soldatov and Borogan (2015), and Stengel (2019) are of interest and easily accessible. The first is an academic practical handbook; the other two are informative, relying on insider information.

Although Putin first mentioned *soft power* in a speech in February 2013 (NATO used the expression for the first time in 1999 [Nye 1999:12–15]), Russians, as Soldatov and Borogan

(2015) document, have been weaponizing information for a long time. According to Stengel (2019: 145):

> The Russian military had been thinking and writing about information war for decades. It was embedded in their military doctrines. There seemed to be an analogy between failed states and disinformation: Putin wanted failed truth.

Four preeminent figures can be considered the major architects of the Russian doctrine: General Valerij Gerasimov, chief of general staff of the Russian Army; professor and former KGB officer Igor Panarin; political analyst and strategist Aleksandr Dugin; and Colonel Vladimir Kvachkov, member of ГРУ/GRU (Russian: Главное разведывательное управление, Glavnoye Razvedyvatelnoye Upravlenie, Chief Intelligence Office, i.e. the Military Intelligence Service) and of Спецназ России (Spetsnaz Rossii, the Russian Special Forces). Kvachkov (2004) theorised the principles of Russian Special Operations, those that Putin, referring to the war in Ukraine, recently rephrased in *Special Military Operations*. His analysis is ruthless and lucid in the best military spirit of the lesson learned. He states the following:

> War is a massive, large-scale organized violent impact on a state, people, social or ethnic group that uses armed struggle and/or non-combat means to achieve political, military, economic, cultural and other objectives. Various forms of struggle can be used in war: informational, armed, economic, financial, diplomatic, cultural and others. . . . A new type of war has emerged, in which armed warfare has given up its decisive place in the achievement of the military and political objectives of war to another kind of warfare – information warfare.
>
> (Kvachkov 2004, my translation)

Reading this definition of war and the forms of struggle foreseen, please note that *informational* is in the first place, followed by *armed*. This explains the importance of the asset *information* for the Russians. Furthermore, Kvachkov's influence has informed, as Giles (2016: 4) points out, the development of Russian doctrine:

> In the Russian construct, information warfare is not an activity limited to wartime. It is not even limited to the "initial phase of conflict" before hostilities begin, which includes information preparation of the battlespace. Instead, it is an ongoing activity regardless of the state of relations with the opponent; "in contrast to other forms and methods of opposition, information confrontation is waged constantly in peacetime". The entry for Information *Operations* (информационная война, informatsionnaya voyna, although voyna means *war/warfare*) in a glossary of key information security terms produced by the Military Academy of the General Staff makes a clear distinction between the Russian definition – broad, and not limited to wartime – and the Western one – which it describes as limited, tactical information operations carried out during hostilities.

Consequently, the assets of this approach to war range from psychological operations to degradation of navigation support, including disinformation and intelligence. Gerasimov's doctrine can be summarised in a sentence: "you have your truth, we have ours". He maintains that in contemporary war

> the emphasis on the methods of fighting moves toward the complex application of political, economic, information, and other non-military means, carried out with the support of military force.
>
> (Giles 2016: 64)

This implies, echoing Kvachkov, that in information warfare, there are no rear areas. Modern warfare is nonlinear with no clear boundary between military and non-military campaigns. According to him, a key feature of modern warfare is "simultaneous effects to the entire depth of enemy territory, in all physical media and the information domain" (Gerasimov 2014: 13). This implies that also deception is one of the elements of this equation since it involves actions executed to deliberately mislead adversary military, paramilitary, or violent extremist organisation decision-makers. The goal is to erode Western public audiences' trust in public discourse and democratic processes. "It is an unconventional threat to our system of beliefs and how we define ourselves" (Stengel 2019: 13). Thus, Russian disinformation does not aim at being objective but rather at creating an alternative reality. Russia has put information operations and psychological operations at the core of its military efforts. The kinetic has become secondary. Pomerantsev summarised the essence of this view:

> Russia's message is about the relativism of everything. The relative truth of the two sides in Ukraine. The relativism of the West. . . . The Russians don't have a view that they are trying to persuade you of, just that everything is relative. Nothing is better than anything else. . . . It's a war on information.
>
> (quoted in Stengel 2019: 137)

This is the effect of Dugin's doctrine. In his 1997 Основы геополитики (Osnovy geopolitiki, Foundations of Geopolitics) he encourages all kinds of "separatism and ethnic, social and racial conflicts". He also supports "extremist, racist, and sectarian groups" to destabilise the internal political processes of adversaries, namely, Western democracies. Dugin's desired outcomes include

> a fractured NATO, the Russian partition and eventual seizure of Ukraine, and the creation of several transnational "axes" of sympathetic antiliberal fronts and states. Dugin anticipated that these axes would attack liberal societies from within while sharing irregular and informational warfare tactics and techniques to fracture democratic governments, especially the U.S., as "payback" for the fall of the Soviet Union.
>
> (Daines 2022)

For Dugin all truth is relative and a question of belief. This is why freedom and democracy are not universal values but peculiarly Western ones. These must be contested since, as Panarin states, Russia is the victim of information aggression by the US. The only way out of this is net-centric warfare. As a consequence, he is sympathetic to the rise of right-wing populist movements in Europe, being its theorist and Russia the funding partner. This kind of support has been thoroughly analysed by a series of three reports, *The Kremlin's Trojan Horses* (2016, 2017, 2018), available at the Atlantic Council website (www.atlanticcouncil.org/).

Within this doctrinal framework, social media are thus exploited by several institutional and non-institutional players to generate divisive narratives that endanger the very roots of public debate. As has been seen, relativization, or denialism, is a key strategy that is empowered by filter bubbles and echo chambers (Khosravinik 2017; Spohr 2017). These reinforce public opinion narratives (Gainous and Wagner 2013; Stromer-Galley 2014) that are far from being rational ones. MIT researchers (Dizikes 2018) have discovered that "falsehood diffuses significantly farther, faster, deeper, and more broadly than the truth, in all categories of information, and in many cases by an order of magnitude". The scholars "found the spread of false information is essentially not due to bots that are programmed to disseminate inaccurate stories. Instead, false news speeds faster around Twitter due to people retweeting inaccurate news items". Schmitt (2021) has specifically investigated Twitter's impact on public opinion and EU foreign affairs.

To achieve these goals, besides the activities of the *Internet Research Agency*, a.k.a. the *troll factory*, based in St. Petersburg, the Kremlin's modern media and information distribution are mainly vested in two closely linked players: disinformation outlet Sputnik and the news outlet RT (formerly Russia Today). Their publicly stated commitment is to secure Russia's national interests through their reporting. Russia's external strategy is less projection of a positive image of the country in favour of sowing discord and chaos in the target country. Recent events have also confirmed that Russia uses military techniques and personnel to obtain a divisive political effect on the American and European public opinion to influence the political debate and decision-making process (Polyakova et al. 2016, 2017; Pomerantsev 2015). Since this is also one of the tenets of the US Public Affairs and Information Operations doctrines, the implications for the European Information Environment are paramount. American investigation led by Special Counsel Robert Mueller's office has proven that 12 Russian military officers belonging to GRU, the Chief Intelligence Office, were involved in hacking activities. Their goal was to influence the 2016 US presidential election. The files also disclosed an intense Twitter activity focused on the hashtag #mattarelladimettiti (#mattarellaresign), the Italian president. It was a delegitimating campaign supported by the Lega Nord and Movimento 5 Stelle parties against Sergio Mattarella because he used the constitutional right to reject a proposed minister, in this case, Paolo Savona, well-known for his anti-Euro and anti-Europe positions. All the traffic was generated overnight by the St. Petersburg's troll factory. Mueller's investigations and the Italian ones highlight the military dimensions of these operations and confirm a state sponsored agenda (Linvill and Warren 2020) that is driven by a specific military strategy.

Infowar and infodemic: two sides of the same coin

As we have seen, modern warfare is nonlinear, with no clear boundary between military and non-military campaigns. The Russians, like ISIS (Conoscenti 2017, 2019), merge their military lines of effort with their information and messaging one, obtaining a tactical and strategic advantage in the control of the European Information Environment. Furthermore, observing the lines of effort and the Russian master narratives used from Ukraine on, an analogy between failed states and disinformation can be drawn: public opinion must perceive reality as if it were a state of failed truth since it is easier to disrupt things than it is to keep them together. It must be remembered that the purposes of psychological operations are achieved by conveying selected information and indicators (themes/narratives) to targeted audiences by employing adapted assets and media. Here is the definition for *narrative* in a document that will soon be part of NATO's Strategic Communications Policy/Doctrine (Chatham House Rule applies here):

> Narrative is a coherent system of stories that creates a cause and effect relationship between an originating desire or conflict, and an actual or desired or implied resolution. In so doing, Narrative has the capacity to express identity, values, moral basis, legitimacy and vision around which entities (organisations or activities) can unite.

This implies that, given that social media are a well-established global phenomenon,

> in order to control and influence populations in "irregular" or unconventional warfare, the incorporation of new media into operations is important to Special Operations.
>
> (Chancey 2013: 47)

Thus, the Information Environment can become a place where influencers use digital or traditional media to amplify rumours that, soon "caught" by unsuspecting members of the public, can help reach the strategic goals we discussed. This operational scenario has been magnified by four recent events: the 2016 and 2020 US Presidential Elections, the COVID pandemic, and the War in Ukraine. These share a common fil rouge: the Russian massive presence in the environment. The Digital Forensic Research Lab (**DFRLab**), an emanation of the Atlantic Council, is a hub of digital forensic analysts whose mission is to identify, expose, and explain disinformation where and when it occurs using open-source research. **DFRLab** has published several reports which expose Russian Information Operations. Those of interest, DFRLab (2021) and Holt (2022), identify and document a continuum, masterfully driven by Russia, that links different narratives with the same goal, that is, polarising Western public opinion: Putin→Trump→ISIS→Populists/Sovereignists→QAnon→Anti-Vax→No-War.

> ISIS and Vladimir Putin and Donald Trump. For all three of them, communications – what we in government called messaging – was not a tactic but a core strategy. They all understood that the media cycle moves a lot faster than the policy cycle, and policy would forever play catch-up. They knew that it was almost always better to be first and false than second and true. One problem with the U.S. government is that we didn't really get that; we saw messaging as an afterthought. . . . All three of them . . . weaponized the grievances of people who felt left out by modernity and globalization. In fact, they used the same playbook: ISIS sought to Make Islam Great Again; Putin yearned to Make Russia Great Again; and we know about Mr Trump. The weaponization of grievance is the unified field theory behind the rise of nationalism and right-wing strongmen.
>
> (Stengel 2019: 15–16)

DFRLab (2021) has demonstrated that rumours about an infection's origins led to a military weaponised narrative. Consequently, the World Health Organisation labelled it an *infodemic*.

The World Health Organisation recognised relatively early in the crisis that the pandemic presented potential information dangers and that mis- and disinformation were spreading quickly. On 2 February 2020, the World Health Organisation released a COVID-19 situation report that described the pandemic as featuring a parallel infodemic:

> An abundance of information – some accurate and some not – that makes it hard for people to find trustworthy sources and reliable guidance when they need it. Due to the high demand for

timely and trustworthy information about 2019-nCoV, WHO technical risk communication and social media teams have been working closely to track and respond to myths and rumours.

(WHO 2020)

Since then, stemming from World Health Organisation's definition of infodemic, "too much information including false or misleading information in digital and physical environments during a disease outbreak", *infodemia* has gained popularity extending its meaning. It is an abnormal flow of information of variable quality on a topic, produced and circulated with extreme rapidity and capillarity, through traditional and digital media, such as to generate disinformation, with consequent distortion of reality and potentially dangerous effects on the level of reactions and social behaviours. This could be a working definition for information operations/psychological operations as well, and this is why it is now an asset of information operations. Kandel (2020) has observed that

many of us may be unknowingly suffering from information disorder syndrome. It is more prevalent due to the digitized world where the information flows to every individual's phone, tablet and computer in no time. Information disorder syndrome is the sharing or developing of false information with or without the intent of harming and they are categorized as misinformation, disinformation and malinformation.

Just like a pandemic, an infodemic can be mitigated by practising a digital form of hygiene – employing scepticism, verifying sources, and the like. And conversely, an infodemic can spread out of control when influencers and the public make no attempts to contain the rumours around them. Influence operations turn into disinformation operations:

During this particular infodemic, Russia, China, and Iran embraced traditional propaganda tactics that leveraged their existing state media infrastructure to push narratives highlighting how well they were handling the crisis while denigrating their adversaries and competitors. While these efforts were not limited to targeting domestic audiences, domestic concerns played a significant role in terms of which narratives were embraced. Narratives originating from the United States also reflected domestic audiences, but in the context of elected officials positioning themselves as part of a competitive, democratic, and open information environment.

(DFRLab 2021: 47)

This represented a shift from 2016 Russia's strategy for the American elections and, later, for the 2019 European Parliamentary Elections. At that time, it created the accounts that posted divisive content to sow distrust. In line with Gerasimov's and Dugin's doctrine, Russian trolls now exploit pre-existing false or misleading COVID-19 narratives in foreign countries by simply amplifying the local voices posting them, including conspiracy theorists and QAnon supporters. It must be remembered that QAnon has national franchisee branches in the UK, France, Germany, and Italy, and their favourite social media is Telegram, founded by Russian brothers Durov, who also developed Russian web twin apps WebK and WebZ. Telegram's secret chats and groups are particularly liked also by jihadists, far-righters, anti-vax, and recently no-war activists. The questionable use of the service has been highlighted when the chairman of the public organisation *Electronic Democracy*, Volodymyr Flents, on 11 May 2020 announced that a Telegram bot appeared on the web, which sold the personal data of Ukrainian citizens.

Although it is not the objective of this contribution to discuss the genesis of the web of relationships between QAnon and the Sovereigntists, it must be observed the overlap of Putin's agenda on sowing discord in the West and Steve Bannon's, Trump's White House chief strategist, one. Among Bannon's initiatives, it is worth remembering *The Movement*, a joint effort between right-wing Belgian politician Modrikamen and Bannon. They had global plans to promote the populist-radical right, and economic nationalism, ahead of the EU parliament elections in 2019. When asked who was paying for his free consultancies to the very same European populists leaders identified in the *Kremlin's Trojan Horses* reports, Bannon did not disclose donors, generically referring to "private individuals from Europe and the United States" (Nielsen 2018). Furthermore,

> the former Trump aide said that the Italian government is an experiment in uniting left and right. "A populist party with nationalist tendencies like the 5Stars, and a nationalist party with populist tendencies like the League . . . it's imperative that this works because this shows a model for industrial democracies from the U.S. to Asia".
>
> (Sciorilli Borrelli 2018)

Again, the similarities between Dugin's and Gerasimov's doctrines and the way they are carried out are evident. QAnon's genesis and goals, a decentralized conspiracy movement whose adherents subscribe to a sprawling web of unsupported beliefs premised around the existence of a *deep state* and a worldwide *shadow elite*, are functional to this information operations strategy. The movement was instrumental in the amplification of the theory that COVID-19 was a Chinese bioweapon.

> The traditional view about conspiracy theories is that they exist along the fringes of the information space, apart from the mainstream and official communications. However, in the United States, these conspiracy theories have permeated all layers of discourse, particularly being embraced by elements of mainstream media and individual conservative policymakers during the Trump Administration.
>
> (DFRLab 2021: 21)

The mechanism is simple but psychologically devastating. It starts with the deliberate spread of false information. Frequently source material for others to do so is provided. Thus, information shared by profiles with large public platforms and inherent clout in spreading unverified information is quickly transformed through amplification by others into demonstrably false information. The key actors spreading false narratives include QAnon and other conspiracy theory communities, right-wing websites, and several high-profile conservative influencers. Here the 1–9–90 rule is at work. The 1% generates the content that is passed to the 9% that will reach 90% of the target population. Maximisation of the information operations with minimum effort. It is interesting to observe that the very same Telegram groups active in spreading the previous narratives have now turned into no-war activists. As Krassen (2022) has noted:

> Since the Russian invasion of Ukraine at the end of February, Bulgaria's anti-vax movement has shifted its focus. Instead of fixating on COVID-19 vaccines and related conspiracy theories, they have become staunch supporters of President Vladimir Putin and Moscow and are nurturing anti EU sentiments.

IFOP (2022), a French research institute, has found that more than half of the French believe in at least one conspiracy narrative about the Ukraine war peddled by Russian president Vladimir

Putin's regime. The figure increased to almost two-thirds for the respondents who voted for the most radical left or right-leaning parties. Many anti-vax also said they believed in the Kremlin's justifications for the war, with 71% of them siding with Putin's rhetoric. At the time of writing, April 2022, the US and their allies, mainly NATO countries, are currently facing a situation where, serendipitously, their language engineering processes, those devised and refined after the Vietnam War, passing through 9/11, Assange's Wikileaks, and the spread of social media (Conoscenti 2004) are less and less effective, but they are not able, as insiders, to explain why. Many blame Russians Information Operations. This is part of the answer. The other possible *key* can be that the US national interests and those of the European NATO collide to the point that their narratives are inconsistent and contrasting. Recently, the doctrine, as we have seen, given the attention of public opinion on these issues, has attempted to sanitise the concept of manipulation, although "this is just another way to name propaganda, Information Operations and Psychological Operations". Chatham House Rule applies here.

Actions against mis-information: Europe and its clay feet

The EU Commission, since large-scale disinformation campaigns are a major challenge for Europe and require a coordinated response from EU countries, institutions, social networks, news media, and citizens, has developed several initiatives to tackle disinformation. In 2016, it was understood that stepping up the cooperation between the EU and NATO in a joint effort to counter hybrid threats was paramount. The European Commission (2018) published a report which tried to set some short and long-term objectives: the first was acting against the most pressing problems, the latter increasing societal resilience to disinformation. Promoting media and information literacy to counteract disinformation was considered a viable solution. This would help users properly navigate the digital media environment. The development of tools for empowering users and journalists to combat disinformation while promoting a positive engagement with fast-evolving information technologies was also recommended. In the same year, the Commission launched the *Actions Plan against Information* to mobilise the private sector to tackle disinformation. Setting aside a few cosmetic actions taken by social media big players, the initiative has gone unheeded. In 2021 (European Commission) it was the turn of the *European Commission Guidance on Strengthening the Code of Practice on Disinformation*. I had the honour to amend the drafts of this document, but it substantially reflects the problem of many EU documents. Despite it declares that it "lays out a set of worldwide self-regulatory standards for the industry", it must compromise with internal political balances, and it dares not press fundamental key players such as the big social media and Hi-Tech companies to act. It all relies on goodwill declarations and actions taken voluntarily. In Conoscenti (2019) I have thoroughly discussed the reasons, and the possible solutions, to this impasse. It is evident that, despite numerous overoptimistic press releases, a little, compared to the importance of the Institution, has been realised, for practical and, most importantly, for contrasting national political reasons and interests that the war in Ukraine has made more evident. Unfortunately, we are still at the starting pole. Better fortune must be credited to two, more practical, contributions which aim to clarify the nature of the problem and have spared you a long list of discussions on its key terms. The first (Council of Europe 2017) tries to establish an interdisciplinary framework for research and policymaking on *Information Disorder*. The report identifies the *Agents*, the *Messages*, and the *Interpreters* involved in the process. It then frames them along the filter bubbles and echo chambers continuum. The sections "Attempts at solutions" and "Recommendations" set a good ground for feasible solutions. UNESCO's *Handbook for Journalism Education and Training* (2018) is rich with practical activities that could be easily adapted for different levels of education. Misinformation, disinformation, and malinformation are correctly framed to provide proper media and information literacy to contrast their spread on differ-ent platforms. Fact-checking and social media verification are also addressed.

Conclusions

Since the European public space is the target of military inform and influence activities, the "les-sons learnt" from the military and political world (Nielsen 2012; McKenna and Hahrie 2014) must be considered to better prepare public opinion for their influence. This should be possible because

> for the first time, people are asking questions about whether constant engagement with digital media is healthy for democracy. They are developing more critical instincts about false infor-mation online and demanding accountability from companies that play fast and loose with personal data and stand aside as organized disinformation operators seek to disrupt democracy.
>
> (Ghosh and Scott 2018: 60)

If the impact of these activities is fully understood, as declared by the EU in 2016, then the de-velopment of synergies with the military should also be considered. This would mean to prioritise contrasting actions against Information Operations by foreign countries that aim to obtain politi-cal effects on the European public opinion. The point has been formulated by Stengel (2019: 13):

> In a democracy, government is singularly bad at combating disinformation. That's in part because most of those we are trying to persuade already distrust it. But it's also not good at creating content that people care about. That's not really government's job. Early on at the State Department, I said to an old media friend, "People just don't like government content". He laughed and said, "No, people just don't like bad content".

The war in Ukraine has made evident in Europe that information operations adversaries are au-thoritarian governments that provide government institutions with the ability to direct a whole-of-nation approach. Each can exercise influence within their public, press, or a sceptical and potentially powerful electorate, to achieve information operations objectives without delay. They are not bound, like democratic countries, to a legal framework to advance information operations in the gray zone (activities by a state that are harmful to another state and are sometimes consid-ered to be acts of war, but are not legally acts of war) that has been described. Western democracies must develop

> a legal framework more closely reflecting rules of engagement consistent with the environ-ment we've found ourselves in . . . the Gray Zone. Having a war, or Gray Zone activities be executed at the speed of legal decisions assuredly leave democratic societies at a clear disadvantage.
>
> (Kiesler 2021: 18)

In June 2018 I lectured at the Italian NATO Rapid Deployable Corps Headquarters on "How to Operationalise the Use of Social Media". I offered the same point already made at a NATO Joint Senior Psychological Operations conference in Tampa, in December 2016, at the NATO-US Special Operations Command, titled "The Psychology of Social Media". It is bizarre, to say the least, that civilians exhort the military to elicit a better and more flexible legal framework to have effective information operations. Working Group 2 at the Tampa Conference worked on the theme: "How Can Psychological Operations Best Leverage Social Media in Peacetime (no Article 5) and During Military Operations?" Among its recommendations to the NATO nations, the working group listed the following: (a) to create a constant presence in social media relevant to current and potential target audiences and (b) to have a NATO shared policy on social media. It is worth noting that the recommendations are addressed to the NATO members and not to the NATO HQs. Is this the evident expression of a hope that national practices will influence NATO doctrine? This could be the case given that section 6 of the Conference Report states the following:

> Specific recommendations were made . . . on how NATO nations can work together to mitigate and counter the negative effects of SoMe that permeate the global information environment and our respective areas of interest. Within the 28 nations of NATO . . . the challenge is that each country must individually determine how they might apply or use the recommendations to the benefit of their nation's interests. Understandably, there are vast differences amongst nations in terms of social media policy, capabilities and capacities.

As we have seen, the military face difficulties keeping pace with this fast-evolving scenario. Despite NATO Allied Command for Transformation efforts to stimulate specific solutions, the political military nature of the Alliance does not allow it to lead the change and transformation proactively. It simply reacts, by trying to adjust and accommodate scenarios within a traditional working model. The result is fragmentary and incoherent communication that is shared and reflected by the European Union as well, as recent comments on the Facebook page *EU vs DiSiNFO* (www.facebook.com/EUvsDisinfo) unmercifully show:

> Given the way governments of the US, UK and various EU countries disseminated vast heaps of disinformation to justify their invasion of Iraq, I'm puzzled as to why this service systematically ignores disinformation coming from our own governments via western media outlets. How can we be well informed if you shield the often very dubious narratives coming out of the US State Department, the Pentagon and the White House from critical scrutiny? (comment by Coilín ÓhAiseadha to post www.facebook.com/photo/?fbid=3484412273083 44&set=a.148103890675413).

Ultimately, this contribution is a cautionary tale, a case study in an escalating competition for primacy over the global information environment and potentially a harbinger of things that already came and that we must be able to interpret and manage.

References

Anand, V., 'Chinese Concepts and Capabilities of Information Warfare'. *Strategic Affairs*, 30(4), 2006. www.idsa.in/strategicanalysis/ChineseConceptsandCapabilitiesofInformationWarfare_vanan d_1006

Chancey, D. L., *New Media: The Key to Influence in Irregular Warfare*. Newport, RI: Naval War College, 2013. Chatham House. www.chathamhouse.org/about-us/chatham-house-rule

Conoscenti, M., 'Europe at the Centre of Military Inform and Influence Activities: Implications for the European Public Debate'. *Problemi dell'Informazione*, Il Mulino, XLIV(1), 2019: 117–144.

Conoscenti, M., 'ISIS' Dabiq Communicative Strategies, NATO and Europe. Who is Learning from Whom?'. In M. Ceretta and B. Curli (eds.), *Discourses and Counter-Discourses on Europe, from the Enlightenment to the EU*. Abingdon: Taylor & Francis, 2017: 238–257.

Conoscenti, M., *Language Engineering and Media Management Strategies in Recent Wars*. Roma: Bulzoni, 2004.

Council of Europe, *Information Disorder: Toward an Interdisciplinary Framework for Research and Policy Making*. Strasbourg: CoE, 2017. https://rm.coe.int/information-disorder-report november-2017/1680764666

Daines, C. J., 'Competing Against Authoritarism', *The Strategy Bridge*, 2022. https://thestrategybridge.org/the-bridge/2022/3/16/competing-against-authoritarianism

Department of the Army, *Army Technique Publication 7–100.3 Chinese Tactics*. Washington, DC: DoA, 2021. https://armypubs.army.mil/epubs/DR_pubs/DR_a/ARN33195-ATP_7-100.3-000-WEB-1.pdf

Department of the Army, *FM 3.05.30 Psychological Operations*. Washington, DC: DoA, 2005. https://irp.fas.org/doddir/army/fm3-05-30.pdf

Department of the Army, *FM 3.13 Inform and Influence Activities*. Washington, DC: DoA, 2013. www.globalsecurity.org/military/library/policy/army/fm/3-13/fm3-13-2013.pdf

Department of Defense, *Annual Report to Congress: Military and Security Developments Involving the People's Republic of China*. Washington, DC: DoD, 2019. https://media.defense.gov/2019/May/02/2002127082/-1/-1/1/2019%20CHINA%20MILITARY%20POWER%20REPORT%20(1).PDF

Department of Defense, *Annual Report to Congress: Military and Security Developments Involving the People's Republic of China*. Washington, DC: DoD, 2020. https://media.defense.gov/2020/Sep/01/2002488689/-1/-1/1/2020-DOD-CHINA-MILITARY POWER-REPORT-FINAL.PDF

Department of Defense, *DOD Dictionary of Military and Associated Terms*. Washington, DC: DoD, 2021. www.jcs.mil/Portals/36/Documents/Doctrine/pubs/dictionary.pdf

The Development, Concepts and Doctrine Centre, *UK Terminology Supplement to NATOTerm*. London: Ministry of Defence, 2022. https://assets.publishing.service.gov.uk/government/uploads/system/uploads/attachment_data/file/1 050322/20220124-JDP_0_01_1_2022_Edition_A.pdf

Digital Foresinc Research Lab, *Weaponized: How Rumors about COVID-19's Origins Led to a Narrative Arms Race*. Washington, DC: Atlantic Council, 2021. www.atlanticcouncil.org/wp content/uploads/2021/02/Weaponized-How-rumors-about-COVID-19s-origins-led-to-a-narrative arms-race.pdf

Dizikes, P., 'Study on Twitter, False News Travels Faster Than True Stories'. *MIT News*, March 8, 2018. http://news.mit.edu/2018/study-twitter-false-news-travels-faster-true-stories-0308.

Dugin, A., *Основы геополитики (Foundations of Geopolitics)*, 1997. https://n01r.com/wpcontent/uploads/2022/01/Foundations-of-Geopolitics-Geopolitical-Future-of-Russia-Alexander Dugin-English-auto-translation-with-appended-original.pdf

Ehlers, R. S., and P. Blannin, 'Core Aspects of the Information Environment'. *Small Wars Journal*, 2020. https://smallwarsjournal.com/jrnl/art/making-sense-information-environment

European Commission, *European Commission Guidance on Strengthening the Code of Practice on Disinformation*. Brussels: Publications Office, 2021. https://eur-lex.europa.eu/legal-content/EN/TXT/PDF/?uri=COM:2021:262:FIN

European Commission, *A Multi-Dimensional Approach to Disinformation: Report of the Independent High-level Group on Fake News and Online Disinformation*. Brussels: Publications Office, 2018. https://data.europa.eu/doi/10.2759/0156

Gainous, J., and K. M. Wagner, *Tweeting to Power. The Social Media Revolution in American Politics*. Oxford: Oxford University Press, 2013.

Gerasimov, V., 'Роль Генерального штаба в организации обороны страны в соответствии с новым Положением о Генеральном штабе, утвержденным Президентом Российской Федерации'. *Vestnik Akademii Voennykh Nauk*, 1, 2014: 14–22.

Giles, K., *Handbook of Russian Information Warfare*. Rome: NATO Defense College, 2016.

Ghosh, D., and B. Scott, *#Digital Deceit. The Technologies Behind Precision Propaganda on the Internet*. Cambridge, MA: Harvard Kennedy School, Shorenstein Center on Media, Politics and Public Policy, 2018. https://d1y8sb8igg2f8e.cloudfront.net/documents/digital-deceit-final-v3.pdf

Holt, J., *After the Insurrection: How Domestic Extremists Adapted and Evolved After the January 6 US Capitol Attack*. Washington, DC: Atlantic Council, 2022.

IFOP, 'Désinformation, complotisme et populisme à l'heure de la crise sanitaire et de la guerre en Ukraine', 2022. www.ifop.com/wpcontent/uploads/2022/03/Rapport_Ifop_REBOOT_VOL_1_2022.03.24.pdf

Kandel, N., 'Information Disorder Syndrome and its Management'. *JNMA*, 58(224), 2020: 280–285. www.ncbi.nlm.nih.gov/pmc/articles/PMC7580464/#:~:text=Information%20disorder%20syn drome%20is%20the,is%20categorized%20into%20three%20grades

Kelly, J., and C. François, 'This is What Filter Bubbles Look Like'. *MIT Technology Review*, 2018. www.technologyreview.com/s/611807/this-is-what-filter-bubbles-actually-look-like/.

Khosravinik, M., 'Right-Wing Populism in the West: Social Media Discourse and Echo Chambers'. *Insight Turkey*, 19(3), 2017: 53–68.

Kiesler, J., *A Next Generation National Information Operations Strategy and Architecture*. Cambridge, MA: Belfer Center for Science and International Affairs, Harvard Kennedy School, 2021. https://www.belfercenter. org/sites/default/files/files/publication/Next%20Gen%20National%20IO%20Strategy%20-%20Kiesler.pdf

Kozinet, R. V., P. Dolbec, and A. Earley, 'Netnographic Analysis: Understanding Culture through Social Media Data'. In U. Flick (ed.), *Sage Handbook of Qualitative Data Analysis*. London: Sage, 2014: 262–275.

Krassen, N., 'Bulgarian Anti-Vaxxers Rally Behind Putin'. *Euractiv*, 30/03/2022. www.euractiv.com/section/ politics/short_news/bulgarian-anti-vaxxers-rally-behind-putin/

Kvachkov, V., 'спецназ россии'. *Voyennaya Literatura*, 2004. http://militera.lib.ru/science/kvachkov_vv/ index.html

Lakoff, G., *The Political Mind*. New York, NY: Viking, 2008.

Lin, H., 'Doctrinal Confusion and Cultural Dysfunction in DoD'. *The Cyber Defense Review*, 5(2), 2020b: 89–106. https://cyberdefensereview.army.mil/Portals/6/Documents/CDR%20Journal%20Articles/Lin_ CDR %20V5N2%20Summer%202020.pdf

Lin, H., 'On the Integration of Psychological Operations with Cyber Operations'. *Lawfare*, 2020a. www. lawfareblog.com/integration-psychological-operations-cyber-operations

Linvill, D. L., and P. L. Warren, 'Troll Factories: Manufacturing Specialized Disinformation on Twitter'. *Political Communication*, 37(4), 2020: 447–467.

McKenna, E., and H. Hahrie, *Groundbreakers. How Obama's 2.2 Million Volunteers Transformed Campaigning in America*. New York: Oxford University Press, 2014.

Michaels, J. H., *The Discourse Trap and the US Military*. New York: Palgrave Macmillan, 2013.

NATO, *AAP-06 NATO Glossary of Terms and Definitions (English and French)*. Brussels: NATO Standardization Office, 2021. https://standard.di.mod.bg/pls/mstd/MSTD.blob_upload_download_routines.download_ blob?p_id= 281&p_table_name=d_ref_documents&p_file_name_column_name=file_name&p_mime_ type_col umn_name=mime_type&p_blob_column_name=contents&p_app_id=600

NATO, *NATO Strategic Communications Handbook*. Brussels-Norfolk: SHAPE-SACT, 2015. https:// dokumen.tips/documents/nato-strategic-communications-handbook-draft-for-nato-is operating-in-an-era-where.html?page=1

Nielsen, N., 'Bannon's the Movement to Launch with January Summit'. *EUobserver*, 22/10/2018. https:// euobserver.com/political/143125

Nielsen, R. K., *Ground Wars. Personalized Communication in Political Campaigns*. Princeton, NJ: Princeton University Press, 2012.

Nye, J. S. Jr., 'Redefining NATO's Mission in the Information Age'. *The NATO Review*, 47(4), 1999: 12–15.

Polyakova, A., F. Splidsboel Hansen, R. van der Noordaa, Ø. Bogen, and H. Sundbom, *The Kremlin's Trojan Horses 3. Russian Influence in Denmark, The Netherlands, Norway and Sweden*. The Atlantic Council, 2018. https://www.atlanticcouncil.org/wp-content/uploads/2021/02/The-Kremlins-Trojan-Horses-3.pdf

Polyakova, A., M. Kounalakis, A. Klapsis, L. S. Germani, J. Iacoboni, F. de Borja Lasheras, and N. de Pedro, *The Kremlin's Trojan Horses 2. The Russian Influence in Greece, Italy, and Spain*. The Atlantic Council, 2017. www.atlanticcouncil.org/images/The_Kremlins_Trojan_Horses_2_web_1121.pdf.

Polyakova, A., M. Laruelle, S. Meister, and N. Barnett, *The Kremlin's Trojan Horses. Russian Influence in France, Germany, and the United Kingdom*. The Atlantic Council, 2016. www.atlanticcouncil.org/images/ publications/The_Kremlins_Trojan_Horses_web_0228_third_edition.pdf

Pomerantsev, P., 'The Kremlin's Information War'. *Journal of Democracy*, 26(4), 2015: 40–50.

Rampini, F., 'Perché l'Occidente è arrivato impreparato all'invasione di Putin?'. *Corriere della Sera*, 22/03/2022. https://www.corriere.it/politica/22_marzo_09/putin-sottovalutato-democrazie-4f53849a-9f1a-11ec-937a-aba34929853f.shtml

Schmitt, L., *What's in a Tweet? Twitter's Impact on Public Opinion and EU Foreign Affairs*. Barcelona: CIDOB, 2021. www.cidob.org/en/content/download/78432/2509011/version/23/file/DOCUMENTS%20CI DOB_11_LEWIN%20SCHMITT.pdf

Sciorilli Borrelli, S., 'Steve Bannon: Italian Experiment "Will Change Global Politics"'. *Politico*, 23/09/2018. www.politico.eu/article/steve-bannon-italy-europe-the-movement-experiment will-change-global-politics/

Soldatov, A., and I. Borogan, *The Red Web*. New York, NY: Public Affairs, 2015.

Spohr, D., 'Fake News and Ideological Polarization: Filter Bubbles and Selective Exposure on Social Media'. *Business Information Review*, 34(3), 2017: 150–160. https://doi.org/10.1177/0266382117722446

Stengel, R., *Information Wars: How We Lost the Global Battle Against Disinformation and What We Can Do About It*. New York, NY: Atlantic Monthly Press, 2019.

Stromer-Galley, J., *Presidential Campaigning in the Internet Age*. Oxford: Oxford University Press, 2014.

UNESCO, *Journalism, Fake News & Disinformation*. Paris: UNESCO, 2018. https://en.unesco.org/sites/default/files/journalism_fake_news_disinformation_print_friendly_0.pdf

WHO, *Novel Coronavirus (2019-nCoV) Situation Report – 13*. New York: WHO, 2020. www.who.int/docs/default-source/coronaviruse/situation-reports/20200202-sitrep-13-ncov v3.pdf

Yadav, D. S. M., *China's Information Warfare Strategy and its Implications for India*. New Delhi: Centre for Land Warfare Studies, 2021. www.claws.in/chinas-information-warfare-strategy-and-its-implications-forindia/#:~:text=The%20basic%20concept%20of%20Chinese,will%20or%20ability%20to%20fight

15

ATTITUDES ABOUT PROPAGANDA AND DISINFORMATION

Identifying discursive personae in YouTube comment sections

Olivia Inwood and Michele Zappavigna

Introduction

YouTube comment sections are rich sources of data, particularly for researchers interested in studying discourse and disinformation. YouTube has been used as a platform for spreading disinformation and extremist views, ranging from terrorist recruitment (Andre 2012; Klausen et al. 2012), state propaganda (Golovchenko et al. 2020), and right-wing extremism (Ekman 2014; Lewis 2018; Levy 2020). Whilst issues of hate speech and disinformation on social media have been studied widely, there is a need to move beyond solely researching platforms such as Twitter that have currently dominated disinformation and racism research (Matamoros-Fernández and Farkas 2021). In comparison to Twitter, YouTube is a less studied platform but one that needs further exploration, particularly in regards to ensuring platform diversity and cross-platform analyses (Matamoros-Fernández and Farkas 2021). Thus, from these continuing discussions in social media research, this chapter focuses on how attitudes about propaganda and disinformation can be researched in YouTube comment sections. In particular, it identifies a method grounded in systemic functional linguistics for identifying discursive personae in YouTube comment sections. By discursive personae we mean how persons and personalities commune in discourse and how this is realised linguistically. The linguistic identification of discursive personae can help us to understand commenters' attitudes towards issues of propaganda and disinformation. In addition, the identification of various discursive personae avoids the homogenisation of propaganda and disinformation, instead illustrating the varied attitudinal targets of commenters, and how commenters approach the same topic with different linguistic resources.

This chapter will firstly provide an overview of research into propaganda and disinformation. It will then introduce the concept of discursive personae and how this concept has been explored in previous literature. The systemic functional linguistics (hereafter SFL) methodology for analysing discursive personae will be explained, followed by a case study on YouTube comments from RT (formerly known as Russia Today) videos for English-speaking audiences on the Skripal poisoning. The Skripal poisoning refers to the poisoning of Sergei Skripal, a former Russian double

DOI: 10.4324/9781003224495-18

agent, and his daughter, Yulia Skripal, in Salisbury, England. The British government accused Russia of instigating the incident, resulting in the expulsion of many Russian diplomats world-wide. The videos investigated for this case study are examples of Russian propaganda, as RT is a news channel funded by the Russian government and has been described as an organisation that engages in disinformation and conspiracist strategies (Yablokov 2015; Elswah and Howard 2020). The purpose of the case study in this chapter is to illustrate the process of identifying discursive personae and how it can illuminate new insights into how propaganda is received by audiences. After explaining the findings from this case study, broader implications for identifying discursive personae in YouTube comments will be discussed.

Defining propaganda and disinformation

In order to understand the conceptual premises of this chapter, it is important to clarify what we mean by disinformation and propaganda. Disinformation originated from the Russian term "dez-informatsiya" (as found in S.I.O.egov's dictionary *Slovar russkogo jazyka* from 1949). The term is defined as follows:

> The dissemination of deliberately false information, esp. when supplied by a government or its agent to a foreign power or to the media, with the intention of influencing the policies or opinions of those who receive it.
>
> (Dictionaries 2001)

"Deliberate" is a key word when considering the definition of disinformation, as the unintentional spread of false information is referred to as misinformation (Wardle and Derakhshan 2017). In addition, in both journalistic and academic discourse, a strong connection has been made with disinformation and Russian interference, as even the term disinformation originated from the Cold War era (Haiden and Althuis 2018). As Karlova and Fisher (2013) write, "The strong association between disinformation and negative, malicious intent probably developed as a result of Stalinist information control policies". Presently, organisations such as the *European External Action Service East Stratcom Task Force*, *EU vs. Disinfo* and *Stop Fake* have all used the term "disinformation" in order to address false information particularly spread by Russian organisations. Many academic articles have also been written relating Russia to disinformation (Yablokov 2015; Mejias and Vokuev 2017; Bennett and Livingston 2018). Thus, the word "disinformation" continues to hold strong connections to Russia, even if the definition of disinformation does not explicitly state this.

There is also a strong connection between disinformation and propaganda. Propaganda from 1929 onwards has referred to "material or information propagated to advance a cause" (Harper 2022). Similarly, Søe (2018) defines propaganda as "information of a biased/misleading nature to promote a political cause". Biddle in *A Psychological Definition of Propaganda* (1931) writes how propaganda has relied on methods including "persuasion", "direct emotional appeal", "direct suggestion", and "indirect suggestion" (Biddle 1931). In addition, he writes that "the emotional pattern of 'we' versus an 'enemy' runs through all propaganda, of war or of peace" (Biddle 1931). This is similar to how disinformation campaigns rely on an enemy such as Russia vs the West (Lucas 2014; Mejias and Vokuev 2017; Polyakova and Boyer 2018). Thus, a lot of disinformation promotes the desire to eradicate a perceived enemy. In considering these definitions there are many similarities with propaganda and disinformation, which also intersect with information manipulation and ideology; van Dijk (2006) writes that manipulation consists of "social power abuse, cognitive mind control and discursive interaction". These qualities can be linked to the intentional harm caused by disinformation. As we can see from this discussion of the definitions of disinformation and propaganda, disinformation is the broader umbrella term referring to any false information that has been deliberately created, whilst propaganda refers to deliberate false information shared to promote a political cause.

Discursive personae

In considering issues of linguistic identity, discursive personae is an important notion to consider because it provides a way of generalising the linguistic patterns observed in social media comment threads, which is particularly insightful when wanting to understand how people engage with disinformation. Discursive personae (also referred to as persona), from an SFL perspective, refers to "persons and personalities communing in discourse" (Martin 2009). Thus, personae does not refer to individual people but rather it is a generalisation of how identities are enacted linguistically. These identities are characterised by particular "coupling dispositions" (Zappavigna 2014a; Zappavigna 2014b; Zappavigna 2018), that is, a tendency to construe particular patterns of values. The linguist Firth (1950) originally referred to the idea of "bundles of personae", that is, how personalities interact in discourse and how one person can enact multiple personae depending on the circumstance they are in. This is similarly supported by the definition of discursive personae as "a function of the acts of positioning that a writer makes, or, in mediated interactive contexts the positioning each contributor makes to a discussion in response to others' comments" (Don 2018). In this sense, discursive personae are distinguished by these positioning acts rather than an individual's self-image or social role ascriptions (Don 2018). It is this history of personae from an SFL perspective that this chapter draws on.

By considering personae in terms of the tendency to negotiate particular values, we can understand the main ideologies that personalities bond around in the context of disinformation. Work considering the function of textual personae in SFL has been explored from various linguistic dimensions. For instance, discursive persona has been examined from the perspective of dialogistic positioning, drawing on the engagement subsystem of appraisal (White and Sano 2006) and authorial persona has been examined through evaluative disposition (White 2008). Textual persona has also been explored from the level of clause, known as discourse semantics (Don 2007, 2016) and from the level of participants in discourse known as tenor (Don 2009, 2018). Identity has been explored from the perspective of iconography (Tann 2011, 2012). Additionally, SFL explorations of personae have been previously explored in terms of shared values in microblogging (Zappavigna 2014a), as an act of impersonation using paralinguistic and dialogic resources (Logi and Zappavigna 2021), and as communal identity in conversational exchanges (Knight 2010b). The work in this chapter interprets personae from the discourse semantic level of SFL, focused on interpersonal meaning enacted by resources from the appraisal and affiliation systems (as will be further explained in the methodology section).

Beyond studies in SFL, personae have been explored in other linguistic fields and in media and cultural studies. In linguistics outside of SFL, researchers have used the term "persona" and have explored it according to phonology (D'Onofrio 2018), dialect style as a type of persona management (Coupland 2002), and as a register of language from a linguistic anthropology perspective (Agha 2005). Goffman's work on the presentation of the self and impression management also aligns with the notion of a persona (Goffman 1959). In media studies, personae have been explored in terms of how one can enact different identities online and offline (Du Preez and Lombard 2014) and from the perspective of "advertising persona", defined as a created character "whose purpose is to persuade an audience to consume" (Stern 1994).

The specific field of "persona studies" takes a cultural studies perspective and connects the study of persona with the "close study of the performance and assemblage of the individual public self" (Marshall et al. 2019: 17). In the move from researching persona to developing the field of persona studies, Marshall, Moore, and Barbour write that the aim of persona studies is "experimenting with and developing a set of approaches for analysing the expansion and proliferation of the development of the public self" (Marshall et al. 2015: 289). The authors acknowledge that this recent interest in studying persona has emerged from studies of social media and micro-celebrity (Senft 2013), where one can present their identity online in multiple ways, thus making the study of persona particularly relevant. In comparison to this chapter, Marshall, Moore, and Barbour refers to "personas" rather than "personae". From their perspective, "personas" refers "to the multiple aspects of an individual's character that are presented and understood by others at certain times and places and in certain roles; a politician, a mother, a celebrity" (Marshall et al. 2015: 302). They interpret "personae" as "reserved by dictionaries" and used to refer to "members of a dramatic work or the multiple characters inhabited by the author over a series of novels" (Marshall et al. 2015: 302). As this example shows, there are some differences in terminology across different disciplines. Overall, personae have been explored from a diverse range of perspectives. Whilst this chapter takes inspiration from how persona has been considered in various disciplines, again, it is focused on personae from a discourse semantic SFL perspective.

Systemic functional linguistics

Systemic functional linguistics (SFL) studies meaning-making resources in language in terms of their social context (Halliday 1978). SFL considers language as both a functional process as its function is to make meanings, and a semiotic process, that is, a process of making meanings by choosing. It is also systemic, as it applies an "analytical methodology which permits the detailed and systematic description of language patterns" (Eggins 2004: 21), foregrounding the analytical power of SFL. Additionally, SFL uses a "system network" to describe the sets of options available for a chosen entry condition. System networks represent paradigmatic organisation, in other words, meaning arising from choice (Matthiessen et al. 2010). An example of a system network is illustrated in Figure 15.1. The curly bracket represents simultaneous systems of "and", whilst a square bracket represents parallel systems of "and" where only one feature can be selected. It is this systematic approach to language that is characteristic of SFL. A core concern of SFL is developing an approach to the study of language that can be applied to many different practical

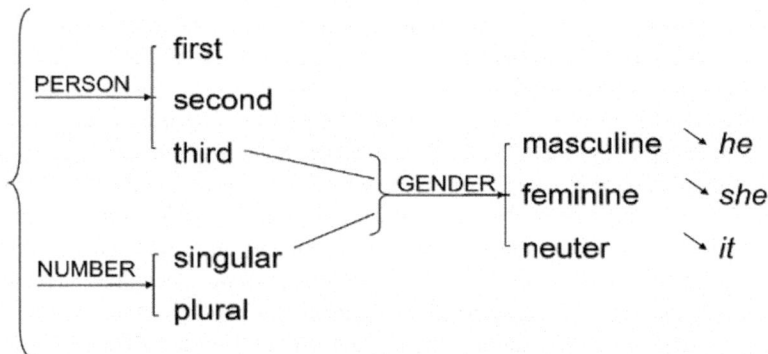

Figure 15.1 Example of a system network (from Martin 2016)

situations and areas of research in order to address particular social issues and problems adhering to Halliday's notion of an appliable linguistics.

Methodology

The methodology for this study is focused upon the appraisal and affiliation frameworks within SFL. The appraisal framework operates at the strata of discourse semantics (clause level) within SFL (Martin and White 2005) and examines the meanings in evaluative language, in terms of "attitude" (feelings and evaluations of people and things), "engagement" (understanding how opinions are placed in discourse) and "graduation" (the grading of feelings) (Martin and White 2005). The appraisal system incorporates polarity between positive versus negative evaluations. Meanings within the "attitude" subsystem are also encoded as either explicit meanings that are clearly evident in the text (inscribed attitude) or implicit meanings that require further context in order to understand (invoked attitude) (Martin and White 2005). In Table 15.1 the subsystems of appraisal are explained. These subsystems are used to code all instances of evaluative meaning in a text.

The ways in which users' bond around certain content online reveals what is actually at stake beyond a simple view of the content of the disinformation. Ideation-attitude couplings are the unit of analysis applied in affiliation theory, as developed by Knight (2010a). This refers to the combination of ideation (what is being evaluated) and attitude (how it is being evaluated) in order to understand the semiotic significance of evaluative meaning (Martin 2008b; Zappavigna 2018). This gives us a way of understanding not only how people express opinion and emotion but how they express opinion and emotion "about people, places and things, and the activities they participate in, however abstract or concrete" (Martin 2008a: 58). Therefore, the ideation-attitude coupling is a useful resource for understanding the key ideas and attitudes that users hold and how these couplings are leveraged as affiliation strategies, in other words, linguistic resources used to bond with others.

This chapter is also focused on the communing affiliation framework. This framework accounts for the ambient aspect of online communication where users do not interact directly. Therefore, ambient affiliation involves communing around values, rather than directly negotiating values in a clearly defined conversational exchange (Zappavigna 2018). The original communing affiliation

Table 15.1 Appraisal subsystems

Appraisal			Explanation of Subtype
Affect	Un/Happiness		Moods of feeling happy or sad
	In/Security		Feelings of peace and anxiety
	Dis/Satisfaction		Feelings of achievement and frustration
	Dis/Inclination		Feelings of fear and desire (irrealis affect)
Judgement	Social Esteem	Normality	How special?
		Capacity	How capable?
		Tenacity	How dependable?
	Social Sanction	Veracity	How honest?
		Propriety	How far beyond reproach?
Appreciation	Reaction		Impact and quality
	Composition		Balance and complexity
	Valuation		Was it worthwhile?

Source: (adapted from Martin and White 2005)

243

framework encompasses three main subsystems: CONVOKING (mustering around community), FI-NESSING (positioning a coupling in relation to other potential couplings). and PROMOTING (inter-personally emphasising a coupling) (Zappavigna 2018; Zappavigna and Martin 2018; Zappavigna 2021). In other versions of the communing affiliation framework, PROMOTING has been renamed TEMPERING in order to account for how a coupling can be emphasised or de-emphasised in order to attract attention (Inwood and Zappavigna 2021). The communing affiliation framework (see *Figure 15.2*) details how affiliation strategies are created, in terms of explaining the particular linguistic resources used in relation to a coupling so that it can be bonded around.

These three systems may further be understood as follows:

- Convoking: mustering together a community by using collectivising resources such as voca-tives, for instance "*guys*" (marshal), and/or establishing a community's parameters by naming or referencing, for instance, "*as a Russian*" (designate).

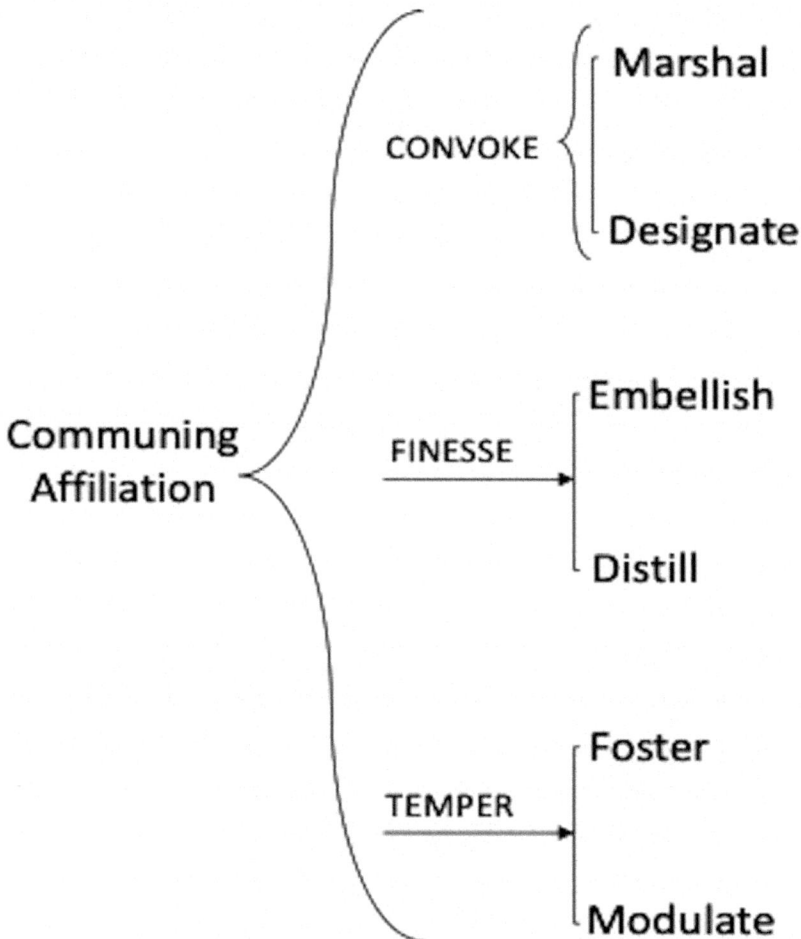

Figure 15.2 Communing affiliation framework (adapted from Zappavigna 2018)

- Finessing: broadening (embellish) or confining (distil) a bond. For example, embellishing opens the bond to various other possibilities offered via heteroglossia ("*I think*") whereas distilling limits this range, often to only one choice ("*It wasn't*").
- Tempering: modifying a bond through upscaled or downscaled graduation, for instance, via quantification "*zero value*" (foster), or adjusting how exemplary it is via emphasis, for example the typographical emphasis of "*LOL*" (modulate).

To summarise, the following conventions will be used in order to explain the results of this study:

- Ideation-attitude couplings will be depicted as [ideation: <<>>/ attitude: <<>>] with how they are tabled as key bonds written underneath in SMALL CAPS
- Arrows represent the examples of affiliative strategies in the text
- **Bold font** indicates ATTITUDE and underlining indicates that target of the ATTITUDE
- SMALL CAPS are used to indicate technical terms and key bonds

Case study: Skripal poisoning

This section will illustrate how an SFL approach to identifying discursive personae can be applied to a particular case study. The case study chosen is based on videos about the Skripal poisoning by RT (formerly known as Russia Today). RT, a news channel funded by the Russian government, is one of the most viewed news channels on YouTube, and has been described as an organisation that engages in disinformation and conspiracist strategies (Yablokov 2015; Elswah and Howard 2020).

The Skripal poisoning case study is interested in how Russian media outlets, and individuals from various nations have spread propaganda to English-speaking audiences. The Skripal poisoning refers to the poisoning of Sergei Skripal, a former Russian spy who emigrated to the UK, and his daughter, Yulia Skripal. It was discovered that the Skripals were poisoned by a Novichok nerve agent (developed by Russia during the latter part of the Cold War), and the British government blamed Russia for the poisoning, expelling many Russian diplomats (Carlsen 2019). The Russian government denied the poisoning and instead blamed Britain for the incident. Various forms of disinformation, propaganda, and conspiracy theories were then spread about the incident.

The dataset for this case study consists of video comments taken from five different RT videos. YouTube Data Tools (Rieder 2015) was used in order to discover all videos related to the Skripal poisoning. From this list, five videos were selected that represented shared propaganda or false information about the Skripal poisoning and had the highest number of views (refer to Table 15.2). *AntConc* software (Anthony 2014) was used to discover the most common word (Russia) in the corpus of comments taken from all videos. A grounded theory approach (Strauss and Corbin 1997) was then taken in order to create a dataset of 500 comments that shared a mix of positive, neutral, and negative views of RT and the Skripal poisoning. These 500 comments were then manually analysed via an appraisal and affiliation analysis. Trends in evaluative meanings and affiliation strategies were then identified and grouped into discursive personae categories. Personae labels were developed by systematically considering the key ideational targets of the attitude in the comment dataset.

In the following section, the different discursive personae that were identified from the Skripal poisoning dataset will be discussed. Each persona will be individually explained with relevant examples shown from the dataset. These examples represent the key evaluative and affiliation strategies in relation to each persona.

Table 15.2 Video dataset

Video Title	Channel Name	Date Published	Views	Comments
Full Skripal case interview with the UK's suspects (EXCLUSIVE)	RT	2018–09–13	98 264	1917
Lavrov: OPCW may've misidentified nerve agent used in Skripal poisoning	RT	2018–04–14	44 303	693
"Skripal case is a carefully-constructed drama" – John Pilger	RT	2018–03–18	201 684	1782
Yulia Skripal gives first media interview since Salisbury Poisoning	RT	2018–05–23	48 487	649
Galloway: Russia could not benefit from Skripal poisoning	RT UK	2018–03–15	45 277	585

Nationalist

The Nationalist persona is concerned with portraying Russia as righteous, innocent, or powerful. With Nationalist persona comments, Russia is treated with positive attitude whilst negative attitudes are directed towards the West, or the Skripal incident is portrayed as false. In addition, the Nationalist persona is characterised by FINESSING affiliation strategies that definitively portray Russia's positive attributes.

In particular, the Nationalist persona emerged in discourses surrounding the impact of RT's reporting. These comments would celebrate RT for their journalism and state Russia's innocence. In this example, we see how RT is positively evaluated:

Full congratulations[1] to RT for interviewing these two citizens that are being **wrongfully accused**[2] in this **false**[3] Skripal case that **wishes to undermine**[4] and make Russia **look like a villain**[4].

[ideation: RT/ attitude: positive VALUATION][1]

Successful RT bond

[ideation: two citizens/ attitude: positive VERACITY][2]

Innocent citizens bond

[ideation: Skripal case/ attitude: negative VALUATION][3]

False event bond

[ideation: Russia/ attitude: positive PROPRIETY][4]

Innocent Russia bond

Finesse: Distil → being

Finesse: Embellish → wishes to, look like

Temper: Modulate → full

RT is celebrated for its news coverage as it exposes the FALSE SKRIPAL CASE. "*Full congratulations*" is an example of TEMPERING affiliation as it emphasises the significance of RT's news coverage. FINESSING affiliation is also evident in this example, where the Skripal case is shown as a FALSE EVENT BOND rallied around with definitive language. This comment ends with an INNOCENT RUSSIA BOND as Russia is positively evaluated because it is caught up in the "*false Skripal case*".

The EMBELLISHING of *"wishes to"* and *"looks like"* speculates on the purpose of the Skripal case. Comments like these followed a similar structure in positively evaluating RT, casting doubt on the VERACITY of the Skripal case, and then emphasising Russia as either innocent or righteous.

In another example of a typical Nationalist persona comment, Russia is portrayed with positive CAPACITY because it *"will make"* the West speak the truth. *"Will make"* is an example of DISTILLING affiliation as it is definitive, leaving little room for negotiation:

Russia **will make**[1] the west **to speak the truth**[2].
[ideation: Russia/ attitude: positive CAPACITY][1]
Powerful Russia bond
[ideation: the West/ attitude: negative VERACITY][2]
Lying West bond
Finesse: Distil → will make

In contrast to the power and truthfulness of Russia, the West is portrayed with negative VERACITY, for refusing to speak the truth. These types of Nationalist comments again emphasise a powerful and righteous Russia in comparison to a deceiving West.

Anti-Elitist

The Anti-Elitist persona negatively evaluates the British elite, globalists, and the UK government. Most commonly, this persona uses negative VERACITY to definitively ascertain that the UK government is lying. In the following example we can see how CONVOKING affiliation is used to strengthen the LYING GOVERNMENT BOND:

I am English and **I don't believe any of the statements made by**[1] my government with regards to Russia/Skripals/WMD. They **lied to us**[1] so many times that we simply don't trust them anymore.
[ideation: government/ attitude: negative VERACITY][1]
Lying government bond
Convoke: Designate → I am English
Convoke: Marshal → us & our
Temper: Modulate → so many
Finesse: Distil → don't trust

By stating that *"I am English"* the commenter implies that what they are saying is not associated with nationalist rhetoric. Instead, they negatively evaluate the UK government as lying, with the CONVOKING affiliation of *"us"* and *"we"* signalling the wider community that they are addressing. In addition, the TEMPERING affiliation of *"so many"* and the definitive language of *"don't trust"* strengthens the LYING GOVERNMENT BOND. Thus, we see here a lot of different affiliation strategies being used in order to strengthen the force of the LYING UK GOVERNMENT BOND.

In other examples, the Russian government and UK governments are directly contrasted, drawing on DISTILLING affiliation to make these contrasts definitive. In this specific example, RT and the Russian government are praised, whilst the UK government is depicted with negative VERACITY:

Full Congratulations[1] for RT/ Russian government for exposing the **baseless claims**[2] of the UK_Government when trying to portray these two common citizens as GRU operatives. The UK is **losing more credibility**[2] every time it tries to make Russia **look like the bad guy**[3] when in reality those inviduals who control the political elite in the US/UK are the **real enemie**[4].

[ideation: RT & Russia government/ attitude: positive CAPACITY][1]

Capable Russia bond

[ideation: UK government/ attitude: negative VERACITY][2]

Lying UK government bond

[ideation: Russia/ attitude: positive PROPRIETY][3]

Innocent Russia bond

[ideation: US/UK political elite/ attitude: negative PROPRIETY][4]

Evil elites bond

Temper: Modulate → full

Finesse: Distil → baseless, is, real & in reality

"Full Congratulations" uses TEMPERING affiliation to strongly praise the Russian government. In contrast, DISTILLING affiliation is used to definitively ascertain the UK government's lying behaviour and the evil behaviour of US and UK elites. These contrasts in negative and positive evaluation, and TEMPERING and DISTILLING affiliation contribute to the stark differences in how the Russian government versus UK government is depicted. Overall, the Anti-Elitist persona is focused on using negative VERACITY to critique the UK government and elites, which can be complemented with contrasting evaluations of the Russian government.

Conspiracist

The Conspiracist persona is distinguished by a focus on negatively evaluating the Skripal case as false. These evaluations were targeted towards the event itself rather than specific people, thus negative VALUATION was the most common evaluation type. In addition, the Conspiracist persona positively evaluated Russia forming an INNOCENT RUSSIA BOND. For example, in the following comment the false event is called out, and then Russia's innocence is explained:

It's **fake**[1] it's **staged by**[2] the EU UK and the UN . . . to **blame**[3] Russia and isolate Russia from the rest of the world

[ideation: it's (Skripal poisoning)/ attitude: negative VALUATION]1

False event bond

[ideation: EU, UK, and UN/ attitude: negative PROPRIETY][2]

Evil West bond

[ideation: Russia/ attitude: positive PROPRIETY][3]

Innocent Russia bond

Finesse: Distil → it's, to blame

The FALSE EVENT BOND is formed from a negative VALUATION of the Skripal poisoning (*it's fake*). The EU, UK, and UN are then negatively evaluated for their evil actions in staging the event. The second part of the comment shifts focus to an evaluation of Russia as innocent (INNOCENT RUSSIA BOND), for it has been blamed by the West for an incident it was not involved in. Throughout this comment, DISTILLING affiliation is used with every evaluative coupling in order to definitively state the message, thus strengthening the perceived VERACITY of the comment's main claims that the Skripal poisoning is fake, the West is evil, and Russia is innocent.

In another example, we see a similar pattern of the FALSE EVENT BOND followed by an INNOCENT RUSSIA BOND:

This was obviously a **staged hoax**[1] deliberately designed to **demonise**[2] Russia

[ideation: this/ attitude: negative VALUATION][1]

False event bond

[ideation: Russia/ attitude: positive PROPRIETY][2]

Innocent Russia bond

Finesse: Distil → obviously & deliberately

In this example, the Skripal poisoning (*this*) is negatively evaluated as a "*staged hoax*", thus forming a FALSE EVENT BOND. The finessing of "*obviously*" strengthens the impact of this FALSE EVENT BOND. In the next part, Russia is treated with positive PROPRIETY because it has been demonised (with the comment implicitly inferring the West is demonising Russia). Again, the FINESSING affiliation of "*deliberately*" strengthens the impact of this statement and makes it appear as a definitive position, without negotiation. The Conspiracist persona is distinguished by this contrasting patterning of a FALSE EVENT BOND (that evaluates a thing rather than a person/country) and an INNOCENT RUSSIA BOND, with DISTILLING affiliation making these bonds appear definitive.

Anti-West

The Anti-West persona explicitly calls out the West and rallies around a CAPABLE RUSSIA BOND. In similarity to the Conspiracist persona, Anti-West comments are made up of contrasting bonds – an EVIL WEST and an INNOCENT RUSSIA. However, what distinguishes Anti-West comments from Conspiracist comments is the use of SOCIAL SANCTION and SOCIAL ESTEEM for evaluations of the West, in comparison to the Conspiracist persona's focus on negative VALUATION for evaluating an event rather than a person or entity. The most typical example of an Anti-West persona comment can be seen here:

Destroy[1] uk and usa, Russia **you can do it**[2].

[ideation: US & UK/ attitude: negative PROPRIETY]l

Evil US & UK

[ideation: Russia/ attitude: positive CAPACITY][2]

Capable Russia bond

Finesse: Distil → destroy

Convoke: Marshal → you

In this example, the UK and USA are negatively evaluated, hence forming an Evil US and UK bond. "*Destroy*" is an example of distilling affiliation as it definitively ascertains the demand that the UK and USA be destroyed. Russia is then evaluated with positive capacity as it has the ability to destroy the West. The convoking affiliation of "*you*" addresses Russia directly as if it is a person. Overall, these Anti-West comments build up a dichotomy of an Evil West versus a capable or righteous Russia, drawing on social sanction and social esteem.

Xenophobe

The Xenophobe persona made explicit comments negatively evaluating Jews. Whilst this persona shares in common some of the qualities of the Conspiracist persona, it is distinguished by its focus on negative propriety rather than evaluating objects or events. In the following example, we see the role of negative propriety in targeting M16, Mossad Zionists, and the UK:

Another **dirty job**[1] of M16 and Mossad Zionists, **failed attempt**[1] to frame Russia. **Shame on**[2] UK.
[ideation: M16 & Mossad Zionists/ attitude: negative propriety][1]
Evil M16 and Zionists bond
[ideation: UK/ attitude: negative propriety][2]
Evil UK bond
Temper: Modulate → another
Finesse: Distil → shame on

These instances of negative propriety form an Evil M16 and Zionists bond and an Evil UK bond. "*Another*" is an example of tempering affiliation as it emphasises the "*dirty job*" of M16 and Mossad Zionists. Whilst distilling also occurs in this comment with "*shame on*" being a definitive statement and not leaving any room for interpretation. This comment emphasises hatred towards M16 and Mossad Zionists with negative propriety, distinguished from the use of negative veracity with the Anti-Elitist persona comments.

In another example, we see again the use of negative propriety towards the Rothschilds (a wealthy Jewish family) and Jews in general:

The Rothschild's are **planting propaganda everywhere**[1] to spark a war to stimulate military borrowing and urban destruction. Jews are **still angry at Russia**[2].
[ideation: Rothschild's and Jews/ attitude: negative propriety][1]
Evil Rothschilds and Jews bond
[ideation: Jews' feelings towards Russia/ attitude: negative dissatisfaction][2]
Attacked Russia bond
Temper: Modulate → everywhere, still

Additionally, this comment evaluates the Jews' feelings toward Russia with dissatisfaction. The two couplings of evaluative meanings are strengthened by tempering affiliation with "*everywhere*" and "*still*" emphasising each bond (Evil Rothschilds and Jews bond, and Attacked

RUSSIA BOND). The Xenophobe persona is distinguished by its focus on negative PROPRIETY towards Jews as a means of spreading hatred and lies towards a particular group.

Sceptic

The Sceptic persona was the most neutral personae identified in the dataset. This persona is distinguished by its use of EMBELLISHING affiliation that broadens the scope of possibilities rather than limiting them. The Sceptic persona also relied on questions with implicit rather than explicit evaluations given. For example, the following comment does not have an explicit meaning:

So this was a <u>Russian lab</u> that **found the bz?**[1]

[ideation: Russian lab/ attitude: negative VALUATION][1]

UNTRUSTWORTHY RUSSIAN LAB BOND

Finesse: Embellish → ?

Rather, it is inferred from the question mark (an example of EMBELLISHING affiliation) that a Russian lab cannot be trusted, as the commenter is questioning the type of lab that found the bz, thus forming an UNTRUSTWORTHY RUSSIAN LAB BOND. In comparison to the other comments analysed, Sceptic persona comments have variable implicit meanings, therefore making it more difficult to decipher from a researcher's perspective.

In another example, this Sceptic persona comment implicitly critiques those who have targeted a commenter for simply questioning more:

It's extremely unlikely that <u>I</u> may be called **Rusky-Botsky (Russian Bot or Troll)**[1] for **questioning more?**[2]

[ideation: Russian troll/ attitude: negative VALUATION][1]

EVIL RUSSIAN TROLL BOND

[ideation: I/ attitude: negative CAPACITY][1]

SUSPICIOUS COMMENTER BOND

[ideation: (those who target the commenter)/ attitude: negative PROPRIETY][2]

EVIL COMMENTERS BOND

Temper: Modulate → extremely

Finesse: Embellish → unlikely & questioning more

The use of TEMPERING affiliation (*extremely*) and EMBELLISHING affiliation (*unlikely* and *questioning more*) casts a sense of sarcasm and ambiguity. Whilst the "*Rusky-Botsky*" has an association with negative VALUATION (Russian bots are bad), this evaluation is then counteracted by the following phrase "*questioning more*" that is also negatively evaluated, shifting the main target away from the Russian bot, instead to the commenter who feels targeted for merely expressing a view. Thus, these examples illustrate how the Sceptic persona utilises implicit meanings that require greater contextual knowledge to understand.

251

Heckler

The Heckler persona directly targeted the Russian people or government. This persona cannot be characterised as explicitly spreading truthful or false information, rather its purpose is to purely ridicule. Take for example the following comment:

RUSSIA NICKNAME IS **THE PAPER BEAR**[1]
[ideation: Russia/ attitude: negative CAPACITY][1]
POWERLESS RUSSIA bond
Temper: Modulate → PAPER

In this instance, Russia is evaluated with negative CAPACITY because *"the paper bear"* has an implicit meaning of being a weak state. Thus, a POWERLESS RUSSIA bond occurs. TEMPERING affiliation is evident with the entire comment being written in capital letters.

In another example, the Russian government is negatively evaluated as unprofessional, thus forming an INCAPABLE RUSSIAN GOVERNMENT BOND:

---

you underestimate **unprofessionalism**[1] of russian government
[ideation: Russian government/ attitude: negative CAPACITY][1]
INCAPABLE RUSSIAN GOVERNMENT BOND
Convoke: Marshal → you

This comment uses CONVOKING affiliation in order to directly address an ambient audience *"you underestimate"*. Again, we see this negative evaluation as a form of ridicule, without any extra comment on RT's propaganda. The Heckler persona ridicules the Russian people or government with negative evaluation but does not add extra bonds that attempt to comment on the VERACITY of the situation.

Critic

The Critic persona directly critiques Russia with negative evaluation. In comparison to the Heckler personae, the Critic does not ridicule Russia (in terms of negative CAPACITY), rather it highlights Russia's negative PROPRIETY. Take for example the following comment:

Russia **just wants to watch the world burn**[1]
[ideation: Russia/attitude: negative PROPRIETY][1]
EVIL RUSSIA bond
Temper: Modulate → just

This comment negatively evaluates Russia for wanting to *"watch the world burn"* hence forming an EVIL RUSSIA BOND. The *"just"* in this instance is a form of TEMPERING affiliation as it adds extra value to what Russia *"wants"* to do.

Similarly, in the following comment, Russia's negative PROPRIETY is highlighted:

<u>He</u> was of **zero value to Russia**1 which is why <u>they</u> **poisoned him**[2].

[ideation: he/ attitude: negative CAPACITY][1]

USELESS SKRIPAL BOND

[ideation: they (Russia)/ attitude: negative PROPRIETY][2]

EVIL RUSSIA BOND

Temper: Foster → zero

Finesse: Distil → which is why

In this comment, Skripal (*he*) is evaluated as useless to Russia (negative CAPACITY). The fostering of "*zero value*" emphasises this particular evaluation. Russia is then evaluated with negative PROPRIETY for poisoning Skripal. The phrase "*which is why*" definitively ascertains this. Overall, the Critic persona evaluates Russia with negative PROPRIETY but is also supported by additional bonds, distinguished from the Heckler persona that predominately uses negative bonds towards Russia without any further explanation.

Anti-Propagandist

The Anti-Propagandist persona is concerned with questions of VERACITY. This persona drew attention to false comments and highlighted RT's status as a Russian-owned propaganda channel. With the first example, we see a common comment used to call out the behaviour of those spreading false information:

Damn sooo many **Russian <u>BOTS</u>**[1] in the comment section

[ideation: Russian bots/ attitude: negative VERACITY][1]

LYING COMMENTERS BOND

Temper: Modulate → sooo many, BOTS

In this comment, Russian bots are evaluated with negative VERACITY as Russian bots are culturally associated with large-scale automated activity on the Internet, typically of a false nature. The TEMPERING of "*sooo many*" and *BOTS* in capital letters emphasises these claims.

The other commonly occurring comment by the Anti-Propagandist persona directly called out RT as a propaganda channel. For example:

LOL, exclusive interview – <u>RT</u> is a **Russian owned and run propaganda channel**[1] and <u>Peskov</u> **is their troll.**[2]

[ideation: RT/ attitude: negative VERACITY][1]

FALSE RT BOND

[ideation: Peskov/ attitude: negative VERACITY][2]

LYING PESKOV BOND

Temper: Modulate → LOL

Finesse: Distil → is

This comment evaluated RT with negative VERACITY for being a *"Russian owned and run propaganda channel"*. Peskov, a Russian diplomat, is also evaluated with negative VERACITY for being a *"troll"*. The TEMPERING affiliation of *"LOL"* laughs off the idea of an exclusive interview, instead evaluating RT as false information. DISTILLING affiliation also has a role in this comment, as the *"is"* makes these claims definitive without room for negotiation. Thus, from these examples we see how the Anti-Propagandist persona is focused exclusively on evaluations of VERACITY as a way of calling out Russian propaganda.

Bond cluster diagram

In order to visualise the key bonds that constitute each persona, a bond cluster diagram is used (see Figure 15.3). The bond cluster diagram illustrates the key bonds that personae share and how these bonds interlink with other personae. These sorts of diagrams are useful for visually mapping out the wide range of comments made across a large YouTube comments dataset and how we can interpret the importance of evaluative language in these comments.

The overall findings of this case study demonstrate the different attitudes towards Russian identity, Russian propaganda, and "fake news" in general. On the left-hand side of the bond cluster diagram, we have discursive personae broadly bonding around an "evil West" and/or "innocent Russia" macro bond, spreading disinformation. On the right-hand side, discursive personae bond around a "false content" macro bond, attempting to highlight the falsity of RT's reporting. Beyond these macro bonds (highlighted in bold), each persona has their unique micro bonds. Due to the short nature of the comments analysed for this case study, each comment represented a specific persona; however, with larger texts, it is possible for multiple personae to be identified within the same text. From the Skripal poisoning case study we see the clear distinction between "Pro-Russia" versus "Anti-Russia" personae, with no overlapping bonds. Whilst the "Pro-Russia" persona are more concerned with highlighting the evils of the West and Russia's innocence, the "Anti-Russia" persona are more focused on calling out RT as propaganda; thus, they are more concerned with

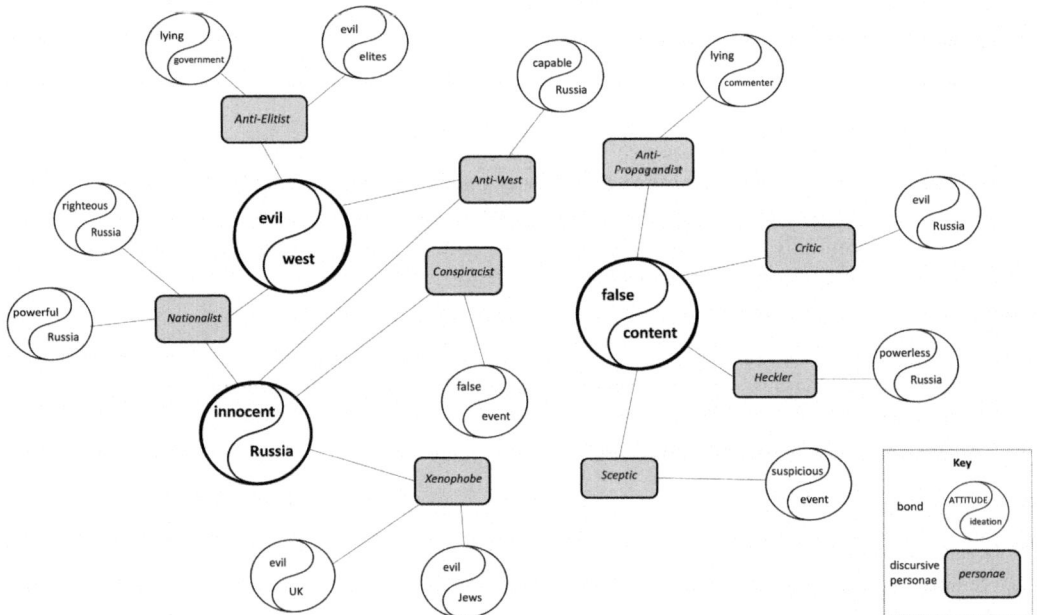

Figure 15.3 Skripal poisoning case study bond cluster diagram

questions of VERACITY rather than PROPRIETY. From this analysis, we see the importance of evaluative positioning that allows different social values to emerge and be considered at a macro level.

Implications for research and conclusion

This chapter has explored the different evaluative and affiliation strategies used by YouTube commenters engaging with Russian propaganda for English-speaking audiences. By considering different linguistic patterns, we were able to identify various discursive personae in the dataset. The various discursive personae discovered highlight the array of different evaluative meanings that can be made and the division among commenters regarding with VERACITY versus PROPRIETY.

In considering the implications of this research beyond the particular case study explored in this chapter, the methodology outlined is beneficial to qualitative and quantitative studies regarding discourses of propaganda and disinformation. By being able to linguistically identify different discursive personae in discourse, this means that tailored solutions can be developed for specific communities, rather than overgeneralising disinformation discourses. As a bond cluster diagram can show, false information can be engaged with in a variety of different ways, and it is important to delve further into these reasons by exploring evaluative meanings in detail. In addition, understanding the personae in comment sections can aid in the creation of manual and automated detection processes for identifying the specific networks of values that charge disinformation discourses. SFL approaches to studying disinformation can also be useful in designing educational materials so that students can linguistically identify the language used by those engaging with propaganda and prevent themselves from becoming radicalised (Szenes 2021).

The methodological approach to discovering discursive personae detailed in this chapter has previously been applied to the genre of Internet hoaxes on YouTube (Inwood and Zappavigna 2021) and COVID-19 conspiracy theories on YouTube (Inwood and Zappavigna 2022). Whilst some personae such as "Sceptics" are shared across these different case studies, other personae categories are different, particularly in comparing political versus non-political discourse. Future research might apply this methodology to more case studies, encompassing a range of different issues. The methodology could also be refined to identify the patterns more closely in language most relevant to these potential domains and further specify the relationships between affiliation strategies and bonds.

Related chapters

- Chapter 10: Investigating the Language of Fake News across Cultures – Nele Põldvere, Elizaveta Kibisova, and Silje Susanne Alvestad.
- Chapter 23: The COVID-19 Infodemic on Twitter: Dialogic Contraction within the Echo Chambers – Marina Bondi and Leonardo Sanna.
- Chapter 5: A Model for Understanding and Assessing Semi-Fake Scientific News Reporting – Paola Catenaccio.
- Chapter 7: Fakespeak in 280 Characters: Using a Corpus-Based Approach to Study the Language of Disinformation on Twitter – Sylvia Jaworska.

References

Agha, A. (2005) *Registers of Language*, Malden: John Wiley & Sons.
Andre, V. (2012) 'Neojihadism' and YouTube: Patani militant propaganda dissemination and radicalization. *Asian Security*, 8, 27–53.
Anthony, L.A. (2014) *Computer Software*, Tokyo, Japan: Waseda University.

Bennett, W.L. & Livingston, S. (2018) The disinformation order: Disruptive communication and the decline of democratic institutions. *European Journal of Communication*, 33, 122–139.

Biddle, W.W. (1931) A psychological definition of propaganda. *The Journal of Abnormal and Social Psychology*, 26, 283–295.

Carlsen, L. (2019) After Salisbury Nerve agents revisited. *Molecular Informatics*, 38.

Coupland, N. (2002) *Language, Situation and the Relational Self: Theorizing Dialect-Style in Sociolinguistics*, Cambridge: Cambridge University Press.

Dictionaries, O. (2001) *Paperback Oxford English Dictionary*, Oxford: Oxford University Press.

Don, A. (2007) *A Framework for the Investigation of Interactive Norms and the Construction of Textual Identity in Written Discourse Communities: The Case of an Email Discussion List*. Unpublished PhD Thesis. University of Birmingham.

Don, A. (2009) Legitimating tenor relationships: Affiliation and alignment in written interaction. *Linguistics & The Human Sciences*, 5.

Don, A. (2016) "It is hard to mesh all this": Invoking attitude, persona and argument organisation. *Functional Linguistics*, 3, 1–26.

Don, A. (2018) Stance-taking and the construal of textual persona in written contexts: Social Contact revisited. *Linguistics and the Human Sciences*, 13, 70–95.

D'onofrio, A. (2018) Personae and phonetic detail in sociolinguistic signs. *Language in Society*, 47, 513–539.

Du Preez, A. & Lombard, E. (2014) The role of memes in the construction of Facebook personae. *Communicatio*, 40, 253–270.

Eggins, S. (2004) *Introduction to Systemic Functional Linguistics*, London: A&C Black.

Ekman, M. (2014) The dark side of online activism: Swedish right-wing extremist video activism on YouTube. *MedieKultur: Journal of Media and Communication Research*, 30, 21.

Elswah, M. & Howard, P.N. (2020) "Anything that causes chaos": The organizational behavior of Russia Today (RT). *Journal of Communication*, 70, 623–645.

Firth, J.R. (1950) Personality and language in society. *The Sociological Review*, 42, 37–52.

Goffman, E. (1959) *The Presentation of Self in Everyday Life*, New York: Anchor Books.

Golovchenko, Y., Buntain, C., Eady, G., Brown, M.A. & Tucker, J.A. (2020) Cross-platform state propaganda: Russian trolls on Twitter and YouTube during the 2016 US Presidential election. *The International Journal of Press/Politics*. http://doi.org/1940161220912682.

Haiden, L. & Althuis, J. (2018) The definitional challenges of fake news. *Report: King's Centre for Strategic Communications*, Department of War Studies, King's College, London.

Halliday, M.A.K. (1978) *Language as Social Semiotic: The Social Interpretation of Language and Meaning*, London: Hodder Arnold.

Harper, D. (2022) *Online Etymology Dictionary*. Retrieved from: www.etymonline.com/

Inwood, O. & Zappavigna, M. (2021) Ambient affiliation, misinformation, and moral panic: Negotiating social bonds in a YouTube internet hoax. *Discourse & Communication*, 15.

Inwood, O. & Zappavigna, M. (2022) The ID2020 conspiracy theory in YouTube video comments during COVID-19: Bonding around religious, political, and technological discourses. In M. Demata, V. Zorzi & A. Zottola (eds.) *Conspiracy Theory Discourses*, Amsterdam: John Benjamins.

Karlova, N.A. & Fisher, K.E. (2013) "Plz RT": A social diffusion model of misinformation and disinformation for understanding human information behaviour. *Information Research*, 18.1, 1–17.

Klausen, J., Barbieri, E.T., Reichlin-Melnick, A. & Zelin, A.Y. (2012) The YouTube jihadists: A social network analysis of Al-Muhajiroun's propaganda campaign. *Perspectives on Terrorism*, 6, 36–53.

Knight, N.K. (2010a) *Laughing Our Bonds Off: Conversational Humour in Relation to Affiliation*. Unpublished PhD Thesis. University of Sydney.

Knight, N.K. (2010b) Wrinkling complexity: Concepts of identity and affiliation in humour. In *New Discourse on Language: Functional Perspectives on Multimodality, Identity, and Affiliation*, London: Continuum, 35–58.

Levy, H. (2020) Grammars of contestation and pluralism: Paulo Freire's action in Brazil's periphery and the rise of right-wing discourse on YouTube. *International Communication Gazette*, 82, 474–489.

Lewis, R. (2018) Alternative influence: Broadcasting the reactionary right on YouTube. *New Data & Society [ebook]*. Retrieved from: https://datasociety.net/output/alternative-influence.

Logi, L. & Zappavigna, M. (2021) Impersonated personae – paralanguage, dialogism and affiliation in stand-up comedy. *HUMOR*, 34.3, 339–373.

Lucas, E. (2014) *The New Cold War: Putin's Russia and the Threat to the West*, New York: Macmillan.

Marshall, P.D., Moore, C. & Barbour, K. (2015) Persona as method: Exploring celebrity and the public self through persona studies. *Celebrity Studies*, 6, 288–305.

Marshall, P.D., Moore, C. & Barbour, K. (2019) *Persona Studies: An Introduction*, Hoboken, NJ: John Wiley & Sons.

Martin, J.R. (2008a) Innocence: Realisation, instantiation and individuation in a Botswanan town. *Questioning Linguistics*, 32–76.

Martin, J.R. (2008b) Tenderness: Realisation and instantiation in a Botswanan town. *Odense Working Papers in Language and Communication*, 29, 30–58.

Martin, J.R. (2009) Realisation, instantiation and individuation: Some thoughts on identity in youth justice conferencing. *DELTA: Documentação de Estudos em Lingüística Teórica e Aplicada*, 25, 549–583.

Martin, J.R. (2016). Meaning matters: A short history of systemic functional linguistics. *Word*, 62(1), 35–58.

Martin, J.R. & White, P.R.R. (2005) *The Language of Evaluation: Appraisal in English*, New York: Palgrave Macmillan.

Matamoros-Fernández, A. & Farkas, J. (2021) Racism, hate speech, and social media: A systematic review and critique. *Television & New Media*, 22, 205–224.

Matthiessen, C.M., Teruya, K. & Lam, M. (2010) *Key Terms in Systemic Functional Linguistics*, New York: A&C Black.

Mejias, U.A. & Vokuev, N.E. (2017) Disinformation and the media: The case of Russia and Ukraine. *Media, Culture & Society*, 39, 1027–1042.

Polyakova, A. & Boyer, S.P. (2018) *The Future of Political Warfare: Russia, the West, and the Coming Age of Global Digital Competition. Report: Brookings – Robert Bosch Foundation Transatlantic Initiative (BBTI)*. Washington: The Brookings Institution.

Rieder, B. (2015) *YouTube Data Tools* (Version 1.11). Retrieved from: https://tools.digitalmethods.net/netvizz/youtube/

Senft, T.M. (2013) Microcelebrity and the branded self. In J. Hartley, J. Burgess & A. Bruns (eds.) *A Companion to New Media Dynamics*, West Sussex: John Wiley & Sons, 346–354.

Søe, S.O. (2018) Algorithmic detection of misinformation and disinformation: Gricean perspectives. *Journal of Documentation*, 74, 309–332.

Stern, B. (1994) Authenticity and the textual persona: Postmodern paradoxes in advertising narrative. *International Journal of Research in Marketing*, 11, 387–400.

Strauss, A. & Corbin, J.M. (1997) *Grounded Theory in Practice*, Thousand Oaks: Sage.

Szenes, E. (2021) Neo-Nazi environmentalism: The linguistic construction of ecofascism in a Nordic Resistance Movement manifesto. *Journal for Deradicalization*, 146–192.

Tann, K. (2011) *Semogenesis of a Nation*. Unpublished PhD Thesis, University of Sydney.

Tann, K. (2012) The language of identity discourse: Introducing a systemic functional framework for iconography. *Linguistics & the Human Sciences*, 8.

Van Dijk, T.A. (2006) Discourse and manipulation. *Discourse and Society*, 17.3, 359–383.

Wardle, C. & Derakhshan, H. (2017) *Information Disorder: Toward an Interdisciplinary Framework for Research and Policymaking* (Vol. 27), Strasbourg: Council of Europe, 1–107.

White, P.R.R. (2008) 20. Praising and blaming, applauding, and disparaging – solidarity, audience positioning, and the linguistics of evaluative disposition. In *Handbook of Interpersonal Communication*, Berlin: De Gruyter Mouton, 567–594.

White, P.R.R. & Sano, M. (2006) Dialogistic positions and anticipated audiences-a framework for stylistic comparisons. In *Pragmatic Markers in Contrast*, Frankfurt: Elsevier, 189–214.

Yablokov, I. (2015) Conspiracy theories as a Russian public diplomacy tool: The case of Russia Today (RT). *Politics*, 35, 301–315.

Zappavigna, M. (2014a) CoffeeTweets: Bonding around the bean on Twitter. In P. Seargeant & C. Tagg (eds.) *The Language of Social Media*, Berlin: Springer, 139–160.

Zappavigna, M. (2014b) Enacting identity in microblogging through ambient affiliation. *Discourse & Communication*, 8, 209–228.

Zappavigna, M. (2018) *Searchable Talk and Social Media Metadiscourse*, London: Bloomsbury Publishing.

Zappavigna, M. (2021) Ambient affiliation in comments on YouTube videos: Communing around values about ASMR. *Journal of Foreign Languages 外国语*, 44, 21–40.

Zappavigna, M. & Martin, J.R. (2018) # Communing affiliation: Social tagging as a resource for aligning around values in social media. *Discourse, Context & Media*, 22, 4–12.

257

16

CITIZENS' PERSPECTIVES ON THE NEWS MEDIA AND DEMOCRACY

A citizens' panel case study from Wales

Philip Seargeant, Donna Smith, and Dylan Moore

Introduction

One of the driving forces behind recent concerns about the impact of "fake news" is the effect it can have on a democratic system which operates on the basis of citizens making informed decisions about how they wish to be governed. Many of the chapters in this handbook discuss the interconnections that exist between "fake news" and the media and fakeness and post-truth, as well as how "fake news" discourse can be counterclaimed and the phenomena which fall under this umbrella term be addressed. The news media plays a pivotal role in creating an environment in which this can happen, and thus a sustainable, trustworthy news media – that is, one which is resilient to the spread of disinformation – is a basic expectation for a well-functioning liberal democracy. From this perspective, trust in the news media is a prerequisite for trust – and engagement – in the political process.

This chapter investigates the relationship between citizens' perspectives on the news media and their beliefs about politics, democracy, and their own sense of political engagement. It examines this within the context of Welsh politics and the various challenges that arise in this context, from both a political, cultural, and media industry perspective and from the nature of the union between Wales and the broader concept of the United Kingdom. For its central case study, the chapter reports on the process and results of a citizens' panel research project conducted in the first half of 2022 by the Open University and the Institute of Welsh Affairs. This research explored how Welsh citizens' access to, and understanding of, the media, news, and information in Wales might be improved, especially in an era of "fake news". The project team worked closely with citizens to make recommendations to inform and influence the work being conducted by the Welsh government and the Senedd (Welsh Parliament) in the areas of broadcasting and media regulation, educational provision, and the strengthening of the Welsh language and culture. The premise behind all the recommendations was that reliable sources of news and information are vital for a flourishing democracy, as they allow people to make informed choices about the issues that matter to them. As well providing insight on Welsh citizens' perspectives on news media and democracy in the era of "fake news", the chapter also outlines the challenges and opportunities of conducting a citizens' panel on a topic of this sort, which academics and policymakers can, we hope, learn from.

DOI: 10.4324/9781003224495-19

Active citizens and citizens panels

As noted in the introduction, the originating principle for the research which comprises our case study is that essential to the democratic system is informed decision-making by the electorate, and that for informed decision-making to take place, citizens need access to reliable information about issues that are of concern to them, as well any contextual knowledge which will allow them to interpret and evaluate this information. In other words, access to trustworthy sources of news, alongside relevant educational or explanatory resources, is of vital importance for allowing citizens to take an active part in the democratic process. It is within this context that disinformation or "fake news" impacts the democratic purpose as it actively attacks the principle of informed decision-making.

The citizen panel format, which is the vehicle for the research reported upon here, is, in microcosm, a model for active democratic practice in that it is structured around a number of key elements which make up informed decision-making within society. Brown (2006) defines citizen panels as "temporary advisory bodies that involve lay people in cooperative deliberation informed by expert advice". Panels consist of a number of "lay citizens" who are brought together over a number of days to learn about and discuss a political topic (usually of a complex and perhaps contentious nature). The learning involves input from a range of experts; the discussion is coordinated by members of the research team, and the process concludes with the panel drawing up recommendations about policy or other institutional interventions which are communicated to those in institutional positions of power. The concept was developed alongside theories of deliberative democracy in the 1980s and 1990s (Crosby et al., 1986; Floridia, 2018), as a way of facilitating new forms of public participation in the political process (Hörning, 1999). Although conventionally the process has taken place in a face-to-face context, panels have increasingly been conducted online (Chwalisz, 2021) due to the impact of the COVID pandemic on society generally.

Brown (2006) outlines several features which distinguish citizen panels from other forms of citizen participation. These include creating the opportunity for dialogue between citizens and a diverse range of experts, the fact that they are advisory only (i.e. they do not have the authority to make legally binding decisions), and that their recommendations are addressed to both institutions/officials and the general public. As a form of political participation, the output or recommendation stage is of great importance in that it feeds directly into the workings of the political system. From a research point of view, however, it is the process and the conclusions from the discussion which are of primary interest, and thus this is what we report on in this chapter.

If we return to the idea of informed decision-making within society, we can break this down into three stages:

1 Accessing and interpreting relevant information;
2 Deliberating via discussion upon the implications of this information;
3 Making decisions about proposed actions based upon these deliberations.

In the terminology of the citizen panel format, these three stages are referred to as (a) the education phase, (b) the deliberation phase, and (c) the recommendation phase.

This format allows for a sort of ideal context in which the practice of informed decision-making can take place in that it provides resources of time, organisation, and management in which these three stages can be carried out. In real life, the stages are likely to be undertaken by people in a far more ad hoc fashion. "Education" comes from exposure to whatever news media one engages with; deliberation as a social practice comes from talking with friends, colleagues, or acquaintances (and perhaps arguing on social media), and recommendations are in the form of engaging with the political process in some form or other, including voting. And each of these can be complicated by a plethora of everyday constraints (such as a lack of time in the normal daily schedule).

Given that the citizen panel format works along very similar principles as informed-political participation does, and that informed-political participation relies on access to trustworthy information, there is an inbuilt synergy between this as a research format and the problem of "fake news". In particular, what the citizen panel approach allows for is research into the reflections of citizens on the role that their current access to news and information has on their sense of political engagement and satisfaction within the political system that regulates the society in which they live. In the Methodology section of this chapter we outline in more detail precisely how the citizen panel was organised to address the topics of news, disinformation, and political participation in Wales. Before that, however, it will be useful to explain a little about the background to the Welsh political environment and the media ecosystem.

The wider context

The Welsh political context

Although the relationship between news media and the political sphere is fundamental to a functioning democracy, and the erosion of public trust in the reliability of media resulting from the challenge of "fake news" and other factors are clearly global, there are a number of specific issues related to Wales that arise from its developing political status within the United Kingdom.

Wales was granted its own devolved administration, then called the National Assembly for Wales, in 1999 following a referendum held in 1997. A previous referendum had been held in 1979, when devolution was rejected by a large majority (4:1). In 1997, on a turnout of 50.22%, Welsh voters were in favour of the proposed Assembly, but by an extremely narrow margin (50.3% in favour, 49.7% against). Since then, further acts of Parliament have strengthened the institution: the Government of Wales Act 2006 created an executive body (Welsh Government), separate from the legislative body, and granted the Assembly further competences. In 2011, a further (non-binding) referendum was held to assess Welsh citizens' views on whether the Assembly should be granted law-making powers in its 20 areas of competence. This referendum returned a much clearer majority, with almost two-thirds in favour of strengthening devolution; however, turnout was much lower, at just 35%. In 2014, another Wales Act granted the Welsh Assembly some tax-raising powers, among other provisions. In 2017, yet another Wales Act strengthened devolution further by ensuring the permanence of the Assembly and paving the way for the institution renaming itself Senedd Cymru/Welsh Parliament in 2020. In 2022, Welsh government set up an independent commission to

> consider and develop options for fundamental reform of the constitutional structures of the United Kingdom, in which Wales remains an integral part . . . [and] to consider and develop all progressive principal options to strengthen Welsh democracy and deliver improvements for the people of Wales.

Therefore we can see that the famous statement made by former secretary of state for Wales Ron Davies, largely credited as a principal "architect of devolution", that "devolution is a process and not an event" has been borne out by the continually shifting constitutional status of Wales within the United Kingdom.

Meanwhile, the party political landscape in Wales has very much diverged from that of the United Kingdom and its other constituent nations during the period since the advent of devolution. In 1997, the Labour Party won a landslide victory at the UK General Election, setting the scene for honouring its manifesto commitments to deliver devolved parliaments for Wales and Scotland. But while Welsh Labour has continued as the main governing party in Wales for the entire period of the National Assembly's and then Senedd Cymru's existence (including various coalition and cooperation arrangements with Plaid Cymru and the Liberal Democrats, as well as periods of overall control), since 2010 the UK Government has been led by Conservatives. This also roughly coincides with the rise of the Scottish National Party, who formed a minority government in Scotland in 2007 and have ruled as a majority party since 2011. Taking into account the very different political landscape of Northern Ireland, this has meant that the four nations of the UK have been ruled for over a decade by parties with very differing ideologies and agendas. Particularly since the referendum on Scottish independence in 2014 and the UK's vote to leave the European Union in 2016, there has also been a rise in indicative support for Welsh independence, and a much more fractious relationship between the Labour-led Welsh Government and successive Conservative governments in Westminster (the UK seat of power).

However, despite all these very significant developments, the media landscape in Wales has not altered at the same pace as its governance. Studies have consistently shown that most Welsh citizens still receive their news from UK sources, which tend towards London-centricity and often report news that is, because of the asymmetric constitutional structure of the UK, only relevant to England. This creates what has been widely identified as a "democratic deficit", whereby Welsh citizens are underinformed about the decision-making institutions and processes that govern their lives. Despite 20 major areas of policy – including health and education – having been in Wales' competence for more than two decades, polls consistently find that up to 40% of people in the country either do not know who makes decisions in these areas or that they believe decisions are made in Westminster. Despite the fact that the COVID-19 pandemic, beginning in 2020, shone a spotlight on devolved politics like never before – with each of the four nations of the UK setting their own, often very different, restrictions – surveys continued to show a lack of knowledge and understanding about devolved decision-making within the Welsh public at large.

Media regulation

The current regulatory landscape affecting Wales is a complicated one – and one that crosses borders. In relation to the press, in 2013 the UK Parliament established the Royal Charter on Self-Regulation of the Press, which in turn established the Press Recognition Panel (PRP), which is tasked with approving press regulators. Most UK newspapers are members of the Independent Press Standards Organisation (IPSO), the UK's industry funded regulator for the newspaper and magazine industry (including online newspapers) in the UK, including those based or active in Wales. IPSO has never applied for PRP approval and is not seen as meeting the relevant criteria. Some smaller titles are members of The Independent Monitor for the Press (IMPRESS) (including, for instance, WalesOnline). IMPRESS has applied for and received PRP approval. Some newspapers are members of IPSO and IMPRESS. Others are not members of any regulator.

Another issue to consider here is regulatory jurisdiction and the fact that Welsh issues may be covered by newspapers sold in Wales but not based in Wales or owned by a Welsh company. It is therefore difficult within the existing devolution settlement and the current media landscape to regulate media in Wales effectively.

Arguments from the press against external regulation usually refer to the importance of a free press for the workings of democracy, which is certainly important. But a free press is undermined if its users feel they cannot trust the information presented, or if a large proportion of the potential audience feels there is a lack of quality in their local and national media. Regulation is thus one way to help restore trust and confidence, as well as a commitment to qualitative standards to enhance media provision for citizens.

Moving on to television and radio, broadcasting is not a devolved function of Wales. Broadcasting is regulated by the Office of Communications (Ofcom), and while there is currently an Ofcom Advisory Committee for Wales, which provides advice about the opinions and interests of the people of Wales, overall Ofcom is a function of the UK government. "Exploring the devolution of broadcasting", a 2021 report by the Culture, Welsh Language, and Communications Committee of the Fifth Senedd, called for Wales to have more powers over broadcasting, including powers over Welsh language public service broadcasting and more content produced in Wales.

In relation to online media, the UK government has declared its intention to regulate digital platform providers, via Ofcom. The Online Safety Bill (2022), as drafted in summer 2022, states an intention to create a duty of care for online platforms, requiring them to protect individuals from certain types of online harm while protecting free speech. This is somewhat controversial legislation, but the bill is an attempt to address the power of large multimedia companies and a recognition of the fact that current legislation has not kept pace with media developments.

Such debates are not unique to the UK. The Open Government Partnership (2021), for instance, an organisation dedicated to transforming how governments serve citizens and which covers 75 countries, has produced a list of action points for transparent and accountable digital governance, including the need to be digitally inclusive, tackle misinformation and disinformation, protect against surveillance and censorship, and prevent online harassment.

What such discussions make clear is that media regulation needs to be considered on a transnational basis. Indeed, there are various tensions at play, such as the one between news produced in Wales (and/or by Welsh citizens) versus that produced outside of Wales but about Wales, the tension between a focus on the local versus discussion of UK-wide and international issues, and the tension between free speech and protection from harm. It is also a fast-moving policy area, in both the UK and internationally, and therefore needs to be treated with some caution about what is possible and over what timescale.

Democracy and citizenship education

A project run by Electoral Reform Society Cymru (ERS) in 2018, called Our Voices Heard, called for a range of interventions to support citizens' understanding of the democratic process, political parties, institutions, and campaigning. As outlined by the ERS in 2020, Welsh Government has supported the creation of political education resources for use in Welsh schools but not mandated political education "as a distinct subject or compulsory topic". It is important to note here that the legacy subjects of PSE (personal and social education) and PHSE (personal, social, health, and economic education) have been incorporated into the Health and Wellbeing "area of learning and experience" (AOLE) of Curriculum for Wales (CfW), and that some aspects of Democracy and Citizenship education are already included in the "What Matters" statements in the Humanities "area of learning and experience".

Under the statement "Human societies are complex and diverse, and shaped by human actions and beliefs", governance – defined as "the systems and ways in which countries, communities and organisations are led and managed" – is listed as a key concept that learners will explore, alongside chronology, change and continuity, diversity, cause and effect, interconnectedness, community, identity and belonging, and authority. Under the statement "Informed, self-aware citizens engage with the challenges and opportunities that face humanity, and are able to take considered and ethical action", there is further statutory guidance that learners will "explore concepts, including citizenship, authority and governance, interconnectedness, justice and equality, enterprise, rights, and social action and responsibility", enabling them to "take committed social action as caring, participative citizens of their local, national and global communities, showing an understanding of and commitment to justice, diversity and the protection of the environment".

Despite this high-level conceptual guidance, the emphasis that CfW places on individual schools' autonomy presents a high risk of variance in the specificity of the Democracy and Citizenship education learners will actually receive. Although CfW is currently being rolled out, qualifications to replace GCSEs are very much still under construction, and it is worth noting that "Reforming qualifications" is a key part of the Co-operation Agreement between Welsh Government and Plaid Cymru.

In "Qualified for the Future" (October 2021) Qualifications Wales communicated its decision to create a new GCSE in history. In paragraph 5.66 "the need for Welsh history to be a key component of the new GCSE History qualification" is noted. There is a clear opportunity here for any new component on modern Welsh history to include the study of devolution, the creation of the National Assembly for Wales and its development into the Senedd, as well as – importantly – the relationships between the different parliaments and jurisdictions of the United Kingdom.

In the same document, Qualifications Wales communicates its decision to create a new GCSE in social studies, a "multi-disciplinary qualification align[ed] with the aims and purposes of the new curriculum". "Qualified for the Future" states that "working groups will be convened at individual subject level to develop proposals for how the content and assessment of each future qualification could support effective curriculum design and teaching practice" (5.78) and that it would ensure progression to further study of "related subjects such as law, sociology, and politics" (5.80).

Although this GCSE would be optional, its widespread adoption in Welsh schools could and should lead to specialist PGCE courses for social studies teachers who could then also deliver specialist democracy and citizenship education lessons to all students at secondary level. All schools in Wales could be mandated to appoint a Democracy and Citizenship education lead, with an attached teaching and learning responsibility. This role would carry with it the responsibility to be the point of contact for elected representatives from all parties and all appropriate levels of governance to visit the school in the spirit of the emphasis within CfW on authentic learning contexts.

Recognising Welshness and the media environment

Another relevant factor for the current media environment in Wales is a well-documented and marked decline of local newspapers, with some areas of Wales described as "news deserts" (see Howells', 2015). It is important to note that "news deserts" are not always geographical and can also relate to particular communities which otherwise appear to be well served (for example, Black, Asian, and Minority Ethnic communities; socio-economically deprived communities, etc.). A recent Welsh government funding initiative through Creative Wales to support BBC Cymru Wales, ITV Cymru Wales, S4C, and Channel 4 aims to "increase opportunities for diverse communities in film and TV in Wales", but the major challenge is the lack of capacity within the current Welsh media landscape to support entry-level journalists from diverse backgrounds. Support from the Welsh government via the Books Council of Wales' New Audiences Fund (2022) was also recently announced, with just under £200,000 made available to develop new opportunities and audiences in the Welsh publishing sector, including community-based projects to collect stories and mentoring underrepresented writers. But it is clear that further substantial and targeted investment is needed to support new routes into the industry.

Current Careers Wales advice on routes into journalism acknowledges that direct entry into the industry via training contracts is becoming rarer all the time, that most entrants are graduates and that competition for jobs is fierce. Perhaps the overall situation is best summarised through the fact that fewer than 1,000 people are employed as journalists in Wales, and that expected future demand for journalist and related jobs is low compared to other jobs in Wales (EMSI, 2022).

There are regional differences within Wales, notably a perceived divide between north and south and a tendency for the capital city Cardiff and the southeast to dominate conceptions of Welshness, as well as for the media to be part of the same "bubble" as politicians. Monoglot English speakers in Wales are particularly underserved in not having adequate access to content produced in the Welsh language.

There is debate about the extent to which it is the purpose of the media to inform citizens about history and culture. Adult education initiatives are a key potential driver of increased media and political literacy within the general population. However, with trust in politicians at its lowest ever level, significant barriers exist to engaging the public in such initiatives, and these would need to be delivered across a diverse range of formats in order to reach a wide range of people.

Methodology

To investigate how Welsh citizens' access to, and understanding of, the media, news, and information in Wales can be improved in an era of "fake news", we established a Citizens' Panel. As well as exploring the relationship between Welsh citizens' perspectives on the news media and their political engagement and understanding, the project team worked closely with citizens to make recommendations to inform and influence the work being conducted by the Welsh Government and the Senedd in the areas of broadcasting and media regulation, educational provision, and the strengthening of the Welsh language and culture, taking into account the context of Welsh politics.

The 15 members of our Citizens' Panel spent 19 hours online together, hearing from experts, discussing the key question, and deliberating about what kinds of recommendations they could make to improve the media in Wales. This Citizens' Panel was designed to reflect (as far as possible within the resources available) a Citizens' Jury, using the developing standards created by a network of practitioners during 2020–2021. Keen to adopt a "test and learn" approach, we used our resources to utilise the principles and the process of a Citizens' Jury on a slightly smaller scale: the panel of 15 reflects the size of a typical Citizens' Jury, but rather than meet for 30–45 hours, the Panel met for 19 hours and received £190 as a gesture of goodwill for their time.

The panel had a single, overarching question to consider – "How well does the news help you understand politics?" – developed over two independently facilitated meetings with a group of professionals drawn from the Open University in Wales and the Institute of Welsh Affairs. The panel was tasked with developing recommendations in response to that question.

Panel recruitment

Citizens' Juries and Assemblies use a process of recruitment called "sortition". This panel used Sortition Foundation to select the 15 participants using national demographic targets as set out here:

- Gender
- Age

- Ethnicity
- Education (level of highest qualifications)
- Geography (location of residence within Wales)
- Urban/rural
- Welsh speaker
- Senedd voter.

Our aim was to slightly "over-recruit" within demographic categories typically underrepresented in democratic deliberative processes, as research shows these groups are also far less likely to volunteer for such activities (Flanigan et al., 2021). For example, we therefore aimed to have slightly more representatives of younger age categories, non-voters, and people from ethnic minority backgrounds. However, given a 100% replacement rate throughout the process, it proved difficult to hit or exceed these targets. Participants received one or more phone calls as well as emails to ensure they were able to fully participate with ease. Any additional needs or digital requirements were supported with the offer of technology and personalised practice sessions.

The participation process

Over the course of three weeks, ahead of the Citizens' Panel synchronous online sessions, the panel heard from speakers with different expertise relating to the media and government in Wales. Each speaker completed a template and short ten-minute interview that was shared with participants. Five of the seven speakers also attended the learning sessions to answer questions live.

This was followed by 19 hours of synchronous online sessions, structured in the following way:

- Information Session: Informing the group what to expect over the sessions and what the purpose of the process was (to receive recommendations from "ordinary" people to inform the media industry, local authorities, and Welsh government of the changes that the public feel are necessary in helping them to understand Welsh politics).
- Learning Phase: two three-hour sessions. Participants heard from experts in the fields of politics, "fake news", alternative media, funding, and regulation to deepen their understanding of how well the news helps people to understand politics.
- Deliberation Phase: two three-hour sessions. This day brought together what participants heard from the experts and their own experiences so that they could identify potential trade-offs and develop their own views and ideas to inform their recommendations.
- Recommendations Phase: a six-hour session where participants held themed discussions based on their deliberations from the previous sessions. Recommendations were drafted, reviewed, redrafted, and rewritten before going to the group vote. For a recommendation to be "approved", it required 80% of the panel's vote.

Creating strong recommendations

The Citizens' Panel were guided through the following process to create strong recommendations:

- The panel agrees criteria for assessing the recommendations;
- They co-create a number of draft recommendations in smaller groups (with two or three other participants);

- Each group then shares their recommendations with the other participants who assess and review the other group's first draft;
- Recommendations are amended to accommodate the views expressed by others and generally strengthen the recommendations;
- Each group shares their final recommendation with the wider panel, and all participants vote for each recommendation on a scale of 1–5 (1 = strongly do not support, 5 = strongly support);
- Recommendations must have a combined percentage of 80% votes in signifying that participants either "strongly agree" or "agree" in order to go forward;
- All recommendations with over 80% support from participants are then presented to the relevant stakeholders.

Challenges

There were two core challenges in this process:

1. Recruitment

With a relatively low response rate, the pool to select from was smaller than was desirable, making the target demographics harder to reach. This was a significant challenge in the process for two key reasons:

- We had an unprecedented 100% panel replacement: 15 replacements were made for a 15-person panel. There was no obvious reason why this happened – people had very different personal and work-related reasons – but when the pool is fairly small to start with, you run the risk of not meeting the targets;
- Age and level of education are often the hardest demographic targets to reach due to relatively low numbers signing up from the youngest age group and those with the lowest level of formal qualifications (Brown, 2006). With a low response rate and high replacement rate, these targets proved even more challenging to meet accurately.

Assembling a group that reflects the broader general population brings with it support challenges. Participants who suffer with conditions that affect participation such as severe anxiety, or those who have never been involved in this type of democratic decision-making require additional dialogue and support prior to and during each session to ensure they feel confident participating. All participants were fully supported, and the success of this approach was reflected in the retention of the group: that is, the process started and finished with 15 participants. In the last session only one person could not attend, for work reasons.

2. Timing

Full Citizens' Assemblies usually take place over the course of several weeks or months (between 30 and 45 hours) (Involve, n.d.). Condensing the 19 hours over the space of two weeks may have affected initial recruitment (availability for participants may have been reduced), and it can also affect the amount of time available to hear from a broader set of speakers. It is good practice to encourage participants to suggest alternative speakers or perspectives. This is possible with space and time to invite others in between sessions, but with a shorter process that time is not possible.

In this case participants' suggestions for speakers from the UK media could not be accommodated. With more space between sessions, it could have.

What does this mean for the strength of the recommendations and robustness of the findings?

By asking the group to create recommendations that would be acceptable to at least 80% of the group, they had to ensure they listened and responded to comments on their first drafts. Everyone was then able to express their support through an anonymous vote.

This Citizens' Panel allowed a diverse set of individuals in Wales to come together, all of whom had different understandings of politics, accessed news through different media outlets, and had different values and political positions based on their experiences of living in different parts of Wales. Whilst it could be argued that "self-selection" takes place in the initial response stage of recruitment, the rationale for that self-selection is largely based on payment rather than the topic or the potential for influence, which might otherwise encourage more active citizens to engage through more traditional techniques.

In this case many of the participants expressed "embarrassment" at not knowing anything about political decision-making in Wales, nor engaging regularly with the news about politics. This view was contrasted with some who were very passionate about how they receive their news about politics. Deliberation and debate that enables those experiences to be better understood results in well-thought-through recommendations that are likely to be acceptable to the general diversity within the population of Wales.

The recommendations

The recommendations that were arrived at by the end of the process address approaches to regulation of the media, the advantages of different sorts of education about politics, and the importance that recognising Welshness plays in creating a distinct and fit-for-purpose media landscape that serves citizens of Wales. In the context of this chapter, this constitutes the findings of the research project and presents a picture of attitudes towards the availability of reliable information which can inform political engagement within the era of "fake news".

We believe that the strength of these recommendations – and the picture they give of attitudes to the media environment and its influence on politics – lies in the very high level of support they received from a wide range of citizens from across Wales. Producing the recommendations was predicated on a process with a very high threshold of agreement, and we have indicated the level of support each recommendation received from the panel, expressed as a percentage. The recommendations broke into three broad categories.

Media regulation

The Citizens' Panel was interested in effective media regulation (at a Wales level, but also UK and international), as a way of making sure that ordinary people can trust what they are reading and watching. At the heart of the discussion was a strong belief that Wales needs more powers, including the power to regulate its own media, to ensure that the issues that matter to Welsh citizens are front and centre in the media, and to strengthen Welsh language media provision.

Generally, there was a feeling that a one-size-fits-all UK approach is inadequate, both in practical terms and in terms of Wales' distinct political reality and linguistic and cultural identity.

Citizens perceived strongly that Wales as a nation as well as its constituent localities are currently being underserved by a media that does not adequately reflect life in its communities, either in breadth or depth – and that this has an impact on political participation.

There was understanding that some of these issues are more easily addressed than others. Indeed, some areas of the Citizens' Panel discussion lie within the powers currently devolved to the Senedd, and some are outside of it. In particular, there was acknowledgement of the fact that media regulation has to be considered in relation to the global nature of the market, and at a national level only so much can be achieved, hence the need for international cooperation and shared oversight. This is likely the situation in many parts of the world at present.

On the basis of their discussions, the Citizens' Panel recommended the following:

- "Establish an effective and powerful regulatory body, covering all media organisations active in Wales, including press, broadcast and online (to make free speech accountable, not to curtail it)" [82% agreed or strongly agreed];
- "to provide independent confirmation of the accuracy of the news" [91% agreed or strongly agreed].

In order to generate final recommendations, the Open University in Wales and the Institute of Welsh Affairs took the panel's suggestions and conducted an analysis against the prevailing political context and media landscape in Wales (as outlined previously) and produced the following final recommendations:

1 We endorse the creation of a Shadow Broadcasting and Communications Authority for Wales and recommend further exploration of a broadened remit for this body, that would include monitoring all media sources in Wales, including print;
2 We further recommend that the Shadow Broadcasting and Communications Authority for Wales should have a representative and diverse membership and should be set up to include a mechanism for consultation with Welsh citizens more widely when creating regulatory policy;
3 We recommend that the Shadow Broadcasting and Communications Authority for Wales develops a made-for-Wales best practice framework against which news outlets active in Wales could be measured (and given a trust rating akin to the food hygiene ratings issued by the Food Standards Agency) and which journalists (including trainees) could use for training and benchmarking;
4 We recommend that the Welsh Government should work with the UK government to improve accountability of Public Service Media organisations (PSMs) to the Senedd, through devolution of specific broadcasting powers, and to create channels through which solutions to the transnational regulatory and non-regulatory issues facing the media in Wales, the UK, and the wider world might be further explored.

Taken together, these reflect public perceptions of the limitations in the current media landscape and how the citizenry feel these could be improved.

Democracy and citizenship education

Democracy and Citizenship education was a strong theme throughout the Citizens' Panel's discussions, being identified very early as a potential solution to the initial conclusion that the news media does not adequately engage the public in understanding politics. From the beginning of the learning phase, most participants said that they felt that their own levels of knowledge about politics, democratic structures, and their own elected representatives were inadequate and that they did not have trusted, easily accessible information to redress this. There was wide agreement that participants had been underserved by their schooling around citizenship and much frustration that Democracy and Citizenship education initiatives are rarely aimed at adults.

There was acknowledgement of some of the difficulties of implementing good quality Democracy and Citizenship education, including the pace of political change, pressures on the school curriculum, and the difficulties around maintaining impartiality, as well as an identification of jargon as a major barrier to the educative function of the media. During deliberation, agreement coalesced around the need for Democracy and Citizenship education for all age groups, with schools identified as an easier path to implementation followed by much more detailed discussion around innovative ideas for how the adult population of Wales might be engaged with high-quality Democracy and Citizenship education (these ideas are outlined further in our recommendations pertaining to "Recognising Welshness").

On the basis of their discussions, the Citizens' Panel recommended the following:

- "Supplement the current life skills/Personal, Social and Health Education (PSHE) syllabus with an additional focus on the current practice and history of politics within school curriculums, by means of a combined compulsory Personal and Social Education (PSE) class" [73% agree or strongly agree];
- "Bring politics to the wider community by promoting and encouraging a deliverable government funded educational service using a variety of accessible platforms" [83% agree or strongly agree];

From this we produced the following final recommendations:

5 We recommend that the Welsh government should take steps to strengthen democracy and citizenship education in schools, including more explicit guidance for the teaching of democracy and citizenship (local, national, and global), as well as the modern history and politics of Wales, within the humanities "area of learning and experience" (AOLE) of curriculum for Wales;
6 We further recommend that the Welsh government should ensure the new GCSE qualifications in history and social studies include significant Wales-relevant components on politics and democratic processes;
7 We recommend that the Welsh government should create appropriate teacher training pathways, including PGCEs and in-service training to allow for specialisation in social studies, including politics.

Recognising Welshness

The Citizens' Panel agreed that a key weakness of Wales' media landscape is that it does not adequately serve individuals and communities in Wales. A strong theme of the discussions was the London-centric nature of the UK news media. Many participants expressed the fact that they were not consciously aware of the lack of a Welsh dimension to the news they consumed and that their involvement in this project had usefully allowed them to see the news differently.

In addition to a developing understanding of the "democratic deficit" caused by a lack of attention paid to Welsh politics by UK news sources, participants also identified a vital information deficit relating to Welsh history and culture, including the Welsh language. Participants expressed surprise that news about Wales is not largely produced in Wales by Welsh journalists, and quickly formed a consensus that Wales should not be neglected by UK media sources. To redress these issues, the panel felt that it was important for Welsh citizens to have easy access to stories about their own local areas as well as about decisions made that affect their lives and a better understanding of where these decisions are taken and by whom. They felt that a solution to this would be specific funding to train journalists who would be embedded in local communities, connected to other local citizens and knowledgeable about Welsh history, culture, and politics.

On the basis of their discussions, the Citizens' Panel recommended the following:

- "Welsh news must be produced in Wales by journalists who live in Wales or know the country" [59% agreed or strongly agreed];
- "The Welsh Government to set up public funding source[s] to support the development of local groups to provide online, accessible local news" [67% agree or strongly agree];
- "Create a readily available information service aimed at adults including online, print and audio resources about Wales' history, culture and political system, through the Welsh Government's education department and universities" [91% agree or strongly agree];
- "Bring politics to the wider community by promoting and encouraging a deliverable government funded educational service using a variety of accessible platforms" [83% agree or strongly agree].

We then produced the following final recommendations:

8   We endorse the commitment in the Welsh government and Plaid Cymru Co-operation Agreement to "fund existing and new enterprises to improve Welsh-based journalism to tackle the information deficit" and recommend that further funding be allocated to support new career entrants from a wide range of backgrounds in localities across Wales to access journalistic training, with a specific focus on improving the media coverage of Welsh matters, Welsh language provision, and addressing underrepresented groups;

9   We recommend that the Welsh government should create a Task and Finish Group to deliver a range of high-quality democracy and citizenship education resources for both school pupils and adults; these should be co-produced with citizens, disseminated through a wide range of community settings and digital channels, and backed by a well-funded public information campaign aimed at a diverse range of groups.

What does this mean for news media and democracy?

In this final section we look at how these recommendations relate to wider discussion about the relationship between Welsh citizens' perspectives on the news media and their beliefs about politics, democracy, and their own sense of political engagement.

Where do people get their news?

Given the aim of the project was to bring together a group of people representative of the whole of Wales, it is perhaps unsurprising that the news sources used by our Citizens' Panel were varied and diverse. Some panel members actively sought out political news from a range of sources, including the BBC, Channel 4 News, and The Economist, but others actively avoided the subject and were only aware of the news through "glancing at the headlines that pop up on my phone" or short bulletins on commercial radio stations such as Heart. The widely remarked upon decline of print was reflected in comments made about newspapers, which were seen as "expensive", and news that is both free and easy to access was popular among the group, with the Telegraph, Times, and Guardian websites mentioned, along with the Guardian app. Those who "prefer the printed word" opted for "the Metro on the train in the morning", the Daily Mail and Mail on Sunday. Welsh sources of news were mentioned, but not always positively, and not always in a way that suggests they are being actively sought out. Some members of the panel used Radio Cymru to help with learning Welsh, while Welsh language speakers suggested they trusted the station more than others because it quite literally "talks our language". Social media was reported as a popular source of news but was widely thought to be "a source of other people's opinions" rather than a reliable source of factual information.

How much do they trust it?

In general, the Citizens' Panel were fairly confident in their own levels of media literacy and readily acknowledged that they did not trust everything they read or saw in the media. Some broadcasters were more trusted than others, such as the BBC, ITV, and Sky News, while one participant said they "wouldn't touch [some news channels] with a bargepole!" Some participants said they thought "we are all aware we've been lied to by the right wing and tabloid press", while others reported the problem of party political "bias" with the Daily Mirror supporting Labour and the Times the Conservatives, leaving readers unable to know whether a given story would be trustworthy. Trust was seen as a particular problem on social media, with negative opinions expressed about Facebook, Instagram, and TikTok, as well as some comments that information on social media could be "true, an opinion, or outright lies". Panel members also expressed frustration that fact-checking on sites such as Facebook and Twitter was not always easy or straightforward. Some panel members said they would always check with "trusted" mainstream media sites after seeing information they doubted on social media, but saw "common sense" – meaning a moderate standard of media literacy – as an issue: "People see a headline, take it as true, and then tell their mates".

How does this affect how they think and feel about politics in Wales?

Again, there were a wide range of views shared about the links between the media and people's views of politics and the democratic process. Broadly, the Citizens' Panel had a low level of confidence in their own knowledge of politics, particularly at a Wales level. Politics was perceived as a difficult subject, and the media was not seen as particularly helpful in providing appropriate information at a level ordinary people could understand. A lack of "evidence" was identified as a problem in political news stories, as was "fluff" that distracted from or obscured necessary key information. There was also an awareness of concepts like "echo chambers" on social media that reinforce people's existing biases and often polarise opinions, particularly over binary or "wedge" issues like Brexit. Some people expressed concern about the influence of powerful media moguls like Rupert Murdoch, while others' lived experiences of dealing with democratic systems and processes also coloured their views, such as difficulties navigating local authority bureaucracies.

It was widely agreed that there is a disconnect between the politics reported on the news and real issues felt to affect people's lives in their local communities. Sometimes this was felt to manifest as a media focused on politicians as a category of celebrity rather than one which was primarily focused on detailed examination of policies. Some participants felt politicians were "savvy" in using the media only when it suited their agenda and that they "only engage the public at election time". Notably, much of the discussion around the link between the news media and concomitant levels of trust in politics was focused at a UK level, with exploration of Welsh and local issues mainly becoming part of the conversation only after the learning phase of the project. Within this discussion, it was widely agreed that decision-making at the Senedd is underreported and that there is a "dearth" of news at the local level.

Conclusion

The project reported on in this chapter had as its aim the cultivation of political participation though a process which mixed informed reflection and decision-making with a forum within which one could communicate the results of this deliberation to those in positions of institutional power. One of the most heartening aspects of this work has been the universally positive response to the process from the 15 citizens who gave up 19 hours of their time to commit to learning and deliberating around a topic on which most had little prior knowledge but felt to be of great importance for the good of society. Twelve of the 15 participants committed to staying in touch with the Open University in Wales and the Institute of Welsh Affairs to be involved in disseminating the research, and all agreed that they had enjoyed and been educated by the process. Even more hopefully, they all felt listened to in a way that they said was rare in today's society, where too often citizens' voices go unheard. All feedback was positive from participants, with agreement that taking part in the Citizens' Panel had provided them with more knowledge on the subject, more confidence in expressing alternate views, and a greater willingness to participate in public engagement initiatives in the future. As noted previously, the citizens' panel format is a somewhat idealised version of the practices which constitute the democratic process, and in real-life situations, access to the range of resources outlined in the previous section is never going to be as apparent. But what this research illustrates, alongside the specific picture it provides of attitudes towards the media environment in Wales, is both the desire for but also the concerns about trustworthy and locally relevant information that citizens have and the way the availability of these can impact their confidence and sense of engagement within the democratic process.

Acknowledgements

This chapter is based on a previously published policy report, *"Citizens' voices, people's news: making the media work for Wales. An IWA report, in partnership with The Open University in Wales"*, written by the chapter authors and published in 2022. In writing this chapter we thank those who inputted into the original report, including Mutual Gain and Sortition Foundation, as well as the Open University in Wales and Institute of Welsh Affairs.

References

Books Council of Wales (2022). Announcing Recipients of New Audiences Grant. Available at: https://llyfrau.cymru/en/announcing-recipients-of-new-audiences-grant/
Brown, M. B. (2006) Citizen Panels and the Concept of Representation, *The Journal of Political Philosophy*, 14: 2, pp. 203–225.

Careers Wales, How to become: Journalist (2022), Available at: https://careerswales.gov.wales/job-information/journalist/how-to-become

Chwalisz, C. (2021) The pandemic has pushed citizen panels online, *Nature*, 589: 7841, p. 171.

Crosby, N., Kelly, J. M., and Schaefer, P. (1986) Citizens Panels: A New Approach to Citizen Participation, *Public Administration Review*, 46, 2, pp. 170-178.

Electoral Reform Society (2020). Teaching politics in our schools should be a necessity not an option, Available at: https://www.electoral-reform.org.uk/teaching-politics-in-our-schools-shouldbe-a-necessity-not-an-option/

EMSI, 2022

ERS Cymru (2018) Our Voices Heard: Young people's ideas for political education in Wales. Available at: https://www.electoral-reform.org.uk/wp-content/uploads/2018/11/Our-Voices-Heard.pdf

Flanigan, B., Gölz, P., Gupta, A., Hennig, B. and Procaccia, A. D. (2021) Fair algorithms for selecting citizens' assemblies, *Nature*, 596, pp. 548–552

Floridia, A. (2018) The Origins of the Deliberative Turn, in Bächtiger, A., Dryzek, J. S., Mansbridg, J. and Warren, M. (eds) *The Oxford Handbook of Deliberative Democracy*, Oxford: Oxford University Press, pp. 35–54.

HM Government (2023). The Online Safety Bill. Available at: https://bills.parliament.uk/publications/49376/documents/2822Hörning, G. (1999) Citizens' panels as a form of deliberative technology assessment, Science and Public Policy, 26: 5, pp. 351–359.

House of Commons (2023) Devolution in Wales: "A process, not an event" – research briefing. Available at: https://researchbriefings.files.parliament.uk/documents/CBP-8318/CBP-8318.pdf

Howells, R (2015). Journey to the centre of a news black hole: examining the democratic deficit in a town with no newspaper. PhD Thesis, Cardiff University.

Institute for Government (2021) Welsh independence Does the Welsh public support independence? Available at: https://www.instituteforgovernment.org.uk/explainer/welsh-independence

Involve (n.d.) Citizens' panels, https://involve.org.uk/resources/methods/citizens-panel

Nation Cymru (2020) Weakness of Welsh media causing 'unacceptable and unsustainable' democratic deficit. Available at: https://nation.cymru/news/weakness-of-welsh-media-causing-unacceptable-and-unsustainable-democratic-deficit/

Open Government Partnership (2021). Actions for Transparent and Accountable Digital Governance. Available at: https://www.opengovpartnership.org/actions-for-transparent-and-accountable-digital-governance/

Qualifications Wales (2021) Qualified for the future: the right choice for Wales – our decisions. Available at: https://www.qualificationswales.org/media/7982/qualified-for-the-future-our-decisions.pdf

Welsh Government (2022a) The Independent Commission on the Constitutional Future of Wales. Available at: https://www.gov.wales/independent-commission-constitutional-future-wales

Welsh Government (2022b) AREA OF LEARNING AND EXPERIENCE: Health and Well-being. Available at: https://hwb.gov.wales/curriculum-for-wales/health-and-well-being/

Welsh Government (2022c) AREA OF LEARNING AND EXPERIENCE: Humanities. Available at: https://hwb.gov.wales/curriculum-for-wales/humanities/statements-of-what-matters

Welsh Government (2023) New funding awarded to projects to improve skills in Wales' creative sector, https://www.gov.wales/new-funding-awarded-projects-improve-skills-wales-creative-sector

Welsh Parliament (2021) Exploring the devolution of broadcasting: How can Wales get the media it needs? Available at: https://senedd.wales/media/vjpf0fi4/cr-ld14207-e.pdf

B. Society

17

(DIS)INFORMATION AND ETHICAL GUIDELINES

A critical discourse analysis of news reporting on violence against women

Sergio Maruenda-Bataller

Introduction

The UN General Assembly (2006) states that violence against women, as rooted in historically unequal power relations between men and women, is inherently structural. UN Women (2019: 95) recognise that gender-based violence (GBV) is a multifaceted, transnational, and transcultural violation of human rights (Council of Europe 2011).[1] In most societies, women – regardless of their ethnic origin, nationality, class, or age – are victims of physical, sexual, and economic violence, or even of femicide. To fight this systemic phenomenon, (inter-)national associations have underscored the responsibility of social, political, and legal institutions in raising awareness, preventing, and combating gender-based violence. Undoubtedly, one of these agents is media industries.

In the last years media have played a decisive role in increasing visibility of gender-based violence inside of the public arena and contributing to sensitization. The proliferation of guidelines for media reporting on violence against women (VAW) attests to the conscious effort of journalists to engage in ensuring greater sensitivity towards gender issues. These codes urge newsrooms to address the broader social context of VAW, its systemic and coercive nature, and its power abuse, rather than spotlight on individual incidents (i.e. mostly femicides) (Pereira 2022: 94). However, feminist research has pointed out that the way media frame VAW often contributes to perpetuating GBV discourses by stereotyping, objectifying, and shaming women for the abuse (López Díez 2002; Ajibola 2022), reinforcing the belief that violence is a natural by-product of women's nonconformance to certain sociocultural expectations.

These deficits in compliance of ethical guidelines are explained as stemming from, among other factors, lack of clear articulation, lack of knowledge and training on the subject, and absence of practical guidelines for implementation (Macharia & Morinière 2012: 21). For López Díez (2002: 27), another axis would be located on routines of the news-making process itself, which is often driven by the urgency to produce content. This forces journalists to reproduce agency news without the necessary time to contextualise, document, and contrast sources; in a word, to produce quality information.

DOI: 10.4324/9781003224495-21

Critical discourse studies and the news

News texts are primary conveyors of shared meanings and images of social reality which contribute to the (re-)configuration, challenging, and transformation of social identities, relations, and orders. Through discourse, media crucially frame particular understandings of culture, politics, and social life (Bell 1998). Therefore, news stories convey cultural scripts and ideologies which guide audience perceptions and representations of events and social actors (van Dijk 1988).

The study of news texts as ideology-bearing discourse(s) has been widely researched in critical discourse studies (CDS) (see, for instance, Bell 1991; Fowler 1991; Bell & Garrett 1998; van Dijk 1998; Richardson 2007). CDS scholars seek to raise critical awareness of the way language (as a form of social practice) plays a role in issues of ideology, power, and inequality (Fairclough 1989; Wodak & Meyer 2016; Flowerdew & Richardson 2018). CDS-informed research is key to understanding the effect of particular discourses on public perceptions of dominant topics, groups, and events (Fairclough 1995).

As part of scholarly research in CDS, "gender-based inequalities have constituted an important research focus" (Lazar 2018: 372). In this regard, the present chapter is concerned with how news reporting on VAW uphold particular narratives that perpetuate gender inequalities. Thus, this chapter adopts a feminist critical discourse studies approach (FCDS), one of whose objectives is "to demystify and challenge discourses that continue to buttress gendered social orders in various ways, which harm and foreclose socially progressive possibilities for individuals and groups" (Lazar 2018: 372). This approach should then be regarded as a form of analytical activism, in so far as it involves the raising of critical consciousness through research.

News discourse on VAW

In recent years, VAW has become a major issue in political, social, and institutional discourses, hence permeating the agenda of the newsroom. While increased media attention has spurred a growing public discourse on gender-based violence (GBV), the nature of media reporting on the subject has often been problematic in several regards. Sutherland et al. (2016) identify the following key themes in scholarly research on news reporting of VAW: failure to contextualize VAW as a wider social issue rather than a string of isolated incidents; sensationalism through inaccurate and inappropriate vocabulary (i.e. tabloidization); perpetuation of myths (e.g. pathologisation of perpetrators' motives; VAW as class- or ethnic-specific); victim-blaming and stigmatisation; "romanticisation" of violence (i.e. a crime of passion); lack of expert voices, etc. News media can then privilege certain angles of VAW while hiding others (Bullock & Cubert 2002; Lloyd & Ramon 2017). While acknowledging that media may play a powerful role in challenging myths and sparking informed public discussion, Sutherland et al. (2016: 2) conclude that reporting tends to "mirror society's confusion and ambivalence about violence against women" and reinforce, rather than challenge, cultural, and social biases about gender, thus contributing to disinformation or the construction of what has been labelled *semi-fake news* (Musi & Reed 2022).[2]

Lack of social context: violence as episodic

Some research on media reporting of VAW has criticised the lack of a broader social context in which male-perpetrated VAW occurs (Meyers 1997; Bullock & Cubert 2002; Carlyle et al. 2008; Monckton-Smith 2012; Fairbairn & Dawson 2013; Gillespie et al. 2013). This is done by providing individual-level explanations as causes for the inflicted violence (e.g. drug abuse, ethnicity, separation, or divorce) other than gender inequality and the abuse of power (see Fairbairn 2015:

84–85; Easteal et al. 2019: 452). Specifically, when reporting femicides, stories are often episodic and focus on particular incidents rather than placing violent encounters within the social context of male patriarchy (Meyers 1997: 109). These episodes are then not reported as the endpoint in an escalating pattern of abuse that has occurred over time (i.e. a previous history of violence) but misrepresent cases as unique and anomalous (Bullock & Cubert 2002; Bullock 2008; Carlyle et al. 2008). This fact denies the widespread nature of VAW (Wozniak & McCloskey 2010: 935) and maintains deeply held cultural beliefs and entrenched patterns of response to male violence. For Fairbairn and Dawson (2013: 151), reporting a history of violence as a relevant contextual factor can help counter VAW as spontaneous instances of a male's loss of control, while the underreporting of such context "is a problematic aspect of news media coverage", as violence ends up rationalised and normalised as unavoidable (Gillespie et al. 2013).

Research has also highlighted the significance portraying VAW episodically. Episodic reporting may also contribute to women's self-blaming, given that expert (feminist) voices are often scarce. Lloyd and Ramon (2017: 129) point out that one of the misconceptions surrounding domestic violence (DV) is that leaving an abusive relationship means safety or the end of violence. In their study of the relationship between DV and mental health, they identify, among others, victim-blaming attitudes, DV stigmatisation, and coercive control as factors that explain women's difficulty in disengaging from a violent partner. As per this fact, media could highlight that a woman is in more serious risks when breaking the cycle of violence (Walker 1979). In doing so, the media may play a fundamental role in reinforcing the social rejection of abusers. By legitimizing the victims, media may spread the complexity of the process and free women from the unfair burden of guilt for the violence (Castelló & Gimeno 2018: 20).

Othering: victim-blaming and pathologisation of perpetrators

Another crucial issue in media framing of VAW concerns their discursive representation of the main social actors involved: victims and perpetrators. Bullock (2008: 48) labels this practice as "othering": the framing portrays them as "ideal" victims and abusers, as they exhibit some deviant behaviour that makes them more susceptible to being victimised or abusive (i.e. mental issues, social marginality, ethnicity, education, etc.).

In the case of perpetrators, reports tend to pathologize violence to justify femicides, resorting to male obsession with the victim or emotional instability (e.g. crime of passion, raptus) (Easteal et al. 2015). This frame diminishes men's accountability and promotes the belief that women cause their own victimisation (Meyers 1997). Sexualising rape is another way in which perpetrators' culpability is downplayed and which detracts from the (feminist) view of rape as an act of power (Lazar 2018: 381). Indeed, media coverage of VAW shows a marked proclivity to portray perpetrators as either invisible actors or dehumanised monsters. While mental health and substance abuse are complex issues that may be relevant to explain VAW, Fairbairn and Dawson (2013: 152) view such news frames as problematic, since they "preclude broader discussions about social, cultural, and systemic roots of violence against women such as patriarchal social structures, tolerance of misogynistic attitudes, promotion of violent masculinities, and/or lack of access to social resources and supports for many marginalised women".

Furthermore, coverage may eclipse the agency of perpetrators by using certain linguistic styles. Adampa (1999: 20) notes that linguistic passivisation (e.g. "a woman was murdered") is an ideological factor that reorients and directs audience's perceptions from the victimizer to the victim. For Frazer and Miller (2009: 80), people's repeated exposure to stories using the passive voice engenders negative attitudes towards abused women and higher acceptance of myths (see also

Tranchese & Zollo 2013). A focus on the perpetrator as a "social outsider" creates the impression that VAW episodes are "deviant" or anomalous actions, which "camouflages the social nature of the attack and diminishes its political significance" (Adampa 1999: 21).

Victim-blaming also resonates in the media narratives of VAW. Shifting the blame from male abusers to female victims is congruent with the mythology that imputes responsibility on the victim for transgressing certain cultural "norms" of behaviour. Thus, for instance, women's desire to divorce or end an abusive relationship is often seen as the cause for violence. In the case of sexual violence, the persistent link between "morally questionable" behaviours (e.g. drinking, seductive clothing, walking alone at night, etc.) and vulnerability to rape allows these myths to be reinforced, perpetuating distorted representations of female blame and trivialising rape (Meyers 2004). These narratives further "act to hamper feminist goal of reducing victim's re-traumatisation" (Easteal et al. 2015: 109), to undermine victim's credibility, and thus, to prevent victims from reporting to avoid stigmatisation and backlash. Besides, in their quest for their most "newsworthy" stories, news reports tend to provide a prevailing storyline of vulnerability, ignoring female agency in actively resisting sexual assault, thus contributing to the typical "gender script" that presents women as powerless victims (Hollander & Rodgers 2014; Lazar 2018).

Sensationalism

News reports on VAW tend to dramatize stories to increase audience's interest (Dobash & Dobash 1992). Sensationalism in VAW can adopt multiple forms – the type of violence covered (with an excessive focus on femicide), the extreme and inappropriate lexis used in articles and headlines (Ehrlich 2001), and the types of details used to describe the abuses. The construction of VAW stories through sensationalism "can publicly humiliate victims by subjecting them to the readers' gaze and undermine the serious realities of gendered violence" (Gilbertson & Pandit 2019: 44).

Lack of expert voices

News reports on VAW primarily resort to "official", easily available sources such as police and justice, typically viewed as objective or neutral. This way, media sustain a frame of VAW as one-off incidents and "fail to take into account either the feminist reality of gendered power imbalances in society or the victims' experiences of a myriad of physical and non-physical abusive behaviours aimed to disempower" (Easteal et al. 2015: 107). Wozniak and McCloskey (2010: 937) note that the use of police or justice sources may dehumanise VAW by omitting sources from the home environment. However, other scholars question the reliability of family or neighbours as they may only seek notoriety, self-interested defence, or focus on morbid details, which may serve to trivialise the crime (Castelló & Gimeno 2018).

Feminist scholarship have called for the inclusion of authoritative sources (women's associations, advocates, researchers, survivors) in news coverage of VAW to offer an alternative narrative to the identified myths, highlight the gendered nature of VAW, reveal the pervasiveness and complexity of this phenomenon, and challenge the sociocultural rules of violence (Fairbairn 2015: 97). Despite their success in increasing visibility and awareness of VAW, these expert sources are included in very low percentages in VAW reporting (see Bullock & Cubert 2002; Carlyle et al. 2008; Bullock 2008; Fairbairn & Dawson 2013). In this respect, the last years witness to some attempts by journalists to provide an agenda of (feminist) experts to consult (Castelló & Gimeno 2018).

In view of this, it seems that, in spite of increased media attention, news framing and coverage of VAW "present significant challenges as well as opportunities for VAW work" and become "an important area of feminist engagement and critique moving forwards" (Fairbairn 2015: 80). Against this background, the present work aims to develop an understanding of how news media construct female victims of VAW through specific discourse practices.

Ethical guidelines on VAW

Media codes of ethics gather regulations of journalistic practice. These mandatory standards concern the social accountability of journalists as mediators between news events and citizens in a given community. As such, these norms play a crucial role in the newsroom's endorsement and spread of ideologies through discourse.

Ethical guidelines can help spotlight the political and social dimension of gender violence by advancing an instructional aspect that may lead to a better understanding of its complexities (Macharia & Morinière 2012: 21). In this respect, gender-focussed media codes of ethics can potentially institutionalise a different kind of practice that makes us cognizant about and responsive to gender concerns and to the way and perspective from which media globally show and position women (Castelló & Gimeno 2018). These tools can catalyse a more professional practice that includes a gender perspective.

However, as seen in the previous section, research has noted that media coverage of gender-based violence still presents a series of distorting elements that deviate attention from the problem itself: the violence or domination exerted by men against women. The way violence and domestic murders are covered in media reveals that gender-based violence is underrepresented, trivialised, or even obscured, given an unbridled focus on femicides or sexual violence; victims are often blamed (and defamed) and held responsible for showing "inappropriate" behaviour, and perpetrators are often excused through false myths (e.g. alcohol abuse, pathologies, jealousy, etc.) (IPSO 2021). These discourses reinforce a moralising drift that curtails women's rights and freedom and drags them into a culture of fear and subjugation, thus contributing to disinformation.

Thus, in the current scenario of social legitimation of feminist demands, the paradox arises that, the discourses of the media contribute to curbing these freedoms and feeding patriarchy. Hence, for some researchers, the adoption of a feminist perspective when reporting on gender-based violence is urgent and essential for a social change to take place (see Castelló & Gimeno 2018: 12). Codes, nevertheless, remain essential to guide media professionals to ethical concerns, to increase professional accountability, and equally important, to enable the public to hold media accountable for their practice (Macharia & Morinière 2012: 21).

The following sections aim to critically appraise the paradox that emerges from the construction of two parallel, contrasting narratives on VAW by news media: one depicted by ethical principles and one rendered by the actual reporting. To do so, a two-tiered analysis was conducted. On the one hand, a detailed scrutiny of 16 guidelines for media reporting on VAW was carried out. These include texts and manuals issued by media groups and (inter-)national associations of journalists (see bibliography), which adds a dimension of transnationalism as an important focus in FCDA research. The study of their principles has resulted in the articulation of the analytical apparatus that informs the subsequent sections, built around three areas which discursively contribute to the construction of a media narrative on VAW: (1) focus (i.e. how VAW is generally conceived and represented), (2) profiling (i.e. how the identity of the victim/survivor and the perpetrator are configured), and (3) sources (i.e. whether expert voices are often found). On the other hand, news reports on VAW are gathered from an ad hoc corpus of gender-based violence news in Spanish.[3] The aim is to analyse these news reports vis-à-vis the narrative endorsed by news media.

A narrative on violence against women: the case of the Spanish press Focus

Frame VAW as gender equality or human rights abuse;
it is not "any other crime"

Guidelines encourage journalists to frame their stories in the broader context of GBV as a structural phenomenon, thus helping readers to understand the significance and complexity of this crime and reflecting on systems of oppression, attitudes, and root causes of violence. Table 17.1 shows the word sketches retrieved for the lemmas *structural, history,* and *patriarchy* in the corpus of study:

These word sketches positively show that news media frame GBV as a structural phenomenon and reflect on the asymmetrical relationships between men and women, which can lead to violence, as in (1). However, a close look at their concordances evinces that all these cases coincide with op-ed pieces, not with actual reports. This concurs with Wozniak and McCloskey's (2010) findings: because journalists often portray VAW incidents as episodic, very few news items include discussions of VAW as a social phenomenon.

1 **EM 08.03.2017**

   Feminicides are the most visible exponent of the violence that women suffer because they are women, a **systemic and structural violence called patriarchy** that not only kills us, but also keeps us in a subordinate position with respect to men in all aspects of life.

Attempts to provide a broader social context in VAW reports are evinced by the use of statistics of the number of victims (469 occurrences in the corpus), which place the incident within the context of violence in the community (IFJ 2014):

2 **EP 21.10.2018**. 966 women have been killed by their partners or ex-partners since 2003 . . . In 2018, there are 41 fatal victims.
3 **ABC 09.01.2011**. A woman strangled in Orense and another killed by knife in Valencia yesterday increased to 34 the number of victims of gender violence in Spain.
4 **EM 06.11.2018**. The steepest rise has been in domestic violence, with 26 murders recorded this year after only 9 last year.

Table 17.1 Selection of collocate lemmas related to broader social contact of VAW (Sketch Engine)

Lemma	Lemma + Modifier Lemma and/or . . .	Nouns Modified by Lemma	Lemma (subj.) + Verb	Verb + Lemma (obj.)
structural	systemic, systematic, global, cultural, personal, social	gender, inequalities, problem, machismo, violence		
history	sad, terrible, personal, tragic, dramatic	start, begin, tell, end, show		tell, narrate, write, relate
patriarchy	heteronormative, benevolent, recalcitrant, indecent, capitalist		predominate, persist, manipulate, impose	exacerbate, assimilate, censor, legitimate, establish

The guidelines also state that it is necessary to provide practical and useful information on support and care services, including emergency telephone numbers victims of abuse can contact (UN 2019; Castelló & Gimeno 2018). Unfortunately, the corpus yields no significant data of the mention of help lines in VAW reports where victims may find legal and institutional support. According to Carlyle et al. (2008: 181), omitting the availability of societal resources (1) diminishes public awareness of these services and (2) leave victims alone in trying to find a solution.

Do not provide a sensationalist view

Feminist scholarly research on VAW reporting have established a connection between the over-representation of femicide and the dramatization of VAW crimes (see Carter & Weaver 2003; López Díez 2005). Vis-à-vis this research, media guidelines on GBV advise reporters against the use or morbid and lurid details for this type of violence as these provide no relevant information, go against victims' dignity, and rely on info-spectacle. Specifically, guidelines highlight the need to be aware of the potential impact of visual or textual messages on sustaining stereotypes and imposing prejudices (Marín et al. 2011). This may be done, for instance, by providing details on the victims'/survivors' clothing, addictions, sexuality, past relationships, etc.

The instances in the next section, extracted from the corpus studied, clearly run counter to the guidelines' advice for an ethical and respectful account of VAW. In these cases, reporters overzeal in presenting victims' extreme suffering through lurid details of the brutality inflicted on the victim's body. The tabloidization of VAW through this kind of reporting leads to women's objectification (there is no mention of women's attempts to resist), routinisation of violence, and consequently, desensitization of audiences by fostering and reinforcing particular perceptions and attitudes towards VAW (Fairbairn 2015).

5   **EP 11.09.2018. A death recorded on a shocking video**

Her 40-year-old ex-partner stabbed her five times – three in the chest, one in the neck and one in the hand. . . . By mid-morning, a video was circulating on social networks showing the blonde-haired, bloodied victim lying on the floor.

6   **EP 12.06.2018.** Picking up his ex-girlfriend as throwing her into the tile tub area in his bathroom, causing her bruises to her head, neck, back, shoulders, arms, legs, elbow and feet; puling her from the tub by her hair; screaming that he would kill her or break her arms . . . placing both his hands around her throat and strangle her while she was on the floor.

7   **ABC 21.07.2018. Women targets of femicide in lawless Mexico**

The methods were increasingly violent. . . . Women who are burnt in acid, women who are raped before being killed. . . . Last September Victoria Salas Martínez was found dead in a motel room in Mexico City, her throat slashed, her breast open, her skin flaked by sores from the hot water.

Consider reporting more fully on the success of many women who have recovered and rebuilt their lives

As shown in the instances in the previous section, the tendency to victimize women as the object of abuse stresses the lack of female agency by focusing on their defencelessness. However, research has questioned this treatment of victimization of women since it contributes "to strengthening the demobilizing construction of the traditional feminine identity" (López Díez 2002: 29). The over-representation of femicide may discourage victims from leaving abusive relationships for fear of being killed (Carlyle et al. 2008). In this respect, research and media guidelines insist on the need to focus on the success of women to survive male violence. Examples (8) and (9) confirm a (positive but) still timid upward trend in the reporting of stories of women survivors (76 occurrences: 1.98 per million tokens). This can have an indicatory effect for other women who are enduring it. From their voices and stories, they help and encourage other women to escape from abusive relationships.

8 **EM 22.02.2019**. This is the story of a **survivor of male violence** protected by the police, one of the 58,092 women with police protection in Spain.
9 **EM 16.03.19**. Since **her story as a survivor** came to light, Mariam Gutiérrez participates in events against gender violence . . . she personally assists certain victims . . . and takes the issue of women's violence as if it were a personal matter.

Profiling

Do not blame the victim. Avoid double victimization. (Avoid using derogatory language or blaming women for becoming victims)

While perhaps victim-blaming in VAW reporting is currently less widespread, the idea that victims can deserve the violence remains commonplace (Bullock 2008; Richards et al. 2011; Fairbairn & Dawson 2013; Fairbairn 2015; Lopes & Pimentel 2016; Gilbertson & Pandit 2019). Media coverage that focuses primarily on presenting women's actions as causes of the received violence seem to distinguish between genuine victims and those who should be considered responsible for their own victimization. Despite the efforts of guidelines to locate the cause of the crime in machismo, news report on VAW still seems to polarise the crimes of VAW by differentiating between good and bad victims (Gius & Lalli 2014: 58).

10 **EP 02.01.2018. The legal service of the Community of Madrid attended 766 women**

It is intended for women residents regardless of whether there is a complaint or protection order and without the need to prove their status as a victim.

In the case of (10), victimization occurs by placing on women the responsibility of leaving the relationship ("regardless of whether there is a complaint or protection order") or proving their status as victims. In (11), the victim's desire to divorce is pointed out as the cause of the murder, instead of providing references to the patriarchal culture whereby the man feels that he is the legitimate owner of the woman's life (Castelló & Gimeno 2018).

11 **EM 12.04.2019. Retired policeman shoots his wife to death in Astorga**

The attack took place in the early hours of yesterday morning at the couple's holiday home . . . when the wife had confessed to her assailant her intention to start divorce proceedings.

In (12), the victim's outfit and underwear are reported as causes of her being raped and discharge the aggressor of the responsibility and place the burden on the woman, who is directly reproached for exhibiting behaviours that put her at risk or are socially reserved for men, and for which she deserved what happened to her. Underlying this discourse of provocation is the belief that abusers are simply "succumbing to a natural tendency that may be inevitable and even understandable in certain circumstances" (Fairbairn & Dawson 2013: 58).

12   TT 17.11.2017. MP protests over rape trial verdict

A 27-year-old man was cleared after his defence lawyer suggested that the jury should consider the alleged victim's clothes and underwear the night of the incident. . . . Does the evidence outrule the possibility that she was attracted to the defendant? You have to look at the way she was dressed. She was wearing a thong with a lace front.

Despite guidelines recommendations, women are still held responsible for their inflicted violence. This reporting seems to uphold a moralizing, paternalistic, and instructive narrative (Castelló & Gimeno 2018), which dictates that women's breaching of the norms of morality the patriarchal culture imposes on them stands as an excuse for men.

Make the perpetrator visible. Avoid pathologizing: alcohol, drugs, psychological problems, jealousy, or earlier abuse as often stated as the causes of the abuse

Scholars have identified various ways news reporting on VAW conceal or excuse perpetrators. One way of eclipsing the role of the perpetrator is through the use of the passive voice, which distances the crime and the perpetrator (see Adampa 1999; Frazer & Miller 2009; Tranchese & Zollo 2013). Guidelines urge reporters to identify the subject of the crime as a way to exert social pressure by allocating responsibility. An analysis of the lemma "woman" as a subject of verbs reveals that this tendency is still too common, as examples (13)–(15) also illustrate:

Table 17.2 Forms of passivisation in the corpus

Lemma	Lemma + Verb	N. of Occurrences	× Per Million Token
Woman	die	750	35.19
	be killed	439	20.4
	pass away	172	8.07

13   **ABC 03.09.2019.** The investigators are awaiting the results of the autopsy and the remains collected to verify the facts. If confirmed, there would be 10 women who have died from gender violence so far this year.

14   **EP 07.08.2018.** Yesterday's murder is the second woman to be killed in Catalonia as a victim of gender violence.

15   **EM 28.09.2014.** The woman died after being stabbed several times with a knife.

Hiding or disguising the perpetrator of an act of violence or femicide with the use of passive formulas or misplacing it in gender violence contribute to erasing responsibility and to diverting condemnation and repudiation of these actions.

Research have also pointed out that news reporting often pathologize VAW by attributing violent acts to the perpetrators' mental health, substance abuse, or jealousy (Bullock & Cubert 2002; Carlyle et al. 2008; Fairbairn & Dawson 2013). Table 17.3 illustrates the significance of this frame in news reporting on VAW, where mental health issues and alcohol consumption are most prevalent.

The following examples from the corpus seem to hold to the news frame that excuses perpetrators for killing their partners and may help create a benevolent opinion:

Table 17.3 Lemmas associated with mental health and drug abuse in the corpus for VAW reporting

Lemma	Lemma + Verb	N. of Occurrences	× Per Million Token
Problem	psychological	83	3.89
	mental	87	4.08
	psychiatric	35	1.64
	emotional	15	0.7
Alcohol	drink (v)	44	2.06
	consume (v)	50	2.35
Drugs	taking (v)	63	2.87
	consumption (n)	170	7.98
	effect (n)	20	0.94
	abuse (n)	14	0.66
	problem (n)	19	0.89

16 **EP 19.10. 2018. "My wife had good things. She cooked very well"**

The abuser *had psychological problems and was alcohol dependent.*

17 **TT 28.05.2018. New domestic abuse law needs to highlight controlling partners**

Her husband, who earned a six-figure salary, *appeared jealous of the attention that Angela paid to her child.*

TG 26.10.2018. Why *XXXTentación's* violent confession matters after his death

18 The alarming details laid out in the victims testimony from January 2017 portrayed Onfroy as "monstruous", *his apparent jealousies and insecurities leading him to repeatedly commit horrific acts of abuse towards her.*

Although these circumstances are complex and may be present in the environment of violence, guidelines suggest that these are not given as causes nor serve as mitigating factors or justifications in the story. Such news frames are problematic to fight against VAW. For Fairbairn and Dawson (2013: 158), the focus on individual qualities or situational circumstances hinder in-depth reflections on the systemic roots of VAW such as "patriarchal social structures, tolerance of misogynistic attitudes, promotion of violent masculinities, and/or lack of access to social resources and support for many marginalized women". In the same vein, framing VAW as a matter of isolated pathology or deviance (monsters; N = 279); beasts; N = 170) contributes to "othering", thus depicting violent men as outsiders and unconnected to the patriarchal structure of domination and control.

19 **EP 12.04.2018.** *When a macho monster murders his partner*, no one dares to raise their voice to demand "political solutions" to such crimes.

20 **ABC 21.04.2018.** Once again, evil in its pure state, *the uncontainable fury of man mutated into an irrational beast*, was present yesterday in Vitoria. . . . Shortly before noon, a woman and her mother were murdered by the ex-husband of the former.

The examples in (19) and (20) show that the depiction of perpetrators as deranged monsters is still present in current reporting on VAW. On the positive side, the results show a downward trend, as most of the occurrences are located before 2014, the year around which the guidelines from the most important media groups were issued. For the remaining years, many of these instances are found in op-ed pieces and attributed discourse. This is not positive by any means, as it evinces the persistence of a narrative that nurtures these false myths.

> Do not blame religion, nationality or culture for GBV and do not assume that one religion is more inclined than others. Represent GV as a cross-cultural phenomenon with no geographical or cultural boundaries.

Guidelines advise against publishing someone's ethnic, cultural, or religious background to prevent the typical association of the abuse of women with marginal environments which distort the news and endorse cultural bias and "othering" (see, for instance, NUJ 2013). These guidelines suggest that GBV must be represented as a cross-cultural phenomenon with no geographical or cultural boundaries. In fact, publicising that VAW exists in all social classes is said to contribute to reinforcing the self-esteem of the victims. Table 17.4 shows, however, that ethnic and cultural background is still pervasive in current VAW reporting. The examples (21) and (22) serve to illustrate the prevailing narrative that some cultures are more inclined to violence than others.

21 **EM 15.08.2018**. The man, 39 years old, of Moroccan origin, with whom the victim had a two-year-old daughter.
22 **ABC 29.05.2017**. When the police arrived, they found the body of V. C., a 38-year-old Romanian woman, with her head covered by a plastic bag, gagged and with her hands tied.

3   Sources

3.1   Mention voices of experts. Neighbours and relatives are not necessarily reliable sources (non-qualified testimonies will not help understand the problem)

Feminist research in recent years have been concerned with the sources cited in VAW reporting, which has traditionally relied on police and lawyers as official voices of authority. These sources are, however, more likely to report on the specific details of the crimes (as individual episodes), which often shrouds the overarching social and political meaning of the crime (Bullock & Cubert

Table 17.4 Top five word sketches for the lemmas "nationality" and "origin" (per n. of occurrences)

Lemma	Modifiers	N. of Occurrences	× Per Million Token
Nationality	Romanian	148	6.94
(2,265)	Moroccan	109	5.11
	Ecuadorian	94	4.41
	Bolivian	53	2.49
	Chinese	49	2.31
Origin	Moroccan	109	5.11
(2,478)	Maghrebi	60	2.82
	Ecuadorian	46	2.16
	Romanian	44	2.86
	Dominican	41	1.92

2002; Wozniak & McCloskey 2010; Gilbertson & Pandit 2019). Research and guidelines reclaim a critical feminist perspective, with the inclusion of the voice of experts, survivors, and feminist organisations, who are more likely to provide broader insights into and knowledge of the social nature of the issue. These sources are, however, rarely cited (Bullock & Cubert 2002; Bullock 2008; Fairbairn 2015).

The results from this case study seem to confirm these research trends. Despite the advocacy of guidelines, the use of police as voices of authority is, in absolute terms, ten times higher than the use of expert sources, as can be seen in Tables 17.5 and 17.6, which record the top five verbal processes and verbs of saying retrieved for the lemmas "police" and "expert". This is also evidenced in the number of occurrences. In light of the data, it can be concluded that the wider use of police sources still corresponds to the episodic, individual nature of VAW in Spanish news outlets.

Finally, media guidelines advise against the use of unqualified testimonies (i.e. neighbours and the family) as solvent and accredited sources, given their proximity and relatively easy access. It is claimed that the use of these voices can damage the story, condition the public, and question the victim. The latter is the case in (23). The voices of neighbours blame her fatality on her allegedly unusual behaviour, thus excusing or showing sympathy for the perpetrator.

23 **EM 06.07.2018**. On Friday, EM spoke to several neighbours in the quite streets where the victim had lived since the marriage broke down two years ago. The interviews revealed snippets of her behaviour before and after the separation. Another neighbour . . . said the atmosphere at the home before the separation "did not seem fine".

Interestingly, as can be seen in Tables 17.6 and 17.7, the use of neighbours as testimonials in the corpus is four times higher than that of experts. This, from a feminist critique, needs urgent revision.

Table 17.5 Top five verbal processes associated with police in the corpus (n. of occurrences)

Lemma	Police + Verb	N. of Occurrences	× Per Million Token
Police (22,718)	investigate	208	9.76
	inform	133	6.24
	believe	67	3.14
	discard	59	2.77
	suspect	55	2.58

Table 17.6 Top five verbs of saying associated with the lemma "expert" in the corpus (n. of occurrences)

Lemma	Expert + Verb	N. of Occurrences	× Per Million Token
Expert (2,739)	coincide	44	2.06
	believe	31	1.45
	consider	29	1.36
	alert	27	1.27
	point out	23	1.08

Table 17.7 Top five verbs of saying for the lemma "neighbour" in the corpus (n. of occurrences)

Lemma	Modifiers	N. of Occurrences	× Per Million Token
Neighbour (8,435)	explain	89	4.18
	say	85	3.99
	tell	57	2.67
	relate	56	2.63
	assure	44	2.06

Conclusions

This chapter has examined the state-of-the-art on the discursive construction of female victims in VAW reporting, while exploring the effect(s) of media ethical guidelines on its reporting through a case study. Relying upon CDS, the analysis of VAW reports (vis-à-vis their ethical guidelines and the extant literature) has identified specific frames that routinise myths that can legitimate and per-petuate anti-feminist ideologies. As seen, these problematic portrayals have an impact on society's perceptions of GBV. This is not without a potential ethical cost.

It is time for the news media to realise the importance of a feminist perspective as a key lens through which WAV reporting must be examined to situate GBV in a global dimension. This is only possible if media factor gender in the news-making process. Media must play a fundamental role in reinforcing the social repudiation of abuse(rs), supporting the victims, spreading the struc-tural and systemic complexity of GBV, and helping women to tell their stories in their own voices. This implies a shift in the discursive practices of media, a revision of the routines, and a stance actively committed to more sensitive reporting.

Notes

1 Although this chapter focuses on violence perpetrated against women (VAW), it acknowledges that GBV, and specifically IPV, also occurs in LGBTI relationships. Despite the limited research on the prevalence of GBV amongst the LGBTQ+ community, the OHCHR (2016) suggests that the incidence of IPV in LGBTI relationships is equal to the one in heterosexual relationships.
2 For Musi and Reed (2022: 5), in contrast to fake news, semi-fake news is not constructed with the deliber-ate intention of disinforming the audience. However, they may contain fallacious propositions or myths supported by partially valid sources which may draw conclusions as factual.
3 The corpus used for the present chapter is an ad-hoc corpus of VAW reporting in Spanish dailies (2014–2021). The newspapers included are *El País* (EP), *El Mundo* (EM), and *ABC*, embodying different ideologi-cal inclinations. The size of the corpus is ca. 10 million words, processed in the software Sketch Engine. The examples for illustration are selected from the analysis of concordances. Examples from Spanish have been translated into English for ease of exposition.

Bibliography

Adampa, V. (1999) "Reporting on a violent crime in three newspaper articles. The representation of the fe-male victim and the male perpetrator and their actions: A critical news analysis", *Centre for Language in Social Life Working Paper Series*, 108: 1–33.

Ajibola, B. (2022) "Understanding journalists' perspective of gender-based violence in Nigeria: A survey analysis", in Centre for Journalism Innovation and Development (ed.) *Gender-Based Violence Reporting Handbook*, CIJD, 1–27.

Bell, A. (1991) *The Language of News Media*, Blackwell.

Bell, A. (1998) "The discourse structure of news stories", in A. Bell & P. Garret (eds.) *Approaches to Media Discourse*, Blackwell, 64–104.

Bell, A. & P. Garrett (eds.) (1998) *Approaches to Media Discourse*, Blackwell.

Bullock, C. (2008) "Framing domestic violence fatalities: Coverage by Utah newspapers", *Women's Studies in Communication* 30: 34–63. http://doi.org/10.1080/07491409.2007.10162504.

Bullock, C. & J. Cubert (2002) "Coverage of domestic violence fatalities by newspapers in Washington State", *Journal of Interpersonal Violence* 17: 475–499.

Carlyle, K.E., M.D. Slater & J.L. Chakroff (2008) "Newspaper coverage of intimate partner violence: Skewing representations of risk", *Journal of Communication* 58: 168–186. http://doi.org/10.1111/j.1460-2466.2007.00379.x.

Carter, C. & C.K. Weaver (2003) *Violence and the Media*, Issues in Cultural and Media Studies, McGraw & Hill.

Castelló, R. & A. Gimeno (2018) *Manual de estilo para el tratamiento de la violencia machista y el lenguaje inclusivo en los medios de comunicación*, Unió de Periodistes Valencians.

Council of Europe (2011) *Convention on Combating and Preventing Violence Against Women and Domestic Violence*. https://rm.coe.int/168008482e.

Dobash, R.E. & R.P. Dobash (1992) *Women, Violence and Social Change*, Routledge.

Easteal, P., K. Holland, M.D. Breen, C. Vaughan & G. Sutherland (2019) "Australian media messages: Critical discourse analysis of two intimate homicides involving domestic violence", *Violence against Women* 25(4): 441–462.

Easteal, P., K. Holland & K. Judd (2015) "Enduring themes and silences in media portrayals of violence against women", *Women's Studies International Forum* 48: 103–113. http://doi.org/10.1016/j.wsif.2014.10.015.

Ehrlich, S. (2001) *Representing Rape: Language and Sexual Consent*, Routledge.

Fairbairn, J. (2015) *Ecologies of Change: Violence against Women Prevention, Feminist Public Sociology, and Social Media*, Unpublished PhD Dissertation, Carleton University.

Fairbairn, J. & M. Dawson (2013) "Canadian news coverage of intimate partner homicide: Analysing changes over time", *Feminist Criminology* 8(3): 147–176.

Fairclough, N. (1989) *Language and Power*, Longman.

Fairclough, N. (1995) *Media Discourse*, Bloomsbury.

Flowerdew, J. & J.E. Richardson (2018) *The Routledge Handbook of Critical Discourse Studies*, Routledge.

Fowler, R. (1991) *Language in the News. Discourse and Ideology in the Press*, Routledge.

Frazer, A.K. & M.D. Miller (2009) "Double standards in sentence structure: Passive voices in narratives describing domestic violence", *Journal of Language and Social Psychology* 28(1): 62–71. http://doi.org/10.1177/0261927X08325883.

Gilbertson, A. & N. Pandit (2019) "Reporting of violence against women in Indian newspapers", *Economic and Political Weekly* 19: 41–48.

Gillespie, L.K., T.N. Richards, E.M. Givens & M.D. Smith (2013) "Framing deadly domestic violence: Why the media's spin matters in newspaper coverage of femicide", *Violence Against Women* 19(2): 222–245. http://doi.org/10.1177/1077801213476457.

Gius, C. & P. Lalli (2014) "'I loved her so much but I killed her'. Romantic love as a representational frame for intimate partner femicide in three Italian newspapers", *ESSACHESS Journal for Communication Studies* 7: 53–75.

Hollander, J. & K. Rodgers (2014) "Constructing victims: The erasure of women's resistance to sexual assault", *Sociological Forum* 29(2): 342–364. http://doi.org/10.1111/socf.12087.

Lazar, M. (2018) "Feminist critical discourse analysis", in J. Flowerdew & J.E. Richardson (eds.) *The Routledge Handbook of Critical Discourse Studies*, Routledge.

Lloyd, M. & S. Ramon (2017) "Smoke and mirrors: UK newspaper representations of intimate partner domestic violence", *Violence Against Women* 23: 114–139.

Lopes, C. & T. Pimentel (2016) "Are we missing half the story? Media reporting on VAW", in C. Lopes & S. Mapker (eds.) *Challenging Patriarchy: Conversations on Violence Against Women*, Heinrich Böll Stiftung, 32–46.

López Díez, P. (2005) "La violencia contra las mujeres en los medios de comunicación", *Instituto Oficial de Radio y Televisión* (RTVE): 21–36.

Marín, F., J.I. Armentia & J. Caminos (2011) "El tratamiento informativo de las víctimas de violencia de género en Euskadi: *Deia, El Correo, El País y Gara* (2002–2009)", *Comunicación y Sociedad* XXIV(2): 435–446.

Meyers, M. (1997) *News Coverage of Violence against Women: Engendering Blame*, Sage Publications Ltd. http://doi.org/10.4135/9781452243832.

Meyers, M. (2004) "African American women and violence: Gender, race and class in the news", *Critical Studies in Media Communication* 21(2): 95–118. http://doi.org/10.1080/07393180410001688029.

Monckton-Smith, J. (2012) *Murder, Gender and the Media*, Palgrave MacMillan.

Musi, E. & C. Reed (2022) "From fallacies to semi-fake news: Improving the identification of misinformation triggers across digital media", *Discourse & Society* 33(3): 349–370. http://doi.org/10.1177/09579265221076609.

Pereira, C. (2022) "Ethical imperatives in media reporting on gender-based violence in Nigeria", in Centre for Journalism Innovation and Development (CIJD) (eds.) *Gender-based Violence Reporting Handbook*, CIDJ.

Richards, T.N., L. Gillespie & M.D. Smith (2011) "Exploring news coverage of femicide: Does reporting the news add insult to injury?", *Feminist Criminology* 6(3): 178–202.

Richardson, J.E. (2007) *Analysing Newspapers: An Approach from Critical Discourse Analysis*, Palgrave Macmillan.

Sutherland, G., A. McCormack, J. Pirkis, P. Easteal, K. Holland & C. Vaughan (2016) *Media Representation of Violence against Women and Their Children: State of Knowledge Paper, ANROWS Landscapes, 15/2015*, Anrows, 1–56.

Tranchese, A. & S.A. Zollo (2013) "The construction of gender-based violence in the British printed and broadcast media", *Critical Approaches to Discourse Analysis across Disciplines (CADAAD)* 7(1): 141–163.

UN General Assembly (2006) *Intensification of Efforts to Eliminate All Forms of Violence against Women*, United Nations: A/RES/61/143.

van Dijk, T.A. (1988) *News as Discourse*, Hillsdale: Lawrence Erlbaum Associates Inc.

van Dijk, T.A. (1998) *Ideology*, Sage.

Walker, L.E. (1979) *The Battered Woman*, Harper & Row.

Wodak, R. & M. Meyer (2016) *Methods of Critical Discourse Studies*, Sage.

Wozniak, J.A. & K.A. McCloskey (2010) "Fact or fiction? Gender issues related to newspaper reports of intimate partner homicide", *Violence against Women* 16(8): 934–952.

Codes of ethics used in this study

Balabanova, I. & A. Kojoyan (2020) *Guideline on Gender Equality and Violence against Women for Armenian Journalists and Media Workers*, Council of Europe.

Castelló, R. & A. Gimeno (2018) *Manual de estilo para el tratamiento de la violencia machista y el lenguaje inclusivo en los medios de comunicación*, Unió de Periodistes Valencians.

Centre for Journalism Innovation and Development (CIJD) (2022) *Gender-based Violence Reporting Handbook*. https://thecjid.org/wp-content/uploads/2022/03/Gender-Based-Violence-Reporting-Handbook.pdf.

Council of Europe (1993) *Ethics of Journalism*. Resolution 1003. Report of the Committee on Culture and Education. http://pace.coe.int.

Equal Press (n.d.) *Reporting on Gender-based Violence: A Guide for Journalists*, Canada.

FAPE (2017) *Código Deontológico*. https://fape.es/home/codigo-deontologico/

Gligorijević, J., S. Pavlović & H. Cvetičanin Knežević (2021) *Guidelines on Media Reporting on Violence against Women*, UN Development Programme.

Guardian (2011) *Editorial Guidelines: Guardian News & Media Editorial Code*. http://image.guardian.co.uk/sys-files/Guardian/documents/2011/08/08/EditorialGuidelinesAug2011.pdf

Independent Press Standards Organisation (2021) *Editor's Code of Practice*. www.ipso.co.uk/media/2032/ecop-2021-ipso-version-pdf.pdf.

International Federation of Journalists (IFJ) (2014) *IFJ Guidelines on Reporting Violence against Women*. www.ifj.org/media-centre/reports/detail/ifj-guidelines-for-reporting-on-violence-against-women-in-english-french-and-spanish/category/gender-equality.html

International Press Service (IPS) (2009) *Reporting Gender-based Violence: A Handbook for Journalists*, IPS.

IORTVE (2002) *Mujer, violencia y medios de comunicación*. Dossier de prensa. Ministerio de Trabajo y Asuntos Sociales. Egraf.

Macharia, S. & P. Morinière (2012) *Resource Kit for Gender-Ethical Journalism and Media House Policy*, WACC/IFJ.

National Union of Journalists (NUJ) (2013) *NUJ Guidelines for Journalists on Violence against Women*. www.nuj.org.uk/about/nuj-code/

OHCHR (2016) *Living Free and Equal: What States are Doing to Tackle Violence and Discrimination against Lesbian, Gay, Bisexual, Transgender and Intersex People*, United Nations.

United Nations (2019) *Reporting on Violence against Women and Girls: A Handbook for Journalists*, UNESCO.

18

ONLINE GENDERED AND SEXUALISED DISINFORMATION AGAINST WOMEN IN POLITICS[1]

Eleonora Esposito

1 Conceptualizing online gendered and sexualised disinformation

Disinformation is growingly shaping political processes on a global scale: phenomena like echo chambers, filter bubbles, and polarisation (Barberá 2020), fuelled by the increasing political influence of digital media, have come to represent new challenges for global democracies. In parallel, there has been a rapid rise in tools and practices of online fact-checking and verification that have gained support from a wide range of policy actors, media outlets, and technology developers alike. However, not all actors in the political processes feel urged to counter the phenomenon, as disinformation has also turned into an established tool for political propaganda. In a populist political era, where politics is being "mediatized", "spectacularized", and "personalised" (Mazzoleni and Schulz 1999) at unprecedented levels, forms of deliberately misleading information are often used to "disparage opposing viewpoints" (Tucker et al. 2018) and effectively discredit one's opponents. In turn, media agents and the general population work, more or less intentionally, as amplifiers in this political disinformation process.

While the most prominent and debated political disinformation campaigns are related to national and international politics, economy and health, the phenomenon has also a striking gender dimension. In particular, a growing number of disinformation campaigns target women in politics (henceforth, WIP), spreading false, inaccurate, or misleading gendered and sexualised narratives against them (Inter-Parliamentary Union 2018). Drawing on widespread misogyny and societal stereotypes, gendered and sexualised disinformation frames women as inherently unfit to participate in the democratic process (Stabile et al. 2019). The impact of this type of disinformation is growingly acknowledged, as it has the power to "alter public understanding of female politicians' track records for immediate political gain, as well as to discourage women seeking political careers or leadership roles" (Di Meco 2020).

In this gendered disinformation process, "a picture paints a thousand lies" (Hameleers et al. 2020). Digital visual images, in fact, make "social identities, processes, practices, experiences, institutions and relations" visible (Rose 2014: 13), especially in light of the advent of fully-fledged image-based platforms such as Instagram, Snapchat, and TikTok. As haters and disinformers capitalize on the role of digital media in the visual (re-)production of our social and political life-worlds, the manipulation of visual information is emerging as one of the most effective strategies

DOI: 10.4324/9781003224495-22

to discredit and attack public figures online (Hameleers et al. 2020). Some emerging visual disinformation strategies, such as deepfakes, seem to target women disproportionately and are often employed to generate fake pornographic content (Wagner and Blewer 2019).

With digital media affordances acting as a "force multiplier", both in terms of sheer quantity and vitriolic quality of interactions, visual content abusive to women is proliferating in the cybersphere (Ging and Siapera 2018). Already in 2012, blogger and feminist activist Anita Sarkeesian discussed her first-hand experience of harassment on her blog *Feminist Frequency*, reflecting on visual misogyny as a prime strategy for sexist violence and conceptualizing the inductive categories of "photoshop harassment", "meme images harassment", and "rape drawings" (Sarkeesian 2012). In the same vein, Powell and Henry (2017) theorised "technology-facilitated sexual violence" as a very broad range of sexual and gender-based aggressive behaviours facilitated by digital technologies, entailing the two semiotic sub-categories of "image-based sexual abuse" and "image-based harassment".[2]

More closely related to the experience of women in the political sphere, "semiotic violence" refers to the mobilization of semiotic resources to injure, discipline, and subjugate WIP, on a continuum with other forms of (physical, sexual, psychological, and economic) gender-based violence (Krook and Sanín 2019). Further elaborating the concept, Krook (2020) highlights how semiotic violence often relies on visual-heavy strategies, including the creation and diffusion of sexually graphic, digitally altered images of female politicians.

This chapter illustrates the role played by image-based user-generated content in perpetrating gendered disinformation and sexist stereotypes. In particular, it illustrates two overarching and highly recurrent strategies, namely, *image manipulation* and *false identity attribution*, characterised by the use of visual affordances to restate, sustain and propagate disinformation and sexist stereotypes against WIP on social media platforms. As such, this chapter's ultimate aim is to contribute to the ongoing conceptualization and problematization of the domain of gender-based hostility as an emerging multimodal digital discursive practice in the era of digital disinformation (KhosraviNik and Esposito 2018; Esposito 2021a).

2 Investigating online gendered and sexualised disinformation

Both data and analysis presented in this chapter form part of WONT-HATE, a wider H2020 project (March 2019–March 2021) on violence against WIP, with a specific focus on the role played by digital and social media in the discursive proliferation of misogynistic hostility and abuse in selected EU countries (Italy, Spain, the UK).

Data collection throughout the project was grounded in an immersive digital ethnographic observation, able to capture the ethos of interactivity and "always-on" connectivity of social media communication. Such an ethnographic, problem-oriented, and discourse-centred stance allowed the identification and location of main debates and discourse concentrations, as well as most relevant and abundant foci of data across a variety of social media platforms, encompassing Facebook, Twitter, and YouTube.

While the analysis of online violence against WIP in the UK were presented in other academic publications (Esposito and Zollo 2021; Esposito and Breeze 2022), this chapter focuses on female political figures selected among the most "followed" in Italy and Spain. The Facebook and Twitter visual data presented in this chapter was purposefully sampled (Patton 2002) from the project corpus with the purpose of exemplifying and systematising *image manipulation* and *false identity attribution* as two overarching multimodal strategies of visual misogyny employed to harass, discredit, and defame the public image of WIP and their reputation.[3]

This chapter draws on theoretical and empirical contributions within the domain of social media critical discourse studies (SM-CDS), an emerging theoretical and methodological framework combining tenets from critical discourse studies with scholarship in digital media and technology (KhosraviNik 2017), and focuses on complex social digital discursive phenomena which require a problem-oriented, multidisciplinary approach. On the one hand, this chapter draws on the scholarly tradition of social semiotics as a "form of enquiry" that "comes into its own when it is applied to specific instances and specific problems" (van Leeuwen 2005: 1) and aims at bringing to the surface what is being communicated by means of visual designs (Kress and van Leeuwen 2006). Additionally, the social semiotic approach is complemented by a critical stance towards the visual, always to be regarded as mediated rather than transparent, as representational rather than depictional, as a carrier of particular "ways of seeing which are socially and historically specific" (Hand 2017: 217). In this vein, my work builds upon existing conceptualizations of gender-based objectification and shaming and on the role played by the creation and diffusion of sexually explicit/pornographic content in the silencing, defamation and subjectivity-denial of women (Nussbaum 2010; Langton 2008; see also MacKinnon 1987).

Readers should be warned that this chapter contains graphic content. Euphemizing data or reporting only the milder examples as a form of self-censorship would be detrimental and may contribute to wrongfully frame gendered and sexualised disinformation as a nonthreatening and/or recreational phenomenon (Jane 2016). Far from being an endorsement, this programmatic choice is framed by a critical, socio-prognostic approach aimed at denouncing an issue with a profound impact on gender equality in digital spaces, in the political arena, and in society at large.

3 Strategies of online gendered and sexualised disinformation

3.1 Image manipulation

A prime strategy of *image manipulation* is to alter WIP's words or message. Figure 18.1a pictures Spanish politician Inés Arrimadas, spokesperson of the centre-right *Ciudadanos* party. The original

Figures 18.1a and 18.1b   Image manipulation – Inés Arrimadas' original (left) and manipulated ("Price List") image

picture was taken on 12 December 2018, as Arrimadas was questioning the president of the Government of Catalonia Quim Torra during a session at the Parliament of Catalonia in Barcelona. As the Catalan independentist conflict was plunging Spain into a deep political crisis, Arrimadas made her intervention in Parliament holding a banner saying "155", alluding to the Spanish Constitution's article on direct rule and suspension of autonomy of self-governing communities. Figure 18.1b shows how the original picture was modified and the "155" banner was photoshopped into a price list for different sexual performances.

Holding a banner or a sign in the era of Photoshop has proven particularly dangerous for one's own reputation. Images like Figure 18.1a can be regarded as a "Speech Process" (Kress and van Leeuwen 2006 [1996]: 68), characterised by an "utterance" (a written message) and a "sayer" (the actor to whom the message is attributed), similar to the composition of a comic strip. *Image manipulation* allows the modification of the content of the "utterance", while the "sayer" stays the same: the result is attributing to the subject, by means of visual juxtaposition, a message which is not their own. In the context of social media communication, this strategy of *image manipulation* has been largely appropriated by meme culture (Milner 2016; Denisova 2019), for it allows the creation of cultural units characterised by core patterns of replicability, modification, and potential virality (Varis and Blommaert 2014). That is to say, the "utterance" can be changed an infinite number of times, allowing every prosumer to enter the conversation on social media platforms and contribute to the collective mockery and derision of the "sayer".

On a related note, the banner can also be modified not by altering the utterance it contains but substituting the object altogether yet maintaining the sexualized, misogynous, and offensive nature at the core of the image modification strategy. In another picture taken during Inés Arrimadas speech in the Parliament of Catalonia, the "155" banner she is holding was substituted with a pair of women's black lace panties (see Figure 18.2a and 18.2b), drawing on a classic comedic trope (the "underwear exposure"), which facilitates the delivery and social acceptance of sexist content.

Figures 18.2a and 18.2b   *Image manipulation* – Inés Arrimadas' original (left) and manipulated ("Lace Underwear") image

Figures 18.3a and 18.3b   Image manipulation – original (left) and manipulated image of Maria Elena Boschi swearing-in ceremony

In Italy, Maria Elena Boschi drew much media coverage back in 2014 when PM Matteo Renzi appointed her, at age 33, as Minister for Constitutional Reforms and Relations with the Parliament. Figure 18.3a pictures the actual moment of the young member of the *Partito Democratico* (PD) being sworn into office. A photoshopped version of the image (Figure 18.3b) portrays a fake "wardrobe malfunction", as if her leaning over the table exposed a purple G-string. The manipulated image was reprised by a large number of Italian and international newspapers, including the *Daily Mail* in the UK, the *Bild* and *Augsburger Allgemeine* in Germany, *20Minuten* in Switzerland. While most articles acknowledged the picture as fake, the image achieved an all-time high circulation compared to the hundreds mushrooming on a daily basis on social media platforms.[4]

Generally speaking, Figure 18.3b may be regarded as convincingly "real" because it is clearly very well executed in terms of composition, proportions, and quality of the image, and the modified part of the image blends in well with the original one. These aspects may have played a role in the wide circulation of the image beyond social media platforms into mainstream media. However, there are at least three considerations to be made that are not strictly related to the high quality of the photoshopped image, but rather draw on wider contextual cues as well as on modality as defined by Kress and van Leeuwen (2006).

Firstly, from the perspective of the context of situation, we could infer that an episode of wardrobe malfunction in an official setting *can* happen and is higher on a probability scale compared to an MP showing a pair of panties in a Parliament session (see Figure 18.2b). Also, accidental wardrobe malfunctions of celebrities have been long attracting the attention of gutter press: one of the most famous examples is how the Duchess of Cambridge Kate Middleton manages to consistently make headline news in her public appearances on particularly windy days. The human taste for spotting the rich and famous in relatable, embarrassing situations, paired with the fetishized attention for the (naked) female body, managed to establish women's wardrobe malfunctions as newsworthy in themselves and as episodes receiving consistent coverage in tabloids and gossip magazines.

Secondly, from the perspective of the wider context of culture, Italy should be regarded as a country still firmly anchored in a patriarchal and gendered societal system order, characterised by a mediatization (and consequent normalisation) of sexism that spans many genres, including variety shows, advertisements, and the ominous *commedia sexy all'italiana* ("sex comedy Italian style"). This representational politics of women in Italian media (as well as of Italian women in international media) is also the by-product of a specific socio-political juncture during the Berlusconi era. Starting in the mid-1990s up until the early 2010s, Italy witnessed the "shift of female figures (many of them procured for Berlusconi) from the entertainment world to that of political candidacy" (Melandri 2019: 57) in Berlusconi's party *Forza Italia*, in a well-oiled exchange of political, economic, and sexual favours (see also Tabet 2002). The Berlusconi era had a profound impact on how Italian WIP have come to be perceived, both on a national and international level and, albeit not true, such exposure could be regarded as *verisimilar* in the Italian political scenario.

Finally, compared to other examples of image manipulation, Figure 18.3b may be regarded as characterised by a *higher modality*, where by modality it is meant the property (or combination of properties) of a representation which is understood as construing it as more or less *real*. Elements like the depth and representation of pictorial detail and the colour saturation and brightness in Figure 18.3b can in fact be regarded as responding to "the kind of visual truth which is preferred in the given context" (van Leeuwen 2005: 167), that is, in a real picture of a current event. However, modality is only partially realised in the material features of the message itself: the sender's representation and the receiver's assessment of modality cues are largely social, "dependent on what is considered real (or true, or sacred) in the social group for which the representation is primarily intended" (Kress and Van Leeuwen 2006: 158). That is, the "issues of representation – fact versus fiction, reality versus fantasy, real versus artificial, authentic versus fake" (van Leeuwen 2005: 160) with which modality is involved are based on criteria that are socially created, negotiated, and normalised, "located in a social setting and a history" and product of a "cultural training" (Kress and Van Leeuwen 2006: 158).

Reflections on Figure 18.3b exemplify how the context of situation portrayed in the image, modality as the complex joint product of the judgements made by communicators and audiences, as well as the broader context of culture in which production and fruition are both embedded are to be regarded as three micro-to-macro considerations for a situated analysis of image manipulation. These are to be taken into account as important epistemological elements, which are particularly relevant to delve into the analysis of an image characterised by an above-average circulation. As further explained in Section 4, such a semiotic construction of Maria Elena Boschi's representation and identity, as well as its socially perceived verisimilitude, should be regarded as profoundly ideological and deeply embedded in the societal perception of WIP at large.

3.2   False identity attribution

Fake identity attribution is a strategy that entails the viral circulation of an unaltered image characterised by a deliberate misattribution of identity aimed at attacking, objectifying, and defaming a WIP. Two core elements can be identified: (a) the subject in the picture will be a woman with a more or less close facial resemblance to the targeted WIP and (b) the woman being depicted will be wearing very revealing clothes (such as her underwear) or will be fully naked. One of the most important semiotic resources of the *fake identity attribution* strategy is the caption and its interplay with the image: the caption, in fact, is intended to persuade social media users that the subject in the picture is actually the WIP being targeted (and not just a woman who may look like her).

In Figure 18.4, the diptych of Zoë Vialet, a Dutch photo model and manager of a high-class escort service, is being presented as Italian politician Maria Elena Boschi with the support of the accompanying caption which reads, "She is our Undersecretary to the Presidency of the Council of Ministers, Maria Elena Boschi. And there are still those who wonder why she got ahead in

Lei è il nostro Sottosegretario alla
Presidenza del Consiglio. Maria Elena
Boschi. E poi c'è ancora chi si meraviglia di
come abbia fatto carriera in politica

Figure 18.4   Fake identity attribution – Lingerie pictures of Zoë Vialet as Maria Elena Boschi

politics!" The underlying argument links the presence of Boschi in the Italian political arena to an alleged sexual availability, which would have allowed her to gain a leading role in the political life of the country (there were rumours of an alleged affair with married PM Matteo Renzi). The caption reprises the aforementioned sexualization of Italian WIP, partly due to the connection between access to political power and sexual favours, which was largely fuelled by the political advent of Berlusconi's party *Forza Italia*, and which came to represent an unfortunate stigma for many women entering the Italian political arena.

Another version of the caption to the same diptych attributed to the Undersecretary Boschi reads: "The photos are from a few years ago, who knows if she thought she would become Minister? Or maybe yes, of course someone like this can aspire to do everything". This caption exemplifies well one of the recurring discursive strategies of the *fake identity attribution*, which involves dating the pictures back to a more or less defined past moment in a WIP's life. This has two main aims: first, by dating the picture back to a "past life", it creates a narrative that presents the picture as the incontrovertible evidence of a secret (and equally immoral) event in the life of the WIP, which is finally being revealed. Second, it aims at flattening the perception of the anatomical differences between the woman in the picture and the WIP being targeted. In line with the argument put to the fore in the caption to Figure 18.4, Boschi's beauty and youth ("someone like this") are highly valued ("can aspire to do everything") in the system of transactional sexual exchange which has allegedly brought her to power.

Figure 18.5 pictures a naked woman in an outdoor setting: the only other element in the picture is a man's arm being placed on the woman's hip, while the man is cut out.[5] The woman is wearing a pair of sunglasses, which serve the purpose of the *fake identity attribution* well, as they allow

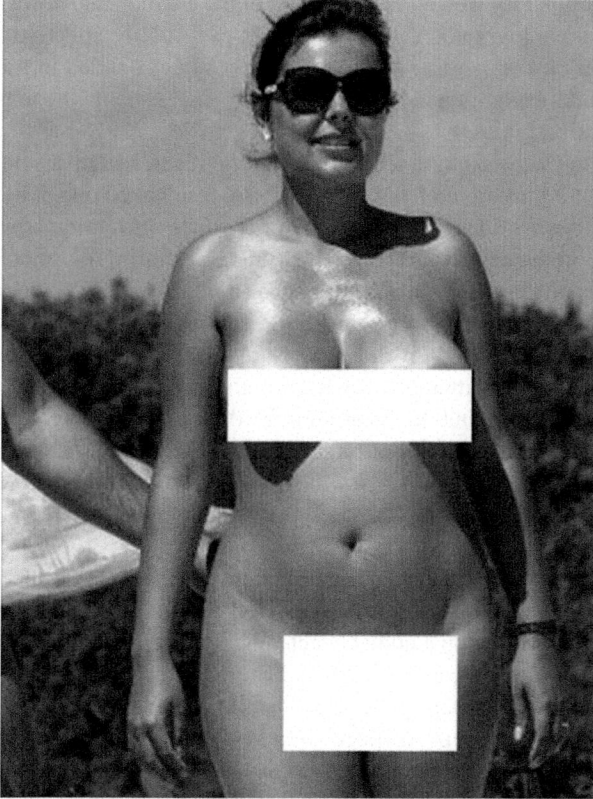

Figure 18.5 Fake identity attribution – porn actress as Laura Boldrini

a higher degree of ambiguity in the identity attribution. As mentioned, this strategy of visual misogyny is characterised by a persuasive caption which accompanies the picture, representing an
essential element and actual discursive core of the attack. Different versions of this picture were
retrieved, characterised by captions that use various strategies all aimed at attributing the identity
of the woman to the president of the Italian Chamber of Deputies, Laura Boldrini.

Caption in Figure 18.5 reads, "Is that Laura Boldrini? The President of the Chamber? Oh wow. . . .
The PD moralizers . . . all had a blast in the past! OMG . . . have you recognized her? Who's she? She
is our beloved President of the Chamber!!!"[6] Some discursive choices in the caption are particularly
salient as they directly engage the audience: the caption opens with a direct interrogative ("Ma è la
Boldrini?") and contains more similar questions ("L'hai riconosciuta?" and "Chi è?") to elicit engagement and response from the reader. Slang interjections ("Acc . . ." and "Me cojoni") and sarcasm ("La
nostra cara presidente") add to the informal, direct, and engaging style.

One of the most relevant elements of the caption, at the core of this strategy of visual misogyny,
is the moral judgement of the WIP: "tutte con un passato allegro . . . le moralizzatrici del PD". The
"sex scandal" is a long-standing strategy to undermine the power of politicians or other powerful
figures traditionally bound to maintain moral conduct and represent model behaviour. Attributing
the identity of "woman with a past" to a WIP is one of the most established and effective ways of
undermining her credibility, and when no "skeletons in the closet" are actually to be found, the

affordances of the participatory web come in support of the creation and diffusion of false information with equally false photographic evidence. This is particularly effective in the case of Laura Boldrini, as it is aimed at dismantling her authority as WIP, grounded in a long-standing active role in the field of gender equality and human rights: an engagement which earned her the title of "moralizer" in the caption.

In another post of the same picture, a different caption reads: "Ministro boldrini nuda spiaggia nudisti Francia 2009 . . . il troiaio non ha fine" ("MP Boldrini naked nudist beach France 2009 . . . the brothel is always open").[7] The core elements of the fake attribution strategy are all present: identifying the person in the picture as the WIP ("Ministro Boldrini"), setting the picture in a specific time that predates office ("2009"), and expressing a negative value judgement ("il troiaio non ha fine"). Not only the identity attribution to Laura Boldrini, but also the date ("2009") and the location ("spiaggia nudisti Francia") of the picture are false, but they are included as contextualizing details with the aim of attributing veracity. Another, slightly modified, version of the same caption changed the date from 2009 to "vent'anni fa" ("Twenty years ago"), in line with the caption in Figure 18.5, which dates back the picture to Boldrini's *passato allegro* ("loose past"). These can be regarded as attempts to increase the degree of truthfulness of the picture by dating it back to an earlier date, in all probability because the woman in the picture may look younger than the 1961-born Boldrini.

Fake identity attribution can have far-reaching consequences, as in the case of the Spanish politician Teresa Rodríguez, member of the Spanish left-wing political party *Podemos*. An alleged picture of Rodríguez fully naked on a nudist beach quickly went viral a few days before the Andalusian regional elections where the politician was a candidate. The composition of the picture features two elements aimed at facilitating the false identity attribution. The first is a smaller portrait of the actual Teresa Rodríguez giving a speech in a *Podemos* assembly in the lower left corner of the image, aimed at promoting the association between the politician and the naked woman. The juxtaposition highlights the only tangible physical trait the two women have in common, that is, the distinctive layered haircut with squared-off bangs, very common among young radical leftists in Spain. The second is a tongue-in-cheek caption reading *Podemos no tiene nada que ocultar* ("Podemos has nothing to hide"), hinting at nudity while also calling into question the party's reputation as a transparent movement founded in the aftermath of the 15-M Movement protests against austerity, inequality, and corruption in Spain (see Figure 18.6).

Sadly, the misogynous and sexist attack against Rodriguez is not the worst aspect of this false identity attribution: the picture, in fact, depicts a private citizen and was surreptitiously taken on a beach and distributed without her consent. While the woman had been long battling to get it removed from the web (Sánchez Juárez 2015), the false attribution to Rodriguez condemned the picture to virality. Widely shared in its uncensored version on social media, the picture was also taken up by the national newspaper *El Mundo* as well as by the TV talk-show *Amigas y Conocidas* ("Friends and Acquaintances") on Spain's national network La1. The publication and distribution of the image only gave further exposure to the anonymous woman, who became collateral damage in the misogynous political attack against Rodriguez (see also the analysis by Moreno Segarra and Anderson 2019).

4   Concluding discussion

When mediated by the social media communication paradigm, gendered disinformation and women's sexualisation comes to be shaped at an extremely complex intersection of multimodal communicative acts. In a context of "constant connectivity" (Keipi et al. 2017) and in the absence

Figure 18.6 *Fake identity attribution* – the nudist beachgoer as Teresa Rodriguez

of gatekeeping practices, terabytes of content with massive social and cultural implications are being "prosumed" as data on a daily basis across the cybersphere. In particular, two extremely well-established and powerful human social practices seem to play a role in the proliferation of the examples of visual misogyny illustrated in this chapter.

On the one hand, *image manipulation* capitalises on humour and is often characterised by the incorporation of an element of comicality and irony, which legitimates the prosumption of sexist, misogynous, and violent content. The blanket of humour plays a crucial, complex (and still under-studied) role in mediating the social acceptance of digital forms of violence as inoffensive and in the broader normalisation of online violence as an integral and harmless act of digital citizenship (Sarkeesian 2015). Such manipulated pictures are also characterised by a considerable amount of multimodal creativity, which contributes to the mainstreaming of such visual misogyny as episodes of "hate-play" or "recreational nastiness" (Jane 2014: 531–532).

On the other hand, *fake identity attribution* capitalises on gossip, grounded in our love-hate relationship with celebrities and our human curiosity for the lives of the "rich and famous" (Breeze 2009). However, while we are bound to acknowledge the unrelenting presence of gossip and rumour-mongering throughout human history, pure fabrications are often treated as real news on digital and social media, and public opinion is likely to be affected by the fruition of such fake visual material. With so-called "post-truth politics" thriving on suspicions, this form of reputational warfare impacts particularly on WIP, who are more likely to be objects of offensive and sexist gossip and have their reputation destroyed beyond repair.

At the same time, the viral spreading and "cascading" (Sunstein 2010) that seem to characterise the digital fruition of visual misogynous content can only partially be explained by the nature of social interactions as mediated by the affordances and contextual features of social media platforms. For example, we have seen how captions, often dating the picture back in time to maximise verisimilitude, contribute to persuade digital prosumers of the authenticity of the content, together with some degree of physical resemblance of the woman in the chosen picture with the targeted WIP. In the same vein, contexts and patterns of use, such as the velocity at which these types of content are being consumed and the relatively small screen size of smartphones, could be taken into account as contributing to the perceived veracity and the viral circulation of the image. However, one of the most relevant points here, where established theories of belief formation can contribute to our interpretation of the phenomenon, is that rumours arise and gain traction largely because they support the idea we have of the people involved and the quality of information exchanged allows to intensify pre-existing beliefs and convictions (Sunstein 2010). That is to say, people believe in misogynous rumours about WIP because they *want to* and that portrayal only fits with the idea they have about WIP (and women in general), grounded in traditional gendered hierarchies and mediatised sexism, and only further contributing to the low degree of social acceptance of women in decision-making roles.

Assessing whether social media prosumers actually believe or not in the veracity of manipulated or fake images is not only beyond the scope of this research but also pointless. In fact, the viral prosumption of naked images attributed to WIP raises a far more critical point to be discussed, such as the colossal objectification (Nussbaum 1995), which characterises the communication process in its entirety. The gendered body still emerges as a prime target and site of repressive power and domination (Foucault 1977), even more so for the primacy of the visual which characterises the digital age. In this respect, both *image-manipulation* and even to a larger extent *false identity attribution* are to be regarded as grounded in a digital representation of the female body, which revolves around reduction: women are no more than their bodies, and the long-standing obsession for women's (naked) bodies is only taken to the next level by the means of a broadly visual medium such as the digital one.

The objectifying nature of visual misogyny strategies can be further elucidated if these are problematized and interpreted as deeply enmeshed in a long-standing obsession with women's (sexual) morality. Morality, and most importantly the lack of it, is particularly at stake when it comes to WIP. In particular, a woman's interest for the political arena may be regarded as "immoral" per se, as it violates and subverts the gendered social order that has always seen men in charge of high-status, decisional roles. As "trespassers to be prosecuted", WIP are often subject to double standards, harsher judgements, and a general "moral suspicion" (Manne 2017: 271), encompassing every possible ground for doubt about competence, character, and accomplishments. With lack of social acceptance and misogyny directed at women pursuing political careers so engrained to the point of "distorting moral and rational judgements" (Manne 2017: 283), "slut-shaming" proves to be an effective restraining and silencing act against women, absolutely regardless of the fact that the violation of societal expectations may be "real, imagined or made-up" (Hanson-Young 2018: 55).

In this respect, the public revealing of a WIP's made-up "immoral conduct" of her past is at the very heart of the *fake identity attribution* strategy but can be regarded as highly relevant also to *image manipulation*. While being characterised by a vast array of semiotic resources being targeted and tampered with, the examples of *image manipulation* discussed in Section 3 draw on a shared representational politics which is fully grounded in the evaluation of a woman's morality: the misogynous trope of the "woman as whore" (Dworkin 1974; Dworkin 1981).

Conceptualizing a WIP as a whore is an immediate and successful strategy of ostracization on the basis of her immorality, drawing on an established way of downgrading and controlling women which has been ingrained in gendered societal values and expectations for centuries.

Mediatised gossip often revolves around a number of public figures' mishaps like their sexual escapades, divorces, or drug use, capitalizing on the human itch for seeing celebrities (usually richer, more famous, and more powerful than us) in deep water. However, for Nussbaum the fruition of misadventures of *female* celebrities (specifically WIP here, but also actresses, sport figures, etc.) is a form of gendered objectification characterised by an element of "pornographic delight" (2010: 76): their autonomy and subjectivity are denied, their morality is questioned, and their reputation is defamed, and most importantly, "pleasure is taken in destroying these things" (2010: 72).

While a WIP's morality is at stake in both gossiping on aspects of her personal life and in the "prosumption" of manipulated and/or fake images, the graphic visual element which characterises strategies of visual misogyny introduces another level of semiosis. The strategies examined in this chapters, in fact, yield a further shade of meaning to the element of "pornographic delight" identified by Nussbaum: when the unclothed woman's body is exposed to the (sexual) gaze of others, it is automatically foregrounded as a sexually consumed product (see also MacKinnon 1987: 176). In the same vein, the digital prosumption of photoshopped and/or fake naked pictures attributed to WIP is a complex phenomenon that cannot be reduced to the mere sexual fantasy of seeing a celebrity naked. "Political pornification" has been identified by Anderson (2011) as the mainstreaming of frames and images from the realm of pornography in the political realm, sexualizing a context where sexuality would not be otherwise highlighted. This pornification, however, does not target male and female politicians alike, but it is largely aimed at discrediting, objectifying, and dehumanising women in politics. Pornification, therefore, would represent a form of Nietzschean "ressentiment", a reactive emotion which is strategically aimed at undermining the power of subjects that we feel weaker or inadequate in comparison to (Nussbaum 2010: 76).

Politics remains a profoundly gendered institution, whose structures, roles, and procedures have been established by men for men, at a time when women were still largely excluded from the public sphere and fighting for the most basic civil rights. As women's active participation in the political sphere is still regarded by some societal segments and in many socio-political contexts as a transgression of gendered societal norms, these forms of manufactured exposure would represent a "shame punishment" (Nussbaum 2010: 76), characterised by the final aim of spoiling and stigmatizing their public figure. As we continue to underestimate the impact of gendered disinformation and the "prosumption" of visual misogynous content across the digital sphere, we end up ignoring (or even worse, normalising) the fact that the cybersphere is not an ideal realm in which all are treated equally, but a forum that has emerged as inherently biased and abusive against half of the world's population. The ongoing proliferation of gendered disinformation also entails continuing to expose existing and emerging generations of voters to content aimed at delegitimizing, objectifying, shaming, and sexualizing WIP. Such content targets WIP's "freedom, agency and good name" (Nussbaum 2010: 72) and the legitimacy of their political power, jeopardising hardfought progress towards closing the gender gap in political institutions on a global level.

Notes

1 This work was generously supported by the Marie Skłodowska-Curie actions (H2020-MSCA-IF-2017 – Grant Agreement ID: 795937).
2 According to the taxonomy developed by Powell and Henry (2017), "image-based sexual abuse" is an umbrella term loosely encompassing five forms of behaviours: relationship retribution, sextortion, sexual voyeurism,

sexploitation, and sexual assault. "Image-based harassment", on the other hand, is a subtype of online sexual harassment that can entail the sending of unsolicited explicit material and the creation and distribution of visual material (or entire pages/websites) designed to sexualize, denigrate, and "slut-shame" women.

3 WONT-HATE's data is open and FAIR, and the sub-corpus of images used for this chapter is available on Zenodo (Esposito 2021b)

4 Not only has Figure 18.3b circulated for years since 2014, but it also managed to gain a second wave of mo-mentum three years later, in October 2017, when it was accompanied by a comment attributing the picture to the new First Lady of the US Melania Trump: "This is YALL'S FIRST LADY!!!AND THEY GOT THE NERVE TO TALK ABOUT FIRST LADY MICHELLE OBAMA wearing sleeveless dresses??? #melani-atrump #pornstar".

5 By means of Google Image search, the original picture was retrieved on an adult "pro-amateur" website, as part of a beach photoshoot: such pictures are commercially produced by professional photographers and pornographic actors, but the media content is characterised by specific stylistic choices aimed at conveying a feeling of watching authentic amateur content, namely "forbidden nudist videos".

6 PD stands for *Partito Democratico* (Democratic Party). The caption wrongly presents Boldrini as a member of the PD. In 2013, Boldrini was elected as an independent member of *Sinistra Ecologia Libertà* (Left Ecology Freedom), which joined the PD and other centre-left parties in the successful coalition *Italia. Bene Comune* (Italy. Common Good).

7 This caption is characterised by a political inaccuracy: Laura Boldrini, in fact, was never a MP ("Ministro") but was elected as the president of the Chamber.

References

Anderson, K. V. (2011) "'Rhymes with Blunt': Pornification and US Political Culture," *Rhetoric & Public Affairs*, 14(2), 327–368.

Barberá, P. (2020) "Social Media, Echo Chambers, and Political Polarization," in N. Persily and J. Tucker (eds.) *Social Media and Democracy: The State of the Field, Prospects for Reform* (SSRC Anxieties of Democracy), pp. 34–55. Cambridge: Cambridge University Press.

Breeze, R. (2009) "Tarnished Stars: The Discourses of Celebrity in the British Tabloid Press," *Odisea: Revista de Estudios Ingleses*, 10, 7–18.

Denisova, A. (2019) *Internet Memes and Society: Social, Cultural, and Political Contexts*. London: Routledge.

DiMeco, L. (2020) "Why Disinformation Targeting Women Undermines Democratic Institutions," *Power3.0*. www. power3point0.org/2020/05/01/why-disinformation-targeting-women-undermines-democratic-institutions/

Dworkin, A. (1974) *Woman Hating*. New York: Penguin Books.

Dworkin, A. (1981) *Pornography: Men Possessing Women*. London: Women's Press.

Esposito, E. (2021a) "Introduction: Critical Perspectives on Gender, Politics and Violence," *Journal of Language Aggression and Conflict*, 9(1), 1–20.

Esposito, E. (2021b) Visual_Misogyny_it_Es [Data Set]. *Zenodo*. http://doi.org/10.5281/zenodo.4717537

Esposito, E. and Breeze, R. (2022) "Online Hostility against UK MPs: Patterns of Digital Intersectionality," *Discourse & Society*, 33(3), 303–323. https://doi.org/10.1177/09579265221076608

Esposito, E. and Zollo, S. A. (2021) "'How Dare You Call Her a Pig, I Know Several Pigs Who Would Be Upset if they Knew' A Multimodal Critical Discursive Approach to Online Misogyny Against UK MPs on You-Tube," *Journal of Language Aggression and Conflict*, 9(1), 44–75. https://doi.org/10.1075/jlac.00053.esp

Foucault, M. (1977) *Discipline and Punish: The Birth of the Prison*. New York: Vintage Books.

Ging, D. and Siapera, E. (2018) "Special Issue on Online Misogyny," *Feminist Media Studies*, 18(4), 515–524. https://doi.org/10.1080/14680777.2018.1447345

Hameleers, M., Powell, T. E., Van Der Meer, T. G. and Bos, L. (2020) "A Picture Paints a Thousand Lies? The Effects and Mechanisms of Multimodal Disinformation and Rebuttals Disseminated Via Social Media," *Political Communication*, 37(2), 281–301.

Hand, M. (2017) "Visuality in Social Media: Researching Images, Circulations and Practices," in L. Sloan and A. Quan-Haase (eds.) *The SAGE Handbook of Social Media Research Methods*, pp. 215–231. London: SAGE.

Hanson-Young, S. (2018) *En Garde*. Melbourne: Melbourne University Publishing.

Inter-Parliamentary Union (2018) *Sexism, Harassment, and Violence against Women in Parliaments in Europe*. Accessed 30 June 2021. www.ipu.org/resources/publications/reports/2018-10/sexism-harassment-and-violence-against-women-in-parliaments-in-europe

Jane, E. A. (2014) "'Your a Ugly, Whorish, Slut' – Understanding E-Bile," *Feminist Media Studies*, 14(4), 531–546.

Jane, E. A. (2016) *Misogyny Online: A Short (and Brutish) History*. London: SAGE Swifts.

Keipi, T., Näsi, M., Oksanen, A. and Räsänen, P. (2017) *Online Hate and Harmful Content: Cross-National Perspectives*. London: Routledge.

KhosraviNik, M. (2017) "Social Media Critical Discourse Studies (SM-CDS)," in J. Flowerdew and J. E. Richardson (eds.) *Handbook of Critical Discourse Analysis*, pp. 583–596. London: Routledge.

KhosraviNik, M. and Esposito, E. (2018) "Online Hate, Digital Discourse and Critique: Exploring Digitally-Mediated Discursive Practices of Gender-Based Hostility," *Lodz Papers in Pragmatics*, 14(1), 45–68.

Kress, G. and van Leeuwen, G. (2006) [1996] *Reading Images: The Grammar of Visual Design* (2nd ed.). New York, NY: Routledge.

Krook, M. L. (2020) *Violence Against Women in Politics*. New York: Oxford University Press.

Krook, M. L. and Restrepo Sanín, J. (2019) "The Cost of Doing Politics? Analyzing Violence and Harassment against Female Politicians," *Perspectives on Politics*, 1–16.

Langton, R. (2008) *Sexual Solipsism*. Oxford: Oxford University Press.

MacKinnon, C. (1987) *Feminism Unmodified: Discourses on Life and Law*. Cambridge, MA: Harvard University Press.

Manne, K. (2017) *Down Girl: The Logic of Misogyny*. Oxford: Oxford University Press.

Mazzoleni, G. and Schulz, W. (1999) "'Mediatization' of Politics: A Challenge for Democracy?," *Political Communication*, 16(3), 247–261.

Melandri, L. (2019) *Love and Violence: The Vexatious Factors of Civilization*. New York: SUNY Press.

Milner, R. M. (2016) *The World Made Meme: Public Conversations and Participatory Media*. Cambridge, MA and London: The MIT Press.

Moreno Segarra, I. and Vasby Anderson, K. 2019. "Political Pornification Gone Global: Teresa Rodríguez as Fungible Object in the 2015 Spanish Regional Elections," *Quarterly Journal of Speech*, 105(2), 204–228.

Nussbaum, M. C. (1995) "Objectification," *Philosophy and Public Affairs*, 24, 249–291.

Nussbaum, M. C. (2010) "Objectification and Internet Misogyny," in S. Levmore and M. C. Nussbaum (eds.) *The Offensive Internet*, pp. 68–87. Cambridge, MA: Harvard University Press.

Patton, M. Q. (2002) *Qualitative Research and Evaluation Methods* (3rd ed.). Thousand Oaks, CA: Sage.

Powell, A. and Henry, N. (2017) *Sexual Violence in a Digital Age*. New York, NY: Springer.

Rose, G. (2014) "On the Relation Between 'Visual Research Methods' and Contemporary Visual Culture," *The Sociological Review* 62: 24–46.

Sánchez Juárez, A. (2015) "La desafortunada historia de la chica desnuda de la foto de Teresa Rodríguez," *Vanitatis*. Accessed 30 June 2021. www.vanitatis.elconfidencial.com/noticias/2015-02-24/la-desafortunada-historia-de-la-chica-desnuda-de-la-foto-de-teresa-rodriguez_717026/

Sarkeesian, A. (2012) "Image Based Harassment and Visual Misogyny," *Feminist Frequency*. Accessed 30 June 2021. https://feministfrequency.com/2012/07/01/image-based-harassment-and-visual-misogyny/

Sarkeesian, A. (2015) "Stop the Trolls. Women Fight Back Online Harassment," *Women in the World*. Accessed 30 June 2021. www.youtube.com/watch?v=BGrlk8_kevI

Stabile, B., Grant, A., Purohit, H. and Harris, K. (2019) "Sex, Lies, and Stereotypes: Gendered Implications of Fake News for Women in Politics," *Public Integrity*, 21(5), 491–502.

Sunstein, C. R. (2010) "Believing False Rumours," In S. Levmore and M. C. Nussbaum (eds.) *The Offensive Internet*, pp. 91–106. Cambridge, MA: Harvard University Press.

Tabet, P. (2002) "La grande beffa," *La Ricerca Folklorica*, 46, 3–17.

Tucker, J. A., Guess, A., Barbera, P., Vaccari, C., Siegel, A., Sanovich, S., Stukal, D. and Nyhan, B. (2018) *Social Media, Political Polarization, and Political Disinformation: A Review of the Scientific Literature*. Hewlett Foundation Report. https://hewlett.org/wp-content/uploads/2018/03/Social-Media-Political-Polarization-and-Political-Disinformation-Literature-Review.pdf

Van Leeuwen, T. (2005) *Introducing Social Semiotics*. London: Routledge.

Varis, P. and Blommaert, J. (2014) "Conviviality and Collectives on Social Media: Virality, Memes, and New Social Structures," *Tilburg Papers in Culture Studies*, N° 108.

Wagner, T. L. and Blewer, A. (2019) "'The Word Real Is No Longer Real': Deepfakes, Gender, and the Challenges of AI-Altered Video," *Open Information Science*, 3(1), 32–46.

19

THE RAINBOW CONSPIRACY

A corpus-based social media analysis of anti-LGBTIQ+ rhetoric in digital landscapes[1]

Giuseppe Balirano and Bronwen Hughes

1 Introduction

The onslaught of disinformation and fictional narratives across social networking sites, specifically targeting minority communities, is particularly common in times of global crisis and uncertainty, such as the ones we are currently enduring. These fabricated accounts offer a more specific target against which to address our fears and hatred, something more tangible and consequently less paralysing. By granting explanations, however improbable, fictional narratives allow "ordinary" people to feel that they can gain greater control over their lives when faced with the unknown, with whatever is different or removed from them. Social media users gain a sense of being "in the know", possessing knowledge about events that other people lack, and this raises their self-esteem and their consideration of like-minded identity groups (see Sternisko et al. 2020). Social networking systems such as Twitter foster a complex of interpersonal bonds which traverse multiple discursive regions creating communities and sub-communities. Making fun of, criticising, discriminating, or in general, expressing negative appraisal of a third party has always been a highly aligning activity which serves to erect in-group/out-group boundaries. As Wilkinson and Kitzinger (1996: 8) state, "'We' use the 'other' to define ourselves: 'we' understand ourselves in relation to what 'we' are not". Maintaining a positive view of oneself and the group to which one belongs is also a vital ingredient when creating online in-group/out-group affiliations through criticism and discrimination. Shyer individuals wary of public exposure in other non-mediatic contexts may well hold back their opinions fearing them to be unpopular or unendorsable; they will however find a sense of safety in numbers on social media platforms due to the visibility of fake content online. Recent research (see Van Prooijen & Douglas 2018; Douglas *et al.* 2019) has illustrated that those who spread misinformation and conspiracy theories tend to stick together and align, and the affordances of social media platforms allow users to circumvent gatekeeping mechanisms. Belief in conspiracy theories concerning gay people is often driven by a desire to maintain control over events or to "other" minority groups in the face of incomplete or conflicting news regarding a specific incident (Balirano & Hughes 2020).

Gay-conspiracy, indeed, thrives on the attribution of evil and hostile qualities, those that need to be ascribed to a given out-group, to someone who does not and could not belong to our cultural setting, often a minority group already weighed down by a number of negative stereotypes; terrorists

DOI: 10.4324/9781003224495-23

are a prime example; the Jewish community, too, benefits from such unrequited attention; as do the members of the gay community dealt with in this chapter.

Conspiracy theories and their relative targets have a vast literature, varied in nature and mainly dealing with how such theories are legitimated (Harambam & Aupers 2021), or how, for instance, they can move from the abstract realm of social media exchanges and become concrete real-life events (Apuke & Omar 2021), or again how they are structured to successfully spread and "stick" and hence ensnare increasing numbers of "believers" (Franks *et al.* 2013). However, specific academic studies regarding conspiracy theories involving members of the LGBTIQ+ community are few and far between (Herman 1996; Woods 2003; Marchlewska *et al.* 2019). Those which do focus on the connection between "gay" and "conspiracy" will progressively emerge as this chapter unfolds.

A red thread connecting the LGBTIQ+ community and latent conspiracy theories does however surface in the popular press. Indeed, as early as 1951, the Conservative magazine *Human Events* issued a warning about the danger that the "Homosexual International posed to the free world", claiming that "This conspiracy has spread all over the globe; has penetrated all classes; operates in armies and in prisons; has infiltrated into the press, the movies and the cabinets and it all but dominates the arts, literature, theater, music and TV".[2] Subsequently, in 1977, the Dade County Commission, a US body responsible for ensuring that federal and state requirements are fulfilled, passed an ordinance in favour of gay rights. To counter such a measure, Anita Bryant, singer and born-again Christian, immediately launched a campaign to repeal the decision and set up an organisation called Save Our Children, based on the idea that "Homosexuals cannot reproduce, so they must recruit". By focusing on the idea of an underlying threat to children by members of the LGBTIQ+ community united in a form of recruitment conspiracy, Bryant had successfully paved the way for an incredibly powerful rhetorical focus for social conservatives. A few years later, in the wake of Bryant's gay conspiratorial outburst, a Baptist pastor and conservative activist, Jerry Falwell, in a letter to his parishioners warned, "Please remember, homosexuals don't reproduce! They recruit! And they are out after my children and your children".[3] By the 1980s, the religious right had made the fight against gay and lesbian liberation one of its primary objectives slowing the advance of gay-rights and fostering an organised anti-gay opposition.

Moving now to current times, on 31 May 2022, *The Intelligencer* published a story predictably titled: "The Long, Sordid History of the Gay Conspiracy Theory. Today's right-wing campaign against 'groomers' is America's latest moral panic". The article outlines the homophobia-linked moral panics that have occurred in rapid succession in the United States from the 1950s until present day: "to comprehend America's latest moral panic, it is necessary to recognize homophobia as not only a form of prejudice like any other but as a conspiracy theory" (*The Intelligencer*, 31 May 2022).

In terms of academic research-based studies, the investigation carried out by Benton *et al.* (2022) at the time of Elon Musk's takeover of the Twitter platform and amnesty of deleterious, violent accounts, examines the visibility of the term "groomer" across the platform. With regard to gay conspiracy theory, the authors confirm as follows:

Perhaps the most essential conspiracy used against marginalized communities is the myth that they are "coming for our children". From the "blood libel" of the Middle Ages which posits children are being abducted by Jews for child sacrifice to conspiracies of hypersexual Communities of Color attacking virginal white girls, the visceral fear stoked by such conspiracies serves a unifying function with the creation of clearly defined enemies. This conspiratorial tendency has historically been used to target the LGBTIQ+ community through the construction of fictional predators harming youth.

(Benton *et al.* 2022: 3)

Over the years, fictional accounts and conspiracy theories related to the publication of misleading information and disinformation have progressively gained more consolidated meanings, though increasingly devoid of truthfulness. In 2006, the Merriam Webster dictionary, following comedian Stephen Colbert's *The Colbert Report* aired from 2005 to 2014, defined "truthiness" as "a truthful or seemingly truthful quality that is claimed for something not because of supporting facts or evidence but because of a feeling that it is true or a desire for it to be true".[4] At that time, the move away from truth as a monolithic, non-negotiable concept still benefited from the softening effects of humour and satire, and truthiness consisted in blurring or fudging reality, not in creating an alternative version. In that prelapsarian era, the concept of truth still defied contention.

Still today, truth has become a rather fuzzy concept to the extent that pseudo-veracious vitriolic campaigns meted out against minority groups still gain considerable consent and support. This is due, in the main, to far-right media campaigns carried out across SNSs (Van Prooijen *et al.* 2015; Balirano & Borba 2021; Cinelli *et al.* 2022; Rasulo 2023), which tax gender activists, gay individuals, and any of their possible allies – left-wing woke culture and/or liberals, for example – with heinous labels such as "paedophiles", "family wreckers", "child groomers", and "hate bearers" as will be shown in our corpus analysis. These pejorative expressions of hostility underlie anti-LGBTIQ+ misinformation, building upon a number of mainstream religious, medical, or moral discourses generally deemed to be an integral part of contemporary ideological *topoi*. Gender bias is connected to anti-leftism wherein leftists, feminists, and queer activists are depicted as responsible for society's decline and the imposition of a new vision of society: "We define gender conspiracy beliefs as convictions that gender studies and gender-equality activists represent an ideology secretly designed to harm traditional values and social arrangements" (Marchlewska *et al.* 2019: 776).

A common feature of gender conspiracy beliefs is the use of the rhetoric of scientific inquiry (Byford 2011; Huneman & Vorms 2018). The fake news we investigate throughout this study seems to progressively morph into gender conspiracy beliefs by means of those bonding practices found across SNSs (Zappavigna 2012), whereby scientific facts become alternative fictional ones (McIntyre 2018). These, in turn, progressively take on authentic "truth" value due to their stance as news-reported items. In June 2021, for instance, CNN reported that the Pentagon had refused to fly the pride flag on any of its military bases: "The Department of Defence will maintain existing policy for the display of unofficial flags". This article then triggered a reaction in an online right-wing newspaper, the *First Thing* – self defined as "America's most influential journal of religion and public life" – which titled "Our rainbow regime". This then generated a domino effect across the Twitter platform with a tweet that turned a fact into a fictional report stating, "The time is coming, perhaps soon, when our elites will suppress the American flag and wave, all the more insistently, the rainbow substitute". In point of fact, in 2017, the Collins dictionary declared that "fake news" was to be their word of the year: "If you describe information as fake news, you mean that it is false even though it is being reported as news, for example by the media".[5]

Besides equating fake news to falsehoods reported in a media context, the Collins definition also underlines the symbiotic relationship between "real" and "false" news, thus questioning our collective knowledge of what news is and somehow touching upon the notions of gullibility and naivety in our systems of belief. As a result, manufactured phrases and neologisms such as *homintern, purple hand, lavender mafia, gay mafia, gay agenda, gaystapo* and *LGBTIQ+ conspiracy* feed into the fake news discourse of anti-LGBTIQ+ rhetoric. Such false terms and labels employed across SNSs inevitably produce a system of "saturated belief" in the Twitter users, and consequently in society at large. Today, fake news regarding the LGBTIQ+ community has also become a hot topic as it

> mimics the form and function of standard news, leveraging our collective notions of what news is or should be to its advantage. Because of this parasitic relationship, we can better understand the problem of fake news by exploring our complicated relationship with news in general.
>
> (Brotherton 2020: 5)

Although misinformation and disinformation regarding minority communities appear to be only a prefix apart, the difference between the terms is abyssal, setting casual, unintentional communication, and deliberate, manipulative meaning-making in stark opposition. It is therefore important to distinguish their meanings. Whereas misinformation about the gay community characterises news or information that may be incomplete, fuzzy, or lacking in detail, it is still fundamentally "true, accurate, and informative depending on the context" (Karlova & Lee 2011: 3). Disinformation, on the other hand, involves the malicious creation and dissemination of news or information devoid of any factual basis.

Fake news and conspiracy theories which often derive thereof thrive on a general lack of information about specific events or understanding of specific knowledge areas (Harambam *et al.* 2021: 1005). Illustrative of this may be the fact that many of us who do not possess any medical training often fall for quack remedies, entirely devoid of authenticity, in the hope of, for example, losing weight rapidly or fixing some minor flaw in the workings of our inner bodies. An innate wish to "go with the flow" and participate in a kind of herd-thinking also explains the rapid dissemination of fake information, particularly across the digital landscapes. After all, it is more comfortable to embrace what so many other people see as a plausible explanation for events rather than contest facts and run the risk of being evicted from our social group of like-minded thinkers (Tandoc *et al.* 2019).

In this chapter, we posit that Internet-based fake news progressively seeps into gay conspiracy theories. This osmotic process may be due to the fact that online users often gaze at the world through apophenic lenses by creating meaningful patterns between seemingly unrelated or random events. Such a cognitive process may eventually lead to a belief in an underlying gay conspiratorial thread destined to hook both the more gullible online producers and consumers and the intentionally malicious. As Introne *et al.* (2018: 2) claim:

> Unlike a piece of fake news that cascades through social media, false narratives are not just passed from person to person. They are also constructed from disparate pieces of information that are drawn from multiple sources, building over time to become part of a plausible reality.

The possibilities offered by social media platforms such as Instagram, Facebook, or Twitter to upload content often in a highly repetitive manner, to distribute one's own content while endorsing others by liking, cross-referencing, re-tweeting, and supporting, increases the visibility and fast dissemination of fake news, allowing it to spread more rapidly than factual accounts and carefully verified information (see Vosoughi *et al.* 2018). Elements of fake news and conspiracy theory necessarily give rise to a badly informed society subjected to erroneous facts and information.

Against this backdrop, the present chapter explores the current discourses of anti-gay activism stemming from conspiratorial accounts which bolster the claim that non-heteronormative sexual orientation runs counter to most mainstream, traditional, or religious values. More specifically, a corpus-based social-media critical discourse (SM-CDS) analysis of a collection of online conspiracy-eliciting texts from the Twitter platform may help detect and interpret the emergence of LGBTIQ+ related conspiracy theories. To this end, a number of discursive categories pertaining to recurrent themes are identified in order to pinpoint dangerous anti-LGBTIQ+ discourses.

2   The gay mafia corpus

For this research, we specifically chose the online micro-blogging Twitter platform as an important stakeholder in today's information ecosystem known for the rapid dissemination of both factual and deceptive accounts. Twitter allows for different forms of information exchanges: hashtagged tweets, following activities and commenting upon them, replying through mentioning and retweeting. All of these exchanges allow for the rapid spread of fake news, and through their tweets, users show interest, express their opinions, seek alliances, and engage in political and social topics. The language used in the microposts by the online prosumers, whose tweets we focused on, is often steeped in intense feelings and emotions which can have a significant effect on public opinion (Balirano & Hughes 2020).

To collect data for our study, we decided to search Twitter posts containing seed words and phrases related to "gay mafia". The corpus was assembled by automatically crawling the Twitter API using the following seed words/phrases: "gay mafia", "lavender mafia", "gaystapo", "homintern", "lgbtiq+ OR lgbtiq OR lgbtqia OR lgbtqi OR lgbt OR lgbtq conspiracy". The online SNS Twitter has in fact made available the collection of popular data sources suitable for the analysis of online social communication (Leetaru *et al.* 2013; Barbaresi 2016). The tweets we collected resulted in a corpus we decided to name the "Gay Mafia Corpus" (henceforth GMC).

The GMC is made up of 1,654,920 tokens from 49,200 tweets and replies to tweets collected in a time span stretching from 2017 to 2022. Twitter data are extremely relevant when carrying out research in the social sciences but quite challenging to handle from the perspective of corpus linguistics. Due to access restrictions, it is often not possible to collect all the tweets one would require, limiting the overall linguistic analysis and positing privacy issues that must be dealt with (Mallinson 2018). This is the reason why XML encodings were used to save the information linked to the individuals tweeting specific messages in the structure of the corpus hiding such metadata to avoid privacy issues. The selection of the words or phrases in order to collect our data was based on a preliminary qualitative investigation of the online discussions linked to topics involving the LGBTIQ+ community. To collect data for our study, we chose to unpack Twitter posts containing seed words and phrases related to the semantic field of "gay mafia". While some scholars select common seed words extracted from lists gathered from pre-existing corpora (e.g. BNC), for specialised corpora or languages that do not have corpora available, these lists do not exist yet, thus requiring that researchers build their own seed word list related to the purpose of their study. Therefore, a semi-supervised model was adopted for the selection of these terms: we started with a simple search on the Twitter Advanced Search using the phrase "gay mafia" and subsequently expanded the list of seed words to include all the terms that were semantically related to our initial search. Table 19.1 reports the raw and the normalised frequencies of the seed words/ phrases searched for to build up the GMC:

As can be seen in Table 19.1, it is immediately evident that the occurrences of the phrase "gay mafia" are higher than the rest of the seed words/phrases featured in the GMC. This suggests that "gay mafia" is obviously more frequently adopted when referring to an alleged "gay conspiracy" compared to any other phrases we selected as seed terms, and no other concomitant terms

Table 19.1 Raw and normalised frequencies of seed words/phrases used in the collection of the GMC

Seed Words	Raw Frequencies	Normalised Frequencies (PMW)
gay mafia	10,625	6,420.25
lavender mafia	1,622	980.11
gaystapo	845	510.6
homintern	240	145.02
lgbtiq OR lgbtqia OR lgbtqi OR lgbt OR lgbtq conspiracy	46	27.8

collocating with conspiracy were found in the corpus. As a matter of fact, from a preliminary analysis of our corpus, the immediate appearance of a hypothetical connection between the LGBTIQ+ community and "mafia" hints at some shared values, although the atypical juxtaposition of the two terms "gay" and "mafia" is not commonly found across social networking sites, nor in everyday contexts of interaction. Indeed, in a quick search of the Corpus of Contemporary American English (COCA, one billion words of text ranging from 1990 to 2019), only 24 occurrences of the phrase "gay mafia" emerged, mostly derived from TV series and reality shows, hence creative contexts of written-to-be-spoken language production. For instance, in *Will & Grace* (Season 5, Episode 10: "The Honeymoon's Over", aired 5 December 2002), there is one of the earliest occurrences of the term: "It's the gay mafia. I'm going to sleep with the fish drizzled with lemon and capers!"; this example is preceded only by another occurrence found in Olivia Goldsmith's book, *Fashionably Late* (1994), in which she writes the following:

They believed that there was some kind of twisted conspiracy among gay stylists to make women look ridiculous. Jeffrey called them "the gay mafia".

As can be seen from this early use of the phrase, the concept of "gay mafia" had already been discursively crafted to indicate a form of underground conspiracy involving a group of individuals plotting against the social order with the intention of achieving personal gains by challenging the normatively dominant group. The discursive construction, therefore, already underlined a reversal of power: the dominant group becomes the victim of a conspiracy plot devised and designed by a minority group (i.e. LGBTIQ+ individuals). Yet rather surprisingly, David Icke (2007), one of the world's better known conspiracy theorists, has never alluded to gay mafia in any of his thematic bestsellers.

Another important aspect linked to our data collection concerns the type of information we were able to retrieve about the geographical areas of the Twitter users. This was automatically extracted from the descriptions provided on the individuals' Twitter accounts and as such is obviously unverifiable. Since geographic metadata are regarded as a significant source for performing linguistic studies, this information was encoded in the XML structure of the GMC and the following visualisation was generated by uploading the corpus to Sketch Engine.[6] Figure 19.1, therefore, shows the geographical areas involved:

Most tweets in the corpus, as Figure 19.1 illustrates, come from accounts that have not disclosed their geographical provenance. However, when this piece of information was actually

311

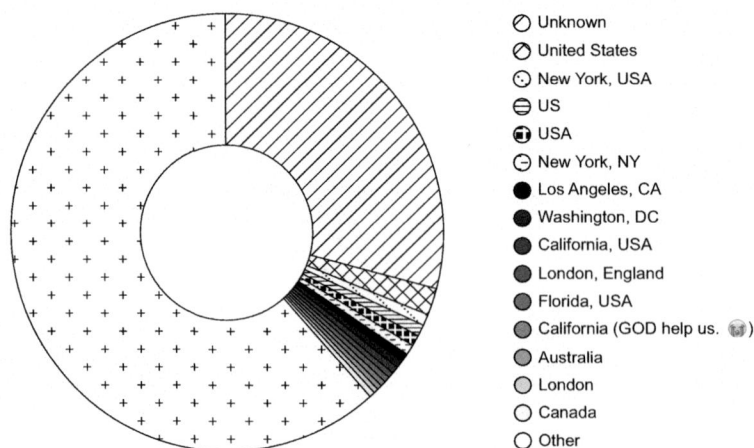

Legend:
- ⊘ Unknown
- ⊘ United States
- ☉ New York, USA
- ⊜ US
- ⊕ USA
- ⊖ New York, NY
- ● Los Angeles, CA
- ● Washington, DC
- ● California, USA
- ● London, England
- ● Florida, USA
- ● California (GOD help us. 🙄)
- ○ Australia
- ○ London
- ○ Canada
- ○ Other

Figure 19.1 Users' geographical areas displayed by using Sketch Engine

provided by our Twitter users, it is possible to attest that the majority of tweets were shared by individuals residing in the US.

As for the analysis of the GMC, a combination of mixed Corpus linguistics and SM-CDS methodologies was used. In particular, concordances of the seed words/phrases were investigated to closely study their context of use from a discursive perspective. In order to do this, Sketch Engine was adopted as the main software for the study of the corpus. Whenever specific patterns were highlighted, collocation analysis was then performed to check the validity of the insights emerging from the qualitative analysis. Collocations were calculated by using two statistical measures to first check the strength of the association (in this case, the MI3 was adopted) and then the frequency/distribution of the association in the corpus (in this case, we switched to logDice).[7] The more quantitative analysis of the GMC was backed by a recently developed approach to the analysis of social media: social media critical discourse studies (KhosraviNik & Unger 2016; KhosraviNik 2017; KhosraviNik & Sarkhoh 2017; KhosraviNik & Esposito 2018). SM-CDS, in particular, approaches the investigation of texts produced on SNSs in order to uncover the sociopolitical and ideological work behind their production. Thus, specific discursive loci emerged from this complex triangulation (Egbert & Baker 2020) of quali/quantitative tools of investigation. Such discourses will be presented in the following section.

3 Analysing the GMC

The methodology so far described has allowed for the identification of a number of discursive strategies pertaining to the GMC corpus. Such strategies have been labelled according to the main semantic domains specific to the lexemes found in the proximate linguistic environment of the seed words/phrases used throughout the corpus collection (Baker 2006). Consequently, for the sake of linear analysis, we looked at four discursive strands, or sets of tweets, pertaining to discursively recurrent themes which we titled: *metaphoric imagery, oxymoronic poles, institutions and the media*, and *ideological colonisation*. These selected strands might obviously differ when analysed across other cultures and languages, depending on the context of linguistic investigation. All strands in the GMC are located at the crossroads of fake news about an LGBTIQ+ conspiracy. As will emerge from the analysis of the corpus, however, it must be said that our strands overlap and intersect with one another in several ways, internally generating a number of very similar discursive stacks.

3.1 Strand 1: metaphoric imagery

The first strand we investigated collects all the tweets which mainly revolve around the metaphorical imagery of stereotypical representations of gay lifestyle, objects, or events which are discursively grafted into new spurious items. Such a fixation with the LGBTIQ+ world imagery could well depend on the fact that whereas half a century ago the community was barely visible in the media, and therefore in pop culture, today lesbian and gay liberation movements have created an entirely new space of representation providing a sense of community and empowerment. This has brought about a marked increase in LGBTIQ+ visibility on the media stage providing numerous role models and sources of inspiration (Hart 2000) for other minority communities enabling them, in turn, to engage in and endorse specific forms of counter-discourse. These novel representations – by crossing cultures, gender boundaries, ideologies, and moral frameworks – have also led to the fabrication of other identities and other sociocultural sites (Balirano 2020) strongly contested by members of the mainstream.

All the tweets in the "metaphoric imagery" strand evoke prototypical, though non-authentic, alleged gay objects and/or events emerging from news sources and, cunningly, stitch them together into a tapestry of fake gay imagery. If one were to illustrate this concept in pictorial terms, one could claim that a piece of fake news disseminated across social media lacks both authorial and situational authenticity, thus corroborating the "fakeness" of the representation. As Susan Sontag (2003: 38) aptly states as follows:

> A painting or drawing is judged a fake when it turns out not to be by the artist to whom it had been attributed. A photograph – or a filmed document available on television or the internet – is judged a fake when it turns out to be deceiving the viewer about the scene it purports to depict.

Rather than simply "deceiving" the tweeps, the gay imagery emerging from the GMC discursively construes a fictional, yet viable, gay mafia resemiotisation hinting at the underlying existence of a gay conspiracy. This pastiche strategy enables the creation of a realistic represented participant, that is, "gay mafia" or rather "gay conspiracist", which haunts and retraces the imagery of the LGBTIQ+ community. The juxtaposition of real and fake scripts serves to muddle discourses and unite disparate genres and adversarial representations, thus creating a chaotic yet fully recognisable blended image. This recurrently employed technique generates false information across Twitter and produces bogus tropes about minority or underrepresented communities.

In our corpus, some of the metaphors employed to construe the gay conspiracy stem from discursive remediations of Mafia folklore [see examples 1 and 2]. In tweet [1], for instance, the expression "Dead dolphins" refers to a gay member of the 'Ndrangheta, Italy's most powerful organised crime syndicate involved in everything from intimidation to vote-buying, drug trafficking to murder. The pastiche technique is at play here when intertextually associating a gay man, an alleged member of the Mafia, with a "dead dolphin" by simply tweeting the title of a by-lined article issued by *The Daily Mail* on 29 November 2021: "Dead DOLPHINS were used to issue Godfather-style warnings by 'Ndrangheta mob" where the guy was killed, just for being gay.

(1) Dead DOLPHINS were used to issue #Godfather style warnings by #Ndrangheta mob who also killed one of their own crew & buried him under tarmac for being gay, mega #mafia

trial hears as more than 300 alleged members being tried #Calabria #Italy So it wasn't totally fictional

(2) It's a fad enforced by the Gaystapo. Much like the Mafia, once you're in, you are not allowed to leave #deaddolphins

Interestingly, some canonically "straight" objects are linguistically and visually woven together with kitsch and cheesy items to recall the stereotypical glamour of a certain kind of gay camp representation such as the use of feathers, glitter, and flamboyancy in general, so dear to drag queens and representations of theatrical camp (Holleran 2019); thus, the police car turns into a rainbow-coloured vehicle driven by a member of the so-called "gaystapo":

(3) @metpoliceuk rainbow cars. LOL!!! 😂 Just add colored chalks, garters and stilettos and you can officially consider yourself the new Gaystapo. 😂 😂 😂 (UK: Police to now use "rainbow coloured" patrol cars to help the LGBT community – Aug 21)

The quasi-homophone "gaystapo", an original blend term whereby the word "gay" is compounded with the ending of "gestapo" (the infamous German secret-police organisation), is a pivotal lemma when defining this metaphoric category. This prefabricated term is able to resemiotise the United Kingdom's past where the mines, from Thatcher's winter of discontent (1978–1979), are "gayfied" into "glitter mines" surveilled by members of the "gaystapo":

(4) oh no the agenda. i must run before the gaystapo makes me work in the glitter mines. you okay there cupcake? Seems you might be a little offended about people existing.

The resemiotisation of terms such as "glitter" or "cupcake" is generally found within highly gendered contexts where such terms can be used to designate affiliation to the gay world by constructing a Disneyfied camp reality (Dallacqua & Low 2021: 72). Furthermore, the term "gaystapo" is also capable of turning a socially recognised symbol of coercion, the police baton – an icon often associated with sexuality and hegemonic masculinity, whereby the raised baton is a clear representation of an erect phallus (Elliott 1995; McGovern 2006) – into a less than virile magic wand, as the following tweet illustrates by mocking and attempting to emasculate the police institution:

(5) @Telegraph Does the Gaystapo use Magic Wands instead of police batons and guns? Or the means of coercion remain the same?

On a culturally more elevated level, again based on discursive reversal, the blend term "gaystapo" is linked to the work of the fashion designer Hugo Boss, an active member of the Nazi party in the early 1930s, who tailored the Wehrmacht uniforms. As Borba (2022: 70) puts it:

> The creation of a register with clear conspiracist content in ways that make it look legitimate and authoritative, however, requires intense semiotic work. Such an endeavor relies on manoeuvres to give credibility and veracity to the apocalyptic future gender ideologues supposedly envisage.

Tweet [6], by means of "intense semiotic work" enacted by the superimposition of numerous layers of interpretation, weaves together language and visual imagery: the evocation of the Wehrmacht uniforms designed by Hugo Boss, the reference to August Landmesser – famous for his anti-Nazi sentiment – and the calling forth of an alleged political supremacy in the hands of the woke/gay crowd. Such a metaphoric soup cunningly shifts the reference to the historical *gestapo* into a conspiratorial queer *gaystapo* by tapping into a wider idea of totalitarianism and new world order conspiracy theories:

(6) You are the opposite of #AugustLandmesser You are part of the new woke supremacy crowd. Gaystapo in Hugo Boss uniforms in your case.

A consistent and recurring aspect of the GMC, as can be inferred by several excerpts in the corpus, derives from the fact that tweets fostered by fake-news often originate from real news feeds, thus validating the truth-value of the information provided. Halliday's interpersonal meaning, here, becomes crucial if one wishes to appreciate the way attitudinal stances can be construed in our tweets (Zappavigna 2012). The fact that the tweeters resort to the use of "@mentions" (cfr.: @ metpoliceuk; @Telegraph), as an introductory social metadata device, points to the creation of dialogic affiliations (Zappavigna 2015; Osterbur *et al*. 2021). This move serves a dual purpose: (1) to highlight the authenticity of the news bearer; (2) more significantly, to create a connection between the content of the tweets and the symbolic attributive meaning deriving from the external authoritative source. As Zappavigna (2018: 135) states when dealing with the issue of gathering community and creating ambient affiliation across SNSs:

> Convoking can, of course, occur directly as part of dialogic exchanges and incorporate inter-locutors in the form of named users. For example, some posts draw on the @ mention convention where the @ character is used to refer to another user account in a manner similar to a vocative in a face-to-face conversation.

Moreover, when analysing Halliday's textual metafunction in this strand, the convoking discursive ploy (@) works as a cohesive semiotic device which, in its exophoric dimension, calls into play validation/truthfulness while granting coherence to the tweets, since it overtly makes reference to something previously mentioned or simply assumed by the Twitter users.

The metaphoric imagery strand also includes a recurring reference to the "rainbow flag" which, created by American artist Gilbert Baker in 1978 as an important symbol of the diversity of the LGBTIQ+ community, became extremely popular during the gay rights protests (mainly 1970s and 1980s). Today, rainbow flags can be found at Gay Pride Parades around the world accompany-ing slogans such as "Gender is Imaginary" (Fisher 2017; Balirano 2020). In our corpus, the noun phrase "rainbow flag", or simply the noun "rainbow" works as a humorous pre- or post-modifying attribute. It can be found specifically in the surroundings of the blend term "gaystapo" or around the ambiguous phrase "gay mafia" [see 3, 9 and 12].

(7) The obsession with the rainbow is just sickening. The @gaystapo crowd is out to force their degenerate lifestyle on all of us

Other interesting references are those connected to the widespread acronym used to label the gay community (i.e. LGBTIQ+ and its variations) which, in our corpus, is often ridiculed by means of the noun phrase "alphabet people" [10] superciliously recalling, of course, the children's alphabet soup. Despite this demeaning mechanism, the LGBTIQ+ group is not seen as a victimised minor-ity ("Victims. HA!"), but rather as an oppressive force, strengthening in this way the process of fake affiliation between the gay community and the gestapo.

The mentions, as a broadcast device aiming to introduce social metadata, also serves to invite authoritative external participants to aggregate in an interactive manner and join in as anti-gay rhetoric supporters. Some of the convoked participants in the strand are in fact eminent journalists such as Quentin Dempster [8] and Bill Kristol [10], or politicians such as Clover Moore [9] and Maxime Bernier [11]:

(8) @Kotaku Kotaku is judge and jury and executioner too. The rainbow propagandists have spoken, so that the #Gaystapo can be justified as they mark with label people who are accused of bad thinking.

(9) @CloverMoore @VoicesForAU It's "the independent effect" Its the gay mafia effect, lol, keep sticking rainbows on everything.

(10) @Mark_Dykes @BillKristol I don't think that in the time of the Gaystapo you can bully any of the "alphabet people". They're the ones doing all the bullying. Victims. HA!

(11) The LGBTQWXYZ mafia is in control @MaximeBernier We cannot turn to any media without seeing their anti-civilization gay/lesbian conversion therapy in our faces. Without family & procuration, civilization ends. A Legal challenge against gov. needs to be put forth.

(12) @Marsha250 @shuna551 The Gaystapo are even more powerful. Every single major corporation has multicolored their logo for the month of June. And for what? Less than 5% of the population.

3.2   Strand 2: oxymoronic poles

The second strand identified across the GMC deals with oxymoronic poles since it construes an improbable overlapping between ideological state apparatuses (cfr.: ISAs in Althusser 1970), such as the police, the media, the Church, and the gay community. This amalgam creates a unique graft-chimaera or simply a "graft" of power and control in the hands of gay people who are therefore depicted as an evil elitist few. These particular tweets [13 and 14], in fact, exemplify the process of grafting (Gal 2018) which consists in an adroit manipulation of language carried out by the anti-gay advocates, parasitically implanting into the gender-favourable discourse, a semblance of the authority of the "esteemed institutions" (ISAs) that the mainstream agenda opposes. This grafting process produces a number of twisted secondary indexicalities through which the anti-gay people chimaera is born of an artfully manipulated scion grafted upon the striving-for-truth rootstock:

(13) @FrogsRevenge This is Gay Mafia, Jewish Mafia, Mossad, and Israel controlling govt and CIA to where CIA will cover for Israel doing 911.

(14) The LGBTQWXYZ mafia is in control @MaximeBernier We cannot turn to any media without seeing their anti-civilization gay/lesbian conversion therapy in our faces. Without family & procuration, civilization ends. A Legal challenge against gov. needs to be put forth. https://t.co/BBBhlM3y5V.

These discursive strategies are once again based on a reverse/counterattack mechanism and employ the same instruments that have been used against the gay community (Borba & Zottola 2022), as will become evident later in our analysis.

The overarching and ubiquitous power of the gaystapo/gay mafia in the corpus is therefore grafted upon a ruling elite to be countered. This strand also includes references to bullying, intimidation, and coercion which serve to construe an elitist totalitarian regime:

(15) @MilatheSulimov I think I just had an aneurism reading the first couple posts on their page. From what I could tell is they basically want big brother to come in and force others Gestapo

style (or maybe I should say Gaystapo) into bending over backwards in every way of life to support the LGBT.

(16) Now that Biden is president I have to take estrogen pills and put on my maid outfit before I get shot by the gaystapo. To be clear I have NO CHOICE on the matter, I am being FORCED to do this.

(17) It doesn't matter how much you grovel before the #LGBTP Gaystapo, they will still hate you. Be a man. Be a conservative. Stand up for normal families for once.

The anti-gay tweets [15, 16, and 17] upon which we focus, portray LGBTIQ+ discourse as extremist and totalitarian stretching across the spectrum from left to right. By means of clever semantic engineering, words and intentions are manipulated, and true objectives are disguised.

The oxymoronic poles strand further exemplifies a certain discursive tendency to lump all political "causes" together, by fictitiously and randomly associating the LGBTIQ+ community with any possible political stance. Due to woke culture, gay mafia in numerous tweets is unsurprisingly associated with left-wing politics:

(18) @gaymafia No, he won't. He's part of the Democrat, Hollywierd, gay mafia cabal. He's protected.

(19) The gaystapo loves its woke inept government. It's not about the vaccine. It's about harassing conservatives.

Figure 19.2 reinforces this concept if one focuses on the concordance lines around the node term "gay" and its collocate "communist*":

However, progressively and unexpectedly, the left-oriented pole gives way to other equally polarised right-wing political positions (e.g. "Trump", "Conservative", "Republican", etc.) resulting in a sort of all-inclusive political soup:

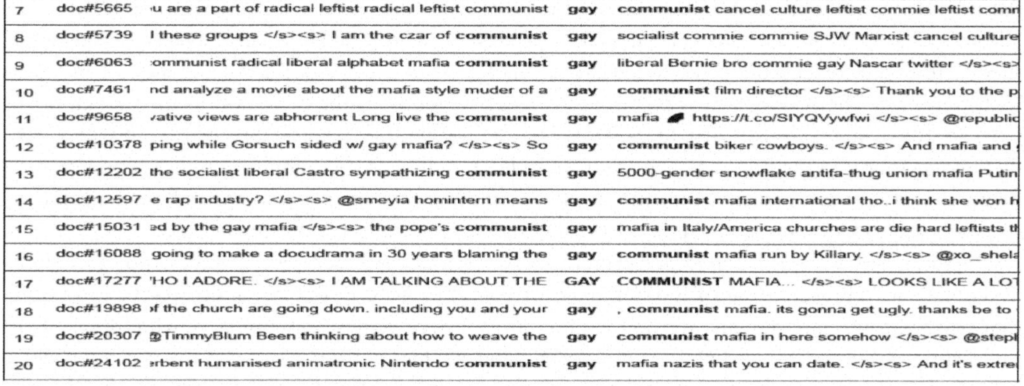
CQL gay + communist • 21
12.69 per million tokens • 0.0013%

	Details	Left context	KWIC	Right context
1	doc#300	1pMIcUC </s><s> @guylinerx Its a struggle being a	gay	**communist** bitch ooc. </s><s> Always having to de
2	doc#370	echnician You're truly there. </s><s> There being a "	gay	**communist** mafia leader" . </s><s> @strausswin
3	doc#580	vill now eat 800 pizzas to fight the leftist **communist**	gay	mafia https://t.co/nAdMkZ0UxB </s><s> @angelgotti
4	doc#5408	ire Marxist cancel culture socialist commie gay woke	gay	**communist** Bernie bro cancel culture woke SJW gay
5	doc#5452	nist leftist alphabet mafia cancel culture **communist**	gay	liberal Bernie bro commie gay leftist woke liberal Nas
6	doc#5665	are a part of radical leftist radical leftist **communist**	gay	communist cancel culture leftist commie leftist comm
7	doc#5665	u are a part of radical leftist radical leftist communist	gay	**communist** cancel culture leftist commie leftist comm
8	doc#5739	l these groups </s><s> I am the czar of **communist**	gay	socialist commie commie SJW Marxist cancel culture
9	doc#6063	ommunist radical liberal alphabet mafia **communist**	gay	liberal Bernie bro commie gay Nascar twitter </s><s>
10	doc#7461	nd analyze a movie about the mafia style muder of a	gay	**communist** film director </s><s> Thank you to the p
11	doc#9658	vative views are abhorrent Long live the **communist**	gay	mafia https://t.co/SIYQVywfwi </s><s> @republic
12	doc#10378	ping while Gorsuch sided w/ gay mafia? </s><s> So	gay	**communist** biker cowboys. </s><s> And mafia and
13	doc#12202	the socialist liberal Castro sympathizing **communist**	gay	5000-gender snowflake antifa-thug union mafia Putin
14	doc#12597	e rap industry? </s><s> @smeyia homintern means	gay	**communist** mafia international tho..i think she won h
15	doc#15031	ed by the gay mafia </s><s> the pope's **communist**	gay	mafia in Italy/America churches are die hard leftists th
16	doc#16088	going to make a docudrama in 30 years blaming the	gay	**communist** mafia run by Killary. </s><s> @xo_shela
17	doc#17277	'HO I ADORE. </s><s> I AM TALKING ABOUT THE	GAY	**COMMUNIST** MAFIA... </s><s> LOOKS LIKE A LOT
18	doc#19898	of the church are going down. including you and your	gay	, **communist** mafia. its gonna get ugly. thanks be to
19	doc#20307	@TimmyBlum Been thinking about how to weave the	gay	**communist** mafia in here somehow </s><s> @stepl
20	doc#24102	erbent humanised animatronic Nintendo **communist**	gay	mafia nazis that you can date. </s><s> And it's extre

Figure 19.2 Concordances of "gay" + "communist*" taken from Sketch Engine

(20) @run_zeke @comedndRichards @greggutfeld @kilmeade @JesseBWatters @Ingraha-mAngle @TuckerCarlson @dbongino @seanhannity @DebraMessing @LandauDave @scrowder Funny how leftist loons w/TDS (Trump Derangement Syndrome) assume anyone not willingly goose stepping to their GayStapo hate "must be a Trump supporter" Speaks volumes about their mental status/maturity. 🤪 Maybe I was a card carrying Democrat before u haters took over? 😂 But u don't even bother to think/ask.

(21) @Timcast We all get it. The MSM & the Leftist GayStapo NeoTrotskie Democrats will spin anything/everything as "White Supremacy" & all Right/Conservative /Republicans/etcetera are Nazis & Blah blah blah. Even most leftist know better. They (willfully) ignore their cognitive dissonance.

3.3   Strand 3: institutions and the media

Our third strand concerns the way in which the "LGBTIQ+ Mafia" succeeds in infiltrating all institutional and media contexts spanning fields as varied as sports, entertainment, music, and movies, and reaching as far as the hallowed sanctuary of the FBI:

(22) There is a Gay mafia that controls what people see on TV, what they wear, and what is popular music.

(23) @Brickenbrick @NBCNews The Hollywood gay mafia offers protection to any gay member who gets abused in any away! And if black!! It's a bonus!

(24) Leftist NeoTrotsky GayStapo loons think they're winning the culture war. The sports and entertainment machines don't make it easy. And the MSM lies make it seem otherwise, but they are losing.

(25) Brother, I love the raps. . . . but I could have ended life without ever seeing this, 😆 Stay strong, friend! I'm just getting by but I'm happy and encouraged to see you and others making it despite the Leftist system GayStapo and paedophiles stranglehold on "entertainment"!

(26) I'd see that movie! Hell, anything other than the propaganda and virtue signaling trash coming from HollyWeird/HollyQueer and their GayStapo. (I was banished to Twitter jail for calling @brianstelter a pansy.)

(27) Queen for a day Queer for a gay (Watch the Twitter GayStapo come after me for saying words that are LITERALLY in the special protectorates' acronym.)

(28) Fuck the FBI Why are people reporting anything to the gaystapo.

An interesting collocational pattern emerging from this strand, when it comes to mainstream institutions, is the co-occurrence of the verb "infiltrate*" with gay Mafia and lavender conspiracy theory, thus reinforcing the pastiche nature of the GMC. A closer look at the agency of the term "infiltrate*", as the KWIC view reveals, shows that "Church" is the main collocating social actor, both in active and passive structures, thus producing another improbable nexus between very distant oxymoronic institutions. The Church, indeed, works as a lynchpin bringing together such disparate categories as freemasons, mafia, socialism, and Marxism, satanism, and paedophilia, all of which are in fact mere cover-ups for the gay community and its nefarious deeds.

Pursuing this strand, we also performed a keyword analysis comparing our corpus to the en-TenTen20[8] as representative of the language of the web. Among the key multiword expressions that emerge from our analysis, we noticed the phrasal occurrence "gay priest*", which reveals an interesting discursive construction in line with what we have observed so far: the lavender mafia infiltrates the church to the extent that those who support its values become its preachers. There is

1. doc#262 with mafia informant Blutrich https://t.co/ZY0pqTesOt https://t.co/NaiqucFpss @Luke_172 the church has been **infiltrated** by the gay mafia @GeminiTayMC Yes!!! We have recruited another one into the mafia!!!! Ok so now we gotta
2. doc#768 present us Real Catholics who are anti:killing babies, gay marriage, climate hoax and the Galvan Mafia that has **infiltrated** Christ's Church . But we pray for him Are you a queer D&D streamer? Would you like to guest as an initiate
3. doc#893 t.co/68IL51axg3 @DonaldW95510616 @GalaRedpill @AdamG52676399 https://t.co/9FAZa98eY7 They clearly **infiltrate** the Catholic Church as well, even if Qanon truly is the real "gay mafia". https://t.co/pLgnTLG9tr I really
4. doc#2982 conservative and was vocally against gay marriage. @PillarCatholic Truth comes out, at the end. The Church is **infiltrated** and ruled by a Gay Mafia that do not believe the Church Teachings on morality, or maybe on anything. I supp
5. doc#9526 PhilHealth mafia but this reinforces elder gay stereotypes. @dermotfinn75 @MrCasey62 The church has been **infiltrated** by a gay mafia. It's time to weed them out. @karanjohar so Mr gay get ready for investigation.... Its not the m
6. doc#10055 I am the gay mafia seokjin is the mafia boss he just isn't aware yet @u4ikst8 @igneiudicium The gay mafia that **infiltrated** the Church . They filtered out good, masculine men - and let the homos w/ distorted minds in. https://t.co/Z7c
7. doc#10575 3, absolutely correct!!!! We definitely need a good house cleaning and scrubbing, to get out ALL those who have **infiltrated** OUR Church , who want/have been destroying the Church!!! The Gay Mafia is one of them!!! NO women De
8. doc#13111 I of leaving a horse head in your bed they leave a horse dildo from Bad Dragon. The Catholic Church has been **infiltrated** by a gay mafia, that is trying its best to change doctrine Send tweet @watchnishwin @jaavedjaaferi Forget th
9. doc#13218 Dear @JamesMartinSJ, stop bastardizing the Catholic Church. Stop with your support of the gay mafia that has **infiltrated** the church . We don't buy your propaganda campaign against the Catholic Church. @Michael_Voris
10. doc#15399 heHarlow @MsBlaireWhite @robsmithonline @JackPosobiec @CCharitiesUSA The Catholic Church has been **infiltrated** by Communists. It's run by a gay mafia. I say this as a Catholic. @awstar11 @tech_faq Gay mafia is taking c
11. doc#23398 xle will WELCOME you with ROTTEN EGGS @NewWaysMinistry He's speaking about the "Gay Mafia" that has **infiltrated** The Church and seeks to validate homosexuality through The Church. Society may bend over, but Catholics
12. doc#30800 urch have been on post pubescent males? this is not about pedophilia, this is about homo sexual predators that **infiltrated** the Church #Gaystapo @just_n0mad I'm fucking losing it at "gaystapo" lmao You have friends who are LGB
13. doc#33207 @VictoriaHagstr2 @sue_lizzy99 Baptism has nothing to do with the lavender mafia pedophiles who **infiltrated** the church and anyone who is a real Christian wants them out and tried and put in jail. unfortunately the Pop
14. doc#33345 Finally... the ROOT exposed. I sincerely mean it- thank you. When the Communists (later the Lavender Mafia) **infiltrated** the Catholic Church in the 1930's, it has caused immeasurable harm. Decades now of destruction, but that i
15. doc#33427 iadn't thought possible. https://t.co/kodgmbB6TS @NickJFuentes Many forget that the lavender mafia sought to **infiltrated** the Church , state, and academia. They succeeded and need to be rooted out. @CatholicDems You know w
16. doc#33688 ave him by the scruff of the neck. @Questio38070692 @GenFlynn @An0n661 We are the true church & were **infiltrated** . Bella Dodd, Montini, Lavender Mafia. Viganò is the ember of truth that is left because the gates of Hell shall
17. doc#33882 ntieso Better of gone from the pedo zone... there corrupt to the core. It's all window dressing. Church has been **infiltrated** and destroyed by the lavender mafia. Not hyperbole. https://t.co/km58GQGcy7 My daily prayer: Plz, deliver u
18. doc#33919 https://t.co/4venyDs21l @beflybadbelly That's wrong Gina. There's a lavender mafia (gays) who **infiltrated** the Church long ago. Some see the Church as a refuge, a safe place to practice their perverse sexual desire
19. doc#33964 iANO is a man of God & Just. He has been persecuted by the corrupt Lavender Mafia & Freemasons who have **infiltrated** the Church of Christ. VIGANO has many letters & confession of who is involved with the abuses & Cardinal
20. doc#33975 iANO is a man of God & Just. He has been persecuted by the corrupt Lavender Mafia & Freemasons who have **infiltrated** the Church of Christ. VIGANO has many letters & confession of who is involved with the abuses & Cardinal
21. doc#34002 https://t.co/4venyDs21l @DeussExxMachina @CatholicArena @CatholicBishops The entire church has been **infiltrated** by the CIA since Vatican II. That's part of what the"lavender mafia" is. @MICHAEL20450555 @ToupsFamily
22. doc#34113 Mafia you will always be one of my favorite #14 Diggs Skol Lavender I got you @RahmelWare The Church was **infiltrated** in the middle of the last century by the "Lavender Mafia". They prey on boys and young men, including semin
23. doc#34286 lavender mafia is stronger than any pope, and the pope is usually a made man. The Catholic Church has been **infiltrated** by Marxists and the Lavender Mafia. RT miamibeachPI Fast paced, great weekend reads. Detective Lavende
24. doc#34404 @gemmaod1 The cover up by the "lavender mafia" . Vatican 2 was brought in and that's when the church was **infiltrated** with the goal of destroying it especially in Ireland, they done a good job didn't they. RT miamibeachPI Fast pa
25. doc#34435 : I can answer. It's all in 2 books: "Good Bye Good Men" and "The Lavender Mafia." Basically, the Antichrist has **infiltrated** the Church and the current Pope is, and John Paul II was, at his beck & call. @GregorisFr When you are co
26. doc#34442 out? @Davidontour1 @HeathenOpinions @Jayy83x The pedophile rings are run by the "Lavender Mafia" which **infiltrated** the Church in the last century. What you're doing here is just being homophobic, tbh. RT miamibeachPI Fast
27. doc#34824 up and actually teach the Faith! #BurndowntheUSCCB Marie... it is not The Church! The true Church has been **infiltrated** by the lavender mafia & they are now in full control of Vatican + ..headed by the false pope Bergoglio who wa
28. doc#35003 xiDonaldTrump @TigerWoods Look into the conspiracy called the Lavender Mafia. For thousands of years. Men **infiltrated** the church to destroy it from the inside. https://t.co/MgXEFivPcoT RT miamibeachPI Fast paced, great weeke
29. doc#35348 @audrawilliams @MrTrickster3 50 years before that a communist activist admitted her task of helping members **infiltrate** the church to destroy the institution from the inside. Look up Bella Dodd... In America, there were Priests orc
30. doc#35481 hy. Perhaps someday Chicago will actually get a Catholic Bishop. People always talk about the Lavender Mafia **infiltrating** the Church after Vatican II, but nobody ever talks about the Freemasons infiltrating American Rad "Trads." @

Figure 19.3 Concordances of "infiltrate*" displayed by using Sketch Engine

no escaping the rainbow mafia since it is discursively construed as permeating traditional spaces which normally do not include such a minority but are linguistically empowered by associating it with institutions of dominance.

3.4 Strand 4: ideological colonisation

The fourth strand we observed in this study includes the ideological colonisation of gender in schools and universities. It comprises all the discursive strategies used to depict the manner through which the LGBTIQ+ community inculcates its gender ideology into the minds of children in educational contexts. Borba and Zottola (2022: 467) state as follows:

> Revamped images of age-old anti-LGBTIQ+ figures such as the threatened child and the endangered heterosexual family populate acrimonious campaigns against sexual education and inclusive school curricula which are viewed as proxies for the sexualization of children and threats to their supposedly natural gender identity.

Also in this case, the reversal and pastiche strategies tend to highlight the anti-gender prosumers' discursive attacks on any form of gender-oriented type of education – placed under the generic label of "gender ideology" – and subsequently vilified, distorted, and ridiculed. So-called "gender

	Details	Left context	KWIC	Right context
1	doc#32853	'en't spending so much time, money and effort on trying to cover up the depredations of its Lavender Mafia (read	gay	priests) it would be fighting for religious freedom. https://t.co/g3r7dF0tXF @Lavender_oil @KONDEiscool
2	doc#17893	Gay aztec vampires Part 3: Gay vampire but with a STAND!! Part 4: David Bowie Part 5: The literal Mafia Part 6:	Gay	priest sad about gay vampire Part 7: The President Of The United States of America Part 8: ROCK PEOPLE @f
3	doc#3626	anse everywhere. I mean have you ever met an anglo catholic? it's the best argument against the secret cabal of	gay	priests thing Gotta say this one more time stonewall wasn't raided for being a gay bar it was raided to arrest maf
4	doc#19813	to the teacihngs of the Catholic faith. This definitely includes the "gay mafia." Explosive new book lifts lid on	gay	priests in the Vatican https://t.co/movqFG30N8 @BlancoIndian Examples: "Oh you better bake the gay wedding
5	doc#34704	of rot. لم ج من @freewitches @stellaomalley3 yes the Catholic priests, the Lavender Mafia, according to Milo	gay	priests are responsible? I don't know my basic prayers by heart. I know things about my religion that do not help
6	doc#35887	ned his high school and the "insane liberalism" of Catholicism in the 1960s. He said the school was "overrun" by	gay	priests – part of the church's "lavender mafia," he later wrote in The Daily Caller – and was infused with alcohol.
7	doc#5863	alphabet mafia woke gay leftist leftist socialist liberal woke Nascar twitter the bruenigs definitely believe in the	gay	priest mafia My sister said the other day "you cant tell when someone is gay" and I thought....see that's how I kn
8	doc#27589	Not in Ukraine, but ROC has established tentacles like Mafia. Just saying it's today a full Checklist tool. Killing of	gay	priests normal. Kentucky Court Rules Christian Printer May Decline Gay Pride T-Shirt Job https://t.co/KZJyrqAMl
9	doc#8484	ating how he berated The President for going to a Saint John Paul's building. https://t.co/cUZFCAMk7O Another	gay	priest for the gay mafia @pizzashakes and netflix made this AD for pride that's narrated by spadino's actor and
10	doc#22526	.Zito never had a fight in his life https://t.co/TyhoZYGr38 https://t.co/NLIh8w9rxc Powerful words from an openly	gay	priest , writing in the Tablet, agreeing with me and @DouthatNYT that the clerical closet – pejoratively called the
11	doc#33196	anse everywhere. I mean have you ever met an anglo catholic? it's the best argument against the secret cabal of	gay	priests thing @Chris_SmithsJ uhhhh don't you know about the LAVENDER MAFIA that secretly runs the Catholi
12	doc#13260	@tfrsegt112 Jesuit pontiff can not be, but they have poisoned the Vatican so much, with pedophilia,	gay	priests , orgies plus cocaine, linked to the mafia, laundering blood money through the Vatican bank,pedophilia th
13	doc#26505	afia Lord Jamar on Tyler, The Creator Kissing White Boys and the Gay Mafia https://t.co/HR765vLNnU @LifeSite	Gay	priests , gay Bishops, gay Popes. I wonder why the church has been overtaken by the lavender Mafia?
14	doc#142	'en't spending so much time, money and effort on trying to cover up the depredations of its Lavender Mafia (read	gay	priests) it would be fighting for religious freedom. https://t.co/g3r7dF0tXF @dnfbreasts Like a fucking mafia
15	doc#20055	Vorsham @POTUS They'll use the current sex scandal against her - ignoring the Lavendar Mafia as a network of	gay	priests .And there will be plenty of "Catholics" against her. too. The idea with the OC group sounds hella you Ga
16	doc#18019	Japanese speaking vampire, bare naked Aztec Gods, a hand fetishist serial killer, a cross-dressing mafia boss, a	gay	priest and the president of the United States... https://t.co/NUBvhSSg1b Suddenly popped in my mind, what if m
17	doc#18469	)Church_Militant Very disappointed in Dolan. At one time, I thought very highly of him. Now, it appears the liberal	gay	priest mafia got a hold of him. More attempts by the Dark Left and Gay Mafia to twist the minds of young childre
18	doc#5888	are sexy mafia vampires, denim, and gay https://t.co/lNqKn8lygM @MoreMore92 Yasssss, I wanna be the official	Gay	priest of the alphabet mafia 🔥🔥🔥 Fellas is it gay to be in the mafia I swear to god I'm gonna start a mafia and
19	doc#36788	aolicthing It takes real arrogance to admit, as Mr. Carlin does, that he has been oblivious to the existence of the "	gay	priest problem" for decades, despite Rose, lavender mafia, et al, finally open his eyes & then immediately recom
20	doc#33383	guilt, and what we used to be ashamed of. https://t.co/E43MFtcbIG @eltonofficial @VaticanNews @Pontifex The	gay	priests in the Lavender Mafia need to be removed, because they are trying to pervert the Church! Just like the D
21	doc#35998	beral Chicago priest and popular movelist Fr. Andrew Greeley. He described the Lavender Mafia as a network of	gay	priests & bishops who promoted & supported one anohter & covered up one another's crimes. Problem is, most
22	doc#21593	ned his high school and the "insane liberalism" of Catholicism in the 1960s. He said the school was "overrun" by	gay	priests – part of the church's "lavender mafia," he later wrote in The Daily Caller – and was infused with alcohol.
23	doc#18215	se of the children in the Polish chuch for about 2 decades. He has also written about the "Lavender Mafia" that is	gay	priests who molest and then cover for each other. PI write him :) EXCLUSIVE: Lord Jamar & Vlad on Mafia Exto
24	doc#35282	is plotting to rot the Church @panhandleheart @CathoConser True. With recent revelations about the number of	gay	priests , this isn't surprising. Its not that homosexual priests can't be morally virtuous, but apparently it's a lot
25	doc#4988	ry and aven lmao but like i get why people like it ig @verlainestan Well you know "some" people think he's in the	gay	priest mafia or something like that...soooo this should really confirm all of their conspiracy theories. 😂
26	doc#36522	a gay community I've come to observe gays are good recruiters whether to a sexual act or political involvement.	Gay	priests are now bishops and cardinals . I also blame Vat 2. I'm going FSSP now We shouldn't be entirely surprise
27	doc#6910	in the priesthood are a problem. There has been a long internal battle in the Church against the "velvet mafia" of	gay	priests colluding. The Stonewall Inn, the gay bar that was raided and birthed the Stonewall riots, was actually ow
28	doc#35430	aryone must follow the teachings of the Church. @USCatholic Someone who hits the mark! Stop speaking about	gay	priests and lavender mafia! This is the problem in the church: too much toxic masculinity as you can see by look
29	doc#24496	4e: "sends a kiss" @Itanimerl Part 5: Gay dude's son becomes leader of the mafia after mafioso like him. Part 6:	Gay	priest who worships gay dude resets the universe. Part 7: Cripple kills the president because Jesus told him to. I
30	doc#18239	@corbydavidson The Roman Catholic Church has the Lavender Mafia which provides cover to the large # of	gay	priests . Pedo priests exploit this haze of secrecy to practice their evil predation. Mostly parallel but some Venn

Figure 19.4 Concordances of "gay priest*" from Sketch Engine

ideology" serves as a contextualisation cue that inevitably triggers interactional stances. In Gal's words (2021: 99) the phrase "gender ideology" was adopted by

> many far right, faith-based groups (Christian and other), by NGOs, journalists and writers in Europe, as well as the World Congress of Families – a US based transnational group – and most recently by nationalist, authoritarian parties and leaders such as the prime minister of Hungary, along with organisations in the US and Latin America.

The public endorsement by so many mainstream institutional and authoritative representatives necessarily attributes truth-value to the phrase "gender ideology" as can easily be inferred from the following tweets:

(29) i cannot believe the Gaystapo is recruiting children into their ranks, literally 1984.

(30) This is why getting your kids for grooming purposes is so important to the Gaystapo.

(31) A 2nd grader at a Christian school was expelled for telling another girl she had a crush on her, mother says [Gaystapo descends].

(32) Gaystapo pushing their lifestyles to people who should be learning math, reading and science. Same thing goes for CRT. Democrat/Marxists pit people against one another.

(33) everyone who thinks it's gay for little boys to play with kitchen sets, I hope all your kids join the #alphabetmafia.

(34) San Francisco Senator, a homosexual, is trying to legalize sodomy between minor children . . . Wiener legislation seeks to end "blatant discrimination" in sex offender registry
laws https://t.co/L2cJf7I6uF #tcot #Parler #gaystapo #ProtectTheChildren #WakeUpPeople
#wakeupAmerica.

(35) The queers and trannies have already infiltrated schools and social media.

As can be deduced from the ideological colonisation strand, gay mafia is portrayed as progressively penetrating traditional family values with a view to polluting the entire human race through
ad hoc gender recruitment, which inevitably begins at school. These boldfaced portrayals across
the Twitter platform should hardly surprise us when such respectable, historical institutions as the
Heritage Foundation, the American conservative think tank, currently host events titled "Protecting
Our Children: How Radical Gender Ideology is Taking Over Public Schools & Harming Kids".[9]

In much the same manner as in the previous discursive strategy, the "gay mafia" therefore
becomes a dominant group in a society that otherwise marginalises it. Through clever reversal
tactics, the gaystapo becomes a hegemonic entity by means of the same linguistic resources used
to challenge traditional institutions.

4 Concluding remarks

In this study, we have focussed on those ideological processes that underlie, pervade, and inform
social action across digital landscapes. Our aim has been not merely to contemplate the sites of
fallacious rainbow conspiracy ideology but also to analyse the discursive strategies employed online to ensnare new adepts and to spread fake news about the LGBTIQ+ community. We therefore
posit that, as previously mentioned, and in line with the affordances granted by SNSs to prosuming
opinion-makers, the LGBTIQ+ community is currently enjoying new-found visibility, for better or
for worse. Being in the limelight transforms the formerly invisible community into a target which
inevitably catalyses the hate, discrimination, and envy usually addressed to powerful institutions
and bodies to the point of creating a present-day Frankenstein's monster, indeed an alphabet soup
to which you can add or detract various bits and pieces.

One fundamental point that has emerged from this study is the fact that in the crafting and grafting of fake news revolving around the gay community, the discursive construction of the rainbow
conspiracy grows and evolves around real news feeds, which validate the truth-value of the information given. This is surprising because if one thinks back to the many conspiracy theories, we are
familiar with (the Illuminati, Jews, anti-vax, climate, COVID, etc.) there are rarely any such triggers. We therefore believe that when the medium is social media (and in our case specifically Twitter), it is precisely the discursive strategies of the medium itself that need to be investigated further.

Our study demonstrates that fake news originating from manipulated news feeds and subsequently woven together by means of the affordances provided by SNSs may progressively lead to
the construction of a conspiracy theory which in the case of the "gay mafia" appears to be gaining
ground rapidly and wreaking further damage upon a sorely tried minority.

Notes

1 The authors have jointly discussed and conceived this chapter. Nevertheless, individual contributions in
writing this research article are identified as follows: Giuseppe Balirano is responsible for Section 2, Sec-
tion 3, Section 3.1, Section 3.2, and Section 3.3; Bronwen Hughes is responsible for the introductory Sec-
tion, Section 3.4, and Section 4.

2 The article is available online at https://nymag.com/intelligencer/2022/05/the-long-sordid-history-of-the-gay-conspiracy-theory.html (retrieved 21 February 2023).

3 Ibid.

4 The definition is available online at www.merriam-webster.com/dictionary/truthiness (retrieved 6 December 2022).

5 The definition can be found online at www.collinsdictionary.com/dictionary/english/fake-news (retrieved 21 February 2023).

6 Sketch Engine (Kilgarriff *et al.* 2004, 2014) is an online corpus analysis software that can be accessed at the following address: www.sketchengine.eu/ (retrieved 7 December 2022).

7 The choice of the statistical measures involved was based on the observations provided by Gablasova *et al.* (2017) and Brezina (2018).

8 The English Web 2020 (enTenTen20) corpus is an English corpus made up of texts collected from the Internet with a genre annotation and topic classification available on Sketch Engine. More information about the TenTen corpus family can be found online at www.sketchengine.eu/ententen-english-corpus/ (last accessed 20 July 2022).

9 7 March 2022 – www.heritage.org/gender/event/protecting-our-children-how-radical-gender-ideology-taking-over-public-schools-harming.

References

Althusser, Louis. 1970. Idéologie et appareils idéologiques d'État, notes pour une recherche, *La pensée. Revue du rationalisme moderne* 151(juin), 3–38.

Apuke, Oberiri Destiny, and Omar, Bahiyah. 2021. Social Media Affordances and Information Abundance: Enabling Fake News Sharing During the COVID-19 Health Crisis. *Health Informatics Journal* 27(3).

Baker, Paul. 2006. *Using Corpora in Discourse Analysis*. London: Continuum.

Balirano, Giuseppe. 2020. Of Rainbow Unicorns: The Role of Bonding Queer Icons in Contemporary LGBTIQ+ Re-Positionings. *Ocula* 21(22), 46–60.

Balirano, Giuseppe, and Borba, Rodrigo (eds). 2021. Re-Defining Gender, Sexuality, and Discourse in the Global Rise of Right-Wing Extremism. *Anglistica AION: An Interdisciplinary Journal* [Special Issue]. Available online at www.serena.unina.it/index.php/anglistica-aion/issue/view/642 (retrieved February 21, 2023).

Balirano, Giuseppe, and Bronwen, Hughes. 2020. Fat Chance! Digital Critical Discourse Studies on Discrimination Against Fat People. In *Homing in on Hate: Critical Discourse Studies of Hate Speech, Discrimination and Inequality in the Digital Age*, ed. by Giuseppe Balirano and Hughes Bronwen. Naples: Paolo Loffredo Editore, 3–50.

Barbaresi, Adrien. 2016. Collection and Indexing of Tweets with a Geographical Focus. In *Tenth International Conference on Language Resources and Evaluation* (LREC 2016), May 2016, Portorož, Slovenia, 24–27.

Benton, Bond, Luo, Yi, Choi, Jin-A, Strudler, Keith, and Green, Keith. 2022. A Preview of Post Amnesty Twitter: Analysis of "Groomer" on Twitter After the Colorado Springs Shooting. *School of Communication and Media Scholarship and Creative Works*, 1–26.

Borba, Rodrigo. 2022. Enregistering "Gender Ideology" the Emergence and Circulation of a Transnational Anti-Gender Language. *Journal of Language and Sexuality* 11(1), 57–79.

Borba, Rodrigo, and Zottola, Angela. 2022. 'Gender Ideology' and the Discursive Infrastructure of a Transnational Conspiracy Theory. In *Conspiracy Theory Discourses*, ed. by Massimiliano Demata, Virginia Zorzi, and Angela Zottola, 465–488. Amsterdam and Philadelphia: John Benjamins Publishing Company.

Brezina, Vaclav. 2018. *Statistics in Corpus Linguistics: A Practical Guide*. Cambridge: Cambridge University Press.

Brotherton, Roy. 2020. *Why We Fall for Fake News*. London, Oxford, and New York: Bloomsbury.

Byford, Jovan. 2011. *Conspiracy Theories. A Critical Introduction*. New York: Palgrave Macmillan. https://doi.org/10.1057/9780230349216

Cinelli, Matteo, Etta, Gabriele, Avalle, Michele, Quattrociocchi, Alessandro, Di Marco, Niccolò, Valensise, Carlo, Galeazzi, Alessandro, and Quattrociocchi, Walter. 2022. Conspiracy Theories and Social Media Platforms. *Current Opinion in Psychology* 47, 394–407.

Dallacqua, Ashley K., and Low, David E. 2021. Cupcakes and Beefcakes: Students' Readings of Gender in Superhero Text. *Gender and Education* 33(1), 68–85.

Douglas, Karen, Uscinski, Joseph, Sutton, Robbie, Cichocka, Aleksandra, Nefes, Turkay, Ang, Chee Siang, and Deravi, Farzin. 2019. Understanding Conspiracy Theories. *Advances in Political Psychology* 40(1), 3–35. https://doi.org/10.1111/pops.12568

Egbert, Jesse, and Baker, Paul (eds). 2020. *Using Corpus Methods to Triangulate Linguistic Analysis*. London and New York: Routledge.

Elliott, Ira. 1995. Performance Art; Jake Barnes and "Masculine" Signification in the Sun Also Rises. *American Literature* 67(1), 77–94.

Fisher, Alice. 2017. Why the Unicorn Has Become the Emblem for Our Times. *The Guardian*, October 15. Available online at www.theguardian.com/society/2017/oct/15/return-of-the-unicorn-the-magical-beast-of-our-times (retrieved December 12, 2022).

Franks, Bradley, Bangerter, Adrian, and Bauer, Martin. 2013. Conspiracy Theories as Quasi-Religious Mentality: An Integrated Account from Cognitive Science, Social Representation Theory, and Frame Theory. *Frontiers in Psychology* 4(424), 1–12.

Gablasova, Dana, Brezina, Vaclav, and McEnery, Tony. 2017. Collocations in Corpus-Based Language Learning Research: Identifying, Comparing, and Interpreting the Evidence. *Language Learning* 67(S1), 155–179.

Gal, Susan. 2018. Registers in Circulation: The Social Organization of Interdiscursivity. *Signs and Society* 6(1), 1–24.

Gal, Susan. 2021. Gender and the Discursive Authority of Far Right Politics. *Gender and Language* 15(1), 96–103.

Goldsmith, Olivia. 1994. *Fashionably Late*. New York: HarperCollins Publishers.

Harambam, Jaron, and Aupers, Stef. 2021. From the Unbelievable to the Undeniable: Epistemological Pluralism, or How Conspiracy Theorists Legitimate Their Extraordinary Truth Claims. *European Journal of Cultural Studies* 24(4), 990–1008.

Hart, Kvlo-Patrick R. 2000. Representing Gay Men on American Television. *Journal of Men's Studies*, 9, 59–79.

Herman, Didi. 1996. (Il)legitimate Minorities: The American Christian Right's Anti-Gay-Rights Discourse. *Journal of Law and Society* 23(3), 346–363.

Holleran, Andrew. 2019. Glitter and Be Gay. *The Gay & Lesbian Review Worldwide* 26(3), 1–12.

Huneman, Philippe, and Vorms, Marion. 2018. Is a Unified Account of Conspiracy Theories Possible? *Argumenta* 3(2), 247–270.

Icke, David. 2007. *The David Icke Guide to the Global Conspiracy (and How to End It)*. Faridabad, India: Thompson Press.

Introne, Joshua, Yildirim, Irem Gokce, Iandoli, Luca, DeCook, Julia R., and Elzeini, Shaima. 2018. How People Weave Online Information into Pseudoknowledge. *Social Media and Society* 4, 1–15.

Karlova, Natascha, and Lee, Jin Ha. 2011. Notes from the Underground City of Disinformation: A Conceptual Investigation. *Asis&t* 48(1), 1–9.

KhosraviNik, Majid. 2017. Social Media Critical Discourse Studies (SM-CDS). In *The Routledge Handbook of Critical Discourse Studies*, ed. by John Flowerdew and John E. Richardson. London and New York: Routledge, 582–596.

KhosraviNik, Majid, and Esposito, Eleonora. 2018. Online Hate, Digital Discourse and Critique: Exploring Digitally-Mediated Discursive Practices of Gender-Based Hostility. *Lodz Papers in Pragmatics* 14(1), 45–68.

KhosraviNik, Majid, and Sarkhoh, Nadia. 2017. Arabism and Anti-Persian Sentiments on Participatory Web Platforms: A Social Media Critical Discourse Study. *International Journal of Communication* 11, 3614–3633. Available online at https://ijoc.org/index.php/ijoc/article/view/6062 (retrieved April 23, 2019).

KhosraviNik, Majid, and Unger, Johann W. 2016. Critical Discourse Studies and Social Media: Power, Resistance and Critique in Changing Media Ecologies. In *Methods of Critical Discourse Studies*, ed. by Ruth Wodak and Michael Meyer, 3rd edn. London: SAGE, 206–233.

Kilgarriff, Adam, Baisa, Vit, Bušta, Jan, Jakubícek, Milos, Kovár, Vojtech, Michelfeit, Jan, Rychlý, Pavel, and Suchomel, Vit. 2014. The Sketch Engine: Ten Years on. *Lexicography* 1(1), 7–36.

Kilgarriff, Adam, Rychlý, Pavel, Smrz, Pavel, and Tugwell, David. 2004. The Sketch Engine. In *Proceedings of the Eleventh EURALEX International Congress: EURALEX 2004*, ed. by Geoffrey Williams and Sandra Vessier. Lorient: Université de Bretagne-Sud, 105–116.

Leetaru, Kalev, Wang, Shaowen, Cao, Guofeng, Padmanabhan, Anand, and Shook, Eric. 2013. Mapping the Global Twitter Heartbeat: The Geography of Twitter. *First Monday* 18(5).

Mallinson, Christine. 2018. Ethics in Linguistic Research. In *Research Methods in Linguistics*, ed. by Lia Litosseliti, 2nd ed. London and New York: Bloomsbury, 57–84.

Marchlewska, Marta, Cichoka, Aleksandra, Lozowski, Filip, Górska, Paulina, and Winiewski, Mikolaj. 2019. In Search of an Imaginary Enemy: Catholic Collective Narcissism and the Endorsement of Gender Conspiracy Beliefs. *Journal of Social Psychology* 156(6), 766–779.

McGovern, Timothy. 2006. Expressing Desire, Expressing Death: Antòn Lopo's Pronomes and Queer Galician Poetry. *The Journal of Spanish Cultural Studies* 7(2), 135–153.

McIntyre, Lee. 2018. *Post-Truth*. Cambridge, MA: The MIT Press Essential Knowledge Series. https://doi.org/10.7551/mitpress/11483.001.0001

Osterbur, Megan, and Kiel, Christina. 2021. Tweeting in Echo Chambers? Analyzing Twitter Discourse between American Jewish Interest Groups. *Journal of Information Technology & Politics* 18(2), 194–213.

Rasulo, Margaret. 2023. *Master Narratives of Hate Speech. A Multimodal Analysis*. Naples: Loffredo Editore.

Sontag, Susan. 2003. *Regarding the Pain of Others*. New York: Picador.

Sternisko, Anni, Cichocka, Aleksandra, and Van Bavel, Jay J. 2020. The Dark Side of Social Movements: Social Identity, Non-Conformity, and the Lure of Conspiracy Theories. *Current Opinion in Psychology* 35, 1–6. https://doi.org/10.1016/j.copsyc.2020.02.007

Tandoc, Edson C., Lim, Darren, and Ling, Rich. 2019. Diffusion of Disinformation: How Social Media Users Respond to Fake News and Why. *Journalism* 21, 381–398.

van Prooijen, Jan-Willem, Krouwel, André P.M., and Pollet Thomas V. 2015. Political Extremism Predicts Belief in Conspiracy Theories. *Social Psychological and Personality Science* 6(5), 570–578.

van Prooijen, Jan-Willem, and Douglas, Karen M. 2018. Belief in Conspiracy Theories: Basic Principles of an Emerging Research Domain. *European Journal of Social Psychology* 48(7), 897–908.

Vosoughi, Soroush, Roy, Deb, and Aral, Sinan. 2018. The Spread of True and False News Online. *Science* 359(6380), 1146–1151.

Wilkinson, Sue, and Kitzinger, Celia. 1996. *Representing the Other: A Feminism & Psychology Reader*. London, Thousand Oaks, CA, and New Delhi: Sage Publications.

Woods, Gregory. 2003. The 'Conspiracy' of the 'Homintern'. *The Gay & Lesbian Review Worldwide* 10(3), 11–14.

Zappavigna, Michele. 2012. *Discourse of Twitter and Social Media*. London: Continuum.

Zappavigna, Michele. 2015. Searchable Talk: The Linguistic Functions of Hashtags. *Social Semiotics* 25(3), 274–291.

Zappavigna, Michele. 2018. *Searchable Talk: Hashtags and Social Media Metadiscourse*. London: Bloomsbury Academic Publishing.

20

THE DISCOURSES OF CLIMATE CHANGE DENIALISM ACROSS CONSPIRACY AND PSEUDOSCIENCE WEBSITES

Isobelle Clarke

Introduction

Despite the growing body of scientific evidence supporting the notion of anthropogenic global warming (AGW) and climate change, there remains a persistent sceptic and denialist movement – comprised of and influenced by the fossil fuel industry, conservative think-tanks, politicians, contrarian scientists, some news media, and self-interested corporations and individuals, among others. The movement's endurance is largely a consequence of their employment of discourses (McCright and Dunlap, 2010). Some of the discourses that have been consistently reported on across studies (e.g. Dunlap and Mc-Cright, 2010, 2015; Washington and Cook, 2011) investigating the denialist movement include (1) stating that climate scientists are in a global conspiracy that they profit from, (2) referring to fake experts that deny AGW, (3) stating calls for action on climate change are unsubstantiated because of uncertainties in climate models and disagreements between climate scientists, and (4) outright denial.

Much attention has been paid to the roots of climate change denial, which has demonstrated the role of the fossil fuel industry (e.g. Lahsen, 2005), conservative think-tanks (e.g. Lahsen, 2005), politicians (e.g. McCright and Dunlap, 2003), contrarian scientists (e.g. McCright and Dunlap, 2003), and the press (e.g. Boykoff and Boykoff, 2004). More recently, research has focused on the role of climate denier blogs, which are blogs by self-described climate sceptics and contrarian scientists dedicated to disputing climate science and questioning the reality and significance of climate change (Dunlap and McCright, 2010, 2015). Denier blogs have passionate audiences with new posts often inciting hundreds of comments expressing contempt for climate scientists, activists, and policy proponents (Dunlap and McCright, 2015). Whilst the community of deniers is smaller than that of science-based bloggers, denier-based bloggers and their community are more closely linked and supportive of one another (Bloomfield and Tillery, 2018). For example, Dunlap and McCright note that

> virtually any claim uttered by a contrarian scientist – whether it be a "finding" that challenges anthropogenic climate change or the discovery of a weakness in a mainstream scientist's work or an allegation of suppression – immediately zooms around the internet via the climate change blogosphere.

> (2010: 253)

DOI: 10.4324/9781003224495-24

In addition to the mechanisms behind the circulation of denial content, research has investigated the content of denier blogs. Harvey *et al.* (2018), for example, compared the representation of polar bears and Arctic Sea ice by science-based and denier-based bloggers. They found that the two groups represent the facts differently. Science-based blogs were found to use the frame of established scientific certainties, drawing on published literature concerning the reduction of Arctic Sea ice extent, which is threatening polar bears, whereas denier blogs were found to emphasise the uncertainties around AGW to cast doubt on the population trends of polar bears.

In another study, Brüggemann et al. (2020) analysed science-based and denier-based blog posts for evidence of the hoax discourse, which they define as calling into question the truthfulness of someone else. In a sample of the posts referring to hoax-related terms, they found science-based posts refer to "denial" and "denier", whilst sceptic blog posts referred to "alarmist" and "fraud". Both groups use "fake", "hoax", "propaganda", and "conspiracy" to refer to the other. Overall, they found that the hoax discourse impeded deliberation and open exchange of arguments. Instead, they argue that it served identity purposes as one was able to situate themselves as supporting a particular group.

The Internet has changed the ways in which science is communicated, enabling "voices to appear equally credible" and "reach many people" (Tillery and Bloomfield, 2022: 1). Climate change denial views are both visible and proliferate on the Internet, meaning that they can have considerable influence. Because the Internet is a hub for science and environmental communication, Dunlap (2013) called for more research into sceptic and denier blogs. While previous research has explored the communication strategies of blogs, existing research is limited to either (1) providing a detailed account of the strategies employed by a single or small number of sites (e.g. Bloomfield and Tillery, 2018; Tillery and Bloomfield, 2022), (2) providing an account of how a larger number of denier blogs frame a small number of entities (e.g. polar bears and sea ice in Harvey *et al.*, 2018), or (3) exploring the use of a single strategy across the denier blogs (e.g. Brüggemann *et al.*, 2020). As a result, there lacks a large-scale exploratory linguistic analysis of the common discourses used across many climate denier websites and blogs. This chapter seeks to fill that gap by analysing the major representations of climate change and global warming across 186 websites and blogs known to promote pseudoscience and conspiracy.

Methodology

Data: the pseudoscience and conspiracy sources (PaCS) corpus

This research reported on in this chapter forms part of a larger project investigating numerous branches of antiscience, including climate change denialism. In this project, a corpus has been built comprising texts (all content on a single webpage – i.e. article and comments) from 235 websites labelled as "conspiracy-pseudoscience" by mediabiasfactcheck.com, which is a comprehensive and continuously updated resource of online media sites which have been rated for various levels of bias. The corpus was then filtered by retaining texts according to "seed" words and phrases associated with the branches of antiscience relevant to the larger project. The present chapter drew on the climate change sub-corpus of the pseudoscience and conspiracy sources (PaCS) corpus, which was filtered according to the seed phrases "climate change" and/or "global warming".

Duplicated texts were removed from the corpus using a Python script to avoid skewing the data. Table 20.1 presents the composition of the climate change sub-corpus before and after the removal of duplicates. This table shows that nearly 27% of texts were reproduced from other sites. Table 20.1 shows that the climate change sub-corpus analysed comprises 19,961 texts, totalling over 38-million-word tokens. These texts come from 186 different sites.

Table 20.1 The climate change denial sub-corpus

	Number of Texts	*Number of Word Tokens*
Before removal of duplicates	27,302	46,739,379
After removal of duplicates	19,961	38,510,518

It should be noted that not all the sites included in this analysis are denying climate change. Some websites are dedicated to antiscience strands, which mention the impact of climate change (e.g. anti-genetically modified organisms). Unfortunately, no further filtering of the data was completed to ensure that the texts analysed are only those which deny climate change. This was in part due to (1) the large number of texts in the corpus and the lengths of some of these, which would take a considerable amount of time to read to assess the presence of denial; (2) the complexity, sophistication, and persuasiveness of denial, which, for a general novice in climatology (such as myself), can make it hard to assess if denial is present in the texts, and; (3) for reasons of replicability. Because of this, it is important to note that while I label the discourses identified as climate change denial (for matters of convenience), they are more specifically characterised as the representations of climate change on pseudoscience and conspiracy websites.

Keyword co-occurrence analysis

To identify the discourses of climate change denialism, this corpus is analysed using keyword co-occurrence analysis (KCA; Clarke, McEnery and Brookes, 2021). KCA is an approach aimed at identifying patterns of co-occurring keywords across a corpus of texts. In corpus linguistic research, keywords are words which occur with a statistically marked frequency in one corpus (focus corpus) when compared with another (reference corpus). Keywords can allow access to discourses associated with some object of study (Baker, Gabrielatos and McEnery, 2013). KCA draws on the notion that keywords point to discourses (Baker, Gabrielatos and McEnery, 2013), as well as the notion of linguistic co-occurrence (Biber, 1988) – that is, that frequent patterns of co-occurring linguistic features tend to reveal an underlying communicative function – to hypothesise that patterns of co-occurring keywords may point to discourses (Clarke, McEnery and Brookes, 2021).

The keyword analysis was completed in Sketch Engine, which uses the simple maths method for the computation of keywords (see Kilgariff, 2009). Specifically, the climate change sub-corpus was uploaded to Sketch Engine and defined as the focus corpus. This focus corpus was then compared to the English Web 2020 corpus (enTenTen2020), which served as the reference corpus. The enTenTen20 corpus is a 38-billion-word corpus comprising online texts collected between 2019 and 2021. This reference corpus was selected as it represents a general sample of web content throughout these years and because the bulk of the focus corpus' texts are from this period (nearly 30% spread across these 3 years, with the remaining 70% spread across 20 years; see Figure 20.1). However, this reference corpus is limited in that the climate change sub-corpus spans a wider timeframe (from 1999 to 2021) and comparisons against it may thus lead to some time-sensitive words being defined as key.

The keyword analysis produced a list of 1,000 keywords. KCA uses multiple correspondence analysis (MCA) to group keywords based on how they co-occur in the texts of the corpus. Very infrequent features are given unfair weight in MCA, and so Le Roux and Rouanet (2010) advise that features occurring in less than 5% of the data are removed. Consequently, the list of 1,000

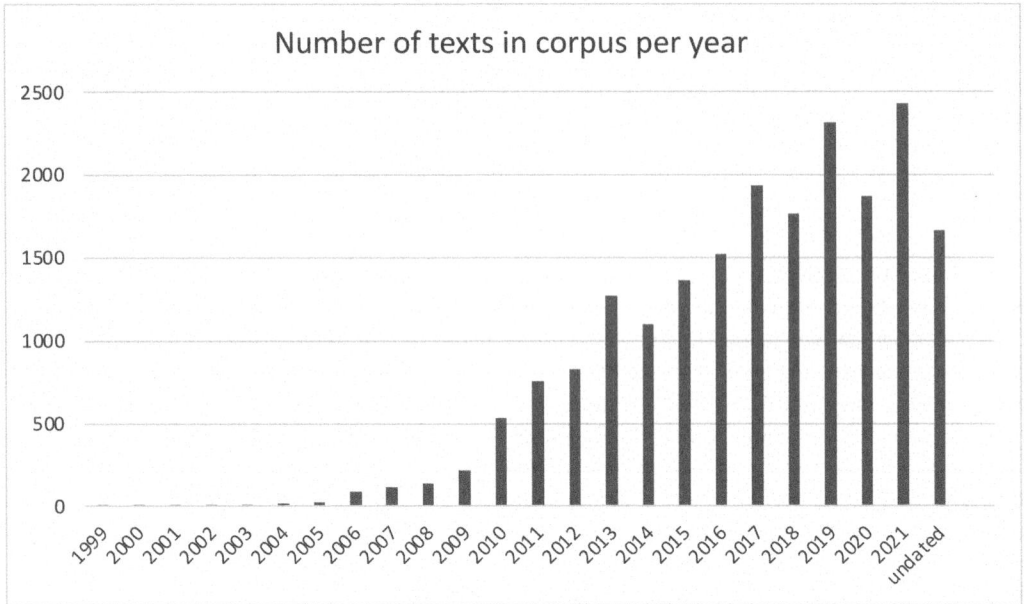

Figure 20.1   The number of texts in the climate change sub-corpus per year

keywords was reduced, retaining only those that occurred in more than 5% of the texts (135 keywords). These keywords can be found in Appendix 1.

To complete KCA, each text in the corpus was analysed for the presence/absence of each of the 135 keywords using a script, written in R, which records this information in a data matrix. This matrix was then subjected to MCA.

MCA is a geometric data analytic method which identifies relationships between three or more categorical variables. In KCA, MCA is used to identify keywords that co-occur often in the texts of the corpus. It also reveals which texts exhibit these patterns of co-occurring keywords. Specifically, MCA produces a series of dimensions where each category of a keyword (e.g. presence of *climate*, absence of *climate*), and each text in the corpus is assigned a coordinate and a contribution for each dimension. Coordinates reflect the nature of the association between the categories of the keywords in terms of proximity, where keywords distributed in similar ways in the texts have coordinates closer to each other on the same side of the origin, and keywords not distributed in similar ways are positioned on opposite sides of the origin (i.e. one will have a positive coordinate and the other a negative one). Hence, coordinates signal co-occurrence patterns. Contributions show which categories of keywords are the most important contributors to the dimensions. Contributions do not have polarity, and so the coordinates of the keywords need to be interpreted in conjunction with their contributions. Specifically, keywords with strong contributions and positive coordinates need to be interpreted in opposition to keywords with strong contributions and negative coordinates. In line with Le Roux and Rouanet (2010), only the categories of keywords whose contribution exceeds the average were analysed, as these represent the most distinguishing patterns of variation. Each dimension represents a distinct pattern of co-variation. Dimension 1 represents the best fit of the data with each subsequent dimension representing the next most common pattern of variation (i.e. set co-occurring keywords).

Each dimension was interpreted until the dimensions were no longer readily interpretable (i.e. it was not possible to make sense of the patterns of co-occurring keywords), beginning with the first dimension. Overall, eight dimensions were interpreted. Like other studies employing KCA (e.g. Clarke, McEnery and Brookes, 2021), the first dimension opposed the *presence* of keywords with the *absence* of keywords and had a strong correlation to the length of the text ($r = .70$). This is a result of investigating the presence/absence of keywords, as opposed to the texts' relative frequency, as text length is not controlled for. The relative frequencies of features are often analysed so that texts of different lengths can be compared reliably. The relative frequencies of keywords in each text are not analysed in this study because most texts (63%) analysed contain under 1,000 words. The relative frequencies of features in texts with less than 1,000 words tend to be unreliable estimates. Moreover, the relative frequencies of keywords are also not analysed in KCA because keywords are typically infrequent in comparison to high-frequency grammatical features, meaning there will be lots of zeros. When datasets comprised of many zeros are analysed by multivariate statistical techniques for continuous data (i.e. not MCA, but techniques such as factor analysis or principal component analysis), then the correlation coefficients can be misleading. As a result, the presence/absence of keywords are analysed using MCA (a multivariate statistical technique for categorical data). However, because text length is not controlled for, and because the length of the text in words is the greatest influence on the presence of keywords (i.e. the more words a text has, the more likely the keywords will be present), the first dimension reflects text length. No other dimensions are associated with text length. For this reason, Dimension 1 is not interpreted further. In the next section, I present the patterns of co-occurring keywords and sample texts that are most associated with Dimensions 2 to 8 and provide my interpretations of the discourses to which the patterns point.

Results

Dimension 2: political versus science discourses

The keywords associated with positive Dimension 2 point to political discourses. Politicians (*clinton, obama, trump*), political ideologies (*socialist, capitalism, activist*), and organisations (*UN, EPA*) are referenced to discuss policies (calls for), political action, and programmes related to AGW, such as calls to control energy production, storage and consumption (*energy, grid, electricity, fuel, nuclear, gas*), limiting the burning of fossil fuels (*fossil, coal, fuel*) due to their effects (*pollution, emission, carbon, dioxide*), and switching to renewable energy sources (*wind, renewable*). These keywords co-occur with keywords signalling hoax discourses (*scam, corrupt, agenda, propaganda, fraud, fake*), ignorance (*ignorant, stupid, ignorance, nonsense*), and cost (*trillion*), frequently to evaluate such political calls for action against the threat of AGW as a scam and stupid, as the actions (e.g. renewable energy) cost a huge amount, profit particular individuals, especially those calling for climate action, and are unreliable. There are also arguments suggesting that limiting the burning of fossil fuels impacts economic growth and is pointless as other countries do not make reductions. For example, Text 1, taken from the corpus, is strongly associated with positive Dimension 2. This text covers various American presidents' actions and policies on AGW. The text describes Clinton's climate change policies as a "weapon" for scaremongering. Additionally, it presents the view that other countries are producing more CO_2, rendering any reductions by America pointless.

Text 1: Green New Deal – Boldest Tactic Yet to Advance U.N. Agenda 21 (https://wattsupwiththat. com/2019/03/29/green-new-deal-boldest-tactic-yet-to-advance-u-n-agenda-21/, 29 March 2019)

> [...]
>
> The main weapon used by *Clinton* for his call for action was the threat of Environmental Armageddon, particularly manifested through the charge of manmade global warming, later to becoming "climate change". It didn't matter if true science refused to cooperate in the scheme, as actual global temperatures are not rising and there continues to be no evidence of any appreciable manmade effects on the climate.
>
> [...]
>
> And even if Americans did stop producing CO_2, Earth's CO_2 levels would continue to rise because China, India, and other countries are building *coal*-fired plants by the dozen, which will like more than offset any reductions Americans make.
>
> [...]

Alternatively, the keywords associated with negative Dimension 2 draw on scientific discourses. There are keywords associated with places and areas (*antarctica, antarctic, greenland, hemisphere, arctic, atlantic, polar, sea, ocean, surface*), changes in state (*warm, warmer, melt, melting, cooling, freezing, snow, ice, temperature*), natural processes (*variability, volcanic, el* (Niño), *winter, weather, tropical, precipitation*), and scientific data analysis (*forecast, trend, graph, satellite, NOAA*). These keywords co-occur in articles to discuss the poor predictions of scientific models on the impact of future climate change, to suggest that they should not be trusted, especially the model's conclusions that man-made CO_2 levels are to blame. These keywords also co-occur in articles suggesting that any changes in temperature, weather, sea level, and ice thickness are not due to man-made carbon emissions, but rather due to natural processes, such as volcanic eruptions, el niño, and natural variability, which occur in periodic cycles. Records of growing ice in Antarctica and Greenland are also referred to as a form of "whataboutery" to disprove global warming, as in Text 2. This text draws on evidence showing ice gain in Greenland to suggest that climatologists are lying about ice loss and fabricating data to align with their theory of climate change.

> Text 2: If The Data Doesn't Match Theory, Change The Data (https://realclimatescience.com/2017/04/if-the-data-doesnt-match-theory-change-the-data/, 25 April 2017)
>
> Professional climate fraudsters claim that *Greenland* is losing *ice* 600% faster than predicted.
>
> As of yesterday, the Danish Meteorological Institute (DMI) showed *Greenland surface* mass gain for the *winter* at a record high. This is a direct contradiction to the lies being spread by climate alarmists.
>
> The DMI data was being widely cited by skeptics as evidence against global warming fraud, so today DMI changed the *graph*. They changed their baseline dates, and no longer show 2017 as being a record high.
>
> We have seen this identical story hundreds of times. Climate data being altered to avoid criticism from global warming alarmists. [...]

This dimension indicates that the second most common pattern of keyword variation distinguishes between texts drawing on political discourses with those drawing on scientific discourses. This demonstrates that climate change and climate change denial are both political and scientific issues.

Dimension 3: the discreditation of public institutions versus the discreditation of renewable energy

The keywords associated with positive Dimension 3 are used in the texts for the purpose of discrediting public institutions. The mainstream media (*msm, mainstream*), politicians (*Clinton, Gore, Trump, Obama, UN*), political ideologies (*socialist, activist*), and scientists (*mann, scientist, met*) are often critiqued in the texts for promoting bias, fake news, and alarmism about AGW (*bias, corrupt, cagw, fraud, fake, alarmism, alarmist, warmist, propaganda, hoax, ignorance, ignorant, scam, scare, stupid, nonsense, agenda*). Such texts emphasise that global warming is a *conspiracy*, that there is no *consensus* on *AGW*, and that they are sceptical (*skeptical, skeptic*) of claims that humans are to *blame* and of graphs and data. For example, Text 3 reports on "Climategate" – a case where hackers broke into email exchanges between researchers within the Climate Research Unit at East Anglia University, which supposedly involved researchers colluding on manipulating data to conceal evidence against global warming – to suggest that man-made global warming is a conspiracy. Some texts reject the common accusation of climate change sceptics/denialists as having capitalist interests (*capitalism*).

Text 3: Climategate: CATO's Pat Michaels and Center for American Progress Dan Weiss on Fox News (https://wattsupwiththat.com/2009/11/25/catos-pat-michaels-and-center-for-american-progress-dan-weiss-on-fox-news/, 25 November 2009)

Hackers broke into thousands of emails and documents from the Climate Research Unit at East Anglia University last week and uncovered the global warming conspiracy.
[. . .]
Calls for an independent inquiry into what is being dubbed "Climategate" are growing as the foundation for man-made global warming implodes following the release of emails which prove researchers colluded to manipulate data in order to "hide the decline" in global temperatures.
[. . .]

The keywords associated with negative Dimension 3 are used to discredit renewable energy. Notably, renewable energy sources (*renewable, solar, wind, sun, gas*) are described as expensive, unpredictable, unreliable, and unable to cope with demand, as in Text 4. Such texts describe fossil fuels (*fossil, fuel, gas*) as being more reliable than renewable energy sources, as the electric grid is described as requiring a constant and stable flow of electrons and is damaged by the unpredictability of renewable energy (*energy, electricity, grid*). There are also keywords associated with atmospheric CO_2 levels (*atmospheric, atmosphere, CO2, carbon, dioxide, heat, pollution, greenhouse, heating, emission*), and these often co-occur to emphasise that natural gas (which has been a solution to burning less coal and can be viewed as a bridge to a clean energy future) still produces a large amount of carbon dioxide and pollution. Additionally, atmospheric CO_2 levels are often mentioned to emphasise that CO_2 is a trace gas and therefore cannot be the cause of climate change.

Text 4: Endless Subsidies For Unreliable Wind & Solar are an Economic Suicide Pact (https://stopthesethings.com/2021/08/01/endless-subsidies-for-unreliable-wind-solar-are-an-economic-suicide-pact/, 1 August 2021)

> Australia's *renewable* energy target has subsidised *wind* and *solar* to the tune of more
> than $60 billion, wrecked its *grid* and driven power prices through the roof.
> [. . .]
> And, in a country heavily reliant upon *wind* and *solar*, power becomes scarce when
> the sun sets and/or calm weather sets in.
> Couple that with a period of peak demand (breathless 42°C days, for example) and
> *energy* intensive industries are simply chopped from the grid under the euphemism
> of "demand management".
> Suicidal doesn't cover it.
> [. . .]

Overall, this dimension indicates that the next most common pattern of variation across the texts in the climate change denial corpus distinguishes texts that are discrediting believers of climate change or discrediting initiatives for combating the effects of climate change. Oreskes and Conway (2010) similarly found that climate denial strategies are designed to question the credibility of mainstream scientists and simultaneously boost the appearance of scientific credibility for the denial countermovement. This dimension marks the overt questioning, undermining, and damaging of the reputation of climate scientists, other public institutions, and renewable energy, suggesting that climate change denial is a kind of smear campaign.

Dimension 4: the discourse of extremism versus the "consensus"

The keywords associated with positive Dimension 4 often co-occur in texts to point to a discourse of extremism. Specifically, there are keywords associated with extreme cold weather (*freezing, snow, winter, storm, cold, forecast, flooding, polar, weather, ice, extreme, atlantic, melt, melting*). These keywords often occur in texts reporting on cold weather to suggest that global warming is a hoax and that an ice age is imminent, as in Text 5. Many texts emphasise that the mainstream media (*msm*) reports are sensationalistic, *extreme* and *stupid* for blaming (*blame*) the cold weather on AGW, as a *warm winter* would indicate AGW, rather than a *cold winter*. The impact of the cold weather on renewable energy sources (*renewable, wind*) is also discussed in some of the texts, where heaters drawing on fossil fuel energy (*grid, electricity, nuclear, coal*) are required during cold weather to pump *warm* air onto the blades, thereby suggesting that renewable energy is unreliable. Plans to curb rising temperatures and extreme weather – for example, as the "Green New Deal", which proposes a reduction of CO_2 emissions by switching to renewables – are deemed *socialist, extreme*, and unrealistic. Additionally, the use of renewable energy in *Germany* is also mentioned and critiqued as extreme and extremely expensive. Political actors (*clinton, trump, obama*) are also referenced, often to report on actions deemed as extreme. For example, Obama shutting down power plants as the country goes into winter.

> Text 5: Polar Vortex of Stupidity (https://climatechangedispatch.com/polar-vortex-of-stupidity/,
> 30 January 2019)
>
> A few years ago, the Washington Post said global warming would cause cherry trees to start
> blooming in January.
> That didn't work out for them, so now they are *blaming* the record *cold* on global warming.
> If the *Polar* Vortex is caused by global warming, why does it mimic the pattern of the last *ice* age?

By contrast, the keywords associated with negative Dimension 4 are used to discuss the consensus of the role of CO_2 in global warming. Notably, many of the texts mention scepticism (*skeptical, skeptic*) of the *consensus* promoted by the Intergovernmental Panel on Climate Change (*IPCC*) – that climate change (*anthropogenic, man-made*) is a result of increasing levels of atmospheric carbon dioxide (*CO_2, carbon, dioxide, concentration, greenhouse, emission, atmosphere, atmospheric*) produced by humans through the burning of fossil fuels. For example, some texts note that there is no *correlation* between *emissions* and *atmospheric concentrations* of CO_2 to suggest that something else is influencing global warming. Additionally, many texts cite scientific articles (*science, NASA, scientist, scientific, radiation, planetary, physics, magnitude, earth, surface, cloud, atmosphere, atmospheric*), observations (*observed*), findings, and principles to demonstrate particular aspects of the climate where there is uncertainty and debate. These conclusions are used to suggest that there is no consensus and that man-made climate change is a *hypothesis*, as in Text 6. Instead, many of the texts emphasise the role of natural influences on the climate (*volcanic, variability, magnitude, surface, radiation, cloud*).

Text 6: On Consensus (https://notrickszone.com/2013/12/18/climate-sciences-constant-appeals-to-authority-only-confirm-its-total-fallacy/, 18 December 2013)

We are constantly told that there is a *consensus* in climate *science* that CO_2 is warming the planet, or the deep ocean, (or something) and that if we do not limit CO_2 something bad will happen. As one can easily see, there is no *consensus* on the two "somethings" in that first sentence. We are told that CO_2 is responsible for warming, cooling, less rainfall, more rainfall, less snow, more snow, less ice, more ice, more hurricanes, fewer hurricanes, more tornados, fewer tornados, and so on. Each of those things can also be good or bad, (but mostly bad) depending on where and when they happen. The "*consensus*" seems to morph to whatever bad thing the writer wants to prove. This isn't climatology, it's calamitology.

[. . .]

This dimension indicates that the next most common pattern of variation in the corpus distinguishes texts that are drawing on the discourse of extremism with texts that are emphasising that there is no consensus. This dimension shows that refutation is an important strategy in climate change denials, as global warming is refuted due to extreme cold weather, and the consensus is refuted by showing areas of climate science which are debated to persuade others to disbelieve human's influence on climate change. Additionally, the seriousness of global warming is downplayed by suggesting green policies are extreme.

Dimension 5: the role of CO_2 versus natural variation

The keywords associated with positive Dimension 5 co-occur in texts to describe the role of carbon dioxide in global warming. Specifically, there are keywords associated with global warming (*global, warming, earth, planet*), its causes (*carbon, dioxide, pollution*), and its effects, such as melting ice in the Arctic, Greenland, and Antarctica (*melting, antarctica, antarctic, melt, greenland, arctic, ice*), leading to sea levels rising (*sea, rise, ocean*) and the extinction of species (*extinction, polar*). Interestingly, some texts with these keywords present research findings which indicate the impact of global warming, but they then go on to criticise the cited report for perceived flaws. This is arguably for the purpose of instilling doubt in parts or all the conclusions (see Dunlap and McCright, 2010). Some texts acknowledge global warming, describing the different explanations for why the globe is warming (including anthropogenic, natural causes, and aliens), and its different effects, often to downplay the role of humans. Some other texts, especially those containing the keywords used to mark deception (*propaganda, agenda, hoax*) emphasise that global warming is a hoax. Some of these texts state that global warming is only partially caused by human production of CO_2, but that the *mainstream* media, politicians, and organisations (*clinton, UN, obama, trump, mainstream, activist*) make it out to be more. Keywords associated with hysteria (*catastrophe, catastrophic, unprecedented*) are used both to ridicule believers of AGW and to emphasise the seriousness of it. Notably, some texts associated with this side of the dimension refer to growing ice cover, as opposed to melting ice and poor model predictions on sea level rise which overstate the actual measurements. Additionally, many texts claim that carbon dioxide plays no role in global warming, as the planet was warmer before industrialised levels of CO_2, or because the global temperatures are not rising, as in Text 7.

Text 7: Highest CO_2 levels recorded in 3 million years still don't budge global temperatures . . . official climate change narrative collapses in the face of real science (www.newstarget. com/2019-05-03-highest-co2-levels-recorded-in-3-million-years-still-dont-budge-global-temperatures.html, 3 May 2019)

Is *carbon dioxide* the driving force behind climate change? That's what many climate change alarmists would have you believe, but when you look at real-world data, that narrative collapses.
[. . .]
Put quite simply, *carbon dioxide* is not a poison that we should fear. Instead, what we should fear is a dramatic reduction in it because it's what gives our planet life. Without *carbon dioxide*, we wouldn't have plants, which means there wouldn't be oxygen and humans would eventually die out.
In the past, *carbon dioxide* levels have been significantly higher than they are now, yet life still managed to exist and plants, not surprisingly, thrived. Indeed, experts say that if *carbon dioxide* levels drop too much, many plants and other vegetal species would become extinct.
[. . .]

The keywords associated with negative Dimension 5 are used to refer to natural processes (*variability, cloud, precipitation, sun, wind, el* (Niño), *physics, heating, cycle, solar, sun, winter, magnitude*) as a cause of climate change, as in Text 8. Additionally, there are keywords associated with AGW (*AGW, CAGW*) and denigrating terms for people who believe in it (*warmist*), which co-occur in texts often stating that there is *zero* evidence for the *hypothesis* of *AGW*. There are also keywords associated with energy (*electricity, grid*). These co-occur in texts that are critiquing renewable energy policies and the shutting down of power plants. According to the authors, these actions are pointless given that climate change is due to natural causes.

Text 8: New Met Office study suggests natural factors, including the sun, are the biggest reason behind "the pause" (https://wattsupwiththat.com/2018/06/07/new-met-office-study-suggests-natural-factors-including-the-sun-are-the-biggest-reason-behind-the-pause/, 7 June 2018)

[. . .]

A team of researchers from the U.K. Met Office, Sweden and Australia has found that three periods of global warming slowdown since 1891 were likely due to natural causes rather than disruptions to the factors causing global warming.

[. . .]

The team asserts that the third slowdown, aka "the pause" which is also the one on which many global warming skeptics like us here at WUWT follow, was likely caused by a combination of La Niña events and volcanism.

They also claim that the third slowdown period wasn't a stopping point, and they say temperatures continued to rise, they just did so at a slower pace.

[. . .]

Overall, Dimension 5 shows that the next strongest pattern of variation distinguishes texts mentioning the role of CO_2 in global warming with texts mentioning natural variation as the reason for climate change. This dimension indicates that climate change deniers often appeal to the fallacy of lack of proportion, where the role of CO_2 in climate change is downplayed, and the role of natural processes in climate change are exaggerated. Both sides of the dimension align with Cohen's (2001) interpretative denial and may be positioned as climate sceptics, given that both repertoires tend to acknowledge climate change as happening but assign an alternative cause to climate change.

Dimension 6: counterevidence versus no evidence

The keywords associated with positive Dimension 6 co-occur in texts to provide counterevidence against the arguments of AGW. In particular, there are keywords associated with Antarctica and Greenland (*antarctica, antarctic, greenland, hemisphere*), which occur in texts to state that the ice sheet is not *melting* but in fact it is growing, despite CO_2 *emissions* and *concentration* levels rising. These texts provide counterevidence, including *satellite* images of growing ice to suggest that there is no relation between CO_2 and global warming. There are keywords associated with scientific analysis (*graph, observed, physics*), which co-occur in texts discussing scientific models predicting the impacts of climate change over time (*decade*), such as predictions of sea levels (*sea, ocean, surface, melt, melting, atlantic*), the extinction of species (*extinction*), and extreme weather events (*tropical*). These texts often provide counterevidence contrasting the scientific models' predictions with observed reality to suggest that the models are wrong. There are also keywords associated with natural variability (*el* (Niño), *cloud, radiation, volcanic, magnitude*), which occur in texts to provide counterevidence against AGW to suggest that climate change is due to natural causes, as opposed to human's production of CO_2. Some texts refer to *Trump*'s actions in pulling out of green policies and the "evidence" that supports these policy changes. Such evidence is positioned as counterevidence against the impact of CO_2 on climate change. The argument that *capitalism* is to blame for AGW is introduced, so as to counter it. Such texts instead emphasise the good of capitalism and reinforce the "actual" causes of climate change. Finally, the keyword *unprecedented* is associated with positive Dimension 6, and this occurs in the texts to critique the "unprecedented" label applied to evidence of AGW. Such texts describe the uses of the word "unprecedented" as hysteria, providing counterevidence, including warmer temperatures in the past (before industrialised levels of CO_2) and natural processes, as in Text 9, which emphasises that the warming in the Arctic is natural and not a result of CO_2.

Text 9: The Real Arctic Story (https://alarmistclaimresearch.files.wordpress.com/2019/02/amo-pdo-solar-and-arctic-v2.pdf, 8 March 2019)

Arctic warming and the *melting* of the arctic ice are not at all *unprecedented* (they happen predictably on multidecadal scales with a period of around 60 years) and are in fact entirely natural.
[...]

The keywords associated with negative Dimension 6 co-occur in texts to indicate that there is no evidence of AGW. Specifically, texts associated with this side of the dimension note that *global warming* is a theory and that claims of the role of *carbon dioxide* in global warming are not substantiated, as in Text 10. Some of the texts use the derogatory labels *warmist* and *alarmist* when referring to those that advocate global warming is *man-made* (*AGW*), to position such views as different to theirs. Such texts suggest that the theory of AGW is a *hoax*, exaggerated and intended to *scare*, as there is no evidence to support the theory. Many of the texts draw on examples of cold weather and temperature (*weather, snow, forecast, temperature, winter, cooling, cold*) to suggest that there is no evidence of global warming. Some of the keywords are used to refer to the individuals emphasising AGW (e.g. *IPCC, gore, science, scientific, scientist*) in order to discredit them. For example, Al *Gore* is referenced to suggest that he is profiteering from climate policies. *Scientists* and the *IPCC* are accused of going against *science* and the traditional *scientific* method by (1) not challenging climate change theory, (2) not publishing dissenting views or counterevidence against AGW, and (3) accepting and promoting that there is a consensus on human's role in global warming. Additionally, some texts mention particular scientists as holding views against the consensus, as in Text 10, which depicts professors, researchers, and scientists who are in support of Senator Roberts report finding that the CSIRO could neither confirm nor prove that carbon dioxide is dangerous or the cause of climate change.

Text 10: Australian Sen Malcolm Roberts Exposes The Climate Change Scam (www.australi-annationalreview.com/state-of-affairs/australian-sen-malcolm-roberts-exposes-the-climate-change-scam/, 19 January 2020)

[...]
The key findings of Senator Roberts' report shows that CSIRO: 1. Refuses to state that *carbon dioxide* from human activity is a danger 2. Does not have empirical evidence proving that *carbon dioxide* from human activity effects climate 3. Have used evidence in their presentation that contradicts the empirical climate evidence. 4. Uses climate computer models that are neither appropriate nor recommended to be used to inform government policy. . . . Those supporting the senator at his press conference were Internationally eminent Canadian climatologist, geographer and environmentalist Professor Tim Ball, expert on the United Nations' unfounded and politically motivated climate claims cited by CSIRO.
[...]

Overall, this dimension indicates that the texts in the corpus can be distinguished according to those providing counterevidence to climate change believers with those stating that there is no evidence for climate change. This dimension reveals common argumentation strategies employed by climate change deniers: rebutting and denying.

Dimension 7: the discourse of weather manipulation versus anti-alarmism

The keywords on the positive side of Dimension 7 co-occur in texts signalling the discourse of weather manipulation. There are keywords associated with weather and weather forecasts (*flooding, drought, storm, weather, forecast, cloud, tropical, cool, extreme, precipitation, sun*), which co-occur in texts often to describe the disparity between the current weather and that which was forecasted. The texts accuse those higher up (*obama, fake, socialist, trump, mainstream, clinton*) of being part of a conspiracy (*conspiracy, corrupt, blame, agenda*), which is aimed at manipulating the earth's (*earth, planet*) climate *cycle*. Notably, they suggest planes are spraying chemicals into the atmosphere (*atmosphere, atmospheric*) to manipulate weather events – often referred to in the texts as geo-engineering. Weather manipulation is described as being, among others, for the purpose of profiting from various climate policies and taxes, which have been enforced at an unprecedented scale, as in Text 11. Weather manipulation is often described in these texts as a threat to life on earth (*extinction, civilization*).

Text 11: Meteorologists And Climate Engineering Denial, Perpetuating The Lie For A Paycheck And A Pension (www.geoengineeringwatch.org/meteorologists-and-climate-engineering-denial-perpetuating-the-lie-for-a-paycheck-and-a-pension/, 22 February 2016)

[. . .] How many so called "experts" have long since sold any shred of honor and honesty they may have once possessed in exchange for a paycheck and a pension? The blatant criminal denial of the climate engineering atrocities so visible in skies around the globe is the greatest deception ever perpetrated on populations of the planet. The majority of the masses have unfortunately so far been all too willing to accept a constant parade of lies from the power structure and their paid minions on an endless list of issues.

[. . .]

The keywords associated with negative Dimension 7 co-occur in articles expressing the discourse of anti-alarmism. Specifically, the texts most associated with this dimension are often critiquing and mocking believers of AGW (e.g. *mann, IPCC*) as *alarmists* (*alarmism, alarmist, CAGW*). The texts associated with this dimension critique sensationalist reports and headlines emphasising that West Antarctica is melting and sea levels are rising (*antarctic, antarctica, greenland, melt, melting, sea, ice, arctic, polar*), as can be seen in Text 12. The texts instead state that it is not melting, despite rising levels of carbon dioxide (*co2*) from the burning of fossil fuels (*fossil, coal*), or they state that it is melting, but due to natural processes. Keywords associated with renewable energy (*renewable, electricity, grid*) and places where there has been a big push for renewable energy (*Germany*) are mentioned. These co-occur in texts to denounce alarmists' impulsion for renewable energy. Such texts describe the unsustainability of renewable energy, due to the cost and shelf life of wind turbines and their impact on birds, as well as the unreliability of renewable energy on the grid.

Text 12: BIAS BY OMISSION: No Mention Of Mother Nature's Undersea Volcanoes In The Latest Antarctic "Global Warming" Scare Story (https://climatism.wordpress.com/2018/05/10/bias-by-omission-no-mention-of-mother-natures-undersea-volcanoes-in-the-latest-antarctic-global-warming-scare-story/, 10 May 2018)

ANTARCTICA has always been a thorn in the side of the Climate Crisis Industry. It simply has not behaved as global warming *alarmists* would have liked or as climate models predicted.

> HISTORICALLY, Antarctica has been cooling and growing ice mass, despite rising carbon dioxide emissions. Emissions that, according to "global warming theory", are meant to effect the poles greater than mid latitude regions due to the lack of humidity enhancing the theorised CO_2 feedback.
>
> [. . .]

Overall, this dimension indicates that the next major pattern of variation distinguishes texts that promote the conspiracy of weather manipulation with texts that mock climate change believers as "alarmists". It can be argued that promoting the conspiracy of weather manipulation serves as a deflection strategy. Proponents of the conspiracy do not deny AGW but instead divert the attention away from human's CO_2 production and instead focus the attention on the dangers of the manipulation of the weather to block solar radiation. Consequently, the impact of human's CO_2 production is arguably presented as less severe than the dangers and effects associated with climate manipulation. The negative side of this dimension marks that name-calling and responding to the tone are common strategies in climate change denials, as climate change believers are accused of exaggerating and being hysterical. This dimension may therefore be seen as opposing texts that are engaged in emphasising an alternative concern, often in a hysterical manner, with those that are de-emphasising a mainstream concern, often by critiquing the manner of climate activists as hysterical.

Dimension 8: extreme weather as climate scaremongering versus global warming is fraud/scam

The keywords associated with positive Dimension 8 are used in texts to criticise reports of extreme weather as climate scaremongering. Specifically, there are keywords associated with extreme weather (*flooding, drought, tropical, storm, precipitation, extreme, weather, forecast, predict*) in specific areas (*atlantic*). There are also keywords that co-occur to critique AGW believers as climate scaremongering (*climate, climatic, alarmism, catastrophe, catastrophic, alarmist*), such as Text 13. Such texts mock scientists' (*EPA, mann*) use of the word *unprecedented* and *blame* the scientists for overstating and exaggerating the impact of *carbon dioxide* (*greenhouse, fossil, fuels, pollution*) and causing alarm and scare. Natural *variability* is also often mentioned in the texts to indicate that the extreme weather is nothing new and just a part of the earth's climate cycle.

> Text 13: "The Science" Proves Extreme Weather Events Are NOT Increasing (www.climatedepot.com/2020/02/20/the-science-that-proves-extreme-weather-events-are-not-increasing/, 20 February 2020)
>
> COGNITIVE BIAS: *Climate* Change *Alarmists* Refuse To Accept "The Science" That Proves *Extreme Weather* Events Are NOT Increasing
>
> [. . .]
>
> COGNITIVE BIAS fuelled by an era of mass hysteria, delusion, groupthink and panic has helped foster dark and far-fetched clichés of a current "*climate* crisis", that is an "existential threat" which will "end civilisation by 2030".
>
> [. . .]

By contrast, the keywords associated with negative Dimension 8 co-occur in texts emphasising that climate change, that data supporting it, and policies and incentives associated with combating it are fraudulent. There are keywords used to mark that climate change is a hoax (*conspiracy, hoax, fake, scam, fraud, propaganda*), that there is *zero* evidence behind CO_2 and global warming, and that people who believe in it are ignorant (*ignorance, ignorant, stupid*) to the other reasons for the *planet*'s (*earth, planet*) *cooling* and *heating* (*cloud, sun, volcanic, solar, cycle, surface, cool, cold, radiation*). *NASA* is often mentioned to accuse them of adjusting graphs to support AGW, such as Text 14, or to describe the views of a *NASA* employee as going against the consensus.

Text 14: 1975 Documentary "The Weather Machine": Climate "Keeps Changing Gear" . . . "Ice Age Now Due Any Time"! (https://notrickszone.com/2018/03/18/1975-documentary-the-weather-machine-climate-keeps-changing-gear-ice-age-now-due-any-time/, 18 March 2018)

A documentary dubbed "The Weather Machine" produced in 1975 – long before *NASA* fiddled with the data – warned of an impending ice age (10:35), and maintained that the globe is *cooling*. Hat-tip: reader The Indomitable Snowman.
The documentary attempted and succeeded at presenting the latest on climate change at the time.
Changing climate accepted as normal
It is true that back in 1975 climatologists already knew that the climate behaved *cyclically*, as evidenced by the ice cores and tree ring sets extracted from the American Southwest.
[. . .]

Overall, Dimension 8 shows that the final major pattern of variation in the corpus distinguishes texts that depict global warming as a scam with texts that critique people who accuse extreme weather events to be a consequence of AGW. This dimension demonstrates that many texts in the corpus are involved in accusing. For example, the texts associated with the positive side accuse people linking extreme weather events to climate change as scaremongering and the texts associated with the negative side accuse people of making up AGW, adjusting graphs to suit the theory, and for being ignorant to the real causes of global warming.

Conclusion

Responding to calls for more research into sceptic and denier blogs (Dunlap, 2013), the present study aimed to conduct a large-scale analysis of 19,961 texts mentioning global warming or climate change, taken from 186 websites/blogs known to promote conspiracy and pseudoscience. Using corpus linguistic tools, a list of keywords that occur with a significantly higher frequency in this corpus in comparison to a 38-billion-word corpus of web texts (EnTenTen20) was computed. Using this list of keywords, the corpus was analysed for the most common patterns of co-occurring keywords across the texts using KCA (Clarke, McEnery and Brookes, 2021; Clarke, Brookes and McEnery, 2021). Previous research has noted that climate science receives "multifaceted, complex, and nuanced opposition" (Bloomfield and Tillery, 2018: 32). Thus, given that KCA is a multidimensional approach, KCA was deemed appropriate for uncovering such patterns.

KCA revealed the most common patterns of keyword variation in the dataset, which were interpreted as pointing to common representations and discourses associated with climate change across these conspiracy and pseudoscience sites. The analysis has not only revealed the common discourses of climate change scepticism, but it has also shown the order of prominence in terms of frequency – which discourses are most common across the blogs, with each dimension representing the next strongest pattern of keyword variation across the texts in the corpus. As a result, it is possible to say that the texts in the corpus most commonly are either critiquing political calls for action against climate change as a scam or they are critiquing scientific research, such as by pointing out faults and flaws with climate models and scientific measurements. In this way, the analysis has provided a richer account of the most common mechanisms and repertoires of climate scepticism by structuring these co-occurrence patterns in order of frequency.

The results indicate that all the tactics and arguments known to have been developed and promulgated by conservative think tanks (funded by the fossil fuel industry) have permeated online blogs and websites promoting pseudoscience and conspiracy. This lends support to Dunlap and Jacques' (2013) observation that, unlike scientific knowledge, which accumulates through testing, rejecting, and modifying hypotheses and theories, the denial literature accumulates – claims are "retained and reused whenever convenient" (2013: 713). Online blogs and websites provide another home for these claims to be repeated. The major goals of social movement activists are to make their causes publicly visible, resonant, and legitimate (Koopmans, 2004). Because the Internet has enabled "voices to appear equally credible" and "reach many people" (Tillery and Bloomfield, 2022: 1), these recycled arguments arguably have a considerable amount of influence, as the Internet affords public visibility, resonance, and to some degree, legitimacy.

Overall, the analysis has revealed the most common discourses and argumentation strategies used for disputing AGW across websites known to promote pseudoscience and conspiracy. These discourses can be compelling. For example, whilst there is evidence of outright denial in texts associated with negative Dimension 6 ("No evidence") and negative Dimension 9 ("Global warming is a scam"), other dimensions show that texts do not necessarily deny climate change. Instead, texts are focused on downplaying the seriousness of climate change. For example, the seriousness of climate change is lessened in texts associated with positive Dimension 4 (the discourse of extremism) when the authors critique climate policies as extreme. Additionally, the seriousness of climate change is downplayed in texts associated with negative Dimension 7 and positive Dimension 8, when the authors label climate activists as "alarmists" and "scaremongers" respectively. These strategies present climate change as being not as bad as climate activists present it, which consequently creates doubt about the reality of climate change. In comparison to outright denial, which is harder to believe in the face of growing scientific evidence of AGW, downplaying the seriousness of climate change is arguably a subtler and more believable strategy. As in law, rather than prove innocence, the defence attorney need only create reasonable doubt in the narrative being promulgated by the prosecutor. In the context of the climate change debate, the climate denial movement has created an exceptional amount of doubt. This doubt has the potential to delay effective climate action, which will likely have disastrous consequences for life on earth. Studies aimed at uncovering and understanding the discourses of disinformation, such as the one presented here in and throughout this collection, are well-positioned to pave the way for the creation of effective counterstrategies to prevent such negative consequences from happening.

Appendix

Keywords occurring in more than 5% of the texts in the focus corpus:

activist, agenda, agw, alarmism, alarmist, antarctic, antarctica, anthony, anthropogenic, arctic, atlantic, atmosphere, atmospheric, average, bias, blame, btw, cagw, capitalism, carbon, catastrophe, catastrophic, civilization, climate, climatic, clinton, cloud, co2, coal, cold, concentration, consensus, conspiracy, cool, cooling, correlation, corrupt, cycle, decade, dioxide, drought, earth, el, electricity, emission, energy, epa, extinction, extreme, fake, flooding, forecast, fossil, fraud, freezing, fuel, gas, germany, global, gore, graph, greenhouse, greenland, grid, heat, heating, hemisphere, hoax, hypothesis, ice, ignorance, ignorant, ipcc, magnitude, mainstream, man-made, mankind, mann, melt, melting, met, msm, nasa, noaa, nonsense, nuclear, obama, observed, ocean, physics, planet, planetary, polar, pollution, precipitation, predict, prediction, propaganda, radiation, renewable, rise, satellite, scam, scare, science, scientific, scientist, sea, skeptic, skeptical, snow, socialist, solar, storm, stupid, sun, surface, temperature, trend, trillion, tropical, trump, un, unprecedented, variability, volcanic, warm, warmer, warming, warmist, weather, wind, winter, wuwt, zero

References

Baker, P., Gabrielatos, C. and McEnery, T. (2013) *Discourse analysis and media attitudes: The representation of Islam in the British Press*. Cambridge: Cambridge University Press.

Biber, D. (1988) *Variation across speech and writing*. Cambridge: Cambridge University Press.

Bloomfield, E.F. and Tillery, D. (2018) 'The circulation of climate change denial online: Rhetorical and networking strategies on Facebook', *Environmental Communication*, 13(1), pp. 23–34.

Boykoff, M.T. and Boykoff, J.M. (2004) 'Bias as balance: Global warming and the US prestige press', *Global Environmental Change*, 14, pp. 125–136.

Brüggemann, M., Elgesem, D., Bienzeisler, N., Gertz, H.D. and Walter, S. (2020) 'Mutual group polarization in the blogosphere: Tracking the hoax discourse on climate change', *International Journal of Communication*, 14, pp. 1025–1048.

Clarke, I., Brookes, G. and McEnery, T. (2021) 'Keywords through time', *International Journal of Corpus Linguistics*, 27(4), pp. 399–427.

Clarke, I., McEnery, T. and Brookes, G. (2021) 'Multiple correspondence analysis, newspaper discourse and subregister: A case study of discourses of Islam in the British press', *Register Studies*, 3(1), pp. 144–171.

Cohen, S. (2001) *States of Denial: Knowing about Atrocities and Suffering*. Cambridge: Polity Press.

Dunlap, R.E. (2013) 'Climate change skepticism and denial: An introduction', *American Behavioral Scientist*, 57(6), pp. 691–698.

Dunlap, R.E. and Jacques, P.J. (2013) 'Climate change denial books and conservative think tanks: Exploring the connection', *American Behavioral Scientist*, 57(6), pp. 699–731.

Dunlap, R.E. and McCright, A.M. (2010) 'Climate change denial: Sources, actors and strategies', in C. Lever-Tracy (ed.), *Routledge handbook of climate change and society*. London and New York: Routledge, pp. 240–259.

Dunlap, R.E. and McCright, A.M. (2015) 'Challenging climate change: The denial countermovement', in R.E. Dunlap and R.J. Brulle (eds.), *Climate Change and Society: Sociological Perspectives*. New York: Oxford University Press, pp. 300–332.

Harvey, J.A., Van Den Berg, D., Ellers, J., Kampen, R., Crowther, T.W., Roessingh, P., Verheggen, B., Nuijten, R.J.M., Post, E., Lewandowsky, S., Stirling, I., Balgopal, M., Amstrup, S.C. and Mann, M.E. (2018) 'Internet blogs, polar bears, and climate-change denial by proxy', *Bioscience*, 68(4), pp. 281–287.

Kilgariff, A. (2009) 'Simple maths for keywords', in M. Mahlberg, V. González-Díaz and C. Smith (eds.), *Proceedings of corpus linguistics conference CL2009*. Liverpool: University of Liverpool.

Koopmans, R. (2004) 'Movements and media: Selection processes and evolutionary dynamics in the public sphere', *Theory and Society*, 33, pp. 367–391.

Lahsen, M. (2005) 'Technocracy, democracy and U.S. climate politics', *Science Technology and Human Values*, 30, pp. 137–169.

Le Roux, B. and Rouanet, H. (2010) *Multiple correspondence analysis*. Thousand Oaks, CA: SAGE Publications Inc.

McCright, A.M. and Dunlap, R.E. (2003) 'Defeating Kyoto: The conservative movement's impact on U.S. climate change policy', *Social Problems*, 50, pp. 348–373.

McCright, A.M. and Dunlap, R.E. (2010) 'Anti-reflexivity: The American Conservative movement's success in undermining climate science and policy', *Theory, Culture and Society*, 26, pp. 100–133.

Oreskes, N. and Conway, E.M. (2010) *Merchants of doubt: How a handful of scientists obscured the truth on issues from tobacco smoke to global warming*. New York: Bloomsbury Press.

Tillery, D. and Bloomfield, E.F. (2022) 'Hyperrationality and rhetorical constellations in digital climate change denial: A multi-methodological analysis of the discourse of watts up with that', *Technical Communication Quarterly*, Ahead-of-Print, pp. 1–18.

Washington, H. and Cook, J. (2011) *Climate change denial: Heads in the sand*. 1st edition. London: Earthscan.

21

REFRAMINGS OF *FAKE* IN ART DISCOURSE

Chiara Degano

1 Introduction

"Yesterday, this painting was worth millions of guilders and experts and art lovers would come from all over the world and pay money to see it. Today, it is worth nothing and nobody would cross the street to see it for free. But the picture has not changed. What has?" These are the words used by Hans van Meegheren at his trial for forgery in 1947 (Pittaway 1999, *The Guardian*, 25 August) after making a fortune selling fake Vermeers to the Nazis. The fact they were fake saved his life, as otherwise he would be sentenced to death as a collaborationist. "Fake" was not "bad" for him. Normally, though, "fake" does not have positive connotations in art discourse, with authenticity being the absolute prerequisite for value, not too differently from what happens with news discourse. Forgery has always attracted attention the way crime does, with narratives about it intriguing readers for breaching law and accepted norms of behaviour, but in the event contributing to reaffirming the value system they breached. However, in recent years, the notion of fake in art discourse has received attention not only in terms of the authenticity vs forgery dichotomy but also in ways that problematise the notion itself and the value-system that underpins art dealing. Exhibitions have been organised openly displaying fake pieces, thus blurring the divide between authentic works of art to be exhibited and the results of forgery to be hidden from sight, once discovered. Still others overtly play on the concept of fake, displaying works of artists who have placed forgery at the centre of their work, either as a form of social critique or challenging common wisdom and judgements about the phenomenon of fake *itself*, so as to invite a reflection on it.

In light of these developments, whose meaning mostly lies in the discourse surrounding the work of art itself, the chapter will explore the way in which discourse contributes to a problematization of the notion of fake in art. Having reference to different genres of digital discourse, a repertoire of frames will be identified, with the attendant ideological positions, while also turning attention to the pragmatic conventions of discourse organisation in this field, as a way to observe the underlying epistemologies. More at large, the chapter contributes to exploring discourses of the "cultural industries", a field of specialised discourse which, like most of the humanities, has received little research attention in the realms of discourse and genre analysis (with the partial exception of academic discourse; cf. among others Bondi 2016 and 2017). However, the humanities have their own epistemologies,[1] methodologies, and forms of communication and argument, all contributing to the creation of expert knowledge of the world (Knudsen 2017: 908), which calls for a definition of their pragmatic conventions of discourse organisation.

2 Theoretical framework

Reference will be had to the notion of framing, as conceptualised from the perspective of communication, where attention is given to the way saliency is created and exploited in message construction, selecting certain aspects of reality and emphasising them "in such a way as to promote a particular problem definition, causal interpretation, moral evaluation, and/or treatment recommendation for the item described" (Entman 1993: 52), with salience mainly relying on linguistic "cues and markers" (Goffman 1981: 156). This is also in keeping with Goffman's (1974: 10–11) view of frames as "definitions of a situation . . . built up in accordance with principles of organization which govern events – at least social ones – and our subjective involvement in them".

Beyond shaping the cognitive representations with which people make sense of issues and information, social frameworks subject individuals to social appraisal of their actions based on values like "honesty, efficiency, economy, safety, elegance, tactfulness, good taste and so forth" (Goffman 1986: 22).

Goffman's frame analysis perspective and its later developments can provide suitable theoretical and analytic tools for a much-wanted exploration of the discourse of and about cultural industry, an umbrella term covering sectors whose core business rests on some kind of aesthetic experience.[2] As Coupland and Garret put it, at "the heart of Goffman's idea of framing is participants' understanding of the organizational premises of symbolic action" (Coupland and Garrett 2010), which in the case of product discourse (be it a book, an exhibition, a monument, or a tourist destination) translates into prompting particular interpretive frames for the intended receivers.

Framing can be brought to bear onto the discourse of cultural industries at least on three levels. There are public discourses about policies meant to support the sector (which clearly fall beyond the scope of this chapter), there is promotional communication about cultural products, produced by artists themselves or by professionals working with and for them who aim to give resonance to their cultural products, and there are hetero-directed discourses, like reviews and critics' discourse at large, meant to allocate or deny value to cultural products.

With regard to the promotional communication about cultural products, Coupland, who approached the issue with regard to tourism (2012; Coupland and Coupland 2014; Coupland and Garrett 2010), conceptualised three layers of framing involved in the process: sociocultural, generic, and interpersonal. Sociocultural framing refers to macro level social frames in which acts of identity are projected by speakers or writers, positioning themselves or others, in relation to social variables such as age, gender, ethnicity, sexuality, and profession. Generic framing concerns meso-level social frames that constrain the shape of a given text and mediate its reception on the part of the receiver. Interpersonal framing operates at the micro-level of the ways in which participants structure their talk and position themselves in relation to each other. Tseng (2018) applies Coupland's model of framing to a promotional genre specific of the creative industries paradigm, that is, Cultural Product Descriptions, Tseng (2018) adding a fourth layer, conceptual framing, which presides over our way of thinking about a product. Conceptual framing is concerned with the particular outlook projected on the product and is the layer of frames which involves creativity, exploiting devices like humour and metaphors, or creates a feeling or scenario associated with the product.

As for third parties' value-attributing discourse, emphasis has been placed on the interconnection of power and value by theories of the social production of the aesthetic (Wolff 1981). Such studies look at how "value" is bestowed on, or denied to, artistic/cultural forms and practices in given social contexts: "Understanding art as socially produced necessarily involves illuminating some of the ways in which various forms, genres, styles, etc. come to have value ascribed to them by certain groups in particular contexts" (Wolff 1981: 7). On a similar tone, Bielby (2011) examines cultural value in the world market for television, asking what criteria are invoked for product appraisal and how aesthetic criteria are deployed to explore the ways in which cultural arbiters and critical appraisal contribute to transnational culture worlds.

In art discourse this evaluative component is constitutive of the value attached to works of art. However well established, cultural value is hardly a factual matter and mostly depends on the ability to construct adherence to value allocation statements. Absent any hard data, crucial to adherence of mind is the choice of interpretative frames against which such statements will be received and made sense of. Established paradigms of artistic value rests first and foremost on the authenticity-forgery contraposition. Discourses that bring fake to the fore as a form of artistic meaning entail the enactment of a change of existing (or primary frames). In this respect, a central concept in frame analysis is keying, which with musical analogy refers to the process whereby "a set of conventions" by means of which a given activity, which already makes sense in the light of some primary framework (i.e. key) is "transformed into something patterned on this activity, but seen by the participant to be something quite else" (Goffman 1986: 43–44). For this ability to overwrite a pre-existing model or script, keying makes activities vulnerable. Another source of vulnerability lies in *fabrication*, whereby an intentional effort is made to induce a false belief in some of the participants to a given activity, thus entailing a "nefarious design . . . a plot or treacherous plan leading – when realized – to a falsification of some part of the world" (Goffman 1986: 83). Both keyings and fabrications presuppose the existence of a model, that is, "something already meaningful in terms of primary frameworks" to be reworked, but keying entails that all the participants are aware of what is going on – a case in point being that of satire – while fabrication relies on the fact that some participants are kept in the dark, as is the case with plagiarism.

It is here assumed that frames of fake in art discourse can be plotted on a continuum that goes from fabrication to keying, and attention is turned on how linguistic indicators are used to signal frames and modulate saliency.

3   Materials and method

The analysis will rely on the close reading of texts collected online, which due to the exploratory nature of the study do not amount to a corpus but are representative of discourse produced at level two and three of the model indicated previously, that is, discourse created for the promotion of exhibitions of work of arts or exhibitions and discourse around artistic work and events, produced by critics, journalists, or experts in general. The texts are taken from the websites of museums, galleries, newspapers, specialised websites and blogs.

4   Analysis

The analysis will now concentrate on the primary frame of fake in art discourse, as the point of departure for the analysis of keyings that variate from that pattern.

4.1   The primary frame: forgery as fabrication

The primary framing against which keyings of the concept of fake in art discourse can be appreciated is that of fake as fabrication, where forgers are the villains and unaware buyers, or museum visitors are the victims of manipulation. Since this frame is well consolidated, just one example is mentioned:

1 An exhibition in Slovenia *claiming* to feature works by Picasso, Van Gogh, and Matisse was abruptly cancelled this week over *fears* some works were *forged*, prompting a police probe on Friday.

The National Museum of Slovenia planned to officially open the show on Wednesday this week, entitled "Travels" and featuring 160 paintings owned by the *little-known* Boljkovac family.
But hours before planned opening, museum director Pavel Car said the show was cancelled after several art experts warned that, having seen the exhibition catalogue, they believed the works were *most likely fakes*.
"These are *clear forgeries* . . . you don't need to be an art history expert to notice it," Slovenian art expert Brane Kovič told news website N1.
The show *promised* works by Pablo Picasso, Vincent van Gogh, Henri Matisse and Marc Chagall, *apparently* owned by the Boljkovac family.
But Kovič said it was *highly unlikely* that so many masterpieces were among a private collection in Slovenia.
. . .
Car insisted he personally had seen the paintings' authenticity certificates, but nonetheless resigned Thursday, admitting he had been "naive" about the works.
The museum's website removed all references to the cancelled exhibition on Friday. (France-Presse 2022 *The Guardian*, 10 June 2022, my emphasis)

Typical traits of this frame are the reference to the semantic area of police investigation but also to the opposite primary frame, that of authenticity, here represented by the mention of a certificate of authenticity as a guarantee of the owners' credibility. Other roles typically distributed by this representation are that of the owners, the natural suspects, the art dealer (here the museum director), who as an expert who failed to unveil the scheme is cast as naïve but also possibly as complicit in the scheme, and third-party experts as authoritative judges with no vested interests in upholding the scheme. The pragmatic organisation of this discourse is therefore that normally applied to crime reports.

Another pervasive trait, however, pertains to the plane of metadiscursive choices, where several elements contribute in creating a low level of epistemic certainty. These include verbs of saying per se indicating high commitment (claiming, promised), but referred to a discredited source, namely, the museum director; the premodifiers "little-known" referred to the owners, adverbs (highly unlikely, most likely, apparently), the noun "fears". On the other hand, the art-expert quotation contains two boosters that intensify the reliability of the judgement therein expressed as (*clear* forgeries, *you don't need to be an art history expert to notice it*). All in all, the discursive constructions cited reveal the eminent role that discourse plays in construction of value in the art field: far from falling in the realm of certainty and objectivity, authenticity can be established on a complex balance of factors, among which are speech acts resting for the great part on the credibility of their locutors.

As a natural conclusion for this frame, the fakes are removed from the scene by hiding them from the eyes of the audience: the exhibition is cancelled, and any trace of it is removed from the museum website.

4.2   Keying 1. Fake exposed to fight the fake, but with a pleasure for it

A slight shift from the primary framing previously is enacted, bringing fake to the fore, as opposed to hiding it, while still construing it as a problem. This is what happens in exhibitions that decide to display such works as have been found to be forgeries. The aim of these exhibitions is to raise collectors' awareness, but alongside the pedagogical intent there seems to be a fascination for famous forgers of the past. Exhibitions of fake pieces of art include "Intent to Deceive: Fakes and Forgeries in the Art World", Springfield Museum 2014, (www.artrights.me/en/art-manager/), whose blurb reads as follows:

2   This *ground-breaking* exhibition explores some of the most *infamous scandals* of the past century and the forgers that *perpetrated* them.

The art world's *most notorious con artists* are profiled, including Elmyr de Hory, the subject of Orson Welles's film *F is for Fake*, and Mark Landis, a serial counterfeiter recently profiled in *The New Yorker*. View masterpieces by Charles Courtney Curran, Honoré Daumier, Philip de László, Henri Matisse, Amedeo Modigliani, Pablo Picasso, Paul Signac and Maurice de Vlaminck alongside examples of *ingenious* fakes that confounded the experts. The techniques and *amazing* skill employed in creating these forgeries are also explored, as well as detailed descriptions of how art experts use the latest technology to reveal these hoaxes.
The exhibit also delves into the mind of the serial forger, including examples of their legitimate original works as well as their personal effects and ephemera related to their lives as master con artists. (https://springfieldmuseums.org/exhibitions/intent-to-deceive-fakes-and-forgeries-in-the-art-world/)

Differently from the text taken as representative of the primary frame, here the crime frame, activated by words that are even more negatively connoted, either per se (infamous scandals, most notorious,) or through semantic prosody (perpetrated), is juxtaposed to terms relating to the fascination that forgers exert on the layperson and experts alike (con artists, amazing skill, ingenious). Even more interestingly, the crime frame is evoked through the expression "serial forger", with saliency placed on their mind, their lives, and even on their personal belongings.

"Close Examination: Fakes, Mistakes and Discoveries" is another exhibition in this thread, organised earlier, in 2010, at London's National Gallery (www.nationalgallery.org.uk/about-us/press-and-media/press-releases/close-examination-fakes-mistakes-and-discoveries). Introduced as the "first major exhibition of its kind", it focuses on state-of-the-art technology used to preserve collections but also to expose deceit, with an equipment similar to that of TV investigative police drama ("Modern scientific methods, including infrared imaging, X-ray images, electron microscopy and mass spectrometry can provide fascinating insights into the materials used by artists, studio practice and the ways paintings can change over time"). One of the rooms was dedicated to attribution mistakes, another to deception and deceit, the latter being introduced as follows:

3   The lengths forgers will go to deceive is shown in *Portrait Group*. This has been identified as the work of an unknown forger of the early twentieth century, imitating the style of Renaissance profile portraits. The National Gallery purchased the painting in 1923, believing it to be an authentic work from the fifteenth century. Scientific analysis *exposed the deception*, revealing that the artist had used pigments not available before the nineteenth century. It also emerged that the top layer had been coated with shellac, a natural resin, to simulate the appearance of age.

Here the "newsworthiness" of the forgery is enhanced either by reference to the amount spent to buy a fake or to the prestige of the museum or gallery that was fooled. The evaluative frame here seems to rest on the principle: the higher the amount and the greater the prestige, the more attractive the forgery. Sheer condemnation, then, partly leads to fascination.

The novelty of such an approach to forgery, which makes a show of it, is represented in the blurbs of such exhibition, with expressions like *first major exhibition of its kind, ground-breaking, pioneering,* or even *taboo-breaking,* as in the headline: "A taboo-breaking exhibition at Cologne's Museum Ludwig spotlights misattributed Russian avant-garde works" (McGreevy 2020, *Smithsonians Magazine,* October 26). While hiding the fake, once forgery is discovered, is considered the norm, the choice of bringing it to the fore is considered enormously innovative, as suggested by these words:

4   When museums discover a forgery in their collections, staff typically remove the artifact from view and stow it away with a mixture of shame and disappointment.

The Museum Ludwig in Cologne, however, *is pioneering* a different approach to fakes, transforming what could have been a mark against the German cultural institution into the focal point of a new exhibition. . . . "We have wonderful paintings in the collection and our visitors expect that what is hanging on the walls here is authentic", Rita Kersting, the deputy director of the museum, tells the *Art Newspaper.* "We have long had suspicions about certain paintings. And this public display is a way of reconciling that".

The exhibition catalogue justified the huge judgement mistake – 22 out of 49 works analysed in the Ludwig's collection were hoaxes – through the genesis of such paintings. Russian avant-garde works have often been misattributed, as these artists (Kazimir Malevich, Alexander Rodchenko and Natalia Goncharova) faced censorship in the Soviet Union, which led to an increase in the trafficking of smuggled art on the black market, where a lack of official documentation made a perfect bedrock for forgery (source: exhibition catalog).

In 2018, the discovery of a number of forged items in Belgium's Ghent Museum of Fine Art exhibition of Russian avant-garde art led to the museum director's resignation and the arrest of the collectors who lent the works. The choice of making fakes the object of exhibitions might actually be a result of changed contextual conditions: as new sophisticated technology makes it easier to disprove the authenticity of paintings, museums would rather construct themselves as intent on studying and exposing the phenomenon than as victims of forgers' schemes or unwitting accomplices:

5   Kersting tells the *Times* that she believes museums are the best place to conduct research on forgeries because they have less of a vested financial interest in the outcome of their studies.

"Museums are the right institutions to be advancing this research, because for us it's about scholarship, not commercial interests", she argues. "We are open to scholarly contributions and new findings. The research is never finished" (McGreevy 2020, *Smithsonians Magazine,* 26 October).

Gallery-wise, a huge uproar was caused by the early 2000s New York scandal that became the object of a Netflix documentary – *Made You Look: A True Story about Fake Art,* telling the story of the biggest art fraud in the American history. The documentary profiles Ann Freedman, the director of then prestigious Manhattan's Knoedler Gallery, whose reputation and career were destroyed as she failed to identify an unprecedented number of abstract expressionist works purportedly painted by artists of the like of Pollock and Rothko, with obscure provenance sold to her by a woman who was unknown into the world of art dealers. What is emphasised in the documentary is how hugely unlikely it is that so many authentic pieces could be in the hands of just one owner, together with what a *Los Angeles Times* review of the documentary refers to as an obliviousness to the cues of fraud that were there.

Also in this case, newsworthiness lies in the amount of the fraud ("a fascinating $80 million con"), as well as on the prestige of the gallery that was taken in. The adjectives describing the events and the characters embroiled in it (*fascinating* and *intriguing*) testify once more to the appeal exerted by stories of forgery, and to the interest in the mind of those involved, as echoing a trend which is well established in the field of narrative and in stylistics.

6 That mindset proves especially persuasive in the new Netflix documentary "Made You Look: A True Story About Fake Art", a *fascinating* depiction of the various dealers, collectors and gallery owners who found themselves embroiled in the *largest art fraud in American history. . . .* Director Barry Avrich – whose previous documentaries profiled Harvey Weinstein, David Foster and Lew Wasserman – paints an *intriguing psychological portrait* of a collective of sophisticates (whether easy marks or unwitting accomplices) so seduced by the sought-after art in question, they had become genuinely oblivious to the not-so-subtle flaws. (Rechtshaffen 2021, *Los Angeles Times*, 23 February).

A parallel here can be seen with blockbuster movies telling the story of masters of con (just to name a few, *Catch me if you can*, 2002, Spielberg; the Oceans' 11 series 2001–2007, Soderberg; the various versions of Lupin). Common to all of them is that the tone used in these representations of events are far from expressing condemnation, and rather emphasise the grandiosity of the con, as something with an aesthetic value in its own respect. The stance of the observer who tells grand stories of fraud varies from intrigued to bewildered by the naivety of those who failed to raise suspicions, with the social standing of the victims of these fraud all belonging to the higher echelons of society, possibly contributing to that.

Interestingly enough, in terms of attitudes to forgery, the documentary features also an interview with the unassuming forger, a Chinese mathematics professor named Pei-Shen Qian, who says that in his culture copying renowned artists' works is a sign of tribute being paid to them and as such is not viewed as problematic or criminal but is approved of. Copying is decoupled from the intent to deceive, which is the essence of forgery. This introduces, in a way, the second keying that will be considered here, where the modulation of attitude goes beyond fascination.

4.3   *Keying 2: challenging the art dealing system at its heart*

Lately, some artists have also placed fake at the centre of their work, either as a form of social critique, targeting champions of the so-called "post-truth" era, or challenging common wisdom and judgements about the phenomenon of fake *itself*, so as to invite reflection on it.

Featuring a selection of look-alikes next to their originals, the exhibition "Seconde main (Second Hand)", at Museé d'Art Moderne de la Ville de Paris (2010 www.mam.paris.fr/en/expositions/exhibitions-seconde-main) invites a reflection on the notions of copy, appropriation and imitation, starting from the notion of the copy "as the basis of artistic apprenticeship and as a constant of artistic creation". In doing so they follow in the footsteps of the artists who in the sixties and seventies separated the question of authenticity from that of originality intended as singularity, vis-à-vis an economy of mass production. By creating works identical to the originals or reinterpreting them, they embodied what would then become postmodernism, and later on "appropriationism" in the eighties, challenging established wisdom about authorship and originality. Thus, for example, a Picasso from the museum's collection hangs next to appropriationist Mike Bidlo's *Not Picasso*. In this essentially metadiscursive endeavour, different framings are enacted than those of the con because the fakeness is overt. Emphasis is placed on the conceptual meaning created through the copies and their juxtaposition with the originals, as illustrated in the excerpt here:

7   In the context of the globalized art market, today's artists are expanding upon these practices to include having their works produced in China or delegating their production to artisans (Jonathan Monk, Zheng Guogu). Furthermore, various strategies of originality (unlike the work of forgers) reveal the formal differences from one copy to another: such as the choice of the work, the title, the technical medium, the scale (Maurizio Cattelan, Richard Pettibone), the presence or absence of a signature (Karina Bisch). These distinctions, therefore, facilitate the emergence of the second "I" or "author", whether individual or collective, who is gradually recognized and integrated into the history of art.

Drawing on the exhibition blurb, the motives behind such practice are essentially critical, aiming to disrupt either "the linearity of official Western art history discourse" or "the often blind and amnesiac way it operates", thus taking a stand that can be seen as philosophical or political "against the male hegemony of the art world or as critical of the art market mechanisms based on the signature, for example". In the era of digital reproduction these positions are meant as a "death sentence of the sacrosanct idea of unicity", as artists increasingly value the idea of "regeneration" by means of "distant and witty citation", a form of intertextuality ranging "between erudition and free reactivation". In so doing, the exhibition aligns the world of paintings with that of other forms of artistic expression, like cinema and music, where movie remakes or different interpretations of a musical score are widely accepted practices.

As suggested by the words in the previous section, the creative project behind this type of exhibition invites a reassessment of established values and criteria of judgment in the art system, centring around the notion of copy, and hence addressing also those of fake and forgery – once more defining it as "one of the most fascinating and taboo topics in the history of art".

A final case will now be discussed, a case of commercialization of artworks that challenges the tenet of unicity as the seat of value. *The Museum of Forgeries* is the latest project, variously defined as "scheme" or "escapade" (Murphy 2021) by Brooklyn-based art Collective MSCHF who had regularly bought a sketch by Andy Warhol for $20,000, made 999 copies of it, destroyed any record that could tell which the original was, and put the copies and the original on sale for a small amount each, with buyers knowing they had one chance out of 1,000 of acquiring of a real Warhol.

The Museum of Forgery frames this project, what they call their "drop #59" (following a number of other posts published weekly on their website) in the following terms:

8   "Possibly Real Copy Of 'Fairies' by Andy Warhol" is a series of 1000 identical artworks. They are all definitely by MSCHF, and also all possibly by Andy Warhol. Any record of which piece within the set is the original has been destroyed.

A long paratext, which is actually part of the work, explains that the conceptual sense of their overt forgery consists in the destruction through duplication of any "work premised on exclusivity, as a radical form of democratization of ownership".

In this way the MSCF collective positions itself outside the "capital-A Art World" which, they allege, values authenticity far more than aesthetics. They take on the notion of Artwork provenance as nothing more than a "record of ownership, appearances, and sales":

9 By forging Fairies en masse, we obliterate the trail of provenance for the artwork. Though physically undamaged, we destroy any future confidence in the veracity of the work. By burying a needle in a needlestack, we render the original as much a forgery as any of our replications.

From a discursive point of view, the reasoning rests on the reversal of commonly accepted norms. In the first place, forgery is not construed in terms that are limited only to the product of copying but is extended to the original as well. Secondly, words and expressions with a negative connotation are proudly appropriated, as is the case of the collective name MISCHIEF, but also of *destroying confidence in the veracity*. Such an act would normally spark condemnation, but since we cannot assume they mean something bad by means of their affirmative action, the only possible conclusion is that the confidence at issue concerns something which is inherently evil. The otherwise positively connotated notion of "veracity" thus becomes fraught with a negative semantic prosody. Thirdly, the logic according to which copies diminish the artistic value of the original is reversed. While normally it is assumed that "all else being equal, an original is worth more than a copy", they prove that "copies reduce value but increase revenue", as demonstrated in practical terms by the net gain of the Warhol sketch sale, as well as by the following theorem:

10 Paradoxically, for artists, successfully merching down an object = consistent, increased revenue. Posters, prints, or easily replicable derivative works turn an artwork into a product line, and when you hit the big time, product lines tend to be net more profitable than a handful of masterworks.

Finally, they make the oxymoronic claim that "Warhol forgeries are MSCHF originals" and "The copies are ours . . . Fairies, 1954, by Andy Warhol, is a MSCHF artwork", where the author's identity is diluted and becomes collective, extending a trajectory that had its origin and in Warhol's work itself:

11 The copies are ours. More accurately, the entire performance of copying and selling is ours. Not 1000 identical artworks, but a single overarching piece with a thousand co-owners and co-participants. The act of creation is the act of upcycling culture into recombinant forms. Fairies, 1954, by Andy Warhol, is a MSCHF artwork. . . . Warhol and the Factory built toward a mass-production of art, equivalent to consumer goods. The replications we produce extend this trajectory.

MSCHF's drop spurred reactions ranging from slight condemnation to an amused appreciation of the kind reserved for the actions of an *enfant terrible*, with a prevalence of the latter, represented in headlines such as "This Prankster Art Collective Is Making an Elaborate Commentary on Authenticity by Hawking 999 Fake Warhols (Plus One Real One)" or "The Mischief-Makers at MSCHF sell 999 Forged (and 1 real) Warhol Sketches For $250 A Pop, Posted in Design News" (www.printmag.com/about/) and in the opening lines of one of these articles:

12 Professional troublemakers MSCHF are back at it with another one of their schemes, this time targeting the bourgeoisie art world as their latest victim.

While the words *troublemakers, perpetual nose-thumbers*, and *schemes* are negatively connotated and just as negative is being cast as a wrongdoer by describing the target of one's action as "victim", all in all the tone and the context point to the contrary. The reference to the role of "victims" seems actually to play with the primary frame of forgery as crime discussed previously. Featuring on an online magazine of design, which is exactly about the commodification of art and aesthetics, the condemnation cannot be taken too seriously, though, and quite tellingly the piece closes by saying "So what would Warhol himself make of all of this? Well, as a famous iconoclast in his own right, I think he'd be able to handle it". In between, the article explains the Museum of Forgeries meaning as follows:

13 Now, they're selling all 999 forgeries along with the original work for $250 each. The kicker? No one knows which one is the original – not even MSCHF. **And that's the whole point**.

Like all of MSCHF's 59 "drops", *"Museum of Forgeries"* deliberately sets out to spit in the face of the powers that be, preciousness, and exclusivity. The group's co-chief creative officers, Lukas Bentel and Kevin Wiesner, have made it their mission to ruffle the feathers of big brands and poke holes in convention.

MSCHF has already sold out all 1,000 of the "Possible Real Copy of 'Fairies' by Andy Warhol" pieces, meaning they've turned a $230,000 profit, though of course, it was never really about the money. "It's always very funny to do pieces that are able to simultaneously spit in the art world's face, and also do what they're trying to do, which is use art as an investment vehicle, but better". MSCHF is orchestrating a commentary on the money-hungry nature of the high-art world through this stunt, with most collectors purchasing pieces not for their beauty or aesthetic value but for their significance as monetary investment pieces that will appreciate with time.

Other commentators on the MSCHF project emphasise the blurring of the concept of provenance and authenticity, quoting the words of the collective itself "they are all definitely by MSCHF, and also all possibly by Andy Warhol. Any record of which piece within the set is the original has been destroyed" (www.designboom.com/art/mschf-andy-warhol-museum-of-forgeries-10-25-2021/). Or again, "Muddying the waters of authenticity by not telling buyers which of the 1,000 editions is the genuine article, the collective created their fakes using a robotic arm", the challenge to the Art system (Murphy MuseumNext).

Another aspect emphasised in comments about *The museum of forgery* is its technological aspect, set in the frame of robotization of labour:

14 Using digital technology and a robotic arm to recreate Warhol's famous strokes, prior to using a special technique that involves heat, light and humidity to artificially age the piece.
15 Creating a sophisticated forgery workshop that could perfectly replicate the artwork. They built a robot that could draw an identical image to the original that Warhol drew, and went back to chemistry class to create a treatment that would age the sketching paper to appear like it was also from 1954.

This aspect is also addressed in relation to the artistic motives behind the work, drawing connections with Andy Warhol's reflection on the industrialization of artistic creation:

16 Now admittedly, the artistic justification for the *Museum of Forgeries* isn't a bad one. Warhol himself was well documented as being concerned with ideas around the industrialisation of the artistic process and the mass-production of art, even nicknaming his studio *The Factory*.

It was the same problem philosopher Walter Benjamin spent time considering, leading to his 1935 essay, The Work of Art in the Age of Mechanical Reproduction.

Less appreciative comments either link the Warhol project to previous more controversial works by the same collective, one of which earned them a lawsuit from Nike, or underline the expediency of the provocation. In the latter case, though, a sort of balance is sought between the suspicion that the escapade was mostly money-driven with the acknowledgement that there is something to it:

17 The gulf between contemporary art and get-rich-quick schemes seems to be shrinking by the day. Just last month a Danish artist turned in a blank canvas to a gallery after receiving $116,000 to produce an artwork, but this month, the Brooklyn-based art collective MSCHF has created an even more provocative work, involving an Andy Warhol sketch (Kenyon 2021).
18 Possibly Real Copies of "Fairies" by Andy Warhol is as rebellious as it is slick. There are certainly art world stunts that that reek of little more than money-grabbing and faux-iconoclasts, but it feels as though a genuine desire drives this scheme. With every participant being a knowing party in agreement to the terms of a painting of questionable validity, there is truly nobody hurt in MSCHF's use of the trappings of swindlers. In a very large way, they've elevated this piece into being more than a rough sketch by a famous name. They've translated into an idea speaking truth to the contexts by which these forgeries were snatched up, and have hopefully had some in the art world stop to think about the forces that drive this industry (Art Critique 2021).
19 MSCHF is known for doing *things* that are even difficult to define and categorize. remember the NIKE shoes injected with holy water? or the ones that followed that had blood? or this rubber chicken bong that squeaks when you smoke it? yes, everything between hilarious and nihilist (Neira 2021).

5 Conclusions

While fake hardly gets positive press in the realm of the news or in politics, art shows a different path. Starting from positions of sheer condemnation for forgery, framed as fraud, and hence as a crime, in relatively recent times exhibitions have started to appropriate the notion to invite a reflection on art and the art system. The practices are seen here as examples of Goffman's notion of keying, as forms of frame rewriting, so as to change perceptions of a given slice of reality. From a discursive point of view, three frames have been identified, each with its own specific pragmatic organisation, and pointing to different attitudes, ideologies, and epistemological claims. The first frame, a primary frame, represents the orthodoxy according to which forgery is bad. Discursive scripts associated with this are that of crime reports, with the crime as its corollary. In this dichotomical value system, authentic works of art have pride of currency, while forgeries must be removed as stains. This frame is underpinned by an untarnished belief in the practice of the art system, with provenance and authenticity as the repository of value, jointly with the dogma of originality as singularity. The first keying marks a shift in the primary frame, as fake becomes the object of exhibitions. Stark condemnation tones are replaced by a fascination with forgery as a "rogue" affair endowed with an aesthetic value of sorts, with salience placed on details like the amount of the fraud (in financial terms), the prestige of the institution that was victim to the scheme, and the technical skills involved, all elements which increase the appeal of the cultural products thus promoted. The underlying ideological position does not hold forgery as legitimate, thus leaving mostly untouched the mainstream art world belief system, but the choice of exhibiting fakes suggests a repositioning of the museum's role and identity with respect to forgery. Possibly as an effect of the enhanced technological capacity to identify hoaxes, the museum might have an interest in being a step ahead of possible scandals, starting a reflection on forgery, which casts it as a protagonist in the discourse about forgery and not as the victims of fraud.

The second keying marks an even greater shift, with forgery overtly carried out as a critique of the art system logic and as an extension of the reflection started by artists such as Warhol on the role of art in the culture of mass production. Discursive practices revealing the forgery become part of the artistic project, which is not limited to the copies produced from an original but encompasses the channel through which these copies are put on sale and the paratexts there featured. Such a complete rewriting of the forgery frame is met with detached amusement by part of the "critics", especially those close to the world of design, with hints at the expediency of such operations which are very lucrative while "spitting in the face of the system", but also with an appreciation of the motives.

The analysis of discourses about art fakes can be brought to bear on the more general issue of misinformation at two levels. At one level, the paradigm shift in the museum approach to fakes – from hiding to displaying them – suggests that fake news should be brought to the centre of the stage, not just among experts' communities but for the public at large. In practical terms, one way to raise awareness might be for online news outlets to regularly publish real examples of fake news juxtaposed to real news on a similar issue, possibly designing such contents as to make them viral. In this way attention would be attracted to differences between the two texts both in their peripheral features and in the body copy. Going beyond differences that can be detected on the text surface, other aspects that could be exhibited are the backstage factors: how fake news are produced, by whom, through what practices. Attention would thus turn to the context, just as is the case with museums displaying the techniques, the tools, and the lives of forgers. Such an approach would follow in the footsteps of TV shows explaining how things are made, exploiting the audience familiarity with infotainment formats that give viewers a behind-the-scenes look. At another level, a contribution to the debate about misinformation comes from the discussion of *The Museum of Forgeries* project, which was aimed at challenging common wisdom – something art can do very well – about one of the tenets of art dealing, that is, the value of unicity. The condemnation of fake news by all the parties engaged in fighting them has created the implicature that, conversely, all news that is not fake is "good", hence "true". This false impression risks blinding people from realising that a good share of what gets into the news is not objectively verifiable. Commentary first and foremost, but also less conspicuous evaluative elements, as well as news reporting the views of politicians or experts do not belong to the realm of the real but of the preferable, where a propositional content may, at best, be accepted or shared, certainly not verified. In other words, critical thinking, which is about testing the validity of claims, and is therefore key to debunking hoaxes, when brought to the extreme, might even challenge its own tenets and their entailments, thus contributing – through self-reflection – to reducing the bias generated by thought conformity.

Notes

1 There is an ongoing debate in philosophy about the relation between epistemology and art. While aesthetic appreciation of works of art is fundamentally cognitive, questions are raised as to the nature of learning that can come from art. "Is there any sort of propositional content that art can provide which resembles the content that we claim to need for other kinds of knowledge claims?" It is a common claim, though, that we learn from art, that art can change the perception of the world, that "works of art, especially good works of art, can engender beliefs about the world and can, in turn, provide knowledge about the world". Likewise, we know, or claim to know, things about art (we say that a given play was good or bad). We tend to hold in

high respect what critics say about art. Irrespective of nuanced philosophical positions, then, art discourse can be considered to have its own epistemologies. James Fieser, Bradley Dowden, Internet Encyclopedia of Philosophy, Ad vocem "Art and epistemology" https://iep.utm.edu/art-and-epistemology/.

2 From the end of the twentieth century, the term was recast as "creative industries", defined as "those industries which have their origin in individual creativity, skill and talent and which have a potential for wealth and job creation through the generation and exploitation of intellectual property" (DCMS 1998; Flew and Cunningham 2010: 114). Deriving from Adorno and Horkheimer's critical approach to *culture industry* (1944), seen as the mass-oriented commodification of art responding to logics of consumerism and disengagement, the term (modified into cultural industries, to acknowledge the complexity and interconnectivity of the different sectors of cultural production) had by the late 1960s lost its negative connotation (Kong 2014). The view of culture as lost to capitalism was progressively replaced by the idea of culture as a site of tension and struggle within the capitalism frame, with capitalism providing resources and technologies for further development and innovation of the creative process. To ward off the risk of a simple return to Adorno and Horkheimer's pessimistic stance (1944), Kong calls for a more nuanced notion of the creative industries and its potential for cultural development. In the first place, she argues, the all-encompassing term "creative industry" should be abandoned in favour of "cultural industries" that better defines the concept boundaries by emphasising the aesthetic component.

References

Adorno, T. and M. Horkheimer (1944) "The Culture Industry: Enlightenment as Mass Deception," In *Dialectic of Enlightenment*, Translated by John Cumming, 120–167, New York: Seabury.

Art Critique (2021) "MSCHF Sells off 1000 Copies of Andy Warhol's 'Fairies'," 1 November 2021. https://www.art-critique.com/en/2021/11/mschf-sells-off-1000-copies-of-andy-warhols-fairies/)

Bielby, D. (2011) "Staking Claims: Conveying Transnational Cultural Value in a Creative Industry," *The American Behavioral Scientist*, 55(5) 525–540.

Bondi, M. (2016) *Chrononyms in Academic and Popular History*, Bern: Peter Lang.

Bondi, M. (2017) "What Came to be Called: Evaluative What and Authorial Voice in the Discourse of History," *Text & Talk*, 37(1) 25–46.

Coupland, B. and N. Coupland (2014) "The Authenticating Discourses of Mining Heritage Tourism in Cornwall and Wales," *Journal of Sociolinguistics*, 18(4) 495–517.

Coupland, N. and P. Garrett (2010) "Linguistic Landscapes, Discursive Frames and Metacultural Performance: The Case of Welsh Patagonia," *International Journal of the Sociology of Language*, 205 7–36.

DCMS (1998). "Creative Industries Mapping Documents," *Department for Digital, Culture, Media & Sport*, 9 April 1998. www.gov.uk/government/publications/creative-industries-mapping-documents-1998

Entman, R.M. (1993) "Framing: Toward Clarification of a Fractured Paradigm," *Journal of Communication*, 43(4) 51–58.

Fieser, J. and B. Dowden, *Internet Encyclopedia of Philosophy*, Ad Vocem "Art and Epistemology," https://icp.utm.cdu/art-and-epistemology

Flew, T. and S. Cunningham (2010) "Creative Industries After the First Decade of Debate," *The Information Society*, 26(2) 113–123.

France-Presse (2022) "National Museum of Slovenia Cancels Art Exhibition Over Alleged Fakes," *The Guardian*, 10 June 2022. www.theguardian.com/world/2022/jun/10/national-museum-of-slovenia-cancels-art-exhibition-over-alleged-fakes

Goffman, E. (1974) *Frame Analysis: An Essay on the Organization of Experience*, Cambridge, MA: Harvard University Press.

Goffman, E. (1981) *Forms of Talk (Conduct and Communication)*, Oxford: Blackwell.

Goffman, E. (1986) *Frame Analysis. An Essay on the Organization of Experience*, Boston: Northeastern University Press.

Kenyon, N. (2021) "How to Make $300,000 with a Real Andy Warhol Artwork (and 999 Forgeries)", 26 October 2021. https://www.bosshunting.com.au/hustle/mschf-warhol-forgeries/

Knudsen, S. (2017) "Thinking Inside the Frame: A Framing Analysis of the Humanities in Danish Print News Media," *Public Understanding of Science*, 26(8) 908–924.

Kong, L. (2014) "From Cultural Industries to Creative Industries and Back? Towards Clarifying Theory and Rethinking Policy," *Inter-Asia Cultural Studies*, 15(4) 593–607.

McGreevy, N. (2020) "Why a German Museum is Displaying Fake Paintings From its Collections. A Taboo-Breaking Exhibition at Cologne's Museum Ludwig Spotlights Misattributed Russian Avant-garde Works," *Smitsonians Magazine*, 26 October 2020. www.smithsonianmag.com/smart-news/new-light-shed-fake-paintings-taboo-breaking-exhibition-180976130/2020

Murphy, A. (2021) "Museum of Forgeries Fakes 999 Warhol's to Sell with Original," 28 October 2021. www.museumnext.com/article/museum-of-forgeries-fakes-999-warhols-to-sell-with-original/

Neira, J. (2021) "MSCHF's possible real copy of 'fairies' by Andy Warhol", 25 October 2021. https://www.designboom.com/art/mschf-andy-warhol-museum-of-forgeries-10-25-2021/

Pittaway, B. (1999) "Forger to the Reich," *The Guardian*, 25 August 1999. www.theguardian.com/culture/1999/aug/25/artsfeatures3

Rechtshaffen, M. (2021) "'Made You Look: A True Story about Fake Art,' A Fascinating $80 Million Con," *Los Angeles Times*, 23 February 2021. www.latimes.com/entertainment-arts/movies/story/2021-02-23/review-made-you-look-true-story-fake-art

Tseng, M.Y. (2018) "Where Cultural References and Lexical Cohesion Meet: Toward a Multi-Layer Framing Analysis," *Pragmatics*, 28(4) 573–597.

Wolff, J. (1981) *The Social Production of Art*, London: Red Globe Press.

355

C. Medical discourses

22
EXPLORING HEALTH-RELATED MISINFORMATION, DISINFORMATION AND "FAKE NEWS"

Roxanne H. Padley

Introduction to "fake news"

Spreading incorrect information through media channels is not a new phenomenon; however, in recent times the term "fake news" has garnered a great deal of attention from a variety of scholars due to the wide-reaching impact that it can have on public opinion. "Fake news" can be identified on any topic and is most certainly more impactful in this day and age with the prevalence and accessibility to Internet as well as social networks. The term was first coined in 1925 in an article in *Harper's Magazine* whose title was "Fake News and the Public" (McKernon, 1925). The essence of the article was that of begrudging the way in which news wires allowed misinformation to spread with such haste, which remains the key issue with "fake news" today, albeit on a much larger scale.

The turning point in "fake news" dissemination can most certainly be linked to the modern digitalised era whereby intentional or unintentional misleading information spreads over the Internet at an uncontrolled rate and with little governance (Wang et al., 2019). Indeed, in 2013 the World Economic Forum described this viral misinformation spread as a series of "digital wildfires" that were extremely difficult to mitigate or extinguish (Howell, 2013; World Economic Forum, 2013). Further interest into the impact of misinformation in the news also grew following the 2016 American presidential elections whereby Donald Trump used the term "fake news" repeatedly throughout his electoral campaign to refer to any news story which was not to his liking. Indeed, rather than applying the term to news stories which had been verified as being misleading or incorrect, the term was used for any news story which Trump wanted to discredit and dismiss (Hunt & Gentzkow, 2017). This communicative strategy was likened to using the term "fake news" for reasons of propaganda and which has also been replicated by other politicians since, with success, such as Bolsonaro (BBC, 2018).

The very nature of the digital era and the possibility for news stories to be spread through numerous channels and mediums of course means that "fake news" related to topics of health is by no means exempt. Indeed, stories which provide non-verified and inexact information are rife and published on a variety of topics, such as vaccinations, cancer, and heart disease, to name but a few. Wang et al. (2019) posit that the most widely diffused "fake news" stories regarding health are in fact related to vaccinations offering scare stories and the like with little or no scientific grounding (e.g. the correlation between autism and the measles, mumps, and rubella vaccination) or

 DOI: 10.4324/9781003224495-27

interpreting scientific publications with a different optic (Padley, 2022). The impact of such stories can be wide reaching and ultimately could impact on people's health with direct consequences, including delaying or preventing effective care.

Defining terminology

Prior to delving further into the ways in which health misinformation exists and impacts on health-care systems and provision on the whole, it is worthwhile clearly delineating the key terminology and its use. The overarching term "fake news" can be considered as problematic, especially following the 2016 presidential elections and its use for signifying any news which is not welcomed, that is, it does not support somebody's beliefs, regardless of its validity (Lazer et al., 2018; Vosoughi et al., 2018). Indeed, "fake news" is generally understood to mean news which is untrue and factually unsound (Ormond et al., 2016). However, there is a certain amount of ambiguity surrounding the term (Molina et al., 2021), and it is suggested that there is no current true consensus on the actual meaning of "fake news" (Rahmanian, 2022), and it cannot solely be considered to mean untruthful news.

Rahmanian's (2022) investigation into the reasons why "fake news" can be problematic to define point to several motivations for consideration of other terminology as more appropriate (depending on the intended meaning of the speaker/writer). There are a number of studies which consider "fake news" to signify simply untruthful information (Ormond et al., 2016; Levy, 2017), which would appear to be the immediate and most common perception of "fake news". Indeed, Rahmanian's (2022) study indicates that this is far too simplistic as this implies that any untrue information (including false satirical jokes) could be considered as "fake news" (Quandt et al., 2019). Thus, the intentionality behind the news story must also be taken into account (Wardle & Derakhshan, 2017) as this aids in ascertaining if a news story has intentionally been created to deceive the reader or the information provided is unintentionally incorrect.

Further to the point of intentionality, some scholars categorise "fake news" as being directly related to the intention of deceiving and that it must be entirely fabricated (Montgomery & Gray, 2017; Allcott & Gentzkow, 2017; Lazer et al., 2018). On that premise, "fake news" can only be perceived as having been created for malicious purposes and certainly does not take stock of the interpretation which was applied to it during the US 2016 presidential elections, nor does it consider that the news story may be unintentionally incorrect (Rahmanian, 2022).

Therefore, considering such ambiguity, the other key terms related to incorrect news online, and which will be adopted henceforth, are misinformation, disinformation, and malinformation. The former is understood to intend any information provided which is inexact or vague in nature with some level of untruth (Cooke, 2018), while disinformation is falsified news which is intended to be so and is deliberately misleading (Shin et al., 2018; Weiss et al., 2020), and malinformation is information which is disseminated with the intention to cause harm and may include taking private information out of context and into the public sphere (Wardle & Derakhshan, 2017). Indeed, this distinction is significant as it aids in clarifying available online information and whether the information is inadvertently incorrect (misinformation) or intentionally so (disinformation or possibly malinformation) with the aim to cause harm and confusion (Howell, 2013).

Misinformation and disinformation through the ages

Misinformation has been used through the ages for a variety of reasons ranging from propaganda to marketing as well as malicious intent. Some of the first examples of misinformation date back to Roman times in 63 BC when Roman Emperor Augustus Octavian developed a slander campaign against Marc Antony by having slogans written on coins in order to slur his reputation (Kaminska, 2017). Other historical examples date back to the fifteenth century when a Franciscan preacher in Italy blamed a Jewish community for a missing child leading to a series of unfounded arrests and torturing of the accused (Soll, 2016) as the message travelled by word of mouth. The sixteenth and seventeenth centuries instead saw the invention and wide use of the printing press, which of course made it possible to disseminate news on a wider scale. However, a fixed feature of the newspapers at the time were the gossip columns, which were often considered as real news and, as such, an example of misinformation or even disinformation when involving more personal details (Common Sense Education, 2017).

An example of the first news hoax disseminated can be identified in 1835 with an article in the *New York Sun*, which later became known as *The Great Moon Hoax*. The paper published a story, complete with illustrations, stating that life had been identified on the moon, and the creatures depicted included bearded blue unicorns and humanoid bat creatures (Thornton, 2000). Finally, more recently in the twentieth century, there was a fake story in 1915 regarding a Corpse Factory in Germany, which was later discovered to be untrue and of course the Nazi propaganda which was rife between 1933 and 1945. In the latter case the Nazi propagandist Joseph Goebbels founded his own newspaper titled *The Attack* specifically to spread lies and malinformation in order to support the Nazi regime (Common Sense Education, 2017). Indeed, the line between disinformation and propaganda is often rather blurred.

As regards historical health misinformation, one of the most prolific examples of misinformation as well as disinformation is the AIDS epidemic which began in the 1980s and led to a series of discriminatory beliefs and behaviours towards homosexuals. The fear which was created around the AIDS epidemic, founded on lack of knowledge and understanding as well as false reports, led many to believe that HIV could be contracted through simply touching an infected person (Cope, 2022). The lack of correct information available along with the abundance of misinformation on the topic had a direct impact on increasing discrimination against homosexuals, leading directly to stringent restrictions and impacting on their access to adequate healthcare assistance (Price & Hsu, 1992).

There was also a prolific case of misinformation which resulted in unjustly laying the blame for the entire AIDS epidemic in the USA on one man, namely, Gaétan Dugas. Dugas was wrongly labelled as patient zero due to his job as a flight attendant and his presumed promiscuity in different continents (Compagnon, 2020). In reality, this news was disseminated due to the letter "O" on his patient records being assigned to his case meaning "out of California". However, this was never clarified in news stories, and he was branded as THE MAN WHO GAVE US AIDS by the *New York Post* in 1987. Even following his death from the disease, there were various resurgences of the story and the blame repeatedly placed on his shoulders (Compagnon, 2020). However, in the case of the AIDS epidemic, some of these negative effects were counteracted by the very public figure, Princess Diana, who campaigned in order to raise awareness about the disease as well as combatting stigma by demonstrating empathy and physical contact with AIDS patients (Cope, 2022). Therefore, her actions were able to influence the beliefs of others and in some way counteract the negative effects.

Information spread

In the previous section, there was mention of the role that people's beliefs play in terms of misinformation and how it is received and thus consequently disseminated. Wang et al. (2019) cite Wardle and Derakhshan's (2017) study as fundamental in comprehending the mechanisms which underpin how misinformation is interpreted and processed. Their study points to three important elements which contribute to the creation, production, and sharing (and resharing) of misinformation, that is, the agent, the messenger, and the interpreter. The agent is the body who creates the news article for whatever purpose (be it for innocent purposes or malicious ones – mis/disinformation creation), while the messenger is the medium chosen in order to share the news content (usually online or through social media). Finally, the interpreter is the person who reads the message and makes their own judgement as to whether they believe the message or not and hence may choose to share it or otherwise.

Thus, the information is managed on both a micro and macro level. The micro level directly involves the psychological concept of belief in the source and trusting its credibility, and works very much on the basis that spreading rumours does (Allport & Postman, 1947). Indeed, Allport and Postman's (1947) study was considered a breakthrough in social psychology as it investigated how rumours spread during World War II and what the impact of these may have been on national security. Therefore, the propagation of misinformation which starts on an individual level, that is, through the interpretation and "acceptance" of the news story they are receiving, which is then passed on either by word of mouth (as with traditional news spreading) or online (as with more modern practice) is comparable to the social phenomenon of rumour spreading. The interpreter of the message may indeed be unaware that they are disseminating mis/disinformation as they believe what they are sharing to be true. This behaviour can of course have grave consequences in many fields but is even more relevant in terms of disseminating health information.

The macro level of misinformation spreading instead is a direct consequence of the micro interpretation. Once the information has been accepted as credible by the receiver (Metzger, 2007), the Internet allows for the news to spread and cascade (through instant accessibility and sharing). The effects of the digital wildfire (Howell, 2013) are immense and relentless, and the impact can be wide reaching. Indeed, the entire way in which social media works enables and encourages the propagation of viral stories (true or otherwise) due to specifically designed algorithms which propose and repropose news articles based on users' search history and preferences (Giansiracusa, 2021). Therefore, if one person searches for a particular piece of information regarding a disease or health issue, there is a possibility that they may come across misinformation, based on their search history, as well as viral stories which circulate. This characteristic is particularly significant during health epidemics and pandemics as the mis/disinformation which is available online may have lasting consequences on effective healthcare, as will be explored in the next section.

An overview of misinformation and health

Within the realm of healthcare, there is an array of misinformation available on a variety of topics which range from vaccinations, cancer, heart disease, other infectious diseases such as Zika and Ebola, the use of stem cells, abortion, and more recently of course the SARS-CoV-2 pandemic. The extent of misinformation regarding vaccinations is extensive and will be addressed in the next section, as will the misinformation regarding vaccinations during the COVID-19 pandemic. This section instead will therefore delineate other types of common misinformation related to health, providing some examples.

The number of articles available online which contain misinformation is so extensive that members of the scientific community feel compelled to counter this information with further publications (Wang et al., 2019). In fact, much of the misinformation which is proposed online and on social media cites scientific articles as the basis of their evidence and often comes about due to the demand for specialised information by the general public, which in turn, can then be wrongly interpreted leading to misinformation (Maci, 2019). Thus, the scientific community may repropose publications offering clarifications which aim to debunk the myths, and so the cycle continues.

Wang et al. (2019) proposed a very comprehensive review of a number of these clarification articles, and the topics have been categorised into Table 22.1.

As can be seen in the table, the highest frequency of articles clarifying misinformation refers to the category of infectious diseases (which also incorporates news related to vaccinations). This is then followed by a miscellaneous group and topics of general health and then cancer, cardiovascular disease, diet and nutrition, and smoking with the same number of hits followed by water safety/quality.

An example of fake news and infectious diseases include both the Zika virus and the Ebola outbreak. The Zika outbreak was first announced in 2016 and was mainly geographically located in Brazil. Shortly after the World Health Organisation's (WHO) announcement, a number of conspiracy theories were generated and circulated the Internet via social media, namely, Twitter (Wood, 2018) and Facebook (Sharma et al., 2017) and related theories, such as the creation of genetically modified mosquitoes, which could also be used as a bioweapon. The Ebola outbreak saw a similar reaction on social media, but in this case was the focus of rumours online regarding treatment speculation as well as misguiding videos, which were issued by influencers with a high number of followers (Pathak et al., 2015).

In terms of misinformation regarding cancer, one of the key sources of misinformation regarding screening, diagnosis, and treatment is YouTube, where there are numerous videos offering "expert advice" which have been proven to be unsound in terms of scientific rigor (Loeb et al., 2019). This is another instance of users searching for specialised information but coming across information which may be either inexact or vague in nature, often leading to a low rate of reliability and a high rate of misinformation or vague information.

The use of stem cells for medical purposes and treatments is another relatively controversial topic which has often been the focus of misinformation as well as conspiracy theories. Indeed, the very nature of obtaining stem cells has automatically garnered opposition, and it is often these opponents who generate imprecise information online (Marcon et al., 2017). Finally, a more recent example of misinformation is the correlation between having an abortion and higher rates of breast cancer. The topic of the right to an abortion has been extremely prevalent in the news in recent times, particularly following the decision of some states in the United States to revoke the right to an abortion (Center for Reproductive Rights, 2022). Indeed, politicians who advocated such a

Table 22.1 Table of scientific studies published in medical journals between 2012 and 2018 addressing issues of misinformation according to type

Table of scientific studies addressing misinformation (2012–2018)	
Type of Health Issue	*Number (%)*
Infectious Diseases	30 (53%)
Others	8 (14%)
General Health	5 (9%)
Cancer	3 (5%)
Cardiovascular Disease	3 (5%)
Diet and Nutrition	3 (5%)
Smoking	3 (5%)
Water Safety/Quality	2 (4%)

Sources: Data sourced from Wang et al., (2019)

move were also heard citing the connection between breast cancer and abortion as a motivating factor. In reality, there is no scientific proof of such a link, and this misinformation was widely propagated in the meantime (Kitchen et al., 2005).

The impact of misinformation regarding health information is significant and wide reaching. Having access to and a proper understanding of health information improves health outcomes in general (World Health Organisation, 2013). If an individual already has a doubt about a particular health issue, the misinformation which is available online may go some way to validating this doubt and lead the information seeker to believe that piece of information rather than the facts, leading to what is known as confirmation bias (Hart et al., 2009), that is, interpreting information in order to affirm our pre-existing beliefs. This concept will be explored in more detail in the following section regarding vaccinations and, in particular, with regard to the COVID-19 pandemic.

Vaccination information frenzy

Information regarding vaccinations is extremely prolific and can be traced back even soon after its introduction in the nineteenth century following Edward Jenner's work. Indeed, the introduction of the *Vaccination Act* (1849–1898) in the UK soon led very quickly to resistance to vaccinations as it was perceived as being a violation of civil liberty (Maci, 2019). This in turn led to different kinds of information dissemination (the first instances of vaccination misinformation) and indeed an anti-vaccination movement commenced. Similar situations also played out in the USA, and despite serious smallpox outbreaks, it was impossible to impose any sort of vaccination mandate (Maci, 2019).

In modern times, anti-vaccination campaigns remain rife, and the 1990s saw an insurgence of stories related to the measles, mumps, and rubella (MMR) vaccination and its potential correlation with autism as well as bowel disease (Wakefield et al., 1998). The study was in fact published in *the Lancet*, which is a prestigious medical journal with an Impact Factor of 202 (at the time of writing). The publication has since been retracted as fellow medics and scientists proved the findings to be unfounded and essentially unsubstantiated. In this case, the misinformation was unwittingly provided by a peer-reviewed scientific journal and, as such, remained even more difficult to debunk as nonfactual. In fact, a search online for vaccinations linked with autism produces an array of articles, which would appear to be founded on truths, and for those who are dubious about vaccinations can serve just the purpose to confirm their bias and opt not to have a vaccination.

Misinformation regarding vaccinations is certainly no exception as regards its proliferation online. In fact, several studies report a high prevalence of MMR vaccinations and autism-related topics online even today (Basch et al., 2017; Donzelli et al., 2018; Porat et al., 2018), despite the original publication having been discredited and retracted. Other topics related to vaccinations which would appear to be very popular online are those related to misinformation regarding side effects as well as mistrust in the government and institutions on the whole (Tustin et al., 2018). Another important factor related to vaccinations was investigated by Krishna et al. (2017), who investigated the type of user who would search and propagate misinformation. The study found that the majority of the propagators were greatly lacking in knowledge regarding vaccines (the MMR vaccine in particular) and that those who adhered to anti-vaccine campaigns were much more active in online searches and, hence, sharing the information found.

Linguistic investigations into vaccination discourses online also revealed the extent to which misinformation is truly widespread and engrained within online communication and spread by those who are either dubious or entirely against vaccinations. Maci (2019) demonstrated the ways in which Twitter is used for the dissemination of misinformation through a corpus linguistic and multimodal investigation. Her work concludes that much of the information available on Twitter is claimed to be constructed on scientific information and provides accessible and comprehensible language. Parents have important decisions to make regarding vaccinations, which are influenced greatly by their online research, and vaccinations on the whole are perceived as cognitively dangerous. She highlights the need for digital-health literacy to be increased in order for misinformation to be curbed and correctly interpreted, which is a crucial point, shared by the scientific community, in having an impact on debunking false health information (Bin Naeem & Kamel Boulos, 2021).

The UK-based research group, the European and Social Research Council (ERSC) Centre for Corpus Approaches to Social Science (CASS) based at the University of Lancaster has also launched a research project into vaccination discourses, namely, the Quo VaDis project (Quo VaDis). Their main aim is to investigate the ways in which vaccinations are written or spoken about in different contexts and to explore the concerns related to this. While they do not investigate misinformation directly, one of their recent studies demonstrates the extent to which vaccinations can be considered as a very heated topic of debate (Coltman-Patel et al., 2022). Indeed, in this study they also used corpus linguistic methodologies to investigate the discussion of vaccinations on the Mumsnet Talk forum, and one of their findings is that there is a high incidence of insults and conflict evident in these discourses, which confirms the level of controversy and disagreement which has plagued vaccinations since their introduction. Their study also highlighted how forums are considered as a reliable source for users seeking information about vaccinations, which was also supported by Campbell et al.'s (2017) survey, stating that 29% of parents use the website in order to garner information about vaccinations.

While the debate and discussion surrounding vaccinations has been ongoing for more than a century, the arrival of the SARS-CoV-2 pandemic definitively renewed the debate surrounding vaccinations and amplified the amount of misinformation which was available online. Indeed, the Oxford English Dictionary named the word *vax* as their word of the year in 2021 (Oxford University Press, 2021). Vaccine hesitancy was quickly identified as a key issue in fighting to contain the pandemic (Lee et al., 2022), and thus one of the subsequent challenges was also that of the effect of misinformation in increasing such hesitancy.

Padley (2022) carried out a fieldwork investigation into the narratives surrounding individuals who were in favour of the COVID-19 vaccines and those who were not. The context of this study was also particularly important as the investigation compared the experiences of the UK and Italy. The latter nation had introduced the vaccination passport (namely, the Green Pass), which essentially served as a pseudo vaccine mandate due to the restrictions which were placed on the citizens who did not have a Green Pass, the so-called *No-Vax*. The conclusions of the study pointed to a certain degree of discrimination towards the non-vaccinated individuals (despite the obvious benefits of a blanket vaccination campaign) but also highlighted how the individuals who were against having the vaccination interpreted official sources of information in order to confirm their own biases and justify their choices (Hart et al., 2009).

The digital effect and the infodemic

The role of the Internet has been mentioned several times throughout this chapter, and its significance in the role it plays regarding misinformation cannot be underestimated. Indeed, the influence of online communication continues to rise, and thus, in turn, so does the complexity level of health-information that healthcare practitioners and communication experts disclose on the web (Sundar et al., 2011). Therefore, this constantly draws into question the concepts of the source of information and the credibility of the information available. These two terms have now become more fluid, and therefore healthcare information which is made available online also needs to take this into account (Sundat & Nass, 2011).

Prior to the extensive use of the Internet, a source of information was much easier to pinpoint as it was more of a physical entity. Currently, a source could be considered the original source (i.e. the words that the doctor used) and then secondary sources are those which take the doctor's words and rework them into an article, which may then be shared and shared again (Sundar et al., 2011). The difficulty in being able to identify the original source can therefore also call into question the credibility of the information. Credibility in relation to the source information has now become much more complicated to evaluate and thus easily renders itself vulnerable to becoming classified as vague or indeed misinformation (Sundar et al., 2011).

Further to the issues with pinpointing the reliability of the information found online, another issue which is leading to an increased amount of healthcare misinformation is the *infodemic*. The *infodemic* is the presence of far too much information, which includes false information, and which makes it much more difficult for the Internet user to distinguish between reliable sources of information and also to find the desired information in general (World Health Organisation, 2020). Indeed, the abundance of information available in the form of an *infodemic* played a key role during the COVID-19 pandemic. The aim of using the Internet was to keep people informed, safe, and up to date on developments during the pandemic, but the deliberate dissemination of disinformation during the pandemic led to a lack of trust in institutions, in some cases, with direct consequences to life (World Health Organisation, 2020). Furthermore, it enflamed public debate regarding COVID-19 topics and amplified hate speech and conflict both in person and online.

Finally, another key digital source of misinformation related to healthcare information is that of videos made available on YouTube. Indeed, the World Health Organisation (2022) stated that the incorrect interpretation of healthcare information negatively affects people's behaviour and can even impact on their mental health. Taking the pandemic as a case in point, the videos made available on YouTube were directly associated with the spread of misinformation but, what is more, is that the comments section below the videos were also found to influence users' behaviour and in turn potentially undermine public policy (Suter et al., 2022). Therefore, the digital effect can be said to be the main culprit behind the current day spread of misinformation.

Countering misinformation and patient literacy: friend or foe

The abundance of health information available online means that patients themselves are transforming into experts, and the vertical hierarchy of knowledge gatekeeping is now reducing due to patients becoming more literate (Sundar et al., 2011). Indeed, the ways in which patients are able to demonstrate their expertise within the online realm varies, and Ancker et al. (2009) proposed four dimensions of behaviour influence in peer communication online: information, emotional support, instrumental support, and peer modelling. The implications of the expert patient's presence online could be interpreted as a double-edged sword. On the one hand, the patients become a valid source of information for other Internet users, and their health literacy can also help to increase that of others, while on the other hand misconceived interpretation of health information can also be easily disseminated and believed to be true by others. Furthermore, the possibilities for either correct or incorrect information to be shared among peers are endless and could take place via forums, tags, comments, as well as links to other links and so on. While these features likely provide a sense of control and even community to the users, in terms of misinformation spread in these informal contexts, there is little or no governance (Sundar et al., 2011).

Therefore, the question arises as to what the most appropriate measures are in order to mitigate misinformation in health information. The World Health Organisation (2022) recognises that the first step is that of fully understanding the role of the Internet and, in particular, social media when it comes to the spread of misinformation. Indeed, the WHO recognises that the fast spread of false information via social media can lead to opinion polarisation, escalating fear and panic as well as decreased access to health care. The erroneous interpretation of scientific knowledge is often the culprit and thus the WHO report proposes "developing legal policies . . . and promoting awareness campaigns, improving health-related content in mass media and increasing people's digital and health literacy". The identification of figures who are best placed to counter misinformation is fundamental, and the WHO report identifies that those who are best suited are indeed experts and healthcare professionals. Therefore, in order for there to be any improvement in the governance of misinformation, local, national, and international mitigation policies would be necessary in order to address the issue on such a large scale.

Conclusions

This chapter served to outline some of the major issues related to misinformation both in a broad sense and also in terms of the consequences to people's health. The digitalised era means that the various different mediums through which misinformation spread are almost ungovernable and, regardless of future policies which may be put in place, it is the personal interpretation of the information which will make the difference as to whether the misinformation can be identified or otherwise. Indeed, in terms of future mitigation strategies, it could be argued that the most effective one is likely to be that of increasing the user's digital health literacy in general in order to be able to gain the necessary tools to recognise misinformation. While further research into this area would be beneficial in order to better understand the mechanisms which underpin misinformation propagation, it is posited that another effective solution is raising awareness of the dangers of health misinformation and aiming to counter as many of the digital wildfires as possible. In this way, user health-literacy would most likely increase, and in turn the number of false news stories which circulate may indeed decrease.

References

Allcott, H. & Gentzkow, M. (2017). Social media and fake news in the 2016 election. *Journal of Economic Perspectives*, 31(2): 211–236.

Allport, G. W. & Postman, L. (1947). *The Psychology of Rumor*. Oxford: New World Publisher.

Ancker, J. S., Carpenter, K. M., Greene, P., Hoffman, R., Kukafka, R., Marlo, L. A. V. & Quillin, J. M. (2009). Peer-to-peer communication, cancer prevention and the Internet. *Journal of Health Communication*, 14: 38–46.

Basch, C. H., Zybert, P., Reeves, R. & Basch, C. E. (2017). What do popular YouTubeTM videos say about vaccines? *Child Care Health Development*, 43(4): 499–503.

BBC. (2018). How President Trump took 'fake news' into the mainstream. *BBC News*. Retrieved from: www.bbc.com/news/av/world-us-canada-46175024

Bin Naeem, S. & Kamel Boulos, M. N. (2021). COVID-19 misinformation online and health literacy: A brief overview. *International Journal of Environmental Research and Public Health*, 18(15): 8091.

Campbell, H., Edwards, A., Letley, L., Bedford, H., Ramsay, M. & Yarwood, J. (2017). Changing attitudes to childhood immunisation in English parents. *Vaccine*, 35(22): 2979–2985.

Center for Reproductive Rights. (2022). *After Roe Fell: Abortion Laws by State*. Retrieved from: https://reproductiverights.org/maps/abortion-laws-by-state/

Coltman-Patel, T., Dance, W., Demjén, Z., Gatherer, D., Hardaker, C. & Semino, E. (2022). 'Am I being unreasonable to vaccinate my kids against my ex's wishes?' – A corpus linguistic exploration of conflict in vaccination discussions on Mumsnet Talk's AIBU forum. *Discourse, Context & Media*, 48: 100624.

Common Sense Education. (2017). *Fake News: Historical Timeline*. Retrieved from: https://www.common-sense.org/sites/default/files/pdf/2017-08/newsmedialit-fakenewstimeline-85x11.pdf

Compagnon, M. (2020). AIDS, from the perspective of "Patient Zero." *JSTOR Daily*. Retrieved from: https://daily.jstor.org/aids-from-the-perspective-of-patient-zero/

Cooke, N. (2018). *Fake News and Alternative Facts: Information Literacy in a Post-Truth Era*. Chicago: ALA Editions.

Cope, R. (2022). How Diana, Princess of Wales was instrumental in trying to stop the stigma against HIV/AIDs. *Tatler*. Retrieved from: www.tatler.com/article/princess-diana-hiv-aids-awareness

Donzelli, G., Palomba, G., Federigi, I., Aquino, F., Cioni, L., Verani, M. & Lopalco, P. (2018). Misinformation on vaccination: A quantitative analysis of YouTube videos. *Human Vaccines & Immunotherapeutics*, 14(7): 1654–1659.

Giansiracusa, N. (2021). *How Algorithms Create and Prevent Fake News*. Berkeley, CA: Apress.

Hart, W., Albarracín, D., Eagly, A. H., Brechan, I., Lindberg, M. J. & Merrill, L. (2009). Feeling validated versus being correct: A meta-analysis of selective exposure to information. *Psychological Bulletin*, 135(4): 555–588.

Howell, L. (2013). Digital wildfires in a hyper connected world. *WEF Report*, 3: 15–94.

Hunt, A. & Matthew Gentzkow, M. (2017). Social media and fake news in the 2016 election. *Journal of Economic Perspectives*, 31(2): 211–236.

Kaminska, I. (2017). A module in fake news from the info-wars of ancient Rome. *Financial Times*. Retrieved from: www.ft.com/content/aaf2bb08-dca2-11e6-86ac-f253db7791c6

Kitchen, A. J., Trivedi, P., Ng, D. & Mokbel, K. (2005). Is there a link between breast cancer and abortion: A review of the literature. *International Journal of Fertility and Women's Medicine*, 50(6): 267–271.

Krishna, A. (2017) Motivation with misinformation: Conceptualizing lacuna individuals and publics as knowledge-deficient, issue-negative activists. *Journal of Public Relations Research*, 29(4): 176–193.

Lazer, D. M. J., Baum, M. A., Benkler, Y., Berinsky, A. J., Greenhill, K. M., Menczer, F. & Zittrain, J. L. (2018). The science of fake news. *Science*, 359(6380): 1094–1096.

Lee, S. K., Sun, J., Jang, S. & Connelly, S. (2022). Misinformation of COVID-19 vaccines and vaccine hesitancy. *Scientific Reports*, 12(1): 13681.

Levy, N. (2017). The bad news about fake news. *Social Epistemology Review and Reply Collective*, 6(8): 20–36.

Loeb, S., Sengupta, S., Butaney, M., Macaluso, J. N., Jr, Czarniecki, S. W., Robbins, R., Braithwaite, R. S., Gao, L., Byrne, N., Walter, D. & Langford, A. (2019). Dissemination of misinformative and biased information about prostate cancer on YouTube. *European Urology*, 75(4): 564–567.

Maci, S. (2019). Discourse strategies of fake news in the anti-vax campaign. In Garzone, G. E., Paganoni, M. C. & Reisigl, M. Discursive Representations of Controversial Issues in Medicine and Health. *Languages Cultures Mediation*, 6(1): 15–44.

Marcon, A. R., Murdoch, B. & Caulfield, T. (2017). Fake news portrayals of stem cells and stem cell research. *Regenerative Medicine*, 12(7): 765–775.

McKernon, E. (1925). Fake news and the public. *Harper's Magazine*. Retrieved from: https://harpers.org/archive/1925/10/fake-news-and-the-public/

Metzger, M. J. (2007). Making sense of credibility on the Web: Models for evaluating online information and recommendations for future research. *Journal of the Association for Information Science and Technology*, 58(13): 2078–2091.

Molina, M. D., Sundar, S. S., Le, T. & Lee, D. (2021). Fake news is not simply false information: A concept explication and taxonomy of online content. *American Behavioral Scientist*, 65(2): 180–212.

Montgomery, L. & Gray, B. (2017). Information veracity and the threat of fake news. In Matarazzo, J. M. and Pearlstein, T. (Eds) *The Emerald Handbook of Modern Information Management*. Bingley: Emerald Publishing Limited, 409–435.

Ormond, D., Warkentin, M., Johnston, A. C. & Thompson, S. C. (2016), Perceived deception: Evaluating source credibility and self-efficacy. *Journal of Information Privacy and Security*, 12(4): 197–217.

Oxford University Press. (2021). *Oxford Languages Word of the Year 2021*. Retrieved from: https://languages.oup.com/word-of-the-year/2021/

Padley, R. H. (2022). Information channels and narratives: To vaccinate or not to vaccinate, that is the question. *Altre Modernità*, 28: 194–216.

Pathak, R., Poudel, D. R., Karmacharya, P., Pathak, A., Aryal, M. R., Mahmood, M. & Donato, A. A. (2015). YouTube as a source of information on Ebola virus disease. *North American Journal of Medical Sciences*, 7(7): 306–309.

Porat, T., Garaizar, P., Ferrero, M., Jones, H., Ashworth, M. & Vadillo, M. A. (2018). Content and source analysis of popular tweets following a recent case of diphtheria in Spain. *European Journal of Public Health*, 29(1): 117–122.

Price, V. & Hsu, M. L. (1992). Public opinion about AIDS policies. The role of misinformation and attitudes toward homosexuals. *Public Opinion Quarterly*, 56(1): 29–52.

Quandt, T., Frischlich, L., Boberg, S. & Schatto-Eckrodt, T. (2019). Fake news. In *International Encyclopedia of Journalism Studies*. Hoboken, NJ: John Wiley & Sons, 1–6.

Quo VaDis. *Questioning Vaccination Discourse*. Retrieved from: www.lancaster.ac.uk/vaccination-discourse/about/

Rahmanian, E. (2022). Fake news: A classification proposal and a future research agenda. *Spanish Journal of Marketing*, 27(1): 60–78.

Sharma, M., Yadav, K., Yadav, N. & Ferdinand, K. C. (2017). Zika virus pandemic-analysis of Facebook as a social media health information platform. *American Journal of Infection Control*, 45(3): 301–302.

Shin, J., Jian, L., Driscoll, K. & Bar, F. (2018). The diffusion of misinformation on social media: Temporal pattern, message, and source. *Computers in Human Behavior*, 83: 278–287.

Soll, J. (2016). The long and brutal history of fake news. *Politico Magazine*. Retrieved from: www.politico.com/magazine/story/2016/12/fake-news-history-long-violent-214535/

Sundar, S. S., Rice, R. E., Kim, H. S. & Sciamanna, C. N. (2011). Online health information. Conceptual challenges and theoretical opportunities. In Thompson, T. L., Parrott, R. & Nussbaum, J. F. (Eds) *The Routledge Handbook of Health Communication*. Milton Park: Taylor & Francis, 181–202.

Sundat, S. S. & Nass, C. (2001). Conceptualizing sources in online news. *Journal of Communication*, 51: 52–72.

Suter, V., Shahrezaye, M. & Meckel, M. (2022). COVID-19 induced misinformation on YouTube: An analysis of user commentary. *Frontiers*, 4: 849763.

Thornton, B. (2000). The Moon Hoax: Debates about ethics in 1835 New York newspapers, *Journal of Mass Media Ethics*, 15(2): 89–100.

Tustin, J. L., Crowcroft, N. S., Gesink, D., Johnson, I., Keelan, J. & Lachapelle, B. (2018). User-driven comments on a Facebook advertisement recruiting canadian parents in a study on immunization: Content analysis. *JMIR Public Health and Surveillance*, 4(3): e10090.

Vosoughi, S., Roy, D. & Aral, S. (2018). The spread of true and false news online. *Science*, 359(6380): 1146–1151.

Wakefield, A. J., Murch, S. H., Anthony, A., Linnell, J., Casson, D. M., Malik, M., Berelowitz, M., Dhillon, A. P., Thomson, M. A., Harvey, P., Valentine, A., Davies, S. E. & Walker-Smith, J. A. (1998). Ileal-lymphoid-nodular hyperplasia, non-specific colitis, and pervasive developmental disorder in children. *Lancet*, 351(9103): 637–641.

Wang, Y., McKee, M., Torbica, A. & Stuckler, D. (2019). Systematic literature review on the spread of health-related misinformation on social media. *Social Science & Medicine*, 240: 112552.

Wardle, C. & Derakhshan, H. (2017). Information disorder: toward an interdisciplinary framework for research and policy making. *Council of Europe Report*, 27. Retrieved from: https://rm.coe.int/information-disorder-toward-an-interdisciplinary-framework-for-researc/168076277c

Weiss, A. P., Alwan, A., Garcia, E. P. & Garcia, J. (2020). Surveying fake news: Assessing university faculty's fragmented definition of fake news and its impact on teaching critical thinking. *International Journal for Educational Integrity*, 16(1): 1–15.

Wood, M. J. (2018). Propagating and debunking conspiracy theories on Twitter during the 2015–2016 Zika virus outbreak. *Cyberpsychology Behaviour Society Network*, 21(8): 485–490.

World Economic Forum. (2013). *World Economic Forum – Global Risks 2013 Eighth Edition*. Retrieved from: www.weforum.org/reports/world-economic-forum-global-risks-2013-eighth-edition/

World Health Organisation. (2013). *Health Literacy: The Solid Facts*. Retrieved from: https://apps.who.int/iris/handle/10665/326432

World Health Organisation. (2020). *Managing the COVID-19 Infodemic: Promoting Healthy Behaviours and Mitigating the Harm from Misinformation and Disinformation*. Retrieved from: www.who.int/news/item/23-09-2020-managing-the-covid-19-infodemic-promoting-healthy-behaviours-and-mitigating-the-harm-from-misinformation-and-disinformation

World Health Organisation. (2022). *Infodemics and Misinformation Negatively Affect People's Health Behaviours, New WHO Review Finds*. Retrieved from: www.who.int/europe/news/item/01-09-2022-infodemics-and-misinformation-negatively-affect-people-s-health-behaviours-new-who-review-finds

23

THE COVID-19 INFODEMIC ON TWITTER

Dialogic contraction within the echo chambers

Marina Bondi and Leonardo Sanna

Introduction

Fake news and misinformation are a key topic when discussing social media analysis research. While they had also been discussed well before the Trump era (Marchi 2012; Saez-Trumper 2014; Frank 2015; Conroy et al. 2015; Zhou et al. 2015), they became a central concern after Trump's election as president of the United States in 2016. The majority of studies on the theme focused on the issue of fake news detection (Conroy et al. 2015; Pérez-Rosas et al. 2017; Shu and Liu 2019), while media studies also contributed a lot with their interdisciplinary perspective (Albright 2017; Vargo et al. 2018; Melchior and Oliveira 2022).

The centrality of these themes has manifested itself not only because of the rise of populist movements, but also because of the key role that information plays in contemporary society. Indeed, we might say that we now live in an information society (Floridi 2009) where the good functioning of us as social beings is ensured by the delivery of a huge amount of information at an incredible speed. The web and the social media have realised a second mass mediatic revolution after that experienced after World War II with the wide diffusion of television. Although the information society has relatively recent origins, as early as the 1980s there was talk of "information overload", with a focus on the cognitive distress brought about by continuous immersion in the media information flow (Wurman 1989).

The rise of digital platforms such as social media, however, has added several layers of complexity to the media environment, intensifying experiences of remediation (Bolter and Grusin 2000), that is, the transfer of typical features of traditional media to digital media and increasing the amount of information available. Notwithstanding this complexity, social media also eased access to this huge amount of information, while at the same time introducing new actors as gatekeepers, sometimes also very different from traditional mass media players. This is the case of emerging (sometimes also called "alternative") media, as well as automated content selection, namely, algorithmic personalization; theoretically, these have been called in to solve the cognitive overload problems caused to us by the enormous amount of information available.

In this context, we have recently experienced information hysteria phenomena for which the term "infodemic" has been coined (Asif et al. 2021; Patwa et al. 2021; Petropoulos and Makridakis 2020; Eysenbach 2020). This rapid spread of potentially harmful information is often fostered on

DOI: 10.4324/9781003224495-28

digital platforms. Linguists have paid increasing attention to this topic since 2016, as the Oxford dictionary chose "post-truth" as word of the year (McIntyre 2018). The term refers to "relating to or denoting circumstances in which objective facts are less influential in shaping public opinion than appeals to emotion and personal belief".

Of course, this definition is rather problematic when dealing with language. In fact, in natural language, we do not have a clear-cut definition of what "objective facts" mean, as we can only deal with representations (or discourses) on objective facts or supposed-to-be objective facts. As rightly pointed out by Russell (1940), "truth and falsehood apply primarily to beliefs, and only derivatively to sentences as 'expressing' beliefs" (Russell 1940, p. 214). This helps us understand the foundation of misinformation spreading as a process of social transformation in which trust boundaries are being renegotiated. In Greimas, for example, the assumption is that communication is an exchange process where there are two kinds of "cognitive doing" (Greimas 1989, p. 659): the addresser realises a persuasive act while the addressee carries out an interpretive act. These two parts do not realise the communicative exchange by that very fact: they need a contract, which does not have a cognitive nature but rather fiduciary; Greimas calls it veridiction contract. We might argue that this perspective is almost too relativistic since, in its strictest interpretation, it would not allow the introduction of any concept of truth outside of a relationship of mutual trust between the two parties involved. Russell, on the other hand, provides a useful tool enabling us to identify textual affordances by highlighting the notion of verifiability as distinct from that of truth: "'true' is a wider concept than 'verifiable', and, in fact, cannot be defined in terms of verifiability" (Russell 1940, p. 227).

The concept of verifiability is crucial as it points to textual structures whose function might be to establish a trusting relationship. We might say then that, when dealing with journalism and fake news, "true" is everything that follows the correct methodology in the verification of sources, while "post-truth" is rather a text aiming to grasp the trust of their readers by other means rather than verifiability.

There are contexts where discourse, while still allowing for correct identification of sources and voices called into question, constructs trust and credibility mostly by emphasising shared identities and positions, usually in opposition to other views. This is what is observed online in echo chambers (Sunstein 2007), that is, particular social structures in which the views of others are systematically rejected and used instrumentally to support one's own beliefs in a polarised debate. Echo chambers are thus contexts in which the ideological-emotional plane plays a much more important role than the truth and verifiability of a text. The notion was introduced by Sunstein in terms of polarisation among groups:

> Group polarization is unquestionably occurring on the Internet. From the evidence thus far, it seems plain that the Internet is serving, for many, as a breeding group for extremism, precisely because like-minded people are deliberating with greater ease and frequency with one another, and often without hearing contrary views.
>
> (Sunstein 2007, p. 69)

An important epistemological distinction can be drawn between echo chambers and divergence of opinion, namely, epistemic bubbles (Nguyen 2020), by highlighting the active dimension of echo chambers in the veridiction process:

> Loosely, an epistemic bubble is a social epistemic structure in which some relevant voices have been excluded through omission. Epistemic bubbles can form with no ill intent,

through ordinary processes of social selection and community formation. We seek to stay in touch with our friends, who also tend to have similar political views. But when we also use those same social networks as sources of news, then we impose on ourselves a narrowed and self-reinforcing epistemic filter, which leaves out contrary views and illegitimately inflates our epistemic self-confidence. An echo chamber, on the other hand, is a social epistemic structure in which other relevant voices have been actively discredited.

(Nguyen 2020, p. 142)

It is thus not the simple opposition between two semantic frames that would define an echo chamber but rather the active rejection of the counterpart.

Echo chambers are often seen as dysfunctions of mass media communication in computational social science (Del Vicario et al. 2016b; Zollo et al. 2017; Di Marco et al. 2021). They are presented as structures that foster the polarisation of debates and the spreading of conspiracy theories. From a linguistic perspective, we might see echo chambers as ideological structures (Eco 1968) that emerge when ideological conflict happens (Rogers 2018). At a lexical level, this would rather produce effects on all those elements of evaluative language that we call dialogic elements, as the distinctive features of an echo chambers are ideological isolation and the extreme polarisation of two irreconcilable positions.

Since echo chambers are essentially the main digital structures in which disinformation and misinformation spread most easily (Del Vicario et al. 2016a), we believe that it is important to explore the role that social media may play in spreading misinformation by looking at evaluative language in their discourse. In order to explore this, we have focused on Twitter. If it is true that affordances like emojis, mentions (@), hashtags (#), retweeting are thought to facilitate dialogue and enhance "connectedness" among people, creating affiliation among people with similar ideological interests (Zappavigna 2011), Twitter has also often been described as having given birth to a new style of news coverage, where users tend to follow politically homogeneous clusters and are unlikely to be exposed to cross-ideological content (Himelboim et al. 2013). In general, there is a large consensus that Twitter may potentially contribute to partisan polarisation (Hong & Kim 2016). Twitter language has been critically explored for ideology construction and dissemination of racist and nationalist ideologies (Boukala & Dimitrakopoulou 2018; Bartlett et al. 2014; Wodak & Boukala 2015; Farkas et al. 2018; Chaudhry 2015). Trump has also been said to use it to establish credibility by denouncing media criticism (Ross & Rivers 2018) in a strategy that Lakoff (2017) defined in an interview as a strategy of "deflection", that is, attacking the "messenger" rather than responding to the accusations.

The focus of our analysis is on the language that manifests the writer's position. Focusing on evaluative language, we adopt Martin and White's (2005) appraisal framework, and in particular the concept of engagement, indicating the speaker's degree of commitment to what is being expressed and manifesting the attitudes projected by authors or speakers. The basic interplay is the one between two major discursive voices, *monogloss* and *heterogloss*. Monogloss voices present facts that tend to concede no room for the negotiation of meaning but rather to elicit confidence in the statement, by presenting themselves as self-evident. Heterogloss' voice, on the other hand, overtly presents propositions as one among others, using a variety of linguistic resources opening or closing options for dialogue (Martin & White 2005, p. 100). This may lead to opening up dialogic space for different positions and arguments advanced by interlocutors (dialogic Expansion) or rather to deflect alternative views (dialogic Contraction) (2005, pp. 102–104). An expression like "I believe that . . ." could then be taken to represent the speaker's acknowledgement of alternative views (expansion), while an expression like "I know that . . ." signals that there is no interest in alternative views (contraction).

Our focus will be on heteroglossic forms of dialogism rather than on monogloss discourse. The presence of a monogloss voice in Twitter discourse would not in itself point to an echo chamber effect but rather to the centrality of positioning oneself on social media. By comparing tweets and news articles we have, for example, already noticed a major disproportion in the space given to reported discourse – inevitably heteroglossic – in the news as against direct claim-making on Twitter (Bondi & Sanna 2022). A focus on the dialogic dimension of Twitter, on the other hand, might provide insights into the nature of the dialogue that takes place on the social medium: how far do tweeters open or close dialogic space in their rhetoric? By looking at how different expressions are used to open up dialogic space or rather to deflect alternative views, we hope to be able to explore the nature of the dialogic space created.

The hypothesis that guides the study is that features of dialogic contraction may characterise Twitter discourse, thus confirming the opinionated, polarised, echo chamber effect that is often attributed to it. If it is true that Twitter now characterises itself as a news site, rather than as a social network, and many Twitter users get news on the site (especially for breaking news), our assumption is that the space given to dialogic contraction on Twitter may be wider than that provided by traditional journalism, even when considering that journalism tends to draw attention to issues of contention and report debates. The hypothesis is that, from a linguistic perspective, echo chambers manifest themselves in the dialogic dimension, restricting the space for external views. However, echo chambers work always in two directions: on the one hand, they restrict the dialogic space leading to ideological isolation, while on the other hand they actively discredit and refuse the counterpart. The study thus explores the hypothesis by comparing the use of dialogic contraction and expansion in Twitter and in news discourse.

The chapter is organised as follows. The next section illustrates the data and the methodology. The results of the overall quantitative analysis are presented in section 3, while section 4 focuses on the role of negation in dialogic contraction and section 5 centres on "know" and "think" as verbs of ideological positioning. Section 6 discusses the results of the different types of analyses and introduces some conclusions.

Data and methods

The study is based on two datasets, namely, a sample of the Coronavirus corpus (Davies 2019), available from English Corpora, and the COVID-19 Twitter dataset. The Coronavirus Corpus includes online newspapers and magazines in 20 different English-speaking countries. Although it is quite varied in sources, occasionally also including comments to the published articles, it is representative of the discourse of online news. It is built from a subset of the NOW Corpus (Davies 2016), a larger corpus of News collected from the daily scraping of more than 1,000 websites. All the articles containing at least two occurrences of the word "coronavirus", "COVID", or "COVID-19" are added to the Coronavirus Corpus.

On the other hand, the Twitter dataset corpus is a repository of an ongoing collection of tweet IDs associated with the COVID-19 outbreak, whose collection started at the end of January 2020. This corpus is collected by searching a set of COVID-keywords via Twitter's search API, as reported by Chen et al. (2020). As recommended by the authors (Chen et al. 2020), we used the software Hydrator to collect the full text of each tweet. Hydrator allowed us to collect the full text starting from the tweet IDs (a unique reference that is used to identify each tweet) provided in our sample of data; in fact, as per Twitter's Terms and Conditions, the sharing of full text is not allowed, but only the sharing of Tweet IDs.

Our analysis is based, for both corpora, on a subset that includes the first seven months of the pandemic outbreak. This choice is dictated by the idea that, at that particular time, it should be possible to observe the emergence of misinformation phenomena and echo chambers, within the neurotic context of infodemics. For the Coronavirus corpus we included all the articles written between January 2020 and July 2020, while we extracted a sample of one million tweets for each month in the same range of time within our Twitter dataset.

From now on we will be referring to our corpora as the News Corpus, for the Coronavirus Corpus, and as the Twitter Corpus for our social media dataset.

The study combines the approach of corpus-assisted discourse analysis (Baker 2006; Baker et al. 2013; Bednarek 2008; Partington et al. 2013; Scott and Tribble 2006) with word embedding as a means to explore the dialogic dimension of echo chambers within the appraisal framework. In particular, corpus-assisted discourse analysis is used to explore the semantic preference and collocations of the appraisal markers in our corpora corpus using Wordsmith Tools 8 (Scott 2020). On the other hand, word embedding (Mikolov et al. 2013a, 2013b) is used to enhance the qualitative exploration of the pragmatic status of the most significant words. Word embedding is a machine learning technique used in natural language processing to create a computational semantic model. Given a word, the semantic model is able to infer words that are most likely to co-occur with the given term. In this study, we are using word embedding as a tool for qualitative exploration (Sanna and Compagno 2020), assuming that the probabilities of co-occurrence could be seen as a semantic frame (Fillmore 1976; Eco 1979) and that therefore this would allow us to infer their pragmatic dimension exploring their semantic preference (Sinclair 2004; Hunston 2007).

The analysis was based on an adaptation of the list of appraisal markers made by Fuoli (2012, 2018). To minimise possible biases due to the nature of the original tagging process, we kept in our checklist only words that were not specifically related to Fuoli's type of data (corporate reports) but were generalisable to our own data, also avoiding multi-words expressions. This allowed us to have a list of common appraisal markers which could be used to compare and quantify the dialogic dimension in our two corpora. As we are interested in ideological structures that are used to express ideological positioning, the most appropriate type of appraisal to investigate is "Engagement", with markers of Contraction and Expansion.

Keeping this list in mind, we looked for the distribution of appraisal markers in both corpora. The idea behind this was to highlight relevant differences between the news and Twitter. We assume that Twitter is characterised by echo chambers but it is also perhaps a preferred space for discussion, and therefore what happens on Twitter is often quite relevant for public debate. If echo chambers do have peculiar characteristics such as the predominance of dialogic contraction, we might be able to highlight these differences using the News Corpus as a reference corpus.

Starting from the quantitative differences between the two corpora, we carried out a qualitative analysis of selected elements, with a view to identifying the lexico-semantic patterns that

Table 23.1 Corpus figures

	N. of Texts/Tweets	*N. of Tokens*	*N. of Types*
News Corpus	650,699	442,252,000	2,086,489
Twitter Corpus	7,000,000	152,468,080	2,638,855

surrounded them and that could help us reconstruct their engagement function, as well as their role in the argumentative dialogue underlying the text. In particular we explored the lexico-semantic dimension by looking at collocation and clusters, while we also used the wider context of concordances to explore the argumentative role of individual occurrences, to see whether these occurrences were actually pointing to instances of positioning with reference to the topic at issue (the debate over COVID). Finally, we also used word embedding to complement the analysis of selected lexical elements.

Analysis

A detailed comparison of the normalised occurrences of our markers, in alphabetical order, is presented in Table 23.2. The lexical elements present in both corpora are many and present significant differences. The higher figures of the pairs, highlighting the word forms that characterise the two corpora in the comparison, are foregrounded in bold.

As shown in Table 23.2, the engagement level is mostly higher – and unsurprisingly characterised by a wider range of word forms – in the news corpus. The Twitter corpus, on the other hand, features a marked preference for a few elements and a decided lack of argumentation markers.

Table 23.2 Normalised occurrence of appraisal markers on Twitter and in the news corpus

Token	Dialogic Function	PTTW Twitter	PTTW News
although	Contract	0.083	**0.762**
anticipate	Expand	0.005	**0.163**
assure	Contract	0.026	**0.113**
belief	Contract	0.044	**0.146**
believe	Contract/Expand	2.180	**2.817**
but	Contract	**8.555**	8.234
Clearly	Contract	0.049	**0.080**
confident	Contract	0.053	**0.367**
convinced	Contract/Expand	0.117	**0.226**
could	Expand	2.517	**5.269**
demonstrate	Contract	0.040	**0.154**
demonstrated	Contract	0.025	**0.164**
Despite	Contract	0.209	**0.658**
did	Contract	2.015	**3.111**
evidence	Contract	0.480	**0.750**
evident	Contract	0.023	**0.118**
expect	Expand	0.313	**0.989**
expected	Expand	0.294	**1.980**
found	Contract	0.778	**1.872**
However	Contract	0.216	**2.247**
Indeed	Contract	0.108	**0.326**
inevitable	Contract	0.068	**0.179**
knew	Contract	0.418	**0.438**
know	Contract	**4.178**	3.050
knowing	Contract	0.160	**0.269**
may	Expand	1.905	**4.689**

(Continued)

Table 2.3 (Continued)

Token	Dialogic Function	PTTW Twitter	PTTW News
might	Expand	0.983	**2.087**
Naturally	Contract	0.005	**0.025**
never	Contract	1.493	**1.560**
No	Contract	**2.242**	1.570
none	Contract	0.154	**0.349**
not	Contract	**12.694**	10.081
nothing	Contract	0.960	**0.797**
obviously	Contract	0.141	**0.325**
project	Expand	0.205	**0.630**
prove	Contract	0.124	**0.301**
recognising	Contract	0.006	**0.040**
recognise	Contract	0.062	**0.213**
reflect	Contract	0.064	**0.490**
reflected	Contract	0.010	**0.154**
reflecting	Contract	0.017	**0.112**
reflects	Contract	0.029	**0.171**
see	Contract/Expand	6.085	**7.162**
should	Expand	3.931	**4.396**
shows	Contract	0.719	**1.131**
stated	Expand	0.094	**0.682**
surely	Contract	0.107	**0.133**
think	Expand	**3.121**	2.403
understands	Contract	0.029	**0.130**
unthinkable	Contract	0.004	**0.028**
While	Contract	0.560	**2.393**
without	Contract	1.154	**2.847**
Yet	Contract	0.226	**0.361**

This emerges by comparing the normalised occurrences of the modal verbs ("could", "may") and other elements typical of the negotiation of the dialogistic dimension, namely, "however" and "although". Certainly, this could be a structural feature of the Twitter environment, where arguing is influenced by the character limit. Twitter also shows a prevalence of five word-forms, namely, a contrastive connector ("but"), two negations ("No" and "Not"), and two verbs ("know" and "think") that are clearly linked to the expression of cognitive processes.

We decided to leave aside a close analysis of "but", for its extremely complex nature, but there is no doubt that its role in "disclaiming" is central to acknowledging a multiplicity of positions, while at the same time rejecting one and taking a stance. We thus decided to take a closer look at the two negations and the two verbs, as they might be interesting markers of ideological conflict within the platform.

A closer study of concordances first of all confirmed the impression that many of the specific elements highlighted are very flexible in terms of their actual value: they do open up to heteroglossia, but whether they are used to enhance the possibility of a continued ne-gotiation of meanings or to fend off that negotiation largely depends on context. Moving away from the proposition to the entire clause complex or to the wider context of the debate helps to see the role they play as responses, either retrospectively (responding to previously expressed opinions) or prospectively (anticipating the interlocutor's response and including counter-responses).

The role of negation in dialogic contraction

Two of the five words identified as characterising Twitter discourse are "not" and "no". If the case of "no" is rather illustrative of a very versatile element which can be found in many different contexts, "not" is more clearly a verb-modifying adverb marking negative polarity, potentially making it easier for us to understand how it is used as a form of dialogic contraction in our corpus in explicit forms of denial. Because of its function in polarity, we can in fact be more precise in our exploration and directly select the most significant verbs that occur with "Not" in our corpus.

We selected the five most significant ones according to t-score (Oakes 1998; Hunston 2002), that is, the verb "to be" in the present tense ("is not"), the verb "to do" in the present tense ("does not"), the verb "should", the verb "to have" in the present tense ("have") and finally the verb "to be" in the past tense ("were not"). In general, it might be noticed that modals are frequently used in their negative form in the corpus, as the modals attested (in order of frequency *will, should, would, could, must, might, can't/cannot* and *shall*) represent approximately 8% (49897/ 625719) of the occurrences of *not*. In terms of collocational strength, however, *should* is definitely the one that most predictably collocates with *not*.

What emerges from an observation of the strongest collocates is that when "not" is used to negate a verb in the third person singular, it is largely part of dialogic contraction processes that point directly to the topics at issue (>90% of cases out of 200 random collocations for both), as clearly shown in the sequence of denials in Example 1:

(1) Just a reminder: Gates is NOT a doctor Gates is NOT an epidemiologist Gates was NOT elected.

In very few other cases, there is no explicit denial, for example when the negation is embedded in a relative clause that simply selects a specific scenario, as in Example 2:

(2) Close the borders. Any citizen not back already frankly needs to accept they should have be back earlier.

In the case of "does not" and "is not", the negation is used in most cases to deny epistemic validity to voices outside the dialogue or the direct counterpart we are addressing (Example 1), sometimes also with a direct reference to veridical aspects:

(3) 5G does not spread coronavirus.
(4) Information circulating on social media on a confirmed case of COVID 2019 Corona Virus is not true.

In the proposed examples, negation of the verbal element is used to position oneself at one of the two poles of the debate, simultaneously narrowing the dialogic space.

Apart from the most frequent collocations with the verb forms mentioned (*is/does/should/have/were*), we further explored the use of the negative element in itself. The study of a randomly selected set of 200 occurrences of "not" can offer insights on its use. The choice of limiting the analysis to 200 occurrences is often the standard in corpus linguistics when numbers are very high (see Groom 2010, pp. 64–65 for a discussion of the measure). Almost 70% of the occurrences in this small random sample (138/200, i.e. 69%) are actually direct forms of denials (Example 5), whereas another 4.5% (9/200) are weakened forms of dialogic contraction, as they are presented in conjunction with an epistemic modal signalling dialogic expansion (Example 6). Other cases, such as those of a few rhetorical questions (6/200, i.e. 3%) might also be considered forms of dialogic contraction, though in the form of a strong (affirmative) claim, implied by the negative question (Example 7):

(5) Seriously people – STOP BUYING MASKS! They are NOT effective in preventing general public from cat.
(6) It might not be a regular respiratory virus.
(7) So yall are NOW washing your hands bc the coronavirus outbreak??? Was this not a thing for yall before??

Of the rest, about 11% (22/200) are forms of reported discourse (mostly reporting decisions) (Example 8), whereas 6% (12/200) are found in conditional clauses presenting a possible case, qualifying a direct or indirect claim (Example 9), 7.5% (15) are found in expressives, manifesting a personal state of mind, which is not in itself subject to any verifiable truth claim (Example 10), and 4% (8/200) are found in imperatives expressing recommendations (Example 11), and another one was an example of a recommendation with the use of "why not":

(8) Trump Administration Says Planned Parenthood Will Not Receive Coronavirus Aid.
(9) Don't worry about the coronavirus, you'll be fine if you're not elderly or vulnerable.
(10) It's 40 days into stay-at-home and I'm not sure I'm entirely sane.
(11) Remember that Covid-19 takes a week to two weeks to incubate. do not let the media fool you when they say these 19,000 cases.

A further level of analysis might want to investigate the nature of the claims and counterclaims involved in the occurrences of "not", looking at their argumentative structures. Given the fragmentary nature of the data, this is of course much more complex to ascertain, let alone quantify. The overall impression, however, is clearly that there are very few cases where the denial is part of a main rejection claim that is also supported by verifiable arguments (Example 12). In some other cases, denials are an unsupported (and unverifiable) subclaim, supporting another conclusion (Example 13), but in most cases they are bare contradictory rejections (Example 14 and 15).

(12) COVID cases are rising and people are getting sick. This is NOT the time to stop social distancing.
(13) China is doing everything right at the moment. Restrictions on travel and major gatherings! The coronavirus could not be anticipated to travel so far so quickly, people didn't know they were infected!
(14) No it's not, pandemic was never what it was reported.
(15) The news regarding the negative test of the coronavirus patient is false. He has not been discharged. He did test positive.

Table 23.3 Top ten three-word clusters of "No" on Twitter

N	Cluster	Freq.
1	THERE IS NO	17,498
2	THERE ARE NO	4,394
3	NO HEALTH CARE	4,257
4	OUT WITH NO	4,179
5	NO TUITION REFUND	4,151
6	WITH NO TUITION	4,148
7	UNEMPLOYMENT NO HEALTH	4,143
8	NO SOCIAL DISTANCING	3,893
9	NO ONE IS	3,386
10	NO AVAILABLE VACCINE	2,554

Table 23.4 Top ten three-word clusters of "No" in the news

N	Cluster	Freq
1	THERE IS NO	49,950
2	THERE S NO	20,773
3	THERE ARE NO	15,623
4	THERE WAS NO	15,421
5	WILL BE NO	6,890
6	THERE WILL BE	6,562
7	WE HAVE NO	6,559
8	THERE WERE NO	6,387
9	IS NO LONGER	6,109
10	NO MORE THAN	5,795

It is worth spending a few more words on the use of "No", the other negative element highlighted in Table 23.2. It may be interesting to look at the top ten clusters in which it occurs in both corpora, to compare Twitter discourse and news discourse.

The data highlight the importance of negative existential patterns. As these existential clauses might be used to contract the enunciation space within the discourse in forms of *denial* (Martin and White 2005), we should not be surprised by their abundance in a context such as the pandemic since most of the discourses are initially centred on the account of the existence of the virus. The most obvious context is one of dialogic contraction, supporting a discourse of denial of the existence of the virus or of the danger of the virus. The word form "no", however, might also be used in other positions, where it is less likely to be a good indicator for dialogic contraction, or at least not explicitly related to the issue that is object of debate.

Taking this possibility into account, we took a sample of 200 occurrences of the top-occurring clusters in both corpora, namely, "There is", to evaluate how many times it was actually used to introduce dialogic contraction in relation to the topic. Again, in the Twitter corpus we found a more marked conflict, with a greater use of "No" as contractor of dialogic space, with 48 occurrences (25%) signalling forms of positioning by denial on the COVID issue, vs 30 occurrences (15%), in the news. In both cases, however, the vast majority of our top-occurring clusters do not act as markers of specific ideological positioning, that is, they do not constitute claims about the (non-)

existence of COVID but may for example simply provide supporting evidence (e.g. "There was no immediate reaction from the White House"). This confirms that our bottom-up approach to appraisal requires analysis of the wider context and might not provide enough elements for any automatic identification of positions in a debate.

Indeed, as suggested by Hunston (2004), we are dealing with a subject that is rather difficult to grasp in a quantitative evaluation since the restriction of dialogic space can also occur by means of allusions that are expressed with complex sequences of words on the discursive level. When these do not occur with regularity, they are difficult to detect by studying the collocations of lexical elements. Moreover, many lexical items on which we are basing our observations on appraisal can certainly occur in contexts where their function is not directly related to the object of debate.

Nonetheless, it is interesting to select some examples from the top occurring cluster in Twitter, that is, "There is no", to illustrate the variety of elements that can be denied. See for example how the expression is used on Twitter to deny the existence of the virus (16), to sum up a position or report it (17), and to reject the validity of a policy (18).

(16) COVID 19 = Exosomes naturally found in all cells. Cells excrete in times of stress or illness There is no virus. Only flu etc.

(17) #CureCancer_By_TrueWorship There is no such disease which cannot be cured by the devotion of Sant Rampal Ji whether it is corona virus or cancer. All diseases can be removed, but true devotion.

(18) There's no point to let unlimited #coronavirus infected patients to enter Hong Kong when we are already running out of medical resources.

It appears that forms introducing a proposition (rather than just the existence of an entity or process), like Examples (17) and (18), are particularly apt at taking distance from this proposition and acting therefore as forms of denial from the point of view of engagement, but also as disagreement from the point of view of argumentative dialogue. In the specific case of the COVID infodemic, forms of denial of existence were also central to the debate, when directly related to the existence of the virus, for example.

It is important to notice, then, that the role of the single markers in determining a contraction of the dialogic space relies on the lexico-grammatical patterns involved, beyond the simple presence of a word. The relevance of these contractions is also determined by the link to specific arguments in the debate. The distinguishing features of Twitter discourse, however, appear to be in line with the definition of echo chambers, as the key strategy is seemingly the rejection of the opponent's view by mere denial.

"Know" and "think" as verbs of ideological positioning

The other two words characterising Twitter discourse are the verbs "think" and "know". While sharing a semantic relationship (i.e. representing a cognitive process), the verbs seem to play different roles in the engagement system, as typically representative of expansion and contraction in combination with the first person singular ("I think"/"I know").

Looking at a small excerpt of 200 concordances for each of these word forms, we notice that "think" is used to introduce a personal standpoint (i.e. "I think") in 30% of the cases, while in the rest of the cases it is used to introduce external voices. The wider context shows, however, that this leads mostly to contexts of contraction (>90%), where external voices are introduced to be discredited, especially when formulating rhetorical questions to negate the counterpart voice ("Do you think you know COVID so well?"), thus confirming a dominant contraction function.

The use of "know" shows a more complex dialogistic dimension, as in the vast majority of the cases (>80%). It is used in combination with negative polarity to express lack of knowledge ("I did not know that this happened") in ways that – in the wider context of the argument – do in fact cast doubt on what others have said. Similarly, when the process is attributed to others ("they don't know if the COVID cases will double"), the argumentative function appears to be that of discrediting external voices.

Beyond the local most obvious heteroglossic function, then, it is important to study the lexico-grammatical patterns around the node word and, even more clearly, the argumentative role that the proposition plays in the debate.

The verb "to know" is obviously linked to information and all the actions connected to bringing new information and knowledge to the debate. However, looking at its general collocates in the whole corpus, it is clear that on Twitter the situation is quite peculiar. Indeed, the most significant verbal element that occurs in the immediate context is a negation, that is, "don't", which obviously adds to the frequency of negations with "no" and "not" that we have already seen in the previous subsection. The significance of the collocates is calculated using t-score (Oakes 1998; Hunston 2002). One of the most recurring patterns is "I don't know who needs to hear that", influenced also by many retweets. What is evident, exploring the concordances (and in particular the propositions introduced by "know"), is that in these negative contexts "know" is almost always used as a means to express a standpoint and very rarely with epistemic intent.

(19) I don't know if I want my hair to come from China. I'm scared.
(20) I don't know if I'm keen to trust data in the middle of a pandemic where adequate testing hasn't been accomplished and attributable death totals are questionably.
(21) I don't know if I've seen anyone say this but my heart goes out to the people of China right now.

As seen in examples (19–20–21), in its most used form, the verb is used with a clear intent to position and almost never as a real recourse to epistemic modalities. A marked willingness to position oneself emerges from its use regardless of debating the veracity of what the stance presupposes. In the examples shown, the potential discussion of an epistemic status in the introductory clause (seemingly opening dialogic space) is only instrumental to strong positioning (narrowing dialogic space) in the second part of the sentence.

Special mention should be made of the locution "Don't know who needs to hear that, but", which is perhaps the clearest example of the use of the negation of the verb "to know" to narrow dialogic space. What this type of formulation implies is a shared knowledge, presenting an epistemic validity that is so shared as to be self-evident; this allows for very strong positioning, as in the case of examples (22) and (23), typically representing the two main positions in this debate, Democrats and Republicans.

(22) I don't know who needs to hear this, but unlike other developed countries, the U.S. really has not flattened the curve.
(23) I don't know who needs to hear this, but Joe Biden is compromised with China. They know Hunter's secrets.

Very similar conclusions might be reached for the verb "to think", often regarded as potentially opening dialogic space. Certainly the verb already naturally appears in contexts where personal beliefs and convictions are expressed, as it is used to refer to our opinions in our cognitive sphere. On the other hand, it is interesting to note how the presence of this cognitive sphere tends to raise the level of ideological confrontation somewhat, especially in negative forms.

(24) You know, I don't think it's too complicated to wear a mask.
(25) You don't think the new world order would exploit something like covid-19 to subjugate us all into slavery, do you?
(26) I don't think coronavirus is caused by 5G. I think it's a complete and total hoax, and there is no new strains of illness.
(27) Raise your hand if you don't think covid-19 is serious. Now, use it to slap yourself because you're an idiot.
(28) Do you think your representative should be getting paid to stay at home and telework? Because that's what Democrats believe.
(29) Do you think Trump woke up today with an ache in his heart for all of the people suffering in the world. Prayed with Melania and her son over breakfast for the families effected by Coronavirus, and then went straight to his office to read the updated briefings to keep us safe?

There are indeed, as in the case of Examples 24 and 25, more or less direct attacks on the other party, either by means of strong criticism (26) or turpiloquy (27), or through an interesting use of rhetorical questions (25). Examples 28 and 29 are in fact questions that reveal ideological positioning. In other words, they are fake questions manifesting denial of the belief attributed to the other party. In this game of extreme positioning, typical of echo chambers, the counterpart is not regarded as legitimate, and their positions are in fact systematically denied at the semantic and morphosyntactic level.

Overall then, these two verbs are used with similar functions on Twitter, that is, representing a precise standpoint or belief. Looking at the word embedding model of both verbs in our corpus (Figure 23.1), we notice that the most similar word for "think" is "know" and vice versa, meaning that they hold a strong semantic and pragmatic relation. Indeed, in both semantic spaces, we do have the word "believe", confirming the hypothesis of representing a precise standpoint.

The semantic frame of both verbs also provides confirmation of their slightly different functions: "think" is used to take a strong position that might also end in an explicit attack to the counterpart, while "know" is used to delimit the ideological space with respect to ideological positioning and is often modulated with a negation, with the aim of excluding from the dialogic space anything that does not adhere to the proposed ideological positioning. The frames of "think" and "know" seem to show overlap of lexical elements afferent to the cognitive ("believe", "understand") and demonstrative areas ("see", "actually"), while differing markedly in other elements. In the case of "know" there are indeed elements related to epistemic modes and knowledge sharing, although we have seen that these are modulated instrumentally to take a position within the debate. In the case of "think", on the other hand, what characterises its pragmatic status is precisely the exaggeration of positioning, with related attack to the other side.

Discussion and conclusions

Our analysis has clearly shown important characteristics of Twitter discourse by contrasting it to traditional journalistic discourse. Twitter certainly cannot be regarded as an informational space, but it is clear that it has now been chosen as the preferred platform for discussion of texts with informational content. However, this discussion does not take place with the tools of

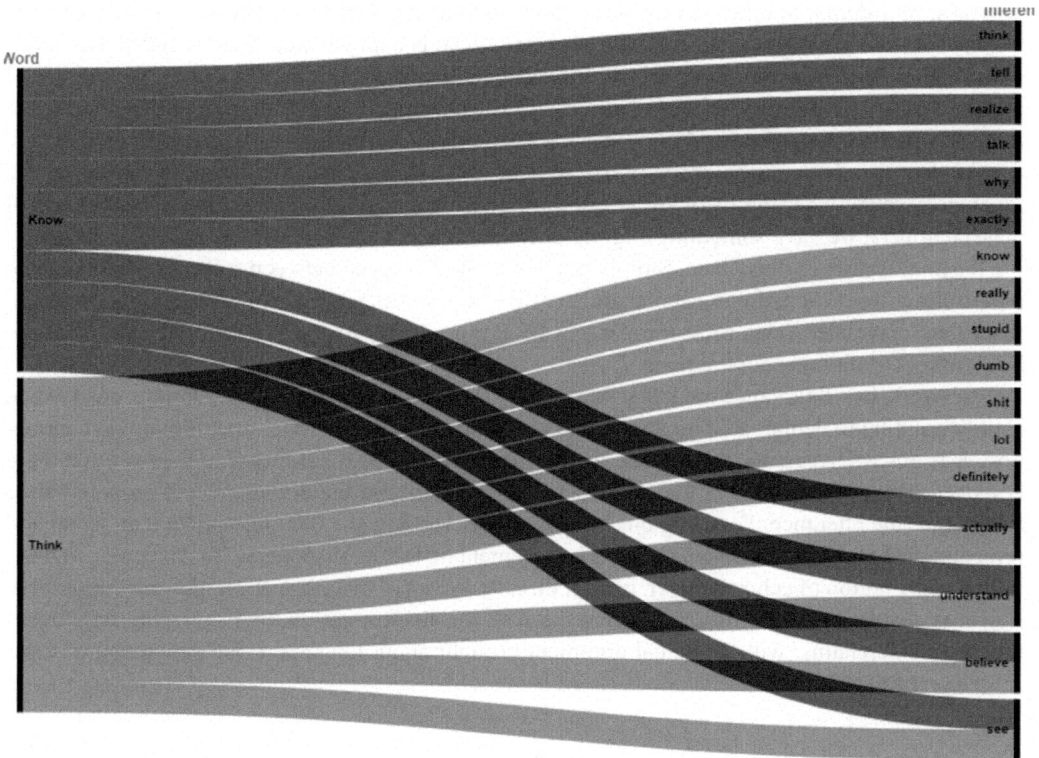

Figure 23.1 Semantic preference visualised in our word embedding model

argumentation but rather with those of positioning. This positioning occurs either by explicit means, with a clear stance of the author of the tweet, or by implicit means, mainly by positioning oneself in a contradictory position to the interlocutor. Nonetheless, the contradiction at the lexical level results in a much deeper division at the semantic level, where there is not a simple negation of the thesis of the other but a contrary positioning. In this case, the contradiction expressed by the negation is instrumental in actually presenting the values of only one of the two parties involved as evident.

In fact, it is precisely on the polarity of "not" and "no" that epistemic modalities are articulated on Twitter, whereas recourse to modal verbs – capable of expressing different nuances with respect to the construction of the discursive space – are comparatively very limited. Twitter positioning is prevalently and explicitly concerned with emphasising contrasting positions. The presentation of this contrast, however, is nothing but a means of reinforcing one's own positioning, with a systematic contraction of the dialogic space actually leading to the negation of dialogue.

This is a typical feature of echo chambers, where polarisation is expressed precisely in this dual nature of ideological reinforcement through the denial of the other. This denial is perhaps something more than a simple divergence of opinion, probably because of the nature of the ideological conflict. As shown previously, the articulation of epistemic modalities onto negation produces, at a lexical level, a contradiction. However, this negation is nothing but a way to present a reinforced standpoint.

The simple denial of other positions is actually a type of polarisation that we might describe as weak, as it subordinates one's own point of view to what is being denied (Lakoff 2004). However, when denial is used, as in our case, with the specific intent of denying the epistemic validity of others in order to reinforce one's own, we are faced with something different. In this case we are in front of a real relation of contrariety, which is then expressed through an articulation of semantic frames that goes beyond the ordinary axiological level, that is, the investment of values on the ideological level, what the ideology in question considers as positive or negative. In the case of echo chambers, we have something slightly different, which may be considered stronger in fostering the polarisation of the debate. Simply put, the main difference between a disagreement and the polarisation of positions in an echo chamber is the robustness with which conflicting axiological planes are contrasted. This robustness might be explored and, partially, measured looking at the key markers of dialogic contraction.

Our work has thus confirmed that individual markers of dialogic construction, even when clearly pointing to denial, are potential markers but not an automatic measure of dialogic contraction. It is always necessary to look at least at lexico-grammatical structures to confirm that there is indeed denial and to look at the wider context to understand the pragmatic and argumentative function of the utterance. Focusing on Twitter as a networking site has also shown that denial and rejection of the opponent's discourse are a key element of Twitter discourse. This of course in itself points to the notion of echo chamber, but not directly to that of disinformation. It is our contention, however, that this kind of discourse paves the way for disinformation, by privileging bare rejection of counterclaims, with no actual argument brought about to support one's own claim or the refutation of the counterclaim.

References

Albright, J. (2017) 'Welcome to the era of fake news', *Media and Communication*, 5(2), pp. 87–89.

Asif, M., Zhiyong, D., Iram, A. and Nisar, M. (2021) 'Linguistic analysis of neologism related to coronavirus (COVID-19)', *Social Sciences & Humanities Open*, 4(1), p. 100201.

Baker, P. (2006) *Using Corpora in Discourse Analysis*, London: Continuum.

Baker, P., Gabrielatos, C. and McEnery, T. (2013) *Discourse Analysis and Media Attitudes: The Representation of Islam in the British Press*, Cambridge: Cambridge University Press. http://doi.org/10.1017/CBO9780511920103

Bartlett, J., Reffin, J., Rumball, N. and Williamson, S. (2014) 'Anti-social media', *Demos*, pp. 1–51.

Bednarek, M. (2008) *Emotion Talk across Corpora*, Basingstoke: Palgrave Macmillan.

Bolter, J. D. and Grusin, R. (2000) *Remediation: Understanding New Media*, Cambridge, MA: MIT Press.

Bondi, M. and Sanna, L. (2022) 'Exploring the echo chamber concept. A linguistic perspective', in M. Demata, V. Zorzi and A. Zottola (eds.) *Conspiracy Theory Discourses*, Amsterdam: Benjamins, pp. 143–167.

Boukala, S. and Dimitrakopoulou, D. (2018) 'Absurdity and the "blame game" within the Schengen area: Analyzing Greek (social) media discourses on the refugee crisis', *Journal of Immigrant & Refugee Studies*, 16(1–2), pp. 179–197.

Chaudhry, I. (2015) '# Hashtagging hate: Using Twitter to track racism online', *First Monday*, 20(2).

Chen, E., Lerman, K. and Ferrara, E. (2020) 'Tracking social media discourse about the Covid-19 pandemic: Development of a public coronavirus twitter data set', *JMIR Public Health and Surveillance*, 6(2), p. e19273.

Conroy, N. K., Rubin, V. L. and Chen, Y. (2015) 'Automatic deception detection: Methods for finding fake news', *Proceedings of the Association for Information Science and Technology*, 52(1), pp. 1–4.

Davies, M. (2016) *Corpus of News on the Web (NOW)*, Available online at www.english-corpora.org/now/

Davies, M. (2019) *The Coronavirus Corpus*, Available online at www.english-corpora.org/corona/

Del Vicario, M., Bessi, A., Zollo, F., Petroni, F., Scala, A., Caldarelli, G. and Quattrociocchi, W. (2016a) 'The spreading of misinformation online', *Proceedings of the National Academy of Sciences*, 113(3), pp. 554–559.

Del Vicario, M., Vivaldo, G., Bessi, A., Zollo, F., Scala, A., Caldarelli, G. and Quattrociocchi, W. (2016b) 'Echo chambers: Emotional contagion and group polarization on facebook', *Scientific Reports*, 6(1), pp. 1–12.

Di Marco, N., Cinelli, M. and Quattrociocchi, W. (2021) 'Infodemics on Youtube: Reliability of content and echo chambers on Covid-19', *arXiv preprint arXiv:2106.08684*.

Eco, U. (1968) *La struttura assente [The Absent Structure]*, Milan: Bompiani.

Eco, U. (1979) *The Role of the Reader*, Bloomington: Indiana University Press.

Eysenbach, G. (2020) 'How to fight an infodemic: The four pillars of infodemic management', *Journal of Medical Internet Research*, 22(6), p. e21820.

Farkas, J., Schou, J. and Neumayer, C. (2018) 'Platformed antagonism: Racist discourses on fake Muslim Facebook pages', *Critical Discourse Studies*, 15(5), pp. 463–480.

Fillmore, C. J. (1976) 'Frame semantics and the nature of language', *Annals of the New York Academy of Sciences*, 280(1), pp. 20–32.

Floridi, L. (2009) 'The information society and its philosophy: Introduction to the special issue on "the Philosophy of Information, its Nature, and future developments"', *The Information Society*, 25(3), pp. 153–158.

Frank, R. (2015) 'Caveat lector: Fake news as folklore', *Journal of American Folklore*, 128(509), pp. 315–332.

Fuoli, M. (2012) 'Assessing social responsibility: A quantitative analysis of Appraisal in BP's and IKEA's social reports', *Discourse & Communication*, 6(1), pp. 55–81.

Fuoli, M. (2018) 'A stepwise method for annotating appraisal', *Functions of Language*, 25(2), pp. 229–258.

Greimas, A. J. (1989) 'The veridiction contract', *New Literary History*, 20(3), pp. 651–660.

Groom, N. (2010). 'Closed-class keywords and corpus-driven discourse analysis', in *Keyness in Texts*, eds. M. Bondi and M. Scott, Amsterdam: Benjamins, pp. 59–78.

Himelboim, I., McCreery, S. and Smith, M. (2013) 'Birds of a feather tweet together: Integrating network and content analyses to examine cross-ideology exposure on Twitter', *Journal of Computer-Mediated Communication*, 18(2), pp. 40–60.

Hong, S. and Kim, S. H. (2016) 'Political Polarization on Twitter: Implications for the use of social media in digital governments', *Government Information Quarterly*, 33(4), pp. 777–782.

Hunston, S. (2002) *Corpora in Applied Linguistics*, Cambridge: Cambridge University Press. http://doi.org/10.1017/CBO9781139524773.

Hunston, S. (2004) 'Counting the uncountable: Problems of identifying evaluation in a text and in a corpus', *Corpora and Discourse*, 9, pp. 157–188.

Hunston, S. (2007) 'Semantic prosody revisited', *International Journal of Corpus Linguistics*, 12(2), pp. 249–268.

Lakoff, G. (2004) *Don't Think of an Elephant! Know Your Values and Frame the Debate*, White River Junction, VT: Chelsea Green Publishing.

Lakoff, G. (2017, January 13) 'A taxonomy of Trump tweets [On the Media]', *WYNC*, Available online at www.wnyc.org/story/taxonomy-trump-tweets/

Marchi, R. (2012) 'With Facebook, blogs, and fake news, teens reject journalistic "objectivity"', *Journal of Communication Inquiry*, 36(3), pp. 246–262.

Martin, J. R. and White, P. R. (2005) *The Language of Evaluation*, London: Palgrave Macmillan.

McIntyre, L. (2018) *Post-truth*, Cambridge, MA: MIT Press.

Melchior, C. and Oliveira, M. (2022) 'Health-related fake news on social media platforms: A systematic literature review', *New Media & Society*, 24(6), pp. 1500–1522.

Mikolov, T., Chen, K., Corrado, G. and Dean, J. (2013b) 'Efficient estimation of word representations in vector space', *arXiv preprint, arXiv:1301.3781*.

Mikolov, T., Sutskever, I., Chen, K., Corrado, G. S. and Dean, J. (2013a) 'Distributed representations of words and phrases and their compositionality', *Advances in Neural Information Processing Systems*, 26, pp. 3111–3119.

Nguyen, C. T. (2020) 'Echo chambers and epistemic bubbles', *Episteme*, 17(2), pp. 141–161.

Oakes, M. P. (1998) *Statistics for Corpus Linguistics*, Edinburgh: Edinburgh University Press.

Partington, A., Duguid, A. and Taylor, C. (2013) *Patterns and Meanings in Discourse*, Amsterdam: Benjamins.

Patwa, P., Sharma, S., Pykl, S., Guptha, V., Kumari, G., Akhtar, M. S., Ekbal, A., Das, A. and Chakraborty, T. (2021) 'Fighting an. infodemic: Covid-19 fake news dataset', in *International Workshop on Combating on Line Hostile Posts in Regional Languages during Emergency Situation*, Cham: Springer, pp. 21–29.

Pérez-Rosas, V., Kleinberg, B., Lefevre, A. and Mihalcea, R. (2017) 'Automatic detection of fake news', *arXiv preprint arXiv:1708.07104*.

Petropoulos, F. and Makridakis, S. (2020) 'Forecasting the novel coronavirus COVID-19', *PLoS ONE*, 15(3), p. e0231236.

Rogers, R. (2018) 'Otherwise engaged: Social media from vanity metrics to critical analytics', *International Journal of Communication*, 12, pp. 450–472.

Ross, A. S. and Rivers, D. J. (2018) 'Discursive deflection: Accusation of "fake news" and the spread of mis- and disinformation in the Tweets of President Trump', *Social Media & Society*, 4(2), pp. 1–12.

Russell, B. (1940) *An Inquiry into Meaning and Truth*, London: George Allen and Unwin LTD.

Saez-Trumper, D. (2014), 'September. Fake tweet buster: A webtool to identify users promoting fake news on Twitter', in *Proceedings of the 25th ACM Conference on Hypertext and Social Media*, New York: ACM Digital Library, pp. 316–317.

Sanna, L. and Compagno, D. (2020) 'Implementing eco's model reader with word embeddings. An experiment on Facebook ideological bots', in *JADT 2020: 15th International Conference on Statistical Analysis of Textual Data*. Available online at https://hal.science/hal-03144105.

Scott, M. (2020) *Word Smith Tools* (Version 8.0), Stroud: Lexical Analysis Software.

Scott, M. and Tribble, C. (2006) *Textual Patterns*, Amsterdam: Benjamins.

Shu, K. and Liu, H. (2019) 'Detecting fake news on social media', *Synthesis Lectures on Data Mining and Knowledge Discovery*, 11(3), pp. 1–129.

Sinclair, J. M. (2004) *Trust the Text: Language, Corpus and Discourse*, London: Routledge.

Sunstein, C. (2007) *Republic.com. 2.0*, Princeton, NJ: Princeton University Press.

Vargo, C. J., Guo, L. and Amazeen, M. A. (2018) 'The agenda-setting power of fake news: A big data analysis of the online media landscape from 2014 to 2016', *New Media & Society*, 20(5), pp. 2028–2049.

Wodak, R. and Boukala, S. (2015) '(Supra)national identity and language: Rethinking national and European migration policies and the linguistic integration of migrants', *Annual Review of Applied Linguistics*, 35, pp. 253–273.

Wurman, R. S. (1989) *Information Anxiety*, New York: Doubleday.

Zappavigna, M. (2011) 'Ambient affiliation: A linguistic perspective on Twitter', *New Media & Society*, 13(5), pp. 788–806.

Zhou, X., Cao, J., Jin, Z., Xie, F., Su, Y., Chu, D., Cao, X. and Zhang, J. (2015) 'May. Real-time news certification system on sina weibo', in *Proceedings of the 24th International Conference on World Wide Web*, New York: ACM Digital Library, pp. 983–988.

Zollo, F., Bessi, A., Del Vicario, M., Scala, A., Caldarelli, G., Shekhtman, L., Havlin, S. and Quattrociocchi, W. (2017) 'Debunking in a world of tribes', *PLoS ONE*, 12(7), p. e0181821.

24

COVID-19 PARODY FAKE VOICE MESSAGES ON WHATSAPP

Dennis Chau and Carmen Lee

Introduction

Since December 2019, the world has been combatting COVID-19. Not only is it a pandemic of a novel coronavirus causing a significant number of deaths and a series of problems, both societal and economic, but it is also a pandemic of information circulating at an alarming rate on social media, an "infodemic", as director-general of the World Health Organization (WHO) Dr. Tedros Adhanom Ghebreyesus put it at the Munich Security Conference in February 2020 (Zarocostas 2020). Much of the information surrounding the coronavirus is, of course, not necessarily true. For instance, at the start of the pandemic, when people were divided on the importance of face masks, there was a Facebook post warning that wearing a mask leads to carbon dioxide toxicity. It was shared many times and subsequently found to have been adapted from a diagram merely illustrating the major symptoms of hypercapnia on Wikipedia (Goodman and Carmichael 2020).

While the topic of disinformation, which has received growing attention since the 2016 presidential election in the US and Brexit referendum in the UK, is nothing new in this "post-truth" era (Lewandowsky, Ecker, & Cook 2017), false or inaccurate health content is arguably "more toxic and more deadly" (Posetti and Bontcheva 2020: 2). For one thing, consuming it may adversely affect one's willingness to engage in health-protective behaviours (Allington *et al.* 2021) and may even result in dire consequences. Just between February and April 2020, thousands of people in Iran poisoned themselves by drinking methanol, a fake treatment for the coronavirus that went viral in the country, and hundreds of them lost their lives (Aljazeera 2020).

In view of the proliferation of online disinformation around COVID-19 and the significant impact it has on consumers, especially the uncritical ones, various parties have taken such measures as fact-checking and debunking claims, removing falsehoods, criminalising the malicious spread of false or misleading messages, as well as enhancing citizens' critical literacy skills (see e.g. Posetti and Bontcheva 2020, Radu 2020). In recent years, applied linguists have also offered insights into this area, even though the research is still in its infancy and much of it is not tied to the pandemic. For example, drawing on a corpus of tweets which former US president Donald Trump posted after the announcement of his victory in an election, Ross and Rivers (2018: 1) examined how Trump accused the media of reporting fake news while being

DOI: 10.4324/9781003224495-29

"a serial spreader of mis- and disinformation". Also using a corpus, Sousa-Silva (2022) identified the linguistic features that authors of fake news written in English and Portuguese tended to employ. Tagg and Seargeant (2021), based on semi-structured interviews with Facebook users, concluded that in order to alleviate problems arising from disinformation, it is crucial to provide critical digital literacies education, one that takes into account how social interactions influence the ways in which social media users engage with information or opinions in their networks.

As can be imagined, many places across the globe have been embroiled in the current infodemic, and Hong Kong is no exception. As with any fake news, COVID-19 disinformation has taken various semiotic forms, including texts, images, videos, and audio messages, the focus of our study. In April 2020, a voice message in which a speaker claimed to be Dr. Pak-leung Ho, a local microbiologist critiquing regularly the government's coronavirus prevention measures, was forwarded to a large number of WhatsApp groups. In the message, the speaker advised recipients to keep their bodies at a slightly alkaline state, to eat more vegetables and less meat, and perhaps more interestingly, to avoid drinking certain bottled water (Sky Post 2020). Shortly after this voice message had gone viral, Ho clarified that he was not the speaker and warned the public on his own social media and in public appearances not to trust the unfounded content. Three months later, unfortunately, another voice message purporting to be recorded by Ho circulated on WhatsApp, and this time Ho said he would consider reporting it to the police. Since then, multiple fake voice messages related to the pandemic have emerged. Here, *fake voice messages* refer broadly to voice-recorded disinformation transmitted on digital media platforms such as WhatsApp. In the remainder of this chapter, *disinformation* will be used instead of *misinformation* to highlight that these false or misleading messages have to be deliberately created in the first place (see Wardle 2017 for the distinction between the two terms).

Central to this chapter, however, is not so much the fake voice messages, like the aforementioned ones, as their *parodies*, which we have from time to time received from our friends and family members as mobile messaging app users, and which we have found worth analysing as applied linguists. In this chapter, we argue that parody fake voice messages are an emerging sub-genre of fake news. Drawing on a purposefully-sampled dataset comprising 21 audio-based parodies about COVID-19 in Hong Kong and adopting a qualitative approach, we characterise this sub-genre by describing its common discursive features with which these parodies are produced. We also probe into the functions of this specific digital genre, about which little is known.

The rest of the chapter is organised as follows: we will first offer an overview of the existing body of literature on parodies on digital media and establish the gaps we wish to traverse. Then, we will outline the methodological design and challenges before presenting and discussing the findings of our exploratory study. The chapter will end with a summary of the findings as well as some suggestions for future directions.

Parody and digital media

Parody, pervasive in artistic works as well as in everyday communication, has taken on an array of meanings over the course of time. There have been book-length discussions about this genre, tracing its history and transformation (see e.g. Dentith 2000, Hutcheon 2000, Rose 1993). For the purposes of this chapter, parody is defined as cultural practices that "are imitative of other cultural forms, with varying degrees of mockery or humour" (Dentith 2000: 193). It is a form of imitation that is humorous, critical, and oftentimes both, with the parodist making use of vari-directional double-voicing, in Bakhtin's (1984[1963]) terms. The critical dimension tends to be implicit. As remarked by Baxter (2014: 31):

> The speaker [parodist] uses the other's voice as a mask to disguise their own intentions; the criticism of the other is made under the cover of mimicry. Yet, at the same time, the semantic intention is clear: the speaker is reproducing the other's discourse in order to mock their target.

As with other texts, parody is a product of intertextuality, a process concerned not only with connections between texts, both prior and future ones (Fairclough 1992), but essentially also with connections between text producers and other users of these texts (Vásquez 2015).

Parody has, no doubt, a long history, but it has been increasingly associated with what can be found on the Internet nowadays. The technological affordances of digital media have facilitated its production, dissemination, and consumption. Of more relevance to our work is research that has studied digital parodies from a discourse analytical perspective. For example, Androutsopoulos (2010: 216) observed that parodies on YouTube were made using a wide range of "techniques of guerrilla double-voicing in the digital age" such as phonetic subtitling, (re-)dubbing, and restaging. He further pointed out that these parodies yield complex interpretations as a result of the multimedia layers and heteroglossic ambiguities they entail. Examining three "buffalaxed videos", consisting of original music video footage and new subtitles, Leppänen and Häkkinen (2012) made similar observations and zoomed in on the multi-layered representation of the oriental Other through entextualisation and resemiotisation. More recently, Lee (2020) studied a parody series titled Google Translate Sings, with a focus on the enregisterment of Googlish as co-constructed by the YouTuber creating the series and commenters. Despite different foci, these studies point to YouTube being a key site for multimodal heteroglossic parodies in which mass media materials can be remixed easily (Jenkins 2006). Importantly, as concluded by Chun and Walters (2011: 268) in their analysis of a video of a stand-up routine, parodies in this digital space "engage in ideological commentary while encouraging sociocultural participation".

Much of the existing research, including what we have just reviewed, centres around parodies in the form of videos on YouTube. It does not mean, however, that it is not worthwhile to scrutinize other forms in other communicative spaces. To this end, Vásquez (e.g. 2016, 2017, 2019) has investigated text-based parodies of consumer reviews on Amazon, an e-commerce platform conceivably different from social media sites in which creative self-expression is expected. In crafting mock narratives, the parodists were found to discursively construct the personae of consumers in bewilderment and to exploit linguistic ambiguity. They rely on and rework not just reviews of parodied products, both genuine and fake, but also other voices, texts, and genres, making their own works highly intertextual and even interdiscursive. Overall, Vásquez's series of studies has provided empirical evidence of and shed more light on the multifunctional potential of this genre of digital communication. In addition to amusing readers and offering social critiques, as may have been expected, some authors of the parodies examined convey overtly political messages. The "authorized transgressions" (Vásquez 2019: 155), that is, parody reviews which deviate in many ways from what is expected but remain on the site without being taken down, may even make otherwise banal products appealing, boosting the sales.

Our study reported in this chapter follows the previous line of enquiry and yet shifts the focus to audio-based parodies of fake voice messages. Another aspect which sets it apart from the existing studies of digital parodies is the platform on which the parodies spread – WhatsApp. According to Statista (2022a, 2022b), it is the most popular mobile messenger app in the world at the time of writing and the second most popular social media platform in Hong Kong with a penetration rate of 83.7% in 2021. The app supports one-to-one and group chats which are end-to-end encrypted. It enables users to send texts, voice messages, images, and videos, to name but a few. Unlike other social media platforms, WhatsApp is characterised by a high degree of privacy and closeness between users. This is evident in the body of research in linguistics and media studies exploring the use of groups. For example, König (2019) examined storytelling practices in German WhatsApp groups and discovered that the users share personal experiences with other participants of the chats primarily through voice messages, which are at times preceded by textual abstracts. In another study looking into Spanish users' news engagement, Masip *et al.* (2021) suggested that news shared on WhatsApp, particularly news shared by users in small groups, is highly social. Its trustworthiness and social endorsement are dependent largely on the senders, rather than on the original source. Through interviews with women faced with Israsel-Gaza violence, Roitman and Yeshua-Katz (2022) found that the group these participants are in serves as a powerful communal coping resource, with its affordances namely immediacy, mobility, multimodality, and reachability. In all these studies, the very act of sharing, which establishes and indexes intimacy, is integral to mobile communication.

The focus of our study on a voice-based genre also extends the existing literature on fake news that is based predominantly on text-based and video-based data. To date, there is a dearth of literature on audio messages of either misinformation or disinformation, let alone literature on the associated parodies. Kischinhevsky *et al.* (2020) analysed viral WhatsApp audio clips produced around the 2018 Brazilian presidential election. Their analysis revealed that the creators utilise features from what they call "radiophonic language" to expedite disinformation campaigns. In another study based in Brazil, Maros *et al.* (2021) compared audio messages containing verified misinformation with other messages, finding that the former ones generally reach more chat groups and users. To the best of our knowledge, the present study is the first one to analyse parody fake voice messages in Hong Kong, contributing to the body of work on audio-based digital parodies with a discourse analytical focus.

Data and methods

The voice messages for the present study were received between February 2020 and February 2022, a period during which Hong Kong experienced a total of five waves of the epidemic. As mentioned in the introduction, our initial interest in this digital genre stems from the relatively high-profile case of Ho's fake voice messages which made its way to mainstream news media. After this incident, we started observing COVID-19-related voice messages we as WhatsApp users received back in early 2020. From this initial observation, we discovered that many of them were parodic in nature. As soon as we decided to carry out the present study, we invited our WhatsApp contacts to forward any pandemic-related voice messages they believed to be parodic and to let us know the time when they first received them. A total of 34 audio files were first collected, saved, and converted to the mp3 format. Duplicate ones were then removed. From there, we eventually selected 21 messages fulfilling two major criteria: firstly, the messages came with a "Forwarded many times" label, indicating that they had reached a considerable number of users in society. Secondly, both of us also agreed that these messages were parodic. That is to say, the messages explicitly mimic and mock the COVID-19 disinformation transmitted via WhatsApp voice notes, and their double-voicing yields complex interpretations. Behind the seemingly serious tone, as we will show in the analysis, these messages contain certain degrees of mockery and humour. Unlike fake voice messages that do aim to deceive recipients, parody messages are not reported as fake and debunked.

The selected recordings lasted between 3 and 53 seconds. All of them were in Cantonese, a major spoken variety in Hong Kong. For the purposes of this exploratory study, the data were transcribed verbatim and coded iteratively for discursive patterns and functions. It is important to note that this is a small and selective sample, which can be attributed to the challenges of compiling a sample of parody fake voice messages. A fundamental challenge is that deciding whether a message is parodic is not a straightforward issue as it inevitably involves subjective interpretation (Hutcheon 2000). Other challenges are concerned with the nature and source of data. As they are audio messages in a closed and private communicative space, keyword search is not feasible, and more efforts have to be made to get access to and obtain them. Notwithstanding the small sample size, the database enables us to provide a rich language-based characterisation of this emerging digital genre. In the analysis that follows, illustrative examples and their English translations will be provided.

Findings and discussion

Discourse features

The parody fake voice messages we collected tend to convey a sense of intimacy, importance, urgency, and credibility through different resources and practices (see Table 24.1).

Intimacy, common in WhatsApp audio messages of disinformation (Kischinhevsky *et al.* 2020), can be created through such resources as pronouns and informal words. In our dataset, this is achieved remarkably through vocatives, particularly familiarizers (e.g. a. 兄弟 *guys*). The vocatives appear in initial position in group messages and enable the speakers to project their identity as someone with whom the addressees are familiar. In addition to maintaining close relationships (McCarthy and O'Keeffe 2003), vocatives in digital communication can serve as what Asprey and Tagg (2019) called "focuser", drawing the recipients' attention to the key message that is to follow. What is striking is that repetition of phrases or clauses is frequently observed. In the present case, it not only facilitates production and comprehension (see e.g. Tannen 2007), but more importantly also highlights "important" information, such as what spreads the coronavirus (b.) and how

Table 24.1 Discourse features of (parody) fake voice messages

Features	Examples
Vocatives	a. 兄弟
	(guys)
Repetition	b. 啲銀紙呢有菌，啲銀紙有菌
	(banknotes carry the virus, banknotes carry the virus)
Adverbs of time	c. 我啱啱呢同我Er嗰個 . . . ICU嗰個即喺個head呢，就傾咗一陣
	*(I've **just** chatted with the head of ICU [Intensive Care Unit] briefly.)*
	d. **而家**啲肥婆係咁比人搶呀
	*(Fat women are highly sought after **now** .)*
	e. 呢個消息一出呢，**好快**衛生巾都會斷市㗎喇
	*(Once the news breaks, sanitary pads will also be out of stock **soon**.)*
Reference to source of information	f. 我喺**醫管局**入面做嘅
	(I work at the Hospital Authority.)
	g. 我收到可靠情報，差唔多有**99%**準確嘅
	(I've got reliable information, which is around 99% accurate.)

to prevent infection. The information is always presented as new and relevant to action that the recipients need to take immediately, with the use of adverbs of time indicating recent past (e.g. c. 啱啱 *just*), present (e.g. d. 而家 *now*), and immediate future (e.g. e. 好快 *soon*). To establish credibility, most speakers make it explicit at the outset that they have the first-hand information (f.) or that the information is from a trustworthy source (g.), despite not having been verified. Since the news comes from the speakers they know and what the speakers believe, the recipients are inclined to believe it, using what Metzger *et al.* (2010) called "endorsement heuristic".

The discourse features discussed previously are to a certain extent reflective of what can be found in fake voice messages, as it is precisely these features that make the parodies recognisable and successful. It should also be noted that they contribute to the feelings of co-presence and immediacy, the affordances of WhatsApp perceived to be crucial in the context of COVID-19 (Costa *et al.* 2022). Despite the linguistic and structural resemblance, parody fake voice messages manifest additional elements of humour, exaggeration, and ridicule to criticise the spread of fake voice messages, their creators, and believers. The functions these parodies serve will be delineated in the following subsection.

Multifunctional nature

What is common to all parodies in our dataset, perhaps not surprisingly, is that they create humour, albeit in varying degrees. The first two examples presented here are explicitly humorous, whether or not the recipients would appreciate the intended playfulness and laugh:

Example 1: "Just run in the playground for 30 minutes"

我都係聽人地講番嚟㗎，佢話想check自己有冇肺炎呢，就係落操場跑30分鐘囉，   如果你有出汗嘅話呢，咁就係冇肺炎囉，如果你冇出汗嘅話呢，咁就係有肺炎囉。因為佢哋話呢er「武漢」肺炎吖嘛，咁你冇出汗咁咪有肺炎囉。

(I was told from someone that if you want to check whether you have pneumonia, just run in the playground for 30 minutes. If you sweat, it means you don't have it. If you don't sweat, it means you have it. It's because, as they said, er, it's called "Wuhan" pneumonia. If you have no sweat, then you'll have it.)

In Example 1, likely produced in early 2020 before WHO named the disease as COVID-19 and when people in Hong Kong saw it as a pneumonia, the speaker claims that running in the playground for half an hour is a way of determining if one has the coronavirus disease. He then adds that the indicator is whether one sweats after running and explains why this is so. The creator employs a number of techniques to make the message entertaining. One notable technique is the creative use of a homophonic pun, as has become apparent in the punchline. The Cantonese pronunciation of 武漢 (*Wuhan*; Jyutping: mou5 hon3), where the first batch of reported cases was found, is almost identical to that of 冇汗 (*no sweat*; Jyutping: mou5 hon6). Another salient technique is the addition of unexpected, absurd ideas to an ostensibly serious, informative message. The beginning leads recipients to believe that they may be able to find something valuable, though not yet widely known, but it turns out that what is followed is a piece of "advice" that is not scientifically grounded at all and is far from reasonable, that is, to run for a somewhat random duration of time, resulting in incongruity, a concept at the heart of humour studies (Forabosco 2008).

Example 2: "Grow nasal hair out"

各位朋友，各位朋友，留心聽住喇。有個方法呢，係可以避呢個Omicron嘅，就係留長啲
鼻毛，記得呀，同大家屋企人講，留長啲鼻毛，因為呢個Omicron呢，係「鼻毛」可避嘅。

(*Friends, friends, your attention please: There is one way to prevent Omicron, which is to grow nasal hair out. Don't forget to tell our family to grow nasal hair out, since nasal hair can prevent the infection.*)

Similar techniques can be observed in Example 2, which circulated at a time when Omicron, a highly infectious variant, arrived and caused the fifth wave of outbreak in Hong Kong. Firstly, the repeated expression 鼻毛 serves as a homophonic pun on the intended expression 避無, both sharing the Cantonese pronunciation bei6 mou4. 鼻毛 denotes *nasal hair* and is creatively employed as a substitute for 避無, the first two characters of a Chinese idiom 避無可避. The substitution results in a completely different expression (「鼻毛」可避), with the last two characters 可避 literally meaning "can" and "avoid" respectively. Taken together, the expression means, in this context, that nasal hair enables one to avoid contracting the virus. In contrast to it, the original idiom 避無可避, meaning unavoidable, interestingly invites an additional reading that it is next to impossible to avoid it and perhaps further suggests that people should not be overcautious. Secondly, the message juxtaposes what appears to be pressing and important with a ridiculous "prevention measure" – to grow nasal hair out.

Humorous discourse has a plethora of social functions, among which, as summarized by Chovanec and Tsakona (2018), are building solidarity and enhancing intimacy. In this case, the senders and recipients are connected through their shared knowledge of the jokes and shared experiences of living with anxiety and uncertainty due to the health crisis. We argue that in many ways these ludic recordings bear resemblance to Internet memes, which refer broadly to "groups of items sharing common characteristics of content, form, and/or stance . . . created, transformed, and circulated by many participants through digital participatory platforms" (Gal *et al.* 2016: 1700). The audio recordings are like memes not just because they are fun and spreadable, reaching a large number of users, but also because they have been playfully reworked. Regardless of whether Example 1, as what we have analysed, provides an inspiration for or is inspired by Example 3, it is clear that one references and almost copies another with only a few changes.

Example 3: "Go running, run for 30 minutes"

啱啱聽個friend講呢，話可以有個方法可以證實到自己有冇肺炎㗎，佢話落去跑步，跑30分鐘，如果有出汗呢，有出汗呀講緊，就er就冇事。如果冇出汗呢，咁就仆街喇。如果冇出汗即係代表係患上咗肺炎，因為佢叫做「武漢」肺炎㗎，所以如果冇流汗呢就仆街㗎喇。

(*I've just learnt from my friend that there is a way of checking whether you have pneumonia. He said one can go running, run for 30 minutes. If you sweat, sweat I mean, then you're er good. If you don't, then you're doomed. If you don't sweat, it means you have been infected with it. As it's called "Wuhan" pneumonia, if you have no sweat, then you're doomed.*)

In times of COVID-19 pandemic, specifically, digital humour in the form of multimodal memes provided relief from anxiety, stress, and other negative emotions (see Aslan 2022). There is no reason to believe that audio memetic messages cannot do the same.

Some parody messages have a more critical and ideological dimension. In Example 4, for instance, the addressees are encouraged to throw away all banknotes because they carry the virus. The exaggeration in terms of the action and quantity makes the "advice" obviously unreal and ridiculous.

Example 4: "Banknotes carry the virus"

Er呢單消息呢未經證實嘅，但都可信程度都好高嘅，嗽就話啲銀紙呢有菌，啲銀紙有菌，叫你揼晒啲錢出街，唔好要啲錢。

(*This piece of news hasn't been verified yet, but its credibility is pretty high. It says that banknotes carry the virus, banknotes carry the virus, and that you should dump all of them in the street and not keep them.*)

Through this parody, the creator possibly makes fun of people who are too scared to be rational. What should not be lost sight of is, however, that the message is simultaneously reflective of a broader ideology which many Hong Kong people have long espoused: money is all one lives for and depends on (Matthews and Lui 2001). Another parody, excerpted in Example 5, deploys a similar ideology in the service of social critique. The creator makes reference to the toilet paper shortage that once affected the city and other parts of the world due in part to panic buying and at the same time satirizes Hong Kong people's money madness.

Example 5: "Place a time deposit of two rolls of toilet paper"

遲啲個啲廁紙呢會值錢過啲銀紙，嗽呢聽日就攞兩卷廁紙入中國銀行，做番個定期，穩陣啲。

(*Toilet paper will be worth more than banknotes. Place a time deposit of two rolls of toilet paper at the Bank of China tomorrow. It's a safer investment.*)

What is also worth noting is that some parodies, such as Example 6, promote the idea that mainland Chinese, be they immigrants or tourists, compete with Hongkongers for resources.

Example 6: "Mainlanders are entering Hong Kong snatching our poo"

我喺醫管局入面做嘅，而家啲大陸人落緊嚟香港搶我哋啲屎呀，因為原來呢美國證實咗呢，食屎喺可以抗肺炎，而家大陸啲屎畀人食晒呀，佢哋落嚟香港我哋啲公共廁所嗰到搶我哋啲屎呀。

(*I work at the Hospital Authority. Now, mainlanders are entering Hong Kong snatching our poo, as the US has already confirmed that eating poo can cure the coronavirus. Having already eaten their own poo on the mainland, they're entering Hong Kong snatching our poo in our public toilets.*)

Throughout the recording, a boundary is demarcated between Hongkongers, who are portrayed as innocent victims with "resources" (*our poo*) being taken away, and mainland Chinese, portrayed as the greedy invaders draining others' resources after having consumed theirs (*their own poo*). It is a clear case of us-them polarisation found in ideological discourse (Van Dijk 2006). In Hong Kong, this polarisation has intensified since an influx of mainlanders bought up luxury goods as well as basic necessities such as milk powder in the late 2000s (Ma 2015) and were regarded by some local netizens as "locusts" (Yam 2016). It is plausible that the parody functions to reinforce the stereotype, perpetuate the othering, and invoke negative emotions such as hatred. The anti-mainlander sentiments are "justified" in this message, for the "resources" are claimed to be cures for a serious disease that has caused many deaths.

The last example to be presented in this subsection (Example 7) demonstrates the multifunctional nature of parodies:

Example 7: Order conscience, rationality, and intelligence

喂er各位同學呀，er我入面呢識得人呀，所以呢大家淨係好share比自己人得喇，仲一 快呀，因為政府入面已經有內部消息講緊呢，佢收到風，大陸呢已經有好多嗰啲工廠同埋公司嗰啲生產線都已經全部停晒喫喇，咁所以呢好多er嗰啲必需品呢er有幾樣嘢呢係幾日內呢已經會斷貨喫喇。嗱，er以下貨物呢，大家收左線之後即刻要去訂，第一樣嘢係良心，第二樣嘢係理性，第三樣好緊要嘅，呢排無晒喫喇，叫智商。咁所以大家快啲落order，落儲備呢，咁遲一日呢係乜Q都無喫喇，所以即刻要落order。

(Hey, schoolmates, I know an insider, so share (the news) only with those around you and do it quickly. The insider heard there's internal news from the government about the shutdown of many factories and companies' production lines on the mainland. It means some necessities will be out of stock in a few days. Order the following immediately after you hang up the phone: first, conscience; second, rationality; third – very important but missing these days – intelligence. So place your order as soon as possible and have these reserves. One day late and you'll have literally nothing! So place your order immediately.)

On the surface, the speaker informs his "schoolmates" of an imminent shortage of supply of "necessities". He further asks them to share the news with only those they are close to as well as to place an order "as soon as possible". What is unexpected but made clear towards the end is, however, that the essentials are not what Hong Kong citizens have been found to stock up on, such as food and toilet paper, but "conscience", "rationality", and "intelligence" – the qualities that the citizens are accused of gradually losing. Similar to previous examples, this parody conveys humour, which has its therapeutic function in times of epidemic. But it does more than that. Through double-voicing, the creator negatively evaluates the anxious shoppers, the behaviour of panic buying, and the ones spreading disinformation about shortages in society. We argue that the recording has its educational dimension as well, as the recipients are reminded to think before they act and be sensible. Last but not least, situated in the wider socio-political context of Hong Kong, where large-scale protests happening just before the outbreak sharpened the (pro-government) "blue" and (anti-government) "yellow" divide and caused an unprecedented level of radicalisation (Lee *et al.* 2021), the message can also be understood as an attempt to ask the recipients to behave according to their "conscience", "rationality", and "intelligence" – words that are commonly found in the recent political discourse.

Conclusion

Based on our exploratory analysis of a dataset of audio-based parodies that spread on WhatsApp, we have discovered that the parodists deploy a range of discourse features such as vocatives that occur message-initially, phrasal or clausal repetition, adverbs of time, and reference to source of information in imitating the fake voice messages. Through these resources, the (parody) messages are designed to be listened to by those with whom the senders are familiar and constructed as important ones containing reliable news and requiring the addressees' prompt action. These messages are therefore suitable for and common in a relatively closed digital space such as WhatsApp.

Our focus is not on disinformation per se but on the creative parodies arising from it. The study has lent support to Vásquez's observation: parodies "tend to present scenarios that are highly unlikely, completely absurd, very funny, sharply critical – and frequently, all of the above" (2019: 128). The parody messages in our dataset display varying degrees of humour created primarily through homophonic puns, juxtapositions of incompatible elements, and exaggeration. The humour enables users to maintain closeness and better cope with the stress and anxiety during the pandemic. As Example 7 has demonstrated, the parody messages can simultaneously be educational, critical, ideological, and political, allowing the creators to remind recipients not to believe whatever they receive blindly, criticise people's reactions to the pandemic, promulgate broader ideologies, and even promote changes.

Overall, the findings presented here have shed light on an under-researched and emerging digital genre, one that resembles the Internet meme and is not merely for fun. Understanding parody and its practice is, in fact, essential in critical media literacy education (Sinclair 2020). Future work will need to draw on a larger dataset, delve into how these parodies are engaged with and responded to using an ethnographic approach, explore how they are made possible by newer technologies, and unfold their complex interaction with disinformation. More attention should be paid to memetic messages that are not multimodal (Chau 2021). While there may be fewer parodies surrounding COVID-19 disinformation when the pandemic comes to an end (hopefully soon), there will certainly be parodies about other kinds of disinformation on digital media worthy of investigation.

References

Aljazeera. (2020) *Iran: Over 700 Dead after Drinking Alcohol to Cure Coronavirus*, 27 April. Available at: www.aljazeera.com/news/2020/4/27/iran-over-700-dead-after-drinking-alcohol-to-cure-coronavirus (Accessed: 24 May 2022).

Allington, D., Duffy, B., Wessely, S., Dhavan, N. and Rubin, J. (2021) Health-protective behaviour, social media usage and conspiracy belief during the COVID-19 public health emergency. *Psychological Medicine*, *51*(10), 1763–1769.

Androutsopoulos, J. (2010) Localizing the global on the participatory web. In N. Coupland (ed.), *The handbook of language and globalization*. Malden, MA: Wiley-Blackwell, pp. 203–231.

Aslan, E. (2022) Days of our 'quarantined' lives: Multimodal humour in COVID-19 internet memes. *Internet Pragmatics*, *5*(2), 227–256.

Asprey, E. and Tagg, C. (2019) The pragmatic use of vocatives in private one-to-one digital communication. *Internet Pragmatics*, *2*(1), 83–111.

Bakhtin, M. (1984 [1963]) *Problems of Dostoevsky's poetics* (ed. and trans. Caryl Emerson). Minneapolis, MN: University of Minnesota Press.

Baxter, J. (2014) *Double-voicing at work: Power, gender and linguistic expertise*. Basingstoke: Palgrave Macmillan.

Chau, D. (2021) Spreading language ideologies through social media: Enregistering the 'fake ABC' variety in Hong Kong. *Journal of Sociolinguistics*, *25*(4), 596–616.

Chovanec, J. and Tsakona, V. (2018) Investigating the dynamics of humor: Towards a theory of interactional humor. In V. Tsakona and J. Chovanec (eds.), *The dynamics of interactional humor: Creating and negotiating humor in everyday encounters*. Amsterdam: John Benjamins, pp. 1–28.

Chun, E. and Walters, K. (2011) Orienting to Arab orientalisms: Language, race and humor in a YouTube video. In C. Thurlow and K. Mroczek (eds.), *Digital discourse: Language in the new media*. Oxford: Oxford University Press, pp. 251–273.

Costa, E., Esteve-Del-Valle, M. and Hagedoorn, B. (2022) Scalable co-presence: WhatsApp and the mediation of personal relationships during the Covid-19 lockdown. *Social Media+ Society*, *8*(1), 20563051211069053.

Dentith, S. (2000) *Parody*. New York: Routledge.

Fairclough, N. (1992) Intertextuality in critical discourse analysis. *Linguistics and Education*, *4*, 269–293.

Forabosco, G. (2008) Is the concept of incongruity still a useful construct for the advancement of humor research? *Lodz Papers in Pragmatics*, *4*(1), 45–62.

Gal, N., Shifman, L., and Kampf, Z. (2016) It gets better: Internet memes and the construction of collective identity. *New Media & Society*, *18*(8), 1698–1714.

Goodman, J. and Carmichael, F. (2020) Coronavirus: 'Deadly Masks' Claims Debunked. *BBC*, 24 July. Available at: www.bbc.com/news/53108405 (Accessed: 24 May 2022).

Hutcheon, L. (2000) *A theory of parody: The teachings of twentieth-century art forms*. Urbana: University of Illinois press.

Jenkins, H. (2006) *Convergence culture: Where old and new media collide*. New York: New York University Press.

Kischinhevsky, M., Vieira, I. M., dos Santos, J. G. B., Chagas, V., Freitas, M. D. A. and Aldé, A. (2020) WhatsApp audios and the remediation of radio: Disinformation in Brazilian 2018 presidential election. *Radio Journal: International Studies in Broadcast & Audio Media*, *18*(2), 139–158.

König, K. (2019) Narratives 2.0: A multi-dimensional approach to semi-public storytelling in WhatsApp voice messages. *Journal für Medienlinguistik*, *2*(2), 30–59.

Lee, C. (2020) Googlish as a resource for networked multilingualism. *World Englishes*, *39*(1), 79–93.

Lee, F. L., Cheng, E. W., Liang, H., Tang, G. K. and Yuen, S. (2021) Dynamics of tactical radicalisation and public receptiveness in Hong Kong's Anti-Extradition Bill Movement. *Journal of Contemporary Asia*, 1–23.

Leppänen, S. and Häkkinen, A. (2012) Buffalaxed super-diversity: Representations of the other on YouTube. *Diversities*, *14*(2), 17–33.

Lewandowsky, S., Ecker, U. K. and Cook, J. (2017) Beyond misinformation: Understanding and coping with the "post-truth" era. *Journal of Applied Research in Memory and Cognition*, *6*(4), 353–369.

Ma, N. (2015) The rise of "anti-China" sentiments in Hong Kong and the 2012 Legislative Council elections. *The China Review*, 39–66.

Maros, A., Almeida, J. M. and Vasconcelos, M. (2021). A study of misinformation in audio messages shared in WhatsApp groups. In J. Bright, A. Giachanou, V. Spaiser, F. Spezzano, A. George and A. Pavliuc (eds.), *MISDOOM 2021: Disinformation in open online media. Lecture notes in computer science: vol. 12887*. Cham: Springer, pp. 85–100. https://doi.org/10.1007/978-3-030-87031-7_6

Masip, P., Suau, J., Ruiz-Caballero, C., Capilla, P., and Zilles, K. (2021) News engagement on closed platforms. Human factors and technological affordances influencing exposure to news on WhatsApp. *Digital Journalism*, *9*(8), 1062–1084.

Matthews, G. and Lui, T. L. (2001) Introduction. In G. Matthews and T. H. Lui (eds.), *Consuming Hong Kong*. Hong Kong: Hong Kong University Press, pp. 1–22.

McCarthy, M. and O'Keeffe, A. (2003) What's in a name? – Vocatives in casual conversations and radio phone-in calls. In P. Leistyna and C. Meyer (eds.), *Corpus analysis: Language structure and language use*. Amsterdam: Rodopi, pp. 153–185.

Metzger, M. J., Flanagin, A. J. and Medders, R. B. (2010) Social and heuristic approaches to credibility evaluation online. *Journal of communication*, *60*(3), 413–439.

Posetti, J. and Bontcheva, K. (2020) Disinfodemic: Deciphering COVID-19 disinformation. *Policy Brief 1*. Paris: United Nations Educational, Scientific and Cultural Organization.

397

Radu, R. (2020) Fighting the 'Infodemic': Legal responses to COVID-19 disinformation. *Social Media+ Society*, *6*(3), 2056305120948190.

Roitman, Y. and Yeshua-Katz, D. (2022) WhatsApp group as a shared resource for coping with political violence: The case of mothers living in an ongoing conflict area. *Mobile Media & Communication*, *10*(1), 3–20.

Rose, M. A. (1993) *Parody: Ancient, modern and post-modern*. Cambridge: Cambridge University Press.

Ross, A. S. and Rivers, D. J. (2018) Discursive deflection: Accusation of "fake news" and the spread of mis- and disinformation in the tweets of President Trump. *Social Media+ Society*, *4*(2), 2056305118776010.

Sinclair, C. (2020) Parody: Fake news, regeneration and education. *Postdigital Science and Education*, *2*(1), 61–77.

Sky Post (2020) 假錄音瘋傳弱鹼性抗疫 何栢良轟無邏輯, 7 April. Available at: https://skypost.ulifestyle. com.hk/article/2611815/假錄音瘋傳弱鹼性抗疫%20何栢良轟無邏輯 (Accessed: 24 May 2022).

Sousa-Silva, R. (2022) Fighting the fake: A forensic linguistic analysis to fake news detection. *International Journal for the Semiotics of Law-Revue internationale de Sémiotique juridique*, 1–25.

Statista. (2022a) *Penetration Rate of Leading Social Networks in Hong Kong as of 3rd Quarter 2021*. Available at: www.statista.com/statistics/412500/hk-social-network-penetration/ (Accessed: 24 May 2022).

Statista. (2022b). *WhatsApp – Statistics & Facts*. Available at: www.statista.com/topics/2018/whatsapp/#dossierKeyfigures (Accessed: 24 May 2022).

Tagg, C. and Seargeant, P. (2021) Context design and critical language/media awareness: Implications for a social digital literacies education. *Linguistics and Education*, *62*, 100776.

Tannen, D. (2007) *Talking voices: Repetition, dialogue, and imagery in conversational discourse*. Second edition. Cambridge: Cambridge University Press.

Van Dijk, T. A. (2006) Discourse and manipulation. *Discourse & Society*, *17*(3), 359–383.

Vásquez, C. (2015) Intertextuality and interdiscursivity in online consumer reviews. In R. H. Jones, A. Chik, and C. A. Hafner (eds.), *Discourse and digital practices: Doing discourse analysis in the digital age*. London: Routledge, pp. 66–80.

Vásquez, C. (2016) Intertextuality and authorized transgression in parodies of online consumer reviews. *Language@ Internet*, *13*(6).

Vásquez, C. (2017) "My life has changed forever!": Narrative identities in parodies of Amazon reviews. *Narrative Inquiry*, *27*(2), 217–234.

Vásquez, C. (2019) *Language, creativity and humour online*. London: Routledge.

Wardle, C. (2017) *Fake news. It's complicated*. Available at: https://firstdraftnews.org/articles/fake-news-complicated/ (Accessed: 27 November 2022).

Yam, S. Y. S. (2016) Affective economies and alienizing discourse: Citizenship and maternity tourism in Hong Kong. *Rhetoric Society Quarterly*, *46*(5), 410–433.

Zarocostas, J. (2020) How to fight an infodemic. *The Lancet*, *395*(10225), 676.

25

THE IMPACT OF COVID-19 REPORTS ON MULTICULTURAL YOUNG PEOPLE'S SOCIAL AND PSYCHOLOGICAL WELL-BEING

Novel experiential metaphors in an ELF-mediated debate on fake news

Maria Grazia Guido

Research focus

This chapter reports on a descriptive case study in cross-cultural cognitive linguistics (cf. Langacker 1991; Lakoff and Johnson 1999) concerned with the socioculturally variable use of English modal verbs which emphasises new COVID-triggered cognitive metaphors conceived by a focus group of young and multicultural participants in an online debate, whose exposure to possible fake news and media disinformation come to modify the perception of their social and psychological state within increasingly changing virtual and multicultural contexts of interaction. The group was composed of Italian, Greek, and migrant subjects from Nigeria, Morocco, and Yemen, all non-native speakers of English that they used as a "lingua franca" (ELF) (cf. Guido 2008, 2018). The study intended to determine whether the group's pragmatic use of modals introducing novel metaphors actually varied in relation to the role played by the participants' different background experiences and values (or *schemata* – Rumelhart 1980), developed within their native sociolinguistic communities,[1] as well as to the particular "emotion-raising" topic chosen for the case study – namely, the probable fake news on the causes of the COVID-19 pandemic. A journalistic text (drawn from a corpus of texts on the same topic submitted to the focus group for an ELF-mediated discussion) represented the trigger for the newly coined metaphors of "seclusion", "inclusion", and "exclusion". The online debate then expanded to encompass topics such as fake news on online communication, as well as on the related issues of gender and ethnic discrimination and empowerment, particularly in relation to the migrant participants' concern for their welfare and healthcare in the host European countries. All such issues acquire an unprecedented momentum because they are contextualized within the so-called "virtual metaverse" (Narula 2022).[2]

DOI: 10.4324/9781003224495-30

Research assumptions, rationale, and hypothesis

The study starts from the observation that the more the participants were emotionally involved in the topic – regarding possible fake news on the causes and the consequences of the COVID-19 pandemic – the more markedly their specific ELF variations emerged in the debate. This is assumed to be due to the fact that the participants unconsciously perceived such ELF variations as more spontaneous and familiar for the immediate expression of their emotions and opinions, insofar as these variations have developed from the natural transfer of the participants' native-language structures into the non-native English language they used (Guido 2008, 2018). Indeed, precisely these ELF variations allowed the conveyance of the new metaphors for the expression of the participants' novel experience of forced lockdown and online communication having an impact on their social and psychological well-being.

At the basis of such an assumption, there is the notion that negative emotions developed with reference to the topic that activated in the participants' minds what is here defined as *high-context schemata*, whereas positive emotions activate *low-context schemata*. Conventionally, the term "low-context" is associated with cultures whose communicative styles are characterised by direct, semantic-based denotative meanings conveyed by words independently from context, whereas the term "high-context" is related to indirect and context-bound pragmatic communication occurring within cultures with strong social values and shared connotative associations (cf. Hofstede 1983; Hall 1990).[3] The rationale in this study is that the increasing COVID-triggered digitalization and dematerialization of both reality (turned into a "virtual metaverse") and the physical bodies of people interacting online (Guido 2021) is affecting the established characteristics of the different socioculturally marked contexts which determine the different conceptualization of events.

The hypothesis is that the sudden imposition of online communication modes as a global health policy with the intent of containing the spread of the pandemic – with the consequent spread of a number of possible fake news on its causes and effects on people's lives – has challenged the pre-existing ways of making sense of contexts and events of reality conventionally accepted within different sociolinguistic communities.[4] In the case study in point, the challenge involves also the conventional attribution of low-context and high-context schemata to the participants in the online interaction who belong to different native linguacultural contexts, to the point of affecting the cognitive metaphors by which they make experiential sense of the new virtual dimension of communication.

The case study

As the case study will illustrate, a deviation from the expected conventional attribution of high/low-context schemata was identified in the participants in the online debate. This group was composed of three Italian university students (one male and two females), two Greek university students (a male and a female), a female migrant student from Yemen and a female migrant student from Morocco (both attending the Greek university involved in the case study), and two migrant students from Nigeria (a male and a female, collaborating with research in the Italian university involved),[5] all in their early/mid twenties. According to the taxonomy of high/low-context cultures by Hall (1990), Nigerian, Moroccan, and Yemeni cultures are ranked among the highest-context ones insofar as the shared contextual knowledge is given for granted and is essential for the disambiguation and understanding of messages. Also Italian and Greek cultures are conventionally ranked – like the cultures of other Southern-European countries – among the high-context cultures (*ibidem*), though less high than the cultures of non-Western countries of Africa, Asia, Middle East, and Latin America. This seems to be due to the influence of Northern European countries and the United States that are ranked, instead, as low-context cultures.

As the analysis reported in the next section will reveal in detail (carried out on the whole corpus of case study data – cf. Guido 2022), with reference to the online context of interaction, Italian and Greek participants in the focus group seemed to strengthen their position among the high-context cultures; whereas, surprisingly, the Moroccan, Nigerian, and Yemeni migrant participants revealed a significant countertrend towards a low-context type of culture in contrast with the native high-context cultures they belong to. More precisely, data analysis showed a high-context schema involvement in the Italian and Greek participants' response to the topic under discussion, signalled by a higher frequency of deontic modals (principally "must"), emphasising "social" obligation and necessity. Such deontic modals occur precisely in relation to novel metaphors related to the Italian and Greek participants' recent distressing experience of "seclusion" in their homes imposed by the lockdown measures introduced worldwide to contain the COVID pandemic, as well as to their personal feelings of "exclusion" from normal social relations, all of a sudden entirely replaced by virtual meetings on online platforms. A low-context schema involvement in the topic was identified, instead, in the Nigerian, Moroccan, and Yemeni migrant participants' responses to the set-topic, signalled by a frequent use of epistemic modals of possibility and deduction (i.e. "can", "could", "may") in relation to the freedom and the surprising sense of "inclusion" offered to them by the new contexts of the online "metaverse", opening unexpected possibilities of emancipation from the strict social rules regulating their native and host high-context cultures.

Before proceeding to an in-depth examination of this high/low-context schema asymmetry between the participants of the focus group, the theoretical grounds of the present study will be introduced to provide the scope and context for data interpretation.

Theoretical framework

In the field of cognitive linguistics, modality is regarded as stemming from a unique categorial prototype stored in the mind as a result of people's experience of external socio-physical force-dynamics (i.e. the experience of forces and barriers that naturally intervene in people's physical and social interaction with the environment and that come to develop as shared cognitive metaphors – Talmy 1988). This force-dynamic prototype is thus a cognitive/affective "core meaning" from which both deontic and epistemic interpretations of modality can be derived by inference (Sweetser 1990; Hinkel 1995). English has grammaticalized its modal notions of possibility, obligation, and volition symmetrically, by deriving them from the same physical force-dynamic experience of a "barrier" to be forced (*will/shall*), to achieve potential (*may*) or complete (*can*) removal (at the basis of the epistemic metaphors of "inclusion"), or to be retained to restrict action (*must, have to, need, ought to, should*) (at the basis of the deontic metaphors of "exclusion" and "seclusion").

Indeed, data from the present case study suggest that the new virtual environments of the "metaverse" – suddenly substituting the actual real contexts of interaction during and after the total lockdown imposed worldwide to contain the COVID pandemic – has undermined every consolidated experience with reference, on the one hand, to the physical world, since communication has occurred through computer/smartphone screens, and on the other, to the expected socially accepted pragmalinguistic uses (cf. Guido 2021).

What seems to be implied in this experientialist view of modality is a notion of modal verbs as grammaticalized emotional patterns (cf. Collier *et al.* 1982) encompassing all the human responses to the physical and social "forces" experienced while interacting with the environment. On these premises, it is here claimed that within a totally unexplored virtual environment, such as the on-line "metaverse", the semantic and pragmatic roots of modal verbs come to be experientially reconverted within situations of intercultural communication, where divergences emerge not only in reference to the perception and interpretation of the same events but also to the emotional involvement of the participants in the discourse topic. The corollary to this is that the participants' low-context schema involvement in the topic they are dealing with can prompt an epistemic exploration of social and experiential possibilities within the new metaphorical space of the "metaverse". On the contrary, the participants' high-context schema involvement in the topic can prompt a deontic resistance to possible new sociocultural and experiential scenarios introduced by online interactions.

Protocol analysis

The case study was ethnographic in orientation with a special emphasis on the analysis of the participants' responses to a number of articles on the possible origin of the COVID pandemic (one of which alone is reported in this chapter as an example) – chosen on the basis of the covert manipulating insinuation strategies implemented by the authors – and their comment on the probable fake news identified in them as they participated in an online debate by using their respective ELF variations (cf. Guido 2022).

In the protocol analysis reported in the next section, participants in the focus group are marked with the following identification labels: *a)* "Italian female participant 1": IF1 (Alessia); *b)* "Italian female participant 2": IF2 (Stefania); *c)* Italian male participant 3": IM3 (Marco); *d)* "Greek female participant 4": GF4 (Despina); *e)* "Greek male participant 5": GM5 (Nikos); *f)* "Nigerian female participant 6": NF6 (Jamilah); *g)* "Nigerian male participant 7": NM7 (Ayo); *h)* "Moroccan female participant 8": MF8 (Najia); *i)* "Yemeni female participant 9": YF9 (Shirin). Next are reported two extracts from the set text,[6] followed by a critical discourse analysis on the argumentative discourse construction (O'Halloran 2003), meant to illustrate how linguistic features in the text may be organised in such a way as to convey the author's intended illocutionary force of his/her discussion, aimed at manipulating the perlocutionary effects of the text on receivers in their interpretation processes, and then by a protocol analysis (Ericsson and Simon 1984) of the participants' recorded comments during the debate in order to observe the effects of the text on them in terms of their cognitive responses and emotional reactions to the textual construction.[7]

The set-text is an article titled *Gain of Function*, written by a US science populariser, Derek Lowe,[8] and published in the online issue of *Science* on 26 October 2021.

Extract 1

Ever since the advent of SARS-CoV-2 in Wuhan, there have been questions about coronavirus work conducted at the Wuhan Institute of Virology. My own view hasn't really changed since the last time I wrote about that particular issue: I think a natural origin for the current virus is *very* much more likely than it being some sort of engineering construct (in fact, I don't give that latter possibility any real credibility at all). But what that doesn't rule out is the general lab-leak hypothesis, because someone could have been studying the wild-type virus and made a careless mistake as well. Clarity in this area is totally lacking, and while I hope the new investigative team . . . can figure some things out, I doubt if that will happen. The Chinese authorities have (so far) shown no interest at all in really cooperating with such an inquiry. They must realize that this just brings on more suspicion, but they have clearly decided that that is better than many of the alternatives.

Critical discourse analysis

The point of view of the US author of Text 1 represents the typical stance of his low-context culture, looking for an unambiguous communication based on the actual meaning of words in a message not marked by specific context-bound connotations – as it is instead typical of high-context cultures (such as the Chinese one) where the meaning of messages is covert and, thus, to be achieved within a sociocultural context. And yet behind such a low-context style, it is possible to perceive a covert high-context biased viewpoint on the topic.

The extract starts with an existential process conveyed by the syntagm "there have been" introducing an agentless passive that is rendered not as a "process" by means of a verb form (such as "to question") but as a "fact", by resorting to the corresponding verb nominalization: "questions", enquiring into the "coronavirus work" at the Wuhan Institute of Virology. Also the human agency in charge of such a "work" is omitted since it is only implied by the use of the past participle "conducted" as an elided form of agentless passive. The author's contention moves, however, are always introduced through declarative clauses and phrases stated in the first person ("My own view"; "I think"; "I don't give . . . any real credibility"; "I hope", "I doubt"), by which he continuously highlights his view on the lack of clarity in the Chinese lab experiments. Initially, the author seems to concede that the origin of COVID does not derive from an "engineering construct" devised by the Wuhan virologists. In stating this, he uses epistemic adverbial and adjectival edges ("my own view hasn't *really* changed"; "I think a natural origin for the current virus is *very* [italicized emphasis] much more *likely* than it being *some sort of* engineering construct"; "*any real* credibility *at all*"). Then, the adversative "But" suddenly conveys a change in the direction of the author's thought by introducing his contention for a possible "general lab-leak hypothesis". The subsequent "concession move" this time regards again the accidental "careless mistake" – caused by an unspecified agent ("someone") – suggested by the epistemic modal "could". Yet the ensuing statement is formulated as an objective "fact" through the use of the present simple of the verb "to be", which represents a serious attack against the ambiguous behaviour of the Chinese authorities and virologists who, however, are not thematized in any grammatical, logical, and psychological subject position within the clause (Halliday 1994). In fact, the clausal subject in a thematic collocation is represented by the abstract medium – that is, "Clarity" – denied by the negative connotation of the non-finite verb phrase marked by an adverbial booster: "is totally lacking". Though the author seems to allow a new – and almost indefinite – epistemic concession by "hoping" for a "new investigative team" that "*can* figure some things out", then he soon denies such a possibility: "I doubt if that will happen". The modal "will" conveys a double implication: a deontic determination – disapproved by the author (cf. Guido 2004) – not to be clear about the nature of the Wuhan experiments, as well as an epistemic belief that "clarity in this area" has never been expected to represent an option.

Finally, the author enacts his defence move by directly attacking "The Chinese authorities" collocated in a psychological, logical, and grammatical subject position within an active clause, thus foregrounding the authorities' responsibility (mitigated by the parenthetic "so far") as agents who "have (so far) shown no interest at all in really cooperating with such an enquiry". The epistemic "must", introducing a logical conclusion and judgment in the argumentation, focuses on the authorities' realisation that their ambiguous behaviour provokes "more suspicion", though the new adversative "but" grants another – and yet still critical – concession to a possible and, this time "clearly decided", favourable opportunity for their choice.

Participants' debate

IF1: I think that the author is not giving fake news. I think (..) I think that China is (.) really hiding information about the virus (..) created in the lab (..) and then escaped from the lab.

GM5: you mean (. . .) accidentally?

IF1: yes

GM5: because (..) I don't think that it was a mistake (.) I think that China is (. . .) is (.) spreading Covid in all the world (..) I mean (.) intentionally.

MF8: why you think this?

GM5: because China has decided that it must to (. . .) impose its power in the world and (. . .) and pandemic is a (. . .) weapon of mass destruction (..) and control (..) because China must submit all humanity to its power.

MF8: but this a racist prejudice (. . .) a lot of people died of Covid in China.

NM7: but also if U.S. and Europe say Chinese scientists bin make mistake (.) and the virus left the lab (..) and spread (.) I think (.) this a racist prejudice because (.) Chinese people are no American (.) or European and so (..) people must think here se [that] they are (.) no serious (.) true scientists.

IF2:   I think that China (..) decided that all people must be (. . .) must be imprisoned in their houses and can communicate only with computer or smartphone (. . .) we are prisoners (..) you understand? (..) China limit freedom (.) and relations to control people.

YF9: well (..) I'm not sure this is a limitation. I feel more free to say what I like if I can speak through a computer screen (..) I mean (..) I can switch off the video and (..) and I'm not judged because I wear the Islamic headscarf (. . .) I'm not judged for my external appear-ance (.) for my modesty (.) because I don't want to follow Western fashion rules (..) so (..) people must focus on what I want to say.

IF1: really? (..) I thought that the veil is symbol of the man's oppression for Islamic women (. . .) also the computer screen must be considered oppression (..) because we cannot be free to be near (.) I mean (.) physically near to other people.

MF8: I think I understand what Shirin [YF9] means (..) and I agree with her (. . .) the computer screen can be like our headscarf (..) it cover women's physical aspect and (.) allow their free expression with nobody that can judge them for their look (..) I mean (.) women can be more powerful when they speak protected by a headscarf or by a computer screen.

NF6: yes (..) the screen can also cover the colour of the skin (. . .) I know (..) I can get more when I ask help online for social services (.) or health services (.) with no video that show I'm black.

GF4: but people on the other side of the screen know that you are Nigerian.

NF6: yes (.) but they can no see me (.) no see I'm black (..) you know? (..) I can be just a migrant like another (..) like a white migrant (..) you understand? (..) they no see me and can no think to the colour of my skin.

NM7: if doctors, or lawyers see we are black (.) they give us just little assistance (..) better if they no see we are black (..) here people think se [that] virus come with African people and we spread the virus in Europe (..) but African people have strong health (..) desert (.) sea (.) prison torture bin no kill us (.) we are strong.

From the participants' debate triggered by this extract, some novel cognitive metaphors emerge. On the one hand, Italian and Greek participants still keep activating their expected high-context schemata to make sense of the new computer-mediated social relations, as they converge on the conventional deontic modal metaphor of the gatekeeping "physical barrier" – represented by the computer/smartphone screen – by which the Chinese totalitarian power covertly imposes an obligation ("must") to stay secluded at home, or denies permission ("cannot") to meet people in the flesh by only giving permission ("can") to socialize online. Such deontic metaphor of "seclusion" represents China as a deliberate antagonist of the democratic lifestyle of Western countries. Hence, GM5 states that China *must* impose its power to submit the whole humanity, so that – IF2 adds – all people *must* be imprisoned in their houses and *can* only communicate through a computer screen that, as IF1 remarks, *must* be considered as an oppression since people *cannot* be free to meet in the flesh. On the other hand, non-Western participants, represented by migrants from the high-context cultures of Nigeria, Morocco, and Yemen, surprisingly find in the new online environment a possibility for freeing themselves from the high-context schema constraints imposed by their native and host social contexts. This allows them to activate in their minds the novel epistemic modal metaphor of "inclusion", according to which the computer/smartphone screen represents no longer a limiting barrier but a possible protection enhancing gender/race empowerment. YF9 remarks that she feels free to say what she likes if she *can* (epistemic possibility) speak through a computer screen by switching the video off and being judged not for her Islamic headscarf and her nonconformity to the Western aesthetic standards imposed upon women but for what she says. To this MF8 adds that the computer screen *can* be like the Islamic headscarf, covering women's physical aspect and allowing their free expression. Furthermore, NF6 remarks that a switched-off video *can* hide the migrants' skin colour, thus allowing them to get more benefits from the social service providers. NM7 upgrades this view by highlighting the connection between being black and receiving less assistance from medical doctors and legal advisors since African people are perceived as a vehicle of virus spread, whereas – NM7 claims – they are strong and healthy, having overcome so many threatening obstacles (i.e. desert, sea, prison, and torture).

What follows is another extract from the same text under discussion.

Extract 2

A particularly hot topic has been "gain-of-function" research, so let's try to define that a bit. . . . In virology, it generally refers to work that would help to understand how a particular virus might be able to mutate in the future under different conditions. . . . Viruses are constantly mutating, and GoF work is an attempt to see around the corner and anticipate what might come next – and how likely (or unlikely) that might be to happen in the real world. I believe that this is very important work, but it's not to be undertaken lightly. In the most dangerous cases – which can also be the most important ones, at times – you may be working with a virus that could acquire (through your work) the ability to spread through the human population. Even further, you may be working with a virus that is *already* capable of doing that, and producing forms of it that are still more infectious or more easily able to avoid the human immune response. This sort of work calls for extremely stringent review and oversight, and it also needs the highest levels of lab safety and containment measures that biomedicine is capable of providing. Those controls apply to any lab that's handling the most dangerous pathogens. There are only a few dozen labs in the world that work at these levels, and very few of those are doing anything like gain-of-function. Some of them, for example, are strictly for diagnostic work. That link provides the less-than-reassuring news, though, that only about a quarter of those labs receive high scores overall for safety and security. And only a handful of countries categorize experiments like gain-of-function research as a separate thing that needs its own regulatory oversight. China does not, nor are the members of the International Experts Group on Biosafety and Biosecurity Regulators.

Critical discourse analysis

This extract is only apparently just informative about the so-called Gain-of-Function research. In fact, since the beginning, the author tries to directly involve his implied readers ("so let's try to define that a bit") with the probable covert purpose of manipulating their interpretation of the "stated facts". The author repeatedly uses "might" – namely, the epistemic modal verb of "improbability" – as an uncertainty marker determining discourse formality and entailing the author's psychological distancing from the aims of the GoF experiments. Furthermore, such experiments are referred to by means of epistemic edging ("likely or unlikely") and the popular metaphor of the "corner" ("GoF work is an attempt to see around the corner and anticipate what might come next"). Indeed, the argumentative structure is quite complex. It introduces the author's first-person endorsement on the GoF research ("I believe") by which he concedes "that this is very important work". Such an apparent unreserved approval is, however, soon downplayed with the introduction of the adversative "but" and the negative specifier "not" by which the author warns against the risk of "undertaking" this type of research "lightly". In this way, he surreptitiously seems to imply that such a "lightness" may in fact be ascribed to the Chinese GoF research. The next hypotactic sentence is a convoluted one, composed of a dominant clause alarmingly introducing the author's negative judgment on GoF, emphasised by an adjectival booster in the phrase "the most dangerous cases". This dominant clause is then split into two separate parts by the incorporation of a dependent relative clause as a mitigating concessive statement of positive epistemic possibility ("which can also be the most important ones"). The second part of the dominant clause is then characterised by the author's direct involvement of his implied receivers through the use of the second-person address term "you" marking a quite informal tenor (Halliday 1994), followed by the epistemic modal verbs of probability "may" and "could". This may be regarded as a strategy of persuasion – if not of audience manipulation – aimed at casting the readers themselves in the role of scientists so as to give them the possibility (introduced by the epistemic modal "may") of experiencing first-hand how likely it is for scientists to make mistakes. This eventuality is made even more probable (as denoted by the epistemic modal "could") and dangerous when readers themselves, virtually experiencing the role of the GoF virologists (as explicitly stated by the parenthetic phrase "through your work") manipulate a virus to the point that it acquires "the ability to spread through the human population". The subsequent repeated epistemic modal "may", once again preceded by the second-person pronoun "you" as the clausal subject, is then emphasised by the expression "even further", as well as by the italicized adverb *"already"*, both alarmingly introducing the 'capability' of the virus to spread more and more, thus becoming "still more infectious" and "more easily able to avoid the human immune response". The series of adjectives in the superlative form and adverbial phrases with negative connotations that follow, together with non-finite verb phrases in the present participle, emphasise the worryingly growing situation of danger insinuated by the author. To be as clear as possible, the author activates, by using the deontic modal "need", the low-context schema that clearly states the necessity for extreme safety and security measures to be adopted, which transcends any lab context in the world "handling the most dangerous pathogens". The frightening news – probably "fake news" – that the author introduces, with the aim of alarming readers even more, regards the fact that very few of "those labs receive high scores overall for safety and security". Then, all of a sudden, he concludes his argumentation with the sharp revelation that "China does not" (receive high scores for lab safety and security), thus placing China in the responsible thematic position of logical, psychological, and grammatical clausal subject, subsequently upgrading such a climax by signalling the highest state of danger in China as he adds that "nor are the members of the International Experts Group on Biosafety and Biosecurity Regulators".

Participants' debate

IM3: this is very dangerous experiments with the virus (..) I don't think they do them "to see around the corner" and understand what can happen in the future (..) I think that they (.) they create in secret weapons of mass destruction.

GM5: exactly (..) their aim is not to save people but to destroy all of them.

IF1: this is really (..) really worry (..) worrying (. . .) I really think that China decided that the world must end.

IF2: I already thought to this when Xylella (.) was created in the lab and killed all the (.) olive trees (.) and I think that it was created just to destroy nature (. . .) someone decided that the olive trees must die (.) maybe for economic reasons (.) competition between olive oil of different regions (.) and I'm so sad (.) when I see all these trees dead (..) like skeletons.

IM3: genetic manipulation is destroying nature (.) you see how are big the fruits and (..) and the vegetables now? (..) enormous! And they have no (..) no taste.

IF1: and also animals! (..) chickens are big like my dog (.) they are full of hormones.

IM3: this is for marketing reason (..) you know? (..) manipulated fruits must (..) to sell for a long time (..) they also treat it with (.) pesticides (.) but they destroy the health of people (.) of animals (.) and plants.

NM7: I think this a fake news (..) genetic manipulation for agriculture can really help solve the problem of people (.) hungry in poor countries (.) like Africa (..) can help produce more food (.) for all them (..) no expensive food.

MF8: and of course genetic manipulation of a dangerous virus (.) like Covid (.) can help (.) develop new vaccines (.) low-cost vaccines (.) for all people in the world (.) to stop the pandemic.

GM5: a virus manipulated in the lab (..) when go out in the real world kill everybody (. . .) like food manipulated in the lab is (.) dangerous for the health.

GF4: and also our relations are manipulated now that we must be online (..) yes (.) and if we can finally go out in the real world (.) we shall not know (.) no more (.) how (.) how we can have (..) normal real relations with other people (..) now I (.) don't really understand no more when I'm in the computer screen where is in or out (.) or (.) where is up and where is down.

GM5: yes, China uses the computer screen like a lab (..) a place for experiments because it must manipulate us (.) we always must fear infection and death and use the mask (.) so we cannot smile no more (..) I also have no more orientation (.) and don't know no more the sense of my life (.) if I live in the screen (.) and I cannot imagine my future.

The participants' debate, at this stage, focuses on the possible outcome of the risky GoF experiments in virology. In particular, they make overt the extent to which they deviate from their conventionally expected high/low schema categorization of sociocultural contexts (Hall 1990). In fact, participants from Italy – who belong to the medium/high-contexts typical of Southern-European countries – once again show their high-context positioning when they let themselves be influenced by the author's alarming tone to the point that they expand the scope of the text argumentation to add their own schema associations with other parallel distressing topics. Such topic correlations are all marked by the use of deontic modals "must" (implying "obligation") and "can" ("permission"), which are here seen to convey a high-context schema metaphor of "exclusion". Indeed, since the beginning of the exchange, a high-context schema metaphor of "exclusion" introduced by the deontic modal "must" is identified in IF1's expansion of the author's shocking statement on the lack of lab safety and security in China to include the possible fake news about China's deliberate criminal decision to doom the world to destruction, "excluding" people from the possibility of a safe life. This metaphor is taken up by the other Italian female participant, IF2, who extends it – again through the use of the deontic modal "must" – to encompass the parallel topic of Xylella, and insinuate the other possible fake news that a ruthless economic warfare is the cause of this special bacterium created in the lab to destroy olive trees, "excluding" them from the perspective of being an economic support for Southern Italy. The metaphor of "exclusion" is even more expanded by the Italian IF2 and IF1 – still through the use of the deontic modal "must" – to encompass the parallel topic of the economic warfare imposing lab research on genetic manipulation of food (i.e. producing "giant" fruit, vegetables, and meat animals) to make it last longer in the market, without any consideration for the harmful effects on people's health.

At this point, non-Western participants from Nigeria and Morocco take an unexpected low-context schema stance deviating from their expected native high-context schema one conventionally suspicious of scientific advances on genetic manipulation (mainly for religious reasons – cf. Guido 2008). The Nigerian participant NM7 introduces a novel low-context schema metaphor of "inclusion" by claiming that genetic manipulation in agriculture actually offers the possibility (marked by the epistemic modal "can") of solving the problem of hunger in poor countries, like many African countries, through the mass production of low-cost food available to everybody. This schema metaphor of "inclusion" is then expanded by the Moroccan participant MF8 who uses it – by employing the same epistemic modal verb ("can") – to encompass the promising benefits of genetic manipulation on a dangerous virus like COVID for the mass production of low-cost vaccines to immunize the entire population in order to impede the spread of the pandemic.

The Greek participants, then, introduce a new turn in the interpretation of the set text by developing the novel high-context schema metaphor of "seclusion" triggered by China's assumed determination – highlighted by the use of the deontic modal "must" – to completely control the existence of humankind. GF4 is the first participant that mentions the new metaphor of "seclusion" when she claims that people are forced to stay indoors in a state of confinement, deprived of freedom of physical movement and social relations in the flesh. Furthermore, she foresees (by using the deontic modal "shall") that if one day people were given the permission (signalled by the deontic modal "can") to leave the virtual online environment and, thus, their houses, then they shall no longer be able to establish not only actual social relationships but even orientational relationships with the surrounding physical environment. GM5 extends even more this metaphor of the "imposed seclusion" – as China's strategy of people manipulation by controlling them through the fear for infection and death (and the use of surgical masks denying the facial expression of emotions) – to include his inability to find the sense and future of his life imprisoned in the virtual environment.

Conclusions

This case study has analysed non-native uses of English modality as they diverge from habitual high/low-context metaphorical schemata within different sociolinguistic communities represented by a focus group of multicultural participants in an ELF-mediated online debate. More specifically, the case study has explored the new cognitive metaphors of "inclusion", "exclusion", and "seclusion" developed by the participants in relation to their social and psychological involvement with the topic under discussion – namely, the probable fake news on the causes of the COVID-19 pandemic, conveyed by the journalistic text submitted to the focus group. The discussion developed further to encompass the positive and negative consequences of pandemic, involving the obligation to stay at home and communicate exclusively online, with the related issues of gender and ethnic discrimination, or rather empowerment.

What stands out in this case study is that the more the participants were emotionally involved in such a topic (and, thus, were induced to seek accommodation to the new context and to the different opinions of the multicultural participants they are interacting with), the more markedly their specific ELF variations emerged in the debate, in that ELF results from the natural transfer of the participants' native-language structures into the non-native English language they used (cf. Guido 2021). Hence, for instance, the typical syntactic and semantic structures of the Nigerian Pidgin English emerged in the ELF variation used by the Nigerian participants NF6 and NF7 – such as the pre-verbal particle "bin" as a past-tense marker; the structure of the negative clause with the sole negative particle "no"; the transfer of the relative pronoun "se" from their native Igbo language used instead of "that"; and the transfer of ergative OVS structures transferred from Igbo, collocating abstract/inanimate objects in animate-subject position ("desert, sea, prison, torture no kill us"). The omission of the copular verb "to be" and of the third-person singular suffix "-s" can be identified in the Moroccan participant MF8's ELF variation ("this a racist prejudice"; "it cover women's physical aspect"), and a normalisation of the structure of the comparative monosyllabic adjective can be found in the Yemeni participant YF9's ELF variation ("I feel more free"). Several deviations from the Standard-English norms can be identified in the Greek and Italian participants' ELF variations. In the Italian participants' ELF uses, deviations range from a lack of agreement between clausal subjects and singular/plural suffixation of verbs, to third-person singular suffix drop; inappropriate use of prepositions; and omission of auxiliaries and auxiliary inversion in formulating questions. These features can be identified also in the Greek participants' ELF uses, where in addition it is possible to notice a double negation in the clausal structure ("I don't really understand no more"; "we cannot smile no more"; "I also don't know no more").

Indeed, precisely these ELF variations allowed the conveyance of the new metaphors for the expression of the participants' experience of forced lockdown and online communication. In this respect, the participants in the online debate who were migrants from the high-context cultures of Nigeria, Morocco, and Yemen unexpectedly developed novel low-context epistemic metaphors of "inclusion" triggered by their sense of freedom from native social constraints offered by communication through a computer/smartphone screen concealing their ethnic and sociocultural features. On the contrary, participants from the middle/high-context cultures of the Southern European countries of Italy and Greece showed a strengthening of the stereotypical high-context deontic metaphors of "exclusion" and "seclusion".

Noticeably, the data collected and analysed in this case study (only partially reported in this chapter) are still too limited to permit generalisations. Yet the case study findings encourage further investigation aimed at verifying whether this novel type of computer/smartphone-mediated communication is undermining not only the consolidated culture-specific schemata by which participants in online cross-cultural interactions make sense of reality dissolved in the "virtual metaverse" – which, indeed, makes it difficult to distinguish true and verifiable news from fake news and deliberate disinformation – but it is also modifying the structures of the participants' respective ELF variations, especially as they try to develop novel strategies of accommodation to new contexts and to the online interlocutors they interact with.

Maria Grazia Guido

Notes

1 The expression "sociolinguistic community" is here meant to define a group of speakers using the same native language and sharing common cultural values (cf. Gumperz 1971).

2 The "virtual metaverse" is represented, in this case, only by the virtual reality of the online university classroom where the multicultural students' interactions took place, which excluded the use of augmented reality technology.

3 Although these theories on high-/low-context-cultures developed some decades ago, before the increasing globalisation of the world, yet they are believed to be not only still valid today (cf. Würtz 2005), but even strengthened and consolidated in today's societies (cf. Burmann and Semrau 2022) as they are threatened by the possible disappearance of national cultures due to the levelling power of globalisation.

4 The accepted ways of making sense of contexts and events of reality are different from culture to culture, and they are reflected in the experiential schemata shared by the different sociolinguistic communities. Such schemata determine the semantic, typological-syntactic, and pragmatic structures of the speakers' native languages – which, eventually, come to be transferred into their respective ELF variations used in intercultural communication (cf. Guido 2008).

5 The Italian and the Greek universities involved in the case study are left unspecified due to the sensitive issues discussed by the participants in the debate, to whom alone the ownership of the opinions expressed is to be attributed.

6 The link to the set-text is www.science.org/content/blog-post/gain-function.

7 Bracketed dots indicate pauses at various length – from one to three dots. Features of the participants' different ELF variations have been retained in transcription.

8 The author was unknown to the participants in the case study – apart from his brief professional profile as an organic chemist outlined at the bottom of the set-text – so they were unaware of his political and cultural opinions probably already expressed elsewhere.

References

Burmann, K., and Semrau, T. (2022) "The Consequences of Social Category Faultiness in High- and Low-Context Cultures: A Comparative Study of Brazil and Germany," *Frontiers in Psychology* 13 1082870. www.frontiersin.org/articles/10.3389/fpsyg.2022.1082870/full.

Collier, G., Kuiken, D., and Enzle, M.E. (1982) "The Role of Grammatical Qualification in the Expression and Perception of Emotion," *Journal of Psycholinguistic Research* 11 631–650.

Ericsson, K.A., and Simon, H.A. (1984) *Protocol Analysis: Verbal Reports as Data*, Cambridge, MA: The MIT Press.

Guido, M.G. (2004) *Mediating Cultures: A Cognitive Approach to English Discourse for the Social Sciences*, Milan: LED.

Guido, M.G. (2008) *English as a Lingua Franca in Cross-cultural Immigration Domains*, Bern: Peter Lang.

Guido, M.G. (2018) *English as a Lingua Franca in Migrants' Trauma Narratives*, London: Palgrave Macmillan.

Guido, M.G. (2021) "Relexicalisation and Decategorialisation Processes in Migrants' ELF-Mediated Online Narratives in the Disembodied Time of the Covid-19 Pandemic," *Textus* 35 87–102.

Guido, M.G. (2022) "ELF-Mediated Modal Metaphors of 'Inclusion', 'Exclusion' and 'Seclusion' in an Online Discussion on Covid-19 Fake News: A Case Study in Cross-Cultural Cognitive Linguistics," *Lingue e Linguaggi* 53 225–252.

Gumperz, J.J. (1971) *Language in Social Groups*, Stanford: Stanford University Press.

Hall, E.T. (1990) *Understanding Cultural Differences*, Yarmouth, ME: Intercultural Press.

Halliday, M.A.K. (1994) *An Introduction to Functional Grammar*, London: Edward Arnold.

Hinkel, E. (1995) "The Use of Modal Verbs as a Reflection of Cultural Values," *TESOL Quarterly* 29(2) 325–341.

Hofstede, G. (1983) "National Cultures in Four Dimensions: A Research-Based Theory of Cultural Differences Among Nations," *International Studies of Management and Organization* 1(2) 46–74.

Lakoff, G., and Johnson, M. (1999) *Philosophy in the Flesh: The Embodied Mind and its Challenge to Western Thought*, New York: Basic Books.

Langacker, R.W. (1991) *Foundations of Cognitive Grammar. Volume II: Descriptive Application*, Stanford: Stanford University Press.

Narula, H. (2022) *Virtual Society: The Metaverse and the New Frontiers of Human Experience*, New York: Random House.

O'Halloran, K. (2003) *Critical Discourse Analysis and Language Cognition*, Edinburgh: Edinburgh University Press.

Rumelhart, D.E. (1980) "Schemata: The Building Blocks of Cognition," in R.J. Spiro, B.C. Bruce, and W.F. Brewer (eds.) *Theoretical Issues in Reading Comprehension: Perspectives from Cognitive Psychology, Linguistics, Artificial Intelligence and Education*, Hillsdale, NJ: Erlbaum.

Sweetser, E. (1990) *From Etymology to Pragmatics: Metaphorical and Cultural Aspects of Semantic Structure*, Cambridge: Cambridge University Press.

Talmy, L. (1988) "Force Dynamics in Language and Cognition," *Cognitive Science* 2 49–100.

Würtz, E. (2005) "Intercultural Communication on Web Sites: A Cross-cultural Analysis of Web Sites from High-context Cultures and Low-context Cultures," *Journal of Computer-Mediated Communication* 11 274–299.

26

MAPPING POLYLOGICAL DISCOURSE TO UNDERSTAND (DIS)INFORMATION NEGOTIATION

The case of the UK events research programme

Elena Musi, Kay L. O'Halloran, Elinor Carmi, Michael Humann, Minhao Jin, Simeon Yates, and Gautam Pal

Introduction

The advent of the Networked Society has radically changed the (dis)information ecosystem. A major aspect is that digital technologies and platforms have enabled new participatory models of news production, such as citizen journalism (Allan and Thorsen 2009), where citizens are both news producers and consumers. In addition, digital media algorithms and affordances constrain the way we access, create, and negotiate information, leading to filter-bubbles and echo chambers. Such a situation fuels media distortions, including polarisation and fake news. Thus, in a society where the medium is more and more the message, there is the need to make citizens active in the news gatekeeping process, exercising critical thinking when accessing, commenting, and creating news discourse. This is especially important in crisis scenarios, such as the pandemic, where major uncertainties might trigger confusing official communications which, in turn, spike diverse sentiments and potential misbehaviours. As discourse analysts, to identify the roots of disinformation and prevent its genesis and propagation, it is first crucial to understand how and why discourse(s) around issues of public interest are shaped. To the latter goal, we propose in this study a scalable methodology to analyse polylogues (Musi and Aakhus 2019) where stakeholders (e.g. citizens, journalists, politicians) advance various positions (news claims) across multiple venues (e.g. social media, broadcast media, discussion fora) and pinpoint potential sources of disinformation across digital media. We apply this methodology to the analysis of discourse(s) around the Events Research Programme (ERP) in the United Kingdom, which was developed to gather evidence on the reopening of events and venues assessing the risk of SARS-CoV-2 transmission, and to pilot risk-mitigation measures in concert with the UK Government's Roadmap for COVID-19 recovery. We then compare the results with those of a questionnaire that participants taking part in the live events were asked to complete.

More specifically, we focus on the first phase of the ERP during which three pilot events took place in Liverpool from 15 April to 15 June 2021. The study constitutes a privileged point of view

DOI: 10.4324/9781003224495-31

to investigate the negotiation of (dis)information because it is centred around a topic of radical un-certainty (is it safe to reopen large event?); it has been announced and advertised in a constrained period, thus allowing for a comprehensive data analysis; and it is geolocated, thus catalysing reactions from local to national communities.

Related work

The awareness of the presence and dangers cast by the infodemic during the pandemic has brought discourse analysts to join efforts countering the spread of disinformation. To better navigate the post-truth scenario, various studies have focused on defining different types of information distortions, distinguishing misinformation from disinformation and malinformation (e.g. Carmi et al. 2020; Wardle 2017). Another research stream has tackled the identification of deception clues in discourse, both adopting a qualitative and a quantitative/computational perspective: Marko (2022) has analysed through the lenses of critical discourse analysis the linguistic features flagging a conspiratorial anti-COVID Facebook group, while natural language processing approaches have focused on building classifiers for automatic fake news detection (Varma et al. 2021). Leveraging on the notions of fallacious discourse, Musi and Reed (2022) and Musi et al. (2022) have proposed a corpus-based taxonomy of misinformation triggers encompassing ten types of fallacies that have recurrently conveyed misleading information about COVID-19. Adopting a distribution-oriented perspective, other studies (e.g. Scannell et al. 2021) have dealt with persuasion techniques used by fake news spreaders to achieve popularity, if not virality. Reversing the perspective, argumentation scholars have published a collective volume centred around how public argumentation has changed in the face of the pandemic from a formal, normative, and functional perspective (Oswald et al. 2022). Despite differences in specific targets of inquiries and methodologies, state-of-the-art studies around discourse in/and the pandemic in relation to disinformation have scope over disinformation as a product. What we propose in this pilot study is to configure a methodology to observe the shaping of discourse in its complexity as a process that might prevent the rise and the spread of disinformation.

Data and methods

To analyse how ERP has been communicated by official sources (Dataset$_{official}$), we collected both news on (1) *UK Government* and *Liverpool City Council* webpages (list of links available in the Appendix) and (2) online local (Liverpool Echo) and national (*The Guardian, The Independent, The Evening Standard, The Metro,* and *The Sun* and *BBC*) news media through web-scraping. We considered 15 April–15 June 2021 as a time span during which the following three events were held in Liverpool: *Good Business Festival,* 19 April; *Circus Nights,* 30 April/1 May; and *Blossoms at Sefton Park,* 2 May 2021 (www.cultureliverpool.co.uk/event-research-project/). As filters to retrieve most relevant information we used a set of relevant event-specific keywords (e.g. "liverpool" AND "gig" AND "pilot"). We obtained a dataset of 23 articles from governmental sources and 44 articles from online news media.

To investigate public reactions on social media (Dataset$_{reactions}$), we have focused on the social media Twitter due to the availability of the API for the academic community. We have collected (i) all the tweets published by the Liverpool City Council official pages (*Liverpool City Council, Culture Liverpool; Visit Liverpool*) in the given time span to monitor public engagement (likes, retweets) with the communicated content, amounting to 125, and (ii) all the public tweets (2,144 + 813 retweets) targeting the live events according to a set of filter-keywords (e.g. "circus" AND "live" AND "test") to get an overview of public stances over the (testing) of the reopening of large events.

To understand whether official communications and public stances resonate with those of aspiring participants who wanted to attend the live events, we have considered pre-event questionnaires data collected as part of a funded evaluation of the ERP (DCMS – www.gov.uk/government/publications/information-on-the-events-research-programme/information-on-the-events-research-programme). It focused on capturing public perception of the events, looking at their expectations, experiences, and overall organisation. (Dataset$_{questioannire}$). This gathered 40,263 responses (*Good Business Festival* = 572; *Circus Nights* = 21,583 and *Blossoms at Sefton Park* = 20,026) from individuals planning to attend. We have focused on the questions (Q2–Q7, see Appendix) aimed at capturing concerns about attending the live events, the arguments behind these concerns, and the perceived risk of catching COVID-19 and spreading it to others.

As far as methodology is concerned, we have combined natural language processing techniques (topic modelling and sentiment analysis) with qualitative content and argumentative analysis. Topic modelling (Nikolenko et al. 2017) and sentiment analysis (Liu 2010) are natural language processing techniques respectively used to uncover hidden topics and positive vs negative vs neutral tone in texts. We have applied both techniques over Dataset$_{official}$ and Dataset$_{reactions}$ through the Multimodal Analysis Platform (*MAP*, O'Halloran Pal and Jin 2021). Sentiment analysis is carried out in MAP using the BERT (bidirectional encoder representation for transformers) model (Hoang et al. 2019). As to topic modelling, MAP gives the option of treating it as a classification problem based on a *Long Short-Term Memory* model (www.tensorflow.org/api_docs/python/tf/keras/layers/LSTM) trained on the News Category Dataset (www.kaggle.com/datasets/rmisra/news-category-dataset).

Getting an overview of the topics discussed across official news informs about how institutions and major news media outlets want to frame the ERP initiative, foregrounding certain aspects of an issue over another (Entman 1993). As underlined by Tversky and Kahneman (2013), frames have the potential to prime decision-making processes, strengthening the force of certain arguments (e.g. reason to join the reopening of a large event) over others (potential deterrents). On the other side, the topics surfaced through the social media analysis shed light on what aspects are felt as relevant to be discussed or raised by communities. It contributes, over the Dataset$_{official}$, to understanding the tone through which the events are announced to the public which might have a strategic communication impact, for example, promoting participation or fearmongering, while the sentiment expressed in the Dataset$_{reactions}$ provides hints as to positive vs negative attitudes entertained by the larger public. To investigate the arguments underlying such sentiments, we have carried out a qualitative content analysis (Krippendorff 2018) of the 100 tweets with the highest sentiment polarity (both positive and negative). The results have been compared with the questionnaire's answers, pointing to a (relative lack) of concern about catching or spreading COVID-19 at the live events. Further statistical measures have been applied to investigate correlations between concerns, gender, and vaccination status.

Results

Governmental and news media sources: the official ERP discourse

Supervised topic modelling over the Dataset$_{official}$ reveals that the official media releases are primarily concerned with science (i.e. the research programme) (30.4%), entertainment (26.1%), impact (e.g. on transmission, reopening of events) (17.4%), sports (8.7%) (e.g. opening of football matches etc), business (4.3%), green issues (4.3%), politics (4.3%), and travel (4.3%) (e.g. parking etc). In a temporal perspective, after the initial media release about the live events programme in early May 2021, the focus moved to science and entertainment which remained a consistent theme throughout, culminating with a focus on science and the impact of the programme at the end of May 2021.

The average sentiment of the online media articles is positive with a value of 0.686, revealing that the UK and Liverpool City Council endorsed and promoted the live events programme in a highly positive manner: the majority of articles (16 out of 23 articles) have a sentiment value within the range of 0.9 to 1.0, which is the highest possible range for positive sentiment scores (i.e. sentiment values range from −1.0 to +1.0). The rhetorical appeal of positive emotions to instil public enthusiasm is confirmed by a coherent use of images. Out of the 19 images that were found on the Liverpool City Council website, approximately half of the images are long shots of Liverpool City, which would typically be found in promotional and tourism materials for Liverpool. The other images are photos of the live events (e.g. the audience, the crowd, the band performing, and promotional shot of the band), in addition to a photo of Kevin McManus, head of Culture Liverpool, Liverpool City Council. The images function as framing devices, reinforcing the entertainment aspect of the live events, while making COVID-19 or testing less prominent topics.

Turning to the news media coverage, national ones are mostly concerned with entertainment (54.5%), arts (11.4%), impact (11.4%), and politics (9.1%). Other articles are classified as business (2.3%), college (2.3%), queer voices (2.3%), science (2.3%), wellness (2.3%), and world post (2.3%). The *entertainment frame* is apparent and in line with governmental sources, with most articles appearing at the time when the live events took place, rather than before-head to promote cautionary measures.

The average sentiment score is positive, with a value of 0.694, suggesting that online news media reported the live events programme in a very favourable light, again in line with the governmental news media sources. As to local newspapers (i.e. *Liverpool Echo*), they do reveal more diversity compared to national newspapers, with a focus on entertainment (27.3%), the impact of the events (27.3%), arts (18.2%), business (9.1%), college (9.1%), and politics (9.1%). The registered sentiment is slightly lower (0. 590) but overall leaning towards positive polarity.

Social media: the public ERP discourse

The longitudinal analysis of the public tweets (Dataset$_{reactions}$) reveals that they were primarily posted during three time periods: (a) when the live events research programme was building up in mid-April 2021 (week starting Monday 19 April 2021), (b) during the week when the live events took place (i.e. week starting Monday 26 April 2021), and (c) when the news that the live events did not lead to an increase in the spread of COVID-19 in the week starting Monday 24 May 2021 was released (www.liverpoolecho.co.uk/news/liverpool-news/liverpool-covid-pilot-events-had-20676455; https://news.liverpool.ac.uk/2021/05/25/liverpool-pilot-events-have-no-impact-on-covid-spread-in-region/; https://twitter.com/lpoolcouncil/status/1397221555567009796). The top 30 days of public tweet posts show that the actual events and the media release on 25 May 2021 attracted most interest on Twitter. As shown in Figure 26.1, the number of retweets and likes was the highest when the news about the results of the live events was released.

The average sentiment score for the public tweets is 0.500 (and 0.633 with retweets removed). The sentiment ranges from − 1.0 to − 0.9 and 9.0 to 1.0, but most tweets have a positive value of 9.0 to 1.0. On the other hand, the average sentiment scores for Liverpool City Council tweets is 0.859. This is the highest sentiment score found in the dataset, stressing the council's overall

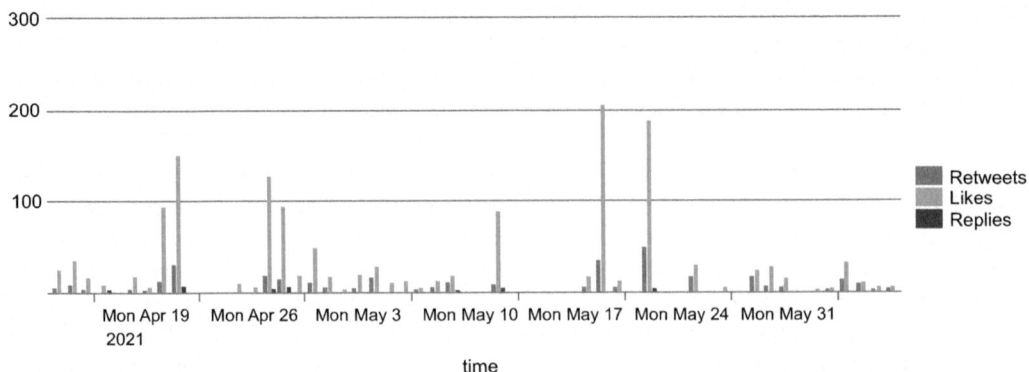

Figure 26.1 Public tweets: average number of retweets, likes, and replies for live events in Liverpool

endorsement of the ERP programme. Such an intention is confirmed by the exclusive use of images (overall 101) to promote features of the live events (e.g. band, crowd, and venue) rather than inciting the use of precautionary measures (e.g. there are no images of COVID-19 tests).

The most liked Liverpool City Council Tweet overall concerns the absence of risk posted by the Liverpool Public Health Officials on 25 May 2021:

> #BreakingNews | #Liverpool Public Health officials and scientists find that the city's 4 pilot events had no impact on #Covid19 spread in the region. Learn more: https://t.co/ f6ZIpEWzeH @DPH_MAshton @LivUni @profbuchan @CIRCUSmusic @FRfestivals

The classification of topics across the public tweets shows a focus on healthy living (21.3%), entertainment (18.8%), business (18.4%), sports (11.2%), travel (7.2%), wellness (3.7%), and politics (3.5%). This marks a shift from the earlier classifications of official and news media articles which are variously focused on entertainment, impact, science, arts, travel, and politics. The classifications for the Liverpool City Council tweets are entertainment (32.5%), travel (27.7%), wellness (10.8%), queer voices (7.2%), and impact (4.8%). The classifications for Liverpool City Council tweets fit with patterns from other media, but with an increase in focus on wellness.

From the content analysis of the 100 top positive and negative tweets, respectively 7 and 10 main underlying reasons have emerged (ordered according to frequency). Those underpinning positive sentiments are mostly evaluative propositions targeting features of the lived events (1, 2, 6) or their positive impact on the urban and cultural environment overall (3, 4, 7) with a few mentions to the of the rationale of the ERP program itself (assisting research, 6). On the other side, COVID-19 related issues are catalysed by reasons underlying negative sentiments (5, 7, 9, 10), next to practical aspects (3, 4, 5, 6), and inclusivity policies from a hospitality perspective (1 and 8):

Positive sentiments

1 Positive feelings about seeing the events on media
2 Positive feelings about attending the events
3 Wishing luck for future opening
4 Happiness towards reopening of culture events

5 Follow health measures to assist research
6 Positive feelings about the artists and music at the events
7 Positive feelings about Liverpool as a city to live in

Negative sentiments

1 Neglecting small venues
2 Complicated process to book
3 Concerns about weather
4 Concerns about fellow event goers' lack of etiquette
5 Criticism against the government
6 Noise complaints
7 Ethical concerns
8 Anger about artists selection to the events
9 Anger at having to take tests
10 Lack of scientific rigor

Questionnaire: the participants' discourse

At the time of completing the survey, 55.5% (22,366) of respondents had not received the vaccine, 15.1% (6,094) had received one dose, and 8.3% (3,333) had received both doses, with 21.0% (8,470) not responding to this question.

The perceived risk of catching COVID-19 at the live events was low, with 35.5% and 31.7% of participants responding that it was "very unlikely" and "fairly unlikely" respectively. The number of people who thought it "very unlikely" increased proportionally over time, suggesting an increased level of confidence about the low-level risk as the live events approached. However, the tendency to not respond to this question increased over time as well.

The perceived low level of risk of catching coronavirus at the live events correlated with a lack of concern about infecting others, as displayed in Figure 26.2. That is, the majority of people who thought it "very unlikely" to catch COVID were "not at all concerned" with infecting others. Those who thought it "fairly unlikely" were largely "not at all concerned" or were only "slightly concerned" about infecting others.

Thus, 63.1% (25,400) of participants were "not at all concerned" about attending the event, with women being slightly more concerned than men. Gender differences in risk perception (Gustafsod 1998) are, thus, not significant across the participants' sample. For example, 29.7% (11,942) of women and 30.9% (12,459) of men were not at all concerned, and 7.7% (3,113) of women and 5.4% (2,188) of men were slightly concerned, as displayed in Figure 26.3.

Participants expressed low levels of concern about attending the event, regardless of whether they had been vaccinated or not, as shown in Figure 26.4.

The reasons selected for being "not at all concerned" are the following (in order of frequency):

More generally, 81.6% (32,855) of respondents did not express any specific concerns about attending the event, such as possibly catching COVID-19, having to self-isolate if tested positive, having others think that the person is being reckless, and social anxiety. The largest single concern was catching COVID-19 (4.4%), though this was coupled with other concerns (e.g. having to self-isolate if tested positive for COVID-19, others thinking I am being reckless) in 8.4% of cases. Most participants considered it "very important" and "moderately important" to resume the events, regardless of gender.

417

Self Infecting

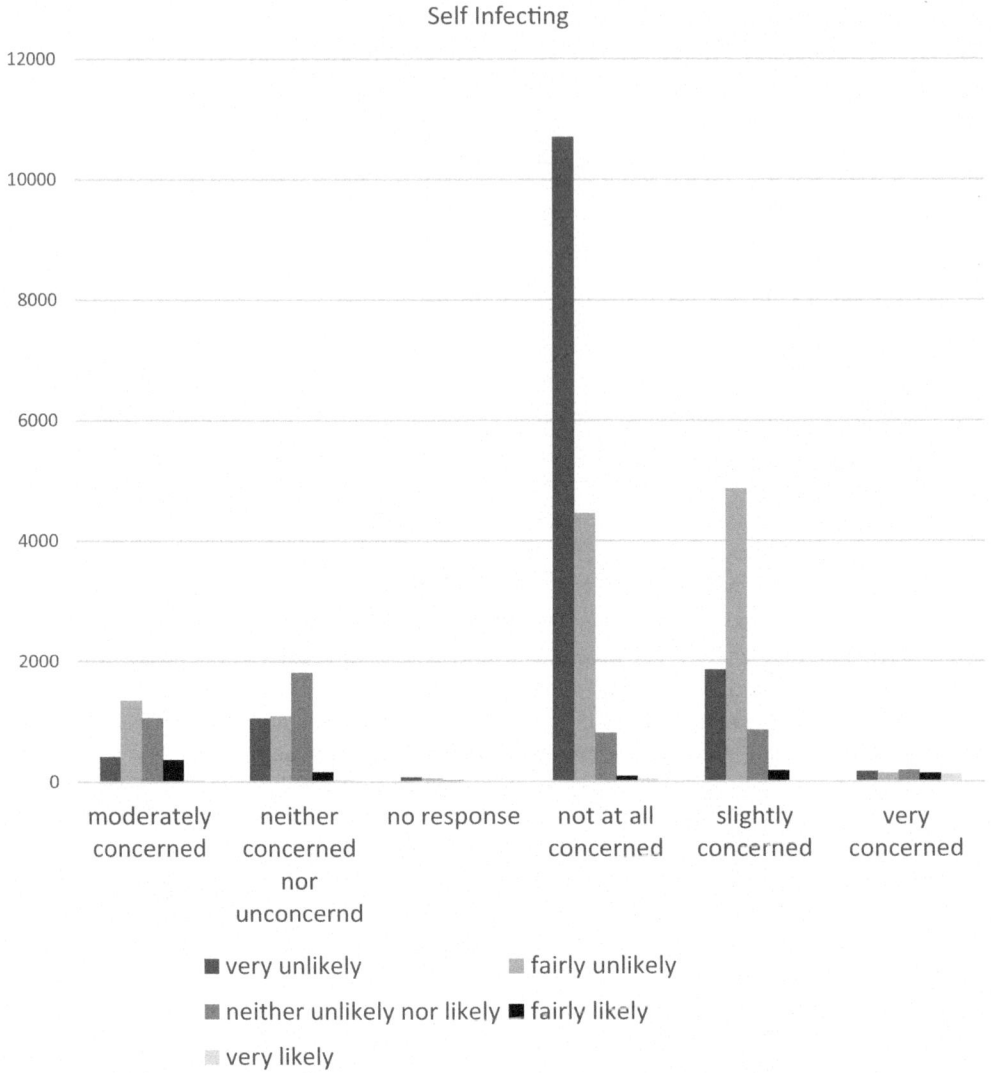

Figure 26.2 How likely do you think you are to catch COVID at the event and infect others

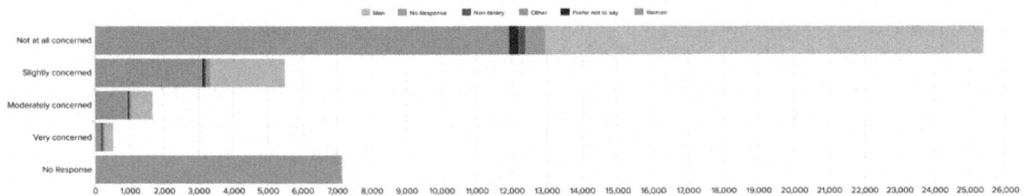

Figure 26.3 Level of concern about attending the event and gender

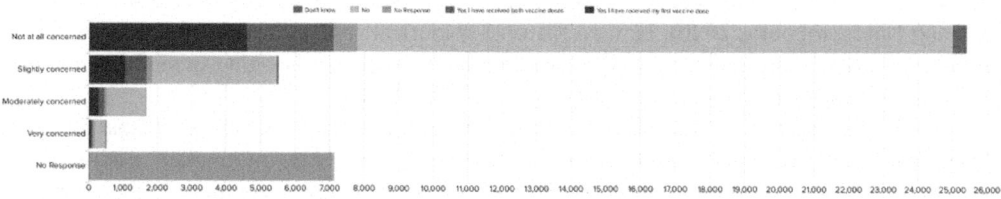

Figure 26.4 Level of concern about attending the event and vaccination status

Table 26.1 Reasons for being "not at all concerned"

Item	Number
Because I have followed guidance on reducing the spread of coronavirus (COVID-19)	3170
Because I've been tested; Because I have followed guidance on reducing the spread of coronavirus (COVID-19)	2190
Because I've been tested; Because I've been vaccinated; Because I have followed guidance on reducing the spread of coronavirus (COVID-19)	2000
Because I've previously had COVID-19	1630
Because I've been tested	1513
Because I've been vaccinated	1566
Because I've previously had COVID-19; Because I've been tested; Because I have followed guidance on reducing the spread of coronavirus (COVID-19)	1322
Because I've previously had COVID-19; Because I've been tested; Because I've been vaccinated; Because I have followed guidance on reducing the spread of coronavirus (COVID-19)	781
Other	2331

Discussion

The analysis of discourse(s) around the pilot live events from different stakeholders (UK government, official national and local media, social media users, and aspiring participants at the large events) across media outlets (official website, news media outlets, Twitter, and questionnaire) reveal common trends as well as mismatches between official communication and public concerns that indicate the presence of/the potential for disinformation to spread.

The official UK government media and the Liverpool City Council messages were concerned with science (i.e. the research programme), entertainment, and the impact of the events, with a high positive sentiment score. The Liverpool City Council posted images of the city and photos of the live events (e.g. audience, band, and bright lights), which promoted the entertainment aspects of the live events programme and Liverpool City itself. Similarly, the UK news media press also focussed on the entertainment and the arts, and to a lesser extent on impact, with a similar positive sentiment score. Overall, the official discourse framed ERP events with the strategic goal of promoting them, downsizing possible risks. As shown by previous studies (e.g. Xu and Guo 2018), the use of positive sentiment words is a successful strategy to increase message popularity. In the case of ERP, message popularity was advocated to guarantee the involvement of a wide spectrum of participants with diverse demographic features. From a media perspective, the strategy of stressing the positive aspects brought about by ERP counterbalances the increasing news avoidance, which has at its core the depressing nature of news, especially during the pandemic (Toff and Kalogeropoulos 2020). However, such a rhetorical strategy brings about opportunities for both intentional and unintentional misleading news to spread, bringing misinformation and disinformation rather than increased literacy (Carmi et al. 2020).

From the close qualitative analysis of tweets with negative sentiment, it is apparent that members of the public were concerned with the partiality and/or lack of accurate information received about the risks, and the measures put in place by the UK government to mitigate them. Criticism ranges from pointing out the bad timing (e.g. "recipe for disaster, and too early for such a socially enclosed event. bbc news – covid: uk clubbers return to liverpool for trial night https://t.co/ixzgaphdyo") to the neglect of the consequences that this might have on vulnerable people (e.g. "@circusmusic remember it's an experiment to see who gets sick, if they pass on to a vulnerable person, and kill them . . . fools rush in. i am in the vulnerable category but it appears any events in liverpool exclude us. if deaths go up, on your hands. can i have my tax back?"). To ascertain the soundness of these critiques, we went through the official communication and news articles about the *Circus Nights*: besides having partial information about the health measures involved in the pilot events, we attested the presence of nonfactual information; namely, that pilots are part of the pilots for vaccine passport, which is not the case. On the contrary, the ERP was conceived as an opportunity to not only monitor public behaviours but also gather public stances over the potential use of vaccine passports to inform future policies. One of the questions in the post-event questionnaire that participants were asked to complete was, in fact, meant as a public consultation over the matter: "If similar events in the future would require attendees to present a 'Covid passport' in order to enter, how likely are you to join such events?". The majority of participants (ca 75%) positively answered either "likely" or "very likely". We, thus, confirm that public reactions on social media rightly point to the presence of misinformation from official sources, which has been identified and discussed by various studies during the pandemic (Kyriakidou et al. 2020; Islam et al. 2021). It must be noted that lack of information can be as detrimental as nonfactual information in triggering misbehaviours (Musi et al. 2022), thus counting as misinformation. Regardless of its type, misinformation opens doors for conspiratorial thinking and, at best, scenarios to decrease trust in institutions, which hinders effective communication in crisis scenarios. Transparent and accurate communication about the institutional goals for setting up the ERP would rule out misunderstandings which are bound to fuel disinformation. Public tweets were, for instance, questioning the motive of the programme, reconducting it to governmental discrimination towards Liverpool (e.g. "liverpool were the first to pilot the lateral flow tests and now we're the first to pilot events without social distancing, masks etc. y'all the government really hates us don't they 😂"). The lack of benevolence from the UK government (Mayer et al. 1995), which is a key pillar of institutional trust, is most likely at the origin of public fears about being involved in an experimental study. A closer scrutiny at the tweets expressing concerns reveals widespread worries about local people being used as "guinea pigs" and "rats" in a government supported scientific experimental study (e.g. "Using scousers as social experiment guinea pigs", "Government social experiment. Using Liverpool as guinea pigs. We've nothing to lose, so lets see how it goes they'll say"; "Liverpool again ! Guinea pigs !!! Not London ???? Wonder why?"). That of inferring malicious intentions as the best possible explanation in absence of others easily accessible constitutes one of the major causes of conspiratorial thought (Moffitt et al. 2021).

The results of the questionnaire show that most aspiring participants were not worried about catching or transmitting COVID-19, being on the other side of the spectrum. Their main rationale is that they have followed guidance on reducing the spread of coronavirus, showing that trust in institutions is at the very basis of a perception of safety. However, detrimental consequences following from the lack of information could highly impact their trust.

Recommendations

The polylogue around ERP events showcases how the analysis of discourse can help not only identifying but also preventing the rise of both misinformation and disinformation. Such an endeavour calls first of all for an awareness of the complexity of the current information ecosystem where information is not communicated top-down from official news media venues, but it is, instead, continuously negotiated amongst different sectors of society. Drawing from our analysis, three key recommendations emerge to craft effective public messages in crisis scenarios:

- Understand public epistemic needs and concerns: social media reactions need to be scrutinised while shaping a communication campaign. As evidenced by public reactions on Twitter, for instance, the safety measures put into place to ensure compliance for the safety of everyone involved should have been provided. At the same time, the rationale behind the live events and their role as a form of public consultation rather than an experiment to enforce governmental decisions should have been clearly stated.
- Develop standpoints and arguments aimed at minimising risks: the communication goals of official media should prioritise public risk avoidance. From the questionnaire, it was clear that people who wanted to attend the live event considered the risk to be extremely low, even though that may not have necessarily been the case in a testing scenario. A negative outcome would have caused a public backlash against institutions as well as fuelled conspiratorial thought.
- Use framing devices as means to achieve communication goals: both natural language and multimodal content (images) shall be used to foreground both advantages and risks (and precautionary means) to guarantee accountability without fearmongering. Thematic content and images shall have emphasised all key issues rather than focussing on the entertainment aspect of the events.

Appendix

Sources: https://liverpool.gov.uk; www.cdc.gov/coronavirus/2019ncov/index.html; www.ecdc. europa.eu;www.gov.uk/coronavirus;www.gov.uk/government/organisations/scientific-advisory-group-for-emergencies; www.independentsage.org; www.nhs.uk/conditions/coronavirus-covid-19; www.who.int/emergencies/diseases/novel-coronavirus-2019

Questionnaire

(Q1) What are the main reasons you decided to join the Events Research Programme?
(Q2) Are you concerned about attending the event?

Not at all concerned
Slightly concerned
Moderately concerned
Very concerned

(Q3) Are there any factors that might contribute to some of your concern about attending the event?

Possibly catching COVID-19
Impact of having to self-isolate if I test positive for COVID-19
Social anxiety
Others thinking I'm reckless
Other

(Q4) How likely do you think you are to catch coronavirus at the event?

Very unlikely
Fairly unlikely
Neither unlikely nor likely
Fairly likely
Very likely

(Q5) How concerned are you about potentially infecting others after attending the event?

Not at all concerned
Slightly concerned
Neither concerned nor unconcerned
Moderately concerned
Very concerned

(Q6) If "not at all concerned" on last question, having stated that you are not concerned, share reasons why

Because I've previously had COVID-19
Because I've been tested
Because I've been vaccinated
Because I've followed guidance on reducing the spread of COVID-19
Other

(Q7) How important do you think it is to resume these kinds of public events as soon as possible?

Not at all important
Slightly important
Neither important nor unimportant
Moderately important
Very important

(Q8) In the past seven days, how often did you wash your hands with soap and water straight away after returning home from a public place?

Always
Often
Sometimes
Not very often
Never

(Q9) In the past seven days, have you used a face covering when outside your home to help slow the spread of the coronavirus (COVID-19)?

Yes
No
Not applicable

(Q10) While you were inside a public space (e.g. shop, public transport) in the last seven days, how often did you wear a protective face covering to help slow the spread of the coronavirus (COVID-19)?

Always
Often

Sometimes
Not very often
Never

(Q11) On average, how often do you follow the guidance on social distance when outside of support/childcare bubbles, maintaining 1–2 metres between yourself and other people?

Always
Often
Sometimes
Not very often
Never

(Q12) In the past seven days, have you had any visitors inside your home from outside your support/childcare bubbles, including tradespeople, carers, or medical staff?

Yes
No

(Q13) When you have had a visitor inside your home, which of the following actions did you take to reduce the spread of the coronavirus (COVID-19)?

Worn a face mask
Asked the visitor to wear a mask
Opened windows or doors
Cleaned touch points
Maintained social distancing
Washed hands regularly
Other
None of the above

(Q14) As part of your condition for attendance to this event, you will be required to complete a test. In case that this test results comes back negative, which statement below best describes what it means to you?

I am definitely not infectious
I am probably not infectious
I am probably infectious
I am definitely infectious
Don't know

(Q15) What gender do you most identify with?

Man
Woman
Non-binary
Other
Prefer not to say

(Q16) Ethnicity

Asian/Asian-British – Indian, Pakistani, Bangladeshi, other
Black/Black British – Caribbean. African, other

Mixed race – White and Black/Black British
Mixed race – other
White – British, Irish, other
Chinese/Chinese British
Middle Eastern/Middle Eastern British – Arab, Turkish, other,
Other ethnic group
Prefer not to say

(Q17) Have you previously been diagnosed with COVID?

Yes, I've had a positive test (antibody or swab)
Yes, most likely but I've not had a test to confirm
No, don't think I've had COVID-19
Don't know

(Q18) Have you received your vaccination?

Yes, I have received my first vaccine dose
Yes, I have received both vaccine doses
No
Don't know

References

Allan, S. and Thorsen, E. eds., 2009. *Citizen Journalism: Global Perspectives* (Vol. 1). Peter Lang.

Carmi, E., Yates, S.J., Lockley, E. and Pawluczuk, A., 2020. Data citizenship: Rethinking data literacy in the age of disinformation, misinformation, and malinformation. *Internet Policy Review*, 9(2), pp. 1–22.

Entman, R.M., 1993. Framing: Towards clarification of a fractured paradigm. *McQuail's Reader in Mass Communication Theory*, 390, p. 397.

Gustafsod, P.E., 1998. Gender differences in risk perception: Theoretical and methodological erspectives. *Risk Analysis*, 18(6), pp. 805–811.

Hoang, M., Bihorac, O.A. and Rouces, J., 2019. Aspect-based sentiment analysis using bert. In *Proceedings of the 22nd Nordic Conference on Computational Linguistics* (pp. 187–196). Linköping University Electronic Press.

Islam, M.S., Mahmud, R. and Ahmed, B., 2021. Trust in government during COVID-19 pandemic in Bangladesh: An analysis of social media users' perception of misinformation and knowledge about government measures. *International Journal of Public Administration*, pp. 1–17.

Krippendorff, K., 2018. *Content Analysis: An Introduction to its Methodology*. Sage Publications.

Kyriakidou, M., Morani, M., Soo, N. and Cushion, S., 2020. Government and media misinformation about COVID-19 is confusing the public. *LSE Covid-19 Blog* https://blogs.lse.ac.uk/covid19/.

Liu, B., 2010. Sentiment analysis and subjectivity. In *Handbook of Natural Language Processing* (Vol. 2, pp. 627–666). CRC Press.

Marko, K., 2022. Extremist language in anti-COVID-19 conspiracy discourse on Facebook. *Critical Discourse Studies*, pp. 1–20.

Mayer, R.C., Davis, J.H. and Schoorman, F.D., 1995. An integrative model of organizational trust. *Academy of Management Review*, 20(3), pp. 709–734.

Moffitt, J.D., King, C. and Carley, K.M., 2021. Hunting conspiracy theories during the COVID-19 pandemic. *Social Media+ Society*, 7(3), p. 20563051211043212.

Musi, E. and Aakhus, M., 2019. Framing fracking: Semantic frames as meta-argumentative indicators for knowledge-driven argument mining of controversies. *Journal of Argumentation in Context*, 8(1), pp. 112–135.

Musi, E., Aloumpi, M., Carmi, E., Yates, S. and O'Halloran, K., 2022. Developing fake news immunity: Fallacies as misinformation triggers during the pandemic. *Online Journal of Communication and Media Technologies*, 12(3), pp. 2–18.

Musi, E. and Reed, C., 2022. From fallacies to semi-fake news: Improving the identification of misinformation triggers across digital media. *Discourse & Society*, *33*(3), pp. 349–370.

Nikolenko, S. I., Koltcov, S. and Koltsova, O., 2017. Topic modelling for qualitative studies. *Journal of Information Science*, *43*(1), pp. 88–102.

O'Halloran, K. L., Pal, G. and Jin, M., 2021. Multimodal approach to analysing big social and news media data. *Discourse, Context & Media*, *40*, p. 100467. https://doi.org/10.1016/j.dcm.2021.100467.

Oswald, S., Lewiński, M., Greco, S. and Villata, S., 2022. *The Pandemic of Argumentation* (p. 371). Springer Nature.

Scannell, D., Desens, L., Guadagno, M., Tra, Y., Acker, E., Sheridan, K., Rosner, M., Mathieu, J. and Fulk, M., 2021. COVID-19 vaccine discourse on Twitter: A content analysis of persuasion techniques, sentiment and mis/disinformation. *Journal of Health Communication*, *26*(7), pp. 443–459.

Toff, B. and Kalogeropoulos, A., 2020. All the news that's fit to ignore: How the information environment does and does not shape news avoidance. *Public Opinion Quarterly*, *84*(S1), pp. 366–390.

Tversky, A. and Kahneman, D., 2013. Choices, values, and frames. In *Handbook of the Fundamentals of Financial Decision Making (In 2 Parts)* (Vol. 4, p. 269). World Scientific Publishing.

Varma, R., Verma, Y., Vijayvargiya, P. and Churi, P.P., 2021. A systematic survey on deep learning and machine learning approaches of fake news detection in the pre-and post-COVID-19 pandemic. *International Journal of Intelligent Computing and Cybernetics*, *14*(4), pp. 617–646.

Wardle, C., 2017. Fake news. It's complicated. *First Draft*, *16*, pp. 1–11.

Xu, Z. and Guo, H., 2018. Using text mining to compare online pro-and anti-vaccine headlines: Word usage, sentiments, and online popularity. *Communication Studies*, *69*(1), pp. 103–122.

INDEX

Note: Page numbers in *italic* indicate a figure and page numbers in **bold** indicate a table on the corresponding page.

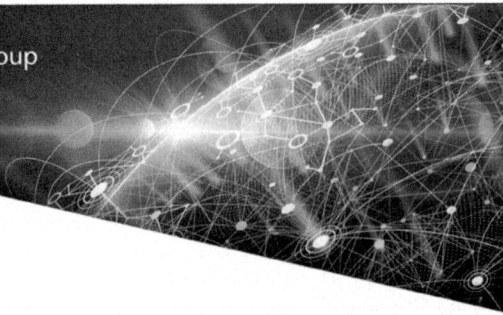